DAVID FELLMAN
Vilas Professor of Political Science
University of Wisconsin
ADVISORY EDITOR TO DODD, MEAD & COMPANY

D1277833

THE POLITICS OF THE
FEDERAL BUREAUCRACY

THE POLITICS OF
THE FEDERAL
BUREAUCRACY

ALAN A. ALTSHULER

MASSACHUSETTS INSTITUTE OF TECHNOLOGY

DODD, MEAD & COMPANY

New York   Toronto   *1968*

PREFACE

I HAVE approached the federal bureaucracy in this reader as a major sub-system of the American political system, one which deserves the closest attention of political scientists both as a fascinating political system in its own right—fully as interesting in this respect as the legislative, judicial, and party systems—and as an actor of fundamental and rapidly growing importance in the American political drama taken as a whole. The selections are predominantly descriptive and analytical rather than normative. At the same time, they have been chosen for the provocative light that they shed on *important* political relationships, and importance, needless to say, can ultimately be measured only in terms of values.*

Most students will be wondering as they approach this volume: why study American public administration? Why consider *it* important? The most fundamental—though certainly not the only answer, it seems to me, is that the bureaucratization of society and government over the past century has radically transformed the nature of American democracy. The countless small private associations that aroused de Tocqueville's wonder have largely been replaced—if we confine our attention to those of political significance—by regional and national organizations of the sort that led Michels to formulate his "iron law of oligarchy." The capitalism of small enterprises struggling constantly for survival against severe competitive threats has been superseded by one of giant corporations able to control their competitive environments in very significant degree, and thus to provide most members of the labor force with nearly perfect cushioning against the instabilities and uncertainties of the market place. The seamy side of this picture is that large bureaucratized associations and corporations tend to escape society's "natural"—that is, non-governmental—control mechanisms. Whether the natural control mechanisms are doing an "adequate" job in any particular situation is, of course, a matter for the political system to determine. In practice, it determines that greater and greater governmental control is required with every passing decade.

Similar developments have occurred in the fields of welfare and national security, though in these the new bureaucracies are predominantly public.

---

* The term "political" appears five times in the above paragraph. What, precisely, does it mean? I have ventured a formal definition in my article, "The Study of American Public Administration," which appears in Section I-C, below. See page 55, footnote 1.

v

In the former, the decline of the extended family as a welfare institution, the demise of the locality as a self-sufficient economy, the increasing mobility of the nation's population, and rapidly rising welfare expectations have produced immense bureaucracies devoted to caring for the poor and helpless, to insuring workers against the financial perils of old age and unemployment, to educating the nation's youth, and to maintaining the national economy on a vigorous upward course. In the latter, the demise of the European balance of power, the declining value of the oceans as protectors, and the Communist revolutions in Russia and China have compelled the nation to maintain huge standing military forces—supplemented by such trimmings as a vast intelligence establishment and a five billion dollar a year space program—for the first time in its history.

Thus, the federal government, though it lagged a bit until the presidency of Franklin Roosevelt, has grown at least as rapidly over the past century as its corporate and associational competitors for national dominance. Laissez faire has been superseded by the "mixed economy," and in it the role of government has become increasingly dominant. Within the public sector, the "old federalism" of states rights has increasingly given way to a "new federalism" of government by contract and grant-in-aid. Within the national government, the scales of dominance have shifted decisively from Congress to the executive branch. In recent decades, moreover, the same threats from abroad that have made defense the nation's biggest business have rendered plausible the idea that many of the fundamental bases of the government's most vital decisions should be kept secret, and that much other information should be released selectively with an eye to manipulating foreign—and by coincidental indirection, therefore, domestic public and congressional—opinion.

In view of these and countless related developments, there are many who believe that American society is moving inexorably toward a situation in which something like the following conditions will prevail: (1) most power will be wielded by a relatively few huge bureaucracies, whose top administrators will be meaningfully accountable only to their own consciences and each other; (2) among these bureaucracies, those which are private institutions, and those which are state and local, will have little power to balance the federal government in genuinely pluralistic fashion; (3) Congress and the public will have little capacity to control the activities of the executive branch, particularly when it is led by a master politician in the presidency; and (4) because of the decline both of the constitution's checks and balances *and* of the widespread diffusion of power in American society as a whole, democracy and liberty will at best remain pale shadows of their former selves.

This picture may or may not be overdrawn. Regardless, the popular definition of democracy as involving fairly detailed control of governmental decision making by the electorate becomes less descriptive each year of the way in which the American political system actually operates. Some would dismiss this observation as too obvious to be worth making. The plain fact is, however, that only the crudest beginnings have yet been made toward building a democratic theory that grapples seriously with the realities of the bureaucratic state—one which explains how "adequate" public control ought to be redefined in the light of modern conditions, and how the public can be rendered capable of exercising such control without the republic being rendered unable to meet the vital challenges that it faces from within and without.

The organization of this reader rests ultimately on my concern with these cardinal issues. They are generally in the background, however. The volume begins and concludes with sections devoted to them, but for the rest of its length it focuses on the most important specific conflicts that have swirled within and around the American federal bureaucracy in recent years. Its primary objectives are simple and four in number: (1) to introduce beginning students of public administration to the main actors in these areas of dispute, their opinions and interests, their sources of influence and weakness; (2) to indicate how the American governmental system typically deals with these conflicts—particularly where these ways differ from those that the average, legally oriented, introductory course in American government might lead one to expect; (3) to present a variety of provocative viewpoints on how it *ought* to deal with them; and (4) to spur students to think seriously about what they, as budding systematic theorists wishing to grasp the essential dynamics of the American political system, ought most to want to know about the federal bureaucracy and its patterns of interaction with the other major forces in American political life.

In short: this book of readings has no methodological or normative axe to grind; its central presupposition, however, is that American public administration can very fruitfully be studied as a branch of American politics. I have developed this latter theme a bit more fully—in the course of analyzing the intellectual history of public administration as a field of study—in a brief essay which appears below (pp. 55). I trust, however, that the utility of this volume will not be confined to those who agree with the opinions there expressed, nor, for that matter, even to those who are explicitly interested in the issues there explored.

ALAN A. ALTSHULER

CONTENTS

ix

I. FUNDAMENTAL ISSUES

A. Bureaucratization and Liberal Democracy

IN his classic essay, "Bureaucracy," * Max Weber (1864-1920) contended that the trend toward bureaucratization in the modern world was irreversible. His brief was simple. Bureaucracies are the most efficient mechanisms for mobilizing men and resources yet devised. Therefore, all nations, businesses, political parties, and other human associations that find themselves in competitive situations are driven to organize themselves bureaucratically. Those that do not tend to fall by the wayside.

This contention was striking enough, but Weber's thesis took on greatly added force from the stark simplicity with which he defined bureaucracy. The ideally efficient bureaucracy (which is to say, the ideally efficient mode for cooperative human activity), Weber wrote, is one characterized by a monocratic authority structure, by the elaborate articulation and recording of decision rules to guide subordinate officials in all their activities, by the making of personnel decisions on a strict merit basis, and by the total dependence of each official upon his job for his social status and livelihood.

Weber's image of bureaucracy and his sense of historic inevitability have dominated serious thought about bureaucracy until very recent years. Developing them, many scholars have concluded that liberal democracy is doomed. If history is characterized by the struggle of nations and lesser institutions for survival, they have reasoned, if the organizational form best adapted to this struggle is autocracy, and if the attribute most to be desired in individual bureaucrats is strict obedience, what basis for optimism about the future of democracy can there be?

In his article which leads off this section, Alvin Gouldner maintains that there is no empirical basis for such pessimism. He argues his case most persuasively, but you will do well to approach it with extreme skepticism. It is characteristically American, after all, to believe that all problems have solutions, that all objectives are compatible (or can be rendered so with a little innovative effort), and that man is master of his fate. These tenets may simply be manifestations of the arrogance of success, however. Other national traditions have been leavened by repeated experiences of failure, and the social analysts produced by them have generally taken very seriously indeed the idea that history has its tragic inevitabilities. Even if one accepts the case for determinism in principle, of course, it by no means follows that the Weberian vision of bureaucracy is valid. No one can say conclusively whether it

* H. H. Gerth and C. Wright Mills, eds., *From Max Weber: Essays in Sociology* (New York: Oxford University Press, 1946), pp. 196-244.

is or not, but it is difficult to imagine anyone writing profoundly about bureaucracy without having reflected long and hard upon that question. Gouldner's article is an excellent starting point for such an analysis.

Norton Long's perspective is very similar to Gouldner's, but his focus is on actual American experience rather than scholarly theories. Long attempts to refute those who have contended that the United States must choose between legislative supremacy and bureaucratic supremacy, or between big government and constitutional democracy. His argument involves a number of unorthodox assumptions about the most meaningful way to define democracy in the current period. The strategy that he recommends for keeping government responsive, and respectful of liberty, in the bureaucratic era appears quite radical at first glance, yet Long contends that American government is already effectuating it. His assumptions, definitions, recommended tactics, and assessments of current American practice all require (and well merit) careful evaluation.

From the beginning of Franklin Roosevelt's Administration to the end of Dwight Eisenhower's, American liberals were generally united in defending the federal bureaucracy against its critics. For much of this time, a public figure could expect that his rhetoric about the bureaucracy would be widely understood as a symbol of his position on most of the other great issues of the day: the welfare state, counter-cyclical fiscal and monetary policy, loyalty-security programs, foreign aid, etc. This situation has changed substantially in recent years. By failing to turn back the clock, the Eisenhower Administration drastically reduced the range of controversy about big government. As this truth gradually sank in, and as just about all of the liberal agenda compiled in the forties and fifties became law in 1964 and 1965, patterns of political conflict began to shift. Many liberals felt free for the first time to take a hard critical look at the ways in which American big government actually operated. Of these, a significant proportion concluded that they had been too sanguine about the efficacy of existing programs and about the relationship between bureaucracy and individual freedom. Without curtailing their support for government efforts to improve upon the market's allocation of national resources, they began to think more and more seriously about administrative means. As their investigations have proceeded, they have "discovered" that a high proportion of contemporary bureaucratic activity is highly burdensome to the ordinary citizen and quite inessential (or even negatively related) to achievement of the government's basic objectives. Their action program has been to spur experimentation with methods of implementing society's collective goals that involve a bare minimum of bureaucratic regulation, discretion, and red tape. James Q. Wilson's article is a highly provocative example of this latest genre of American thought about bureaucracy.

METAPHYSICAL PATHOS AND THE THEORY
OF BUREAUCRACY *
Alvin W. Gouldner

THE conduct of a polemic focusses attention on the differences between two points of view to the neglect of their continuity and convergences. No modern polemic better exemplifies this than the controversy between the proponents of capitalism and of socialism. Each tends to define itself as the antithesis of the other; even the uncommitted bystander, rare though he be, is likely to think of the two as if they were utterly alien systems.

There have always been some, however, who have taken exception to this sharp contrast between socialism and capitalism and who have insisted that there are significant similarities between the two. One of these, the French sociologist Emile Durkheim, maintained that socialism like capitalism involved an overbearing preoccupation with economic interests. In both socialist and capitalist societies, Durkheim argued, economic concerns were at the center of attention. In Durkheim's view, neither capitalism nor socialism deemed it necessary to bridle materialistic ends; neither society subordinated pecuniary interests to some higher, governing, moral norms. Therefore, "from Durkheim's point of view," writes Talcott Parsons, "socialism and laissez-faire individualism are of the same piece." [1]

Bertrand Russell came to similar conclusions on the basis of a trip to the then newly-established Soviet Republic: ". . . the practical difference between socialism and capitalism is not so great as politicians on both sides suppose. Certain features will appear in the early stages of industrialism under either system; and under either system certain other features will appear in its later stages." [2]

Without doubt, though, the most sophisticated formulation of this view was that conceived by the German sociologist, Max Weber. To Weber, the distinguishing characteristic of modern capitalism was the "rational organization of free labor." The pursuit of private gain, noted Weber, was well known in many earlier societies; what distinguishes present-day capitalism, he held, is the peculiar organization of the production unit, an organization that is essen-

* From the *American Political Science Review*, Vol. 49 (June 1955), pp. 496–507. Reprinted by permission of the author and publisher.

1. Talcott Parsons, *The Structure of Social Action* (New York, 1937), p. 341.
2. Bertrand and Dora Russell, *Prospects of Industrial Civilization* (New York, 1923), p. 14.

tially bureaucratic. This conception of capitalism, writes Parsons, "has one important concrete result; in contradistinction to Marx and most 'liberal' theories, it strongly minimizes the differences between capitalism and socialism, emphasizing rather their continuity. Not only would socialistic organization leave the central fact of bureaucracy untouched, it would greatly accentuate its importance."[3]

While Marx had dwelt largely on the interrelations *among* production units, that is, their market ties, Weber focussed on the social relations *within* the industrial unit. If social relations inside of socialist and capitalist factories are fundamentally alike, in that they are both bureaucratic, then, asked Weber, does a socialist revolution yield very much of an improvement for the capitalist proletarian?

If Marx argued that the workers of the world had nothing to *lose* by revolting, Weber contended that they really had nothing to *gain*. "For the time being," he declared, "the dictatorship of the official and not that of the workers is on the march." Capitalism and socialism are thus placed under the same conceptual umbrella—bureaucracy—with the important practical result that the problem of choosing between them loses much of its point.

It is for this reason that the discussions of bureaucratic organization which are heir to the Weberian analysis must be understood as being, in part, a displacement of the controversy over socialism. Weber made it clear that questions of economic choice could no longer be treated in isolation from questions of administration. From Weber's time forward, administrative and economic choices were seen to be but two facets of the same hard problem. This has been recognized even by socialists, at least when they have been unencumbered by Communist party orthodoxy. For example, Oskar Lange once remarked, with a frankness that we hope he will never be compelled to regret, ". . . the real danger of socialism is that of bureaucratic organization of economic life. . . ."[4]

It is sometimes assumed today that the Weberian outlook is at bottom anti-socialist. In effect, the argument runs, Weber's viewpoint devitalizes the myth-like appeal of socialism, draining off its ability to muster immense enthusiasms. Weber's theses are therefore held to be an "ideology" serviceable for the survival of capitalism, while Weber himself is characterized as the "Marx of the bourgeoisie."

Now all this may be true, but it is only a partial truth; for, in actuality, Weber's theories cut two ways, not one. If it is correct that his theory of bureaucracy saps the fervor of the socialist offensive, it also undermines the stamina of the capitalist bastions. If socialism and capitalism are similar in being bureaucratic, then not only is there little *profit* in substituting one for the other, but there is also little *loss*.

3. Parsons, p. 509.
4. Oskar Lange and Fred M. Taylor, *On the Economic Theory of Socialism*, ed. Lippincott (Minneapolis, 1948), p. 109.

Considered only from the standpoint of its political consequences then, the Weberian outlook is not anti-socialist alone, nor anti-capitalist alone, it is both. In the final analysis its political slogan becomes "a plague on both your houses." If Weber is to be regarded as an "ideologist," he is an ideologist not of counter-revolution but of quiescence and neutralism. For many intellectuals who have erected a theory of group organization on Weberian foundations, the world has been emptied of choice, leaving them disoriented and despairing.

That gifted historian of ideas, Arthur O. Lovejoy, astutely observed that every theory is associated with, or generates, a set of sentiments which those subscribing to the theory could only dimly sense. Lovejoy called this the "metaphysical pathos" of ideas, a pathos which is "exemplified in any description of the nature of things, any characterization of the world to which one belongs, in terms which, like the words of a poem, evoke through their associations and through a sort of empathy which they engender, a congenial mood or tone of feelings." [5]

As a result, a commitment to a theory often occurs by a process other than the one which its proponents believe and it is usually more consequential than they realize. A commitment to a theory may be made because the theory is congruent with the mood or deep-lying sentiments of its adherents, rather than merely because it has been cerebrally inspected and found valid. This is as true for the rigorous prose of social science as it is for the more lucid metaphor of creative literature, for each has its own silent appeal and its own metaphysical pathos.

Furthermore, those who have committed themselves to a theory always get more than they have bargained for. We do not make a commercial contract with a theory in which we agree to accept only the consignment of intellectual goods which has been expressly ordered; usually we take also the metaphysical pathos in which the theory comes packaged. In the end, the theory reinforces or induces in the adherent a subtle alteration in the structure of sentiments through which he views the world.

So too is it with the theory of organization. Paradoxically enough, some of the very theories which promise to make man's own work more intelligible to himself and more amenable to his intelligence are infused with an intangible metaphysical pathos which insinuates, in the very midst of new discoveries, that all is lost. For the metaphysical pathos of much of the modern theory of group organization is that of pessimism and fatalism.

I. EXPLANATIONS OF BUREAUCRACY

Nowhere does the fatalism of the theory of organization become more articulate than in its efforts to account for the development of bureaucratic behavior. One of the less challenging explanations, for example, premises a supposedly invariant human nature. Thus in an otherwise illuminating analysis, one

5. Arthur O. Lovejoy, *The Great Chain of Being* (Cambridge, Mass., 1948), p. 11.

political scientist remarks: "Civil servants are ordinary mortals; they have the defects and weaknesses typical of human nature. Each loves, as Shakespeare said, 'his brief moment of authority.'"

This, however, is difficult to reconcile with recurrent complaints, from civic leaders or business managers, that it is often hard to persuade people either to run for political office or to accept positions as foremen. Apparently there are some people who do not hanker after their brief moment of authority.

In any event, it does not seem possible to account for bureaucracy in any of its forms as an outgrowth of "human nature." This explanation cannot cope with the rudimentary fact that in some times and in some places there is much bureaucracy, but in other times and places there is little. Leaving aside the question of the validity of the argument, its practical results are again all too evident. For if bureaucracy is rooted in human nature then all hope for a remedy must be abandoned.

Much more serious as goads to pessimism are theories explaining bureaucracy as the end-product of increased size and complexity in organizations. This is by far the most popular of the interpretations. Marshall Dimock and Howard Hyde, for example, in their report to the Temporary National Economic Committee (TNEC), state: "The broadest structural cause of bureaucracy, whether in business or in government, is the tremendous size of the organization. Thus with capital or appropriations measured in hundreds of millions and in billions of dollars and personnel in tens and hundreds of thousands, it is difficult to avoid the obtrusion of the objectionable features of bureaucracy." [6]

While suggesting varied causes for the development of bureaucracy, Max Weber also interpreted it as a consequence of large size. For example, in discussing the ubiquity of bureaucratic forms Weber adds: "The same [bureaucratic] phenomena are found in the large-scale capitalistic enterprise; and the larger it is, the greater their role." He underscores the role of size by emphasizing that "only by reversion in every field—political, religious, economic, etc.—to small-scale organization would it be possible to escape its influence." [7] Despite his consideration of other possible sources of bureaucracy, these comments suggest that Weber regarded organizational size as the controlling factor in the development of bureaucracy.*

Weber's emphasis on size as the crucial determinant of bureaucratic development is unsatisfactory for several reasons. First, there are historic examples

---

* [Ed. Note: It should be mentioned that Weber can also be read as a kind of Social Darwinian, contending that bureaucracy more and more holds sway because of its greater efficiency by comparison with alternative modes of organization. Consequently, those who pursue their aims bureaucratically tend to prevail in the never-ending social, economic, and political competition for survival. By the same token, it may be inferred, resourceful leaders of threatened organizations turn to bureaucratization as a highly useful tactic.]

6. Monograph #11, Temporary National Economic Committee, *Bureaucracy and Trusteeship in Large Corporations* (Washington, D.C., 1940), p. 36.

7. *Max Weber: The Theory of Social and Economic Organization*, translated and edited by A.M. Henderson and Talcott Parsons (New York, 1947), pp. 334, 338.

of human efforts carried out on an enormous scale which were not bureaucratic in any serious sense of the term. The building of the Egyptian pyramids is an obvious example. Second, Weber never considers the possibility that it is not "large size" as such that disposes to bureaucracy; large size may be important only because it generates other social forces which, in their turn, generate bureaucratic patterns.

Of course, in every analysis there are always intervening variables—the unknown "x"—which stand between any cause and effect. Scientific progress depends, in part, on moving away from the gross causes and coming closer to those which are more invariably connected with the object of interest. The point is that when a social scientist accepts "size" as an explanatory factor, instead of going on to ask what there is *about size* that makes for bureaucracy, he is making an analytic *decision*. It is not a formulation unavoidably dictated by the nature of the data itself.

Significantly, though, it is a decision that leads once again to bleak pessimism. For to inform members of our society that the only way out of the bureaucratic impasse is to return to the historical past and to trade in large for small-scale organizations is, in effect, to announce the practical impossibility of coping with bureaucracy. Moreover, many people in our society believe that "bigness" symbolizes progress; to tell them that it also creates bureaucracy is to place them on the horns of a dilemma which gores no matter which way they turn. In such a position the most painless response is inaction.

Underlying this conception of the matter there is a Hegelian dialectic in which "good" and "bad" are viewed as inseparably connected opposites; bureaucracy, "the bad thing," is represented as the inescapable price that has to be paid for the good things, the efficiency and abundance of modern life. One social scientist clearly puts it this way: "Assembly line techniques offer marked advantages over those of custom craftsmanship. They also have their price. They entail the imposition of an order of progression, the fixing of a rate or rhythm of operation, and the discipline of a regular routine. Set order, fixed pace, and adherence to routine—these are the very stuff of which red tape is made. Yet they are of the essence of system, too." However true or false, there can be little doubt that this is an outlook which is convenient and comfortable for bureaucrats—if not for many others.

II. THE STRUCTURAL-FUNCTIONALISTS

The fuller ramifications of this approach to bureaucracy can best be explained by turning to the analyses of industrial organization made by some of the "structural-functionalists." This is a comparatively new and vigorous school of American sociologists, which has grown directly out of the theories of Durkheim, Weber, and others, and whose most elaborate expression is to be found in the work of Talcott Parsons.

Parsons' recent analyses of industrial bureaucracy are of sufficient importance to be quoted in full. "Though with many individual exceptions [which he does not examine], *technological advance* almost always leads to increasingly *elaborate division of labor* and the concomitant requirement of increasingly elaborate organization." He continues:

> The fundamental reason for this is, of course, that with elaborate differentiation of functions the need for *minute coordination* of the different functions develops at the same time. . . . There must be a *complex organization of supervision* to make quite sure that exactly the right thing is done. . . . Feeding the various parts into the process, in such a way that a modern assembly line can operate smoothly, requires very *complex organization* to see that they are available in just the right quantities at the right times and places. . . . One of the most important phases of this process of change is concerned with the necessity for *formalization* when certain points of complexity are reached. . . .
>
> *Smaller* and simpler organizations are typically managed with a high degree of particularism (i.e., personal consideration) in the relations of persons in authority to their own subordinates. But when the "distance" between points of decision and of operation increases, and the number of operating units affected by decisions with it, uniformity and coordination can be attained *only* by a high degree of formalization. . . .[8]

Surprisingly enough, this is an atavistic recurrence of technological determinism in which characteristic bureaucratic traits—such as an elaborate division of labor, complex organization, and formalization—are held to stem directly from technological advance. This is a form of *technological* determinism because bureaucracy is seen as the result of technological change, without inquiring into the motives and meanings which these changes have for the people involved, and without wondering whether technological change would have a different impact on the formal organization of a group that had a high motivation to produce and therefore did not require close supervision. This is a form of technological *determinism,* because no alternative solutions are appraised or deemed possible and coordination is seen as attainable *"only* by a high degree of formalization. . . ."

Here once again we are invited to draw the conclusion that those who want modern technology must be prepared to pay for it with a minute and even stultifying division of labor.

All this, though, is a theoretical tapestry devoid of even the plainest empirical trimmings. Even on logical grounds, however, it is tenuous indeed. For it is evident that organizational patterns, such as a high division of labor, are found in spheres where modern technology has made comparatively little headway. This, in fact, is a point that Weber was at pains to insist upon. And if, as he maintained, bureaucratic forms are also found in charitable, political, or religious organizations—and not solely in industry—then they certainly cannot be explained as a consequence of modern machine technology.

Beyond these logical considerations, there are also some *empirical* grounds for questioning the adequacy of Parsons' analysis. Peter Drucker, for example, became extremely doubtful about the necessity of a minute division of labor

8. Talcott Parsons, *The Social System* (Glencoe, Illinois, 1951), pp. 507–8. Italics added.

while observing large-scale American industry during World War II. (This is crucial for Parsons' argument, because he holds that it is through increased specialization that technology evokes the other elements of bureaucratic organization.) Drucker comments that "we have learned that it is neither necessary nor always efficient to organize all mass production in such a manner as to have the majority of workers confine themselves to doing one and only one of the elementary manipulations. . . . It was impossible [because of wartime shortages of skilled labor] to 'lay out' the job in the usual assembly-line fashion in which one unskilled operation done by one unskilled man is followed by the next unskilled man. The operation was broken down into its unskilled components like any assembly-line job. *But then the unskilled components were put together again with the result that an unskilled worker actually performed the job of a highly skilled mechanic*—and did it as reliably and efficiently as had been done by skilled men." [9]

In short, lower degrees of specialization than those normally found in large-scale industry are not necessarily forbidden by modern technology. Drucker's observations must, at the very least, raise the question as to how much of the minute division of labor is attributable to technological causes. Parsons, though, gives no consideration to other factors contributing to an extreme division of labor. However, Carl Dreyfuss, a German industrial sociologist, has advanced an array of keen observations and hypotheses which meet this question directly. He writes: "the artificial complication of the rank order . . . permits numerous employees to feel that they hold high positions and are to a certain extent independent." Moreover, he notes that a complicated division of labor is "with its unwarranted differentiations, telescoped positions, and ramifications, diametrically opposed to efforts of rationalization." In other words, Dreyfuss suggests that much of the complex division of labor today is not to be explained by technological requirements, but rather in terms of the prestige satisfactions, the "psychic income," that it presumably provides workers.

In Dreyfuss' view, the "minute division of labor" also stems from management's needs to *control* workers and to make themselves independent of any specific individual or group of workers. A high division of labor, said Dreyfuss, means that "individual workers and employees can be exchanged and replaced at any time." Through its use, "dependence of the employee upon the employer is greatly increased. It is much more difficult for today's employee, trained in only one particular function, to find reemployment than it was for his predecessor, a many-sided, well-instructed business man, able and fitted to fill a variety of positions." [10]

A similar view is advanced in the more recent studies of industrial organization in Yankee City, which were made by W. L. Warner and J. O. Low. "While machine processes were adopted by shoe factories primarily to reduce costs and to speed the processing, the machine has other great advantages over

9. Peter Drucker, *Concept of the Corporation* (New York, 1946), pp. 183–84.
10. Carl Dreyfuss, *Occupation and Ideology of the Salaried Employee,* trans. Eva Abramovitch (New York, 1938), p. 17, 75, 77.

the human worker from the managerial point of view," comment Warner and Low.

> Control problems are simplified . . . on two counts through mechanization: (1) machines are easier to control than human beings, and (2) mechanization tends to disrupt the social solidarity of the workers, who thereby become easier to control than they would if they were able to maintain close social relations during working hours . . . these factors tend to increase the subordination of the individual worker to management; from the management's viewpoint they are valuable means of social control over workers. . . . The routinization of jobs also simplifies control of workers in another way. The individual operative today does not have the feeling of security that the oldtime craftsman derived from his special technical abilities. In most cases, today's operative is aware that only a comparatively brief training period protects him in his job from a large number of untrained individuals. The members of the supervisory hierarchy are also well aware of this fact. The psychological effect of this result of the division of labor is to intensify the subordinate position of the individual operative and to make him submit the more readily to the limitations on his behavior required by the supervisory group.[11]

It is unnecessary for our purpose here to resolve this disparity between Warner and Dreyfuss, on the one hand, and Parsons, on the other. What may be suggested, however, is that there is considerable reason for holding Parsons' position to be both logically and empirically inadequate and to recognize that it has, without compelling scientific warrant, accommodated itself to the metaphysical pathos of organizational theory, which sees no escape from bureaucracy.

III. THE TRADITION OF MICHELS

There is another offshoot among the structural-functionalists which is distinguished by its concern for the problems bequeathed by Robert Michels and, as such, it is even more morosely pessimistic than others in the school. Michels, it will be remembered, focussed his empirical studies on the Social Democratic parties of pre-World War I Europe. He chose these, quite deliberately, because he wanted to see whether groups which stood for greater freedom and democracy, and were hostile to authoritarianism, were not themselves afflicted by the very organizational deformity to which they were opposed.

Michel's conclusions were, of course, formulated in his "iron law of oligarchy," in which he maintained that always and everywhere a "system of leadership is incompatible with the most essential postulates of democracy." Oligarchy, said Michels, "derives from the tactical and technical necessities which result from the consolidation of every disciplined political aggregate. . . . It is the outcome of organic necessity, and consequently affects every organization, be it socialist or even anarchist."

In concluding his study, Michels remarks with a flourish of defensive

---

11. W. Lloyd Warner and J. O. Low, *The Social System of the Modern Factory* (New Haven, 1947), pp. 78, 80, 174.

pathos, ". . . it seemed necessary to lay considerable stress upon the pessimist aspect of democracy which is forced upon us by historical study. . . ." "The democratic currents of history resemble successive waves. They break ever on the same shoals. . . . It is probable that this cruel game will continue without end." [12]

Focussing, as Michels did, on an apparently democratic group, Philip Selznick examined the TVA, which many Americans had long believed to be an advanced expression of democratic values. Like Michels, Selznick assumes that "wherever there is organization, whether formally democratic or not, there is a split between the leader and the led, between the agent and the initiator. The phenomenon of abdication to bureaucratic directives in corporations, in trade unions, in parties, and in cooperatives is so widespread that it indicates a fundamental weakness of democracy."

Selznick's study concludes that the TVA's emphasis on "decentralization" is to be best understood as a result of that agency's needs to adapt to suspicious local communities and to survive in competition with older governmental agencies based in Washington. "Decentralization" is viewed as a "halo that becomes especially useful in countries which prize the symbols of democracy." In its turn, the TVA's emphasis on "participation" is explained as a catchword, satisfying the agency's needs to transform "an unorganized citizenry into a reliable instrument for the achievement of administrative goals. . . ."

Selznick, like Michels, is impressed with the similarity in the organizational devices employed by different groups, whether they are democratic or authoritarian in ideology. He asserts ". . . there seems to be a continuum between the voluntary associations set up by the democratic (mass) state—such as committees of farmers to boost or control agricultural production—and the citizens' associations of the totalitarian (mass) state. Indeed the devices of corporatism emerge as relatively effective responses to the need to deal with the mass, and in time of war the administrative techniques of avowedly democratic countries and avowedly totalitarian countries tend to converge."

In Selznick's analysis human action involves a commitment to two sets of interests: first to the *goals* intended, and second to the organizational *instruments* through which these goals are pursued. These tools are, however, recalcitrant; they generate "needs" which cannot be neglected. Hence if men persist in their ends, they are forced to satisfy the needs of their organizational instruments. They are, therefore, as much committed to their tools as to their ends, and "these commitments may lead to unanticipated consequences resulting in a deflection of original ends."

For these reasons, organizational behavior must be interpreted not so much in terms of the *ends* that administrators deliberately seek, as in terms of the organizational "needs" which their pursuit engenders. "The needs in question are organizational, not individual, and include: the security of the organization as a whole in relation to social forces in its environment; the stability of

12. Robert Michels, *Political Parties* (Glencoe, Ill., 1949), p. 400. Michel's work was first published in 1915, pp. 401, 402, 405, 408.

the lines of authority and communication; the stability of informal relations within the organization; the continuity of policy and of the sources of its determination; a homogeneity of outlook with respect to the means and role of the organization."

"In general," writes Selznick, "we have been concerned to formulate some of the underlying tendencies which are likely to inhibit the democratic process. Like all conservative or pessimistic criticism, such a statement of inherent problems seems to cast doubt upon the possibility of complete democratic achievement. It does cast such a doubt. The alternative, however, is the transformation of democracy into a utopian notion which, unaware of its internal dangers, is unarmed to meet them." This, however, is an argument that rests upon assumptions which are not transparently self-evident and are acceptable without dispute only by those who are susceptible to its metaphysical pathos. Despite demagogic appeals to democratic symbols, there seem to be few places in either the Eastern or Western worlds in which there is a real and present danger of the "transformation of democracy into a utopian notion." Surely this is not to be expected among the class-conscious working classes of Europe, the laborite masses of England, the untutored peasants of China, or among the confused and often apathetic American electorate to whom politics is something of a dirty game, to be periodically enlivened with scandals and investigations. And if this appraisal is correct, then just who is there to be "armed" with this knowledge of the internal dangers of democracy?

For some reason Selznick has chosen—and this was not forced upon him by the data—to focus on the things which harry and impede democratic aspirations, rather than on those which strengthen and energize it. It is for this reason perhaps that he is led to reiterate Michel's apologia: "Attention being focussed on the structural conditions which influence behavior, we are directed to emphasize constraints, the limitation of alternatives imposed by the system upon its participants. This will tend to give pessimistic overtones to the analysis, since such factors as good will and intelligence will be de-emphasized."[13]

Selznick chose to focus on those social constraints that *thwart* democratic aspirations, but neglected to consider the constraints that enable them to be *realized,* and that foster and encourage "good will" and "intelligence." Are these, however, random occurrences, mere historic butterflies which flit through events with only ephemeral beauty? Or are they, as much as anything else, often the unanticipated products of our "commitments"? Why is it that "unanticipated consequences" are always tacitly assumed to be destructive of democratic values and "bad"; why can't they sometimes be "good"? Are there no constraints which *force* men to adhere valorously to their democratic beliefs, which *compel* them to be intelligent rather than blind, which leave them *no choice* but to be men of good will rather than predators? The neglect of these possibilities suggests the presence of a distorting pathos.

It is the pathos of pessimism, rather than the compulsions of rigorous analysis, that lead to the assumption that organizational constraints have stacked

13. Philip Selznick, *TVA and the Grass Roots* (Berkeley and Los Angeles, 1949), pp. 9, 220, 252, 259, 265.

the deck against democracy. For on the face of it there is every reason to assume that "the underlying tendencies which are likely to inhibit the democratic process" are just as likely to impair authoritarian rule. It is only in the light of such a pessimistic pathos that the defeat of democratic values can be assumed to be probable, while their victory is seen as a slender thing, delicately constituted and precariously balanced.

When, for example, Michels spoke of the "iron law of oligarchy," he attended solely to the ways in which organizational needs inhibit democratic possibilities. But the very same evidence to which he called attention could enable us to formulate the very opposite theorem—the "iron law of democracy." Even as Michels himself saw, if oligarchical waves repeatedly wash away the bridges of democracy, this eternal recurrence can happen only because men doggedly rebuild them after each inundation. Michels chose to dwell on only one aspect of this process, neglecting to consider this other side. There cannot be an iron law of oligarchy, however, unless there is an iron law of democracy.

Much the same may be said for Selznick. He posits certain organizational needs: a need for the *security* of the organization, for *stable* lines of authority and communication, for *stable* informal relationships. But for each of the organizational needs which Selznick postulates, a set of contrary needs can also be posited, and the satisfaction of these would seem to be just as necessary for the survival of an organization. If, as Selznick says, an organization must have security in its environment, then certainly Toynbee's observations that too much security can be stultifying and corrosive is at least as well taken. To Selznick's security need, a Toynbee might counterpose a need for a moderate *challenge* or *threat*.

A similar analysis might also be made of Selznick's postulated need for homogeneity of outlook concerning the means and role of the organization. For unless there is some *heterogeneity* of outlook, then where is an organization to find the tools and flexibility to cope with changes in its environment? Underlying Selznick's need for homogeneity in outlook, is there not another "need," *a need that consent of the governed be given—at least in some measure—to their governors?* Indeed, this would seem to be at the very core of Selznick's empirical analysis, though it is obscured in his high-level theoretical statement of the needs of organizations. And if all organizations must adjust to such a need for consent, is there not built into the very marrow of organization a large element of what we mean by democracy? This would appear to be an organizational constraint that makes oligarchies, and all separation of leaders from those led, no less inherently unstable than democratic organization.[14]

14. See Arthur Schweitzer, "Ideological Groups," *American Sociological Review,* Vol. 9, pp. 415–27 (Aug., 1944), particularly his discussion of factors inhibiting oligarchy. For example, "A leadership concentrating all power in its hands creates indifference among the functionaries and sympathizers as well as decline in membership of the organization. This process of shrinkage, endangering the position of the leaders, is the best protection against the supposedly inevitable iron law of oligarchy" (p. 419). Much of the research deriving from the Lewinian tradition would seem to lend credence to this inference.

These contrary needs are just as real and just as consequential for organizational behavior as those proposed by Selznick. But they point in a different direction. They are oriented to problems of change, of growth, of challenging contingencies, of provoking and unsettling encounters. Selznick's analysis seems almost to imply that survival is possible only in an icy stasis, in which "security," "continuity," and "stability" are the key terms. If anything, the opposite seems more likely to be true, and organizational survival is impossible in such a state.

Wrapping themselves in the shrouds of nineteenth-century political economy, some social scientists appear to be bent on resurrecting a dismal science. For the iron law of wages, which maintained that workers could never improve their material standards of life, some sociologists have substituted the iron law of oligarchy, which declares that men cannot improve their political standards of life. Woven to a great extent out of theoretical whole cloth, much of the discussion of bureaucracy and of organizational needs seems to have provided a screen onto which some intellectuals have projected their own despair and pessimism, reinforcing the despair of others.

Perhaps the situation can be illuminated with an analogy. For many years now, infantile paralysis has killed and maimed scores of people. For many years also doctors, biologists, and chemists have been searching for the causes and cure of this disease. Consider the public reaction if, instead of reporting on their newest vaccines, these scientists had issued the following announcement: "We have not reached any conclusions concerning the causes of the disease, nor has our research investigated defenses against it. The public seems to have perfectionist aspirations of flawless health, they have 'utopian' illusions concerning the possibilities of immortality and it is this—not the disease—that is the danger against which the public needs to be armed. We must remember that the human animal is not immortal and that for definite reasons his lifespan is finite." It is likely, of course, that such scientists would be castigated for having usurped the prerogatives and functions of clergymen.

This, however, seems to parallel the way in which some social scientists have approached the study of organizational pathology. Instead of telling men how bureaucracy might be mitigated, they insist that it is inevitable. Instead of explaining how democratic patterns may, to some extent, be fortified and extended, they warn us that democracy cannot be perfect. Instead of controlling the disease, they suggest that we are deluded, or more politely, incurably romantic, for hoping to control it. Instead of assuming responsibilities as realistic clinicians, striving to further democratic potentialities wherever they can, many social scientists have become morticians, all too eager to bury men's hopes.

BUREAUCRACY AND CONSTITUTIONALISM *
Norton E. Long

THERE is an old aphorism that fire is a good servant but a bad master. Something like this aphorism is frequently applied to the appropriate role of the bureaucracy in government. Because bureaucracy is often viewed as tainted with an ineradicable lust for power, it is alleged that, like fire, it needs constant control to prevent its erupting from beneficent servitude into dangerous and tyrannical mastery.

The folklore of constitutional theory relegates the bureaucracy to somewhat the same low but necessary estate as Plato does the appetitive element of the soul. In the conventional dichotomy between policy and administration, administration is the Aristotelian slave, properly an instrument of action for the will of another, capable of receiving the commands of reason but incapable of reasoning. The amoral concept of administrative neutrality is the natural complement of the concept of bureaucracy as instrument; for according to this view the seat of reason and conscience resides in the legislature, whatever grudging concession may be made to the claims of the political executive, and a major, if not the major, task of constitutionalism is the maintenance of the supremacy of the legislature over the bureaucracy. The latter's sole constitutional role is one of neutral docility to the wishes of the day's legislative majority.

The source of this doctrine is found in part in a reading of English constitutional history and in part in the political metaphysics of John Locke. The drama of English constitutional development may be seen as first the concentration of power in the Norman kings, with the suppression of feudal anarchy, and then the gradual attainment of parliamentary supremacy. Because the bureaucracy was created by the kings as an instrument of national unification, it became identified with them and was envisaged as a monarchical rather than a popular element, and one which required control. At a later date the class monopoly of the upper hierarchy of the civil service reinforced liberal suspicions of the bureaucracy, and it seemed especially clear that the most bureaucratic part of the bureaucracy, the military, had to be placed firmly under civilian, i.e., legislative, control.

John Locke, writing the apologia for the Glorious Revolution and its ac-

* From the *American Political Science Review*, Vol. 46 (September 1952), pp. 808–818. Reprinted by permission of the author and publisher.

companying shift in political power, held that "there can be but one supreme power, which is the legislative, to which all the rest are and must be subordinate. . . ." To be sure, Locke conceived of the legislature only as the fiduciary of the people, from whom all legitimate power ultimately stemmed. But since the legislature was considered the authentic voice of the people changeable only by revolution, this limitation could be forgotten in practice. Despite Locke's qualifications, the latter-day exponents of his views have given currency to what Jackson called the "absurd doctrine that the legislature is the people." Professor Charles Hyneman, accepting the majority will metaphysics of Willmoore Kendall, has ably expounded the consequence of that point of view in his recent *Bureaucracy in a Democracy*. It is his position that in a democracy the people should get what they want, and that what the legislature wants is the best approximation of what the people want; ergo, we should fashion our institutions for legislative supremacy, at least with respect to the bureaucracy.[1] Acceptance of the principle of legislative supremacy by practicing administrators is, of course, more a counsel of expediency than an article of faith. It pays for the administrator to call Congress our board of directors, whatever his private conviction may be.

Unfortunately for the simplicity of the theory that democracy means giving the people what they want and that this means giving the legislature what it wants, the legislature is divided into two branches and the President is an independently elected official. In case of conflict between any or all of these, who should be supreme as the authentic representative of what the people want? Professor Hyneman has his uneasy moments between President and legislature. Realism compels some doubts as to the validity of the voice of congressional committees, and closer examination bogs the theory down in exceptions and qualifications. . . .

Dissatisfaction with the view of bureaucracy as instrument and Caliban has grown among students of government as first-hand experience in government and historical research have undermined accepted dogma. Professor C. J. Friedrich has pointed to the beneficent role of bureaucracy as the core of modern government. Dr. Fritz Morstein Marx has described the vital role of the Prussian bureaucracy in developing the *Rechtsstaat*. The studies of Pendleton Herring, John M. Gaus and Leon O. Wolcott, Arthur W. MacMahon and John D. Millett have illustrated the genuinely representative part played by the bureaucracy in American government. And in a widely used text Professor J. A. Corry has not hesitated to refer to administration as the mainspring of government and to the administrative, as distinguished from the political, executive as a fourth branch of government. An assessment of the vital role of bureaucracy in the working American constitution seems to be overdue.

The most ardent advocate of legislative supremacy can no longer blink the fact of administrative discretion and even administrative legislation. Nor does any one seriously suppose that the clock can be turned back. Improvement there may be in the capacity and willingness of the legislature to exercise gen-

1. See Part 1 of *Bureaucracy in a Democracy* (New York, 1950).

eral policy superintendence, but anything approaching the conditions necessary to achieve a separation of policy from administration is highly doubtful. The bureaucracy is in policy, and major policy, to stay; in fact, barring the unlikely development of strong majority party legislative leadership, the bureaucracy is likely, day in and day out, to be our main source of policy initiative. The role of the legislature and of the political executive may come to consist largely of encouraging, discouraging and passing on policy which wells up from the agencies of administration. All of this is because the bureaucracy is not just an instrument to carry out a will formed by the elected Congress and President. It is itself a medium for registering the diverse wills that make up the people's will and for transmuting them into responsible proposals for public policy.

Growth in the power of the bureaucracy is looked upon as a menace to constitutionalism. By some it is seen as a dangerous enhancement of the power of the President, by others as an alarming accretion of power to a non-elective part of the government. The logic of *either-or* sees a cumulative process in which the supremacy of the elected legislative is replaced by the supremacy of an appointed bureaucracy. Given the alternative, the choice of the supremacy of an elected legislature would be clear, but that choice is an unreal bogy. To meet our needs, we have worked out a complex system in which the bureaucracy and legislature perform complementary and interlocking functions. Both are necessary, and the supremacy of either would be a constitutional misfortune. We sometimes forget that the authors of the *Federalist* and Jefferson alike were aware of the danger of legislative tyranny.

Professor Friedrich and others have argued that the essence of constitutionalism is the division of power in such a way as to provide a system of effective regularized restraints upon governmental action. The purpose of this division of power is not to create some mechanical equipoise among the organs of government but so to represent the diversity of the community that its own pluralism is reflected in a pluralism within the government. As Mosca has well said, "the only demand that is important, and possible, to make of a political system is that all social values shall have a part in it, and that it shall find a place for all who possess any of the qualities which determine what prestige and what influence an individual, or a class, is to have." Now it is extremely clear that our Congress fails to do this and that the bureaucracy in considerable measure compensates for its deficiency. Important and vital interests in the United States are unrepresented, underrepresented, or malrepresented in Congress. These interests receive more effective and more responsible representation through administrative channels than through the legislature.

In considerable part this is due to the nature of the presidency and its constituency. Responsible behavior in the sense of sensitivity to long-range and broad considerations, the totality of interests affected, and the utilization of expert knowledge by procedures that ensure a systematic collection and analysis of relevant facts, is more characteristic of the executive than of Congress. Despite the exceptions, and there are many, this kind of responsible behavior is more expected, more politically feasible, and more frequently practiced in the administrative branch. The bureaucracy headed by the presidency is both compelled and encouraged to respond to, and even to assist in the development of broad publics (e.g., the public for Ewing's Health Insurance Program); but broad publics seldom emanate from the organization and the geographic concentration necessary for effectiveness in the congressional committee process. The public's conception of the President as national leader creates an expectation as to his role that differs markedly from any stereotype of Congress or Congressman. This general conception of the presidency not only imposes itself on the incumbent of the office, enforcing a degree of responsibility for playing a national part, but also provides the political means for its performance by organizing a nationwide public. As one President has remarked, the presidency is the best pulpit in the land. It has a nation for its congregation. But what is important here is the expectation that the President should offer a national and party program which provides a degree of synthesis for the agencies of administration. Imperfectly effective as are the organs of coordination—Cabinet, Bureau of the Budget, National Security Council, interDepartmental committees, and the rest—they are far more effective at ensuring integration than is even the well-disciplined House Appropriations Committee, with its stubbornly fragmented procedures.

In addition to the broader constituency represented by the presidency and the national concern imposed by this office on the subordinate agencies of administration, there is another factor to account for the vital role of these agencies in supplementing congressional representation. It is simply that the shield of presidential power permits the development of the agencies of administration into institutions to mediate between the narrow and the broad interests at work in the subject matter of their concern. The presidency provides a balancing power that permits and sustains a perspective which the overwhelming concentration of narrow interests in the congressional subject matter committee makes difficult in the legislative process. Representation of consumer interests in the Bureau of Agricultural Economics, for example, depends upon presidential protection. Under this same shelter, agencies may develop organizational codes, stereotyped in public expectations, that permit the continuance of broader representation and encourage responsibility in the range and manner in which problems are considered and solutions sought.

To the modern student of government, Aristotle's characterization of an election as an oligarchical device always comes somewhat as a shock. Nonetheless, its implications for representative democracy are significant. If one were to set forth in law the facts of life of the American Congress, it would appear that, to be eligible, overwhelmingly a candidate had first to be in the upper upper-income bracket or second, either personally or through his associates, to be able to command substantial sums of money. Expressed as custom, such conditions are passed over save for the carping criticism of Marxists; yet if they were expressed in law, they would clearly characterize our constitution as oligarchic.

While the Jacksonian conception of the civil service as a domain for the common man was not expressly designed as a balance to the inevitably oligarchical aspects of an elected legislature, it has been influential in that direction. Accustomed as we are to the identification of election with both representation and democracy, it seems strange at first to consider that the non-elected civil service may be both more representative of the country and more democratic in its composition than the Congress.

As it operates in the civil service, the recruitment process brings into federal employment and positions of national power, persons whose previous affiliations, training, and background cause them to conceive of themselves as representing constituencies that are relatively uninfluential in Congress. These constituencies, like that of the presidency, are in the aggregate numerically very large; and in speaking for them as self-appointed, or frequently actually appointed, representatives, the bureaucrats fill in the deficiencies of the process of representation in the legislature. The importance of this representation lies not only in offsetting such defects as rural overrepresentation, the self-contained district, and other vagaries of our system of nominations that leave many without a voice, but in the qualitative representation of science, the professions, the institutions of learning, and the conscience of society as it is expressed in churches, civil liberties groups, and a host of others.

The democratic character of the civil service stems from its origin, income level, and associations. The process of selection of the civil service, its contacts, milieu, and income level after induction make the civil service as a body a better sample of the mass of the people than Congress. Lacking a caste system to wall them off from their fellows, the members of this sample are likely to be more responsive to the desires and needs of the broad public than a highly selected slice whose responsiveness is enforced by a mechanism of elections that frequently places more power in the hands of campaign-backers than voters. Furthermore, it is unlikely that any overhauling of our system of representation in Congress will remove the need for supplementary representation through the bureaucracy. The working interaction of President, Congress, courts, and the administrative branch makes the constitutional system a going concern—not the legal supremacy of any one of them.

Given the seemingly inevitable growth in the power of the bureaucracy through administrative discretion and administrative law, it is of critical importance that the bureaucracy be both representative and democratic in composition and ethos. Its internal structuring may be as important for constitutional functioning as any theoretical or practicable legislative supremacy. That wonder of modern times, the standing army possessed of a near-monopoly of force yet tamely obedient to the civil power, is a prime example of the efficacy of a balance of social forces as a means to neutralization as a political force. A similar representation of the pluralism of our society in the vitals of the bureaucracy insures its constitutional behavior and political equilibrium.

It is not by any means sure that the people think that what they want is the same as what Congress wants. In fact, there is considerable evidence that the ordinary man views Congressmen, if not Congress as an institution, with considerable skepticism. The retort that the people elected the Congress falls somewhat wide of the mark. Given the system of parties and primaries, rural overrepresentation, seniority rule, interest-dominated committees, and all the devices that give potent minorities a disproportionate say, it should occasion no surprise if Congress' claim exclusively to voice what the people want be taken with reservations.[2] Skepticism of the exclusiveness of the claim, however, is no warrant for denying the vital contribution of the representative legislature to the maintenance of constitutionalism. Without it bureaucratic absolutism would be well-nigh unavoidable.

If one rejects the view that election is the *sine qua non* of representation, the bureaucracy now has a very real claim to be considered much more representative of the American people in its composition than the Congress. This is not merely the case with respect to the class structure of the country but, equally significantly, with respect to the learned groups, skills, economic interests, races, nationalities, and religions. The rich diversity that makes up the United States is better represented in its civil service than anywhere else.

While it has distressed those who see in the bureaucracy merely an efficient instrument for executing policy framed elsewhere, its persistent refusal to block the path of the common man by educational qualifications beyond the reach of the poor has made the civil service a democratic *carrière ouverte aux talentes*. Like Napoleon's soldiers, the humble clerk carries a marshals' baton in his knapsack. And the open avenue of opportunity in the government has meant much in providing substance to the forms of democracy. At a time when administration has become a towering fact, the significance of our recruitment process for a democratic and representative bureaucracy overshadows an academic preoccupation with the objective of a merely technical proficiency. One has only to consider seriously the role of bureaucracy as formulator of the bulk of the policy alternatives for legislature and political executive alike—as rule-maker-in-chief—to recognize that representativeness must be a prime consideration in the recruitment process.

It can hardly be denied that, despite the attempt to achieve it by the recruitment process, representativeness in the agencies of government is seriously inadequate. The capture of commissions such as the I.C.C. by the regulated interests has often been charged, not without persuasive evidence. In his pioneering work, *Public Administration and the Public Interest,* Pendleton Herring has documented the problem. Yet however crassly one-sided an agency of government may become, few indeed will be found so completely under the dominance of a single interest as the subject matter committees of Congress.

2. Hyneman is aware of these misgivings; "If there is widespread and serious doubt that Congress can make the major decisions—including the decision as to what authority the President shall have—in a way that the American people as a whole will find acceptable, then we had better get busy with the improvement of our political organization, our electoral system, and the organization of Congress so that the grounds for such doubt will be removed" (*op. cit.,* p. 217). [James MacGregor] Burns and others have pointed out the road blocks in the way of such reform. Compensation for congressional deficiencies through the presidency and bureaucracy seems the normal course of our development. Had Professor Hyneman considered the possibilities of moral restraints, . . . this road might not have seemed so perilous.

And those that are so dominated have a bad conscience not shared by their brethren on the Hill.

The Department of Agriculture is probably as clearly a clientele department as any in the United States government. Nevertheless, it compares most favorably with the Senate and House Agricultural Committees in the breadth of its conception of the public interest. (In point of fact, the luckless Bureau of Agriculture Economics incurred congressional wrath for daring to act on the assumption that it had a responsibility to the consumer.) As mediator, moderator, and synthesizer of the raw demands of the agricultural pressure groups, the Department works to attain a feasible national farm policy in a context of political and group demands. The structure of the Department in itself ensures some consideration of the many aspects of the nation's agriculture in the formation and formulation of policy alternatives. Agronomists, soil chemists, nutritionists, economists, market analysts, and a host of others organized in bureaus and divisions bring together and into focus the elements necessary for responsible decisions. The point of view of personnel trained to think of a national economy and to utilize a scientific outlook is a needed counterpoise to the immediacy of political demands and the narrowness of pressure group perspective. In addition, the very permanence of the Department and the comparative permanence of many of its personnel provide a range of vision that at least partially transcends the headlines of the moment. Of course, it is true that sometimes, as in the Forest Service, the interest of the Department seems to be a bureaucratic contemplation of its own navel. Still the Department institutionalizes, however inadequately in its bad moments, the long view and the broad look on the nation's agricultural problems. While occasional Congressmen and occasional pressure groups also may take the long view, in the main such behavior is exceptional and little reliance can be placed on it.

Responsibility is a product of responsible institutions; and with all their deficiencies—which are many indeed—the departments of administration come closer than any other organs of government to achieving responsible behavior by virtue of the breadth and depth of their consideration of the relevant facts and because of the representative character of their personnel. As continuing organizations, they can learn from their mistakes. They can even make their mistakes meaningful. That is, they can make explicit to themselves the hypotheses on which they act and so make failure itself a source of knowledge. In however limited a form, these agencies are organized to make self-corrective behavior possible.

The difficulties of arriving at self-corrective behavior in the disorganized and heatedly partisan atmosphere of Congress are all too apparent. Legislatures such as the British Parliament have at times developed wisdom and perpetuated it in a sound tradition workably related to the problems confronting the nation. But in the absence of a disciplined party system with reasonable continuity of leadership, conditions are too anarchical in our Congress to permit that body to try to organize its experience for the production of knowledge.

The conditions of political success do not encourage the cooperative corporate endeavor that characterizes our successful disciplines dedicated to the discovery of fact and the testing of hypotheses. One must hasten to admit that few agency heads willingly admit failure and search for its causes. The extraordinary but explicable overestimate of the magnitude of reconversion unemployment by the O.W.M.R. after World War II was regarded less as an opportunity and a first-rate challenge to reëxamine some fundamental economic thinking than as a botch to be dealt with by the palliative arts of propaganda. Even the eminently sane strategic bombing survey was frequently imperiled by an expediential urge to color the facts. Nonetheless, for the Air Force to undertake a strategic bombing survey at all is an encouraging instance of the recognition of the need of self-corrective behavior. Similarly, the State Department may undertake a review of China policy not simply to provide a brief for the defense but to examine the causes of past failure and to extract the lessons that may lead to future success. Given the current situation, such a review is beyond the capacity of Congress to undertake. In addition to the anarchic conditions already noted, a major reason for this lies in a phenomenon pointed out by Roland Young: the members of Congress, majority as well as minority, do not identify themselves with administration. Law in action is administration—and it is the work of the bureaucrats from whom and from whose works Congressmen instinctively dissociate themselves. Policy in practice thus is never the responsibility of Congress. The "foul up" is always the fault of the Administration, and Congress is well-nigh in the position of the British King who can do no wrong. Yet the penalty for the failure to accept responsibility for the test of legislation in administration is blindness to the possible lessons of experience. It may be that if government is ever to learn from its experience, the learning process will in large measure depend on the functioning of the bureaucracy.

Through the breadth of the interests represented in its composition, the bureaucracy provides a significant constitutionalizing element of pluralism in our government. Through its structure, permanence, and processes, it provides a medium in which the conditions requisite for the national interpretation of experience can develop. Thus it has a substantial part to play in the working constitution as representative organ and as source of rationality.

Returning now to Aristotle's suggestive analysis of the real components of a constitution, it is interesting to consider the ethical constitution of the bureaucracy. What is the prevailing ethos of the leading elements in the bureaucracy and how does it compare with those of the other branches of government, notably that of Congress? A detailed analysis of working attitudes toward the rule of law, civil liberties, and due process would be illuminating. A powerful case might well be made that in practice the bureaucracy shows far more concern and respect for each of these constitutional fundamentals than does the Congress. Certainly no agency shows such blatant disregard for due process as is customary with congressional committees, while the entire body's acquiescence in the abuse of congressional immunity bespeaks a disregard for constitutional safeguards that goes beyond committee excesses.

It was the bureaucracy, acting through the Department of Justice, that drafted Truman's unsuccessful veto of the McCarran Act, despite the potentially great power which the administration of this act could place in the hands of reputedly power-hungry bureaucrats. And if the executive branch has a sorry record on a loyalty program whose procedures give less opportunity to the accused than to a common felon, the explanation lies in a pusillanimous attitude to Congress rather than in a lack of scruples. One may search the records of Congress for a wigging administered to the F. B. I. similar to that frequently administered to the Home Office by the British Parliament. It is the nation's good fortune in having a man of the character of J. Edgar Hoover heading the F.B.I. rather than careful congressional scrutiny that has thus far secured us from the danger inherent in a national police.

Clearly the difference in ethos in the congressional and administrative branches of the government is not due to any mysterious vice in the one or virtue in the other. The difference must relate to the backgrounds and education of the personnel recruited for each and the seemingly wide difference in what constitutes successful practice in each as well as to the forces that bear upon them. Both branches are products of the effective political sentiments bearing upon them; they are rivals in political competence, varying according to their respective patterns of representativeness and responsibility. (For example, criticism of law schools and law reviews wrings the withers of no Congressman; it does have effect upon the bureaucracy and the courts.) Altogether, the climate of influential opinion is different, and the working of the group structure through the relevant institutions of selection and election produces a different result.

Given the views and composition of Congress, it is a fortunate fact of our working constitution that it is complemented by a bureaucracy indoctrinated with the fundamental ideals of constitutionalism. This varied group, rooted in the diversity of the country, can be counted on to provide important representation for its pluralism. In a real and important sense, it provides a constitutional check on both legislature and executive.

It is no neutral instrument like the German bureaucracy, available to Nazi and democrat alike, pleading its orders from *"die höhe Tiere"* as an excuse for criminal acts. Be it noted that this plea of duty to carry out orders neutrally met short shrift at Nuremberg. Facing the facts should lead to some interesting changes in the theory of the desirability of administrative neutrality. It is the balance of social forces in the bureaucracy that enables it both to perform an important part in the process of representation and to serve as a needed addition to a functioning division of power in government. Were the administrative branch ever to become a neutral instrument, it would, as a compact and homogeneous power group, either set up shop on its own account or provide the weapon for some other group bent on subverting the constitution.

A candid review of the causes leading to the overthrow of constitutional governments in recent years will show few, if any, examples where prime responsibility can be placed on the bureaucracy. With the exception of the military in Spain and South America, one must look elsewhere. Indeed, the very weakness of bureaucracies incapable of maintaining order has been a major chink in the constitutional armor; but anarchical legislatures incompetent to govern, accompanied by the rise of totalitarian political parties, have been the political causes of the debacle of constitutionalism. It is high time that the administrative branch is recognized as an actual and potentially great addition to the forces of constitutionalism. The advice of the devotees of Locke would make it a neutral instrument, a gun for hire by any party. Fortunately, such advice cannot be taken. Far better would be to recognize that, by appropriate recruitment, structure, and processes, the bureaucracy can be made a vital part of a functioning constitutional democracy, filling out the deficiencies of the Congress and the political executive. The theory of our constitution needs to recognize and understand the working and the potential of our great fourth branch of government, taking a rightful place beside President, Congress, and Courts.

THE BUREAUCRACY PROBLEM *
James Q. Wilson

THE federal bureaucracy, whose growth and problems were once only the concern of the Right, has now become a major concern of the Left, the Center, and almost all points in between. Conservatives once feared that a powerful bureaucracy would work a social revolution. The Left now fears that this same bureaucracy is working a conservative reaction. And the Center fears that the bureaucracy isn't working at all.

Increasing federal power has always been seen by conservatives in terms of increasing *bureaucratic* power. If greater federal power merely meant, say, greater uniformity in government regulations—standardized trucking regulations, for example, or uniform professional licensing practices—a substantial segment of American businessmen would probably be pleased. But growing federal power means increased discretion vested in appointive officials whose behavior can neither be anticipated nor controlled. The behavior of state and local bureaucrats, by contrast, can often be anticipated *because* it can be controlled by businessmen and others.

Knowing this, liberals have always resolved most questions in favor of enhancing federal power. The "hacks" running local administrative agencies were too often, in liberal eyes, the agents of local political and economic forces—businessmen, party bosses, organized professions, and the like. A federal bureaucrat, because he was responsible to a national power center and to a

* From *The Public Interest*, No. 6 (Winter 1967), pp. 3–9. Reprinted by permission of the author and publisher.

single President elected by a nationwide constituency, could not so easily be bought off by local vested interests; in addition, he would take his policy guidance from a President elected by a process that gave heavy weight to the votes of urban, labor, and minority groups. The New Deal bureaucrats, especially those appointed to the new, "emergency" agencies, were expected by liberals to be free to chart a radically new program and to be competent to direct its implementation.

It was an understandable illusion. It frequently appears in history in the hopes of otherwise intelligent and far-sighted men. Henry II thought his clerks and scribes would help him subdue England's feudal barons; how was he to know that in time they would become the agents of Parliamentary authority directed at stripping the king of his prerogatives? And how were Parliament and its Cabinet ministers, in turn, to know that eventually these permanent undersecretaries would become an almost self-governing class whose day-to-day behavior would become virtually immune to scrutiny or control? Marxists thought that Soviet bureaucrats would work for the people, despite the fact that Max Weber had pointed out why one could be almost certain they would work mostly for themselves. It is ironic that among today's members of the "New Left," the "Leninist problem"—i.e., the problem of over-organization and of self-perpetuating administrative power—should become a major preoccupation.

This apparent agreement among polemicists of the Right and Left that there is a bureaucracy problem accounts, one suspects, for the fact that non-bureaucratic solutions to contemporary problems seem to command support from both groups. The negative income tax as a strategy for dealing with poverty is endorsed by economists of such different persuasions as Milton Friedman and James Tobin, and has received favorable consideration among members of both the Goldwater brain trust and the Students for Democratic Society. Though the interests of the two groups are somewhat divergent, one common element is a desire to scuttle the social workers and the public welfare bureaucracy, who are usually portrayed as prying busy-bodies with pursed lips and steel-rimmed glasses ordering midnight bedchecks in public housing projects. (Police officers who complain that television makes them look like fools in the eyes of their children will know just what the social workers are going through.)

Now that everybody seems to agree that we ought to do something about the problem of bureaucracy, one might suppose that something would get done. Perhaps a grand reorganization, accompanied by lots of "systems analysis," "citizen participation," "creative federalism," and "interdepartmental coordination." Merely to state this prospect is to deny it.

There is not one bureaucracy problem, there are several, and the solution to each is in some degree incompatible with the solution to every other. First, there is the problem of accountability or control—getting the bureaucracy to serve agreed-on national goals. Second is the problem of equity—getting bureaucrats to treat like cases alike and on the basis of clear rules, known in advance. Third is the problem of efficiency—maximizing output for a given expenditure, or minimizing expenditures for a given output. Fourth is the problem of responsiveness—inducing bureaucrats to meet, with alacrity and compassion, those cases which can never be brought under a single national rule and which, by common human standards of justice or benevolence, seem to require that an exception be made or a rule stretched. Fifth is the problem of fiscal integrity—properly spending and accounting for public money.

Each of these problems mobilizes a somewhat different segment of the public. The problem of power is the unending preoccupation of the President and his staff, especially during the first years of an administration. Equity concerns the lawyers and the courts, though increasingly the Supreme Court seems to act as if it thinks its job is to help set national goals as a kind of auxiliary White House. Efficiency has traditionally been the concern of businessmen who thought, mistakenly, that an efficient government was one that didn't spend very much money. (Of late, efficiency has come to have a broader and more accurate meaning as an optimal relationship between objectives and resources. Robert McNamara has shown that an "efficient" Department of Defense costs a lot more money than an "inefficient" one; his disciples are now carrying the message to all parts of a skeptical federal establishment.) Responsiveness has been the concern of individual citizens and of their political representatives, usually out of wholly proper motives, but sometimes out of corrupt ones. Congress, especially, has tried to retain some power over the bureaucracy by intervening on behalf of tens of thousands of immigrants, widows, businessmen, and mothers-of-soldiers, hoping that the collective effect of many individual interventions would be a bureaucracy that, on large matters as well as small, would do Congress's will. (Since Congress only occasionally has a clear will, this strategy only works occasionally.) Finally, fiscal integrity—especially its absence—is the concern of the political "outs" who want to get in and thus it becomes the concern of "ins" who want to keep them out.

Obviously the more a bureaucracy is responsive to its clients—whether those clients are organized by radicals into Mothers for Adequate Welfare or represented by Congressmen anxious to please constituents—the less it can be accountable to presidential directives. Similarly, the more equity, the less responsiveness. And a preoccupation with fiscal integrity can make the kind of program budgeting required by enthusiasts of efficiency difficult, if not impossible.

Indeed, of all the groups interested in bureaucracy, those concerned with fiscal integrity usually play the winning hand. To be efficient, one must have clearly stated goals, but goals are often hard to state at all, much less clearly. To be responsive, one must be willing to run risks, and the career civil service is not ordinarily attractive to people with a taste for risk. Equity is an abstraction, of concern for the most part only to people who haven't been given any. Accountability is "politics," and the bureaucracy itself is the first to resist that (unless, of course, it is the kind of politics that produces pay raises and greater job security). But an absence of fiscal integrity is welfare chiseling, sweetheart deals, windfall profits, conflict of interest, malfeasance in high places—in short, corruption. Everybody recognizes *that* when he sees it, and none but a few misguided academics have anything good to say about it. As a result, fiscal scandal typically becomes the standard by which a bureaucracy is judged (the FBI is good because it hasn't had any, the Internal Revenue Service is bad because it has) and thus the all-consuming fear of responsible executives.

If it is this hard to make up one's mind about how one wants the bureaucracy to behave, one might be forgiven if one threw up one's hands and let nature takes its course. Though it may come to that in the end, it is possible—and important—to begin with a resolution to face the issue squarely and try to think through the choices. Facing the issue means admitting what, in our zeal for new programs, we usually ignore: *There are inherent limits to what can be accomplished by large hierarchical organizations.*

The opposite view is more often in vogue. If enough people don't like something, it becomes a problem; if the intellectuals agree with them, it becomes a crisis; any crisis must be solved; if it must be solved, then it can be solved— and creating a new organization is the way to do it. If the organization fails to solve the problem (and when the problem is a fundamental one, it will almost surely fail), then the reason is "politics," or "mismanagement," or "incompetent people," or "meddling," or "socialism," or "inertia."

Some problems cannot be solved and some government functions cannot, in principle, be done well. Notwithstanding, the effort must often be made. The rule of reason should be to try to do as few undoable things as possible. It is regrettable, for example, that any country must have a foreign office, since none can have a good one. The reason is simple: it is literally impossible to have a "policy" with respect to *all* relevant matters concerning *all* foreign countries, much less a consistent and reasonable policy. And the difficulty increases with the square of the number of countries, and probably with the cube of the speed of communications. The problem long ago became insoluble and any sensible Secretary of State will cease trying to solve it. He will divide his time instead between *ad hoc* responses to the crisis of the moment and appearances on Meet the Press.

The answer is not, it must be emphasized, one of simply finding good people, though it is at least that. Most professors don't think much of the State Department, but it is by no means clear that a department made up only of professors would be any better, and some reason to believe that it would be worse. One reason is that bringing in "good outsiders," especially good outsiders from universities, means bringing in men with little experience in dealing with the substantive problem but many large ideas about how to approach problems "in general." General ideas, no matter how soundly based in history or social science, rarely tell one what to do tomorrow about the visit from the foreign trade mission from Ruritania or the questions from the Congressional appropriations subcommittee.

Another reason is that good people are in very short supply, even assuming we knew how to recognize them. Some things literally cannot be done—or cannot be done well—because there is no one available to do them who knows how. *The supply of able, experienced executives is not increasing nearly as fast as the number of problems being addressed by public policy.* All the fellowships, internships, and "mid-career training programs" in the world aren't likely to increase that supply very much, simply because the essential qualities for an executive—judgment about men and events, a facility for making good guesses, a sensitivity to political realities, and an ability to motivate others—are things which, if they can be taught at all, cannot be taught systematically or to more than a handful of apprentices at one time.

This constraint deserves emphasis, for it is rarely recognized as a constraint at all. Anyone who opposed a bold new program on the grounds that there was nobody around able to run it would be accused of being a pettifogger at best and a reactionary do-nothing at worst. Everywhere except in government, it seems, the scarcity of talent is accepted as a fact of life. Nobody (or almost nobody) thinks seriously of setting up a great new university overnight, because anybody familiar with the university business knows that, for almost any professorship one would want to fill, there are rarely more than five (if that) really top-flight people in the country, and they are all quite happy—and certainly well-paid—right where they are. Lots of new business ideas don't become profit-making realities because good business executives are both hard to find and expensive to hire. The government—at least publicly—seems to act as if the supply of able political executives were infinitely elastic, though people setting up new agencies will often admit privately that they are so frustrated and appalled by the shortage of talent that the only wonder is why disaster is so long in coming. Much would be gained if this constraint were mentioned to Congress *before* the bill is passed and the hopes aroused, instead of being mentioned afterward as an excuse for failure or as a reason why higher pay scales for public servants are an urgent necessity. "Talent is Scarcer Than Money" should be the motto of the Budget Bureau.

If administrative feasibility is such a critical issue, what can be done about it? Not a great deal. If the bureaucracy problem is a major reason why so many programs are in trouble, it is also a reason why the problem itself cannot be "solved." But it can be mitigated—though not usually through the kinds of expedients we are fond of trying: Hoover Commissions, management studies, expensive consultants, co-ordinating committees, "czars," and the like. The only point at which very much leverage can be gained on the problem *is when we decide what it is we are trying to accomplish.* When we define our goals, we are implicitly deciding how much, or how little, of a bureaucracy problem we are going to have. A program with clear objectives, clearly stated, is a program with a fighting chance of coping with each of the many aspects of the bureaucracy problem. Controlling an agency is easier when you know what you want. Equity is more likely to be assured when over-all objectives can be stated, at least in part, in general rules to which people in and out of the agency are asked to conform. Efficiency is made possible when you know what you are buying with your money. Responsiveness is never easy or wholly desirable; if every person were treated in accordance with his special needs, there would be no program at all. (The only system that meets the responsiveness problem squarely is the free market.) But at least with clear objectives we would know what we are giving up in those cases when responsiveness seems necessary, and thus we would be able to decide how much we are willing to tolerate. And fiscal integrity is just as easy to insure in a system with clear objectives as in one with fuzzy ones; in the former case, moreover, we are less likely to judge success simply in terms of avoiding scandal. We might even be willing to accept a little looseness if we knew what we were getting for it.

The rejoinder to this argument is that there are many government functions which, by their nature, can never have clear objectives. I hope I have made it obvious by now that I am aware of that. We can't stop dealing with foreign nations just because we don't know what we want; after all, they may know what *they* want, and we had better find out. My argument is advanced, not as a panacea—there is no way to avoid the problem of administration—but as a guide to choice in those cases where choice is open to us, and as a criterion by which to evaluate proposals for coping with the bureaucracy problem.

Dealing with poverty—at least in part—by giving people money seems like an obvious strategy. Governments are very good at taking money from one person and giving it to another; the goals are not particularly difficult to state; measures are available to evaluate how well we are doing in achieving a predetermined income distribution. There may be many things wrong with this approach, but administrative difficulty is not one of them. And yet, paradoxically, it is the last approach we will probably try. We will try everything else first— case work, counseling, remedial education, community action, federally financed mass protests to end "alienation," etc. And whatever else might be said in their favor, the likelihood of smooth administration and ample talent can hardly be included.

Both the White House and the Congress seem eager to do something about the bureaucracy problem. All too often, however, the problem is described in terms of "digesting" the "glut" of new federal programs—as if solving administrative difficulties had something in common with treating heartburn. Perhaps those seriously concerned with this issue will put themselves on notice that they ought not to begin with the pain and reach for some administrative bicarbonate of soda; they ought instead to begin with what was swallowed and ask whether an emetic is necessary. *Coping with the bureaucracy problem is inseparable from rethinking the objectives of the programs in question.* Administrative reshuffling, budgetary cuts (or budgetary increases), and congressional investigation of lower-level boondoggling will not suffice and are likely, unless there are some happy accidents, to make matters worse. Thinking clearly about goals is a tough assignment for a political system that has been held together in great part by compromise, ambiguity, and contradiction. And if a choice must be made, any reasonable person would, I think, prefer the system to the clarity. But now that we have decided to intervene in such a wide range of human affairs, perhaps we ought to reassess that particular trade-off.

B.   Hierarchical Control vs. Decentralized Initiative

MAX WEBER's analysis (see p. 3) of the trend toward bureaucratization, and of the characteristics of efficient bureaucracy, had little direct influence on American scholarship until after the Second World War, but almost without exception American writers on administration had reached similar conclusions. They had not submitted to pessimism about the future of democracy, though. Rather, they had postulated that a strict dualism could be maintained, with democracy setting the public bureaucracy's tasks but having nothing to say about the ways in which they were executed. Similarly, they had assumed that democracy could flourish in the public sector while being excluded systematically from the lives of most nonpublic organizations. In view of the national commitment to such concepts as federalism, the separation of powers, checks and balances, and the free market economy, one might have expected these propositions to come in for vigorous critical attack. They did not, however, perhaps because "common sense" told American students of administration that formal organizations had little in common with whole societies, perhaps because they lacked the imagination to conceive either an alternative to the corporate (monocratic) model of organizational efficiency or the demise of American democracy.

As Gouldner's and Long's essays reprinted in Section I-A make clear, contemporary American analysts of administration remain optimistic about the future of democracy. They no longer believe that the line between goal determination and goal implementation can be neatly drawn, however, and they recognize that the most "rational" way to organize human behavior will vary with the objectives being pursued and with the society's overall structure of values and habits. It follows that they include much more under the intellectual rubrics of "organized" and "rational" behavior than did their predecessors. By way of illustration, consider the argument of Robert A. Dahl and Charles E. Lindblom in their landmark volume, *Politics, Economics, and Welfare.** Dahl and Lindblom developed the theme that four broad types of sociopolitical processes had been developed for coordinating the activities of large groups of men. Which of these four it was most rational to employ in any particular situation, they wrote, depended on an enormous variety of considerations—which they devoted several hundred pages to merely outlining. This is no place to review their analysis in detail. The points of greatest relevance to the present discussion that they made, however, were the following: (1) that

* (New York: Harper and Row, 1953).

monocratic bureaucracy was a pure organizational form of extremely limited applicability to real administrative situations—if one's aim were the efficient ordering of cooperative activity rather than the satisfaction of a chief executive's neurotic ego demands; (2) that in many circumstances the bureaucratic form worked more effectively when mixed with (and therefore modified by) other cooperative modes than when employed alone; and (3) that for many purposes it was almost totally inappropriate.

Dahl and Lindblom labeled their four major sociopolitical processes hierarchy, bargaining, polyarchy, and the price system. They defined the price system as one in which a central authority is dispensed with, and in which a large number of persons trade on the basis of money prices set (and responded to) in accord with their own values and calculations. They defined hierarchy—i.e., monocratic bureaucracy—as "a process in which leaders control nonleaders," bargaining as "a process in which leaders control each other," and polyarchy as "a process sometimes called democracy in which non-leaders control leaders." They emphasized that these pure types could be blended to produce an infinite variety of alloys, and that even so they did not exhaust the subject of social control. The four sociopolitical processes were ways of reaching collective decisions; when it came to controlling individual behavior, they required numerous supplements. Dahl and Lindblom stressed that individuals are controlled only marginally by commands; except in cases of rule by terror, other influences tend to be far more important: for example, internalized moral norms, perceptions of legitimacy, the opinions of peers, and environmental signals indicating the probable costs and risks of particular lines of endeavor.

Thus, the question of what organizational modes are most "rational" has taken on greater and greater complexity as the study of administration has proceeded. Far more issues have been opened than resolved. As thought about administrative issues has become more sophisticated, it has concurrently become less dogmatic. Most contemporary scholars would argue that objective analysis alone can never provide "right" answers, even for particular cases. It can only set out the major requirements, consequences, and value implications of alternative organizational modes. Weighing the significance of these disparate variables, making appropriate allowances for risk and uncertainty, and judging when to pass from analysis to decision remain largely the domain of art and intuition.

There is no space here for more than a sampling of the great range of "open questions" that preoccupy modern administrative analysts. To permit a fairly leisurely exploration, I have opted to focus this section on only one. It is, however, perhaps the single issue that has most preoccupied students of administration over the years: namely: to what extent does "rational" organization require an extreme centralization of decision-making authority?

Alexis de Tocqueville (1805–1859), whose *Democracy in America* remains perpetually relevant, approached the centralization problem in terms of the role of local government in the American political system. He assumed that local government should operate within a broad national policy framework, and that within the sphere of national responsibilities power should be sufficiently concentrated so that the government could act decisively and with dispatch whenever necessary. What is most relevant in the present context, though, is that he took great pains to consider the benefits to the nation of leaving local matters to the discretion of local authorities. His discussion in the selection which follows is marred by two assumptions: first, that it will normally be clear which issues require national handling and which do not; and second, that local authorities should be considered parts of the "administration" rather than semiautonomous governments in their own right. In addition, he fails to consider other means of decentralization than the delegation of responsibilities to local authorities. He does place the centralization issue in broad and profound perspective, however; and if you are receptive, the flaws in his presentation may simply challenge you to think independently about how his principles might be applied in ways he himself failed to perceive.

Philip Selznick considers decentralization in a much narrower context. He assumes the perspective of a corporate chieftain whose aim is simply to maximize the effectiveness with which his own policy decisions are executed. Selznick's policy maker is unconcerned with such national values as liberty, democracy, and citizen self-reliance. The question to which Selznick addresses himself is: under what conditions will even such a policy maker be well served by a high degree of decentralization? His analysis is highly suggestive but extremely sketchy. Its appreciation demands a special effort on the reader's part to imagine how it might look as a fully elaborated theory, able to provide answers to such questions as the following: how should the foreign service be run so as to obtain an optimal combination of decentralized initiative with a deep sense of common purposes and perspectives? to what extent does modern corporate decentralization rest upon the development of "group cohesion" as opposed to the objective nature of profit as a measure of subunit effectiveness? how ought one to go about deciding for a particular organization what functions should be decentralized, to what extent, and how?

Charles Lindblom contends that those responsible for managing national economies do well to plan very selectively, leaving the vast majority of economic decisions to be made by private economic actors in free markets. He believes that even in an underdeveloped country like India the market has a great contribution to make, and that for most planning purposes it is a far more effective administrative device than direct bureaucratic controls. You may judge that Lindblom has overstated his case—or, what amounts to the same thing, that he has failed to specify what the market cannot do as carefully as what it can—but even so, you will almost surely find it rewarding to evaluate his arguments with care.†

DECENTRALIZATION IN AMERICA *
Alexis de Tocqueville

. . . THERE are two methods of diminishing the force of authority in a nation. The first is to weaken the supreme power in its very principle, by forbidding or preventing society from acting in its own defence under certain circumstances. To weaken authority in this manner is the European way of establishing freedom.

† For a much more elaborate statement of Lindblom's viewpoint, see his book, *The Intelligence of Democracy* (New York: The Free Press, 1965).

* First published 1835. Reprinted here from *Democracy in America*, the Mentor edition (New York, 1956), pp. 62–72.

The second manner of diminishing the influences of authority does not consist in stripping society of some of its rights, nor in paralyzing its escorts, but in distributing the exercise of its powers among various hands, and in multiplying functionaries, to each of whom is given the degree of power necessary for him to perform his duty. There may be nations whom this distribution of social powers might lead to anarchy; but in itself, it is not anarchical. The authority thus divided is, indeed, rendered less irresistible and less perilous, but it is not destroyed.

The Revolution of the United States was the result of a mature and reflecting preference of freedom, and not of a vague or ill-defined craving for independence. It contracted no alliance with the turbulent passions of anarchy; but its course was marked, on the contrary, by a love of order and law. . . .

. . . Centralization is a word in general and daily use, without any precise meaning being attached to it. Nevertheless, there exist two distinct kinds of centralization, which it is necessary to discriminate with accuracy.

Certain interests are common to all parts of a nation, such as the enactment of its general laws, and the maintenance of its foreign relations. Other interests are peculiar to certain parts of the nation; such, for instance, as the business of the several townships. When the power which directs the former or general interests is concentrated in one place or in the same persons, it constitutes a centralized government. To concentrate in like manner into one place the direction of the latter or local interests, constitutes what may be termed a centralized administration.

Upon some points, these two kinds of centralization coincide; but by classifying the objects which fall more particularly within the province of each, they may easily be distinguished.

It is evident that a centralized government acquires immense power when united to centralized administration. Thus combined, it accustoms men to set their own will habitually and completely aside; to submit, not only for once, or upon one point, but in every respect, and at all times. Not only, therefore, does this union of power subdue them compulsorily, but it affects their ordinary habits; it isolates them, and then influences each separately.

These two kinds of centralization mutually assist and attract each other; but they must not be supposed to be inseparable. It is impossible to imagine a more completely centralized government than that which existed in France under Louis XIV.; when the same individual was the author and the interpreter of the laws, and the representative of France at home and abroad, he was justified in asserting that he constituted the state. Nevertheless, the administration was much less centralized under Louis XIV. than it is at the present day.

In England, the centralization of the government is carried to great perfection; the state has the compact vigor of one man, and its will puts immense masses in motion, and turns its whole power where it pleases. But England, which has done so great things for the last fifty years, has never centralized its administration. Indeed, I cannot conceive that a nation can live and prosper without a powerful centralization of government. But I am of opinion that a centralized administration is fit only to enervate the nations in which it exists, by incessantly diminishing their local spirit. Although such an administration can bring together at a given moment, on a given point, all the disposable resources of a people, it injures the renewal of those resources. It may insure a victory in the hour of strife, but it gradually relaxes the sinews of strength. It may help admirably the transient greatness of a man, but not the durable prosperity of a nation. . . .

The partisans of centralization in Europe are wont to maintain that the government can administer the affairs of each locality better than the citizens could do it for themselves: this may be true, when the central power is enlightened, and the local authorities are ignorant; when it is alert, and they are slow; when it is accustomed to act, and they to obey. Indeed, it is evident that this double tendency must augment with the increase of centralization, and that the readiness of the one and the incapacity of the others must become more and more prominent. But I deny that it is so, when the people are as enlightened, as awake to their interests, and as accustomed to reflect on them, as the Americans are. I am persuaded, on the contrary, that, in this case, the collective strength of the citizens will always conduce more efficaciously to the public welfare than the authority of the government. I know it is difficult to point out with certainty the means of arousing a sleeping population, and of giving it passions and knowledge which it does not possess; it is, I am well aware, an arduous task to persuade men to busy themselves about their own affairs. It would frequently be easier to interest them in the punctilios of court etiquette, than in the repairs of their common dwelling. But whenever a central administration affects completely to supersede the persons most interested, I believe that it is either misled, or desirous to mislead. However enlightened and skilful a central power may be, it cannot of itself embrace all the details of the life of a great nation. Such vigilance exceeds the powers of man. And when it attempts unaided to create and set in motion so many complicated springs, it must submit to a very imperfect result, or exhaust itself in bootless efforts.

Centralization easily succeeds, indeed, in subjecting the external actions of men to a certain uniformity, which we come at last to love for its own sake, independently of the objects to which it is applied, like those devotees who worship the statue, and forget the deity it represents. Centralization imparts without difficulty an admirable regularity to the routine of business; provides skilfully for the details of the social police; represses small disorders and petty misdemeanors; maintains society in a *status quo* alike secure from improvement and decline; and perpetuates a drowsy regularity in the conduct of affairs, which the heads of the administration are wont to call good order and public tranquillity; in short, it excels in prevention, but not in action. Its force deserts it, when society is to be profoundly moved, or accelerated in its course; and if once the co-operation of private citizens is necessary to the furtherance of its measures, the secret of its impotence is disclosed. Even whilst the centralized power, in its despair, invokes the assistance of the citizens, it says to them: "You shall act just as I please, as much as I please, and in the direction which I please. You are to take charge of the details, without aspiring to guide the system; you are to work in darkness; and afterwards you may judge my work by its results." These are not the conditions on which the alliance of the human will is to be obtained; it must be free in its gait, and responsible for its acts, or (such is the constitution of man) the citizen had rather remain a passive spectator, than a dependent actor, in schemes with which he is unacquainted.

It is undeniable, that the want of those uniform regulations which control the conduct of every inhabitant of France, is not unfrequently felt in the United States. Gross instances of social indifference and neglect are to be met with; and from time to time, disgraceful blemishes are seen, in complete contrast with the surrounding civilization. Useful undertakings, which cannot succeed without perpetual attention and rigorous exactitude, are frequently abandoned; for in America, as well as in other countries, the people proceed by sudden impulses and momentary exertions. The European, accustomed to find a functionary always at hand to interfere with all he undertakes, reconciles himself with difficulty to the complex mechanism of the administration of the townships. In general, it may be affirmed that the lesser details of the police, which render life easy and comfortable, are neglected in America, but that the essential guaranties of man in society are as strong there as elsewhere. In America, the power which conducts the administration is far less regular, less enlightened, and less skilful, but a hundred-fold greater, than in Europe. In no country in the world, do the citizens make such exertions for the common weal. I know of no people who have established schools so numerous and efficacious, places of public worship better suited to the wants of the inhabitants, or roads kept in better repair. Uniformity or permanence of design, the minute arrangement of details, and the perfection of administrative system, must not be sought for in the United States: what we find there is, the presence of a power which, if it is somewhat wild, is at least robust, and an existence checkered with accidents, indeed, but full of animation and effort.

Granting, for an instant, that the villages and counties of the United States would be more usefully governed by a central authority, which they had never seen, than by functionaries taken from among them,—admitting, for the sake of argument, that there would be more security in America, and the resources of society would be better employed there, if the whole administration centred in a single arm,—still the *political* advantages which the Americans derive from their decentralized system would induce me to prefer it to the contrary plan. It profits me but little, after all, that a vigilant authority always protects the tranquillity of my pleasures, and constantly averts all dangers from my path, without my care or concern, if this same authority is the absolute master of my liberty and my life, and if it so monopolizes movement and life, that when it languishes everything languishes around it, that when it sleeps everything must sleep, and that when it dies the state itself must perish.

There are countries in Europe, where the natives consider themselves as a kind of settlers, indifferent to the fate of the spot which they inhabit. The greatest changes are effected there without their concurrence, and (unless chance may have apprised them of the event) without their knowledge; nay, more, the condition of his village, the police of his street, the repairs of the church or the parsonage, do not concern him; for he looks upon all these things as unconnected with himself, and as the property of a powerful stranger whom he calls the government. He has only a life-interest in these possessions, without the spirit of ownership or any ideas of improvement. This want of interest in his own affairs goes so far, that if his own safety or that of his children is at last endangered, instead of trying to avert the peril, he will fold his arms, and wait till the whole nation comes to his aid. This man, who has so completely sacrificed his own free will, does not, more than any other person, love obedience; he cowers, it is true, before the pettiest officer; but he braves the law with the spirit of a conquered foe, as soon as its superior force is withdrawn: he perpetually oscillates between servitude and license.

When a nation has arrived at this state, it must either change its customs and its laws, or perish; for the source of public virtues is dried up; and though it may contain subjects, it has no citizens. Such communities are a natural prey to foreign conquests; and if they do not wholly disappear from the scene, it is only because they are surrounded by other nations similar or inferior to themselves; it is because they still have no indefinable instinct of patriotism; and an involuntary pride in the name of their country, or a vague reminiscence of its bygone fame, suffices to give them an impulse of self-preservation.

Nor can the prodigious exertions made by certain nations to defend a country in which they had lived, so to speak, as strangers, be adduced in favor of such a system; for it will be found that, in these cases, their main incitement was religion. The permanence, the glory, or the prosperity of the nation were become parts of their faith; and in defending their country, they defended also that Holy City of which they were all citizens. The Turkish tribes have never taken an active share in the conduct of their affairs; but they accomplished stupendous enterprises, as long as the victories of the Sultan were triumphs of the Mohammedan faith. In the present age, they are in rapid decay, because their religion is departing, and despotism only remains. Montesquieu, who attributed to absolute power an authority peculiar to itself, did it, as I conceive, an undeserved honor; for despotism, taken by itself, can maintain nothing durable. On close inspection, we shall find that religion, and not fear, has ever been the cause of the long-lived prosperity of an absolute government. Do what you may, there is no true power among men except in the free union of their will; and patriotism or religion are the only two motives in the world which can long urge all the people toward the same end. . . .

It is not the *administrative,* but the *political* effects of decentralization, that I most admire in America. In the United States, the interests of the country are everywhere kept in view; they are an object of solicitude to the people of the whole Union, and every citizen is as warmly attached to them as if they were his own. He takes pride in the glory of his nation; he boasts of its success, to which he conceives himself to have contributed; and he rejoices in the general prosperity by which he profits. The feeling he entertains toward the state is analogous to that which unites him to his family, and it is by a kind of selfishness that he interests himself in the welfare of his country.

To the European, a public officer represents a superior force: to an American, he represents a right. In America, then, it may be said that no one renders obedience to man, but to justice and to law. If the opinion which the citizen entertains of himself is exaggerated, it is at least salutary; he unhesitatingly confides in his own powers, which appear to him to be all-sufficient. When a private individual meditates an undertaking, however directly connected it may be with the welfare of society, he never thinks of soliciting the co-operation of the government; but he publishes his plan, offers to execute it, courts the assistance of other individuals, and struggles manfully against all obstacles. Undoubtedly he is often less successful than the state might have been in his position; but in the end, the sum of these private undertakings far exceeds all that the government could have done. . . .

I believe that provincial institutions are useful to all nations, but nowhere do they appear to me to be more necessary than amongst a democratic people. In an aristocracy, order can always be maintained in the midst of liberty; and as the rulers have a great deal to lose, order is to them a matter of great interest. In like manner, an aristocracy protects the people from the excesses of despotism, because it always possesses an organized power ready to resist a despot. But a democracy without provincial institutions has no security against these evils. How can a populace, unaccustomed to freedom in small concerns, learn to use it temperately in great affairs? What resistance can be offered to tyranny in a country where each individual is weak, and where the citizens are not united by any common interest? Those who dread the license of the mob, and those who fear absolute power, ought alike to desire the gradual development of provincial liberties.

I am also convinced, that democratic nations are most likely to fall beneath the yoke of a centralized administration, for several reasons, amongst which is the following.

The constant tendency of these nations is to concentrate all the strength of the government in the hands of the only power which directly represents the people; because, beyond the people, nothing is to be perceived but a mass of equal individuals. But when the same power already has all the attributes of government, it can scarcely refrain from penetrating into the details of the administration, and an opportunity of doing so is sure to present itself in the long run, as was the case in France. In the French Revolution, there were two impulses in opposite directions, which must never be confounded; the one was favorable to liberty, the other to despotism. Under the ancient monarchy, the king was the sole author of the laws; and below the power of the sovereign, certain vestiges of provincial institutions, half destroyed, were still distinguishable. These provincial institutions were incoherent, ill arranged, and frequently absurd; in the hands of the aristocracy, they had sometimes been converted into instruments of oppression. The Revolution declared itself the enemy at once of royalty and of provincial institutions; it conformed in indiscriminate hatred all that had preceded it,—despotic power and the checks of its abuses; and its tendency was at once to republicanize and to centralize. This double character of the French Revolution is a fact which has been adroitly handled by the friends of absolute power. Can they be accused of laboring in the cause of despotism, when they are defending that centralized administration which was one of the great innovations of the Revolution? In this manner, popularity may be united with hostility to the rights of the people, and the secret slave of tyranny may be the professed lover of freedom.

I have visited the two nations in which the system of provincial liberty has been most perfectly established, and I have listened to the opinions of different parties in those countries. In America, I met with men who secretly aspired to destroy the democratic institutions of the Union in England, I found others who openly attacked the aristocracy; but I found no one who did not regard provincial independence as a great good. In both countries, I heard a thousand different causes assigned for the evils of the state; but the local system was never mentioned amongst them. I heard citizens attribute the power and prosperity of their country to a multitude of reasons; but they *all* placed the advantages of local institutions in the foremost rank.

Am I to suppose that when men, who are naturally so divided on religious opinions and on political theories, agree on one point, (and that one which they can best judge, as it is one of which they have daily experience,) they are all in error? The only nations which deny the utility of provincial liberties are those which have fewest of them; in other words, those only censure the institution who do not know it.

DECENTRALIZATION AND SOCIAL INTEGRATION *
Philip Selznick

IN the design of decision-making procedures, much attention is devoted to the maintenance of policy without overly concentrated or multiplied controls. Various patterns of administrative decentralization have been developed to achieve this balance. Here too, however, diagnosis and prescription should heed the

* From Philip Selznick, *Leadership in Administration,* pp. 112–116. Copyright © 1957 by Harper & Row, Publishers, Inc. Reprinted by permission of the publishers.

life-cycle conditions that affect the application of administrative principles. Precepts regarding the value of administrative decentralization will be more adequately formulated and more intelligently applied if they take account of organizational evolution.

The need for centralization declines as the homogeneity of personnel increases. A unified outlook, binding all levels of administration, will permit decentralization without damage to policy. When top leadership cannot depend on adherence to its viewpoint, formal controls are required, if only to take measures that will increase homogeneity. On the other hand, when the premises of official policy are well understood and widely accepted, centralization is more readily dispensable. Hence we shall expect that a relatively high degree of centralization will be required in the early stages of institutional development. Later, when homogeneity has been achieved, decentralization will be feasible without undue loss of control. . . .

Decentralization requires a preparatory period of training, in which leadership has the opportunity to influence deeply the ideas that guide decision-making at lower levels. This influence may take the form of indoctrination, including the informal promotion of an official philosophy or even formal schooling. Educational measures are especially important where circumstances impose barriers to close contact. More useful is the collaborative development of plans and policies by as many levels of the organization as possible, so that a unified view, or at least understanding of the controlling viewpoint, will be achieved. This entails the participation of top leadership in low-echelon decisions and the participation of subordinate staff personnel in high-level planning. . . .

Perhaps the best-known example of decentralization in American industry is found in General Motors. Yet historically the period of decentralization was preceded by a decade of tight control. Centralization was required in order to reorient the organization after the DuPont interests took over the company. The significance of this experience for administrative analysis is (1) that decentralization would have been an unfeasible policy during the stage of reorientation; and (2) that the period of tight control probably created precisely those social conditions essential to a later policy of decentralization.

Participation is a way of deepening communication and developing group cohesion. (This is sometimes associated with democratic doctrine, but need not be so understood.) Yet a given level of communication and cohesion may be adequate to the circumstances at hand. Hence maximal participation is not always required. It should be prescribed only when there is a problem of cohesion, when cohesion cannot be taken for granted and must be reinforced. Among the general conditions generating such problems is the newness of organizations. We expect, therefore, that leadership will attend to the problem of cohesion before techniques of administration that presume its solution are instituted. At least it will be understood that this problem must be solved before the full promise of these administrative methods can be fulfilled. . . .

ECONOMICS AND THE ADMINISTRATION
OF NATIONAL PLANNING *
Charles E. Lindblom

THE contribution of economics to national economic planning is obvious and overwhelming. Regulation of national output and employment requires that plan administration be interlarded with competence in fiscal policy, aggregative economic theory, and the economics of industrial organization, to mention only a few areas in which public administration draws directly on economics. The development of investment projects to implement planned production targets requires economic analysis of benefits and costs. The design of complex plans calls for calculation of capital-output ratios, intersectoral relations, and domestic savings. The market mechanism, a central concern of the economist, is equally significant in the duty of planning administration.

HISTORICAL AND CONTEMPORARY CONTRIBUTIONS

The original economist seems to have been an administrator. He was called an *oikonomis* in ancient Greece, from *oikos,* a house, and *nemein,* meaning to manage. Even today, it does not strain ordinary usage very much to think of economics as the administration of society's wealth, or resources, or work force.

To find, however, a contribution of economics to *governmental* or *public* administration, one looks perhaps to the thirteenth century in which it is thought that double-entry bookkeeping first came to use. If one can claim accounting as a part of economics, one cannot think of anything that matches in breadth, power, and specificity, the contribution to public administration made by the development of accounting. If through amnesia we could rob public administration of most of what it now *knows* about accounting or most of what it now *knows* about such topics as span of control, line and staff functions, decentralization, authority, and responsibility, we might choose to protect accounting and let the others go. In these days, public administration without sophisticated accounting is nearly inconceivable.

In recent times, accounting has been employed for transactions in the national product and income for entire economies rather than only for the transactions of governmental units or private business and households. It is in large part through the development of national income accounting that public administration has achieved an acceptable level of control over the key variables

* From the *Public Administration Review*, the Journal of the American Society for Public Administration, Vol. 25 (1965), pp. 274–283. Reprinted by permission of the publisher.

in the economy—output, employment, the price level—that all nations now seem to wish to plan. This is largely a post-World War II development. It has in a short time, however, revolutionized the possibilities for successful planning of the general level of economic activity in a nation.

As the beginning of a new era both in economics and in public administration, the development of national income accounting has not been sufficiently celebrated. It was an extraordinary development in economics because it represented a welding together of observable fact and theoretical concept such as economics had never before achieved. The theoretical or conceptual revisions which underlay drew heavily on those introduced in the 1930's by Keynes. Through his new or revised concepts and his patterning of the relationships among the variables he conceptualized, it became possible for the economic administrators of any economy—central bankers and treasury officials, for example—to analyze and to plan by reference to variables for which there were real-world, empirical, usually statistical, approximations. The development of national income accounting represented a dual movement: one toward constructing a set of accounts that made use of the new concepts; the other toward refining the statistical approximations. The result of the development was to give to economic administrators a piece of social science that was scientifically operational and in a form serviceable for social control. In its combination of theoretical elegance and practical usefulness, there may be no comparable contribution to administration from any other social science, or, for that matter, any comparable second contribution from economics.

Other contemporary contributions from economics to public administration, especially to the administration of economic planning, are represented by statistics, input-output analysis, systems analysis and operations research, decision theory, bargaining theory, game theory, and the study and theory of economic planning. Most of these developments, it should be noted, represent convergences of a number of disciplines, including philosophy and mathematics, and do not represent therefore an exclusively economic contribution to public administration.

Some of these highly formal and specialized contributions to public administration, like input-output analysis or game theory, are today much in vogue, for they promise—and sometimes have already delivered—exciting new practical competences in the management of economic systems. To put them in perspective: probably none of them has yet accounted for as powerful an effect on administrative competence in national economic planning as that of old fashioned monetary theory alone.

For 19th century England and the U.S., a major aim of then embryonic national economic planning was the avoidance of acute instability; yet, the inadequacies of central banking repeatedly frustrated fiscal and monetary management to that end. Only slowly did economics and administration succeed in overcoming the economic instability produced by poor monetary systems. In more recent times, one of the most conspicuously successful forms of technical assistance the developed nations of the world have been able to export to the developing nations has been for monetary reform. The input into this technical assistance program is economics; the output is administrative capacity for managing essential components of national economic planning. This—the development of competence in central banking and in managing the money supply—is the clearest, least arguable, specific technical contribution of economics to the administration of national planning.

THE MARKET MECHANISM AND PUBLIC ADMINISTRATION

A contribution of economics to public administration of a different order from any so far mentioned has to do with the market mechanism as an administrative device.

The world is apparently now in a new stage in the renaissance of appreciation of the market mechanism as a fundamental technique of social organization. The new stage is signalled by the turn toward the market mechanism in the communist economies. It has finally become clear that the market mechanism and private enterprise, often confused with each other, are not at all the same thing and that the market mechanism is serviceable in an extraordinary variety of circumstances not limited to Western economies or to the private sector.

The market mechanism has gained strikingly in repute since World War II. In the United States, a country bound by ideology to faith in the market mechanism, only a shadow of disrepute fell on the market as a result of the market disorganization and prolonged unemployment of the 1930's. With relative economic stability since World War II and an embarrassing degree of affluence, Americans are as likely to speak with enthusiasm of the market mechanism as they were to be stricken by doubt in the 30's. It is in Europe, however, that the renaissance is conspicuous.

To begin with, the English socialists, with a pronounced antimarket bias in the 30's—stemming not simply from their experience with unemployment, but also from socialist principle—finally opted to discipline their newly nationalized industries largely through market forces rather than through the administrative devices of post-office socialism. They also joined with the Conservatives in withdrawing after World War II from forms of central planning, like industrial licensing, control of transactions in land, and import controls that were antagonistic to as heavy a reliance on the market as has in fact emerged in the United Kingdom.

Continental socialists took the same direction; and Western Europe became, by agreement among nearly all parties and schools of thought, a pioneering area in market organization. No less noteworthy than the eventual spread of new appreciation of market mechanism to the communist economies is the fact that Western Europe took its first great step toward unification not through a common language, common flag, common government, or common political aspiration, but through a Common Market.

Just what is the market mechanism—or price mechanism, or price system, as it is sometimes called? The Soviet Union has always employed money and prices in its economic planning; yet we say that only recently it shows a new interest in the market mechanism. Similarly, the U.S. Army employs money and prices in administering its affairs; yet we do not suggest that the military deploys its resources through the market mechanism.

We mean by the market mechanism a system of cueing, signalling, and providing incentives for desired action by prices, price movements, price differentials, and flows of money income. A contrasting system is the control of action by prescription. For the control of the inputs and outputs of an economic system, a market mechanism constrains inputs, allocates them, and regulates output by prices, price movements, and price (or price-cost) differentials. Without a market mechanism, inputs are administratively allocated through a quota system or a priority system, as is generally the case in the USSR; and outputs are regulated by prescription to achieve physical targets, although there may be monetary rewards for hitting the targets.

It may clarify the distinction between the market mechanism and its absence to note that, although the USSR has traditionally minimized the use of the market mechanism for the control of production, it has usually employed it for the distribution of consumer goods, the prices of which are varied in order to increase or decrease their rates of consumption. Even those nations most sceptical of the usefulness of the market have shrunk from attempting a direct allocation of consumer goods to masses of consumers, except in time of war, acute shortage, or in the case of certain critical commodities like housing. In those cases, consumer supplies are administered through a ration card system or some other form of administrative allocation.

The distinction between a market mechanism and direct controls over production is, however, on the whole sufficiently familiar to dismiss without further detailing. Given the distinction between the market mechanism and other forms of control, what is the relationship between plan administration and the market mechanism?

Planning vs. the Market. The market mechanism was of course once widely regarded as an instrument not of planning, but of planlessness; that is, of laissez-faire. In the tradition of classical economics, an administered economy is one thing, a market-regulated economy another. Even so, classical economics could make a substantial contribution to public administration, and Adam Smith's *Wealth of Nations* can be read as a treatise on certain fundamentals of public administration. Read as a treatise in public administration, Smith's first prescription was: Decentralize! His concern for the evils of over-centralization carried him beyond the now conventional case for administrative decentralization (to lower levels in the hierarchy or to field offices) to an argument for decentralization of a vast number of decisions to private buyers and sellers in a market. That he consequently jumped out of the field of public administration should not obscure the fact that he began with a classical problem in public administration and a now conventional solution for it.

But why decentralize? One reason, he thought, was that some tasks of public administration were beyond human competence. In sounding the theme that administrative task and organization have to be matched with human intellectual capacities, he hit upon an obvious fundamental principle of administrative science which has only lately begun to receive the attention it deserves in the literature of public administration and the theory of decision making.[1]

Decentralization, Smith also saw, is a method of tapping powerful incentives; and it is, of course, this theme that is predominant in Smith's case for carrying decentralization to the extreme of decision making by individual buyers and sellers. Smith took the relationship between decentralization and incentives much more seriously than it has since been taken in the literature of public administration, where incentive effects of decentralization are taken to be only secondary arguments for decentralization. But the strength of the Smithian tradition on decentralization and incentives is illustrated in recent years by Albert Hirschman's work on development planning. Hirschman shows that incentives are often enormously strengthened where orderly plans give way to decentralization—of a degree that sometimes approximates administrative disorganization.[2]

Another fundamental principle of public administration—and of social organization more generally—that became a linchpin in Smith's theoretical system is that the complex organization can be designed to achieve results not intended by any participant within the organization. The view he was opposing is that desired results are typically achieved only by persons intending to achieve them. He did not, however, pause to work out the implications of this for the organization of a governmental administrative system. Instead, he rushed on to shoot what he thought was bigger game, showing how in the market mechanism masses of buyers and sellers intent on their own private interests could systematically produce useful social results (such as a more or less systematic allocation of national resources, a systematic organization of these resources for cooperative production, and a systematic distribution of the population of a productive output). His fundamental principle—that intention and result can be systematically disassociated in useful ways—remains, however, a pregnant principle, still deserving further exploration for its applicability to public administration.

Market Socialism. The antithesis between plan and market mechanism was much later sounded again by an atypical school of democratic socialists who paradoxically chose to identify socialism with the market mechanism rather than with economic planning. Many are familiar with the challenge put to the socialists, conspicuously by Ludwig von Mises in 1920, in which the question is raised as to whether socialists actually have in mind any system or method for the actual administration of economic affairs under democratic socialism.

While most socialists ignored the challenge, a few went back to the 1908 work of the Italian economist Barone to demonstrate that a market mecha-

---

1. See, for example . . . David Braybrooke and Charles E. Lindblom, *A Strategy of Decision* (The Free Press, 1963), Chapter III.
2. Albert O. Hirschman, *The Strategy of Economic Development* (New Haven, Yale University Press, 1958), and Hirschman and Lindblom, "Economic Development, Research and Development, Policy Making: Some Converging Views," *Behavioral Science* (April, 1962), pp. 211–222.

nism was possible without private enterprise; that is, with universal public ownership of enterprise.[3] They made their case, but only by describing a highly decentralized, relatively unplanned socialist economy, guided by consumer tastes as expressed through the market, and relatively uninfluenced by central decisions about social priorities. So far as their brand of socialism made a place for centrally determined priorities, priorities were for the most part to be given effect through the same fiscal and monetary techniques and general regulatory devices that characterize a regulated private enterprise economy. Hence, they met the challenge by surrendering the central planning or collective determination of economic priorities that most socialists held to be the distinguishing elements of socialist economic organization.

What is significant here is that the idea of market socialism gained currency as a reply to the allegation that for large and complex economic systems there was no way to *administer* the economy in the absence of market relations among private enterprises. The theory of market socialism is therefore a piece of theory about public administration, about the fundamental economic tasks of public administration, and how they can be discharged under the condition of universal or widespread public ownership of business enterprises.

Planning the Market Mechanism. Meanwhile, an alternative view of the relationship between the market mechanism and planning had become dominant. It came to be widely accepted in all the market economies of the West that a very loose kind of planning could improve the performance of the market mechanism itself. Through taxation and redistributive devices such as free public education or social security, the market mechanism's distribution of income could be much improved. The degeneration of competitive markets into monopoly could be blocked by regulation of trade practices and of combinations among sellers. Instability of employment and income in market mechanisms could be dampened by the central regulation of the money supply and by the manipulation of the government surpluses or deficits.

This new view of planning and market mechanism in the Western democracies was the thesis of a number of books and articles by professional economists in the months and years immediately following World War II. They argued for this much planning and no more. An eloquent statement of the position was James E. Meade's *Planning and the Price Mechanism* which grew out of an earlier review of Sir Oliver Frank's *Central Planning and Control in War and Peace,* which Meade took to be representative of a postwar line of thought insufficiently appreciative of the role of the price mechanism in democratic planning.

Meade asked himself, "Am I a planner?" His answer was:

If a planner necessarily believes in a quantitative program of output, employment and sales for particular industries, occupations and markets and the exercise of such direct controls by the State as are necessary to carry this out, I am certainly no planner. If an anti-planner necessarily denies that the State should so influence the

3. For a survey of socialist economics of this stripe, see Abram Bergson, "Socialist Economics," *A Survey of Contemporary Economics,* ed. H. S. Ellis (Blakiston, 1948).

working of the price mechanism that certain major objectives of full employment, stability, equity, freedom and the like are achieved, then I am a planner. The thesis of this book is that a large measure of state foresight and intervention is required to guide the economy from war to peace, to prevent inflationary and deflationary pressures, to ensure a tolerably equitable distribution of income and property, and to prevent or to control the anti-social rigging of the market by private interests, but that these objectives can be achieved in an efficient and a free society only if an extensive use is made of the mechanisms of competition, free enterprise and the free market determination of prices and output.[4]

To understand the implications of this kind of planning for public administration, it ought to be remembered that it was a new wide agreement on the feasibility of regulating employment and distribution of income through manipulating the market mechanism that finally undercut the appeal of the 19th century socialist slogan, "Abolish the wages system!"—a slogan that implicitly proposed mountainous burdens for public administration. In short, it was the possibility of planning the market mechanism itself that in Western Europe destroyed the traditional socialist vision of direct governmental administration of economic affairs. Planning the market mechanism became a method of achieving the important old objectives with a vast simplification of the administrative apparatus once believed to be necessary for the achievement.

It should be noted in passing that the tasks of public administration necessary for planning the market mechanism require expertise in economics, especially in price theory, aggregative theory, and monetary theory, beyond or in addition to general administrative skills. If administrators are to implement employment and income policies through so complicated and delicate an instrument as the market mechanism, they have to know a great deal about it.

Central Planning through the Market Mechanism. Meanwhile, neither the Soviet Union nor its satellites showed much interest in using the market mechanism except for the distribution of consumer goods. Both production and distribution of producer goods, as well as production of consumer goods, were to be responsive to central, collective, or governmental preference instead of to the market preferences of individual buyers. Communists rejected the idea of planning or manipulating the market in the style dominant in the Western democracies, for this kind of soft planning improved rather than replaced decentralized consumer control of production and distribution. They wanted it replaced.

The search for effective administrative implements of central control over inputs and outputs has driven the communist countries from one unhappy expedient to another. It is impossible to write a central plan that specifies in detail a production target for every one of the multiple products of every enterprise and also specifies the quantity of each input to be made available to each enterprise. But, then, how to control an enterprise's outputs and inputs? To

---

4. J. E. Meade, *Planning and the Price Mechanism* (Macmillan, 1949), pp. v, vi. Sir Oliver Franks, *Central Planning and Control in War and Peace* (Harvard, 1947).

characterize only roughly and briefly the typical difficulty of physical planning as practised in the communist countries: If, in the absence of detailed prescription of each input and output of the firm, output targets are aggregated in, for example, weight, the firm is tempted to specialize in heavy products; if its targets are aggregated in terms of numbers of output, the firm chooses to make many small products, each as small as it dares.

The result of communist dissatisfaction with physical plan administration is that in varying degrees the communist countries of Europe have been exploring the possibility of replacing specific instructions in physical terms with some form of the profit motive. In 1957, for example, the Hungarian economist Kornai carefully explored Hungary's difficulties with physical planning and pointed to the advantages of the market mechanism *as an instrument of central direction* of the economy.

He could point out that reforms in that direction had already taken place.

. . . . Since then [1955–6], a great deal of change has taken place as a result of the measures affecting methods of economic administration which were put into effect in 1957. In 1955–6, the initiative of enterprises was severely hampered by the long list of obligatory plan index numbers prescribed for them by higher authorities. By now, the number of indices which have binding force has been reduced to 4–6 in light industry. In 1955–6 the exact amount of every article to be produced by each enterprise was prescribed for them centrally in the greatest possible detail. At present, product-mixes and detailed production programmes are, very largely, the outcome of direct contacts between industrial enterprises and the distributive trades. This has made industry far more sensitive to the real requirements of its customers. Again, in 1955–6 profits were ignored by both the top managements and the other employees of enterprises. At present the financial incentives offered to top managements are, to a large extent, made to depend on profits realized, and the general body of employees receive a part of these profits. . . .[5]

Yugoslavia has actually gone further, it appears, in the direction of the market mechanism than any of the other communist countries, consequently has to some extent weakened central direction of the economy, but on the other hand, has made the market mechanism, rather than detailed administrative instructions, the principal mechanism for administering centrally chosen priorities and policies.

In the Soviet Union the most conspicuous spokesman for production planning with the use of the market mechanism is Professor Evsey Liberman. He says:

At present, there are many indices, apart from profit, that serve to assess the work of Soviet enterprises—gross output, production costs, productivity of labour, wage bill, the number of workers, among them. In my opinion, this restricts the freedom of enterprises to choose and employ the most efficient methods and interferes with their questing for and finding of the most adequate ways and means of economic management. That is why we suggest that Soviet enterprises draft their

5. Janos Kornai, *Overcentralization in Economic Administration* (Oxford University Press, 1959), p. vi.

plans themselves, being guided, first and foremost, by the contracts they have concluded with their "customers." If these contracts have been fulfilled, the estimation of efficiency and incentive for its results must depend only on profit, or rather on the profitability of the enterprise.[6]

He goes so far as to suggest—in defense of what he fears may expose him to attack—that the distinction between capitalism and socialism is not, after all, in the role of profits in controlling production, but in the disposition of profits to income receivers!

The distinction between capitalism and socialism is not in that capitalism asserts profits while socialism refutes them. With both systems, as with commodity production in general, profits are made use of, in so far as they are the monetary expression of the surplus product essential to the development of society. But the basic distinction is: Who gets this product and what uses it is made of? Under socialism, profits are not spent on unproductive luxury, nor on excessive publicity, nor on bribes to officials in order to get profitable government orders. In the USSR, profits are not spent for anything but socially useful purposes.[7]

But how can the market mechanism serve the needs of centrally made plans when it has so long been believed that the market mechanism is an instrument for controlling production and distribution according to the preferences of private buyers and sellers in the market place? Without going into the answer in detail and without specifying precisely what aspects of the market mechanism are not adapted to the needs of central planners, it can be said generally that central planners can give effect to their production programs by manipulating prices and incomes, in much the same way that Western democracies have given effect to their desire for full employment, economic stability, and an improved distribution of income through manipulation of prices and market incomes. It is possible for central government to increase or decrease the production of a commodity at its will, rather than at the will of the masses of consumers, by increasing or decreasing the price that the producing enterprises receive for the product. It is possible, again, for central planners to increase or decrease the rate of use of a natural resource like petroleum by increasing or decreasing the price at which it is made available to the refineries. And the necessary manipulation of prices—of prices of inputs or prices of outputs—can be achieved through taxes and subsidies, as in the Western democracies, or by outright control of prices by fiat.

As a marginal phenomenon in American or Western European economic organization, central decisions to override decentralized consumer preferences with respect to the control of production are well established. Historically, for example, the desires of the central government for expanded production of communication and transportation services have established a tradition of subsidies to railroads, ocean transportation, and airlines. Conversely, some of the support for the high excise tax on liquor reflects a governmental intention to curb its consumption. What the communist countries are now increasingly ex-

6. Evsey Liberman, "Profit in the USSR," *Eastern Economist* (June 4, 1965), p. 1273.
7. *Ibid.*, p. 1275.

ploring is the possibility of generalizing a familiar though marginal Western technique of central direction of inputs and outputs through the manipulation of prices as a substitute for straight administrative prescription of input quotas and production targets.

Hence, to comment again explicitly on the contribution of economics to the administration of national economic planning, it is fair to say that part of the world has now discovered that the most significant *administrative* advance that has come to attention in many a year is the market mechanism.

A case for using the market in planning in communist countries has had to be made in the face of ideological opposition. It is a case that can be won only if there are concrete practical virtues in the market mechanism so great as to justify distorting an established ideology in order to accommodate the required reform. But the concrete and practical difficulties of physical plan administration and the market mechanism's potential for meeting these specific administrative difficulties have been conspicuous enough to effect the change.

Development Planning through the Market Mechanism. The new view of the usefulness of the market mechanism, especially of its serviceability as an instrument of central production planning, represents a revolution in practical economic thought and in the understanding of possibilities of plan administration. The new view has not encompassed the world, however; and that there is a new wave of thought about the market mechanism is either unnoticed or resisted in some nations where the desire to plan might have been expected to stimulate an eager search for good methods for plan administration. Resistance to the new wave of thought is in some part attributable to the influence of turn-of-the-century socialist thought on the intellectual and administrative traditions of some of the new or newly freed developing nations. For that brand of socialism in Europe, especially in England, was fiercely antagonistic to the market mechanism because that mechanism was at the time identified with a system of competitive private enterprise. If, as pointed out, the English socialists have come to draw the distinction between the market mechanism and private enterprise—and drawn a very sharp distinction between the market mechanism and unregulated private enterprise—the students of their fathers, now in important governmental positions in the developing nations, perpetuate the older tradition.

India is an example. It has made great gains in capital growth and inputs since independence; it boasts what is by any reasonable standards an excellent civil service; and no developing country surpasses it in the sophistication of its planners and their plans. But the new appreciation of the market mechanism does not greatly stir in India, and Indian administrators sometimes wrestle with opportunities to use the market as though with a dangerous beast.

Even so, the practical virtues of the market mechanism seem to be turning India somewhat in its direction. India is embarked on a developmental program marked by a great degree of central direction of the economy. In one field after another, the questions whether and how much to use the market mechanism for implementing that central direction are important issues. India's experience is illustrative of problems and possibilities in the use of the market mechanism for development planning.

A first illustrative question in plan administration in India is how to hit centrally determined targets for foodgrain production. India has established a vast bureaucracy for exhortation and instruction in the use of fertilizer, irrigation, and new seeds. If it had chosen to use the market mechanism as well, it would presumably either have secured or even raised the prices of foodgrain output and/or lowered the price of some critical farm input like fertilizer in order to create a powerful financial incentive for output expansion. Instead, it has held down foodgrain prices for the benefit of consumers, especially urban consumers; and it has held up the price of imported fertilizer to protect domestic high-cost fertilizer producers.

Only within the last year or so does the Indian government seem to have decided that the market mechanism might, after all, be a powerful administrative device for implementing farm production targets. It has made a bold attempt to maintain relatively high and secure minimum prices for foodgrain producers and is apparently moving simultaneously to lower fertilizer prices. This represents a great break in Indian foodgrain policy; it has raised the explicit question of the administrative usefulness of the market mechanism to the highest levels of policy, where it is still being debated with respect to other questions on the administration of food policy.

Another practical question in plan administration has been how to achieve the export targets set in the Five Year Plans. Again, India has established a substantial administrative apparatus for stimulating exports in various direct ways: inspection and quality control, assistance in marketing overseas, foreign exhibition of Indian products, and so on. Judging, however, by the unsatisfactory results of the administrative devices, a root of the export problem remains the relative profitability of the home market as against the relative unprofitability of selling overseas. Not until 1962 did India somewhat generalize an earlier small program of awarding extra allocations of controlled scarce imports to exporters—thus, in effect, raising the price of exports. Exports then took the kind of jump that indicated that India had finally hit upon an effective administrative device for reaching export targets. This particular device for increasing the profitability of foreign markets is insufficiently general, but its success has been impressive enough to stimulate further consideration of the market mechanism through more general devices for raising the profitability of selling abroad. Again, therefore, the usefulness of the market mechanism for implementing Indian planning is today an explicit issue in high level policy making.

A third illustrative practical problem in Indian plan administration is how, aside from the special problems of the export industries, to direct industrial production in conformity with planned targets. Currently, the government of India leans heavily on direct prescriptive controls. In the first place, it directly undertakes through public enterprise certain desired lines of production. Secondly, through industrial licensing for the private sector, it permits large new firms or major expansions of old firms only when they conform to the plans of the central government. Thirdly, it achieves a comprehensive and detailed control over industrial production by direct administrative allocation of imported raw materials, intermediate goods, components, and spare parts for industrial enterprises.

Is there any room for the market mechanism in this area of plan administration? In India it is increasingly coming to be appreciated that there is. For one thing, industrial licensing is not a very satisfactory administrative device. It is a veto but not an activator; hence, Indians are coming to recognize that an administrative device that would provide a positive incentive for the establishment of new productive capacity would be superior to one that is capable of nothing more than thwarting any inappropriate intention. Moreover, the direct administrative determination of what should or should not be produced is quite unsatisfactory for commodities whose relation to planned targets is unclear. Targets are established for relatively few major commodities. That leaves the administrator in the position of trying to decide whether high-tensile nuts and bolts are more important than welding electrodes, when neither are targeted. He knows that market forces might work out the answer to his question better than he can, provided, of course, that the market is generally constrained somehow to pursue planned targets.

Difficulties with direct control over lines of production are most widely recognized for import controls. There the possibility of rationing of scarce imports through a high price for them rather than through prescription seems to be gaining ground simply because of the practical difficulties of the latter. As in the Soviet Union, the practical virtues of the market mechanism are already recognized in "unofficial" official approval of black market transactions to rectify the administrative errors of the direct input control system.

One could cite many other examples of problems in plan administration in which India had the option to exploit the market mechanism—in motivating a vast extension service in agriculture, for example; in choosing and designing capital projects; in achieving an effective flow of fertilizer, new seeds, and credit to millions of small farmers; and so on. A common judgment on Indian development efforts is that India implements less well than it plans. Another formulation of roughly the same criticism is that India has been weak in tapping incentives. The use of the market mechanism as an instrument of central planning is of course a device to strengthen implementation, where the mechanism can be used, by tapping incentives rather than by authoritatively prescribing desired actions.

A few years ago, when he was still Minister of Commerce and Industry, the present Prime Minister gave typical expression to Indian vexation over failures of plan administration, when he said, on export promotion difficulties:

I do not completely rule out the possibility of introducing some kind of compulsion, which may help in the stepping up of exports. . . . Compulsory export will also lead to some sort of compulsory quality control.[8]

8. *Hindustan Times* (July 7, 1959), p. 5.

The resort to stronger measures—at the extreme, coercion of the desired responses—has been a frequent note in plan administration in India. It is symptomatic of the extent to which Indian plan administration has been inadequately aware of many opportunities for structuring a system of incentives through the market mechanism so that responses desired by central planners are freely forthcoming.

If the potential of the market mechanism is seriously undervalued in India, it is yet not fully explored in the communist economies in Western Europe, and in the U.S. itself, despite advances in employing it skillfully.

If the special view that economists bring to the investigation of the market mechanism as an instrument of plan administration could be supplemented by additional insights from political science and public administration, the exploitation of this fundamental administrative device would be still further advanced.

C.　The Study of American Public Administration

THE two essays in this section deal with various aspects of the intellectual history of public administration as a scholarly discipline. They are included here on the premise that the contemporary literature can only superficially be understood without some knowledge of the context from which it has emerged.

Alan Altshuler addresses himself primarily to the following questions: What subjects have preoccupied students of American public administration over the past eighty years? Why? And how well have these subjects meshed with the changing concerns of professional students of American politics? After reviewing this history, he concludes that a bold effort to redefine the boundaries and central questions of the subject "American public administration" is called for; and he endeavors to relate the organization and content of this volume to his ideas on the form that the redefinition ought to take.

Herbert Kaufman considers the normative doctrines on governmental organization and personnel policy that have typified the discipline at different stages in its history. He contends that "the administrative institutions of this country . . . have been organized and operated in pursuit successively of three [core] values." Students of public administration and career public officials have traditionally emphasized two of these, which they have viewed as complementary: neutral competence and executive leadership. Recently, Kaufman writes, a conflict between some of the requirements of these two values has become apparent, and has begun to split the discipline. Kaufman explores the contours of this division, and suggests that it is generational: an older group is still thinking in terms of creating a highly professionalized bureaucracy, while a younger one has turned to the problems of controlling it. Other observers have suggested that whatever split on these normative issues exists in the profession is largely occupational: that academics oriented toward political control are increasingly arrayed against practitioners, the latter desiring to maximize the stability and predictability of their working environments. After reading Kaufman's article, you may wish to consider: (1) how the core values that he postulates are in fact balanced within contemporary American government, (2) which major groups in American society would like to increase the stress placed on each of them, (3) what broader political issues are at stake in these disputes, (4) which you believe ought to be stressed more strongly, and (5) what kinds of specific administrative reforms might be necessary to implement your views.

THE STUDY OF AMERICAN PUBLIC ADMINISTRATION *

Alan Altshuler

THE study of American public administration developed in the late nineteenth century as a branch of American political science, then preoccupied with legal relationships, strongly oriented toward reform rather than research, and conceived simply by most of its tiny band of practitioners as "the study of goverment." It seemed obvious enough to political scientists of the day what governments were, and it was also clear that governments performed many noncontroversial service functions at any time in addition to their cardinal function, the management of social conflict.

By contrast, modern political scientists devote little attention to legal forms; they aim at understanding; and they concentrate on the study of distinctly political phenomena. Indeed, they have increasingly considered it irrelevant whether the institutions and processes chosen for analysis have been "governmental" in the formal sense at all; the test of relevance has become the significance of the political functions performed.[1]

Students of public administration have abandoned legalism, reform, and

* Written especially for this volume.

1. A definitional note may be helpful. I understand "politics" to be those activities in a society having to do with the expression of conflicts among social groups within it, and with attempts to resolve or manage such conflicts. I specify "group" conflict (1) on the premise that one ought to exclude from a definition whatever one can without severely aggravating the difficulty of relating actual phenomena to it, and (2) because it seems clear that conflicts among individuals rarely challenge the governmental capacities of a society unless fairly large groups (measured against the standard of the society under consideration) begin to take sides. The group conflicts which I term *distinctly* political are those which in the time period being analyzed are deemed (by at least some of the interested groups) unsuitable for resolution by the mere application of legal or

simple-minded notions of which institutions they ought to consider suitable for study. But they have regularly resisted the overall disciplinary trend toward concentration on politics. My purpose in this essay is to ask why, and to suggest a few highly tentative answers.

At the birth of public administration as an academic discipline, quite naturally a need was felt to explain with the greatest possible clarity what distinguished it from other subjects within the broad field of government. The constitutional distinction between legislative and executive institutions—which the post-Civil War Supreme Court was in process of reifying, and developing into a theory of distinct functions—provided an obvious foundation on which to build. The formulation that quickly won general acceptance was stated with stark simplicity by Woodrow Wilson. In his celebrated 1887 essay, "The Study of Administration," Wilson argued as follows:

The field of administration is a field of business. It is removed from the hurry and strife of politics. . . . It is a part of political life only as the methods of the counting-house are a part of the life of a society; only as machinery is part of the manufactured product . . . [In other words], administrative questions are not political questions. Although politics sets the tasks for administration, it should not be suffered to manipulate its offices. . . . Policy does nothing without the aid of administration; but administration is not therefore politics. . . . This discrimination between administration and politics is now, happily, too obvious to need further discussion.[2]

The object of public administration as a field of study, Wilson went on, should be to improve—through the application of scientific modes of analysis —the performance of public administrative activities. Another way of putting this might have been to say that public administration should follow the reformist bent of the rest of political science, but should focus on the noncontro-

technical expertise—both of which assume the preexistence of authoritative, applicable and clear decision rules.

Three related points deserve to be made.

First, the political importance of any dispute is a matter for judgment, not measurement. It depends on opinion about the significance of the issues at stake. A political scientist does not have to depend solely on his own opinion, however. He can seek also to ascertain the opinions of active participants in the dispute, members of the general public, governmental officials, and panels of expert outside observers.

Second, political science is concerned with potential as well as actual conflicts. The sources of consensus in a society on issues that have disrupted other societies is a typical and highly legitimate subject for political analysis.

Third, my inclination is to specify that "political" means are nonviolent, though they often involve the threat of violence unless compliance is forthcoming. There is nothing political about securing compliance by direct physical force; political science departments do not offer courses in jujitsu, or even in military tactics. One hastens to add that two of the most vital functions of any society's political system are (1) to determine the purposes for which violence may be used in the society, and (2) to determine the procedures by which it should be called upon and applied in appropriate circumstances. One certainly cannot grasp the essential character of a political system without having a profound understanding of its provisions for the regulation of violence. It should be kept in mind, nonetheless, that the actual use of violence indicates a failure of politics.

2. Woodrow Wilson, "The Study of Administration," reprinted, *Political Science Quarterly*, XVI (December 1941), 481–506. The quotations are from pages 493–495.

versial activities of governments, those which political analysts had hitherto ignored.

Having thus defined the focus of public administration rather narrowly, Wilson made clear that his own interests were extremely broad. He placed his call for a science of administration within an analysis of the growing complexity and consequent bureaucratization of the function of governance. For the first time in history, he declared, "it is getting harder to *run* a constitution than to frame one." He wrote, moreover, as a partisan in a *political* movement: that for reform of the nineteenth century spoils system and substitution of a civil service merit system in its place. After issuing his call, Wilson did not consider devoting his scholarly life to the refinement of administrative techniques. He left that to more prosaic minds.

Many did take up where he had left off, however. For fifty years after he wrote, the dominant theme of writings on public administration was the pursuit of principles which, when applied sensitively, would produce "efficient" administration. Without seriously asking why, moreover, nearly all professional students of administration assumed that the "value-free science" of administration should take as its fundamental orientation the perspective of an organizational chief who, knowing his goals clearly, desires only additional knowledge of how to manipulate his subordinates and "customers" more effectively.[3]

Some of the most sophisticated writers of this period—for example, Leonard D. White and Luther Gulick—did regularly remind their readers that the discipline was still in its infancy, that the "principles of administration" discovered to date set only very general constraints, and that therefore the practice of administration remained predominantly art rather than science. About the aim, however, they rarely wavered. Gulick articulated the consensus of the profession when he concluded a seminal volume of essays in 1937 as follows:

In the science of administration, whether public or private, the basic "good" is efficiency. The fundamental objective of the science of administration is the accomplishment of the work in hand with the least expenditure of man-power and materials.[4]

This consensus was already beginning to be challenged as Gulick wrote, however. From Wilson's day to the early 1930's, the study of public adminis-

3. My language here follows Chester Barnard, who noted that many of the essential contributors to any organization's survival and prosperity are not employees. The organization is a system of cooperative activity which must induce possessors of money and materiel to participate as well as workers. Barnard emphasized that the buyers of a business organization's product were fully as important members of its cooperative system as employees. I employ the term "customer" a bit more broadly, to include the investors in and creditors of a business enterprise as well as those to whom it sells, the constituencies (all whose political support is important to it) of a political organization, and the contributors (of energy, time, and materiel as well as money) to a voluntary association.

4. Luther Gulick, "Science, Values and Public Administration," in Luther Gulick and L. Urwick, eds., *Papers on the Science of Administration* (New York: Institute of Public Administration, 1937), p. 192. These were not the volume's final sentences, but they were the key sentences of its concluding essay.

tration had been unambiguously allied with the ideal—to use Herbert Kaufman's nomenclature [5]—of "neutral competence" for the public service. The experience of the early New Deal suggested, however, (1) that patronage might be of great value in aiding a vigorous President to push through programs of social and economic reform, and (2) that such a President might be justifiably reluctant to entrust his new programs to career bureaucrats who —though merit appointees—had grown deeply attached to the philosophies and procedures of the old order. FDR often chose to press for the establishment of new agencies to carry out programs that represented sharp breaks with the past,[6] and it was difficult for professional students of administration to fault him compellingly on "efficiency" grounds for doing so. Many were critical, of course, but others chose to reassess the academic dogmas on which they had been reared.

Thus, beginning in the mid-1930's a body of scholarship began to develop on the constant and apparently irrepressible penetration of administration by politics in the United States.[7] These studies were bound to be, and were, followed quickly by at least a few analyses hypothesizing the "functions" of the patterns observed. From here, particularly in view of the sympathy with which most members of the profession viewed the New Deal, it was only a brief step to extolling the virtues of these patterns. Some, at least, took that step. Even more significantly, no serious student of public administration could ignore the impact of these new descriptions and justifications. Even Gulick, in the very passage cited several paragraphs back, went on as follows:

But both public administration and politics are branches of political science, so that we are in the end compelled to mitigate the pure concept of efficiency in the light of the value scale of politics and the social order.

There are, for example, highly inefficient arrangements like citizen boards and small local governments which *may* be necessary in a democracy as educational devices. It has been argued also that the spoils system, which destroys efficiency in administration, is needed to maintain the political party, that the political party is needed to maintain the structure of government, and that without the structure of government, administration itself will disappear.

While this chain of causation has been disproved under certain conditions, it nonetheless illustrates the point that the principles of politics may seriously affect efficiency. . . .

To illustrate the full extent of the discomfort that—as a theorist anxious to fit the new perspective into the context of the old—Gulick apparently felt during this transitional period, it should be added that after admitting the above he

5. See his article, "Emerging Conflicts in the Doctrine of Public Administration," which immediately follows this essay.

6. By way of illustration, see Arthur Schlesinger, Jr.'s comments which appear in Section II-D, below, and Grant McConnell's case study which appears in Section III-A.

7. See, for one of the earliest and finest examples of the genre, E. Pendleton Herring's *Public Administration and the Public Interest* (New York: McGraw-Hill, 1936).

immediately pulled back to more orthodox ground. His next two sentences but one ran as follows:

These interferences with efficiency [do not] in any way eliminate efficiency as the fundamental value upon which the science of administration may be erected. They serve to condition and to complicate, but not to change the single ultimate test of value in administration.[8]

The confusion might have been resolved, it seems clear today, by recognizing frankly that the objectives actually pursued by any administrative agency —the proper criteria against which to measure efficiency—were often not simply its stated objectives. They might, for example, include satisfying the psychological needs of individual employees, mollifying client interest groups, and providing jobs for members of the political party in power. A profession devoted for fifty years to defining efficiency in terms of universally acceptable, explicitly stated goals—and, in particular, to defining patronage and efficiency as polar opposites—was bound, however, to find this point extremely difficult to accept. Moreover, acceptance of it would only have brought Gulick (and the profession) to two even more embarrassing questions: (1) is it possible to construct a science of efficiency around organizations whose goals are in significant part unknowable? and (2) is the term "efficiency" meaningful even when organizational goals so elude attempts to define them with certainty and precision?

Despite this "crisis of the old order" in public administration, the controversies swirling around such epithets as "big government" and "the bureaucratic state" during the Roosevelt era fascinated American political scientists. Probably in consequence, this period was not only one in which "political" analyses of administrative subjects became fashionable; it was also one in which public administration attracted an extraordinary number of the ablest minds in political science. V. O. Key, Robert Dahl, Pendleton Herring, Herman Pritchett, Harvey Mansfield, Avery Leiserson, David Truman, Charles Hyneman, Norton Long, and Roland Pennock: all were beginning their careers in the thirties and early forties, and chose to focus at least major portions of their research energies on administrative subjects. They were joined, of course, by such as Herbert Simon. Dwight Waldo, Philip Selznick, and Reinhard Bendix—who carried their concerns with problems of bureaucracy into the fifties and sixties (though in progressively less "political" form), but who chose their specialties in the period under consideration.

Even as some students of administration were discovering and being provoked by "politics," however, others were attacking the traditional literature with a more orthodox end in view: that of pursuing efficiency more scentifically. Herbert Simon, who was to be its foremost spokesman and strategist, launched this school with a 1946 article entitled "The Proverbs of Administra-

8. *Op. cit.,* p. 193.

tion".[9] "It is a fatal defect of the current principles of administration," he wrote:

that, like proverbs, they occur in pairs. For almost every principle one can find an equally plausible and acceptable contradictory principle. Although the two principles of the pair will lead to exactly opposite organizational recommendations, there is nothing in the theory to indicate which is the proper one to apply.

He went on to document this apparently devastating charge with reference to four of the administrative literature's most frequently cited "principles."

He cited, for example, the doctrine that: "Administrative efficiency is increased by grouping the workers, for purposes of control, according to (a) purpose, (b) process, (c) clientele, or (d) place." These were clearly alternative criteria, Simon noted. The principle as stated offered administrators no help in deciding how to weigh or choose among them. Moreover, the terms themselves were ambiguous. Thus: "A health department conceived as a unit whose task it is to care for the health of the community is a purpose organization; the same department conceived as a unit which makes use of the medical arts to carry on its work is a process organization." Similarly: "A unit providing public health and medical services for school-age children in Multnomah county might be considered as (1) an 'area' organization . . . ; (2) a 'clientele' organization . . . ; (3) a purpose or process organization. . . ." And these, Simon made clear, were typical rather than unusual cases. The other principles discussed fared no more favorably.

Was the need, then, for a completely new beginning? Simon denied that it was. "Almost everything can be salvaged," he contended. What had been called "principles" of administration were in fact no more than criteria. As criteria, they were useful and important. The aim of the science of administration henceforth had to be to define them precisely, to list them exhaustively, and to weight them scientifically. In Simon's own words:

A valid approach to the study of administration requires that *all* the relevant diagnostic criteria be identified; that each administrative situation be analyzed in terms of the entire set of criteria; and that research be instituted to determine how weights can be assigned to the several criteria when they are, as they usually will be, mutually incompatible.

In fact, Simon was being unfair to the most sophisticated among the students of administration who had written before him. Gulick, for example, had fully recognized the proverbial nature of the "principles of administration." In the course of the most authoritative exposition of them ever written, he had emphasized that:

There is apparently no one most effective system of departmentalization. Each of the four basic systems of organization is intimately related to the other three, be-

9. The article appeared originally in the *Public Administration Review*, Vol. VI (1946), pp. 53–67; and subsequently as chapter two of Simon's book, *Administrative Behavior* (New York: Macmillan, 1947). The quotations which follow (in the text) are from *Administrative Behavior*, pp. 20, 21, 28, 30, 35, 36.

cause in any enterprise all four elements are present in the doing of the work and are embodied in every individual workman. Each member of the enterprise is working for some major purpose, uses some major process, deals with some persons, and serves or works at some place.

If an organization is erected about any of these four characteristics of work, it immediately becomes necessary to recognize the other characteristics in constructing the secondary and tertiary divisions of work. For example, a government . . . divided in the first instance by purpose, may well be divided next by process and then by place. While the first or primary division of any enterprise is of very great significance, it must none the less be said that there is no one most effective pattern for determining the priority and order for the introduction of these interdependent principles.

He had then discussed at length the kinds of circumstances in which each of the four "principles of departmentalization" might profitably be given top priority. And he had begun the section on these principles by confessing frankly that: "Unfortunately, we must rest our discussion primarily on limited observation and common sense, because little scientific research has been carried on in this field of administration." [10] The difference between Simon and Gulick, then, was not that the former could tell a proverbial from a scientific principle. It was rather that the latter considered some proverbs very useful—as checklists of factors worth considering, as handy cores around which to organize one's thoughts, and as the closest brief approximations of wisdom available in many circumstances. Gulick's thought had unquestionably been based on intuition and experience rather than science, but he had presented his observations with such clarity and elegance that even today, when one knows his arguments to be dated, one can almost count on remembering the "principles of administration" for years on the basis of one careful reading of his paper.

It should be kept in mind, moreover, that the "principles of administration" remain alive and kicking. Though scholars stress their limitations, no substitute body of normative ideas on how to organize a bureaucracy has taken their place. Consequently, consultants and committees charged with recommending large governmental reorganizations still regularly fall back upon them.

Simon undoubtedly served the profession well, however, by exposing the inadequacies of the "principles" in such memorable fashion. For most students of administration, they had become sacred dogmas, to be taught and applied rather than developed. They were stultifying thought rather than stimulating it. To cite one outstanding example, the "principles" focused almost exclusively on coordination as the key to efficiency; in consequence, virtually nothing had been written about the problems of infusing large bureaucracies with intelligence, innovative capacity, and zeal.

More generally, concentration on the goal of efficiency had long diverted attention from political phenomena. As noted previously, however, quite a few political scientists had attacked the politics-administration dichotomy by the

10. Luther Gulick, "Notes on the Theory of Organization," in Gulick and Urwick, eds., *op. cit.*, pp. 1–45. The above quotation is from page 21. The previous quotation was from pages 31–32.

time Simon wrote, and some had gone on to explore the patterns of political-administrative interaction that characterized the American system in detail. Simon ignored their work completely. His only major concession—and it was implicit—to their critique was to substitute for the politics-administration dichotomy a "fact-value" dichotomy.

While noting that one could not meaningfully distinguish political from administrative *decisions,* Simon emphasized that all decisions rested on both factual and value *premises.* Only the former, he contended, had any relevance to administrative science. Moreover, most values or goals were not "ends-in-themselves," but were rather "intermediate ends." That is, they were valued on the *factual* premise that they were instrumental to the achievement of ultimate ends. Thus, the applicability of science was extremely wide. One could ask scientifically whether intermediate ends were efficiently conducive to the ends-in-themselves from which they drew their appeal, even though scientists could have nothing to say about the "goodness" of these ultimate values themselves.

So long as the discussion remained abstract, these points contributed to conceptual clarity and were indisputable. When it came to practice, however, the fact-value dichotomy suspiciously took on the hue of the politics-administration dichotomy. For example, while disclaiming any wish to discuss the controversial issue of administrative responsibility at length,[11] Simon contended that democracy, which nearly all Americans considered "good," would be strengthened by:

procedural devices permitting a more effective separation of the factual and ethical elements in decisions. . . . The allocation of a question to a legislator or administrator for decision should depend on the relative importance of the factual and ethical issues involved, and the degree to which the former are controversial. . . . Though the function of making value judgments may often be delegated to the administrator, especially where controversial issues are not involved, his complete answerability, in case of disagreement, must be retained.[12]

These sentences certainly appear to imply that *decisions,* and perhaps even *governmental functions,* can be divided into (1) those that are predominantly concerned with factual and intermediate value decisions, and (2) those that are predominantly concerned with ultimate or controversial value decisions. No sophisticated scholar had ever believed that the conceptual politics-administration distinction should be interpreted for practical purposes as suggesting more.[13]

Over the years, as it happens, Simon himself seems to have abandoned the

11. The dimensions of this issue are explored in Section IV-B.

12. *Administrative Behavior, op. cit.,* pp. 57–58.

13. Frank Goodnow, for example, whose book, *Politics and Administration,* published in 1900, occupies as prominent a place in the history of public administration as Wilson's essay cited previously, emphasized with great clarity that he understood the politics-administration dichotomy to be one of ideal type "functions," not of governmental activities or agencies. Goodnow never used the phrase "ideal type," but he distinguished politics from administration as follows: ". . . Politics has to do with the guiding or influencing of government policy, while administration has to do with the execution of that policy. . . The use of the word 'administration' in this connection is unfortunately somewhat misleading, for the word . . . means popularly the most important executive or administrative authorities. 'Administration,' there-

idea that theorists of administration should focus on efficiency. In the index to *Organizations,* an analytical survey of the literature that he and James G. March published in 1958, the word "efficiency" appears only once—where it refers to the work of Gulick. This is quite understandable. The obstacles to building a science of administration upon the concept of efficiency have proven thus far to be insurmountable. In particular, as rigorous studies have been attempted, it has become increasingly apparent that:

(1) To be meaningful, evaluations of efficiency must rest upon a consideration of all an organization's values, not merely those which have been publicly stated, or those on which attention focused as any particular sequence of decisions was made.

(2) It is impossible to ascertain the true—as opposed to the explicit and announced—goals (together with appropriate weights thereof) of any organization with great precision or certainty.

(3) Decision-makers themselves discover many of their value priorities only in the course of choosing among concrete alternatives.[14]

fore, when used as indicative of function, is apt to promote the idea that this function of government is to be found exclusively in the work of what are commonly referred to as executive or administrative authorities. . . . Such, however, is rarely the case in any political system, and is particularly not the case in the American governmental system."

He considered a rigid separation of powers along these abstract functional lines, moreover, to be clearly unfeasible:

". . . The separation of powers and authorities has proven . . . to be unworkable as a legal principle. The courts have made many exceptions to it, all in the direction of recognizing what one of them calls 'a common vicinage' bordering on the domains of each authority, in the occupancy of which each authority must tolerate the others. Thus, the organ of government whose main function is the execution of the will of the state is often, and indeed usually intrusted with the expression of that will in its details. . . . That is, the authority called executive has, in almost all cases, considerable ordinance or legislative power.

"On the other hand, the organ whose main duty is to express the will of the state, i.e., the legislature, has usually the power to control in one way or another the execution of the state will by that organ to which such execution is in the main intrusted. That is, while the two primary functions of government are susceptible of differentiation, the organs of government to which the discharge of these functions is intrusted cannot be clearly defined."

At the same time, like Wilson and Simon, Goodnow believed *normatively* that Congress should confine its control of the executive branch to matters of general policy interest. His reasons were less formalistic and more interesting, I believe, than Simon's. If political controls were extended further than was absolutely necessary to ensure the execution of the "state will," he thought, the administration was likely to become an instrument of the party in power. To the extent that this occurred, he wrote, "the spontaneous expression of the real state will tends to become more difficult and the execution of that will becomes inefficient." "On the other hand," he noted:

"if the attempt is made to strengthen the administrative system unduly in the hope of securing efficient administration, there is danger that, if the party organization is weak, the administrative organization may be made use of to influence the expression of the will of the state through its power over elections."

He concluded that the only solution lay in "frankly recognizing" that a balance between the conflicting ideals of political control and administrative independence had to be sought. Involved political man that he was, he then went on to specify in detail what he thought would constitute a desirable balance for the American governmental system of his day.

The above quotations are from Frank J. Goodnow, *Politics and Administration* (New York: Macmillan, 1900), pp. 14–16, 28, 92–93.

14. The most provocative analyst of this phenomemon has been Charles E. Lindblom. See his article, "Decision-Making in Taxation and Expenditures," which appears in Section II-C, below, and his book, *The Intelligence of Democracy* (New York: The Free Press, 1965).

(4) It would be an extraordinarily foolish administrator who searched endlessly for the absolute optimal alternative in any situation.

In view of (4), Simon has suggested, reasonable decision-makers "satisfice" rather than "maximize." To put it more simply, they cease searching for proposals when they come across "satisfactory" alternatives. So stated, the satisficing concept expresses a significant and frequently neglected insight; and it is a truism. Simon has sought to develop it into more, however. He has defined "satisficing" in operational terms and written of it as an important scientific hypothesis to be tested. "An alternative is *satisfactory*," according to Simon, "if: (a) there exists a set of criteria that describes minimally satisfactory alternatives, and (b) the alternative meets or exceeds all these criteria." [15] Thus, an administrator can be said to have satisficed if he has listed his minimal criteria exhaustively and then chosen the first alternative presented to him which met them.

This is certainly an operational definition. It is unlikely, however, to provide the operational criterion of efficiency that might make possible a genuine "science" of administrative efficiency. Rare indeed, after all, is the administrator who decides by going through the formal steps of listing criteria exhaustively and then comparing alternatives with them. Moreover, anyone who wished meaningfully to evaluate the efficiency of an administrator seeking "satisfactory" solutions would have to begin by judging whether the criteria that he listed were sufficiently ambitious or imaginative—in view of the obstacles to greater optimality facing him. In this age of innovation, quite clearly, the "efficiency" of the unimaginative and unambitious administrator who achieves all the goals he sets for himself can lead quickly to the decline of his organization.

With considerations such as these no doubt in mind, Simon formally abjured his program of raising the old "principles of administration" from proverbial to true scientific status in his 1957 introduction to the (otherwise unrevised) second edition of *Administrative Behavior*. "Organizations," he wrote:

are complex structures, and the importance of any particular factor in the design of such a structure will depend on many circumstances. Hence we can hardly hope for a set of invariant "weights" to apply to the design problem. I expect that for a long time to come, research in administration will be more concerned with identifying and understanding the basic mechanisms that are present in systems of organizational behavior than with assigning numbers to designate the importance of these mechanisms.[16]

Simon's vigorous reaffirmation of the ideal of a value-free science of administration has had a tremendous impact, nonetheless, probably because it coincided with the postwar behavioral revolution in American social science. Controversy still rages about the proper way to define behavioralism, but clearly its single most significant *influence* has been to enhance the valuation placed

15. James G. March and Herbert Simon, *Organizations* (New York: John Wiley and Sons, 1958), p. 140.
16. *Op. cit.*, Second Edition, 1957, p. xxxiv.

upon certainty—as opposed, for example, to provocativeness and profundity —as a quality of research conclusions. Scholars who have wished to earn the esteem of their behaviorally oriented colleagues have been spurred to define their concepts operationally (which is to say, so as to be susceptible of measurement), and to base their conclusions upon the measurement of observed actions or characteristics. Those *most* sensitive to the behavioral influence have been driven to do controlled experiments; others have been content to control their data analyses through the use of reputable statistical techniques; still others have tried by a variety of review procedures to reduce the element of arbitrariness in the writing of case studies to an absolute minimum.[17]

Of these three techniques, the first is almost never applicable to subjects of high political interest. The second, statistical analysis, is applicable most notably to political processes in which voting is an important factor. Thus, the past two decades have witnessed a flowering of studies of elections, legislative roll call patterns, and even judicial voting consistencies. They have also witnessed the production of numerous sophisticated studies of the opinions and background characteristics of all sorts of groups in American society, including, of course, both public and private bureaucratic leaders.

The third technique, case description, has also been employed in a great number of works. It has had its greatest impact, however, when complementing rather than substituting for more general analyses.[18] The major deficiency of the case study is that it necessarily deals with a very limited set of facts. Statistical research findings are also reliable only for the data with which they

17. I should add that there had been another—and less precisely describable, but more indisputably healthy—impact of the drive to make the study of politics more genuinely "scientific." This has been to spur all the social science professions to do more research and less armchair theorizing, to refrain more scrupulously from offering recommendations unaccompanied by careful analyses of the unintended consequences they may entail, and in general to evaluate evidence more critically. David Truman elegantly stated the case for defining social "science" with reference to values such as these in his 1965 Presidential address to the American Political Science Association:

". . . To specify that 'science' requires the hypothetico-deductive procedures and the integrated form of systematic explanation exemplified by the science of mechanics . . . is probably to deny that the discipline can be scientific or at best to confine it to problems of the most trivial character.

"It is not necessary, however, so to restrict the definition or even to espouse that form of science as a goal or an ideal . . . If one accepts Nagel's characterization that . . . 'The practice of scientific method is the persistent critique of arguments, in the light of tried canons for judging the reliability of the procedures by which evidential data are obtained, and for assessing the probative force of the evidence on which the conclusions are based,' then the recommitment in the discipline becomes sensible and, at least presumptively, manageable.

"Science so conceived requires generality of statement but not in a specified degree, nor does it require a particular level of precision, or a limited set of techniques. It does not assure the truth of every conclusion that it reaches or the absence of bias deriving, for example, from the value commitments of the investigator. It does not suggest that a precise line divides knowledge or beliefs that can be labelled 'common sense' from knowledge that claims to be 'scientific' . . . "

David Truman, "Disillusion and Regeneration: The Quest for a Discipline," *American Political Science Review*, LIX, No. 4 (December 1965), pp. 865–873. The quotation is from pages 870–871.

18. See, for example, Raymond A. Bauer, Ithiel de Sola Pool, and Lewis Anthony Dexter, *American Business and Public Policy* (New York: Atherton Press, 1963) and Robert Dahl, *Who Governs?* (New Haven: Yale University Press, 1961).

deal, of course, but these data may be of wide scope and immense intrinsic interest: national voting or opinion patterns, patterns of cohesion and conflict in Congress or the Supreme Court, background differences between the nation's political and business leaders, and so on. If one tries to deal with comparably large subjects via the case method, it obviously becomes impossible to interview all important actors, to give all a chance to read the case and have their reactions reported, or to examine all the publications, memoranda, and files that might shed light on the action described.

In other words, as the subject becomes larger, the aim of exhaustiveness in research becomes more clearly elusive. Moreover, as the subject matter becomes more controversial, charges that the researcher observed with biased eyes become progressively more difficult to refute. Hence, those anxious to enhance the case method's reputation for scientific reliability have been driven to describe quite small decision-making sequences or systems; and the case studies themselves have generally been most useful for illustrative and teaching rather than theory-testing purposes.

What has been the impact of the behavioral revolution on the study of public administration? One cannot be at all certain, but I believe it has been two-fold. First, it has contributed to the decline of public administration as a sub-field within political science. Second, it has encouraged a boom in social psychological studies of men in organizations. Let us consider these two developments in order.

Public administration has become a rather peripheral subfield of political science, lingering in the teaching curriculum but having little impact on advanced scholarly thought. Those highly oriented toward the "scientific" study of politics have turned to studies of opinions, elections, communications, legislative roll call patterns, etc. They have been diverted from public administration by the fact that statistical analysis of administrative decisions is unusually difficult, for such reasons as the following.

First, most administrative decisions are informal. Second, a large proportion, even in the domestic agencies, are secret. Thus, one can almost never feel confident that the sample of decisions which can be analyzed is typical. Moreover, even where records of decisions are available, their classification for purposes of policy analysis often presents insoluble problems. Administrators normally stress the unique and technical—as opposed to the general policy—determinants of each decision, so as to maximize their future flexibility and to minimize the danger of broad press and congressional interest coming to center on their work. When analyzing congressional decisions, one can often bypass this problem by using the evaluations of particular roll call votes issued by easily labeled organizations, or by looking for voting patterns among the Congressmen themselves. Administrative decisions rarely have obvious labels, however, nor do large groups of administrators vote regularly on common sets of questions. (In contrast to their decisions, of course, the background characteristics and the opinions of administrators are highly amenable to statistical analysis, and numerous studies have focused on them in recent years.)

Even those willing to base their analyses upon case studies find public administration a particularly frustrating field in which to work. Case writers who describe major political disputes at least have intrinsically interesting and important stories to tell. Those who examine congressional processes or election campaigns can use their cases to complement rather than substitute for statistical analyses. Those who examine the politics of a particular city can hope to cover most of the major issues active in it during a given time period, thus eliminating much of the sample problem.[19] Moreover, major political disputes occur largely in the open; in the course of being blown up they come to symbolize general policy issues; and most of the leading participants in them (politicians, interest group leaders, etc.) tend to be anxious to help the case writer get their sides of the story in full.

By contrast, administrative agencies deal with enormous numbers of matters and, as noted previously, tend to minimize the symbolic importance of each. It is quite clear to all that research ought to deal with the great mass of secret, routine, and informal decisions as well as the few that become subjects of widespread public controversy. Thus, after investing several years preparing case studies in a given administrative area, a researcher is likely to find that the stories he has to tell are important only to the extent that they are typical, and that he has no basis for refuting charges that they are not.

So much for the reasons why highly behavioral students of politics may have turned away from public administration. Many other political scientists, however, have continued to choose research topics solely on the basis of political importance. Why have so few of these focused on public administration in recent years?

In part, of course, the answer is obvious. The research boom of the thirties in public administration was significantly due to the fact that this was the period in which big bureaucratized government came to America. Its potential impact on American democracy was one of the hottest intellectual issues of the day. Since World War II, on the other hand, the interest of American intellectuals has increasingly shifted to such subjects as international relations and the politics of the underdeveloped areas.[20] Within the United States, the main focus has been on such "new" issues as race and the impact of the Cold War.

Quite clearly, however, this is only a partial answer. The Cold War has vastly accelerated the bureaucratization of American society and government,[21] and in fact the subject of national security policy making (including

19. Critics will still argue that the issues which are active in a stable political system at any time may be less relevant to a profound understanding of it than those which have been resolved, those which have been tabled, and those which no one has ever thought to raise. One of the historic functions of social science, of course, has been to point up general issues and trends where the active participants in social processes had previously seen only masses of detail.

20. Increasingly in recent years, it should be noted, political scientists concerned with underdeveloped countries have written about their administrative problems and institutions. This is an important development, and it would deserve a prominent place in any comprehensive history of the study of public administration. The present essay, however, is concerned with public administration as a branch of the study of *American* politics and society.

21. National security spending—defined here to include the U.S. budget categories of National Defense, International Affairs and Finance, and Space Research and Technology—rose from one-eighth of the federal administrative budget in 1939 to three-fifths in 1965. The absolute increase was fifty-six times. National security employment increased from two-fifths of total federal em-

such attendant subtopics as science and government, news management, loyalty-security programs, and government contracting) has been the focus of substantial and constantly increasing research activity over the past fifteen years. The interesting question is why so few writers on national security policy making—even those dealing with such subjects as budgeting, inter-agency rivalries, the inner workings of the National Security Council, and the development of the position of Secretary of Defense—have chosen to present their work as falling within the traditional rubric of public administration.

One suspects that they have been put off by the traditional emphasis of public administration on efficiency, and that they have seen little reason in any event to associate with a specialization so widely considered moribund. Whatever their motives, however, their choice has had at least two unfortunate effects. First, it has served to discourage syntheses of the old literature with the new, and of the literature on domestic politics with that on national security politics. Second, it has served to delay incorporation of the new research on national security policy making into the teaching curriculum. Although it constituted the most interesting body of work published in the postwar period on American public administrative processes, many teachers of public administration have yet to make a significant place for it in their syllabi. Consequently, its presentation to students has often had to await the introduction of special courses on national security policy making. Such courses in turn have typically been taught as though their subject matter were *sui generis,* neither drawing sustenance from nor contributing to any larger body of theory about American governmental processes.

Before going on, a brief recapitulation may be helpful. Two major reasons for the decline of public administration as a political science subfield have been suggested. First, the increasing behavioral influence in American social science has spurred students of American politics to move from public administration into the study of subjects more amenable to "scientific" analysis. Second, public administration itself has failed to replace "efficiency"—a term which appears increasingly less precise, and a goal in which students of government are progressively less interested—with a set of concerns more closely related to the central concerns of modern political science. The problem, it should be emphasized, is not that contemporary students of public administration remain unswervingly devoted to efficiency. It is rather that, taken collectively, they have failed to become identified in the eyes of their colleagues with any more compelling set of governmental problems.

So much for the neglect of administration in recent years by students of American politics. One of the striking phenomena of the postwar period, however, has been a burgeoning of administrative research that is not politically (or even publicly) oriented. The interdisciplinary field of organiza-

ployment (civilian and military combined) to three quarters in the same period. The absolute increase was seven times. These employment figures are artificially deflated, it should be noted, because they fail to take into account the millions of civilians now employed in the private sector under government contracts. Government by contract is essentially a postwar phenomenon.

tional behavior, with its focus on the social psychology of men in organizations, has enjoyed a boom of truly major proportions since World War II. Nearly all of the organizations examined have been nongovernmental, however, and few scholars working in the field have considered political relevance a noteworthy criterion of research significance. Formal organizations have been seized upon for their character as relatively well-defined social systems. Attention has focused predominantly on their internal lives, especially their relations with individual employees, small work units, and "customers."

The new discipline of organizational behavior has not emerged primarily, or even very significantly, from public administration. Three major "schools" of administrative study thrived in the first four decades of this century. Of these, only one, that exemplified by Wilson, Goodnow, and Gulick, focused mainly on public bureaucracies. It is today remembered as the "administrative management" school. The other two, which are remembered as the "scientific management" and "human relations" schools respectively, focused primarily on corporate bureaucracies—and the lowest levels of corporate bureaucracies at that.

Members of the scientific management school aimed at making optimal use of the human body in the performance of repetitive mechanical tasks. They produced numerous ingenious studies purporting to specify (1) how specific tasks could be done with minimal expenditures of time and effort, and (2) how maximal production could be obtained from well-motivated workers with minimal expenditures of time for eating, resting, and other nonproductive activities.

During the twenties and thirties a reaction to "scientific management" developed in the name of "human relations." Human relations theorists contended that the fundamental obstacle to industrial efficiency was the difficulty of motivating workers to strive for good performance. The scientific management school had assumed that the human material of bureaucracies was psychologically inert—that is, simply and almost limitlessly susceptible of being manipulated by those at the top charged with prescribing formal structures of authority and systems of compensation.[22] It had followed that the problem of motivation in manual work situations could be dealt with by any competent technician. The solution was to determine scientifically the rate at which "good" men could produce, and what they "deserved" to earn if they worked to capacity. Price rates could then be set accordingly. Human relations theorists, by contrast, maintained that men were primarily seekers after acceptance and approval, particularly from their peers, rather than money. They perceived the answer to the motivation problem to lie mainly in the area of cultivating

22. It should be noted that this assumption was borrowed from classical economics, and that it was shared by the administrative management school. Administrative management theorists carried it to less absurd limits than their scientific management counterparts, however, and by the mid-1930's the more subtle among them were endeavoring to take account of recent writings on both "human relations" and American Administrative politics. The result, as noted previously, was never a genuine reconciliation of old and new, but it *was* a tempering of the old with a good deal of sophistication about its limited applicability.

group life within the factory—conceived ideally as a "community"—and influencing group social and moral norms.

The scientific management and human relations schools still flourish. The problems of showing manual laborers how to use their bodies efficiently and then of inducing them actually to do so remain of great interest to businessmen. Both schools, moreover, have made significant practical contributions to industrial efficiency in a wide variety of situations. In consequence, American corporations have increasingly provided them with testing grounds and money for their research. Over the past fifteen years the two schools have strengthened themselves by gradually integrating their orientations and theories. Their research has increasingly attracted the interest of sociologists and social psychologists interested solely in understanding (as opposed to practical applications). Out of this amalgam has come the half pure—half applied discipline, organizational behavior.

How is this relevant to an understanding of what has happened to public administration? The answer is simply that most of those in the "administrative management" tradition who have not left the study of administration altogether have progressively in recent years taken their bearings from the literature on organizational behavior. Herbert Simon himself has led the way in this direction, and indeed he had indicated in *Administrative Behavior* that he might. On page two of that volume he had declared that "the construction of an efficient administrative organization is a problem in social psychology." On its final page he had returned to this theme, contending that the science of administration might take either of two paths. On the one hand, it might pursue knowledge "as to how men would behave if they wished their activity to result in the greatest attainment of administrative objectives with scarce means." On the other hand, it might simply describe and analyze "the way in which human beings behave in organized groups." These alternatives, he concluded, found their analogies in other sciences, such as economics:

First, economic theory and institutional economics are generalized descriptions of the behavior of men in the market. Second, business theory states those conditions of business behavior which will result in the maximization of profit.

Administrative Behavior had dealt with both, because its concern was the entire science of administration.

It was not surprising, then, that as the pursuit of principles of efficiency to guide top-level administrators came to appear fruitless, scholars who wished to achieve a high degree of certainty and yet to remain students of administration would turn to social psychological analyses of human behavior "in organized groups." This alternative was the more attractive because such scholars who happened to have received their training in political science could take their new bearings from, and more or less join, the growing fraternity of psychologists and sociologists already studying human behavior in organizations. They did not, in other words, have to strike out wholly on their own. They had simply to shift reference groups.

This is not to disparage the field of organizational behavior. Some of its recent fruits have been extremely interesting, and some of the older classics which are today accounted part of its literature are remarkably fruitful sources of hypotheses about the causes and political consequences of bureaucratization.[23] My purpose is rather to venture an explanation of the fact that those political scientists (defined in terms of graduate training and academic appointments) who have continued to specialize in administration have more and more taken their bearings from sociology and psychology—the most "behavioral" social sciences—rather than from the rest of political science. Their research has, no doubt in consequence, been of less and less *political* relevance.

It is not at all clear that the teaching of introductory public administration has followed suit to any great extent. Nonetheless, recent textbooks and books of readings have tended to replace or supplement the old material (left over from the thirties) on the techniques of financial and personnel administration primarily with new material on small group dynamics. The major exception to this picture is that there has been a great resurgence of interest during the 1960's in rational (now termed "cost effectiveness") budgeting. The new theories of budgeting are an outgrowth of economics, and behavioral students of administration feel at home with them. Part of their attraction is that they call for rigorous attempts to quantify and to employ mathematical techniques of analysis in the budget process. Unquestionably, they do constitute an important administrative innovation. In another sense, however, they are a throwback. Their aim is to aid organizations rationally to pursue explicit values determined at the top. They assume implicitly that pluralism and bargaining relationships within an organizational system are unfortunate (except, perhaps, as they are sources of ideas). In other words, they greatly resemble the principles of administrative management. What is politically interesting about them is the ways in which their application can alter bargaining relationships within a political system. Textbook treatments to date, however, have simply expounded the theory. Analyses of its political consequences have been rare even in the scholarly literature.

With the history reviewed in this essay as background, permit me to conclude with a few words on the aims of the present volume. Few contemporary texts or readers focus on the political issues surrounding American public administration. (I have endeavored in these pages to explain why.) These few, moreover, are without exception abbreviated volumes aimed more at the basic American government course—which typically includes a week or so devoted to administrative subjects—than at the full-semester course in public administration. Hence, the first of this volume's aims is simply to make life a bit easier (1) for students, and (2) for those colleagues around the country who believe that public administration should be taught as an integral part of the study of American politics. The second is to serve and reinforce the still em-

---

23. See, for example, the relevant works of Henri de Saint Simon, Emile Durkheim, Max Weber, Robert Michels, and Karl Mannheim.

bryonic trend toward incorporating the literature on national security administrative politics into the public administration curriculum. Third, and finally,
some hope is entertained that this volume may have a modest influence on research, by reminding political scientists specializing in administration of the
need for politically oriented studies, and by reminding students of American
politics more generally of the potential for vital and exciting research that remains in public administration.[24]

EMERGING CONFLICTS IN THE DOCTRINES
OF PUBLIC ADMINISTRATION *
Herbert Kaufman

AS a self-conscious discipline among the cluster of specialties or "fields" encompassed by political science, public administration came late and grew fast.
Its recent arrival and rapid growth sometimes obscure the fact that its origins
are to be found in a process of experimentation with governmental structure
that long preceded the appearance of public administration as a subject of systematic study and is likely to continue as long as the nation exists. This process of experimentation goes on vigorously today, and the development of new
forms is generating discord more profound and far-reaching than any that has
ever hitherto divided students of public administration. It is with the sources
and significance of that discord that this paper is concerned.

I. THREE CORE VALUES

The central thesis of this paper is that an examination of the administrative
institutions of this country suggests that they have been organized and operated in pursuit successively of three values, here designated representativeness,
neutral competence, and executive leadership. Each of these values has been
dominant (but not to the point of total suppression of the others) in different periods of our history; the shift from one to another generally appears to

* From the *American Political Science Review*, Vol. 50 (December 1956), pp. 1057–1073. Reprinted by permission of the author and publisher.
24. Is it totally fanciful to imagine a textbook (broadly defined) influencing research? I think
not, and I suspect that they do quite regularly. Most scholars are teachers, and their ideas for research emerge significantly out of their teaching experiences. These experiences in turn are shaped
significantly by the material that they assign their students to read. Textbooks at times purport
merely to summarize the literature on a subject, but their authors unavoidably make numerous
decisions about what to highlight and what to leave out entirely. When a consensus on many of
the judgments emerges among the textbook writers, the neglect of certain subjects by researchers
may be greatly reinforced. For a forceful statement of much the same point in another context,
see Lawrence J. R. Herson, "The Lost World of Municipal Government," *American Political Science Review*, LI, No. 2 (June 1957), pp. 330–345.

have occurred as a consequence of the difficulties encountered in the period preceding the change. Much of the early literature commonly identified as within the province of public administration was written during the transition from the first to the second of these values, and the great flood of materials produced after World War I often reflected both the second and third values when these for a time (and for reasons to be explained) pointed in the same direction for governmental improvement. Lately, however, the courses of action indicated by the second and third values have been not only different, but contradictory; the cleavage is becoming increasingly apparent in the doctrines of public administration. What the effects will be on the fraternity of practitioners and on their aspirations to professional status is difficult to say, but it seems clear that commitments to values that have become incompatible can produce only gulfs in the realm of ideas and confusion in proposals for governmental reform.

The Quest for Representativeness. The earliest [1] stress was placed on representativeness in government, the quest for which clearly had its roots in the colonial period, when colonial assemblies were struggling with royal governors for control of political life in the New World and "No taxation without representation" was a slogan that expressed one of the principal interests and anxieties of the colonists. The legislatures thus became the champions of the indigenous population, or at least of the ruling elements in the colonies, against what was regarded in many quarters as executive oppression. When the Revolution drove the British out, the legislatures in the new states were, with but a couple of exceptions,[2] enthroned in positions of leadership of the new governments, and, although the franchise continued to be limited to a relatively small proportion of the people, it was through the legislatures that governmental policy was formulated and legitimated. Even in the states that continued to operate under their colonial charters in the post-Revolutionary years, the governors were reduced to figureheads with little influence in the making of governmental decisions. In ten of the states, the governors were elected by the legislatures, most of them for only one-year terms; in just one state did the governor have a veto, and even that was limited by present-day standards. Governors had few powers of appointment and removal, or of administrative supervision and control. They did not function as legislative leaders. Lacking in status and in constitutional and administrative strength, governors had no source of political strength, and they therefore remained subordinate to the legislatures in every respect; they had no leverage with which to exert influence even if they had been so inclined. Hence, the office was regarded as primarily ceremonial and a symbol of honor rather than as a seat of power, and it therefore rarely attracted men of distinction in the early days of the Republic. Consequently, as late as the opening years of the Twentieth Century, the

1. It is impossible to date any of the periods with precision, except arbitrarily, and it is probably unnecessary to do so for most purposes, but their origins can be identified, and so, roughly, can their zeniths.

2. New York and Massachusetts. These states provided important models for the federal executive, which ultimately was set up as an even stronger—and perhaps better—office than its prototypes.

governorship was a dead-end road. As one authority has remarked, they served their short terms and returned to private life with few accomplishments behind them and nothing before them but the pleasure of being called "Governor" for the rest of their days.[3] The legislatures ruled virtually unchallenged.

In local government, too, collegiate bodies were in charge. Whether they were truly "representative," and whether one ought to refer to the governing organ of a community that is not "sovereign" as a legislature, are questions we need not consider here. Suffice it to say that local executives labored under the same or perhaps greater handicaps than their state counterparts and therefore presented no more of a challenge to the local institutions corresponding to legislatures than did the governors to the state bodies.

The constitutional specifications for the Presidency constituted a countertrend to the apparent value system of governmental designers in early America. For the President was invested with greater authority than almost any other chief executive of the time. Yet even at the federal level, there were clearly widespread expectations that the Congress would provide the primary motive power for the government, a view shared, according to Binkley, even by many incumbents of the White House whose "Whig conception" of the presidency as subservient to the legislature may be contrasted with the "stewardship theory" of independent presidential authority to be enunciated much later in history. While Washington and Jefferson fought to protect and extend executive power from the very first, it is probably not stretching the facts to argue that Presidents for a long time had an uphill struggle in this effort, and that many chose to yield to the sentiment of the day and the strength of the giants in Congress. Whether or not the legislatures were actually the most representative institutions need not be explored here; there is ample evidence that they were thought to be so.

The enthronement of the legislature was one of the two major tangible indications of the value placed on representativeness; the other was the rather uncritical faith in the electoral principle. It began with the extension of the franchise and a thrust toward universal adult suffrage. But the faith in elections also took the form of an increasing number of official positions filled by balloting. The first half of the Nineteenth Century saw the number of elective offices sharply increased, especially after the Jacksonian Revolution burst upon the country. The ballot grew in length until almost every public official from President down to dogcatcher came to power via the electoral route. Moreover, with the rise of the party organizations to new influence as a result, even those positions which were not made elective were filled by party faithful; the spoils system came into its own. By the time of the Civil War, voters found themselves confronted by hundreds of names on their ballots, and each change of party brought with it a change in virtually all government employees.

3. There were notable exceptions of course. Cleveland became President after serving as Governor of New York, Hayes and McKinley had both been Governors of Ohio before moving to the White House, and other governors became influential in national politics. As a general rule, however, the governorship was not a springboard to power or prominence.

The Quest for Neutral Competence. As early as the middle of the Nineteenth Century, it had become clear to some people that legislative supremacy, the long ballot, and the spoils system did not in fact increase representativeness; as a matter of fact, they often seemed to have just the opposite effect. For one thing, they tended to confuse both voters and interest groups and thereby opened the way to power to political bosses who, while providing a measure of integration in the bewildering pullulation of government, often utilized their positions to advance their personal interests and the interests of the organizations they headed without regard for the interests of many of the governed. For another thing, legislators and administrators at every level of government proved themselves peculiarly vulnerable to the forces let loose by the burgeoning industrial system; corruption beset legislatures from county boards and city councils right up to Congress itself, and the venality and incompetence of many public officers and employers were common knowledge.

Disillusionment with existing governmental machinery was a result. State and local constitutions and charters grew longer and more detailed as reformers tried to reduce the discretion of legislative bodies. Limitations on the length and frequency of state legislative sessions were imposed to limit the amount of harm they could do. And at every level, reformers began to cast around for new governmental machinery that would provide a high level of responsible government service while avoiding the high costs of unalloyed representative mechanisms.

Thus began the quest for neutral competence in government officials, a quest which has continued to the present day. The core value of this search was ability to do the work of government expertly, and to do it according to explicit, objective standards rather than to personal or party or other obligations and loyalties.[4] The slogan of the neutral competence school became, "Take administration out of politics."

This school produced its own rationale and mechanisms for this purpose. The rationale was the now-familiar politics-administration dichotomy, according to which politics and administration are distinct and separable processes

---

4. Proponents of this value generally did not demean representative institutions; on the contrary, they claimed their programs would strengthen those institutions by rationalizing governmental operations and improving their quality to such an extent that elected officers would be in a position to exert greater control over policy than they ever could hope to do in the prevailing political jungle. The case for neutral competence has normally been made not as an alternative to representativeness, but as a fulfillment of it.

The disillusionment of some was so thorough, however, that they lost faith completely in representativeness, in the capacity of a people to rule themselves, and returned to advocacy of rule by an aristocracy of talent. Civil service reform was, in fact, a movement which found its leaders among the grandsons and great-grandsons of the "Patricians" of early days, among the "Old Whigs" and their sons, among those who had been enamored of, or grew up under, British or German or French institutions (for example, the Adamses, Godkin, Schurz, Villard, Rosengarten), and among the urban mercantile and older businesses or professions rather than among the new industrialists. Distrust of the populace may still be observed in some modern writers and even in some current supporters of the neutral competence idea, but, for the most part, the concept of representation was so deeply ingrained in American thinking—and, indeed, in American emotions, for the word has become a revered one—that few dare to attack it openly whatever their beliefs may be.

that should therefore be assigned to separate and distinct organs. The mechanisms were independent boards and commissions and the merit system, which were designed to insulate many public officials and public policies from political pressures.

The movement gathered momentum after the Civil War, although the first agitation for some of its objectives goes back even further. In local and state governments, library boards and park boards and police boards and boards of health and finance boards and utilities commissions and boards of education and boards of assessment and equalization and boards and commissions for a dozen other purposes mushroomed up all over the governmental landscape. At the federal level, the Interstate Commerce Commission came into being, to be followed in the Twentieth Century by a host of like bodies. These agencies, at every level, differed from each other in details, but had the same underlying structure: their members were appointed for overlapping terms supposedly on the basis of their reputations for general ability and character and specialized knowledge. They were granted wide discretion and secure tenure for substantial periods, and were expected to formulate policy on nonpolitical premises. Objectivity was reinforced in some instances by mandatory bipartisan membership on the boards. The exigencies of the times made it necessary for legislatures to delegate power to administrative agencies; the advocates of neutral competence deflected delegation from the chief executives and the departments under their control to what was later to be branded "the headless fourth branch of government."

The merit system, peculiarly, made its greatest advances where boards and commissions were slowest to gain a foothold—the federal government. Pressure for the merit system began before the Civil War; its first fruit was the federal Civil Service Act of 1883. Initially, the objectives of the program were confined principally to controlling the selection of government workers by taking the power to hire staff from the hands of executive heads (who were politicians) and lodging it with experts who, if they did not actually appoint personnel, at least could screen out all but those who could pass tests of one sort or another. This aspect of the program spread rapidly in the federal government; despite the subsequent growth of the federal service, about nine out of ten government employees today are under some form of merit appointment. But the process did not stop with the removal of the appointing power from politics; over the years, the Civil Service Commission extended its surveillance to dismissal, promotion, and position classification; eventually, with the aid of new legislation, the political activities of civil servants were reduced to little more than voting. A wall was erected between the government bureaucracy and the politicians, a wall policed by the Civil Service Commission.[5]

The quest for neutral competence, though it began about a century ago, has

5. The states and localities were slow to follow suit. By the turn of the century, only two states had enacted civil service legislation and only a few of the largest cities. Even today, the formal merit system still has a long way to go at these levels: states and localities remain the prime targets of the civil service reformers. But they have made some impressive gains during the last quarter-century, and the idea is still spreading.

never waned. The training of civil servants became steadily more formal and systematic as time passed; courses, departments, and even schools of administration appeared in universities. Organization and methods analysis became a profession in itself. Boards and commissions are still common modes of handling administrative problems—witness, for example, the Atomic Energy Commission. Supporters of the merit system continue unabated their efforts to extend it "upward, outward, and downward." The desire to make government employment an attractive career service was given new voice by the Commission of Inquiry on Public Service Personnel a generation ago, and by the Task Force on Personnel and Civil Service of the Second Hoover Commission more recently. The city manager plan—and even the town, county, and state manager plans—have continued to score successes. Neutral competence is still a living value among students of government, career civil servants, and, perhaps more significantly, among much of the general populace.

The Quest for Executive Leadership. Just as the excessive emphasis on representativeness brought with it bitterly disappointing difficulties unforeseen by its advocates, so too the great stress on neutral competence proved to be a mixed blessing. And just as the failures of the machinery established with an eye primarily to representativeness helped produce the reaction toward neutral competence, so too the weaknesses of the governmental arrangements devised by the latter school—or, more accurately, the weaknesses of government resulting from the work of *both* schools—gave impetus to the supporters of a third value: executive leadership.

For both earlier philosophies, and the mechanisms to which they gave rise, created a thrust toward fragmentation of government, toward the formation of highly independent islands of decision-making occupied by officials who went about their business without much reference to each other or to other organs of government. Neither elected administrative officials nor independent boards and commissions welcomed direction from the chief executives; the former were supported by constituencies in much the same way as governors and mayors, and their tenure was linked largely to their vote-getting prowess, while the latter generally remained in office longer than the chief executives and depended very little on them for support. Besides, as these officials and agencies became more accomplished in their respective areas of specialization, they tended to resent efforts of "laymen" and "amateurs" to intervene; this tendency revealed itself even in some civil servants nominally under the chief executives, who, though formally subject to dismissal, turned out in practice to have quite secure tenure, and who, by adept maneuvers in negotiating bureaucratic armistices ("memoranda of agreement") and in forming alliances with legislative committees and clientele groups, succeeded in carving out for themselves broad areas of discretion free of real supervision by their political chiefs.

The drive toward fragmentation could not be effectively countered by legislative bodies, despite their vast statute-making, financial, and investigative powers. Even Congress can exercise only a general and intermittent oversight over administrative agencies, and has had to confine itself to providing general standards guiding the exercise of administrative discretion and to occasional intervention to correct abuses or to force specific changes in policy. And state legislatures and city councils and county boards operate under still greater limitations; many of these bodies are in session for only brief periods out of each year (or biennium), and administrative officials conduct the business of government with great latitude in the long intervals between meetings. Moreover, even if legislatures met often enough and had enough technical assistance of their own to exert control over administration, their composition and procedures would render them incapable of providing integration; working through tens of committees, reaching decisions through processes of compromise and concession among representatives of small territorials units, functioning increasingly as reviewing bodies for proposals placed before them by executive and administrative agencies and by interest groups, they are generally too slow and too fragmented to perform this function effectively.

Neither have the courts been able to integrate the component elements of American government. They were not designed for this responsibility, and they are completely unable to discharge it. Limited to refereeing disputes between contending parties, formal in procedure and deliberate in method, they could not play this role even had they been willing. In fact, they have increasingly moved toward acceptance of findings of fact by administrative organizations and toward restriction of their own activities to review of questions of jurisdiction and procedure.

The centrifugal drives of the representativeness and neutral competence institutions thus found no important counter-force in the legislatures or in the courts. So the efforts to maximize these values brought with them the dispersion of governmental policy-making processes.

There were widespread criticisms of this fragmentation.[6] It bred chaos; agencies pursued contradictory policies in related fields. It fomented conflict; agencies engaged in bitter bureaucratic warfare to establish their spheres of jurisdiction. It opened gaps in the provision of service or of regulation; clienteles were sometimes denied benefits or escaped supervision because they fell between agencies. It was costly; many agencies maintained overhead organizations that could have been replaced more cheaply and effectively by a common organization, and citizens had to make their own way through bureaucratic labyrinths. And, most important of all, it led to irresponsibility; no one quite knew how the pattern of organization and program came into existence or what could be done to alter it, each segment of the fragmented governments became a self-directing unit, the impact of elections on the conduct of government was minimized, and special interest groups often succeeded in virtually capturing control of individual agencies. No one seemed to be steering the governmental machinery, though everyone had a hand in it. At best, it seemed

---

6. Criticisms, that is to say, of the fragmentation "in general." When it came to the particular fragments over which they exerted their greatest influence, legislators, bureaucrats, party organizers, and interest groups were often defensive of their special positions and hostile to integrating remedies which might disturb their control.

to be drifting (and just when the growth of the economic system appeared to make greater direction necessary), while at worst it showed signs of flying apart or grinding to a stop. These were among the forces that persuaded many students of government that chief executives had to be built up to take charge of the machinery.

The office of the chief executive became their hope because it furnished the only available means of achieving the end sought.[7] Movement toward strengthening chief executives began long before there was an explicit body of doctrine to explain and justify it. In the federal government, it took the form of struggles between Presidents and Congress for control of policy. Since the Presidency was set up with strong constitutional powers at the very start, the battle raged over the breadth of the powers conferred rather than over formal constitutional changes. Those powers were firmly defended, liberally interpreted, and gradually expanded under the strong Presidents from Washington on. The governors, on the other hand, having been granted few powers at the start, gained strength slowly, largely through constitutional amendment, in the course of the Nineteenth Century. In the same period, many city executives developed from mere chairmen of councils to weak mayors and then to strong mayors, and there was even an occasional step in this direction among the rural units of government. These things were taking place even while the emphasis on representativeness was predominant; they continued after the pursuit of neutral competence became the order of the day; but the Twentieth Century was well on its way before executive leadership became a systematic quest supported by articulate theories, and before it really began to gather speed.

One of the first signs of the new emphasis was the rapid spread of the executive budget in government. For a long time, agency requests for funds were considered individually, and there was no central point at which total expenditures were reviewed and the competing claims balanced against each other in the light of the resources available; indeed, very often, the only way governments could figure out how much they were spending was to add up the appropriation bills after they had been passed. The reformers turned to the chief executives to rationalize the spending process, and out of it came the now familiar phenomena of executive review and adjustment of agency requests, and the submittal of a comprehensive budget supposed to make it possible to see the overall spending pattern. The practice was often far short of ideal, but, for the first time, chief executives were given a powerful instrument with which to control administrative behavior; it was a major advance in striving to equip them to integrate American government. A few large cities and states adopted budgetary legislation during the first two decades of the Twentieth Century, and the Taft Commission on Efficiency and Economy in 1912 urged such a measure upon the federal government. By the middle of the

7. Party bosses occasionally did serve this function, but *only* occasionally, for it must be remembered that our political parties are really congeries of smaller organizations in most places and therefore hardly equipped to provide governmental integration. Besides, they were phenomena from which governmental designers were seeking to deliver the governmental process.

third decade, many of the largest cities, virtually all of the states, and the federal government had budget laws on the books. Since then, in general, the tendency has been toward continued increase in the budgetary powers of chief executives, and toward adoption of the process by those jurisdictions in which it did not previously obtain. A large body of literature now backs up this practice, and, though the lack of a *theory* of budgeting (as contrasted with beliefs about the appropriate *machinery* for budgeting) has been pointed out, the executive-budget doctrine is widely accepted and rarely challenged.

Another indication of the concern with executive leadership is the administrative reorganization movement. It is frequently described as having begun in 1917, when Illinois adopted a sweeping change in its administrative structure, although such measures had been unsuccessfully urged in other states several years earlier. Under this plan, the number of agencies was reduced, and they were grouped into comparatively few departments headed by officials appointed by the governor; an administrative pyramid, with the governor standing at the apex, was the goal, and if it was rarely achieved completely, the extent to which it was approximated is indeed remarkable considering the degree of fragmentation prior to the changes. The number of elected administrative officials was sharply diminished, and ballots became correspondingly shorter. The appointing and removal power of the governor was also increased. In a single vast upheaval, the reorganizers sought to elevate him from an almost impotent exhorter to a powerful leader; if their efforts did not—as they could not—*immediately* produce the consequences sought, it was not very long before they began to bear fruit. Administratively and politically, the Illinois governor ascended to new eminence and influence. And more than half the states, some cities, and a few counties and towns, followed Illinois' lead. All during the 'twenties and 'thirties, surveys of government machinery were commonplace, and they became even more so after World War II as the first federal Hoover Commission touched off a wave of "little Hoover Commissions" in the states and many cities. "Concentration of authority and responsibility," "functional integration," "direct lines of responsibility," "grouping of related services," "elimination of overlapping and duplication," and "need for coordination" echoed through state capitols, city and town halls, and even through some county courthouses as chief executives became the new center of governmental design.

At the federal level, there were occasional adjustments and readjustments in the machinery of government in the early part of the century, and the President was even invested with broad powers of reorganization during the emergencies of World War I and the depression. But it was not until the mushrooming agencies of the New Deal strained that machinery to its limits that the practices and supporting dogmas of the reorganizers made their appearance in strength in Washington. Few clearer statements of the executive leadership value than the *Report of the President's Committee on Administrative Management* have ever been published; with its recommendations on pulling the administrative functions of the independent regulatory commissions back under the President, on drawing the government corporations back into the hierarchy, on bringing personnel management under close direction by the President, on strengthening the White House staff, on getting the General Accounting Office out of the pre-auditing field and returning this operation to the executive branch, and in the tightly reasoned explanations of these recommendations (which were tied to the peg of the separation of powers), the Committee offered the classic presentation of the reorganization aspects of the executive leadership school.[8]

The Reorganization Act of 1939, which reversed one formal relationship of the President to Congress by conferring initiatory responsibility for reorganization plans on the former and authorizing the latter in effect to veto such proposals, reflected in practice the theory of the Report; even the frequent use of the legislative veto does not reduce the significance of this expansion of executive power, and the fierceness of the periodic battles over renewal of the Act suggests both Congressmen and Presidents are conscious of this significance. In the course of the years since the Report, without much fanfare, other recommendations of the Committee have been put into practice, too; the influence of the Committee continued to make itself felt for a long time.

The first Hoover Commission was considerably less emphatic about strengthening the chief executive than its predecessor, and the second Hoover Commission has displayed, if anything, some coldness (if not outright hostility) to the concept. It is conceivable, therefore, that the reorganization movement has for the time being run its course in the federal government. But it would probably be an error to write off entirely this phase of the quest for executive leadership.

A third index of this quest, an index related to, but distinguishable from, the developments in budgeting and administrative reorganization, is the increase in the size of executive staffs. The archetype is the Executive Office of the President with its hundreds of specialists providing the President with advice on every aspect of policy, reviewing legislative proposals to work out the Presidential attitude, studying administrative management from the President's point of view, planning, researching, furnishing legal counsel, serving as a source of information alternative and supplementary to the formal hierarchy, and studded with "the President's men," responsible and loyal to him and him alone. This is a far cry from the days when a President's secretariat consisted of a few aides who helped him with his official correspondence; it has helped to give the chief executive the means with which to direct the administration he heads and to formulate programs and press them into statute and then into operation; it has helped make him a real center of political and administrative power. In like fashion, the executive offices of many of the governors have been transformed into instruments of leadership, and some local executives

8. To be sure, the Committee also advocated expansion of the merit system, and restated the argument that stronger executive leadership would mean greater popular control of government (i.e., representativeness), thus indicating how deep-seated these parallel values were. But this cannot obscure the basic premises of the Committee's Report, nor negate its general impact: it is overwhelmingly for executive leadership in sentiment.

have been similarly equipped; at these levels, the evolution has been somewhat less dramatic, but not much less effective. The tendencies may be uneven in their fulfillment, but they are pronounced.

Doctrinally, the sharp conceptual cleavage between politics and administration, which gained currency during the years when neutral competence was ascendent, and which served as such a useful philosophical prop for the machinery favored in those years, became an impediment to the justification of executive leadership. For one thing, chief executives, in whom administrative responsibility and power were to be lodged, were also partisan politicians. Moreover, one of the main reasons advanced for seeking integration was elimination of the fragmentation resulting from acceptance of the idea of the separability of politics and administration. Gradually, therefore, the politics-administration dichotomy fell out of favor in public administration, and the doctrine of the continuity of the policy-formulating process, better suited to the aims of executive leadership, began to replace it. Before long, the traditional orthodoxy became old-fashioned and found few defenders.

By every measure, then, the years from 1910 to 1950 were characterized by the rise of the quest for executive leadership to a place of pre-eminence in administrative thought and action.

The Concurrence of Values. For expository purposes, the quest for the three values has here been treated as sequential, and, to be sure, each had a different high point in time. Nevertheless, it is worth pausing to reiterate that at no point was any of them pursued to the complete exclusion of one or both of the others; evidence of interest in all three can be found at any stage of our history, sometimes in a single document by a single author. As has been observed, the defense of any one was often framed in terms of advancement of the others simultaneously. The story is thus one of changing balance among the values, not of total displacement.

II. THE COALITION

For many years, the proponents of neutral competence and the partisans of executive leadership were able to make common cause, and their alliance became so imbedded in their thinking that the differences between them were hardly recognized. The divisive factors beginning to emerge today then lay hidden beneath the mutual striving after a shared goal—a merit system to replace the spoils system.[9] Much of the standard literature of public administration was written during this honeymoon period and therefore embraced both values at once.

That the members of the neutral competence school should support the merit system as against the spoils system is not at all surprising; this reform lay at the core of their program for redesigning governmental organization. But it does require some explanation to account for the position of the execu-

9. "Merit system" and "spoils system," as used in this section of this paper, include, but are not restricted to, personnel management. Patronage, it will be seen, is but one aspect—albeit the principal one—of spoils, which includes contracts, purchases, and other "favors." The remedies of the reformers were aimed at every aspect.

tive leadership people, since spoils were allegedly one of the most effective devices through which executive influence could be exerted. There would seem to be a contradiction between advocacy of measures to strengthen executives on the one hand and endorsement of a system that appeared to reduce executive influence on the other.

The contradiction is more apparent than real. The spoils system had its uses for chief executives, but, as it operated in this country, it never really gave these officers control of the administrative hierarchy. As a source of inducements to persuade legislators to support executive-sponsored measures, it was quite helpful at times. It was also valuable in providing incentives to attract workers for the parties. But it never furnished the executives with loyal, enthusiastic, capable, disciplined administrative machines; it did not make them chief administrators.

Federal patronage, for example, about which more is known than has been revealed about patronage practices at any other level of government, was distributed largely through Senators and Representatives, hopefully in return for the legislators' votes on issues in which the Presidents were interested. But Congressmen ordinarily had to farm out their patronage to the party organizations in their states and districts, and even dissident wings of Presidential parties which did not give Presidential measures consistent support in the legislative chambers could often count on nominating some federal appointees. During election campaigns the Presidents needed the support of all segments of the parties and could not, therefore, afford to weaken them for their legislative defections. In short, the patronage system strengthened party leaders and legislators more than it did executives. Thus the appointing power of the Presidents was bargained away—shrewdly sometimes, to be sure, from the point of view of legislation and of political survival, but at some cost from the standpoint of administrative management. Moreover, if a President's own nomination was itself the result of bargaining in which he was the chosen rather than the chooser, then his appointing power was largely taken away at the start.

It was not just a matter of creating "ten enemies and one ingrate" with every appointment. Equally important, patronage tended to fragment the executive branch as much as did election of administrative officers. For the loyalty of appointees who owed their positions only formally to the appointing official, but in fact to the state and local party units that nominated them, lay with the nominating powers. In the exercise of their legal authorizations, the appointees tended to be as responsive to individual legislators, local and state party leaders, and local community pressures as to their nominal superiors in the hierarchy. Moreover, since their tenure was sure to be cut short as soon as the opposing party won an election, they tried to squeeze all they could out of their posts while they occupied them; their own personal interests, therefore, were likely to take precedence over official directives when the two conflicted. Trying to lead such a staff was like trying to play croquet in Wonderland; subordinates, like the mallets, balls, and wickets of the fairy tale, operated with a high degree of independence.

To the supporters of executive leadership, it was clear that the lateral pulls of political parties and individual legislators had to be reduced, and the incentives for public employees to exploit their offices for personal advantage eliminated. Only then could the other means of building up executive influence be made effective; only then could the President assert his authority over administration. So the executive leadership supporters joined the defenders of neutral competence in the drive toward a merit system of appointment, expecting that a bureaucracy chosen by objective standards would be at least as responsive to Presidential direction as to party and legislative pressures. A merit system of appointment controlled by a Civil Service Commission thus served the ends of two schools of thought; for different reasons, and in pursuit of different goals, they united behind it.

Similar factors apparently operated to promote the adoption of objective standards of practice for other activities corrupted by the spoils system. Political discrimination in public contracting, public works, government purchasing, granting of charters and franchises, distribution of benefits and subsidies, and the enforcement of the law, provided a harvest mainly reaped by state and local party and government leaders. These practices, too, gave a bit of leverage to executives in their legislative and political roles, but they did nothing for executive control of the executive branch. So the executive leadership school approved and worked for the adoption of rigorous statutory limitations, cutting party and individual legislators out of these processes as far as possible just as the civil service system freed the appointing process from their depredations. Here, too, though apparently striving for different objectives, the neutral competence and executive leadership groups joined hands.

Consequently, the flood of literature on public administration after World War I unanimously applauded many of the measures designed to take government out of politics. By the 'thirties, however, as the emphasis on executive leadership increased, evidences of discord grew more persistent.

III. THE EMERGING CONFLICT

In thirty years the number of federal civilian employees has more than quadrupled. If power were measurable, the federal bureaucracy's power would probably turn out to have increased by an even greater factor: Governmental policy is now formulated in administrative regulations and orders, as the growth of the Federal Register vividly attests; judicial proceedings before administrative agencies probably exceed in quantity those before the courts; licensing and administrative decisions regarding benefits and subsidies are the order of the day; and all of this is handled by administrative officials under the very broadest of mandates from Congress and the President. Much of our legislation originates in administrative agencies, and most proposed legislation is submitted to such agencies to determine what the President's position on it ought to be. A corresponding growth of administrative influence has taken place in all large-scale organizations, both governmental and private, but few have a record as dramatic in this respect as the federal government.

The growth of governmental bureaucracy in size and importance was subjected to vehement attacks in this country and abroad. For the most part,
however, the attacks were disregarded, especially by political scientists, because
it was clear that they were not aimed at the bureaucracy *per se,* but at the governmental *programs* administered by the civil servants. The programs themselves were too popular for their critics to assail directly with any real hope of
success; the assault therefore took an oblique approach, hitting at what appeared to be a more vulnerable target. The criticism was therefore not taken
very seriously in the study of public administration. Students of this subject
became ardent and sometimes uncritical defenders of bureaucrats. Now that
the controversy over the New Deal has subsided, however, the bureaucracy itself is more or less taken for granted, and attacks upon it are less frequent, less
vehement, and less publicized than they once were. This has helped students
of public administration to take a somewhat more dispassionate view of the
bureaucracy, and some second thoughts may be at hand.

For though the mechanisms of neutral competence were remarkably successful in reducing the influence of the political parties on the administrative hierarchy, they did not necessarily increase the President's control over administration. Rather, they encouraged the development of "self-directing" groups
within the bureaucracy, and these groups in turn cultivated their own sources
of support among professional groups concerned with the subject matter over
which the services have jurisdiction, among their clienteles, and among appropriate Congressional committees and subcommittees. The components of the
"neutral" bureaucracy, by virtue of their expertness and information and alliances, have become independent sources of decision-making power, and Presidents will probably find them no easier to direct—indeed, perhaps even more
intractable, than their partisan predecessors.

As a consequence, some of the standard devices for promoting neutral competence have been openly questioned in the literature of public administration.
As noted earlier, the independence of regulatory commissions and government
corporations has been vigorously criticized. The Brownlow Committee also
sought to make personnel management an arm of the White House and to
confine the Civil Service Commission to quasi-judicial functions and a role as
"watchdog" of the merit system. This principle was endorsed recently by the
staff of the Temporary (New York) State Commission on Coordination of
State Activities, by a minority (comprising 11 members) of the Mayor's
Committee on Management Survey of the City of New York, by the Sixth
American Assembly, and, implicitly, by the present administration in Washington, under which the chairman of the Civil Service Commission serves as
administrative head of that agency and is located in the executive mansion. A
rising chorus of voices has also begun to call for decentralization of authority
for personnel management to line departments, a position stated with particular clarity and force by Commissioner James K. Pollock of the first Hoover
Commission in a minority report on personnel. The establishment of Schedule
C in the federal government service in 1953, rolling back merit system protec-

tions from a number of positions of a policy-making and confidential character, despite the partisan components of the impetus behind this move, was in large measure an effort to preserve the power of the President over policy. More recently, the arguments of the second Hoover Commission for extension of civil service protections to the very highest administrative officials (in the form of a "senior civil service") have been sharply questioned. Recommendations for an institutionalized corps of political executives have been assailed as likely to weaken the President. The premises of the city-manager plan have been described as inapplicable to large cities, and some spirited defenses of elected mayors have appeared. And all of these views have been reflected in the kinds of administrative improvements adopted in many jurisdictions in recent years. Other similar defections from the coalition between the neutrality and the leadership camps can be found in current literature and practice, but it is not necessary to labor the point; patently, these straws in the wind are examples of the growing divergence between the two philosophies that makes it increasingly doubtful that their adherents will continue to support the same governmental theories or reforms.

Moreover, the philosophical divisions over structural values among the scholars have been intensified by differing political—i.e., program—views. Many of the champions of increased governmental activities, in the realms both of services (welfare, financial, industrial) and economic regulation, tend to rally behind chief executives and especially behind the President. The reason is fairly obvious: Demands for expansion of government service and regulation originate frequently (though not exclusively) in urban areas, and urban areas have their greatest political effect on the election of chief executives and their smallest impact on the state legislatures and Congress, where they are substantially underrepresented. So executives tend generally to be more sympathetic to those demands than do the legislators, and those who favor an expanding role for government look to elected executives, as a rule, when they want to impress their preferences on governmental policy. Quite apart, then, from the concern about the organizational problems created by fragmentation of government, there are considerations of political preference and strategy that generate support for executive leadership.

By the same token, there are issues of political attitudes and tactics that engender enthusiasm for legislative bodies regardless of questions of representativeness. Legislatures, because of the composition and the sources of their political strength, offer the greatest leverage to those who resist the growth of governmental activities—or, more accurately, who oppose those governmental activities sought by urban populations. Not, then, because legislatures are more representative, but because this is where the backers of a particular political attitude can exert their greatest political strength, many individuals recommend in their proposals for governmental reform that these bodies be strengthened both relatively and absolutely.

Finally, it might be inferred that some reformers distrust all politicians and electorates and pin their hopes on the expertise and efficiency of a professionalized bureaucracy. They seem to be moved not merely by a concern for governmental structure but by political values that include an implicit contempt for what we ordinarily understand to be the democratic process and an explicit respect for an aristocracy of talent that borders on a latter-day faith in technocracy.[10]

So the tendencies toward division reinforce each other, and there are no visible factors thrusting toward alliances like that fortuitous one developed by a peculiar conjunction of circumstances during the infancy of public administration as an academic and occupational specialty. As a result, the language of public administration is likely to become increasingly strategic and tactical in tone rather than "scientific." Just as the naked power issues of the legislatively oriented groups came to the surface in the recent efforts to weaken the Presidency—viz., the Twenty-Second Amendment, which reduces the leadership potential of a President in his second term; the efforts to strip away Presidential reorganization authority in 1953; the fight over the proposed Bricker Amendment; the continuing efforts to revamp the Electoral College in such a way as to reduce the political effectiveness of the urban-labor-liberal entente that has been partly responsible for the aggressive and expansive use of Presidential power—so too, many of the reorganization issues will be discussed in power terms in the future as the public administration groups aligned with the executive and with the bureaucracy, respectively, pull apart. The question that will be asked about suggested reorganizations is not, "What, according to the canons of management science, is the best organization?" but, "What will be the effect of this measure on the institution we support?" The differences in the answers will sharpen the theoretical distinctions between the wings of the public administration group and hasten estrangement of the factions.[11]

To many students of public administration trained in the 'twenties, 'thirties, and 'forties, the new atmosphere will be a strange and perhaps a bewildering one, fraught with hostilities. To students trained in the 'sixties, the literature of the earlier period, with its "principles," may seem quaint and even naive. Political scientists of the remoter future, looking back, may well conclude that it is not easy to bridge the gap between a generation seeking to encourage the growth of a professional bureaucracy and a generation in turmoil over how to control it.

10. There would seem to be an emergent split within this group. Some backers of professionalized public service are apparently thinking in terms of a corps of administrative generalists to occupy the top levels of administrative agencies regardless of agency subject matter. Others seem to conceive of an administrative elite of occupational specialists—engineers, lawyers, doctors, social workers, foresters, etc.

11. One may even hazard the guess that the American Society for Public Administration will remain firmly in the hands of the neutral competence group while the executive leadership school in public administration looks more and more to the American Political Science Association as its forum.

II. THE INSTRUMENTS
OF CONTROL

PART II deals with the people and procedures on which the President and Congress depend most heavily in their never-ending struggle—partly with each other—to control the vast bureaucracies that execute national policy. The ways in which the top leaders of any large organization strive for control, and their subordinates for independence, are myriad. In the case of the federal government, we are dealing with a bureaucracy which employs more than six million people (including the armed forces), which spends more than $175 billion annually (fiscal 1968, estimate as of January 1968), which pursues multitudes of disparate objectives, and which is part of a national political system that distributes fragments of power probably more widely than any other in the world. An adequate definition of the federal administrative system, moreover, must take notice of the government's increasing tendency to "contract out" the implementation of large program elements to state, local, and nonpublic agencies. The obstacles to generalized description and analysis are most formidable, therefore, and the coverage of this section cannot be otherwise than highly selective. Fortified by these disclaimers, let us plunge in.

A. The Political Executives: Individually

TOP-LEVEL officials in the federal bureaucracy whose positions are not covered by career civil service regulations are generally labeled "political" executives. They currently number about one thousand, of whom roughly half are "Schedule C" appointees.* Upon their capacity and loyalty the President's control of the bureaucracy ultimately depends, though of course they themselves depend heavily on such factors as Presidential support and the loyalty of civil service professionals to enable them to rule their own houses. This section deals with the recruitment and the roles of individual political executives. Section B will focus on the two best known committees of political executives: the Cabinet and the National Security Council.

Dean Mann reports on the recruitment of subcabinet political executives in the Truman, Eisenhower, and Kennedy administrations. His analysis is particularly useful in that it considers differences between administrations, variations among departments, and changes in recruitment criteria from the beginning of an administration to subsequent stages of its life. Mann's care in documenting these distinctions should put you on your guard against oversimple generalizations about the orientations and loyalties of federal bureaucrats.†

Richard Neustadt has probably written more perceptively than anyone else about the obstacles to effective leadership (of the electorate and Congress along with the bureaucracy) that a President faces, and the strategies that he may follow to maximize his influence. His article reprinted here focuses on the efforts of Franklin D. Roosevelt and John F. Kennedy to make optimal use of the personal and institutional staffs of the Presidency. His most striking thesis is that both Presidents wanted all their personal assistants to be generalists, and that consequently a pattern developed under both in which presidential assistants specialized in "action forcing processes" rather than programs. Neustadt's discussion should provoke you to think about such questions as the following: If a President is this wary of the potential biases of his personal aides, how much more suspicious must he be of all other

* Schedule C positions carry civil service ratings (e.g., GS-17, GS-18), but are defined as involving policy determination, confidential working relationships with top "political" appointees, and/or advocacy of Administration policies in the public arena. In fact, it is often impossible to say on the basis of logic why one position is classified Schedule C and another is not. More than half the occupants of Schedule C positions have come from civil service careers. They have the right, if removed on political grounds, to return to their prior civil service ranks. In practice, however, they almost never do. Schedule C officials who have been drawn from outside the civil service have no more tenure rights than ordinary political appointees—which is to say, none at all.

† No study of cabinet selection comparable to Mann's has been conducted. Richard Fenno, however, has reviewed the vast memoir literature on this subject in his book, *The President's Cabinet* (Cambridge: Harvard University Press, 1959), Ch. 2. For an intimate portrayal of President Kennedy choosing his cabinet, see Arthur Schlesinger, Jr., *A Thousand Days* (Boston: Houghton Mifflin, 1965), pp. 124–145.

sources of information and advice? What kinds of strategies can help a President to evaluate communications from others than his personal assistants effectively, and to delegate authority beyond the White House with confidence that its use will further his ends? In what ways are the obstacles to effective evaluation and delegation that face an American President more challenging than those which face the chief executive of a large corporation?

As you read Neustadt's article, it will be helpful if you keep the distinction between the White House staff and the Executive Office of the President clearly in mind. The former exists to serve the President's personal needs; it has no routinized duties or obligations except as the President assigns them; and all of its members are political appointees chosen for their compatibility with the President. The latter serves the Presidency as an institution; the agencies within it have many of their jurisdictions and obligations specified in law; and the great majority of its personnel are career civil servants. The President's intimate staff aides are very few —roughly a score; the Executive Office is roughly three thousand strong.*

Harlan Cleveland attempts a general portrayal of the federal political executive's world. His central point is that political executives must champion the interests of their subordinates and of client pressure groups at least as much as they concentrate on serving the President. Citing former President Truman, he argues that no one considers the public interest but the President, and that the President is more accurately described as a broker than as an authoritative decision-maker. Richard Fenno focuses specifically on cabinet-level political executives, those whose responsibilities to the President are most immediate and personal; but his conclusions are similar. Fenno emphasizes the limits on a Secretary's power, the multiplicity of forces impinging upon him, and the extent to which he is left "on his own" by the President. Cleveland's characterization of the political executive's world as a jungle fits Fenno's analysis well. Both writers see uncalculating loyalty (even to the President) as a suicidal virtue in a political executive. You may wish to compare their clearly etched picture with the far more complex one suggested by Mann. In addition, you may wish to consider whether there is a trend toward greater loyalty to the President on the part of political executives, whether you believe that there should be, and in both cases, if so, why?

---

* Its major elements are the White House Office, the Bureau of the Budget, the National Security Council, the Council of Economic Advisors, the National Aeronautics and Space Council, the Office of Science and Technology, and the Office of Emergency Planning. The Central Intelligence Agency is also formally a part of the Executive Office, as it is by statute attached to the National Security Council. Its personnel figures are secret, however, and were not taken into account above. This is no doubt just as well, because the C.I.A. is a large operating—as well as staff—agency, and it is many times the size of the whole Executive Office proper. Lumping its personnel totals with those of the Executive Office's other components would, therefore, radically distort one's picture of the size of the Executive Office.

THE SELECTION OF FEDERAL POLITICAL EXECUTIVES *

Dean E. Mann

CENTRAL to the problem of obtaining intelligent and effective management and policy direction in the federal government are the sources and procedures used in the selection of federal political executives. These executives, occupying positions usually subject to presidential appointment and senatorial confirmation, constitute the "key group in making representative government work within the executive branch." Through them the President directs and controls his administration, creates political support, and establishes lines of defense for his political program. . . .

The information available on the backgrounds of men who have served as political executives, the duration of their terms, the procedures used in their selection and their reactions to the prospect of government service—in short, the information to substantiate these charges—has hitherto been highly impressionistic, based on inadequate data, out of date, or tinged with ideological preferences. To cite but a few examples, C. Wright Mills characterized the second team of the political directorate in his *Power Elite* on the basis of a relatively brief period at the beginning of the Eisenhower administration, alleging that they were the product of big businessmen fathers, Ivy League colleges, large corporations or big law firms, and country clubs, all of which made them "representative of the corporate rich." In their landmark study of *Federal Administrators,*[1] now 25 years old, Macmahon and Millett said that "appointments to assistant secretaryships have been political in most connotations of that word, with little regard for qualifications or the needs of the posts. Few of the occupants of these positions have been conspicuous individuals.". . .

For the present study, several approaches were taken in obtaining information on the process of selecting political executives. First, we secured biographical information on all political executives who had served in the federal government between 1933 and 1961.[2] Using standard biographical sources and in-

* From the *American Political Science Review,* Vol. 58 (March 1964), pp. 81–90, 99. Reprinted by permission of the author and publisher.

1. New York, Columbia University Press, 1939, p. 302.

2. As defined in this study political executives are limited to under secretaries and assistant secretaries in major departments and deputies in several other agencies: Bureau of the Budget, Veterans Administration, General Services Administration, Housing and Home Finance Agency, Office of Civil and Defense Mobilization, United States Information Agency, International Cooperation Administration and predecessors.

formation supplied by the federal agencies, we assembled profiles of these executives, including information on place of birth, education, occupation, residence, party affiliation, age at the time of appointment, and length and kind of previous public service. Second, using a modified random sampling procedure we chose 108 cases of appointments during the Truman, Eisenhower, and Kennedy administrations for an intensive investigation to learn the procedures followed in the recruitment and selection of political executives. Interviews were conducted with the appointees, with the officials chiefly responsible for their appointment—usually the agency heads—and with any others who may have played a role in the selection process. We asked not only about the procedures but also the perspectives and values of each of the participants in the recruitment process, including the appointees themselves. . . .

PATTERNS OF RECRUITMENT AND SELECTION

The selection of federal political executives is a matter of interest to virtually every major participant in the political struggle, not only to the aspirant himself. The President is interested in staffing his administration with people personally and politically loyal to him, who will at the same time bring competence and support to the programs he espouses. The Secretary often looks for individuals who will similarly serve him, with perhaps greater emphasis on administration and program execution. Party interests tend to center on rewards for support or hopes for future political effort. The goals of senators and congressmen are varied, but often relate to personal interests in particular candidates or to policy commitments. Interest group stakes in administration are almost exclusively programmatic. Each has his own perspective from which to view the process and each uses his influence as he can; but the contest is hardly one of equals.

In general, the agency head is the central figure in the selection process, although his precise role varies from case to case. . . . In most instances he, or someone he appoints, is directly involved in unearthing eligible candidates and examining their qualifications. In fewer instances, the Secretary may play a more passive role, recognizing a legitimate claim on a particular position by a member of Congress, or the President, or a member of the President's staff. Very frequently, the Secretary plays a vital role in negotiating with interested parties, both inside and outside the government, agreement being arrived at by mutual consent. At the beginning of an administration particularly, the President may fill one or more of the subordinate positions before choosing the agency head, making acceptance of his action a condition under which the agency head accepts his position. Sometimes an individual opens the campaign in his own behalf. Included in the sample of 108 cases . . . are 17 who actively sought appointments and thus exerted their own pressures on the selecting officers. The self-initiated cases divided nearly equally among the three administrations—seven occurring in the Kennedy administration, five in the Truman and five in the Eisenhower.

Scope of Search. The agency head has the most direct interest in the selection of his subordinates, although his active role may be slight in some cases. It is useful to examine, therefore, the methods he uses in recruiting candidates for a particular position. These range all the way from the consideration only of personal friends and close associates to extended searches among many groups and among individuals whom he does not know personally. And in some instances he allows or is forced to permit others to control every aspect of the recruitment process.

In general there is a tendency for the recruiter to rely most heavily on personally conducted searches among his friends and associates, although some differences were found in the scope of search in the three administrations. . . . The most notable departure from this pattern was at the beginning of the Kennedy administration when agency heads relied in many instances on candidates supplied by the "Talent Hunt," or when the President directly intervened to place men in whom he had personal confidence or to whom he was politically in debt. Heavy reliance on personal contacts in selecting political executives in the Truman administration is related to a strong tendency to promote men already serving in the federal government to higher positions. With willing men already available within an agency or in another agency, extensive recruiting outside the government appeared to be unnecessary or futile, especially in view of the great resistance to government service in the postwar period.

Over two-thirds of the agency heads whose recruiting methods were examined took primary responsibility for finding suitable candidates, either through personal contacts or by a broader search. The remainder allowed or were expected to accept leadership from some other source, although usually reserving the right to object and even veto individuals who were not acceptable to them.

The type of search conducted did not necessarily dictate the type of candidate finally selected, although there was clearly some relationship. The instances where the agency head relinquished control of the process were usually those in which party and interest considerations became paramount in the selection. The criteria for selection tended to be related to geographical representation, party service, or access to some other power-holder in the political system. When the agency head retained control, there was often—although not always—an emphasis on past administrative experience, policy objectives, or substantive knowledge of operations for which an appointee would be responsible on the job. Furthermore, the agency head operated under certain restraints in many departments. Where the clientele groups were powerful, his scope of search tended to be narrow and he tended to lose discretion in choosing among candidates. Where the clientele groups were more numerous, disunited, or had interests which did not entirely parallel agency activities, the discretion of the agency head increased.

To a certain extent, the character of the agency head and his perspective on the process predetermined what process would be followed in recruiting. Those with long experience in electoral politics were often inclined to recognize broader needs of the political system, rather than strictly administrative needs within an agency. They could see wisdom in accepting candidates who wore the *imprimatur* of a particular congressman or an interested group.

Finally, the character of the times was occasionally determinative. A crisis situation, or periods when the attractions of private life are paramount, may lead to reliance on career government employees who are promoted into the ranks of political executives. On the other hand, at the beginning of an administration there may be a tendency to consolidate party gains by granting favors, including high position, to party members and interest group functionaries.

Regardless of the process followed, the specific candidate selected may sometimes be the result of coincidence or desperation. There is no assurance that an extended search for *the* most qualified man necessarily results in finding him or finding him available; and failure to find or get him may lead to the appointment of a man who has little more to commend him than his own enthusiasm.

Criteria of Selection. For the various kinds of political executive posts that must be filled, and for the various kinds of functions which circumstances and agency head expectations may require, quite varying standards must be used in measuring the qualifications of those being considered for appointment. Some recruiters have clear ideas of what they consider are the qualities necessary for successful performance in a job. These may relate to personal skills, to substantive backgrounds, or in some instances only to symbolic values. In other cases, the agency head has only an indefinite notion of "getting the best man" for the job. He looks for successful experience of some sort and tends to attribute success in any line of endeavor to some innate capacity to perform well in all positions, including those in the executive branch. It is not exceptional to find, moreover, that an agency head will begin recruiting with one idea in mind and will end up selecting a person with characteristics quite different from those he originally looked for.

The case studies reveal a much greater concern for administrative skill and substantive experience than might be expected. . . . Membership in the administration party is an almost invariable requirement, but within that context more professional standards are applied. There is usually an implicit assumption that only those who have an orientation on policy similar to that of the President or his agency heads will be seriously considered for an appointment. But for some recruiting officials, policy considerations are of less concern than administrative capacity, substantive acquaintance with specific problem areas, and the political significance of an appointment. The self-promoters and the individuals who appeared on the lists of the Talent Hunt were almost automatically qualified on policy grounds since they were usually sympathetic with the new administration. Obviously, however, general sympathy with the new administration did not necessarily mean conformity in policy views on specific issues arising in any particular agency.

The classification of certain appointments as based on "political factors" requires some explanation since all political executive appointments are predicated on some calculation of political advantage, depending on who does the calculating. "Political" criteria were those related primarily to prior political party service or to some party advantage in the future. Seldom were appointments "purely" political, although there were instances of this. Usually, appointments which could be based on compensation for past services could also be justified in some measure on experience and talents which the men brought to the job. Thus, about one-third of all appointments were based on mixed criteria, while less than ten per cent were based solely on political considerations. . . .

Recruitment at the Beginning of an Administration. At the beginning of an administration the President-elect faces a formidable array of tasks which must be carried out with both dispatch and care. One of the most important of these is to fill the high-level positions with men who are responsible, loyal, and experienced, who will give the proper "image" to his administration and also give him the assistance he needs in policy development and management. The pressures of time are severe and the anticipations of both participants and observers are high. With innumerable candidates to choose from, he must carefully sort out the wheat from the straw.

To assist in this operation, the President gathers about him a corps of trusted aides and personal friends to give him guidance and extend his reach into the many institutions of society with which he may be only dimly acquainted. Thus, at the beginning of his administration President-elect Eisenhower relied on two of his most intimate advisers, Herbert Brownell, who had served as his principal strategist in the 1952 campaign, and General Lucius Clay, a lifelong military associate and personal friend. At a somewhat greater distance, but nevertheless working closely with the President and his chief advisers, were Sherman Adams, who later became the President's principal assistant in the White House, and businessmen such as Sidney Weinberg and Harold Boeschenstein who had long been active in recruitment for government positions. In addition an informal group of Eisenhower supporters had hired McKinsey & Company, a management consulting firm, to study the executive recruitment problem. McKinsey had identified 131 high policy positions which should be filled as quickly as possible, and also prepared a list of thousands of potential candidates for these positions.

At the outset, Brownell and Clay and their assistants were primarily concerned with helping the President select his cabinet officers. President-elect Eisenhower was remarkably quick in making these decisions; his entire Cabinet was selected in less than four weeks. Inevitably in the process of looking for cabinet officers, the searchers were led to consider the qualifications of a great many others whom they eliminated for the top positions but kept in mind for subordinate posts. Little was done about appointments at the sub-cabinet level, however, until the chief positions were filled.

The Eisenhower recruiters looked for individuals who had been active in the 1952 campaign and who were from the liberal wing of the Republican

Party. But they recognized the necessity of weighing the competing demands of the Citizens for Eisenhower and the regular party organization. Campaign activity and political persuasion therefore became important factors. At the same time they undertook an extensive search for men qualified for high executive posts on the basis of their experience and competence in particular lines of endeavor. They made use of their numerous contacts in the business world, the professions, universities, and politics to locate likely candidates.

Through business and professional associations, through boards of directors, and an infinite number of personal ties, these men could drop a net over a large segment of the successful men in America. It was clear that the net was designed to bring in successful businessmen more than any other type. Added to these names were the names of candidates from political sources—members of Congress, national committeemen, state officials, etc.—and the aforementioned McKinsey lists.

Once a cabinet officer or agency head had been selected, Sherman Adams reports, "Eisenhower gave [him] complete responsibility for his department and almost never intervened in the selection of their assistants and other key personnel."[3] Each cabinet member could establish his own criteria for selection, search out his own candidates, and present his preferred choice to the White House for the President's approval. This degree of independence in selecting subordinates was consistent with President Eisenhower's unusual propensity for delegating authority to the point of even accepting views and actions which deviated from his own preferences. He was unwilling to exercise his prerogatives in order to blunt the criticism from congressional sources that they were being short-circuited in the appointment process. Undoubtedly the presidential assistants in the Commodore Hotel pressed such considerations on the new agency heads; but lacking the influential support of the President, there was little they could do to enforce their views.

The beginning of the Kennedy administration offers an unusual opportunity for comparing the characteristics of the recruitment process under conditions of some similarity: pressures of time, use of centralized machinery, and marked interest in the character of the appointments by the public, members of Congress, and other parties with something at stake. But other factors in the situation were different: a president with an entirely different background, a party that had been out of power only eight years but which had to weld together perhaps even more disparate elements than those which composed the Republican Party in 1953.

As soon as victory was assured, while President-elect Kennedy vacationed in Palm Beach and in Georgetown, he and his chief advisers spent the major part of their time talking with prospective candidates and evaluating the qualifications of those who had been recommended or who were recommending themselves. The President-elect took an active role in the early consideration of candidates—consulting with the elders of the Democratic Party, with his chief political aides, and with likely candidates for cabinet positions.

Kennedy and his advisers had two important criteria in mind in settling

3. *First-Hand Report* (New York, 1961), p. 59. Our findings essentially confirm this view.

high-level presidential appointments: recognition of those who deserved appointments on the basis of service to the party; and recognition of the need to obtain the "best talent" to serve in these demanding positions. To make these criteria operative in fact as well as in theory, it was decided to divide the recruitment task between two groups of Kennedy aides, with each group focusing primarily upon one of these two criteria. In the words of one member of the staff, one of these groups sought "deserving people" and "hoped they were bright enough," while the other group reversed this order of priority. Together, these two groups became known popularly as the "Talent Hunt."

Heading up these two operations were the President-elect's brother, Robert, and his brother-in-law, Sargent Shriver. Robert Kennedy worked mainly through the nation-wide network of contacts he had developed during the 1960 campaign, while Shriver drew upon his contacts in the business, professional, and university world. The operation under brother Robert was staffed by the President-elect's campaign and senatorial aides: Lawrence O'Brien, Richard Donohue, and Ralph Dungan. The Shriver operation was primarily in the hands of young lawyers who had also been active in the campaign, such as Adam Yarmolinsky and Harris Wofford. In spite of this informal division of labor, the allocation of responsibilities was hardly distinct. In time, in fact, "everyone got into everyone else's business," as one staff member expressed it.

Of particular interest were the criteria the recruiters tried to use in assessing the candidates' qualifications. Persons suggesting candidates and other respondents were asked to assess the qualifications of the candidates in terms of "judgment," "toughness," "integrity," "ability to work with others," "industry," and "devotion to the principles of the President-elect." The evaluator was also asked to say whether the candidate had a wide or limited acquaintanceship with qualified people in his field of specialty or "only local contacts"; and to estimate whether the candidate's appointment to a high-level government position would enhance the administration's standing "nationally," "in his professional group," "in his state," or "in his community." Under pressure of time, however, the staff members found it increasingly difficult to get careful ratings on candidates on each of these discriminating criteria. Instead, the interviewer was more likely to ask a respondent, "What do you know about this guy?" When all of the evaluated material was gathered together, the staff member added a summary evaluation that included general ratings that ranged from "highly qualified," "qualified," and "some qualifications" on the competence side; and "good Democrat," "politically neutral," "Republican," or "politically disqualified" on the political side.

President-elect Kennedy was relatively slow to announce his first appointments. His first selection, that of G. Mennen Williams as Assistant Secretary of State, indicated both a desire and a will to participate actively in sub-cabinet appointments. It also became known that the President had offered the post of Ambassador to the United Nations to Adlai Stevenson long before Dean Rusk and Chester Bowles were selected as Secretary and Under Secretary. These actions suggested that in cases where he had a direct and compelling interest

Kennedy would be willing to make his selections independently of his Secretaries, and expected them to acquiesce in his selections.

In some instances where the President-elect and his chief aides felt themselves inadequately grounded to form a sound judgment both politically and professionally in making selections, they were willing to give a much freer hand to the agency head. But where the appointments required a sensitive balancing, as in the agencies attempting to promote a bipartisan approach, and where the President had a strong commitment to particular policies or political values, he was unwilling to delegate the responsibility. It is clear, for example, that the President-elect and his aides took a much greater interest in the Department of State and the Department of Defense than they did in appointments in the Departments of Labor, Agriculture and Interior.

Within a few days after the appointment of each agency head the Talent Hunt recruiter assigned to that agency met with him and reviewed the list of names in the recruiter's file. At this point the role of the Talent Hunter could follow any of several patterns but almost always along the line of diminished responsibility. In the case of two or three agencies the recruiter was given no further responsibility, the cabinet member preferring to conduct his search by other channels. This was particularly true in agencies whose heads were themselves acutely aware of political considerations and could be relied upon to make selections which would reflect them. In other agencies the Talent Hunt members continued to assist by screening the available candidates and conducting further searches.

In both the Eisenhower and Kennedy pre-inaugural periods members of Congress were active in suggesting the names and promoting the causes of candidates, often men from their own states. They displayed a wide range of attitudes, however, from those who aggressively sought out the Commodore or Talent Hunt recruiters and the newly appointed agency heads to those who did nothing more than transmit the names of men who had been suggested to them. Their vigor varied also with the qualifications of the individuals in question. Republican senators, in particular, were dissatisfied with the early reception that their candidates received at Republican headquarters, since few of the appointees up to the Eisenhower inauguration appeared to come from the more conservative congressional wing of the party. Congressional leaders met with President-elect Eisenhower and received assurances that their recommendations would be given consideration, although he continued to reserve the right of final choice for himself and his agency heads. Democratic members of Congress voiced little open criticism of the procedures and appointments in the Kennedy administration, although there was occasional private grumbling that clearances had been ignored or wrong choices made. The Kennedy recruiters were more conscious of congressional interests and sensitivities than the Republican recruiters, and generally observed clearance procedures before announcing appointments.

In both administrations the special recruiting groups discontinued their operations after inauguration. Some of the participants themselves received appointments and were distracted by their new duties. Top recruitment responsibilities then shifted to the White House—to Sherman Adams and his assistant Charles Willis in the Eisenhower administration, and to the group of aides President Kennedy brought with him from the Senate. But a large part of the function had already devolved on the departments and agencies, with the White House constituting an important clearance point for anyone who recommended a candidate.

Recruitment During an Administration. The intense concern with appointments that characterizes a new administration fades rapidly a few weeks after Inauguration Day. By summer of the first year practically all of the political executive positions are filled. But with the beginning of the second year of a new administration, the problems of political executive recruitment again began to assert themselves. Some appointees have committed themselves only for a limited period of time and therefore prepare for departure. A few unfortunate choices are nudged into early resignation. Others, finding new, attractive, and what may appear to be once-in-a-lifetime opportunities resulting from their new visibility, feel compelled to move on. Still others achieve immediate success in public life and are shifted into other positions in the national government or are encouraged to run for elective office. As the departures begin, the agency heads again must devote a fair amount of their valuable time to canvassing potential appointees.

But by now the recruiting environment has changed markedly from the early days of the administration. The central staff operation that produced long lists of eligible candidates for the President-elect's consideration is largely dismantled, although a few vestiges may remain, usually located in the White House office. In any event, the sense of urgency and determination to obtain the best qualified men have diminished. The President is heavily involved in the other responsibilities of his office and usually can concern himself only with the selection of the highest level officers directly responsible to him. Consequently the decentralization of personnel decisions which is apparent at the beginning of an administration becomes even more pronounced as an administration ages.

At the beginning of an administration, the fervor engendered by the political campaign creates an attitude in both political activists and passive supporters which is favorable toward government service. The large majority may not actively promote themselves for political executive positions, but their commitment to the success of the new administration predisposes them to consider favorably the prospect of an appointment. But as time passes those who have not been selected—whether approached or not, whether disappointed or not—turn to their private concerns and give a smaller share of their time and attention to public affairs, particularly those in Washington. They may continue to participate in party councils, contribute money, and cast their votes for the administration, but everyday activities tend to crowd out public issues which seem less pressing and less immediate. Fewer and fewer are actively seeking positions or are "available" when contacted.

Many of those who supported the victorious presidential candidate may have had strong programmatic commitments and looked to the new administration to bring radical changes in existing policies. But as an administration matures it often becomes disappointingly evident that radical changes either are not possible or can be accomplished only with persistent, strenuous efforts. Potential candidates now may make a more realistic assessment of the constraints of the situation, leading to disillusionment about the possibility of major changes. This reduces the receptivity of some potential recruits for the administration.

Finally, as the second year's congressional elections come and go, uncertainty over the future of the administration is apt to mount. The possibility that the President will not be re-elected and his appointees will have to seek other employment tends to reduce ardor for public office. The prospect of coming to Washington for what may turn out to be only a few months or at the most a year or two, when accompanied with heavy financial losses as a consequence of moving, operates to dissuade men from seriously considering political executive service.

These circumstances lead agency heads and other recruiters increasingly to seek their candidates inside the government rather than in private activities. Having encountered difficulty in getting replacements from private life, they become wary of having their offers rejected or their veiled approaches rebuffed. Moreover, with less time to devote to recruitment than they had at the beginning of the administration they have a stronger tendency to take the easier way in filling vacancies. The easiest solution is usually to select replacements from among those who are already in or closely associated with the government. This also makes sense because the agency heads by this are able to make more accurate evaluations of men already serving in the agency than of "unknowns" from outside. They are less dependent on the evaluation of others. With experienced and proven executives on the scene there is a strong tendency to give them preference.

Turnover in the highest echelons of the major agencies also leads to expectations and hopes on the part of subordinates that they will be advanced to the more prestigious and influential positions. Those who have strong public commitments are often ambitious for promotion to positions where they can have a greater impact on policy decisions, where they can share in the emoluments of high office, and where they can gain recognition for their accomplishments. An expectation naturally develops among subordinate officials that successful performance will be rewarded by advancement to higher office when vacancies occur. Failure to be recognized or seriously considered for promotion has been a critical factor in the decisions of some executives to leave the government.

The case studies reveal clearly this pattern of more reliance on government men in recruitment for positions during an administration. In a total of 62 case studies of appointments after the first year of an administration (including all of the Truman administration), 37, or 60 per cent, of the appointees were already in positions in the federal government. For the Truman administration the insider-outsider ratio was 65 to 35 per cent; for the Eisenhower administration it was 52 to 48. (See Table I.)

The Truman preference for men already in the government partly reflects the continuity between his administration and the Roosevelt administration. Since the two administrations shared the same party allegiance and avowed generally similar policy orientations, the Truman recruiters felt no strong urgency to seek men outside the government who might introduce new policy viewpoints. Moreover, many Truman executives had had long experience in the government previously and were acquainted with men in their agencies who were considered capable of assuming high level responsibilities. Younger men who had served their apprenticeship during the New Deal and World War II had strong hopes that they might be considered for leading political positions as rewards for their faithful service. Finally, the Truman administration was faced with widespread public antipathy toward governmental service and a desire by most men to return to or continue in essentially private pursuits. The years subsequent to World War II were probably the most difficult years for recruiting men to public service.

TABLE I. SOURCE OF POLITICAL EXECUTIVE APPOINTEES
DURING AN ADMINISTRATION

	Per Cent under Truman	Per Cent under Eisenhower
Promotion of political appointees	22	32
Promotion of career officials	35	8
Transfer of political appointees	8	12
Appointment of former federal appointees	11	4
Other appointments	24	44
	100	100

Major differences between administrations show up in the extent to which men with varying kinds of backgrounds rose into the higher ranks of the political executive service during an administration. . . . The case studies tend to confirm the view that the Truman administration had a strong inclination to advance men with *careers* in the public service to political executive positions. Often these men had already moved into politically sensitive positions as confidential assistants or personal aides and it was no major step to go on to a presidential appointment. The Eisenhower administration was much more inclined to bring newcomers into the federal government, and subsequently to promote them to still higher political positions. . . .

Variations among Agencies. Both the biographical information and the case studies reveal important differences among agencies in the sources of executives, the style of recruitment, and the criteria used in selection. Although the following generalizations require considerable refinement and qualification, they highlight the variable context of political executive recruitment.

State and Defense: Professionals and Professional Amateurs. In the Departments of State and Defense, the emphasis on previous service and relevant experience is more pronounced than in other agencies. Political executives are chosen for their expertise and sympathy with presidential programs, but previous governmental service—either at the political executive level or below—in these agencies or the military services is the factor that conspicuously distinguishes recruitment in these agencies from the others. The predominance of this kind of appointment suggests that the men who serve in these agencies may be characterized as "professional amateurs," in that they spend a considerable portion of their mature lives within the government or, if in private life, operate in the environment of that policy area. While not professionals in the sense of being committed and dependent on government service as a career, they are nevertheless remarkably well prepared to assume the duties of office.

In our case studies some agency heads and others responsible for recruitment in the Departments of State and Defense showed a measure of deference to party in making appointments, but the strongest opposition to party influence, particularly by the national committees, but also by the White House, was found in these two agencies. Agency officials often tried to suppress knowledge of a probable vacancy, hoping to find a suitable candidate to present to the President before the national committee or the White House staff could propose alternatives. White House and national committee officials testified that they received less cooperation from these two departments than from any other agencies in the government.

The Department of State has developed a practice of balancing appointments between foreign service officers and non-career appointees. Most frequently, foreign service officers are found heading the bureaus with responsibility for policy development and coordination in particular regional areas, and also in some important administrative positions at the secretarial level. Over one-third of all political executive appointees during the Truman, Eisenhower and Kennedy administrations were foreign service officers, the largest percentage appointed during the Eisenhower administration.

Treasury: The Technicians. Recruitment for the Department of the Treasury has been predominantly a search for bankers and lawyers who appear to have specific experiences and skills required for particular functions within the Department. The Treasury political executives included the second highest percentage of businessmen (chiefly bankers) of all domestic agencies and was second only to the Department of Justice in the percentage of lawyers serving in domestic agencies. These two occupations accounted for 78 per cent of all appointments in the Treasury. Furthermore, Treasury had the lowest percentage of political executives whose primary occupation was in the public service.

The appointments at the beginning of both the Eisenhower and Kennedy administrations indicate this emphasis on technical competence. Both Marion Folsom and Stanley Surrey were experts in taxation, Randolph Burgess and Robert Roosa had had long experience in debt management; and Andrew Overby and John Leddy were both intimately acquainted from practical experience in international finance.

These appointments show a marked departure from the pattern of earlier periods. Macmahon and Millett found that three-quarters of the Treasury appointments were accounted for by political considerations, and that few of these were prominent either before or after serving in the Treasury. Nor was there the striking emphasis on technical qualifications in making these earlier appointments.

In recent administrations, Treasury recruitment has been largely conducted by the Secretary himself with the assistance of his chief aides who obtained useful material in evaluating candidates. The secretaries in the Truman, Eisenhower and Kennedy administrations—Snyder, Humphrey, Anderson, and Dillon—all had extensive experience in the business, banking and financial world and could rely on a wide range of contacts to provide them with a supply of candidates. In most instances, it appears that the secretary went directly to individual acquaintances to obtain their services. On occasion, a departing political executive was able to recommend another candidate in his own special area and even assist in getting him to accept.

Justice: Politics and the Law. By the nature of its function as the chief legal agency of the federal government, the chief officers of the Department of Justice are required to be lawyers. It has seldom been enough, however, for an appointee to have only the technical qualification of a legal background or experience in the practice of law. Far more than the State Department, the Defense establishment, or the Treasury, political executives in Justice have had active experience in public affairs, often in elective office. From 1859 through 1938, some 125 men served as assistant attorneys general; nine-tenths of them had held some political office prior to their appointment. In the Roosevelt, Truman and Eisenhower administrations, over 50 per cent of the assistant and deputy attorneys general were serving in the federal government at the time of their appointment. Three out of four in the Truman administration were in that category.

Appointments in the Truman administration were characteristically advancements from lower non-career positions, often on the basis of merit, but it must be recognized that the procedures which brought the appointees into the department initially were usually highly political. Moreover, the political background of the attorneys general made party considerations of more than routine consequence. Partly as a reaction to the low state into which the Department had fallen as a result of scandals at the end of the Truman administration, Eisenhower officials had a greater tendency to recruit outside of governmental and even outside of active political circles, although political considerations still ranked comparatively high.

Post Office: Politicians and Businessmen. No agency has experienced such sharp reversals in the character of the men appointed to political executive positions as the Post Office Department. Traditionally, this Department has been the harbor for deserving party officials. The Postmaster General usually has held a high level post in the party and his appointments, according to Macmahon and Millett, have been "prevailingly political."

In general, Post Office appointees during the Truman administration were

Democrats who had performed some service for the party, or who could be expected to do so while in the government and subsequently. The Kennedy administration resumed this pattern of appointment.

In sharp contrast with Democratic practice in recruiting for the Post Office stands the record of the Republicans during the eight-year period of the Eisenhower administration. Although Postmaster General Summerfield followed the traditional route from the chairmanship of the national committee to the Cabinet, at President Eisenhower's insistence he resigned from the national committee upon taking office. Summerfield selected only Republicans as his aides, but he defied tradition in not filling the subordinate posts in the Post Office with individuals whose primary claims were based on partisan political service. Some of the initial appointees, such as Charles Hook, had taken part in the campaign but in no sense could be considered professional politicians. With two exceptions—one a career official in the Department and another a former Civil Service Commissioner with extensive service in the federal government—all of the Summerfield appointees were businessmen. In most instances, they were selected because of some specialty they had developed in their business careers which was considered applicable to Post Office operations.

Interior and Agriculture: Politics, Pressure Groups, and Policy. Of all the major domestic departments or agencies in the national government, Interior and Agriculture are probably the most deeply involved in controversy over public policy. The impact of these policy controversies bears directly on the recruitment of high level executives in these two departments. The department heads are guided by the policy views of the individuals they are considering and the organizations they represent. The recruiters tend to rely on the recommendations of those who have policy viewpoints corresponding with their own. Groups with opposing viewpoints are deliberately avoided in the recruitment effort and seldom given oportunities to pass judgment on the merits of individuals who are under consideration.

The search for executives with acceptable views for policy positions in the Department of Agriculture seems to lead to the interest groups and the party organizations. For a reason not clear, the same problem tends to lead executives in the Department of the Interior either to the bureaucracy or to members of Congress. In no other agency of the federal government did the members of Congress play a more significant role than here. Because the department represents interests located primarily in the West, the western senators and congressmen expecially were involved in the selection process.

At least part of the explanation for their role lies in the conflict among the western states over policy and the western sense of proprietorship toward the Interior Department. Representation of a particular area has both a symbolic and a practical value in assuring consideration of its interests in the councils of the Department.

Commerce and Labor: Clientele Politics. In recruiting for the Department of Commerce, secretaries since the beginning of the Eisenhower administration have relied almost exclusively on businessmen, with the occasional addition of a lawyer. Of the fifteen men appointed to under secretary and assistant secretary of Commerce in the Eisenhower administration, thirteen were businessmen in private life, one was a lawyer, and another a former member of Congress who had been a lawyer before running for elective office. Similarly, at the beginning of the Kennedy administration all initial selections were of businessmen, although the creation of a new assistant secretary post for science and technology will undoubtedly bring into the Department men with primary backgrounds in the natural sciences who may not have been associated formerly with business. However, the Eisenhower administration placed a heavy reliance on men without previous experience in any level of government. This is understandable, considering that the Republican administration entering in 1953 was the first in 20 years. Nevertheless, the relative lack of public service stands in sharp contrast with many other agencies during the Republican administration whose political executives had had rather extensive service during World War II, the Korean War, in state government, or in federal career positions.

The relationship between the governmental recruiters and the trade unions in the selection of political executives for the Department of Labor was carefully structured, particularly during Democratic administrations. During the Truman administration the chief clientele groups for the Department, the American Federation of Labor and the Congress of Industrial Organizations, tended to receive equal representation in the Department as a kind of gesture toward their equality in the union movement—or else as a measure of prudent neutrality.

The initial selections in the Kennedy administration clearly followed the typical Democratic practice, with one appointee coming from the AFL background, and another from the CIO.

The appointment process during the Eisenhower administration was of a different nature because of the relatively distant relationships between labor and the Republican Party. At first, the new Republican administration tried to woo labor through appointments from the labor movement such as Martin Durkin and Lloyd Mashburn. The impasse over one union candidate, however, resulted in a tacit agreement that there would be no attempt to provide direct union representation in the high ranks of the Labor Department. As a result, from 1954 on, the appointees in that Department were men with professional or business backgrounds; some of them had strong political connections. Several had been appointed on a political basis to subordinate positions within the Department, later moving up into secretarial posts. . . .

CONCLUSIONS

Significant changes have occurred both in the character of the process by which political executives are recruited and in the sources relied upon. Far from depending merely on "haphazard political reasons," their selection is increasingly related to some experience factor which qualifies them for office above and beyond the qualifications achieved through party membership or service. Selection appears to depend on the personal confidence of the cabinet officer or the White House aide in the capacity of candidates to perform adequately in dealing with substantive problems of an agency, as well as the significance of the appointment in the total political context. The precise specifications for availability vary markedly with time and agency and even position. Party factors rank high at the beginning of an administration but the numerous instances where they are disregarded even at that period make even such a generalization suspect. Clearly some appointments are "political" in the traditional sense—to placate a wing of the party, to satisfy a group interest, etc. —but these tend to be restricted to positions which are—rightly or wrongly— considered less consequential.

The point of view that political executives are part of a "political directorate" is hardly justified. While tendencies exist in certain departments to recruit from an eastern industrial, financial class, they appear chiefly to reflect the interest such groups have taken in the issues of national security. Thus special qualifications of experience and interest again play important roles in selection decisions. When the appointees to domestic departments are considered it is obvious that the ranks of political executives are representative of a wide range of interests, experience, localities and talents from the more mobile elements of the American population.

APPROACHES TO STAFFING THE PRESIDENCY:
NOTES ON FDR AND JFK *
Richard E. Neustadt

IT has been a quarter century since the President's Committee on Administration Management, chaired by Louis Brownlow, blessed by Franklin Roosevelt, heralded a major innovation in our constitutional arrangements: substantial staffing for the Presidency distinct from other parts of the executive establishment—in Edward Corwin's phrase an "Institutionalized Presidency." The Executive Office, which throughout our prior history had been essentially a "private office" in the English sense, was to become a "President's Department." So it did. Presidential agencies have filled the building which in 1937 housed the State Department (and in 1913 had housed War and Navy, too). Presidential aides outrank in all but protocol the heads of most executive departments.

* From the *American Political Science Review*, Vol. 57 (December 1963), pp. 855–863. Reprinted by permission of the author and publisher.

I. THE BROWNLOW REPORT

We date this development from Brownlow's *Report*. In the sphere of presidential staffing, its proposals for the most part were put into practice with promptness and fidelity. And practice, for the most part, has been kind to the proposals, has sustained—indeed has vindicated—key ideas behind them. What a rare experience for an advisory report! . . .

As Brownlow cheerfully acknowledged, his group was in effect a White House "chosen instrument." The Committee urged what Roosevelt wanted. They wrote, he edited. In the election year of 1936 he gave them a "non-political" assignment, "administrative management." After his reelection they couched their response in appropriate terms, PODS-CORB terms, Gulick-and-Urwick terms (shades of Taylorism), with "administration" set apart from "policy" and "politics." Roosevelt thought it politic that they should do so. But he took care that their proposals met his purposes which were emphatically, essentially political. He wanted to enhance his own capacity to rule. And when he undertook to implement what they proposed, the product seemed to fit him like a glove, to be but an enlargement and refinement of his style of operation circa 1936. So I think it was.

The Brownlow *Report* and what followed, the first stages of the institutionalized presidency, must be taken to reflect this President's matured approach after a term in office—to say nothing of his seven years in Wilson's Washington. . . .

To characterize the FDR approach we cannot rest content with the Brownlow *Report*. Its language is too "managerial." . . . For the sake of analysis— and comparison—it becomes necessary to construct a characterization out of what they and their colleagues *did,* as revealed piecemeal by memoirs, by case studies, and by retrospective conversations.

For eighteen years I have made something of a hobby of such conversations. Let me draw on these, and on the published works as well, to characterize as best I can. In doing so I grant the risks of retrospection, still more those of oversimplification. . . .

II. THE ROOSEVELT APPROACH

So far as I can find, Roosevelt did not theorize about the principles which underlay his operating style in later years. But he evidently had some principles, or at least premises, or touch-stones, or instincts, for his practice was remarkably consistent in essentials.

The first of these "principles," I suggest, was a concern for his position as *the* man in the White House. If he began the institutionalized presidency, he did not for a moment mean that it should make an institution out of *him*. The White House was *his* House, his home as well as office. No one was to work there who was not essential for the conduct of his own work, day by day. "This is the White House calling" was to mean *him,* or somebody acting intimately and immediately for him. The things he personally did not do from week to week, the troubleshooting and intelligence he did not need firsthand, were to be staffed outside the White House. The aides he did not have to see from day to day were to be housed in other offices than his. This is the origin of the distinction which developed in his time between "personal" and "institutional" staff. The Executive Office was conceived to be the place for "institutional" staff; the place, in other words, for everybody else.

Not only did he generally try to keep second-string personnel out of his house, he also shied away from second-string activities which smacked of the routine (except where *he* chose otherwise for the time being). This seems to be one of the reasons—not the only one—why he never had "legislative liaison" assistants continuously working at the White House. Reportedly, he foresaw what came to be the case in Eisenhower's time, that if the White House were routinely in the "liaisoning" business, Congressmen and agencies alike would turn to *his* assistants for all sorts of routine services and help. "It is all your trouble, not mine," he once informed his Cabinet officers, with reference to the bills that *they* were sponsoring. This was his attitude toward departmental operations generally, always excepting those things that he wanted for his own, or felt he had to seize because of personalities or circumstances.

For routine, or preliminary, or depth staffwork that his White House aides could not take on (or should not, in his view), Roosevelt usually looked to the Budget Bureau or, alternatively, to a man or group he trusted in the operating agencies. In many ways the modern Bureau was his personal creation. And in most of his later years it was, as well, the only "institutional" staff of substantial size under his own control.

Conceivably, he might have looked instead to interdepartmental mechanisms, to standing committees and secretariats. Indeed, he had begun his presidential career by doing so. He created our first "cabinet secretariat" with the National Emergency Council of 1933. But after experimenting elaborately in his first term, Roosevelt lost taste for interagency committees. Thereafter, he never seems to have regarded any of them—from the Cabinet down—as a vehicle for doing anything that could be done by operating agencies or by a staff directly tied to him. This left small scope for such committees *at his level*. He used the Cabinet as a sounding board *sometimes,* and sometimes as a means to put his thinking, or his "magic" on display. Otherwise, his emphasis was on staffs and on operating agencies, taken one by one or in an *ad hoc* group.

The second "principle" I would note is FDR's strong feeling for a cardinal fact in government: that presidents don't act on policies, programs, or personnel in the abstract; they act in the concrete as they meet deadlines set by due dates—or the urgency—of documents awaiting signature, vacant posts awaiting appointees, officials seeking interviews, newsmen seeking answers, audiences waiting for a speech, intelligence reports requiring a response, etc. He also had a strong sense of another fact in government; that persons close to presidents are under constant pressure—and temptation—to go into business for themselves, the more so as the word gets out that they deal regularly with some portion of his business.

Accordingly, he gave a minimum of fixed assignments to the members of his personal staff. Those he did give out were usually in terms of helping him to handle some specific and recurrent stream of action-forcing deadlines he himself could not escape.

Thus, before the war, he had one aide regularly assigned to help him with his personal press relations and with those deadline-makers, his press conferences: the Press Secretary. Another aide was regularly assigned to schedule his appointments and to guard his door: the Appointments Secretary. Early in the war he drew together several scattered tasks and put them regularly in the hands of Samuel Rosenman as "Special Counsel" (the title was invented for the man; Rosenman, a lawyer and a judge, had held a similar title and done comparable work for FDR in Albany): pulling together drafts of presidential messages, speeches, and policy statements, reviewing proposed Executive Orders, Administration bill drafts, and action on enrolled bills—in short, assisting with the preparation of all public documents through which Roosevelt defined and pressed *his* program.

These fixed assignments, and others like them in the Roosevelt staff, were sphere-of-action assignments, *not* programmatic ones. They were organized around recurrent presidential obligations, not functional subject matters. They were differentiated by particular sorts of actions, not by particular program areas. This had three consequences:

1. The men on such assignments were compelled to be generalists, jacks-of-all-trades, with a perspective almost as unspecialized as the President's own, cutting across every program area, every government agency, and every facet of *his* work, personal, political, legislative, administrative, ceremonial.

2. Each assignment was distinct from others but bore a close relationship to others, since the assigned activities themselves were interlinked at many points. Naturally, the work of the Press Secretary and the Special Counsel overlapped, while both had reason for concern and for involvement, often enough, with the work of the Appointments Secretary—and so forth. These men knew what their jobs were but they could not do them without watching, checking, jostling one another. Roosevelt liked it so. (Indeed, he liked it almost too much; he positively encouraged them to jostle. He evidently got a kick out of bruised egos.)

3. Since each man was a "generalist" in program terms, he could be used for *ad hoc* special checks and inquiries depending on the President's needs of the moment. So far as their regular work allowed, the fixed-assignment men were also general-utility trouble shooters. No one was supposed to be too specialized for that.

All this, by the way, applied not only to the men with fixed assignments in the *personal* staff, but also to the Budget Director, Harold Smith, the head in effect of the institutional staff—which was organized around that notable stream of actions-with-deadlines-attached, the budget process.

There were some spheres of recurrent action, of activities incumbent on the President, where Roosevelt evidently thought it wise to have *no* staff with fixed, identified assignments. One was the sphere of *his* continuing relations with the leaders and members of Congress. Another was the sphere of his own choices for the chief appointive offices in his Administration. A third was the sphere of his direct relations with department heads, both individually and as a Cabinet. Every Roosevelt aide on fixed assignment was involved to some degree in all three spheres. These and other aides were always liable to be used, *ad hoc,* on concrete problems in these spheres. But no one save the President was licensed to concern himself exclusively, or continuously, with FDR's congressional relations, political appointments, or Cabinet-level contacts.

The third thing I would emphasize is Roosevelt's sense of need for mobile manpower and multiple antennae. In addition to his aides with fixed assignments, FDR took full advantage of the Brownlow *Report's* proposal for a number of "Administrative Assistants" on his personal staff, each with a "passion for anonymity." After 1939 and on into the war years, he had several men so titled—and so enjoined—about him, all of them conceived as "generalists," whom he could use, *ad hoc,* as choreboys, trouble shooters, checker-uppers, intelligence operatives, and as magnets for ideas, gripes, gossip in the Administration, on the Hill, and with groups outside government. These men were also used, as need arose, to backstop and assist the aides who did have fixed assignments.

FDR intended his Administrative Assistants to be eyes and ears and manpower for *him,* with no fixed contacts, clients, or involvements of their own to interfere when he had need to redeploy them. Naturally these general-purpose aides gained know-how in particular subject-matter areas, and the longer they worked on given *ad hoc* jobs the more they tended to become functional "specialists." One of them, David Niles, became so involved in dealings with minority groups that Truman kept him on with this as his fixed specialty. Roosevelt's usual response to such a situation would have been to shake it up before the specialization grew into a fixed assignment.

The "passion for anonymity" phrase, which caused such merriment in Washington when Brownlow's *Report* came out, did not seem funny in the least to FDR. He evidently thought it of the essence for the men inside his House whom he would use as general-purpose aides. Fixed, functional assignments interfered with anonymity as well as with his freedom of deployment.

Roosevelt had never wanted in his House more general-purpose men for *ad hoc* missions than he personally could supervise, direct, assign *and reassign.* During the war, however, as his needs and interests changed, his White House staff inevitably tended to become a two-level operation, with some aides quite remote from his immediate concerns or daily supervision. How he might have met this tendency, after the war, we have no means of knowing.

It never seems to have occurred to FDR that his only sources of such *ad hoc* personal assistance were the aides in his own office. He also used Executive Office aides, personal friends, idea-men or technicians down in the bureaucracy, old Navy hands, old New York hands, experts from private life, Cabinet officers, "Little Cabinet" officers, diplomats, relatives—especially his wife—

toward the end, his daughter—as supplementary eyes and ears and manpower. He often used these "outsiders" to check or duplicate the work of White House staff, or to probe into spheres where White House aides should not be seen, or to look into things he guessed his staff would be against.

He disliked to be tied to any single source of information or advice on anything. Even if the source should be a trusted aide, he preferred, when and where he could, to have alternative sources.

Put these three operating "principles" together and they add up to a *fourth:* in Roosevelt's staffing there was no place for a Sherman Adams. Roosevelt made and shifted the assignments; *he* was the recipient of staff work; *he* presided at informal morning staff meetings; *he* audited the service he was getting; *he* coordinated A's report with B's (or if he did not, they went uncoordinated and he sometimes paid a price for that). Before the war, reportedly, he planned to keep one of his Administrative Assistants on tap "in the office," to "mind the shop" and be a sort of checker-upper on the others. But he never seems to have put this intention into practice. From time to time he did lean on one aide above all others in a given area. In wartime, for example, Harry Hopkins was distinctly *primus inter pares* on a range of vital matters for a period of time. But Hopkins's range was never as wide as the President's. And Hopkins's primacy was not fixed, codified, or enduring. It depended wholly on their personal relationship and Roosevelt's will. In certain periods their intimacy waxed; it also waned.

III. FDR IN WARTIME

This brings me to the matter of wartime innovations, unforeseen in 1937, which profoundly changed the atmosphere and focus of the pre-existing White House operation.

From 1941 to 1943 Roosevelt brought new staff into the White House. Superficially, the new men and their new assignments made the place look different. But as he dealt with wartime staff, he operated very much as he had done before. He let his prewar pattern bend; despite appearances, he did not let it break.

The principal new arrivals were Hopkins, Rosenman, Lubin, Leahy, a "Map-Room," and Byrnes. Rosenman, as Counsel, has already been mentioned. Hopkins evolved into a sort of super (very super) administrative assistant, working on assignments without fixed boundaries in the conduct of the wartime Grand Alliance, and collaborating with Rosenman on major speeches. Lubin, nominally a Hopkins assistant, was Roosevelt's counterpart to Churchill's wartime Economic Section, the President's personal statistician, an independent source and analyst of key data on production of munitions, among other things. Leahy, as Chief of Staff to the Commander-in-Chief, became an active intermediary to and from the services, and kept an eye upon the White House Map-Room. This was a reporting and communications center, staffed by military personnel, in direct touch with the services, with war fronts, with intelligence sources, and with allied governments. As for Byrnes, he left the Supreme Court to be a "deputy" for Roosevelt in resolving quarrels among the agencies concerned with war production and the war economy. Byrnes' assignment was relatively fixed, but limited, temporary and entirely at the pleasure of the President, dependent on their personal relationship. In 1944, when Congress turned his job into a separate, statutory office (OWMR), Byrnes soon resigned. . . .

The striking common feature in these wartime innovations is that none of the new aides, from first to last, had irreversible assignments, or exclusive jurisdictions, or control over each other, or command over remaining members of the peacetime staff. Regarding all of them, and as he dealt with each of them, Roosevelt remained his own "chief of staff." And he continued to employ outsiders for assistance. Winston Churchill, among others, now became an alternative source. Anna Boettiger became a window to the world of personalities and politics beyond the terribly confining realm of war-making.

The war, in short, brought new men and new facilities into the presidential orbit, reflecting the new needs and new preoccupations of the President. Compared with 1939, the staff of 1944 had far more scope, more varied skills, incomparably better technical resources, a wider and a *different* range of interests, wider reach for policy, and on the part of leading members an enormous although variable share in exercising presidential powers. To members of the pre-existing peacetime staff it often seemed that everything had changed, that Roosevelt's operation was transformed. But from his standpoint—looking down, not up—nothing had changed save his preoccupations. Despite the surface differences—and making due allowance for the differences in substance, risk, and process—Roosevelt ran the war in the same way, with the same style, responsive to the same instincts or "principles" as during those preceding years when he and Louis Brownlow educated one another about "management." Or so it seems to me.

IV. WARTIME COMPLICATIONS

. . . This is not to say that his approach to staffing brought the same results in wartime as in peacetime. On the contrary, his war experience exposed a host of difficulties which had been undreamed of—or at least left unexplored— when he and Brownlow started their collaboration.

Wartime, for one thing, changed the size and pace of executive operations. We have got used to the Pentagon, but it was then the symbol of a new dimension. The New Deal had substantially enlarged and quickened the executive establishment of Hoover's time. War government towered over the New Deal. With the change in scale came changes in physical proximity, in direct contact, in human scope, in ease of interchange. Rooseveltian staff work called for intimacy, informality, word-of-mouth, walking-through, not only in the White House but around the town. War made it a much bigger town.

Wartime also imposed secrecy and censorship. No longer could the President look anywhere and everywhere for scraps of information and advice on his preeminent concerns, his most compelling choices. No longer could he pick up any aide or friend he chose to spy out the terrain of his official advisers. His instinct for alternative sources, his avid curiosity, his reach for information and ideas, now had to be confined to men with a "need to know."

Moreover, his instinct for competitive administration had to be confined—at least in cardinal spheres of policy—to men whose quarrels with one another were imperfectly observable to him through press reports, men whose opposing views, alternative approaches were veiled from public notice, public argument. As Schlesinger has pointed out, Roosevelt in peacetime relied on contention underneath him to produce a show and test of bureaucratic stresses, congressional reactions, interest-group alignments, political pressures, which he could weigh *before* he chose *his* timing and *his* course. Rooseveltian staffing obviously was designed to help him make full use of competition in these terms. But that peacetime practice took one thing for granted: an open field, a visible arena, with affected interests in the stands and audience-reactions audible to him. Secrecy—and censorship—shadowed the field, reduced the audience, blunted reactions.

In a closed arena, competitive administration gave Roosevelt less protection, fewer clues than it had given before. The inhibitions secrecy imposed upon staff services but added to the problem. Harold Stein's case-books, the new one and the old, provide us classic instances of the pain in that problem. Roosevelt never solved it. Nor—to anticipate—has Kennedy.

Secrecy did something more: it put the President into a world of knowledge *different* from the world the press inhabited. And not the press alone but his old friends, his political associates, many of his aides, the bulk of his bureaucracy, most members of his Cabinet knew less of what was happening and knew it differently, in different sequence, at a different time than he did. Now that we have lived with secrecy for a full generation, all of us have got accustomed to it and some of us have come to discount it.

Numbers of my academic colleagues seem to think that if one reads the *New York Times* with care one misses nothing of importance, secrecy or not. Numbers of Washingtonians appear to share this view. But this, I submit, is an illusion even now. Certainly it was so then when secrecy was new and censorship in force.

Roosevelt's approach to staff-work had assumed a wide array of "knowledgeable men," outside the White House as well as in, communicating freely with the President. But when most of them know less than the President, or know it differently, communication scarcely can be free and often is not useful in his business. So Roosevelt evidently found.

Not only was the President removed from most of his associates by what he knew—and when—but also by the nature of his personal responsibility. This had always been the case to a degree; wartime made it more so. FDR was spared the burden of a Kennedy that his choice, or the lack of it, might devastate a hemisphere; for the most part he was even spared the burden of a Lincoln that his judgment, or its lack, might lose a war. But in the winning of the war the burden of his choices was severe enough to chain him to his desk, exhaust his energy, cut short his life. The perspective he acquired with that burden on his back was not shared fully, could not be, by even his most intimate assistants. He remained his own "chief of staff," but tended less and less to put his mind on this assignment. Toward the end, he seems a man apart from all his principal associates. Neither individually nor collectively were they abreast of his preoccupations and intentions. When Truman later asked what Roosevelt meant to do, the answers were as speculative as the question.

The war had still a further consequence: the great bureaucracies it fostered, in their tangle of arms-length relationships, felt evermore compelling need—the more compelling with each increment of size, distance, impersonality, and "brass"—for service from the White House as a source of arbitration in their combats with each other. Wartime responsibility entangled bureaucratic jurisdictions even as it added scope and scale. The war power, meanwhile, enhanced the presidency as a court of ultimate appeal. But Roosevelt's presidential institution had been built to serve his purposes in mastering the bureaucrats, not theirs in getting service out of him. Orderly procedure, dutiful response, written records binding on the signer, firm decisions in behalf of others at *their* option—these were not often easy to obtain from Roosevelt's White House, and were not meant to be. Grudgingly, belatedly, he yielded ground sector by sector, when and as he felt impelled by bureaucratic and congressional politics, or by strained limits on his own attention. So Hopkins became arbiter-by-delegation on the inter-allied sharing of munitions; so Byrnes became, in time, an arbiter for the home-front economy; so Smith was handed privately, complete control of budgeting for Fiscal 1946.

But in the most important spheres of all, Roosevelt was adamant. On main matters in the conduct of the war and of allied relations he kept White House decision-making intimate, personalized, *ad hoc,* "disorderly," and in *his* hands. This suited him but caused great pain at the Pentagon and State.

The pain Roosevelt inflicted in the war years has left a lasting imprint on our government. Officialdom retaliated, after he was gone. To some degree or other—oftener than not to a large degree—organizations at the presidential level which were written into statute in the later 1940s were intended to assure against just such Rooseveltian free-wheeling. "Never again." It is no more than mild exaggeration to call NSC "Forrestal's Revenge," or NSRB (now OEP) "Baruch's Revenge" with Eberstadt as agent. Even in the 1950s White House organization was, in part, the product of reactions against Roosevelt. Eisenhower, too, had been a victim.

There was no need for Roosevelt to face squarely the pain his practice caused to his officialdom. Their difficulties never grew so great as to block his own ability to function, to make use of them. The war itself, while sharpening their hurt, provided its own palliatives. The White House might be loath to settle a dispute, decide on policy, clarify authority, or choose priorities, but warfare and the aim of winning helped enormously to keep issues in focus, and in bounds. Money helped as well; officials operating in the cardinal spheres of policy had ample funds. As students of the Pentagon are well aware, nothing is more conducive to rational behavior, orderly discussion, give-and-take. Talent helped too; the best of the New Deal, mingled with the best of Wall Street, gave officialdom as much ability, as widely spread, as we have ever seen. Meanwhile the war power kept the various congressional committees relatively united; congressional tempers relatively checked. And wartime unity drove underground, much of the time, the clash of interests and of parties in our politics.

The war, in short, did much to ease usual tensions among "separated institutions sharing powers," much to enhance and clarify the President's central position. With so many peacetime pains removed, or lightened, Roosevelt's wartime bureaucrats could well afford increased discomfort from his persistent "untidyness."

But suppose a President whose operating instincts were not unlike FDR's faced complications of the sort I have ascribed to wartime Washington without the wartime benefits I have just mentioned? There is no need to be supositous. This, roughly speaking, is John Kennedy's plight.

V. THE KENNEDY APPROACH

President Kennedy has been in office a year and a half less than Roosevelt when the latter reviewed Brownlow's proposals; he has worked inside the White House four years less than Roosevelt when the latter fully implemented those proposals. To speak of Kennedy's "approach" to presidential staffing is to deal with something which no doubt is still evolving in his practice and his mind. One cannot characterize what has not happened. Yet Kennedy moved swiftly to create a staffing pattern, to show an operating style, and he has held to these with quite remarkable consistency for some two years. In retrospect this may turn out to have been an interim approach. But this, at least, one can attempt to characterize. Let me try.

There are some obvious affinities between the operating "principles" in Kennedy's own mind and those I earlier ascribed to FDR. His staffing demonstrates this rather plainly. He evidently shares Roosevelt's concern for the distinction between "personal" and "institutional" staff. From Administration to Administration, White House staff has grown inexorably; "this is the White House calling" has less meaning every decade. But Kennedy quite consciously has tried to slow the trend; he cut back Eisenhower's growth and started small.

Kennedy, moreover, has run his personal staff with a feeling as keen as Roosevelt's (or was it Brownlow's?) for organizing around action-forcing processes. Like FDR, this President has operated with a small core of senior aides on relatively fixed assignments, and as with Roosevelt's men these have been action-sphere, not program-area assignments. Theodore Sorensen, as Special Counsel, is a Rosenman-writ-large. McGeorge Bundy is a sort of pinned-down Harry Hopkins, standing astride the stream of operational actions in the conduct of diplomacy and of defense which now flow to a President routinely with no less intensity or volume than had been "exceptional" as late as 1940.

And so it goes for Kenneth O'Donnell, for Pierre Salinger, for Lawrence O'Brien, for Ralph Dungan—each handles a distinctive aspect of the work-flow which the President must get through, day-by-day. Like their Roose-veltian counterparts these men also do other things, *ad hoc*. And as in Roose-velt's day their general-purpose services are supplemented by the services of others who do not have comparable fixed assignments—our commentator for one.

Titles have changed but the style is similar. "Administrative Assistant" has less novelty and dignity; almost everyone is now a "Special Assistant." The fine old title "Secretary" is now held only by Salinger. But do not be confused by nomenclature. The pattern is much the same. So are the operating conse-quences for the staff. And Kennedy is very much his own chief-of-staff.

This personal staff is *unlike* FDR's in one particular: thirty-two months have passed without much feuding. These men have managed the deliberate overlapping of their work and their bilateral relations with the President in re-markably self-disciplined fashion. The lack of "personalities" is striking; the lack of bureaucratic paranoia even more so. This presumably reflects the Presi-dent. His taste for competition, for alternative sources, is stronger than in any President since Roosevelt. But he seems to have no taste for ego-baiting and low tolerance for egoism, even perhaps his own. Comparing presidential styles is tricky business. In this respect, as obviously in others, the Kennedy White House is not simply Roosevelt's reproduced.

The differences grow greater as one moves beyond the personal staff toward the realms of institutional staff and departmental relations. Roosevelt was lucky; he wrote on a clean slate and then he got a second slate "war govern-ment." Roosevelt innovated, Kennedy inherited.

From Truman he inherited an Executive Office larger and much more diffuse than Roosevelt's Budget Bureau, encompassing by statutory mandate NSC staff, CEA, and what we now call OEP. From Eisenhower he inherited a complex "staff system" and cabinet-committee structure, as well as a variety of specialized staff units. From both his predecessors he inherited classic and unresolved dilemmas of relationship between a President and certain key de-partments, notably Defense, State, Justice, Treasury. Kennedy's approach to staffing has been shaped in major part by his attempts to cope with this in-heritance. The outcome naturally resembles Roosevelt's pattern less then does the White House staff, *per se*.

Commotion over Kennedy's deliberate dismantling of his predecessor's staff and cabinet system has obscured the fact that he retained and has elaborated on four features of the Eisenhower era. For one thing, Kennedy disposes of his time with much the freedom Eisenhower painfully acquired from a heart attack. It is only thirty years since Hoover, once a week, received whatever citizens desired to shake hands. It is little more than a decade since Truman's days were crowded by obligatory interviews with Congressmen, with lobbyists, with spokesmen for good causes. One of Eisenhower's greatest contributions to the Presidency—and to the sanity of future Presidents—lay precisely in this: the gift of time.

But Eisenhower's cut-back on the set-appointments list is not the only way in which his practice has been carried forward. Kennedy has also kept, indeed enlarged upon, the White House staff for legislative liaison, a notable departure from Rooseveltian practice, which Eisenhower was the first to introduce in a serious way. Similarly, Kennedy has followed and indeed elaborated Eisenhower's staff for science and technology. The Executive Office now has a new component, OST, and its Director keeps the White House status Eisenhower had conferred. Further, the Special Projects Fund which Eisenhower added to White House resources has been used by his successor, very much as he had done, to bring assorted special staffs with special purposes—including status-recognition for an interest-group or program—into the presidential orbit as need be from time to time. This evidently has become an indispensable adjunct of presidential life as it will be lived from now on.

In his relations with departments and department heads, JFK has evidently sought to steer a course between Roosevelt's "disorder" and Eisenhower's "system." Kennedy appears to view the formal meeting-with-fixed-membership and ponderous procedures much as Roosevelt did: a waste of energy and time and a restriction on the President. But Kennedy also appears far less inclined than FDR to keep his senior ministers at arms length, or at odds with one another, or in the dark about his plans and interventions. On the contrary, with those of his department heads whose work is most bound up with his from day to day—State, Defense, Justice, above all—he has sought a relationship as close and confidential and collegial as with his staff, and he has delegated tasks to them and their associates as though they all were members of his staff. With Justice and Defense, especially, he has devolved on Cabinet members staff-work which a Roosevelt almost surely would have held within the White House. Evidently this is Kennedy's preferred course; if he has not done it everywhere or equally the signs are that he does it where and as he finds he can.

Incidentally, if one looks for Kennedy equivalents of Brownlow's proposals on the budget process and Harold Smith's implementation, one looks not to the Budget Bureau now but to Defense, one-half the budget. As innovators it is McNamara and Hitch who are in the line of succession to Brownlow and Smith.

What all this suggests is not merely that Kennedy's own personal proclivities depart in these respects from FDR's. Their situations differ, their options differ; personalities aside, their approaches could not be the same. Roosevelt, we are always hearing, was his own Secretary of State. To the same degree he also was his own Secretary of Defense, insofar as such a role existed in his time. But no President, not excepting Roosevelt if he were to reappear (which the two-term amendment was enacted to prevent), could manage this under contemporary conditions. This is not Roosevelt's wartime, nor is it what he knew before as "peacetime." It is, instead, a time when government exhibits disadvantages of both with few of the advantages of either. It is, indeed, late in the second decade of that disadvantaged time.

In governmental terms, Kennedy's time (to date) is marked by what I once tried to encompass in the phrase "emergencies in policy with politics-as-usual." It is a time marked also by the presence of intractable substantive problems and immovable bureaucratic structures. A Kennedy must operate from day to day under restraints upon administrative free-wheeling as tight as the restraints upon large policy departures.

On neither score has he a Roosevelt's freedom from maneuver. Kennedy's approach to presidential staffing suggests that he has found this out.

VI. CONCLUDING NOTE

Where do we go from here? A quarter-century ago, members of our profession dealt with presidential staffing as a problem in "management" which the President in question took to mean scope for himself through control over others. Those students of administration and that politician found themselves quite able to agree, despite implicit differences in terms of reference. But their agreement rested on a shaky base: the premise that both democratic theory and constitutional prescription put the President, by right, "in charge" of the executive establishment as though it were a business corporation and he its chief executive. "All power to the boss" was thus a principle of "good administration" which the students could endorse and FDR could hide behind.

But neither as a document nor as accreted precedent does the American Constitution give the President of the United States exclusive warrant to be "boss" of the executive establishment. It gives him but a warrant to contest for that position, agency by agency, as best he can. Congress and its committees have their warrants too; so do department heads and bureau chiefs. And every bureaucrat swears his *own oath* to preserve and defend the Constitution. . . .

Nor would I claim that any sort of presidential staffing—personal or institutional—or any sort of operating style can meet, at once and equally, a President's own needs for service from officialdom and bureaucratic needs for service from the President. What wartime Washington experienced is with us still, in aggravated form: to a degree the needs of bureaucrats and Presidents are incompatible. The better one is served the worse will be the other. Yet each is bound to have a stake in satisfaction for the other. So each is bound to be dissatisfied.

In Kennedy's Washington, as in Eisenhower's and Truman's, to say nothing more of FDR's, honorable and able men inside departments fume in frustration at White House "unwillingness" to be "decisive," while their White House counterparts fume in frustration at bureaucracy's "unwillingness" to be "responsive." Why do these feelings persist (and grow)? For answer one must probe beneath the surface of "machinery," even beneath the surfaces of "personality," to the perspectives and compulsions generated by the combination of "big government" and "separated powers" in a period when foreign and domestic crises coexist as customary features of our daily life.

SURVIVAL IN THE BUREAUCRATIC JUNGLE *
Harlan Cleveland

THE JUNGLE HE INHABITS

A DISCUSSION of that political animal, the government executive, should start with some picture of the jungle in which he lives and works and, if he is fit enough, survives. We can agree, I am sure, that government is a mixture of politics and administration, accommodation and logic, consent and decisions. . . .

We instinctively demand that our Presidents be "double firsts"—that they be great politicians and great administrators too. Of course they don't usually succeed on both counts. Franklin Roosevelt, who is possibly unsurpassed in this century as a builder of consent in war and peace, was as casual an administrator as ever hit Washington. Harry Truman, whose reputation and training were in politics, proved himself an able and orderly administrator, but when it came to building consent for a government program he can hardly be rated better than fair. President Eisenhower, whose forte was military administration, has combined a remarkable talent for evoking consent with an equally remarkable tendency to appoint as administrators of his policies men who disagree with them.

Yet if we seldom or never get quite the perfect Presidential blend, we continue to pine for that rare amalgam—the man who can run the Executive Branch and still get along with most of the other Americans, in and out of Congress, who think *they* are anointed to run the government too.

What is not so clear in much of the literature of public administration is the fact that every official of the Executive Branch must in some measure combine the two qualities we look for in a President—the ability to manage and the talent to build political support for what is managed. Government is a mixture of administration and politics all the way up and down the line, not merely at something called the political level where people called political executives get jobs by a process called political appointment.

THE DIFFUSION OF POWERS

What is it about our government that makes it so political a jungle? The standard explanation is the Constitutional separation of powers, the built-in

* From *The Reporter* (April 5, 1956), pp. 29–32. Copyright, 1956, by The Reporter Magazine Company. Reprinted by permission.

checks and balances, the fact that everybody is in every act but nobody seems to be in charge of the performance.

Woodrow Wilson called this "administration by semi-independent executive agents who obey the dictation of a legislature to which they are not responsible." He was sure that Congress ran the show, described legislation as "the originating force," and complained that the "blind processes" resulting from the division of power made that power irresponsible. But Wilson was too pessimistic about the ability of the government to function in spite of this division of power and purposes—or better, perhaps, because of it. He was certainly overimpressed with the power of the legislature in his academic days, though as President he later underestimated its veto power when it came to getting the League of Nations ratified. The legislature is powerful and can do a massive job of wreckmanship, as we know from our own recent history. But the men who wrote our Constitution were clear about the "dangers from legislative usurpations." "One hundred and seventy-three despots would surely be as oppressive as one," Madison said in one of the Federalist papers. ". . . An elective despotism was not the government we fought for."

Despite the periodic flurries of legislative usurpation, we don't have an elective despotism. But we do have a Congress that participates with appalling vigor in the task of running the Executive Branch of the government. We have, indeed, a system that not only separates the general Constitutional powers but diffuses the power of decision on quite specific matters. One of the very first things I ever had to do in Washington, as an "intern" in the office of Senator "Young Bob" La Follette, was to stand in for the Senator at a hearing in the Veterans Administration on a compensation case. I recall being struck at the time by the distortion of functions thus dramatized: Here I was, a legislative bureaucrat, horning in on the efforts of executive bureaucrats to perform a judicial function.

Each official in each branch of the government has a chance to exercise two (and occasionally even three) of the Constitutional powers at once; and by the same token, each of the three branches gets a crack at nearly every major public issue.

The result of this diffusion of power is not merely as Odegard says, that "Congress has . . . found ways and means for interposing itself between the President and his executive subordinates and thus confusing the clear line of bureaucratic responsibility." Each executive official, whether politically appointed or not, has to spend an unconscionable amount of his time and energy telling Congress what he is doing, and why. In my last year with the Mutual Security Agency, I figure that I spent the equivalent of six months out of the twelve preparing and presenting on Capitol Hill the detailed exposition of the program I was supposed to be helping "administer."

Nor is it enough for an administrator to defend a program from political attack. He finds himself actively promoting a political coalition in its support. For our Congress, which I have heard described to a group of visting Frenchmen as a model of party discipline, is of course as choice an example of coalition government as the notorious French Assembly.

If there is any doubt that Congress is managed by complex, *ad hoc* coalitions which shift with every issue, look for a moment at the record of the Eighty-third Congress. In this supposedly Republican Congress, the fluctuating balance of power swung against the Administration on foreign aid and public housing, but supported the President on farm price supports and (by one vote) the Bricker amendment. A coalition majority could be put together for confirming the New Deal, reducing taxes, cutting slightly the funds for defense, continuing the 1950 version of U.S. foreign policy, and allowing some of its committees to trample on Executive toes. On hardly any of these issues could one party get its way solely with the votes it could deliver from its own side of the aisle.

We see the same pattern operating in the Eighty-fourth Congress, which is theoretically led by the Democrats. There was an excellent example in the Senate when thirty-one Republicans and twenty-two Democrats beat twenty-four Democrats and fourteen Republicans and sent the natural-gas bill to Thomasville, Georgia, to be vetoed by a Republican President.

Because Congress is the way it is, every executive must help splice together the particular coalition that will pass *his* appropriation and protect *his* program and *his* reputation from damage. (His coalition may be very different from another one being fashioned for a different purpose by a colleague in the next office.) If every executive has Congressional relations as an important segment of his duties—even though he may not himself carry a bulging briefcase up Pennsylvania Avenue to "the Hill"—every executive has to have some of the instincts of a politician.

It is usually said that there are seven to eight hundred "political executives" in the national government. But by my definition there are thousands of government executives engaged in 'politics." Under our Constitutional diffusion of powers, the Federal government would hardly operate at all if they were fewer.

THE INSIDE TRACK

Many distinguished writers have pondered whether the American Congress adequately represents the American people, but this is an academic question about which I have never been able to get excited. For the American people do not limit their representation in Washington to electing half a thousand Congressmen. The people are directly represented in the Executive Branch, too.

When I say "the people," I mean what David Riesman intends by the phrase "veto groups." In *The Lonely Crowd,* Riesman observed that political leadership has passed from businessmen as a class to "a series of groups, each of which has struggled for and finally attained a power to stop things conceivably inimical to its interests and, within far narrower limits, to start things.

. . . Among the veto groups competition is monopolistic; rules of fairness and fellowship dictate how far one can go." The tidelands group refrained from going too far; the natural-gas lobby, consisting of some of the same people, so outraged the public conscience that a President thought to be favorable to its objectives had to turn against the natural-gas bill. The farm group's effective power is enormous; the smaller effectiveness of the labor group may be traced, at least in part, to the fact that it overplayed its hand during the New Deal.

What Riesman did not mention is the fact that the power of these new-style lobbies can be roughly measured by the strength of their surrogates *within* the Executive Branch of the government. The Department of Agriculture has long been regarded, both by the farm organizations and the rest of the government, as a farmers' defense league inside the Federal bureaucracy. Organized labor, particularly the CIO, substantially controlled the National Labor Relations Board during the period (in the 1930's) when the Board was clearing the way for the rapid expansion of the CIO. The housing program, created by the New Deal for the purpose of getting houses built, placed itself in the hands of the speculative builders and the savings-and-loan associations to such an extent that moral corruption shaded over into pecuniary corruption. The organized veterans have their own preserve in the Veterans Administration. The Commerce Department has for some years had a Business Advisory Council whose function, in effect, is to bring to bear on internal government decisions an organized business opinion. Defense contracts are habitually given out by men recruited from the businesses that are getting the business, and regulations are drafted by surrogates of the industries to which they apply. The National Recovery Act was declared unconstitutional early in the New Deal, but "self-government of industry" is an established practice with a venerable tradition behind it.

During the Korean War, as John Corson has said, "The Office of Price Stabilization official in charge of price regulations for the apparel industry [in 1951] was borrowed from a leading firm in this industry. His aide, who specializes in women's woven underwear, is 'on loan' from Barbizon, one of the principal competing manufacturers in this field. A succession of five or more chiefs of the Iron and Steel Division in the National Production Authority have been loaned by their companies, the major companies in the steel industry. The acting director of the Equipment and Materials Division of the Defense Transport Administration for most of 1951 was on loan from the American Car and Foundry Company. He actively promoted, for the Defense Transport Administrator, a plea that the NPA make available sufficient steel to build ten thousand freight cars a quarter; his firm . . . is engaged in the production of freight cars."

From time to time this sort of thing gets out of bounds, as in the recent cases of Air Force Secretary Talbott and Chairman Hugh Cross of the Interstate Commerce Commission, both of whom admitted error in using their official positions to advance their private interests. Much more often, there is no formal "conflict of interest." It is considered normal and natural for a steel man to lubricate with government contracts the growth of steel production; for a housing man to get more housing built by having the government absorb a good part of the risk; for a farmers' representative to promote aid for farmers from inside the Department of Agriculture; for a labor organizer temporarily in the government to promote the right of labor to organize. We have institutionalized the inside track.

The political executive consequently has to do more than run his shop and deal with Congress. He has to maintain a complex network of horizontal relations with the veto groups whose interests his actions may affect, with others who think their interests might be affected, and with the surrogates of these groups in *both* the Executive and Legislative Branches of the government.

I am trying hard not to pass any moral judgment on this system, but merely to describe how it seems to work. Given the nature of our society, it is almost bound to work this way. The government is, after all, the least bureaucratic of the major interest groups with which it has to deal. Turnover of government personnel is high, especially at the top. Even if this were not true for other reasons, we make sure of it by having reasonably frequent elections. The same is not true of the major aggregations of veto power outside: In business, labor, agriculture, and a good many other categories, elections are often a façade for maintaining the same leadership from year to year and even from decade to decade. If you don't like the President of the United States, you can vote against him every four years. If you don't like the president of General Motors or the head of a labor union, you can only wait for him to die.

This difference in tenure between government and outside interest groups is critical. If the outside leaders know more about the subject than their opposite numbers inside the government, if they are providing key experts, advisers, and sometimes even the political executives themselves, the views of the regulated are likely to be pretty influential with the regulators. In the United States, the road to the riskless society that Europeans call socialism is paved with the incestuous intention of nearly every major economic interest to bring in the government as the risk-taking partner.

Where, in this picture, does the "public interest" appear? Not, certainly, through the organized political parties, which inflate like balloons at election time and are of small consequence in governmental decision making the rest of the time. No, the defense of the public interest rests in the hands of the people as a whole, who can't do anything much about it, and of the President they elect, who can.

THE BUCK PASSES UP

Whether, under our system, the government ultimately serves the public interest, or merely obliges the private and sectional Trojan horses encamped inside the walls of the Federal bureaucracy, depends on the President to an extraordinary and alarming degree. He is the chief mediator among the veto groups, the one political executive whose whole job is to consider the situation as a whole. He is the one remaining safety man available to stop a specialized interest which breaks through the normal line of checks and balances and threatens to gain too much yardage at the expense of other groups.

In a revealing passage of his autobiography, Mr. Truman regarded it as quite natural that nobody should consider the public interest but the President. "I was always aware," he wrote, "of the fact that not all my advisers looked at the . . . problem in the same manner I did. This was nothing unusual, of course. It is the job of the military planners to consider all matters first and always in the light of military considerations. The diplomat's approach is—or in any case should be—determined by considerations of our relations to other nations. The Secretary of the Treasury thinks in terms of budget and taxes. Except for the members of his personal staff, each Presidential adviser has and should have a departmental outlook."

Though we sometimes make gods or supermen of our Presidents, they have not generally been more moral than most of us. The difference is that in the White House they are compelled to stand a little higher on the mountain than anybody else, and they consequently see farther at the horizon. It is this unique and lonely vantage point that lends grandeur to the American Presidency.

Yet the President's high rank does not necessarily mean that he makes more "decisions" than other political executives below. Indeed it is arguable that in our government, the higher one's rank the fewer decisions one makes. The man who buys paper clips makes a number of unreviewed decisions without consultations—what size and shape of paper clip, from whom to buy, at what price. As you go up the ladder of authority each official is beset with more committees, more horizontal clearances, more veto groups and political personalities whose views must be reconciled or discounted before the "final decision" is reached.

I once tried to get this important idea across to a very bright businessman who had just been appointed a division director and had promptly started to operate as if he were solely responsible for the program coordinated by that division. One day, months after he had taken office, I knew he would survive the transition to becoming a public servant. For he came to me and said: "I'm director of this program, but that doesn't mean I direct anybody, does it? I mean I don't make any *decisions*. I'm really a sort of broker, I guess."

The President's role as chief broker makes possible a certain order in the bureaucratic jungle. It is no accident that matters that frequently get to the White House are often better handled than matters that do not. The Housing Agency worked off in a corner by itself for years, dealing direct with the housing industry and hardly ever creating a crisis requiring Presidential attention. As a result, corrupt practices like "mortgaging out" under Section 608 came to be regarded by some as the natural order of things until Congress finally made a political scandal of them. The foreign-aid program, on the other hand, has spent more than $50 billion since the Second World War, with hardly a trace of scandal. Why? Could it be because so many departments and agencies were always fighting for the right to manage foreign aid that the program was a matter of monthly, even weekly, concern to the President himself? . . .

THE CABINET MEMBER AND DEPARTMENTAL ADMINISTRATION *
Richard F. Fenno, Jr.

WE must . . . resist the temptation to over-personalize organizational activity and to exaggerate the influence which an individual Secretary can have on his department. The most ambitious and talented department head confronts a formidable complex of situational limitations on his activity. The new appointee finds himself amid a framework of established relationships, of goals already fixed and of forces long since set in motion. He faces an impersonal bureaucratic structure with great resistance to change. Most of his organization is staffed with career personnel, relatively unaffected by changes in high-level policy. Power relationships among constituent elements of the department, or between departmental units and clusters of interest outside the department, tend to be in an equilibrium which reflects an optimum adjustment for all concerned. Their desire to survive may confront the Secretary with serious limitations. He has, of course, some formal controls with which to countervail departmental resistances, but these are frequently minimized by the very forces he is trying to combat.

One control, for instance, which is a prerequisite to successful departmental management is the power of appointment. Yet the Secretary frequently operates under considerable restriction—statutory or otherwise. Harold Ickes complained that, "Without the power to appoint subordinates there is no power of control at all. I think this power should lie with the Secretary because, at least in the public mind, he is charged with the responsibility. As it is now, he has the responsibility without any authority, and that makes for bad administration, bad morale, and misunderstanding."

The appointments of the Under Secretary and Assistant Secretaries are subject to many non-Secretarial influences. During party turnovers these positions are eminently suited for the payment of political rewards. Both President and Congressmen may press personal favorites upon the department head. In any case, the result may be unfortunate from the standpoint of internal administration, as, for example, Stimson's experience with Under Secretary Castle will attest. Or, interested groups may lay claim to some of these positions. The desire of the AFL and the CIO for one Assistant Secretaryship of Labor apiece

* From Richard F. Fenno, Jr., *The President's Cabinet* (Cambridge, Mass.: Harvard University Press, 1959), pp. 226–234. Copyright, 1959, by the President and Fellows of Harvard College. Reprinted by permission.

is a case in point. With regard to Bureau Chiefs, the Secretary operates under severe statutory handicaps. Inability to remove these officials follows where the power of appointment is lacking.

The department head's formal managerial weapons may be further blunted by organizational inflexibilities. We have already noted the historical evolution of the so-called "holding company" type of department, which includes Interior, Defense, Commerce, and Health, Education and Welfare. Many constituent units of these departments have their own separate statutory bases, thereby helping to establish an authority with non-departmental roots. Since built-in unity is lacking, it can come to the "holding company" organization only by super-imposition from above, yet it is part of the organizational pattern that such authority is hard to come by. In an "integrated" type of organization the Secretary has substantive grants of authority over the constituent units, whereas in the more loosely structured department he has a vaguely defined responsibility to "direct and supervise" them. In practice, however, such a mandate is "an almost meaningless generality."

This limitation is most obvious in terms of authority to reorganize the relationships of the subordinate units. Frequently, he cannot transfer activities from one unit to another, make adjustments in his field organization, or alter the budget so as to make organizational changes possible. Congress may want to exercise minute supervision over all such organizational changes. When Chairman Carl Vinson of the House Armed Services Committee proposed that the Secretary of Defense should consult his Committee before making any organizational changes, Secretary Louis Johnson exclaimed, "Why, you would become the Secretary of Defense. That completely ties the hands of the Secretary." Said Vinson in reply, "We don't want Congress by-passed."

What appear, from a bird's-eye view, to be limitations on the Secretary's managerial discretion appear from another perspective as the phenomenon of "bureau autonomy." Hoover described the Commerce Department as "a congeries of independent bureaus . . . all old establishments created prior to the Department itself. . . . Each was an inbred bureaucracy of its own. There was little department spirit or *esprit de corps*. Some of the bureaus even placed their own names on their letterheads, without mentioning the Department." Franklin Lane described the Interior Department as "a rather disjointed department [in which] the bureaus have stood up as independent entities." The independence of the Army Corps of Engineers is a classic instance of the pattern of relationships which may develop, and it has been admirably related in another place. The important thing to be noted about bureau autonomy, for our purposes, is that its dynamics are by no means explainable in wholly organizational terms. An administrative organization like a bureau does not hang motionless in a political vacuum waiting to be directed according to statute and hierarchy. In order to gain and hold any degree of autonomy, its position must be shored up by sufficient political support. This usually derives from those groups in the political system to whose advantage it is to maintain such autonomy. In addition to bureau personnel, these groups will ordinarily include the clientele for whom the bureau provides services, and members of the legislature who have an interest, corporate or otherwise, in controlling the activities of an administrative agency. The intimate *rapprochement* which the Corps of Engineers have established with local organizations and with influential Congressmen is a key to their continued administrative independence.

Considered in these broad situational terms, the problems raised by bureau autonomy may arise to some degree in every executive department. Even though a departmental executive may possess considerable authority, a bureau will possess its own independent base of support to which it may appeal. In fact, and this is the point, it must do so in order to get the power to operate. Regardless of statutory relationships with Congress (though these help), direct bureau-legislature relationships will be legion, including appropriations, investigations, appointments, etc. Every governmental bureau has one vested interest, one constant preoccupation—survival. And in the interests of survival, it must cultivate sympathetic attitudes and support on the part of those who can do it harm, which most often means the legislature. In the interests of control, the legislative unit whose relations with the agency are most frequent will encourage and attempt to enforce responsibility to it. This mutuality of interests may create a concentration of power which can undermine the authority of the Secretary over his department.

Interwoven with the bureau-legislature "sub-system," and operating on both parties to it, are the interested private groups. Regional labor groups interested in employment may work with both bureau admirals and pork-barreling Congressmen to keep the control of naval shipyard and supply contracts out of the hands of an economy-minded Secretary of the Navy. In the process of administration, policy is made by the operating bureaus. Each bureau develops its own clientele—people interested in the policy questions within the bureau's area of discretion. Thus, "a structure of interests friendly or hostile, vague and general, or compact and well defined encloses each significant center of administrative discretion." If the bureau is to survive and develop a program, it must have support from these sources. To the private groups, on the other hand, the bureaus "represent the institutionalized embodiment of policy, an enduring organization actually or potentially capable of mobilizing power behind policy." Here again, mutual dependence dictates a close relationship, one which may not be logically consistent with the policies or desires of the Secretary. Little can be known about these informal power clusters by studying the formal intradepartmental hierarchy, yet they may be in direct competition with it. Where this is so, they impair the Secretary's ability to manage his department and to provide the President with good administration just as surely as any lack of adequate formal authority.

Time is still another complicating factor for every Cabinet official. If he wishes to help the President by rendering him good departmental administration, he must focus his energies downward into the department. But as he provides this kind of negative assistance, he has little time left for positive and constructive assistance. Men of large vision and extra-departmental enthusiasms like Secretary of the Interior Franklin Lane will often leave, like him, a testament of frustration in office: "Ability is not lacking, but it is pressed to the point of paralysis because of an infinitude of detail. . . . Every man is held to details, to the narrower view which comes too often to be the departmental view or some sort of parochial view . . . there was little opportunity to think of anything more than the immediate." William Redfield, the man who received Wilson's letter of praise for efficient departmental administration, admitted that "I looked at my duties too much as a business matter—too little as the creative counsellor." But, he explained in defense, "My nose is kept closely to the grindstone in my own Department." The tendency to become sucked in and submerged by routine or detail or immediacy has been called "the most insidious hazard both to the executive and his organization." He cannot lift up his head often enough to look at things from a government-wide, i.e. presidential, standpoint. If he is to be of help to the President, his time is a precious resource, easily exploited and difficult to conserve.

Department Secretaries live in a world which has many extra-presidential dimensions. We have seen the multiplicity of forces within the political system which impinge upon him—forces built into his department by its history, by forces of the appointment process, by forces emanating from Congress, and by forces generated by the publics which the department serves—forces of interest, of authority, and of partisanship. Up to this point in our discussion we have discussed what might be called a series of objective factors which affect departmental administration, with potentialities for lightening or increasing the President's burden. They are objective factors in the sense that the assumption is made that the overriding concern of the Secretary is to manage the internal affairs of his department in the interests of the President. The implicit image of the Cabinet member thus far has been something akin to that of a person whose administrative life history is one ceaseless struggle to surmount a veritable network of obstacles, personal and situational, in an effort to act as the agent and servant of his superior. Such may, indeed, be the case. The Secretary may be exclusively President-oriented, and instances where he fails to help the President may be written off as the result of forces which he cannot bring under control. But it is an equally likely possibility, in view of the department head's problems of success and survival, that he may deliberately assume postures and adopt positions that are department-oriented, and which may not accord with presidential desires.

Secretaries of Agriculture have frequently faced the problem of reconciling the views of the Farm Bureau with their loyalty to the Chief Executive. Secretary of Labor James Mitchell has lived amid similar cross-pressures from his union constituency and from President Eisenhower on such matters as right-to-work laws and FEPC legislation, and he has taken positions on them which the President himself refused to take. There is present, almost always, this dilemma of competing responsibilities, loyalties, and demands, bringing with it the potentiality of conflict. Conflict may, of course, be avoided, but its presence colors the Secretary's whole pattern of behavior. Every department head finds himself caught and torn between alternatives of action—President-oriented or department-oriented—in an environment where the rationale, the means, and the incentives for pursuing either are readily available.

His very position as head of one executive establishment among several carries with it certain attitudes and organizational necessities non-presidential in character. He inherits an immense bureaucratic structure with its own traditions, its own *raison d'être,* and its own operating methods. None of these depend on him, nor will he be able to alter them very significantly. He cannot help but become a part of this particular organization, supporting its vested interests, concerned for its *esprit de corps,* and speaking for it in all of its conflicts.

A Secretary of the Interior will predictably contest the location of the Forest Service (now in Agriculture) with the Secretary of Agriculture. He will do it not because it is a personal or partisan matter, but because it is a long-established, organizational tenet within Interior that the Forest Service belongs there. Secretaries may "defend or [be] governed by bureaus they themselves do not control," which in turn may lead them to "take positions hostile to presidential needs and policy."

The department head is not to be viewed as the unwilling captive of his organization or as someone who "fronts" for bureaus against his own subjective inclinations. . . . If a Secretary is to accomplish any of his goals, he must cultivate the support of his own organization. He cannot, as the Hoover Commission seems to think, trade exclusively on the influence of the President in his operations. Beyond his own organization, he must locate his support within the legislature and with interested private groups. Without non-presidential support of this kind, his department may be decimated—as the Secretary of Labor lost some of his bureaus by congressional action in a period when these units and the department in general had insufficient support from organized labor.

Harold Ickes' attempt to change the name of his Department from "Interior" to "Conservation and Public Works" illustrates how impotent a Cabinet official can be when he operates on the assumption that presidential support is all that he needs to run his department. Relying on Roosevelt's assurances that he was interested, that he would request other executive departments (Agriculture, War, and Navy) not to oppose it, and that he would urge congressional leaders to take favorable action, Ickes introduced his measure. When the bill failed to pass even a congressional subcommittee, Ickes was shocked, and interpreted the result as an act of personal perfidy by the President. What happened, actually, was that other executive departments which felt their interests threatened by the change were able to muster congressional support in the person of the Chairman of the subcommittee, and external support from the farm organizations. The President could not have made the difference in any event. More than this, it is not realistic to expect the President to give strong support to those pet projects of a Cabinet member which affect so many of his fellows. The Cabinet member is left on his own most of the time simply because the

President, for most of his time, must remain relatively detached as between competing departments. And where Congress is concerned, if the President exerts his power too frequently he may, by virtue of a familiar political paradox, lose it.

In the interests of effective departmental administration, most Cabinet members will be led at one time or another to exploit the presence of the competing lines of authority, running vertically to the President and horizontally to the Congress. The spectacle of Secretary of War George Dern supporting the Corps of Engineers in their autonomous operations is explainable only by looking behind the vertical, hierarchical rationale. Dern did everything he could to resist integrated planning on water resources because he felt it would dilute the functions of one of his bureaus. He even went so far as to claim that the Corps was "an agency of the legislative branch," thereby protecting his department by renouncing his own control over it! Many Secretaries, like him, have nourished the notion of horizontal responsibility in order to preserve their organizations. The point is that conflict between President-oriented actions and department-oriented actions inheres in the American political system. It is as evident in the administrative realm as in the legislative. . . .

B.   The Political Executives: In Committee

INDIVIDUAL political executives have specialized responsibilities, perspectives, and loyalties. Collectively, however, the responsibilities of the political executive class are nearly as broad as those of the President himself. It is relevant to ask, therefore, whether (and, if so, in what ways) committees of political executives can provide a President with better advice than their individual members otherwise would.

Committees are flourishing, of course, in all modern bureaucracies. At their best, they provide efficient mechanisms for bringing multiple interests, perspectives, and intellectual disciplines to bear on the evaluation of proposals; they help bind related organizations together by enhancing their awareness of interdependence and common purpose; and they broaden the perspectives of the individual specialists who sit on them. At their worst, on the other hand, committees may smother innovative and independent critical thought; they may paper over program conflicts without doing anything to resolve them; and they may absorb enormous numbers of manhours that could more fruitfully be expended elsewhere.

The Cabinet and National Security Council are the two highest-level continuing committees in American government, and the only two whose perspectives might be thought to compare in breadth with the President's. To what extent, let us ask, are they in fact able to perform the following functions for the President: focus the loyalties of their members on the President by enhancing their sense that the Administration is a single collective enterprise; provide the President with advice from which specialized enthusiasms and loyalties have been filtered out; and/or provide him with a convenient forum in which to force all agencies interested in specific matters to confront each other's arguments directly in his presence?

Richard Fenno maintains that the typical Cabinet meeting is an exercise in non-communication, and endeavors to explain why. Paul Hammond traces the history of the National Security Council, reviews two laudatory "inside" reports on its effectiveness, and speculates provocatively on its uses and limitations. Unlike the Cabinet, the National Security Council deals with a highly interdependent set of policies and it has developed in response to *recent* felt needs. One might expect it, therefore, to be a far more significant institution. Hammond believes that in some ways it is, but most of his analysis explores the ways in which (and the reasons why) it is not. Theodore Sorenson, who served as Special Assistant to the President throughout the Kennedy Administration, notes that President Kennedy considered full meetings of the Cabinet and National Security Council a waste of time, and reports on what he substituted for them.

THE CABINET MEETING *
Richard F. Fenno, Jr.

IT is evident . . . that forces beyond the Chief Executive-Cabinet nexus condition Cabinet-meeting activity. The most significant of these are the centrifugal forces which come into play through the actions of individual Cabinet members. . . . The members have a participant's-eye view of the meeting, with a non-presidential, non-Cabinet logic quite its own. It is a logic the compelling assumptions of which are rooted in the pluralism of the American political system. The pattern of development for the several departments was one of great diversity in purpose, structure, and clientele. The atmosphere of their growth encouraged a free-wheeling independence among the Cabinet's constituent units. Each Cabinet member, moreover, is the product of an appointment process characterized by the inter-determination of many variables—a process designed to build diversity into the Cabinet.

The objectively pluralistic conditions of departmental growth and of Cabinet appointment nourish their own subjective counterparts. Each Cabinet member has his own particularistic, departmental *raison d'être*. His attitude tends, likewise, to be particularistic and departmental. He develops much less of a group feeling than an individualistic one, and he more readily identifies with his department than with the Cabinet. His lack of group identification is

* Richard F. Fenno, Jr., *The President's Cabinet* (Cambridge, Mass.: Harvard University Press, 1959), pp. 131–141. Copyright, 1959, by the President and Fellows of Harvard College. Reprinted by permission.

aggravated, furthermore, by all the personal differences—temperamental and philosophical—which give rise to interpersonal friction with the "official family." The American Cabinet has, of course, no formal collective responsibility, but the psychology of departmentalism even militates against the establishment of what might be called mutual responsibility—a state of mind which stresses group concerns rather than separate and particular concerns. The subjective attitude hardest to come by among Cabinet members is this sense of corporate unity and common purpose, on which basis alone the potentialities of the institution can be realized.

The reaction of the Harding Cabinet, in the face of scandals which sent one member to the federal penitentiary and found another under extraordinarily severe pressure for malfeasance, is illustrative. The disclosures of Teapot Dome, coupled with the mismanagement and face-saving suicides which rocked the Department of Justice, were sufficient to have toppled any responsible European ministry. Yet, from the American Cabinet nothing but silence —"a distant, frigid, and unhelpful silence"—was forthcoming. Only one member was directly involved, and he took the entire blame and the full brunt of the criticism. The rest of the group said simply that it had never been called to their attention and that it was none of their business.

"The question of the legality or the propriety of the oil leases [said Hughes] . . . were never brought before the Cabinet for its discussion." Since Secretary of the Navy Denby and Secretary of the Interior Fall felt it was no one else's affair, this was good enough for their colleagues. Yet Hughes' biographer calls him "astonishingly tolerant of misconduct toward which he bore no responsibility," and the others (Hays and Mellon, for instance) behaved similarly. No one thought of resigning or even of decrying the scandal publicly, and only the rankest opposition newspapers interpreted this as any reflection at all on the whole Cabinet. These events and the attitudes of all concerned reflect a lack of responsibility, collective and mutual, which is characteristic of the Cabinet in action.

The American Cabinet does not fall together, but neither does it stand together; the lack of mutual responsibility is but the obverse side of the departmental attitude. Each Cabinet member maintains his aloofness from his fellows. As an epitome of the attitude, one might take Jesse Jones' blunt statement that "I made no other suggestions to other Cabinet members about their departments and asked none from them." For this official, as for many others, a fellow member's worth was judged in direct proportion to the extent to which he minded his own business. David Houston likewise said, "I have made it a rule not to take the initiative in any matter falling under the jurisdiction of another department and to try to be of assistance only when my aid was sought." Secretary Hughes' colleagues "could not get him interested in matters outside of his department, although by so doing he could help to promote the spirit of cooperation."

When Henry Wallace once sought financial aid for the Department of Agriculture, the reply of his colleague, the Secretary of the Treasury, bespoke a common attitude—"Henry, that's your cross, you bear it." On those occasions when the energies of a department head carry him across departmental lines, the serious charge of "interference" or "meddling" is usually leveled against him—as Cordell Hull frequently charged his cohorts. Secretary of War Garrison replied to Secretary of the Navy Daniels' offer of interdepartmental cooperation: "I don't care a damn about the Navy and you don't care a damn about the Army. You run your machine and I'll run mine." An observer of the Wilson Administration concluded that, "The members of the Cabinet do not seem to have the habit of frankness with one another. Each lives and works in a water-tight compartment."

The particularistic, departmental attitude of the Cabinet member manifests itself in his behavior at the Cabinet meeting. Ideally, the Cabinet meeting is the point at which the various department heads come together to work as a team, to cooperate and to coordinate and by so doing to help the President with his government-wide concerns. The effect of departmentalism militates against all these assumptions about teamwork. The Cabinet meeting tends to become a diplomatic assembly in which the departmentalism of the ambassadors replaces nationalism as the psychological bar to unity and cooperation. There is too often a lack of any sustaining desire within the group to function as a group, and a lack of the will to carry on serious business at the Cabinet meeting.

As Louis Brownlow says, "Each feels his responsibility—as indeed it is—personally to the President and not to the President in Council, nor to the President and his Cabinet, *and above all not to his Cabinet colleagues.*" Jesse Jones stated the canon of behavior perfectly when he said, "My principal reason for not having a great deal to say at Cabinet meetings was that there was no one at the table who could be of help to me except the President, and when I needed to consult him, I did not choose a Cabinet meeting to do so." This attitude converts the meeting into a joint enterprise, in which "joint" denotes a common determination to suppress vital issues and "enterprise" consists in the great variety of devices for doing so.

By all odds, the most important pieces of domestic legislation in Woodrow Wilson's first term were the tariff and federal reserve bills. Since Wilson made it a practice not to bring domestic issues before the group, it was left to the member concerned to raise these two vital questions for discussion. Mr. McAdoo, the Secretary of the Treasury, did not choose to do so, and his behavior effectively cut off this whole area, so vital to the success of the administration, from Cabinet discussion. As one of his colleagues wrote, "The truth is that the two important domestic issues, the tariff and the currency, are under the Treasury and that McAdoo is a solitaire player. He is self-reliant and has dash, boldness, and courage, but he does not cultivate Cabinet teamwork and does not invite discussion or suggestion from the Cabinet as a whole." Multiplied by the number of individuals and problems, the departmental feeling can keep those issues which depend on Cabinet-member initiative from ever coming to the attention of the Cabinet.

Attempts to raise touchy interdepartmental issues may meet with resentment from a colleague and may founder on that account. Early in the Roosevelt administration, Miss Perkins precipitated Cabinet discussion on a public works bill being prepared in the Labor Department. She drew support for her measure from several members, but strong opposition from Budget Director Douglas. Rather than express his views, however, Douglas presented, according to Miss Perkins, "a mild and polite version in terms which he considered suitable for the Cabinet." He informed the group that he was working on a better plan, yet he would not tell them anything about it until "the time came." Even when Henry Wallace stumbled onto the plan and raised it in the Cabinet meeting, Douglas would not say anything specific about it. Yet, he was pressing his views with the President in private. In the same Cabinet, Harold Ickes once raised the subject of the post-war disposition of the Japanese-held islands, a subject which had been the source of an "old feud between Navy and Interior." From Secretary of the Navy Forrestal, Ickes received a facetious rebuke which terminated discussion: "the Navy's suggestion [is] that Mr. Ickes be made king of Polynesia, Micronesia and the Pacific Ocean Area." In private, Forrestal's comments were far more bitter. Under conditions like these the group could not come to grips with, or settle, policy.

When Secretary of State Hull brought up in Cabinet the impasse between State and Interior over the sale of helium to Germany, the shoe was on the other foot for Mr. Ickes. He only stiffened his attitude in the face of adverse comment from several of the members. Roosevelt himself inquired "Well, Harold, what do you say? The army assures me that the gas will not be used for military purposes. Can't you let them have the helium?" To which Ickes replied simply, "Mr. President, I can't surrender my conscience to the Army." Ickes' general contention that it was no one else's business received some confirmation by Roosevelt's refusal to overrule his Secretary of the Interior. A few experiences like this in any single Cabinet would soon convey the impression that it is not considered acceptable to criticize or interfere with one's fellow members. And more than this, they would cause the Cabinet member to turn away from the Cabinet as a coordinating body to dig other, more private channels. Some time later Ickes wrote to Roosevelt, "As a matter of fact, since the helium incident I have been reluctant to communicate in any way with the Department of State on account of the hostility that is all too apparent in that department toward me. . . . Frequently, I have sent to you communications that, in ordinary course, I would have sent directly to the Department of State."

Without doubt, departmentalism is aggravated by the traditional method of transacting the Cabinet's business. Without doubt, an agenda can encourage unity. But with respect to the Eisenhower reform, the roots of departmentalism are sunk too deep for technique to change. One reason why Eisenhower meetings at their best exhibit characteristics of Roosevelt meetings at their worst is the persistence of departmentalism. But in the Eisenhower system, where Cabinet business is screened through a planning process and where the President's presence is a strong influence for harmony, the most impressive manifestations of this force will not be found in the meeting itself. More important for our purposes here, they will be found in the natural reluctance of the department head to place controversial or sensitive items on the agenda in the first place. This problem manifests itself further in the nature of Cabinet discussions.

The Department of the Interior, whose power and water resources programs are among the most publicly and interdepartmentally debated ones of the Eisenhower period, places only four or five items a year on the Cabinet agenda, and these are virtually always informational items or policy presentations such as "Mission 66." Other members do not look upon the Cabinet as a forum for the discussion of knotty problems in their particular field—except to brief the group on some *fait accompli*. The Cabinet Secretary or the Assistant to the President has succeeded in persuading and cajoling some items out of the department head's grasp, but very few of the ten line departments have been reasonably good contributors to the agenda. Here, admittedly and predictably, is *the most vulnerable link* in the Eisenhower Cabinet reform. The problem of overcoming departmentalism constitutes the real nub of the Cabinet Secretary's work, and it is a deep-rooted political problem rather than a procedural one.

Beyond these considerations of willingness, and less purposeful than they, is one concerning the basic competence of the members to discuss matters outside of their own jurisdiction. Secretary of State Hughes delivered a scathing indictment of Secretary Albert Fall's inability to contribute in the field of foreign affairs: "He would discourse at length on foreign affairs, showing neither acumen, discretion, nor accurate knowledge. But he thought he was an authority. His flow of words without wisdom was very boring to me at least, and I think to others. I had little to do with him, but I did not suspect him of having anything worse than vanity and mental indigestion." Frequently time out must be taken in meetings to explain things to members that lie outside their jurisdiction. With his energies devoted to his own department, its problems and its sources of strength, a Secretary may not, with or without agenda, be equipped to participate in many general discussions. This is to some extent a dilemma of departmental management; it is also a psychological attitude which is firmly ingrained. It may also be simply a matter of personal ability, which can many times be traced back to the vagaries of the appointment process. The net result is that even if a member is interested in dealing with matters beyond his immediate baliwick, he may not be capable of adding anything to the group conference.

In addition, it is by no means certain that all members will be interested in their fellows' problems—or at least in the problems which are raised in Cabinet meeting. When each man keeps his own counsel and carefully guards departmental information and interdepartmental issues from the group, the cumulative result may be widespread boredom during routine Cabinet reports. Here, with Miss Perkins talking, one can catch the withering effect of departmentalism on a Cabinet "at work." Harold Ickes writes,

As usual, only the President listened to her. Harry Hopkins wrote me a note something to the effect: "Elementary course in government from four to five by Professor Frances Perkins." Later he passed this to Jesse Jones who was sitting next to Perkins. I looked at Jim Farley on one occasion and saw him with his eyes closed. Bob Jackson was nodding from time to time and at intervals he and Morgenthau were joking about something. Hull sat with the air of an early Christian martyr, with his hands folded, looking at the edge of the table without seeing it or anything else. I think that he was totally oblivious to what was going on. As usual, I studiously avoided being caught by Perkins' basilisk eye. Henry Wallace was contemplating the ceiling.

The logically complementary aspect to the uninformative Cabinet meeting is the business-like manner in which members line up to see the President privately as soon as the meeting is over. After Wilson's Cabinet meetings, individual members remained for "a series of engagements . . . in which (frequently) more important subjects were discussed than at the Cabinet meeting itself." In the Harding Cabinet, Hughes would say, "I have nothing to say now but I should like to see you after the meeting." Jesse Jones, sphinx-like during the Roosevelt Cabinet conference, used to stay behind after every session for what was called "prayer meeting" at "Amen corner." For Henry Stimson, the chief value of the Cabinet council was its usefulness "as a way in which to get into the White House to have a word with the President in private after the meetings were over." President Truman's Cabinet members could accomplish the same end at the regular Cabinet luncheons which preceded meetings. The reluctance to raise issues in Cabinet meetings, to expose programs, difficulties, or plans to a fellow member, leads inevitably to the post-Cabinet (or pre-Cabinet) traffic jam. This phenomenon is, in turn, one hallmark of the Cabinet's own shortcomings.

Perhaps the capstone of mutual irresponsibility is the Cabinet "leak." Members do not acquire a sense of unity sufficient to deter them from revealing to outsiders the contents of the meeting. If the Cabinet were more of a corporate entity, in spirit at least, all members would feel (as many do) a compulsion to keep the proceedings to themselves. The results of the leak are clear. Both the President and the individual officials refrain from bringing important matters before the group. This pulling-in of horns adds cumulatively to the other centrifugal influences and fosters a further retreat from the Cabinet meeting. The Wilson, Harding, and Roosevelt Cabinets (at least) were all beset by this difficulty, and it helped none of them. (The unprecedented publication of Eisenhower Cabinet discussions in Robert Donovan's book may have a similarly harmful effect on the future deliberations of that group.) With the threat of public embarrassment suspended over their heads, the participants will view their conference all the more as a safe forum only for banalities and straightforward reports, instead of a forum for a controversial exchange of ideas, opinions, and projected plans. The Cabinet leak, like departmentalism itself, is both cause and effect. It discourages Cabinet unity and activity, but it flows, too, from the lack of both.

The effects of departmentalism are, of course, subject to modification. Through conscious presidential effort and preliminary staff work, they can be minimized in the Cabinet meeting and in the public press, as has been the case under Eisenhower. Cabinet Secretary Rabb has said that in the Eisenhower Cabinet "The question is not 'What will be best for my department' or 'for me' but now always 'What will be best for the whole Executive Branch—for the President—for the nation?'" This must be taken as an exercise in political hyperbole and not as a statement of fact. Departmentalism cannot be put to death by executive fiat nor can the frequent professions of allegiance to "the team" be taken as its death certificate. Cabinet members may be more privy to the President's views and more conscious of the virtues of harmony, but they are still department-oriented individuals, subject to the same centrifugal pulls as their predecessors. Secretary of the Treasury Humphrey's damaging public criticism of the President's 1958 budget is proof enough. After the Secretary at his budget press conference had stated, "I think that there are a lot of places in this budget that can be cut," the following exchange took place:

QUESTION: Could you tell us a little something about why this strong call for economy comes from you rather than from the President himself and the budget? Has this been a result of consultation? Is this your view or are you speaking for the administration or the President? Just what is the background of that?

SECRETARY HUMPHREY: *I am speaking for the Treasury Department largely.* We are responsible for the federal finances. . . .

If the more obvious symptoms of departmentalism are absent from the meeting, and if observers of the meeting can say that "the Cabinet isn't a clashing Cabinet and has an amazing lack of differences," it does not follow that there are none. Intra-Cabinet controversies involving Messrs. Weeks and Durkin, Mitchell and Weeks, Stassen and Humphrey, and Dulles and Stassen have reached the public press. Others may have been driven underground. Or they may have been transferred to an interdepartmental committee, like those on Water Resources or Transportation Policy. Though its effects may be modified and its surface manifestations altered, departmentalism cannot be eliminated. It will always constitute a serious limitation on the effectiveness of the Cabinet meeting.

In the light of departmentalism, one can understand more fully why the Cabinet exhibits such a low degree of institutionality. Cabinet members, like the President, and for similar reasons of self-interest, may find a flexible system more congenial. The very life of the Eisenhower system as far as the Cabinet members are concerned depends on the retention of its flexibility. Let one department head be *told* that a particular item under his jurisdiction *had* to go on the agenda against his will, and the whole framework would collapse like a house of cards. Given departmentalism, it is not difficult to see why Presidents may be anxious to cancel meetings, or why a basically neutral procedure may fall subject to crippling influences, or why the Cabinet meeting tends to become a series of banal reports. One can also find here forces that may erode the President's power over his Cabinet, forces against which his countervailing power is limited because their origins are non-presidential. The President cannot shape the Cabinet completely in his own image in spite of the basic power-responsibility relationship. And this is one reason why he will seek help elsewhere, from an inner cabinet or a kitchen cabinet, or from some other agency. Considering the impact of departmentalism, it may be as great a cause for wonderment that Presidents use the Cabinet as much as they do, as it is that they use it so seldom.

THE NATIONAL SECURITY COUNCIL:
AN INTERPRETATION AND APPRAISAL *
Paul Y. Hammond

THE National Security Council constitutes the most ambitious effort yet made to coordinate policy on the cabinet level in the American federal government. An examination of the experience of the NSC, together with the assumptions and expectations that went into proposing, establishing, and developing it, should help to clarify the problem of policy coordination under the President.

I. ORIGINS IN AMERICAN NAVAL AND BRITISH CABINET TRADITIONS

Various proposals for a special war cabinet in the United States, usually called a Council of National Defense, date back as far as 1911. The National Defense Act of 1916 established a body by such a name, headed by the Secretary of War. The statute was so watered down from the original proposals, however, that its uses were negligible, except later as a convenient peg for the National Defense Advisory Council (NDAC) and its subsidiaries that Roosevelt called into being in 1940. After World War I, both armed services revived the idea of a more powerful Council in an effort to find some base of support for their military policies, and as a counter to proposals for unification, proposals which they both opposed because these were founded on unrealistic expectations about the sums of money that could be saved through reorganization of the service departments.

When at the close of World War II unification threatened again, the Navy Department turned back to that earlier defense against it, proposing, instead of a single department, secretary, and military chief, several interdepartmental

* From *American Political Science Review*, Vol. 54 (December 1960), pp. 899–910. Reprinted by permission of the author and publisher.

committees capped by a National Security Council which would coordinate the services with each other and with the civil departments and agencies which played important roles in our external relations. The basis of the Navy proposals for postwar reorganization was the Eberstadt Report, a series of studies and a set of proposals commissioned in the summer of 1945 by the Secretary of the Navy, James Forrestal, and prepared under the direction of Ferdinand Eberstadt. The Eberstadt Report assumed that the proposed National Security Council could be a kind of war cabinet in which the responsibilities of the President could be vested. This assumption was not immediately apparent from a reading of the record, for the premise arose not out of any lack of awareness of the Constitutional power of the President, but out of an inclination to modify the Presidency as an institution. The National Security Council (NSC), the report noted, would be only advisory to the President, for it was also an accepted premise of the Eberstadt group, as well as of Forrestal and the Navy protagonists in the unification controversy, that the President could not be forced to share the Constitutional responsibilities of his office. Their failure to understand the Presidency lay in assuming that the President could choose to share those responsibilities without incurring substantial losses to his status as President.

Eberstadt's proposals actually included both a National Security Council for national strategic planning and a National Security Resources Board for national mobilization planning, and both are involved in this misconception of the Presidency. The misconception began with its British origins. "In the opinion of the many qualified British authorities," Myron P. Gilmore concluded in his study of foreign and military policies for the Eberstadt Report, "it has been proven once more that the peace-time machinery of the Committee of Imperial Defense," which had been transformed in both World Wars into a War Cabinet, "could be well adapted to the conduct of a major war." Ignoring the difference between cabinet and presidential government, Gilmore went on to recommend a national security council, the duties of which "would be formally described as advisory." He made clear that only in a formal sense would it be advisory: "The fact that the President himself heads the Council would for all practical purposes insure that the advice it offered would be accepted." The Council would, moreover, supersede the Bureau of the Budget, for it would be the final reviewer of the State Department and military budgets prior to their submittal to Congress, and would advise the President "in writing" regarding them—"in writing" being specified presumably in order to make formal and final the NSC decision, and also make it available to Congress.

In his own report, Eberstadt followed the same lines laid out by Gilmore. The NSC should make annual reports to the President, which should be published when secrecy considerations permitted, as would undoubtedly be the case with most budget matters. Someone more concerned with Presidential prerogatives, or willing to recognize that an NSC decision was in fact confidential executive branch advice to the President, would never have suggested publication as a general rule on any grounds. If, as Eberstadt asserted, the

NSC was to be advisory to the President, then he was in effect proposing to waive the Constitutional tenet that advice to the President is privileged, and to confine the claim for executive secrecy to matters classified in the interest of national security. Such a change was not the intention: Eberstadt evidently did not think of NSC decisions as advice, or of the NSC as advisory, but as a war cabinet which carried a kind of collective responsibility. . . .

Furthermore, within an essentially British conception of cabinet government other persistent problems of Executive Branch relationships were apparently expected to dissolve. The confusion of the President's relationship to the NSC was never clarified. Similarly, although Eberstadt argued for "an intimate, active, and continuous relationship between those responsible for our foreign and our military policies" through the NSC, he did not examine whether such a relationship was possible with the closed staff system of the Joint Chiefs of Staff (JCS). Indeed, even the Chief Executive's relations with Congress were to be dealt with by diffusion rather than definition: following an approach to Congressional relations stylish in the early post-World War II period—not to speak of other times—Congress was to be kept in line by the participation of key Congressmen in the handling of national security matters in the Executive Branch rather than by the more formal relations with Congressional committees (although he did not specify that they would participate in the deliberations of the NSC). This short-circuit approach to Congressional relations, along with the council idea, was strikingly parallel to the early Council of National Defense proposals—which, in fact, Gilmore described in his study.[1]

In both Eberstadt's and the Navy proposals, the image of the President as Chief Executive was blurred. Irrespective of any connections with British or Navy Department traditions, an imperfect vision of the Presidency was a necessary outcome of attempting to cope with the dilemma in which Eberstadt and Forrestal were caught of their own choice. At once they wished to assert that the problem of coordinating national security policy was very broad, and to deny the necessity for the executive power to coordinate. So long as they were concerned with the government as a whole, their dilemma was not too uncomfortable; but when it came to dealing with the military establishment, the discomfort grew. It is easy to state their problem in retrospect, or in contrast with the Army proposals: they accepted as necessary a single military establishment, but denied that there had to be a Secretary of Defense. The duties which would normally be performed by the head of a major executive department they expected to be discharged collectively by the National Security Council.

1. *Eberstadt Report,* pp. 51–52. Eberstadt recommended that the participation of key Congressmen was preferable to formal committee reorganization. This would have left a Military Affairs and a Naval Affairs Committee in each house of Congress to consider the substantive legislation concerned with national security. Beyond the advantages to the Navy in this approach (particularly since the Eberstadt Report recommended the establishment of a separate Air Force Department), the weak position in which each of these committees would be placed when attempting to deal with "coordinated" military policies should be obvious. For comparison, see D. S. Cheever and H. F. Haviland, *American Foreign Policy and the Separation of Powers* (Cambridge: Harvard University Press, 1952).

The NSC, the most remarkable and enduring element in the Eberstadt Report, was to become the king-pin of Forrestal's hopes, and only a little less important in the reorganization legislation of 1947. Yet it was thus based on a misconception about the Executive Branch in the American government. Whether the NSC "germinated" out of the British Committee of Imperial Defense, as Forrestal told Churchill, and as the Eberstadt Report indicates, or was derived from long-standing Navy views about a Council of National Defense, makes little difference because both were inappropriate. Cabinet solidarity may be the cement of the British government, and interdepartmental committees may have certain uses, but the American Executive Branch is held together, if at all, by the authority of the President. The Eberstadt Report treated the powers of the President as something which could be embodied in a committee.

Viewed in terms of Navy traditions, the NSC represented two important characteristics, the Navy perception of its role in national policy-making, as expressed in its Council of National Defense proposals in the Wilson era, and the reliance on horizontal organizational structure—on voluntary coordination, so to speak. The latter was the major characteristic of the old Navy Department organization that had miraculously worked in World War I, but required substantial reconstruction in World War II; it was the assumption that people responsible only for segments could nevertheless produce a whole—a whole military policy in this case, a coordinated naval policy in the earlier one. In contradiction to the traditions of War Department administration, it asserted that a policy program could be achieved by an organization without a unified command structure at the center.

II. EARLY PRACTICE AND APPRAISAL

Once the NSC was established, the divergent purposes which had brought it into being all yielded, of necessity, to one: the Presidential purpose. For while the NSC could be less, it could be no more than what the President wanted it to be, if he knew his mind. No doubt some of its supporters had wanted to devise an arrangement which would prevent a President from running things in the disorderly fashion that seemed to characterize Franklin D. Roosevelt's performance in the White House as an administrator. In this sense, it was supposed to mold Presidential behavior. President Truman answered a fundamental question of defense policy-making concerning the NSC by making it a practice not to sit with the NSC during its first three years, until the Korean War began. Forrestal had anticipated that he would not attend simply because the burdens of the Presidency made the delegation of his responsibilities necessary. Yet, that was not the reason. Rather, it was because Truman felt his presence on the NSC might imply a delegation of authority which he did not intend.[2]

2. The reason has been explained variously: He did not want to stifle free discussion in the NSC; he wanted to be free to accept or reject the outcome of its deliberations; or more generally, he was concerned that the NSC might encroach upon Presidential powers, and this was

The first appraisal of the newly instituted NSC was conducted a year after its establishment. The Hoover Commission Task Force on National Security Organization, chaired by Ferdinand Eberstadt, reported in November, 1948. Its . proposals promised considerable invigoration of the Secretary of Defense and the JCS as centers of initiative in the military establishment, not so much because of proposed changes in formal powers as by virtue of the fact—or was it only a dubious premise?—that more adequate staff arrangements would allow them both to get away from the excessive details with which they were overburdened.

These recommendations, however, or even those of Forrestal himself, could not surmount the difficulties the committee revealed by its own exposition. The National Security Act of 1947 had arranged the military establishment to work properly only if it had adequate policy guidance flowing from the NSC, which was to be, to modify Elihu Root's phrase, the "source of politico-military energy." However, the NSC did not prove to be such a source before the Korean War (or, indeed, after it). As will be explained later, there were fundamental reasons why it was not likely to be.

The committee acknowledged the fact that the flow had not occurred, and that it was needed. It called for a fuller utilization of the NSC to provide the necessary guide-lines for defense policies. Yet it tended to overlook both the need for these guide-lines for a proper functioning of the organization and the difficulties involved in obtaining them. In effect, therefore, it went on to hedge against the possibility that the NSC would continue to prove disappointing. In two major areas, budget integration and economizing, and strategic planning by the JCS, what the committee recommended amounted to going on without NSC guidance. In both cases the implications of such a course of action, as well as the way the role of NSC guide-lines was minimized, are worth noting.

The Task Force had reported that

The President's directive of July 26, 1948, placing a ceiling of $15 billion on the National Military Establishment budget for fiscal year 1950 was apparently issued without the formal advice either of the Joint Chiefs of Staff (his "principal military advisers") or of the National Security Council, whose statutory function it is "to advise the President" in regard to foreign and military policies.

This account misses the point concerning the Joint Chiefs. The ceiling had been set at least a month before the President's directive was issued, which in turn was only a matter of weeks after the JCS had asked for $9 billion as a supplement to an $11 billion fiscal 1949 budget. They had accepted Forrestal's cut on economic grounds. Later, in their fiscal 1950 estimates, they could not

a device to keep it from doing so. Truman mentions in his *Memoirs*, Vol. 2, *Years of Trial and Hope 1946–1952* (Garden City, 1956), p. 60, with disapproval that "there were times during the early days of the National Security Council when one or two of its members tried to change it into an operating super-cabinet on the British model . . . [by assuming] the authority of supervising other agencies of the government and seeing that the approved decisions of the Council were carried out."

bring themselves under $30 billions, or at least $23.5 billions if the McNarney Committee's figures are taken into account. Under these circumstances, which the Task Force committee acknowledged, the fact that the President had not obtained their "formal advice" on a defense budget ceiling is meaningless. In the first place, he knew quite well how much they wanted; and in the second, their figures were so far from what was possible (as the Truman Administration then saw it) that they were practically irrelevant. That the Task Force committee ignored these difficulties was an indication of its tendency to overlook the problems and limitations of political leadership in defense policy-making.

Furthermore, because it overlooked them, it went on to compound those difficulties. Since the agencies concerned with national security "are not performing their respective functions adequately, either individually or in sound relation to each other," the committee observed,

. . . national policy is not emanating, clearly and firmly, from above and descending effectively through the chain of agencies for translation into an efficient and economical military establishment measured against our national needs. As a result, the military have picked up the ball of national policy and are starting down the field with it. Justly concerned about our national security—but at the same time with an eye to individual service ambitions—they have sometimes made their own assessments and appraisals of our "objectives, commitments, and risks" and have translated them into their own ideas of our proper military strength.

The Task Force Committee's solution, however, encouraged the procedures it condemned by making the operation of the military establishment easier in the absence of NSC guidance. Undoubtedly the solution was a responsible one. Making defense policy *more* dependent on a source of guidance which had thus far proven disappointing, in the hope that greater dependence would force improvements, could hardly have been considered seriously. Nevertheless, accommodating the military establishment to the absence of policy guidance was bound to encourage the dominance of military operational—or business management—imperatives over strategy and, ultimately, over policy.

III. NSC STRUCTURE AND OPERATIONS: A RECENT VIEW

Organization. Because of the limited amount of information available about the National Security Council, it is all the more important to keep the objectives of our inquiry in mind. Our concern is with the NSC as a source of coordinated policy guidance. It should be apparent, however, that this is a particular case of a more general problem, the relationship of policy planning to executive leadership—for evidence on which we need not be restricted entirely to the sparse data on the record about the operations of the NSC itself. Since the evidence suggests that Truman was sensitive to the possible effects which this legislation might have on the powers of his office, and would certainly not have convened and used the NSC simply because Congress had told him to, one might well wonder whether the statutory basis for the NSC had any significance whatsoever. While it would be easy to exaggerate that significance,

the long-run value of the statute is quite clear. As Ernest R. May has suggested, it stood as evidence of Congressional approval for the idea that the
President should obtain guidance from a secret council regarding national security matters.

The statutory membership of the National Security Council consists of the
President and Vice President, the Secretaries of State and Defense, and the
Director of the Office of Civil and Defense Mobilization. The Chairman of
the Joint Chiefs of Staff and the Director of Central Intelligence are statutory
advisors to the Council. Since the President may choose his own counsellors,
however, this number has normally been augmented during the Eisenhower
Administration by three principal officials and several lesser ones. The principal ones are the Secretary of the Treasury, the Director of the Bureau of the
Budget, and the Chairman of the Atomic Energy Commission. The others include four special assistants to the President—for National Security Affairs,
Security Operations Coordination, Foreign Economic Policy, and Science and
Technology; the Assistant to the President—the "chief" of his White House
staff—and the White House staff secretary; the Under Secretary of State and
the Director of the United States Information Agency; and the two ranking
officials of the NSC Staff, the Executive Secretary and the Deputy Secretary.
In addition, the President from time to time invites other officials to participate on an *ad hoc* basis.

The principal subsidiary organs of the Council are the Planning Board, the
NSC Staff, and the Operations Coordination Board (OCB). The NSC Staff
remains essentially a secretariat. The OCB is a follow-up mechanism to see
that NSC decisions are executed. Since it is an interdepartmental committee, it
is largely a reporting and monitoring device. (Technically, it is not a part of the
NSC structure.) The Planning Board consists of representatives of assistant
secretary rank for the statutory members of the NSC, plus the Bureau of the
Budget. "Observers" from other agencies may attend as their interests require.
The Central Intelligence Agency and the Joint Chiefs of Staff regularly provide advisors. The President's Special Assistant for National Security Affairs
chairs the Board. Its function is to conduct a thorough preliminary examination of all subjects before they are considered by the Council. Sometimes
knowledgeable private citizens are appointed as informal advisors, called Consultants, who may, individually, work with the Planning Board, or, as a committee, present their views directly to the Council.

The most crucial question about the National Security Council is bound to
be what kinds of decisions it is capable of making—not in the sense of what
subjects it deals with, but as an appraisal of what it accomplishes. At the outset we should distinguish between two elements here: the quality of the decision as a rational process and its practical effects. One could conceive, for instance, of a brilliant exposition of the preventive war thesis, based on a devastating logic, which is never refuted, yet which has negligible effect because it
cannot be the policy of the American government. Of course, rationality and
practicality are really related to each other. The hypothetical preventive war

plan could probably be shown to be either rationally unsound because it ran counter to the values of the state and society which was supposed to support it, or impractical because it could never command the necessary support to make it effective. But the distinction between rationality and practicality will be useful for analytical purposes, providing its limitations are kept in mind.

Two sides have become distinguishable in appraising the practicality and rationality of NSC decisions. The supporters of NSC are best represented by two of the men who have served as President Eisenhower's Special Assistant for National Security Affairs, Robert Cutler and Dillon Anderson, both of whom have published accounts of NSC operations.

Between them, Cutler and Anderson have indicated that the sources for subjects and proposals in the NSC are many and varied enough so that we might be assured that important matters are not overlooked. The working committee for the NSC is the Planning Board. It is the function of the Planning Board, we are told, to reconcile differences when possible, to find the common ground of agreement, and to put its finger on illusory disagreements. Then, "when an irreconcilable disagreement arises between the departments represented, the Planning Board must identify clearly the elements of the disagreement and spell out the alternative policy courses and reasons therefor so that they may be presented fully to the National Security Council." "In the acid bath of the Planning Board," Cutler has written, "all points of view are represented, heard, explored and contested. There is in this process a guarantee against *ex parte* judgments, against imprecise guidance to the Chief Executive and against suppression of conflicting views."

The picture we are given of NSC deliberations themselves is also of a searching examination of issues:

When he became President, General Eisenhower transformed the Council into a forum for vigorous discussion against a background of painstakingly prepared and carefully studied papers. He likes nothing better than the flashing interchange of views among his principal advisers. Out of the grinding of these minds comes a refinement of the raw material into valuable metal; out of the frank assertion of differing views, backed up by preparation that searches every nook and cranny, emerges a resolution that reasonable men can support. Differences of views which have developed at lower levels are not swept under the rug, but exposed.

The Cabinet Status Problem. What Anderson and Cutler have said about the NSC is reassuring. The other side in the appraisal, however, is not. From a variety of sources, some of which obviously have access to members of the Planning Board and the NSC itself, have come the same criticisms: that the Planning Board, in its pursuit of "common grounds," is inclined to "plaster over" significant issues and differences with carefully chosen ambiguities, or language plagued with equivocations expressive of the lowest common denominator of agreement. In the NSC itself as well, it is claimed, there is a reluctance to exacerbate differences of view and opinion, with the result that discussion is inclined to be more courteous than probing. Finally, it is sometimes claimed that agencies are reluctant to bring issues before the NSC, that they even try to keep some important matters out of it. Franklin Lindsay of the Hoover Commission's Procurement Task Force staff observed in June, 1955, that "in recent months there have been situations reported in which policy formulation in vital and urgent issues has been seriously hampered by a lack of free exchange among the Departments represented on the Council."

Undoubtedly there is some substance to these complaints. Among other things, they fit the larger pattern of behavior of the President's cabinet over the years. It is a well documented fact that cabinet meetings have seldom amounted to much because cabinet officers prefer to transact their business with the President without the interference of other executive department heads. The more a President actually refuses to discuss and decide anything that does not go through his cabinet system, the more likely it is that the real issues will come up there. No doubt the determination and professional inclinations of President Eisenhower have stood him well in his resolve to strengthen the performance of his cabinet and of the NSC.[3] Yet it seems unlikely that he has stopped off all channels for maneuver. To begin with, the existence of two different "cabinets," the traditional one which is intended to deal primarily with domestic affairs and the NSC, which is supposed to specialize in national security, or foreign, affairs, with dual membership for some, has left an obvious means of maneuver—the choice of the most favorable forum—with results about which we can at least speculate. Furthermore, there are disadvantages as well as advantages to choking off the individual contacts which weaken the cabinet system: independent and timely information, and informal and candid advice, to name only some. No Presidential prerogative is defended with greater consistency by *all* Presidents than the right to secret counsel. If the right has any validity *vis-à-vis* Congress, the press, or the public in general, it must also be valid within the executive branch. Yet any exercise of it there undermines the cabinet system by allowing individual officials the alternative of bypassing the Cabinet or the NSC and transacting business directly with the President.

While it is clear that President Eisenhower has taken seriously the implications of his staff procedures, it is equally clear that he has continued to allow a number of administration officials direct access to him. Indeed, it may be that the preeminent influence in their time of the former Secretary of the Treasury, George F. Humphrey, and the late Secretary of State, John Foster Dulles, within the Eisenhower Administration, was due in part to their special privilege of access to President Eisenhower; as the converse was certainly the case. Even if that is true, however—if the President has been willing to talk busi-

3. So, "The President has determined that he will not assign an area of national security policy formulation permanently as the responsibility of a department, agency, or individual outside the NSC mechanism or make decisions on national security policy—except in special cases or urgency—outside the framework of the Council." Gordon Gray, "Role of the National Security Council in the Formulation of National Policy," in Senate Government Operations Committee, *Organizing for National Security: Selected Materials*, 86th Congress, 2d sess., p. 64.

ness with a certain few of his cabinet members, but, quite consistently, not with the rest—that situation would not assure that those who were not intimates of the President would be forced to submit their problems to the cabinet process; for, as an alternative, they could make their arrangement with those who were.

Furthermore, the required access need not be given a literal interpretation. President Eisenhower may have been remarkably effective in avoiding *ex parte* presentations and decisions outside of his established staff procedures, yet have allowed that same thing to have resulted from his following those procedures. If Humphrey and Dulles, or anyone else, were the dominant forces in the NSC meetings, it could not matter whether they in fact saw the President privately very much or not. Their special "access" to the President in those meetings would provide, as an alternative to drag-out debates in the NSC, another way for agency heads to advance their interests with the President. The crucial act for them would then be the persuasion of Humphrey or Dulles, rather than an effective presentation in the Planning Board or the Thursday morning White House meetings of the NSC.

This analysis is not intended as a harsh judgment of public officials. We are not entitled to treat lightly the particular perspectives of public officials which derive from the responsibilities of their positions. President Eisenhower has directed that the members of the NSC and the Planning Board should forsake their agency perspectives and advise him from a government-wide viewpoint. It is doubtful, however, that he has been successful in wiping out by directive the agency perspectives of his cabinet or council members. If the NSC operates as has been described, it does so not because of the bad faith or scheming nature of its members, but despite their best efforts, and because of the very forces which have made the NSC seem necessary. The heavy responsibilities and work loads of conscientious men determine in some degree what they will know and think about issues and proposals related to their duties. Moreover, whatever the value of NSC work, the statutory responsibility of each member of it is for the proper operation of his department. His first loyalty may be to the President, but he is responsible to the President for administering an agency in a way that he is never responsible for NSC actions.

Concern with the protection of the agency program or viewpoint does not end with the success or failure of the effort to gain access to the forum most favorable to the agency. Once the forum is chosen, the agency will wish to maximize the achievement of its interests there, an objective which may not be identical with the systematic exposure and preliminary exploration of all issues and problems on their merits in the Planning Board, or the free and frank discussion before the President in the NSC of issues and problems not resolvable on their merits in the Planning Board. Indeed, expediency could dictate the withholding of pertinent information which might weigh against the agency's interest or established position, the avoidance of some issues and the suppression of others in the Planning Board, and finally, the settlement for some kind of half-of-a-loaf in the Planning Board because of an estimation that a better bargain can be struck there than in the Council. And the same kinds of considerations could inhibit debate in the Council itself. Always the alternative may be available of assuring that in fact no decision is really made in either the Planning Board or the NSC by settling for language in the staff paper which is sufficiently ambiguous so that in effect it preserves the latitude of choice desired by one's agency.

The President's Special Assistant has attempted to enforce standards of precision in the drafting of NSC papers, which seems to suggest that he would oppose any such efforts to "plaster over" issues with the language of the draft. But an ambiguous draft agreement is only one of several tactics available for avoiding decisions by committee. Representative councils must depend to a large degree upon their members for access to, and even the interpretation of, the relevant facts, while the ability to eliminate ambiguity will depend upon a mastery of the facts. Those upon whom the Planning Board and the NSC depend for information are therefore in a position to influence, and in some cases to control, the degree of precision with which a problem is presented, discussed, and settled, despite the best efforts of the President's Special Assistant, or of anyone else, to achieve precision in the settlement.

Moreover, the Special Assistant is himself likely to contribute unintentionally to the ambiguity which he seeks to avoid. He is responsible for expediting the work of the Planning Board and the NSC. In carrying out the two functions of the Planning Board, to identify the area of agreement, and to explore the area of disagreement on any matter to be considered by the NSC, his objectives of precision and expeditiousness may conflict. We are assured that the Special Assistant does not desire to suppress disagreements, and we may take that assurance on its face. Yet, unavoidably, he must expedite the processes which distinguish between real and superficial disagreement and between ambiguous and clear language. In deciding when a draft is sufficiently precise, and when the differences it covers are "illusory" or non-existent, he cannot resolve all doubts against precision and illusion. And when he does not, like the department which seeks to avoid an NSC decision, he may be condoning ambiguity and the suppression of important issues.

There can be, finally, the problem of third parties. The subjects of NSC deliberations involve some departments more than others, and sometimes one of them most of all. At any rate, the questions of jurisdiction, expertise, and authority are not likely to be absent from the deliberations of the Council. The President's directive referred to above was probably intended to encourage "third-parties"—that is, departmental representatives in the Planning Board or the Council—to voice their opinions on questions before them even when their particular agency provides them with no special knowledge or expert judgment, and has no special concern about the question at hand. Surely the implications of the staff work done in connection with NSC operations suggest this interpretation of the President's directive if there is any room for doubt as to its meaning. It appears, however, that under the pressure to accomplish its work, the Planning Board has been quite resentful of "third party" contributions, and that in fact it has operated with unwritten rules of jurisdiction on this score which, when violated, have caused considerable friction.

There is no reason to doubt that the same pressures have operated to some degree in the Council. One reason for the effectiveness of this kind of inhibition upon frank discussion, it should be noted, is that it may appear as only the desire of modest men not to sound foolish, or to interfere with matters which would suggest a lack of confidence in their colleagues. Once the third party is eliminated from the discussion in this manner, however, and the field is left to the agencies most directly involved, they will be the ones which are, by definition, working most closely together anyway on the matter, and will have every advantage in cooperating to bring the problems to the NSC when and how they, by agreement, want to.[4]

While some of the foregoing analysis has been speculative in the sense that it has not been based upon knowledge of specific events, it is nevertheless based upon assumptions about loyalty and perspectives which are well established, and which have, for instance, long been evident in the operation, or lack of operation, of the President's cabinet and in the JCS. They are intended to suggest that there are some inherent difficulties in the operation of the NSC—particularly in the making of clear-cut decisions, which lend credence to the continuing criticisms of the NSC on that score.

The Democratic Policy-Making Problem: The Required Range of Consensus. The dimensions of consensus and commitment necessary for policy-making in a democracy constitute a further limitation on the value of NSC "decisions" for the administration of the military establishment. The neo-realism in American foreign relations of the post-World War II period showed how artificial was the American propensity to consider official pronouncements to be foreign policy. Policy, it was asserted, is more than words: it is also the power and determination to achieve one's objectives. The extraordinary faith in secret plans involved in the higher evaluations of the NSC may be another version of that "legalistic" or "moralistic" fallacy in American foreign relations which the neo-realists seemed to have destroyed so effectively.

The President's setting his signature to an NSC document does not make it policy. What does is his will and capability to get it executed, coupled with effective support from Congress. How much of the last is necessary, of course, may vary, and in any case is not precise. Yet the requisite support is not likely

---

4. With this in mind it may be worth speculating about the way the NSC deals with foreign aid matters. The State Department's dominance in the making of policy has statutory origins. Its relations with its major potential rival in policy-making are of a particular character. The office of the Assistant Secretary of Defense for International Security Affairs (ISA) is in this area something of a State Department outpost in the Defense Department. ISA also happens to represent the Defense Department on the Planning Board. It is doubtful that in the Planning Board either the State or the Defense Department is much interested in exploring in front of other officials, in particular normally hostile ones like the Bureau of the Budget or the Treasury Department, the merits of the foreign aid programs in anything like a candid or searching way. If this is true, then consideration of foreign aid matters in the Council itself would be severely limited in its value by the inadequacy of the staff work upon which the Council undoubtedly relies so heavily.

to be obtained for any but the most exceptional cases through, for instance, the secret briefing of a handful of Congressmen. The members of the two houses are inclined to be suspicious of the judgment of their own kind when the latter appear to have been "captured" by the executive branch. Even if that were not so, the necessity for Congressmen to come to terms with their constituencies would still limit strictly the usefulness of such devices as secret briefings and special liaison arrangements. Unless an NSC "policy" happens to coincide with a general public viewpoint, sooner or later it must run the gamut of public discussion. In this respect, the NSC got off to a bad start. The first general policy statement attributed (somewhat inaccurately) to it, NSC-68, which was completed in April, 1950, advocated substantial increases in expenditures in a variety of programs connected with national security, a policy which was clearly at variance with prevailing conceptions of public opinion held contemporaneously in Congress and in the Administration. As to what the Administration might have done to bring the secret policy paper and the public consensus closer together had the Korean War not occurred, we can only speculate. As it was, the war made them converge. Once the war started it was necessary only to make general references to the larger picture of the Soviet threat and to a consequent need for a build-up of a far more general character than the Korean War required, and, privately, to read the document in the light of the entirely new situation, in order to close the gap completely. Even if it were a reasonable expectation, one should not hope that history would again solve in this manner the problem of translating a secret "policy" into a national commitment.

The problem, it should be emphasized, is not properly seen in the terms by which early advocates of a Council of National Defense, and, later, the NSC visualized it: how to gain wide support, through the "non-rational" channels of politics, for "rational" defense policies constructed by a few men privately where they are free from political pressures. If it were indeed possible to construct a security council for the nation which was free from political pressures yet powerful enough to be useful, the NSC is not it. Nor have we evidence that it has always had the edge in rationality. The political vacuum in which the NSC operates is not caused by a total lack of politics in its atmosphere, but only by barriers which prevent the continuing readjustment of atmospheric pressures within the NSC to those outside it. The Eisenhower Administration's commitment through NSC procedures to the massive retaliation doctrine announced by Secretary of State Dulles on January 12, 1954, in a widely publicized (and criticized) speech was evidently the acceptance of a favorite and long-held notion of Mr. Dulles (which he had shared with other Administration officials). Its acceptance was a device for reconciling both the somber security perspectives of NSC-162, the annual survey of American strategy which had been approved the previous October, and the disappointing failure of the new JCS team to cut the defense budget, with demands to cut the federal budget substantially, pressed by Budget Director Joseph Dodge, and the Secretary of the Treasury, George Humphrey.

In the face of powerful and numerous criticisms of the massive retaliation doctrine, including, we may presume, the private counsel received at a foreign ministers' conference in Berlin that winter, Dulles' further "clarifications" of the meaning of his original speech in fact substantially modified it. One of the most important "clarifications" of it was published in *Foreign Affairs* in April, 1954, just as the Administration was learning the inadequacy of the massive retaliation doctrine in the hard test posed by Dienbienphu. On the one hand, the publication of the doctrine by Dulles had exposed it to critical comment sufficiently persuasive so that Dulles chose to modify his public statements rather than defend it publicly, although the military posture the Administration continued to maintain was substantially that of reliance upon a massive retaliation capability. On the other hand, in the clutch of the crisis in Indo-China, the Administration had shown itself not strongly enough committed to its newly adopted strategic concept to attempt the rescue of Dienbienphu. It had flinched in two most significant respects. First, apparently the President in the NSC rejected Admiral Radford's proposal to break the siege of the doomed fortress with massive air strikes, being persuaded by General Ridgway that American military commitments could not stop there. Eisenhower was evidently convinced that ground forces would be needed, and that supplying them would be extremely difficult. At least, it appears, he was so far convinced as to insist on encumbering his commitment to Radford's proposal with heavy qualifications: the United States would assist the French in Indo-China provided we could gain the support of allies in this undertaking.

At the same time, the Administration was evidently willing to carry out its NSC "policy" towards Indo-China if it could gain privately the support of powerful members of Congress, but it was unwilling to do so if it had to make the strong public commitments which would be required to obtain formal Congressional support,[5] a condition the subtleties of which undoubtedly were missed in the phraseology of the NSC paper. Thus what was perhaps the most important decision made through the NSC machinery during the first term of the Eisenhower Administration did not stand the test of either its first public exposition or its first application. Each test, it should be noted, assayed some aspect of its rationality as well as probed the depths of the Administration's commitment. The least we can conclude from what is known about the NSC's role in the Indo-China crisis and the formulation of the massive retaliation doctrine of the Eisenhower Administration is that in this case its freedom from partisan political considerations did not assure it a greater rationality than the more public channels of government decision-making would permit it.

Furthermore, this account is illustrative of the fact that there can be no entirely workable separation between the planning and the operational stages of national security policy, for in politics ends and means must be tested against

5. Chalmers M. Roberts, "The Day We Didn't Go To War," *The Reporter*, XI (September 14, 1954), 31–35. The NSC deliberations are described in Marquis Childs, *The Ragged Edge: The Diary of a Crisis* (Garden City, 1955), pp. 153–58.

each other: it is in the interaction of that testing that consensus becomes wide enough and commitments strong enough for policy to become a reality. Put more prosaically, defenders of the NSC are on sound enough ground when asserting the President's right to confidential counsel from his appointees, for it is the only way he can be sure of getting frank advice. They are also reasonable in insisting that the NSC, as they conceive it, must operate in secret for security reasons as well. But they are misled if they believe that the result is the government's policy. It may be the President's policy, although that is doubtful: What President is so infallible that he can predict in the political isolation of the NSC what will be politically possible in the future, or so rigid that he will never change when he is wrong? The give and take of the NSC chamber, in which, so we are told, all the issues are brought out and tested, the advantages and disadvantages weighed—including the fiscal and the program viewpoints—must be repeated for the interested public in the Congressional-Executive dialogue and the other forums of our public life. The quality of the public performance may be considerably inferior to the Thursday morning meetings in the White House. Undoubtedly public discussions must be carried on without the benefit of access to a considerable amount of relevant information because of security reasons, although they in turn will make use of information which was not available or considered in the privy councils of the White House. But the relative quality of the public and the secret debates over foreign policy has nothing to do with whether the latter will or ought to occur, for they are a political necessity.

Despite these obstacles to effective NSC operation it would be unwise to conclude that the NSC is inoperable, or that its acts must be insignificant. Departmental heads are not simply prisoners of their situations. Indeed, their status within their own agency can be enhanced by their participation in the NSC. The fact that the department head has demands placed upon him in the NSC to rise above departmental viewpoints can be a part of that enhanced status, for all the more must he be reckoned with as the President's spokesman within his own agency. Furthermore, the staff mechanisms of the NSC can make substantial inroads upon the obstacles to effective NSC operation described above. The momentum of staff work, by having available facts and arguments from the previous consideration of the same or similar subjects, can the more effectively evoke current information from the departments and evaluate current departmental judgments and arguments. For instance, simply to record and keep the positions of an agency on file, together with the evidence it provides on a particular subject over time, can build up a record which would at least limit its freedom of maneuver and might force it, increasingly, to discuss the subject on its merits. At the same time, the determination of the Chief Executive to make use of the NSC can in some cases force his agency heads to make use of it also. Finally, there is a *prima facie* argument that the greater the speed and flexibility which the NSC and its staff mechanisms develop—specifically, the more continuous their review of established policies becomes—the more the gap between secret plans and political realities is likely to be closed.

But all of these prospects for overcoming difficulties in the operation of the NSC are substantially limited in what they can accomplish. While it would be unwise to overlook the potentialities of the NSC, or of a cabinet, it would be foolish to ignore their limitations. Like any balance, this one cannot provide the assurance of stability.

Those who praise the NSC are likely to underrate its limitations, even while paying deference to the notion that it is imperfect and can be improved. On the other hand, those who find it wanting conclude too readily that it is dispensable. As real as are the inherent limitations on the effective operations of the NSC which have been mentioned above, the need for it, or for something very much like it, is equally unavoidable. While the mind of one man may be the most effective instrument for devising diplomatic moves and strategic maneuvers, and for infusing staff work with creative purpose, its product is bound to be insufficient to meet the needs of the vast organizational structures and the military, economic, and diplomatic programs which are the instruments of foreign policy. The most sensitive and subtle mechanism is ineffective when overloaded. And as ponderous in comparison with a single mind as are the actions of a large-scale organization, or even a committee, nevertheless coming to terms with the requirements of the bureaucracy is as much a necessity as is flexibility and speed in foreign policy-making.

Since this accommodation to the operational aspects of national security is unavoidable, it only remains to determine the means for accomplishing it. Aside from trivial variations of either, there is only one real alternative to the NSC type of coordinative machinery, a Presidential staff in the Executive Office of the President with no operating responsibilities. While it would avoid the loyalty conflicts (and their many ramifications) of a council of responsible operators such as the NSC, a Presidential staff would have its own inherent difficulties: It would be outweighed in any serious dispute with a department, unless it destroyed the President's confidence in his department head. Its "plans" would lack the sense of reality and the prestige which comes with responsibility. It would have information-gathering problems of its own. It would not necessarily identify itself with the President's viewpoint. And it could become as much or more isolated from political realities than the NSC.

In the end, the question of how best to achieve interdepartmental coordination of national security policy must be answered by weighing these two major alternatives against each other, or by finding the optimum mixture of them. As the query can be put in the more practical terms of increments, should the NSC staff be strengthened with a view to its becoming an independent force in NSC deliberations? Or should civilians without administrative responsibilities be added to the Council? Put in this form the problem is one of the most persistent and universal questions posed in administrative organization: Is coordination to be achieved through lateral clearance or line command? The disadvantages and impossibilities of line-command solutions are usually more visible than the obstacles to effective lateral accommodation. The Eisenhower Administration can be credited with having developed the capabilities of both methods by improving the staff mechanisms of the NSC along with its increasing use of the Council. Yet it seems to have been much more aware of the limitations of staff agents than of advisory councils to a presidential executive.

THE DECISION-MAKING PROCESS *
Theodore C. Sorensen

KENNEDY brought to the White House unusual firsthand knowledge of the foreign, domestic, legislative and political arenas but no experience in the Executive Branch. He was always more interested in policy than in administration, and would later admit that "it is a tremendous change to go from being a Senator to being President. In the first months it is very difficult." He continued to reshape executive procedures throughout his term, but from the outset he abandoned the notion of a collective, institutionalized Presidency. He ignored Eisenhower's farewell recommendation to create a First Secretary of the Government to oversee all foreign affairs agencies. He abandoned the practice of the Cabinet's and the National Security Council's making group decisions like corporate boards of directors. He abolished the practice of White House staff meetings and weekly Cabinet meetings. He abolished the pyramid structure of the White House staff, the Assistant President-Sherman Adams-type job, the Staff Secretary, the Cabinet Secretariat, the NSC Planning Board and the Operations Coordinating Board, all of which imposed, in his view, needless paperwork and machinery between the President and his responsible officers. He abolished several dozen interdepartmental committees which specialized in group recommendations on outmoded problems. He paid little attention to organization charts and chains of command which diluted and distributed his authority. He was not interested in unanimous committee recommendations which stifled alternatives to find the lowest common denominator of compromise.

He relied instead on informal meetings and direct contacts—on a personal White House staff, the Budget Bureau and *ad hoc* task forces to probe and define issues for his decision—on special Presidential emissaries and constant Presidential phone calls and memoranda—on placing Kennedy men in each strategic spot. Particularly in 1961 and particularly on National Security mat-

* From Theodore C. Sorensen, *Kennedy* (New York: Harper & Row, 1965), pp. 281–285. Copyright, 1965, by Theodore C. Sorensen. Reprinted by permission of Harper & Row, Publishers.

ters, he talked at the White House or by telephone to lower-level officers and experts with firsthand knowledge or responsibility. (At least one State Department subordinate was embarrassed by the profanely skeptical reply he gave when the voice on the other end of the line announced itself as the President's.) "The President can't administer a department," Kennedy said when asked about this practice,

but at least he can be a stimulant. . . . There is a great tendency in government to have papers stay on desks too long. . . . One of the functions of the President is to try to have it move with more speed. Otherwise you can wait while the world collapses.

Abolishing the Operations Coordinating Board, he made clear his intention to strengthen departmental responsibility "without extensive formal machinery" and to maintain

direct communication with the responsible agencies, so that everyone will know what I have decided, while I in turn keep fully informed of the actions taken to carry out decisions. We of course expect that the policy of the White House will be the policy of the Executive Branch as a whole, and we shall take such steps as are needed to ensure this result.

A reporter compared the Eisenhower-Kennedy methods of obtaining teamwork with the differences between football and basketball. The Eisenhower football method relied on regular huddles and rigid assignments. In the Kennedy administration all team members were constantly on the move.

Kennedy called huddles, but only when necessary and only with those necessary, those whose official views he required or whose unofficial judgment he desired, regardless of protocol or precedent. Attendance varied with each subject, but it was not haphazard. McGeorge Bundy made certain that no responsible officer or point of view was omitted from meetings on foreign policy, and I tried to do the same on domestic. For example, if Walter Heller and George Ball wanted to meet with the President on the balance of payments, I made certain Dillon was also invited. The President's own accessibility, and his insistence on dealing with subordinates as well as chiefs, made certain that he was not denied any relevant counsel or criticism, and both he and his staff improved our ability to use channels and coordinate decisions during those first crucial months. But he never altered his view that any meeting larger than necessary was less flexible, less secret and less hard-hitting.

As a result, with few exceptions, he held Cabinet meetings only because "I suppose we should—it's been several weeks since the last one," and with few exceptions these meetings bored him. He rarely made any attempt at such sessions, as President Roosevelt had, to engage Cabinet members in light banter, to seek their political advice, to suggest that they volunteer problems or to call on them one by one for discussion.

No decisions of importance were made at Kennedy's Cabinet meetings and few subjects of importance, particularly in foreign affairs, were ever seriously discussed. The Cabinet as a body was convened largely as a symbol, to be informed, not consulted, to help keep the channels of communication open, to help maintain the *esprit de corps* of the members and to prevent the charge that Kennedy had abolished the Cabinet. There were no high-level debates, or elaborate presentations, or materials circulated in advance.[1]

Kennedy relied considerably on his Cabinet officers, but not on the Cabinet as a body. On the contrary, he thought

general Cabinet meetings . . . to be unnecessary and involve a waste of time. . . . All these problems Cabinet officers deal with are very specialized. I see all the Cabinet officers every week, but we don't have a general meeting. There really isn't much use spending a morning talking about the Post Office budget and tying up Secretary Freeman, who has agriculture responsibilities. . . . If we have a problem involving labor-management . . . it is much better for me to meet with Secretary Hodges from Commerce and Secretary Goldberg from Labor. . . . I think we will find the Cabinet perhaps more important than it has ever been but Cabinet meetings not as important.

He also felt, but could not add, that he usually had little interest in the views of Cabinet members on matters outside their jurisdiction. He summoned former Under Secretary of State Dillon to most major meetings on foreign policy and former Ford President McNamara to advise on the steel price dispute. But he did not want McNamara's advice on debt management or Dillon's advice on Nike-Zeus. In his opinion, that only wasted his time and theirs.

Problems involving all Cabinet members, and thus appropriate to Cabinet discussion, were few and far between: Civil Service and patronage, the Budget outlook, legislative relations and somewhat superficial briefings, not consultations, on administration policy and current events. Occasionally more important matters appeared on the agenda—the responsibility of Cabinet officers for advancing civil rights or accelerating Federal projects during the recession, for example—but most typical by far was this Cabinet agenda for December 10, 1962, set forth here in its entirety:

1. Review of Foreign Situation—The Secretary of State
2. Review of Economic Situation and Outlook—Honorable Walter Heller
3. Status Report on 1963 Legislative Program—Honorable T. C. Sorensen

While Heller and I were often asked to make presentations of this kind—as were O'Brien, the Budget Director and the Civil Service Chairman—only the ten department heads (and Ambassador Stevenson, when in town) sat at the long Cabinet table. None of them brought any staff or subordinates with them and most of them said comparatively little. The Cabinet Assistant, the Budget Director, the Science Adviser, the Economic Adviser and I sat behind the President, who kept the meetings as brief as decorum permitted. Often he

1. In the first few months of 1961, Fred Dutton tried valiantly but in vain to make meaningful his role of "Cabinet Assistant" by promoting an impressive agenda, detailed planning, an outline for the President and some of the other characteristics of the Eisenhower Cabinet. But Dutton, and Ted Reardon who succeeded him to these duties, soon gave up.

would cut discussion short. Occasionally he would ask the Vice President to "chair" the meeting during his temporary absence—and then disappear permanently into his office.

Much the same was true of the large formal meetings of the National Security Council, which dealt exclusively with foreign affairs. It had a more significant agenda prepared by McGeorge Bundy, papers were circulated in advance and the meetings were more interesting to the President. He ran them in every sense of the word, first asking the CIA Director for the intelligence summaries on the situation under study, then asking the Secretary of State to give his recommendations, and then throwing it open to Defense and others. (Usually the senior official was addressed by the President as "Mr. Secretary" or "Mr. Dulles," but his own aides by their first names.)

At times he made minor decisions in full NSC meetings or *pretended* to make major ones actually settled earlier. Attendance was generally kept well below the level of previous administrations, but still well above the statutory requirements. He strongly preferred to make all major decisions with far fewer people present, often only the officer to whom he was communicating the decision. "We have averaged three or four meetings a week with the Secretaries of Defense and State, McGeorge Bundy, the head of the CIA and the Vice President," he said in 1961. "But formal meetings of the Security Council which include a much wider group are not as effective. It is more difficult to decide matters involving high national security if there is a wider group present."

For brief periods of time, during or after a crisis, the President would hold NSC meetings somewhat more regularly, partly as a means of getting on record the views of every responsible officer (who might otherwise complain that he wasn't consulted and wouldn't have approved), but mostly to silence outside critics who equated machinery with efficiency. "The National Security Council," he said, when asked about various positions reportedly taken by its members in the Cuban missile crisis, "is an advisory body to the President. In the final analysis, the President of the United States must make the decision. And it is his decision. It's not the decision of the National Security Council or any collective decision." This he meant quite literally, for he often overruled the principal NSC members and on at least one occasion overruled all of them.

There were some complaints about the Kennedy approach to organizational machinery. Secretary Hodges grumbled publicly that there should be more Cabinet meetings. State Department aides grumbled privately that their prestige suffered if they were not present for key decisions. Secretary Rusk complained that he did not like to offer his views in meetings at which "people like Sorensen and Kaysen with no responsibility were making academic comments." He preferred to save his arguments for the President's ear only. But in general the department heads concurred with Willard Wirtz's conclusion that, without many formal meetings, there had been an "extraordinary degree" of close communication, both ways, "between the President and his Cabinet . . . and among the Cabinet members."

C.   The Budget

WHERE constitutionalism has emerged, it has generally done so from parliamentary demands for a veto over taxation and expenditure decisions. Although modern constitutionalism is generally defined in civil libertarian terms, it should not be forgotten that the originally demanded civil liberty was the right not to have one's money taken or spent by the government without the consent of one's representatives. The budget remains the most fundamental instrument for allocating priorities among government programs. Money is for all practical purposes infinitely divisible; the most delicate gradations of emphasis can be expressed with it. One who controls the budget thus possesses a remarkably sensitive instrument for inducing the cooperation of those responsible for any program.

For these reasons, Congress has always been extremely wary of permitting budgetary control to become a Presidential prerogative. From 1802 to 1921, it even denied the President authority to revise agency budgetary requests before transmitting them. Nor was budgetary decision making centralized within Congress itself. By the second decade of this century, fourteen House committees and fifteen Senate committees were authorized to initiate appropriations bills. Jurisdiction over each year's fourteen *regular* appropriations bills was divided among eight committees in the House. (Remarkably, the Senate Appropriations Committee had retained jurisdiction over all but one.) James Bryce discussed the situation in his classic study, The American Commonwealth, as follows:

> The office of Finance Minister is put into commission, and divided between the chairmen of several unconnected committees of both Houses. A mass of business which specifically needs the knowledge, skill, and economical conscience of a responsible ministry, is left to committees which are powerful, but not responsible, and to Houses whose nominal responsibility is in practice sadly weakened by their want of appropriate methods and organization.*

Bryce's ideal was the British system, of course, and by "appropriate methods and organization" he meant party discipline, which could enable the leaders of the majority party to determine, and thus to take clear responsibility for, everything that occurred.

Congress finally authorized the President to draft the national budget in the Budget and Accounting Act of 1921. The same statute established a new agency, the Bureau of the Budget, to aid him in performing this task. By this time budget-drafting was a prerogative of the chief executive in nearly all leading corporations, and the issue of Presidential responsibility for the federal budget had been a live

---

* James Bryce, *The American Commonwealth* (New York: The Macmillan Co., 1910), Vol. I, p. 182.

one in national politics for more than a decade. The immediate development which rendered passage of the Budget and Accounting Act feasible, however, was the rapid growth of the national debt during the First World War. Between 1916 and 1919, the gross debt of the federal government had risen from $1.2 billion to $25.5 billion. Concern about achieving annual budgetary surpluses so as to reduce that debt remained one of the dominant themes of American politics at least until the great depression. The case for businesslike budgetary management therefore had an unprecedented political impact in this period.

More recently, other factors have operated to enhance the feasibility of central budgetary planning. Among these the most notable are probably the following.

First, federal revenues have increasingly come from direct taxes on American citizens. By contrast, nineteenth century revenues came predominantly from tariffs upon foreign goods. Although tariffs resulted in higher prices to American consumers, the domestic interests which most noticed and cared about them were businesses threatened by foreign competition. "Tax" increases were politically quite popular, therefore; few worried in this period about their impact upon the world economy or American foreign relations. The most common form of federal subsidy in the nineteenth century, moreover, was the grant of public land, which also appeared costless to most taxpayers.

Second, the disparity between politically feasible revenue levels and the level of demand for public services has fairly constantly widened. It was vital to the nineteenth century budgetary approach that demand for public services increase very slowly. As it happened, this condition was handily met. American views on the proper role of the state changed at a glacierlike pace until the great depression, and the nation escaped continuous involvement in world affairs until the 1940's. More recently, as *laissez faire* ideology, isolationism, and antimilitarism have fallen as barriers to increased public spending, the case for priority planning has become more and more readily apparent. During this period, parenthetically, budgeting has increasingly come to be considered a substantive planning tool rather than simply a device for holding down federal expenditures.

Meanwhile, the national debt has remained a live issue in many quarters. Mainly as a result of war and inflation, it has risen by twenty-three times since 1930—from $16 billion to $370 billion (June 30, 1968, estimate as of January 1968). Those interests which would be most likely to oppose central budgetary management because of their distaste for concentrated government power happen also to be the ones most concerned about the national debt (not to mention high taxes). Probably in consequence, their opposition to the centralizing trend has been sporadic, disunited, and relatively ineffective.

Congress remains—by comparison with the world's other national legislatures— extremely jealous of its power to authorize expenditures, nonetheless; and it has organized itself to deal with the budget in characteristically fragmented fashion. Revenue and expenditure decisions fall within the jurisdictions of separate committees in each House, and the expenditure (appropriations) committees are broken up into twelve subcommittees in each House. In practice, these subcommittees act independently and are almost never overruled by the full appropriations committees. Their general policy orientations can be shaped by the process of appointing committee and subcommittee members, but neither of these processes is subject to regular Presidential control. American budgetary practice thus remains highly pluralistic, despite the strength of the drift toward central management.

Charles Lindblom believes that it should remain so. Writing in response to most of the literature on budgeting published through the mid-1950's, he maintains that central allocation is far from the same as rational allocation. The existing American budgetary process, Lindblom asserts, probably produces more "rational" policy outputs than any of the proposed alternatives to it would. The central allocation model of rational decision, he states, fails to deal adequately with the complexity and special value problems involved in national decision making. His own preferred model of rational decision is one characterized by "incrementalism and mutual adjustment."

Lindblom has been expounding and elaborating this model in numerous publications over the past decade, and he applies it to nearly all kinds of collective decision making, not just budgeting. On the whole, American social scientists have received it warmly. Some critics have contended, however, that it is applicable only to situations in which consensus is strong, resources are plentiful, and there is no premium on responding quickly to changing circumstances. Others have remarked that Lindblom's model is belated, that it would have been more persuasive had it appeared before the great depression dealt laissez faire a mortal blow as the preeminent theory of how to manage a national economy. In the same vein, some have wondered whether Lindblom's logic does not lead to the conclusion that the American budgetary (not to say entire political) system would operate better without the President and the Budget Bureau.

Lindblom himself, however, eschews extreme conclusions. He is, in fact, a Burkeian conservative *par excellence,* endeavoring to explain how historical evolution has produced a system far more "rational" than anything the reforming mind might substitute for it. To note this is not to disparage his thesis. On the contrary. It is to warn you as you begin to evaluate it that you are dealing not with an ivory tower reform proposal but with the most persuasive defense of traditional American budgetary practice yet advanced.

The 1950's were a period of reaction to the era of Franklin Roosevelt in both American politics and American social science. The incumbent President sought to reeducate the American people in the virtues of individual self-reliance (as an alternative to the welfare state), states' rights, and weak executive leadership. Economists rediscovered the genius of the market. And political scientists turned from emphasizing the need for greater centralization in the American system to celebrating the virtues of pluralism. Lindblom's decision model developed in this context, and by the early 1960's it had pretty well carried the day insofar as political and administrative analyses of the budget process were concerned. Some economists and applied mathematicians continued to elaborate central decision models, but political scientists tended to consider their efforts irrelevant to the realities of social and political decision making. The profession's attitude was *déjà vu.* Before achieving some sophistication about the complex workings of the political system, it too had expended its energies constructing neat and logical proposals for reform. Now it knew better.

History's stock of ironies is never exhausted, however. Just about the time that this conservative tide in political and administrative analysis reached its peak, Robert McNamara became Secretary of Defense. One of his first acts was to appoint Charles Hitch Comptroller of the Defense Department. Hitch had been one of the foremost scholars of the 1950's among those working to perfect the theory of rational central allocation. William Kaufmann describes the planning-programming-budgeting system (PPBS) that McNamara and Hitch instituted. He concludes that it is far more conducive to rational allocation decisions than the system it replaced, and that in political terms it has amounted to a functional substitute for unification of the armed services.

This new approach to budgeting has become highly fashionable, outside as well as within the government. In the summer of 1965, President Johnson ordered all agencies to prepare for submitting their fiscal year 1968 budget requests on a PPBS basis. (This was not as much lead time as it sounds; rough estimates of fiscal 1968 needs were due at the Budget Bureau in May 1966). Despite this record of rapid acceptance, however, the system is not without its critics. There are, in fact, quite a few skeptics who doubt that Secretary McNamara's record on substantive issues would have been significantly different if traditional budgetary practices had been in operation; and there are many more who doubt that the system will have a great effect on nondefense decision making. William Capron reviews the major criticisms that have been made of PPBS, and attempts to answer them. Capron, it should be noted, was a pioneer in the development of PPBS, and served as Assistant Director of the Budget Bureau from 1963 to 1965.

DECISION-MAKING IN TAXATION AND EXPENDITURES *
Charles E. Lindblom

INTRODUCTION

THE planners of this conference believed that it might be possible eventually to formulate more workable standards for government tax and expenditure decisions by interweaving a search for clarification of actual decision processes with a search for workable norms. In undertaking such a project as they proposed, I am accordingly pursuing a refinement of normative economics in a roundabout way. Most of what I have to say will be positive, not normative and, for that matter, will be more derived from political science than from traditional economics. The facts to be alluded to are on the whole familiar. The norms sought are of two kinds: for taxers and spenders and for designers of decision-making machinery. Given the purposes of such Universities-National Bureau conferences as this one, I take it that in the interpretation of facts, hypotheses will often be welcome. If at critical points in the argument I fall back on the plea for additional research, I assume I am within my scholarly rights.

I. CONTEMPORARY PRACTICES AND NORMS

Beginning then with facts, let us take note of some characteristics of govern-

* From Charles E. Lindblom, *Public Finances: Needs, Sources, and Utilization,* a report of the National Bureau of Economic Research, pp. 295–311, 325–329. Copyright © 1961 by Princeton University Press and reprinted with their permission.

ment expenditure and taxation decisions in the United States, especially in the federal government, that are significant to economists.[1]

1. Legislative decisions that authorize expenditures are typically made without benefit of any formal machinery that brings budgetary considerations to bear on them. The authorization committees of the Congress on one hand, and the appropriations committees, on the other, are relatively independent of each other and not locked in close cooperation.

2. The costs and benefits of authorized programs are not typically weighted against each other, systematically and explicitly, when legislative decisions are made.

3. Policy-making is not systematically and explicitly viewed as a problem in the choice among alternative means for the achievement of desired ends. Even in decisions in which the necessity of allocating scarce funds might appear to make the means-ends problem especially acute, decision-making is not typically marked by explicit comparison and deliberate choice among means. The military's penchant for the "best" of everything—the best planes, the best mess kits, the best gloves—is coming to be the classic example of reluctance to evaluate means in the light of ends. Points 2 and 3 are, of course, merely two aspects of the common failure of government decision-makers to employ an adequate concept of cost.

4. Some major expenditure or taxation policies are set or altered as an accident or by-product of other decisions. That is to say, a policy is not always a decision; it is often simply upon us without deliberate and explicit choice. A "decision" to run a surplus or deficit is, for example, often not a decision at all but simply an outcome.

5. More generally, many of the financial and other implications of a decision are ignored when a decision is made. The decision-maker, whether administrator or legislator, permits pressure of work and limits on his own concerns to confine his attention to less than all of the important relevant variables.

In the budgetary process, most of us see a partly realized, partly potential, technique for making expenditure and taxation decisions more rational. This brief list of characteristics of financial decisions can be extended to note certain aspects of budgeting.

6. Many major explicitly financial decisions are outside the budgetary process. Tax decisions are, of course, wholly outside; so also deficiency appropriations. And in wartime, as might be expected, appropriations to the military are so generous that availability of physical supplies, not budgetary considerations, set expenditure rates.

7. As many economists have noted, there is in the federal budgetary machinery no explicit provision for coordinating revenues and expenditures.

8. Formal congressional review of the budget is concentrated in appropriations subcommittees whose interests are focused on segments of the budget considered largely in isolation from other segments.

1. Most of the characteristics of decision-making to be listed are familiar. All can be documented in Arthur Smithies, *The Budgetary Process in the United States*, McGraw-Hill, 1955.

9. Neither the appropriations committee as a whole nor the Congress as a whole gives extended formal consideration to the budget as a whole, nor does the appropriations committee as a whole play a strong coordinating role for the subcommittees.

10. Moreover, even in considering segments of the budget, the subcommittee members are repeatedly drawn into scrutiny of details rather than of the major expenditure alternatives, although this phenomenon varies from one subcommittee to another.

11. Being torn between two possibilities—using budgetary scrutiny for detailed administrative control or using it for planning broad public policy—legislators are drawn toward the first to a degree that reduces significantly their explicit attention to the latter.

12. Congress does not enact the budget as a whole at the termination of budget review but instead enacts a series of appropriations bills.

13. Budgeting is marked by conflict between President and Congress, between the two houses of Congress, and among subcommittees.

Familiar as these provisions are, they are essential to what follows.

The accepted contemporary norms for the budgetary process reflect widespread dissatisfaction with the characteristics of the budgetary process just summarized. I would expect widespread agreement on such a list of norms as the following, taken from Smithies (page references are to Smithies) though altered somewhat in emphasis and presentation. Some are norms for taxers and spenders; some are norms for designers of decision-making machinery. Some are general norms, and some are norms pertaining to coordination, which is a special aspect of decision-making.

1. Governmental objectives should be as clearly and explicitly defined as possible (25ff.).

2. Alternative policies should be explicitly regarded as alternative means toward the achievement of objectives (28).

3. Specifically, expenditure decisions should be made explicitly and deliberately in the light of all of the objectives they are intended to achieve (16).

4. In the interests of a rational comparison of alternatives, final expenditure decisions should not be made until all claims on the budget can be considered (16).

5. Revenue and expenditure decisions should be deliberately coordinated (192).

6. For each expenditure, some systematic and deliberate appraisal of benefits and costs should be made (12ff.).

7. Policy-making, including budgetary policy making, should achieve a unified policy (23).

8. A comprehensive overview of policy-making on expenditures and revenues should be attempted (16, 25).

9. All taxation and expenditure decisions should be somehow embraced in the budgetary process (175ff.).

10. Specifically, the legislature should undertake a comprehensive, unified, rather than segmented, review of the budget (164, 169, 193).

11. Decisions should be made on the basis of a cooperative division of function between the legislature and the executive (45).

For present purposes, it does not matter that some of these norms overlap others and that some are more specific statements of others. It is important, however, to observe that a few central principles run through this and similar lists to be found elsewhere in the literature. In such lists economists reveal themselves as esteeming, not surprisingly, such conventional principles as:

1. A comprehensive overview of factors relevant to a decision
2. Clarity of definition of social objectives
3. A means-end approach to policy
4. Deliberate and explicit choice among policies
5. A calculation and minimization of cost
6. Reason and cooperation rather than arbitrariness, coercion and conflict
7. A unified decision-making process for decisions that are highly interdependent.

Most, perhaps all, of the listed norms are applications in varying degrees of specificity of these more fundamental principles.

2. DISCREPANCY BETWEEN PRACTICES AND NORMS

For all the immediate appeal of both norms and underlying principles, an objection to them is that they do not emerge from a skeptical analysis of the actual decision-making process, good and bad, in government but appear instead to be derived from a paradigm of a rational decision process. They stem from criticisms of government decision-making that take the form of observations that the process is not what one would suppose a rational process to be.

Reconsider now in this light the characterizations of decision-making with which this paper opened. They are invariably read as shortcomings of decision-making, although I did not present them as such. They are thought to be shortcomings, I suggest, not on a demonstration of their effects but by implicit or explicit appeal to obvious standards of rationality. Or look again in this light at the seven underlying principles on which the norms rest. Why are they as persuasive as they are? Because, again, they represent almost universally accepted ideas on how to be rational in any kind of problem-solving.

It is possible that we are all betrayed by these obvious standards for rational problem-solving. Perhaps they are more limited in their applicability than we have thought. Although one's ideas of what is rational suffice to predict that using a milk bottle to drive spikes into 4 x 4's will ordinarily be inferior to using a hammer, one cannot be confident for such a complex process as governmental decision-making that such principles of rationality as comprehensiveness of overview, explicitness of choice, means-ends calculations, and clarity of definition of objectives are appropriate. These are standards drawn largely from our own intimate experiences with small scale, relatively more simple, problem-solving.

That conventional norms do indeed follow paradigms of rational processes rather than reflect independent diagnosis of decision-making and that they may lead us astray can be illustrated. It is a commonplace norm that revenue and expenditure decisions should be coordinated through some formal congressional machinery now lacking. Why? Because fiscal policy is a powerful device for economic stabilization, from which it seems "logically" to follow that Congress should have formal machinery for taking account of the fiscal consequences of a prospective surplus or deficit. But is it in fact true that Congress is without methods for coordinating revenue and expenditure decisions? No, it is only without *formally prescribed* procedures, and we should know by now that informal operating procedures are often superior to formal. And is Congress typically unaware of a deficit when it occurs? No, except to the degree that fact-collecting cannot keep up to date in any organization. Do such deficits and surpluses as do occur (other than those justified by stability considerations) appear at random? No, they are probably the result of a combination of congressional attitudes toward fiscal policy and pressures upon Congress. Do then "economically unwise" surpluses and deficits demonstrate a need for formal coordination? No, not unless formal coordination can be shown to be an intermediate step to the achievement of changed congressional attitudes and to the restructuring of pressures on congressmen.

What is it about government decision-making that might make "obvious" principles of rational choice inappropriate? A first answer is that complex decision-making is molded by limitations on human problem-solving capacities not taken account of in the conventional picture of rational choice.

Consider man's limited capacity to undertake usefully a comprehensive overview of the variables relevant to a complex decision. If sufficiently ambitious, all attempts at a comprehensive overview run into two major limits: first, man's limited intellectual ability, that is, his limited ability to grasp, calculate, and remember; and, second, limited information. Some problems lie so far beyond these two limits that it would be irrational for man to attempt an informed and reasoned solution to them; better he flip a coin, adopt a rule of thumb, or decide by any of several "arbitrary" means.

Commonplace though not trivial decisions as to whether to marry, what occupation to choose, or how many children to produce are not so much comprehensively calculated as resolved through a limited evaluation; or they are drifted into, unthinkingly decided, taken as by-products of other decisions, or settled by rule of thumb. While the role of what might be called "reason" in such decisions might well be increased for some people in some circumstances, I see no evidence that these decisions would always be more rational (unless "rational" is defined as "reasoned") if approached through an inevitably only partly successful comprehensive overview of the relevant variables. I would not be so foolish as to make the attempt myself and did in fact satisfy myself with a very limited view of the variables.

If these relatively simple personal decisions call for intellectual capacities and knowledge beyond our reach, all the more so do complex governmental decisions. The federal budget document runs to 2,000 pages, and prints of committee hearings on it cover many thousands more. It is not at all obvious, and indeed doubtful, that any man or committee can achieve a sufficiently intimate understanding of the budget as to make the thousands of comparisons and evaluations required in a genuinely comprehensive overview, even if these printed materials were all one were required to master. In fact, of course, one cannot understand the variables relevant to budgetary decisions without knowing, grasping, remembering, and relating to the decisions a prodigious amount of information about government, the economy, and the wishes of the citizenry.

These difficulties do not mean that men think and express conspicuously irrational thoughts when faced with the budget, or that they flee in panic, or that the budgetary process comes to a grinding stop. They do mean, however, that most budgetary decisions are in fact made in ways economists are accustomed to call arbitrary, that thousands of important comparisons are never in fact made, that many major issues never come to the attention of decision-makers, and that such agreement as various decision-makers reach is less owed to the exhaustiveness of their scrutiny of the budget than to common ideology, prejudice, or even common ignorance when they all miss the same relevant issues that might have divided them.

If this is true, as can easily be documented and as I should like to see documented by research, then it does not at all follow that even more ambitious attempts at comprehensiveness of overview, as is conventionally recommended, will increase the elements of rationality in government taxation and expenditure decisions. It is quite possible that overtaxing man's limited capacities still further will make the situation worse.

An objection to this line of argument springs to mind. It is that limits of man's capacities have been pushed back by dividing up the decision-making process, that is, by factoring out subdivisions of the decision tasks. It is true, everyone agrees, that limits on man's problem-solving capacity can indeed be pushed back by factoring out parts of problems and enlisting the cooperation of a number of individuals or groups, each of whom attacks its own assigned part of the problem. If it were not for this possibility, even the small federal budgets of earlier decades would have been beyond our grasp. But pushing back the limits is not the same as eliminating them. Hence, even with subdivision of the decision-process in the administration and in Congress, a $70 billion budget presents a staggering decision-making problem. Is it not obvious that, even with subdivision, thousands of important comparisons are not made and many major issues are not brought to the attention of decision-makers?

We can see why subdivision only pushes back but does not remove limits by looking at subdivided decision-making processes. Observers report such familiar difficulties as the following: (1) coordination of subdivisions is a continuing task of top decision-makers; (2) substantial interdependent elements that cannot be factored out remain the responsibility of top decision-makers; (3) appropriate lines of division are unstable, as changing conditions create new patterns of interdependency; (4) difficulties of communication, many of which are intended by subordinates, misrepresent to top decision-makers the facts required for their decisions; (5) motivational difficulties, illustrated by divergence between organizational goals as seen by top decision-makers and as seen by subdivisions, inevitably distort decisions. If this last point is not clear, it predicts, for example, that appropriations subcommittees take a segmental view of the budget not only because they lack a strong central coordinating committee, but also in large part because a subdivision or subcommittee inevitably takes on goals and attitudes of its own.

Now, again, these difficulties in subdividing the task of comprehensive overview do not mean that decision-making becomes chaotic when subdivided. They simply represent specifications of *limits* on man's capacities to carry off successfully a comprehensive overview of a complex problem. And to return to our main point, they buttress the allegation that government decision-making is molded by limits on man's capacities that are not taken account of in contemporary conventional norms and principles.

Another illustration of the failure of conventional norms and principles to take sufficient account of the facts is that government officials often cannot cast a policy problem into a means-ends framework, as the norms require.

An immediate and obvious difficulty on this score is that decision-makers, to say nothing of the electorate, do not in fact wholly agree on objectives or values.[2] To be sure, on many they agree roughly; but the scope of government decision-making is not limited to their areas of agreement. Nor do men generally aspire to universal agreement on objectives of social policy, prizing instead diversity and change. Still, it may be questioned, do we not agree that governments shall take as their working objectives those preferred by the majority? Do we not consequently enjoy a working agreement on objectives of governmental policy?

This is a question of fact, and for several reasons the answer is no. In the first place, it has been shown that majority rule is a process through which it is not usually possible for citizens to indicate preferences on specific policies. If a winning candidate differed from his defeated opponent on, say, an issue in foreign policy (among other issues that divided them), it does not follow that those who voted for him favored his stand on the foreign policy issue. Hence, neither the winning candidate nor anyone else can say what policy objective is to be taken, by majority rule, as the government's objective.

Second, most policy choices open to government, including almost all budgetary choices, are never even raised during election campaigns as campaign issues. Again, therefore, a public official is without a clearly defined governmental objective. Third, even in abstract principle we do not in fact agree on majority rule as a basis of working agreement. For in a large number of decision-making situations, citizens differ as to how far the equality principle implicit in majority rule ought to be compromised to take account of differences in intensity of preference among citizens and differences in their circum-

2. For present purposes, I shall use interchangeably such terms as "values," "objectives" (including "constraints"), "goals," and "ends."

stances. We have even gone so far in the United States as to subject some policy decisions to a vote in which only farmers in particular categories participate. And, of course, the United States Constitution makes numerous systematic provisions for inequality, as in its basis for representation of senators and the bicameral legislature. On all these counts, it is clear that government decision-makers are often without clear instructions from the electorate on policy objectives.

At one extreme, the impossibility of a means-end approach to policy is clear when one decision-maker's mean is another's end. To one decision-maker or citizen, for example, tax reduction comes to play such a role in his thinking that we can only call it an end or objective for him. To another, tax reduction is considered simply as one of several means to an objective like full employment. A government such as ours survives because it takes advantage of agreement among two such individuals where it finds it; to require them to agree with each other on which is end and which is means and then ask for their agreement on both ends and means is not only to pose insuperable problems of calculation to them but also to endanger political stability. The political scientists tell us democracies cannot be fussy about the terms on which their citizens reach agreement.

I should like these specific failures of the conventional principles to take account of the character of government decision-making to be taken as illustrative of two more general failures that will become clearer as we move through succeeding stages of the analysis. The failure to account for man's limited capacities and for the frequent impossibility of casting a problem into a means-end framework is sufficient to reveal the possibility that conventional norms and principles have not taken sufficient account of either (1) the sheer complexity of government decision-making or of (2) the special problems of handling values or objectives. Almost any other specific aspect of decision-making we might have looked into will reveal the same two underlying problems: complexity and special difficulties in evaluation.

It was suggested above that our ideas of what is rational in problem-solving are derived in large part from introspective observation of our own problem-solving processes from which many of the complexities of collectivities, including certain value problems, are absent. In addition, recent new insights into decision-making carry a powerful bias. With few exceptions, the formal theory of decision-making has not faced up to the possibility that complexity can outstrip limited intellectual capacity. And the success of conventional principles in such sophisticated application as operations research have perhaps tempted us to forget the limited competence of these applications and the possibility that extremely complex rational decisions have to be approached quite differently. Aware of this, Charles Hitch writes:

I would make the empirical generalization from my experience at RAND and elsewhere that operations research is the art of suboptimizing, i.e., of solving some lower-level problems, and that difficulties increase and our special competence diminishes by an order of magnitude with every level of decision-making we attempt to ascend. The sort of simple explicit model which operations researchers are so proficient in using can certainly reflect most of the significant factors influencing traffic control on the George Washington Bridge, but the proportion of relevant reality which we can represent by any such model or models in studying, say, a major foreign-policy decision, appears to be almost trivial.

3. INCREMENTAL DECISION-MAKING

We need now to pause to make clear and rather exact the significance of the fact that conventional principles do not face up to either the complexity of decision-making or its special value problems. A common but too quickly despairing inference is that we have no alternative but to press on as far as possible toward comprehensive overviews of our collective problems, toward clarification of objectives, toward structuring each decision as a means-end problem, toward deliberateness and explicitness of choice, and the like. Those who make this inference will grant that man's capacity to employ these methods successfully is indeed limited, that government expenditure and taxation policies, therefore, will at best be none too good; but they may somewhat paradoxically take heart from the discrepancy between practice and norm by believing that the only continuously serviceable norms are those impossible to reach.

But *if* for rational decision-making there is any alternative to comprehensiveness, the means-end approach, deliberateness and explicitness, and the like, the more sensible inference would be to employ these methods only when their limits permit and to employ an alternative when available. A big "if," it will be replied. Let us see. A fundamental characteristic of the literature on expenditure and taxation decisions is that is has not explored the possibility of alternatives, as I now propose to do.

There are a number of ways in which a decision-maker, within government or out, can approach a rational decision that departs considerably from the practice of the conventional principles outlined above.[3] Herbert Simon, for example, has constructed a model of "satisficing" rather than maximizing. It takes account of limits on man's cognitive capacities, by simplifying both the welfare or pay-off function and the process of search for a satisfactory solution. Its implications for government decision-making procedures remain to be explored but are not, I should think, trivial.

Problems of resource allocation in wartime led E. A. G. Robinson to the hypothesis: "The golden rule of all planning is that it must be done in terms of the scarcest of the resources." This, the "bottleneck principle," is hardly more than a hint at still another model of rational decision-making; but it may be the germ of a principle for drastically simplifying a complex problem so that it can be as rationally decided, for all the makeshift appearance of the decision, as through an inevitably futile attempt to comprehend all the complexities of the problem.

3. It is apparent by now that I am not going to define rationality. The reader is invited to supply his own definition, for I think what I have to say about rationality is as true for one concept of it as for another among the common definitions.

Still other ways of simplifying decision-making tasks to avoid irrationalities might be mentioned. Among them is one I have elsewhere described in some detail under the label of the incremental method. I suggest that it is actually the most common method through which public policy decisions, including decisions on taxes and expenditures, are approached. That it is a method commonly practiced has led us to take it for granted rather than formalize it in terms like those that formalize incremental consumer choice, to which it is obviously related.

The incremental method is characterized by its practitioner's preoccupation with: (1) only that limited set of policy alternatives that are politically relevant, these typically being policies only incrementally different from existing policies; (2) analysis of only those aspects of policies with respect to which the alternatives differ; (3) a view of the policy choice as one in a succession of choices; (4) the *marginal* values of various social objectives and constraints; (5) an intermixture of evaluation and empirical analysis rather than an empirical analysis of the consequences of policies for objectives independently determined; and (6) only a small number out of all the important relevant values.

Of these six characteristics, the first three are recognizable characteristics of political decision-making, as practiced by both officials and most policy-minded academic analysts. I shall not linger over them except to point out that anyone whose approach meets the first three conditions has enormously simplified his policy problems compared to what they would be if he literally and strictly followed the conventional prescription to attempt a comprehensive overview. The fourth and fifth strike at the value problem in policy-making; and the sixth strikes at the general complexity of policy analysis, although in what appears to be a shocking way.

Let us first consider problems of handling values. In the incremental method, political decision-makers handle values through marginal comparisons in the same way that consumers do. Although economists describe rational consumer behavior by reference to utility surfaces, indifference curves, demand schedules, and the like, a rational consumer need know nothing about them. He need not first determine his indifference curve for oranges and apples and subsequently decide his purchase policies accordingly. Nor need he first try to comprehend all possible product mixes (or even a few alternative product mixes), then decide which one he prefers, and only then make those purchases necessary to attain the preferred mix. The rational consumer proceeds directly to marginal comparison of alternative specific purchases. The way in which we economists can, for our own professional purposes, conceptualize consumer choice obscures the great difference between what the consumer can be conceived of as having done but does not actually do—ascertain a function, then choose so as to maximize it—and what he actually does— simply compare policies at the margin and choose directly the preferred policy.

Like the consumer, the incremental decision-maker in governmental affairs does not make use of a utility function, in his case a social welfare function. He does not think in terms of "all the variables that might be considered as affecting welfare: the amounts of each and every kind of goods consumed by and service performed by each and every household, the amount of each and every kind of capital investment undertaken, and so on." He can hardly be said to know even a point or two on such a function because he does not think in terms of alternative social states; and, if he can be said to value one social state higher than another, this fact is more to be inferred from his choices than said to control them. He makes specific choices, as does the consumer, at the margin.

Similarly, incremental decision-makers closely intermix empirical and value elements in choice as do consumers. We may describe a consumer who buys a car as having decided upon such a purchase policy in order to attain such objectives or values as speed of movement, ready accessibility of transportation, improved status, and conformity, as well as the pleasures of novelty, display, color and form, and acquisition itself. To decide whether to buy a car and, if so, which car, requires then that he both choose among combinations of such values as these and empirically investigate the consequences of alternative purchase policies for the attainment of each of these values. Thus he must make two kinds of choices: (1) the preferred value-mix and (b) the purchase best suited to the attainment of the preferred value-mix. In actual fact, however, he makes these two choices simultaneously when he decides upon his purchase; he does not in one choice determine the preferred value-mix and then make his purchase in its light.

Moreover, he would find it difficult to describe, even to himself, his preferences among the objectives except by pointing to the purchase made and those rejected. Furthermore, he would confess that many of the objectives or values served by his purchase appeared to him as relevant only after alternative purchase policies began to compete in his mind. He did not, for example, first consider buying a car in order to satisfy his esthetic senses, but esthetic values quickly became relevant once he contemplated buying a car.

Although it is customary to analyze values as a first step in policy-making, it is a characteristic of the incremental method that such an analysis is cursory, short-lived, and only a prefatory clarification of a few of the many goal-values that will be affected by policies to be considered. Sometimes such an analysis is omitted entirely. Either at once or very quickly in incremental decision-making, the analysis turns directly to alternative policies. *Predicting* consequences of alternative policies and *evaluating* the consequences then become intertwined to the degree that, as in consumer choice, only in the final choice among policies is the final choice among objectives or values itself made.

For example, many policy analysts find it extremely difficult to decide how much inflation they are willing to tolerate in order to achieve some specified reduction in unemployment except in contemplation of some particular set of policy alternatives offering marginally different prospective amounts of inflation and unemployment. Or, again, none of us do very well in describing to others—or even to ourselves—the relative value of economic security and rapid economic growth. But we make the choice when confronted with alternative policies offering different increments of the two values. Again, we do not determine our welfare function, then choose, but instead choose directly and, in so doing, simultaneously both indirectly define a part of a welfare function and maximize it.

It is also a characteristic of the incremental method that the decision-maker is much more tentative about his objectives or values than he is considered to be in conventional models. He counts on policy choices to lead him to fresh perceptions about values, he expects to learn about his values from his experiences with pursuing and enjoying them, and he is inclined to think that in the long run policy choices have as great an influence on objectives as objectives have on policy choices.[4]

If incrementalism is a method through which a single decision-maker can rationally evaluate alternative policies, it also offers a solution to the problem of disagreement among decision-makers on values. Incrementalism sidesteps problems posed by disagreement on values because decision-makers deal directly with policies, as has just been explained; no virtue attaches, as it does in the conventional method, to prior discussion of and agreement on objectives or values.

This characteristic of incrementalism makes agreement possible in at least three distinguishable ways. First, ideological and other differences in values that loom large when considered abstractly do not necessarily stand in the way of agreed marginal values. Second, the practice of evaluating only in actual choice situations often leads decision-makers to reconsider values in the light of practical constraints, and reconsideration often moves them toward agreement. Third—and much more important—individuals can often agree on policies even if they hold conflicting values. A group of decision-makers can agree, for example, on the desirability of a sales tax without agreeing on objectives; they may have quite different values and reasons in mind. It will be shown in a later section that incrementalism makes still another attack on the problem of disagreement: sometimes incremental policy-makers are coordinated by methods that do not require them to agree with one another on either values or policies.

As for the general problem of complexity in policy-making, the most drastic simplification of complex problems achieved in incremental decision-making is, as already indicated, through outright neglect of important consequences of policies. Neglect of important variables is so widely preached against that it may be worthwhile to make the point that all policy analysts

4. How then distinguish, it might be asked, a rational and irrational decison? The conventional model defines a rationally chosen policy by its relaton to a set of objectives. A rational policy, for example, is one that attains its objectives, or maximizes the probability of doing so, or is, by warranted beliefs, best suited to attainment of its objectives. But since for complex public policy decisions, the decision-makers' objectives are defined by the policy choice he makes, the principal characteristic of the rational decision—perhaps the defining characteristic—turns on the accuracy of the decision-maker's predictions about the outcome of his policies. . . .

practice such neglect and intend to go on doing so. In academic policy analysis, we economists routinely leave a mound of unfinished business for the political scientist, sociologist, or psychologist to attend to; and we only sometimes remember to qualify our results accordingly. We leave to the psychologist, for example, the appraisal of malingering when we analyze the desirability of liberalizing benefits under unemployment compensation. Less obvious but no less common is every policy analyst's neglect of imponderables, even when they are considered to be important. Beyond these omissions are many others, some of which appear at least superficially to be arbitrary or random, others of which are traceable to our ignorance. Examples are extremely long-run consequences for family solidarity of increasing urbanization achieved as a result of agricultural expenditures (or restrictions of expenditures) that induce farmers to leave the land; short-term consequences for corporate concentration of military procurement decisions; and consequences for the development of socialized medicine of liberal expenditures on veterans' medical care.

If important consequences are neglected, can the method still be described as one suitable for rational decision-making? Or is omission of important consequences a proof of irrationality? Whatever one's concept of rationality, I suggest that the answer in principle is clear. If the consequences are not neglected in the processes by which policies are determined, then that they are neglected by any given decision-maker is not evidence of irrationality in decision-making. Less cryptically, if values neglected by some decision-makers are the concern of other decision-makers, public policies taken together can be rational. We often permit the fallacy of composition to obscure this insight. Or, to put it another way, we often miss this point because we have applied to politics a confusion of partial and general equilibrium analysis.

Consider a hypothetical example. The President and some of his advisers agree on a greatly expanded program of highway expenditures. Their objectives are national defense, reduction of highway congestion for civilians, and economic development. Consequences of the program for the parity of the 50 states as recipients of federal funds are ignored, as are possible consequences for auto fatalities, design of automobiles, profits of existing toll roads, destruction of homes and recreational areas, sales of automobiles, sales of home furnishings, character of home life, participation in organized religion, and so on.

When the program is presented to Congress, if not before, some of the neglected values will be spoken for by, say, representatives of the states or of toll-road authorities. These interests may come to terms immediately with the original proponents of the program, not necessarily by each representative's taking into account each other's values but by agreement directly on modifications of the program. Other interests will wait until congressional consideration of the program is underway, and still other interests will be brought to bear on the administrative officials eventually responsible for implementing the program. And years later, when it becomes apparent to churchmen that too many people are out driving on Sunday rather than attending religious services, they will stir themselves to find ways of combating the tendency. When they do so, they will not necessarily associate the tendency with the earlier highway program, and it is not at all necessary that they do so in order to deal with their problem.

I intend the example to do no more than show the possibility that decisions can be rational even if each decision-maker ignores important values, if only the values neglected at one point are attended to at another. It is not necessary to show that all values are given equal consideration; they are not in the conventional method. Nor is it necessary to show that their inequalities are systematic or are understandable in terms of some formula; they are not in the conventional method. Nor is it necessary to show that all important values are brought somehow to bear on each decision, even if not on each decision-maker. For sometimes a neglected value will move no one to action until a decade later when it becomes clear that it is being endangered.

The example I chose was not after all very hypothetical; the processes illustrated are familiar. . . .

4. IMPLICATIONS FOR NORMS AND PRINCIPLES

Let us now look . . . first to the allocation in the large of federal expenditures and then to the budgetary process. Consider such a choice as that between social welfare and defense expenditures. How to choose?

We must first distinguish sharply, as conventional approaches to this problem do not, between the problem of the individual decision-maker and the problem of coordinating individual decisions, which may or may not be a decision-making problem itself. It follows from all the foregoing that, for the individual decision-maker, whether Director of the Bureau of the Budget, the President, a cabinet member, or congressman, it is a possibility much to be considered that he cannot make a reasoned decision between defense and welfare when they are both aggregated. It is true he can think he is thinking; but whether there is anything for the mind to seize upon when faced with a choice of some marginal increase in the defense budget as against a 10 per cent increase in welfare expenditures is problematical. Faced with aggregates which it must compare and among which it must choose, it is possible that the mind does not so much calculate as default—in some quite capricious or arbitrary way turning up a choice, or leaving the mouth or the hand to make its own decision. And if the mind tries to break the aggregates down and calculate the value of their components, it seems clear that it cannot encompass and interrelate more than a fraction of components at the level of specificity to which it must descend.

Conceding a considerable looseness in my description of mental processes, I nevertheless want to make the point that to sit in a chair and try to think about defense and welfare is not to guarantee that the mind will do anything with the problem that could properly be described as systematic calculations. It is quite likely that more rational decisions can be reached by an individual who tries to compare some fairly specific, concrete—and newly proposed—

military expenditure with some similarly specified innovation in welfare expenditure, making his choice on specifics and letting the aggregates be determined almost wholly as a by-product or residual decision.

Gross determinations of military or welfare expenditures the decision-maker can make, I believe, by calculating in aggregates. But gross determinations are not the repeated business of government decision-makers; each year presents them instead with choices among relatively small variations.

There are, however, so many small choices to be made that the legislature cannot possibly attend to them. As a result the making of expenditure policy has to pass in large part to civilian and military administrators, who can attend to the specific kind of comparisons in which the mind can successfully engage. But these administrators can at best make rational comparisons of specifics within their own agency's field, not between them. Hence, without substantial administrative reform, it would appear that a congressman would do well to become a specialist in interdepartmental and interagency program comparisons. Since even this assignment is too large, ideally a congressman ought to ask each major subdivision of government to identify a small variety of marginal expenditure programs, permitting the congressman then to approach expenditure allocations as a specialist in marginal comparisons among the lowest valued increments to programs of various major subdivisions.

Although I have not qualified this prescription adequately, it serves to emphasize the probable desirability of specific rather than aggregate marginal comparisons in Congress and of a highly selective policy with respect to the specific comparisons to be made. Some of Congress' much deplored refusal to deal with the larger issues in expenditure policy and its preoccupation with haphazardly selected detail is, I think, a laudable even if fumbling attempt to proceed by such a prescription.

As for the coordination of decisions reached by individual administrators, politicians, and others, it is only necessary to state again that debate on the objectives of the military and the objectives of welfare programs will ordinarily accomplish relatively little. Similarly, debate on policy alternatives conceived of in large aggregates of expenditures will help relatively little. If agreement can be reached through debate on specific comparisons and marginal choices, agreement is sufficient, assuming that the individual comparisons of specific alternatives have been well done. Agreement failing, all we should ask is that the processes through which mutual adjustment will produce policy as a by-product meet certain conditions yet to be defined by research.

What then is the appropriate role of the budgetary process in expenditure and tax decisions? I think the answer requires an investigation of the budgetary process from a point of view that has not been taken by previous writers. The literature on the budget, I think it fair to say, has not given extended consideration to the implications of incrementalism and partisan mutual adjustment; were it to give such extended consideration, many firmly held beliefs would turn out to be either erroneous or undemonstrated. My view of the conventional norms for the budgetary process is, therefore, that of an agnostic, except for my explicit rejection of certain budgetary norms listed in the first pages of this paper.

To indicate what might follow from verification of the hypothesis that incrementalism and mutual adjustment are major avenues to rational decision-making, let me speculate as follows, limiting, however, my examination of the budget process to its expenditure programing functions.

It appears possible that the formulation of a comprehensive federal budget as a strong recommendation to Congress for its expenditure decisions should be abolished. As a proposal for expenditure programs, the budget document is not very helpful to the kind of rational decision-making we have been describing; and, as a recommendation from the President and Budget Bureau that the expenditures-mix for the coming year should be as presented rather than slightly different, it is not very convincing. The circumstances of its formulation do not generate much confidence in it as an incremental program proposal, even if its formulation in some ways is well suited in congressional eyes to congressional control over the administrative branch.

In any case, a formal, comprehensive congressional overview of the budget should not be attempted, for it would only drive congressmen into the kind of abstract comparison of aggregates that we have argued is less satisfactory than highly selective comparison of specific programs. I might even suggest that the submission of the budget to Congress as a program for appropriations is made more defensible the less Congress is induced by its presentation to attempt to comprehend it in the large.

A comprehensive budget is best used, it may follow, as a background document to which any decision-maker can refer for reference and such guidance as he can take from it, playing a role in decision-making much like the role, as I understand it, of the Indian Five-Year Plan. A frequently revised budget, embodying both a report on prospective expenditures already authorized and recommendations of the Budget Bureau and President for programs not yet authorized might well always be available to but never thrust upon Congress.

Accordingly, congressional appropriations practices would be altered to permit Congress to make many successive appropriations for relatively limited numbers of functions or agencies, without a concentration of budgetary decisions at any one time of the year and, it might be hoped, to provide for automatic renewal of a very large number of expenditures so as to permit Congress to revise its programs in these fields only when it wished. . . .

Granted that this line of prescription for the budgetary process flies in the face of a sustained movement toward increasing dependence on the budget as a major coordinating instrument, no one has yet made a convincing case that the budgetary process is today an effective and rational coordinator; it has largely been assumed to be so. It is quite possible that the present line of budgetary reform, which goes back at least as far as the Taft administration, was suited to the much smaller government programs of earlier years. But when the Department of Defense alone uses roughly a tenth of the national product, when it spends more than the national product of some nations, when it purchases forty times as many products as marketed by Sears Roebuck, it is no longer safe to assume that the budgetary problem is still basically the same old problem.

Without raising any questions about budgeting within agencies, I suggest in short that comprehensive budgeting for the American government may be a prerevolutionary method of programing the expenditures of a government that has indeed gone through a revolution in its size, complexity, and involvement with citizens' values.

THE McNAMARA STRATEGY *
William W. Kaufmann

. . . WHEN President Eisenhower took office in 1953, the need for a disciplined approach to the military establishment seemed particularly acute. As a result of the Korean war, the Armed Forces had burgeoned from 1.4 million to 3.6 million men and women. Defense expenditures had also shot up; they stood at $49.3 billion as against $14.3 billion in 1950 and were now consuming 13.5 percent of the Gross National Product compared with 5 percent in 1950. As a result of these expenditures, the Army commanded 20 divisions and 18 regimental combat teams, the Navy possessed 1,130 ships together with 3 Marine divisions and their 3 supporting air wings, and the Air Force had reached its interim goal of 95 wings. Although this was a balanced force, there seemed no end to its possible growth. To the new President such a prospect was intolerable. In his view, "the foundation of military strength is economic strength. A bankrupt America is more the Soviet goal than an America conquered on the field of battle." With the Korean war drawing to its end, moreover, he could see no point to the retention of so large a ground force. The Soviets were credited with an active army of 175 divisions and were believed capable of expanding it to 300 divisions in the first month or so of a war. On this assumption, whether the United States Army stood at 20 or 10 divisions did not make a great deal of difference. The security of the United States in future would have to rest primarily on nuclear weapons. As the President was to say later: "Where these things are used on strictly military targets and for strictly military purposes, I see no reason why they shouldn't be used just exactly as you would use a bullet or anything else." Starting with this premise, it seemed entirely feasible to bring the Pentagon under close control.

The President used four major instruments in his campaign. The first was a

* From William W. Kaufmann, *The McNamara Strategy*, abridgment of pp. 21–23, 28–32, 169–189. (New York: Harper & Row, 1964). Copyright, 1964, by William W. Kaufmann. Reprinted by permission of the publishers.

National Security Council document called *Basic National Security Policy* (and known more familiarly to veterans of its drafting as BNSP). Issued annually, and purporting to set forth the basic strategic concept for the United States, BNSP has been described by General Maxwell D. Taylor as "a broad outline of the aims of U.S. national strategy and a more detailed discussion of the military, political, economic elements to support the over-all national strategy." In it, the Eisenhower Administration announced that the United States henceforward would place main but not sole reliance on nuclear weapons. With this guidance, the Joint Chiefs of Staff were expected to prepare a Joint Strategic Objectives Plan (JSOP) which would project force requirements five years into the future.

BNSP and JSOP obviously were not enough. General Taylor, testifying in 1960, threw further light on the Eisenhower approach:

> The NSC members hear the debate on the language of the "Basic National Security Policy," which is in general language which only the experts really understand. That debate takes place usually about May. Then the budget guidelines are issued which should produce military forces compatible with the strategic concept of that basic document.

The technique of the budget ceiling was, of course, the most powerful tool at the disposal of the Administration. President Truman had used it regularly between 1945 and the Korean war and purportedly had decreed that, after the fixed charges on the budget were met, military activities would receive one-third of the remaining revenues. President Eisenhower followed a similar practice. According to one reporter, there was "only one hard-and-fast restriction that the President . . . imposed upon the Pentagon in its development of forces: that the cost of the forces be financed on a pay-as-you-go basis—that is, within a balanced budget." In fact, once defense expenditures had been brought down from their Korean war heights, they remained remarkably constant as a percentage of the Gross National Product. For the six-year period between 1955 and 1960, the amount varied between 9 and 10 percent. Moreover, the New Look, as it became known, stabilized the allocation of funds among the three Services. The Air Force received about 47 percent of the budget, the Navy approximately 29 percent, and the Army about 22 percent. . . .

The technique of the budget ceiling . . . was reasonably successful in holding defense expenditures within ranges that the President found acceptable. In that sense it worked.

In another sense, however, it produced some very odd consequences. The budgetary tool can be a scalpel or a much blunter and less discriminating instrument. As General Taylor saw it in operation:

> . . . economic and budgetary factors have come to play an overriding part in determining military posture. Each year the services receive rigid budget guidelines which control the growth, direction and evolution of the Armed Forces. These guidelines are often set with little knowledge of their strategic implications.

As a matter of fact [Taylor went on], it is very difficult to determine their implications because of the way in which the defense budget is constructed. In spite of the fact that modern war is no longer fought in terms of separate Army, Navy, and Air Force, nonetheless we still budget vertically in these service-terms. Yet if we are called upon to fight, we will not be interested in the services as such. We will be interested rather in task forces, these combinations of Army, Navy, and Air Force which are functional in nature such as the atomic retaliatory forces, overseas deployments, continental air defense forces, limited war expeditionary forces, and the like. But the point is that we do not keep our budget in these terms. Hence it is not an exaggeration to say that we do not know what kind and how much defense we are buying with any specific budget.

General Taylor's conclusion from these observations was somewhat startling.

As a result of the foregoing conditions [he said], we have the strange phenomenon of the partial loss of control of the military in a Government where all parties, including the military, are dedicated to the principle of civilian control.

The difficulty was essentially twofold. BNSP was a remote and general document which really did not provide guidance on how the Administration wanted its defense dollars spent. Moreover, those dollars were appropriated directly to the Services, and neither the President nor the Secretary of Defense exercised very much control over what was being done with them. Despite BNSP and the budget ceiling, the Services enjoyed considerable latitude as to how they spent their funds. McNamara, when he came into office, was appalled.

. . . we found that the three military departments had been establishing their requirements independently of each other. I think the results can fairly be described as chaotic: the Army planning, for example was based, largely, on a long war of attrition, while the Air Force planning was based, largely, on a short war of nuclear bombardment. Consequently, the Army was stating a requirement for stocking months of fighting supplies against the event of a sizable conventional conflict, while the Air Force stock requirements for such a war had to be measured in days, and not very many days at that.

In one instance, McNamara discovered that the Army, "while in general far short of its stated requirements, had 270% of its requirements for 105 mm. towed howitzers, 290% of the requirements for 4.2 inch mortars; we had ten times as many 2.75 inch rockets as were required.

The field of research and development was particularly rich in examples of independent and frequently competitive Service initiatives. One of the most notable cases was the development of the Thor and Jupiter intermediate-range ballistic missiles. There was also the competition between the Nike and the Talos surface-to-air missiles. And duplication abounded in jet aircraft engine development. McNamara's favorite example of this prodigal development concerned fighter aircraft. As he informed a subcommittee of the Congressional Joint Economic Committee:

One of the most costly areas of duplication has been that of fighter aircraft. For example, in the 1955–58 period there were no less than four aircraft under development to perform the fighter mission—two in the Navy and two in the Air Force. The Navy aircraft were the F4H-1 and the F8U-3. The Air Force aircraft were the F-105 and the F-107. One might argue that there were special requirements associated with Air Force and Navy missions which necessitated basically different aircraft. Even so both the F4H-1 and the F8U-3 were, as the House Appropriations Committee noted in its report on the 1958 Defense Appropriation Bill, "all-weather fighters with approximately the same mission and operational characteristics." Accordingly, the Committee directed the Navy to "take prompt action to decide which of these aircraft it will place in production. This should be accomplished at an earlier date and with fewer test and evaluation aircraft than is presently scheduled." The Navy eventually chose the F4H-1 for production, but by the time the F8U-3 development was terminated, it had cost the Government over $136 million.

In the case of the Air Force, the F-107 was terminated at a cost of about $85 million. Even so, two of the four aircraft, the F4H and the F-105, were actually placed in production.

As the House Appropriations Committee noted, as early as May, 1957: "Each service, it would seem, is striving to acquire an arsenal of weapons complete in itself to carry out any and all possible missions."

Budget ceilings managed, in short, to keep expenditures under a degree of control. But by themselves they did not guarantee that the funds would be sensibly allocated. In fact, lacking firm strategic guidance, the Services became more competitive than ever. Since money was in relatively short supply, the battle for the budget intensified. In the field of research and development, each Service launched its own projects independently of the others in the hope of laying claim to some future mission and thereby increasing its share of available funds. Without sharper budgetary controls, the Administration found itself obliged either to increase its expenditures or to engage in a periodic but belated trimming of research and development projects. As in the case of the multiple fighters, the trimming usually occurred only after a great deal of money had already been spent.

Under the reorganization schemes instituted by the President, the Chiefs should have been able in theory to resolve some of these difficulties. But, as General Taylor noted, "in effect we put a sack worth $40 billion in front of four very earnest men and ask them to agree how to split it. That is asking almost the impossible whether the men are in or out of uniform." There remained the Secretary of Defense who, by 1958, had had his authority to run the Department reaffirmed in no uncertain terms. But the lack of clearly defined strategic objectives and the unwillingness to challenge the judgment of the military lingered on. Wilson shied away from "all that military stuff" and concentrated on trying to introduce efficiencies into arms production and procurement. Neil H. McElroy, Wilson's successor, looked at the "stuff" but seemed unable to decide what to do about it. When Senator Stennis asked whether the Secretary would welcome a Congressional decision on a choice among overlapping air defense systems, McElroy replied:

This is one area where we have not done very well in making a decision. As far as I am concerned, it would not bother me if you held our feet to the fire and forced us in connection with this budget.

Thomas S. Gates, when he became Secretary, revived the practice of sitting with the Chiefs when they disagreed on major issues. During the first six months of 1960 he participated in twenty-one such meetings and made decisions on six unresolved issues. General Lemnitzer noted this as a "great advance . . . in dealing with controversial problems and issues more quickly, resolving them, providing a decision, and getting on with the business." Even so, the Secretary remained an arbitrator of disputes rather than an initiator of policies. . . .

The determination of budgetary needs and the achievement of efficiency in the expenditure of resources for the requisite types of military capabilities is an intrinsically difficult task. It has been complicated in the Pentagon by several important conditions. Although the sheer magnitude of the defense organization cries out for decentralized decision-making and management, Service traditions and rivalries make a large measure of decentralization in budgetary and disbursement practices very difficult indeed. The problem is complicated still further by the fact that neither the Services nor the unified and specified commands embody distinct and noncompetitive combat functions. Each has claims which are related in important ways to those of the others. These competing claims have become greatly magnified with the impact of a rapidly changing technology on the weapon systems of the Services. Thus, to take a familiar example, the Polaris submarine with its sixteen ballistic missiles, a Navy system, can perform the same function as the Air Force's Minuteman missle in its protected silo. How much to purchase of each is in itself a hard decision; its difficulty is not reduced by rivalries between the Air Force and the Navy. Nor can the problem be satisfactorily resolved by letting each Service decide independently the procurement policies for its preferred systems. That road is bound to lead to great redundancies in some types of capabilities and serious shortages in other categories. An over-all view and centralized responsibility is required for this kind of decision.

The Eisenhower system of budgeting did not embody these essential characteristics. According to Alain Enthoven, Deputy Assistant Secretary of Defense for Systems Analysis:

It had several important defects, perhaps the most important of which was the almost complete separation between planning and decision-making on weapon systems and forces, on the one hand, and budgeting on the other. . . . In other words, the long-range plans for weapon systems, forces, and all of their supporting elements were made by the Services on the basis of their estimates of the forces required to assure our national security. Generally speaking, costs were not introduced systematically, either to test the feasibility of the whole program or for purposes of evaluating the efficiency of the allocation.

Budgeting, on the other hand, had as its point of departure the guideline dollar totals laid down by the Administration and based on estimates of the burden the economy could or should bear. The result was a gap. The "required forces" always cost much more than the Administration and the Congress were willing to pay. The process by which the conflicting interests were resolved was unsystematic and wasteful because it led to unbalanced programs.

Furthermore, the Secretary of Defense did not receive adequate cost data. The budgetary system identified cost by object classes—Procurement, Military Personnel, Installations, etc.—the *inputs* to the Defense Department, rather than by weapon systems and forces, such as B-52 wings and Army divisions, which are the tangible *outputs* of the Department. . . . Moreover, cost data were presented and financial management was conducted at the Defense Department level on a year-at-a-time basis. The full time-phased costs of the proposed forces were not presented to the Secretary of Defense. Because the costs of most programs are small in their first years, this led to the starting of many programs that could not be completed at anything like existing budget levels. Although a certain amount of this is a desirable hedge against uncertainty, it is clear that there were a great many wasteful stretch-outs and cancellations of programs that would not have been started if the costs of all of the approved programs had been anticipated.

This kind of procedure was unacceptable to McNamara. Not long after his arrival in the Pentagon, he described generally the role he visualized for himself. "I see my position here," he said, "as being that of a leader, not a judge. I'm here to originate and stimulate new ideas and programs, not just to referee arguments and harmonize interests. Using deliberate analysis to force alternative programs to the surface, and then making explicit choices among them is fundamental." Nearly two years later he characterized his basic management philosophy in the following terms:

It is a philosophy based on a decision pyramid and a system of administration in which all possible decisions are pushed to the bottom of that pyramid. But for intelligent decisions to be made at the bottom of the pyramid there must be a framework within which those decisions can be made. Basic policies must be established against which a decision-maker at the lower levels can compare his decision and gain some confidence that he is acting in accordance with a pattern of decisions elsewhere in the organization. This will lead to unity and strength rather than an imbalance, which can only lead to weakness.

And it is the establishment of these policies that can only be done at the top.

The basic policy that we have established is a policy that shifts from a reliance on massive retaliation to the option response or capability. . . . Now, this is a shift required, we believe, because of a change in the character of Soviet military forces in the world environment in which we find ourselves as a nation operating. It is a shift, however, that requires a complete rebalancing of the military forces of this Nation, and it is not something, therefore, that could be simply turned over to the Services for them to decide unilaterally how they should proceed.

We must insure that the Army is balanced to the Air Force, that the Navy is balanced to the requirements of the Army, that the financial budget is balanced to the military force structure required as a foundation for our foreign policy.

It is this type of decision that comes up to my level and, until we translate this basic policy into a balanced force structure, I really know of no other way to follow.

This isn't because I like to make decisions, and I don't happen to like to work six or seven days a week, twelve hours a day, but I don't know any other way to do it when passing through this transitional period.

The method which McNamara chose to assist him in making these decisions was the planning-programming-budgeting system—largely the work of Charles J. Hitch, his Comptroller. McNamara described the system's function briefly as he expanded on his management philosophy.

It is through this system that we look at the defense effort as a whole. Major program priorities can be meaningfully determined only in terms of the total program, and a proper balancing of all the elements of the defense effort can only be achieved at the Department of Defense level. For example, the size of the Polaris force cannot be determined in terms of the Navy shipbuilding program or even the entire Navy program, but can be validly judged only in relation to all of the other elements of the strategic retaliatory forces—the B-52's, the Atlas, the Titan, and the Minuteman ICBM's. Similarly, the requirement for Air Force tactical fighters cannot be determined independently of the requirement for Army ground forces. All such interdependent decisions must be made at one place in the defense organization, and in this process the Joint Chiefs and the Secretary must play a major role. Alone among the elements of the Department, they have the overall vantage point from which to reach sound recommendations on balanced military forces.

While I believe that unified planning, programming, and decision-making are indispensable to the effective management of the defense effort, I am equally convinced that the actual operation of the program should be managed, to the maximum extent possible, on a decentralized basis. The defense effort is entirely too big, too complex, and too geographically dispersed for its operations to be managed from a single, central point.

Thus, the organization and management of the Defense Department must be based on the principle of centralized planning and decentralized operation.

The planning-programming-budgeting system has become the device by which to do the centralized planning; through it, national security objectives are related to strategy, strategy to forces, forces to resources, and resources to costs. As described by Enthoven, the program "consists of a five-year projection of all forces, weapon systems, and other activities described in physical (or non-financial) terms, together with their costs, all as approved by the Secretary of Defense, plus a set of regular procedures for modifying the plan." Hitch has gone into some detail about the process by which this five-year projection is maintained and modified.

The first phase of the decision-making process—military planning and requirements determination—involves the participation of all appropriate elements of the Defense Department in their respective areas of responsibility. This is the phase in which the Joint Chiefs of Staff organization and the planners in the military departments play a particularly important role. Although the system provides for specific changes in plans and requirements at any time during the year, there is a need for a comprehensive review and analysis, at least once a year, of the entire longer-range military plan and the forces required to support it. The product of this effort is the Joint Strategic Objectives Plan (JSOP) which is prepared by the Joint

Chiefs of Staff with the assistance of the planners in the military departments. The military plans and force requirements are developed on the basis of broadly stated national security policies and objectives, and intelligence assessments of our opponents' likely future capabilities. This is a dynamic process. Plans are continually being modified as old assumptions are tested, new data are integrated, new intelligence information becomes available, and alternative ways of accomplishing specific military tasks are examined and new choices made.

Hitch now came to a critical part of the system: program packaging. The force requirements are directly related to the major military missions of the Defense Department; thus, whatever the Service origin of the forces—whether Army, Navy, or Air Force—where they perform the same functions they are put in the same package (of which there are nine), and displayed for purposes of comparison as to cost and effectiveness. As one example, all these forces which would perform the retaliatory mission in a strategic nuclear war appear in the first program package. According to Hitch, the Secretary then makes his decisions about forces in terms of the program packages. As Hitch describes the process:

> During this programming phase we try:
>
> First, to develop our programs on the basis of broad military missions which cut across traditional organizational lines, rather than on the basis of unilateral plans and priorities of the Military Services;
>
> Second, to relate resource "inputs"—manpower, materiel and installations—together with their costs, to military "outputs"—strategic retaliatory forces, general purpose forces, and others;
>
> Third, to coordinate our long-range military planning with short-range detailed budgeting by projecting our detailed programs at least five years into the future;
>
> Fourth, to appraise our programs on a continuous basis;
>
> Fifth, to control approved programs through a system of progress reporting;
>
> And sixth, to provide both physical and financial data in forms suitable for making cost-effectiveness studies of alternative force structures.

McNamara, testifying in 1962, explained further the reasoning behind the program packaging approach and the five-year projections.

> Because of the great technical complexity of modern-day weapons, their lengthy period of development, their tremendous combat power and their enormous cost, we believe that sound choices of major weapon systems in relation to military tasks and missions have become the key decisions around which much else of the defense program revolves. But the full cost implications of these decisions, present and future, cannot be ascertained unless both the programs and their cost are projected over a period of years, ideally over the entire life cycle of the weapon system. Since such long-term projections are very difficult to make with any degree of accuracy, we have fixed on a 5-year period, which is short enough to assure reasonably accurate estimates and long enough to provide a good approximation of the full cost.

Hitch points out the magnitude of the decisions and describes how they are approached:

We break down the cost of each program element into three categories—Research and Development, Initial Investment, and Annual Operating—each of which has its own particular significance in the decision-making process.

The first category, Research and Development, . . . represents the cost of bringing a new weapon or capability to the point where it is ready for operational use. Since the cost of development alone may run into very large sums, making a commitment to development is in itself a major management decision. For example, over $1.3 billion has already been committed to the Nike-Zeus anti-ballistic missile program, and another few hundreds of millions of dollars will be required just to complete the research and development phase. The decision to go ahead with only the development of the more advanced Nike-X represents an additional outlay of well over a billion dollars.

The Investment category represents the costs beyond the development phase required to introduce a new capability into operational use. These decisions many times involve outlays of 4, 5, and even more billions of dollars. Our investment in the B-52 force over the years is estimated at well over $7 billion, excluding the cost of tankers, air-to-surface missiles, etc.

The Operating costs are the annual recurring costs required to man, operate, and maintain the capability. Quite often the cost of operating a system over its expected life is more important than investment costs. For example, it costs us as much to operate and maintain an infantry division for one year as it does to equip it in the first place. Thus, operating costs can be crucial to the initial management decision to produce and deploy one weapon system as compared with another.

Therefore, wherever possible we try to estimate the total cost, including R&D, investment and operating costs through what we call the "first line life" of the weapon system before any decision is made to proceed with a major development.

The third phase of the system, after planning and program packaging, is the preparation of the annual budget estimates. The military departments submit their budget estimates early in October. They are reviewed by the Office of the Secretary and then passed on to the President for recommended inclusion in his annual budgetary submission to the Congress. As Hitch points out, the actual submission takes the traditional form.

The Five-Year Force Structure and Financial Plan is an internal Defense Department tool and does not represent an approved program of the U.S. Government. The Congress . . . reserves unto itself the right to authorize and appropriate funds, year by year, against this proposed program, and even the President . . . is not unalterably committed to the five-year program in detail. It is essentially a planning tool—a road map, if you please—of where we hope to move over the next five years.

The first five-year program was developed in connection with preparations for the fiscal year 1963 budget. Thereafter, with the original program as the starting point, the Department concentrated each year on projecting the plan by a year and on introducing changes and refinements into the program. According to Hitch, changes in the program were made as necessary, at any time during the year.

However, the majority of the important changes are concentrated in the three-month period, June, July, and August, following the completion of the annual JSOP by the Joint Chiefs of Staff. We hope that by the middle of August the Secretary will have substantially completed his program review so that the military departments can be furnished an approved program for the next five fiscal years 1965–69, upon which to base their budget estimates for fiscal year 1965.

The specific administrative procedure for making these changes is known as the "Program Change Control System." The basic elements of this procedure involve the submission of program change proposals by any major component of the Department of Defense, their review by all interested components, the Secretary's decision and finally, the assignment of responsibility for carrying out this decision to the appropriate military agency.

Hitch argues that this formal change procedure helps to ensure:

1. that there is only one channel for major decision-making;
2. that proposed changes receive a rapid, but complete, review by all parties concerned;
3. that program decisions are made on the basis of the best information available, including a validation of their long-range cost implications;
4. that all major changes are made only after approval by the Secretary of Defense; and
5. that there is always available an up-to-date, approved five-year program for U.S. defense activities.

It should be noted that the program change control system does not operate at quite the stately pace that one might expect on the basis of its formal description. McNamara, who has now been exposed thrice to the workings of the system, described, early in 1963, what happened on the first occasion.

This year, in contrast to last year when we had to develop a 5-year program from the ground up, we started the budgeting cycle with an approved program projected through fiscal year 1967. This was essentially the same program I presented . . . last year. We realized, of course, that changes in this program would be needed as time went on; first, to reflect the action of the Congress on our fiscal year 1963 budget, and then to take account of all the numerous changes which are bound to occur in the international situation, in our requirements for military forces, in technology, and in costs. Accordingly, we established last summer a program change procedure designed to provide an orderly method for proposing, reviewing, and approving program changes. The procedure affords all elements in the Defense Department concerned with a particular proposal a full opportunity to present their views. For example, an Air Force proposal to modify its airlift fleet would be referred to the Army for comment as a user; to the Navy because of its impact on the sealift requirement; to the Joint Chiefs of Staff as representatives of the using commands, as well as to appropriate parts of my office. When all of these views have been assembled, Mr. Gilpatric or I review each proposal and render a decision or, in some cases, ask for further study. Where major issues are involved we discuss the matter in greater detail with our principal military and civilian advisers. Indeed, such major issues as the RS-70, Nike-Zeus, strategic forces, and so forth, were given individual and extensive study by the Chiefs, and their views were considered before the decisions were made.

The program change procedure went into effect last July and, up until the time the budget estimates were submitted in early October, several hundred program change proposals were received. These program changes would have added about $40 billion to the previously approved 1964–67 program base. The sizable sums requested were by no means unexpected, inasmuch as we had eliminated the arbitrary budget ceilings which had been used prior to 1961.

The program change procedure has unquestionably increased the workload on the Office of the Secretary of Defense, but I was particularly anxious that nothing should be done to discourage the military departments from submitting any program change they felt was necessary for the defense of the Nation. This was consistent with President Kennedy's instructions to me to (1) develop the force structure necessary to meet our military requirements without regard to arbitrary budget ceilings; and (2) procure and operate this force at the lowest possible cost.

The total of the fiscal year 1964 programs and budgets submitted by the Services and defense agencies amounted to $67 billion. All of the budgets were carefully reviewed jointly by the budget examiners of my office and the Bureau of the Budget, as has been the custom in the past. The analyses resulting from this review were forwarded to me for decision. In consultation with our principal advisers, Mr. Gilpatric and I then thoroughly reviewed all of the outstanding issues. Our decisions were transmitted to the respective Services and, in the final step of our review, outstanding differences were resolved. As a result of this review, we were able to reduce the approximately $67 billion requested by the Services to the total of $53.7 billion in new obligational authority recommended in the President's budget.

Although the five-year force projection and the program change procedure placed an extraordinarily heavy responsibility on McNamara, they also provided him with a more precise and integrated picture of American combat power than any previous Secretary of Defense had received. They also displayed for him in an orderly way the kinds of choices—expressed in terms of capabilities and costs—that he had available and must make in order to determine the shape of the military establishment. But neither five-year projection nor program change proposals could tell McNamara what automatically were the preferred choices. For that kind of advice he turned to another set of devices.

Perhaps the most important technique is that of operational research or systems analysis. Here, the war game or the exercise, with its vital military inputs, is wedded to considerations of cost so that the policy-maker can obtain some knowledge about the degree of military effectiveness that can be achieved with a particular capability for a given expenditure. As Hitch has pointed out,

there is a need for . . . detailed and intensive analyses of special problem areas such as conventional vs. nuclear-powered aircraft carriers, the need for a new long-range interceptor aircraft, the use of aircraft to enhance Army mobility, etc.

Many of these special requirements studies are initiated by the Secretary of Defense to help solve particular problems which arise during his program and budget review or to fill gaps in the data available to him. Others are initiated by the military departments, the Joint Chiefs of Staff, or other elements of the Office of the Secretary of Defense.

In each case we are interested not only in the military worth of the proposed requirement but also its cost. In our view, military effectiveness and cost are simply two sides of the same coin and must be considered jointly in the decision-making process. For example, the value to our national security of a five per cent increase in our capability to destroy a given target system can be decided only in relation to the cost of acquiring it—so long as we live in a world in which resources are limited.

We do not use systems analysis or cost/effectiveness studies as a substitute for sound and experienced military judgment but rather as a method to get before the decision-maker the relevant data, organized in a way most useful to him. There are and there should be many other inputs to the decision-maker, particularly in those areas which are not susceptible in whole or in part to quantitative analysis. While no important military problem is ever likely to be wholly susceptble to quantitative analysis, properly applied analytical techniques help to minimize the areas in which unsupported judgment must govern in the decision-making process.

McNamara has described a typical case in which he found this type of analysis relevant.

Now, one of the pertinent factors in the presentation of a Navy program is the Air Force program that is proposed to accomplish the same objective. And the only way I found to make an intelligent decision on the proposals of one service is to consider the actions of other services that relate thereto.

I can give the illustration of the Polaris. Whether we should have a 45-boat Polaris program, as the Navy has suggested, or a 29-boat program, as the Air Force thinks, is in part affected by the decision we make on the Air Force Minuteman missile program.

Exactly how this particular problem of choice should be resolved, McNamara did not go on to say. But he did describe in surprising and lucid detail the analysis which would precede the decision.

A major mission of these forces is to deter war by their capability to destroy the enemy's warmaking capabilities [deleted]. With the kinds of weapons available to us, this task presents a problem of reasonably finite dimensions, which are measurable in terms of the number and type of targets or aiming points which must be destroyed and the number and types of weapon delivery systems required to do the job under various sets of conditions.

The first step in such a calculation is to determine the number, types, and locations of the aiming points in the target system.

The second step is to determine the numbers and explosive yields of weapons which must be delivered on the aiming points to insure the destruction or substantial destruction of the target system.

The third step involves a determination of the size and character of the forces best suited to deliver these weapons, taking into account such factors as—

1. The number and weight of warheads that each type of vehicle can deliver.

2. The ability of each type of vehicle to penetrate enemy defenses.

3. The degree of accuracy that can be expected of each system, i.e., the CEP, which we know as circular error probability.

4. The degree of reliability of each system, i.e., the proportion of the ready operational inventory that we can count on getting off successfully within the prescribed time.

5. The cost/effectiveness of each system, i.e., the combat effectiveness per dollar of outlay.

Since we must be prepared for a fast strike by the enemy, allowances must also be made in our calculations for the losses which our own forces would suffer from the initial enemy attack. This, in turn, introduces a number of additional factors into our calculations, including:

1. The size, weight, and effectiveness of a possible enemy attack—based on estimates of the size and character of the enemy's long-range strategic offensive forces and the warhead yields, reliability, and accuracy of their weapon systems.

2. The degree of vulnerability of our own strategic weapon systems to such an attack.

Clearly, each of these crucial factors involves various degrees of uncertainty. But these uncertainties are not completely unmanageable. By postulating various sets of assumptions, ranging from optimistic to pessimistic, it is possible to introduce into our calculations reasonable allowances for these uncertainties. For example, we can use in our analysis both the higher and lower limits of the range of estimates of enemy ICBM's and long-range bombers. We can assign to these forces a range of capabilities as to warhead yield, accuracy, and reliability.

With respect to our own forces, we can establish, within reasonable limits, the degree of reliability, accuracy, and vulnerability of each type of offensive weapon system and we can establish its ability to penetrate the enemy defenses under various modes of operation. Obviously, the last factor also involves an estimate of the size and character of the enemy's defenses.

This is, admittedly, a rather oversimplified version of the actual studies and calculations we made to help us determine the size and character of the Strategic Retaliatory Forces required, now, and over the next 5 or 6 years—to assure that we have at all times the capability to destroy any nation which might attack us, even after we have absorbed a first blow from that nation.

Despite the fortunate absence of data about a strategic nuclear war, the problem and the requirements lent themselves, as McNamara pointed out, to relatively straightforward analysis. Making choices with respect to systems like Polaris and Minuteman, or the B-52, Skybolt, and the RS-70, could proceed with some confidence. Where limited war and the forces required for it were concerned, however, difficulties proved substantially less tractable. McNamara gave a number of reasons for this comparative lack of precision:

1. The great diversity of units and capabilities included in these forces;

2. The relationship between our general purpose forces and those of our allies around the world;

3. The wide variety of possible contingencies that they must be prepared to meet;

4. The important role that the Reserve components play in these forces, the Reserve and National Guard components; and

5. The sheer number and diversity of weapons, equipment, and supplies involved.

McNamara nevertheless persisted in his search for useful analyses. As he informed the Congress in 1963:

Last spring I asked the Chairman of the Joint Chiefs of Staff to establish a working group to study the requirements of U.S. general purpose forces to meet a number of possible non-nuclear combat situations in various oversea potential trouble spots. This group was headed by Vice Adm. H. D. Riley, the Director of the Joint Staff, with Lt. Gen. T. W. Parker, now Army Deputy Chief of Staff for Military Operations, serving as Vice Director, and included about 110 officers from all the services. Parallel studies were conducted in the military departments. The group was given considerable freedom to develop study situations which took the form of several different sets of assumptions and objectives. Then the group was provided with the latest intelligence data and was asked to examine the general purpose forces requirements to meet various kinds of enemy attacks in four broad geographic regions—Europe, the Middle East, southeast Asia, and northeast Asia. Including those examined by the military departments, some 16 different situations were studied.

In each of these situations, the specific requirements for ground forces and tactical air forces were examined in considerable detail. Requirements for naval forces, because of their special character, were examined primarily on a worldwide basis. This latter study proved to be particularly complex and difficult to define, and we will be giving it much more intensive study in future months.

McNamara found the resulting analyses highly useful; but, he cautioned,

in an effort to keep them manageable, a certain degree of over-simplification was inevitable. We are under no illusion that any of these situations would actually develop exactly as postulated for purposes of the studies. They never do and we know it. Furthermore, each situation, of necessity, had to be examined solely within its own context and no attempt was made to evaluate its effect on the world situation as a whole. Conversely, the interaction of other likely world events on the particular situation under study was also omitted from consideration.

Nevertheless, with all of these limitations, the general purpose forces studies constitute a very useful approach to the problem of determining the force requirements for limited war.

They have been of great assistance in assessing the capabilities of our land and tactical air forces to cope with situations short of general war occurring in various parts of the world, in some cases in more than one place at the same time.

They have also given us a much better idea of what we could do with our non-nuclear forces in these kinds of situations, and a much better grasp of the size and composition of the forces—both our own and the enemy's—that would most likely be involved.

Although this kind of analysis did not allow the comparison of alternative weapon systems and strategies to nearly the degree that characterized the war gaming of strategic nuclear conflict, it could take advantage of the experience that the Services had accumulated in conventional war. Consequently McNamara found it valuable—provided always that his advisers could support their judgments with data from that experience. If he became somewhat intransigent it was usually where he thought that advice and evidence had failed to coincide.

Such a failure had occurred, in his view, with respect to the Navy's requirements. As he told Congress:

We do not yet have acceptable situation-by-situation analyses of naval require-ments comparable to those now available for ground and tactical air forces. Until such analyses become available we are accepting the Navy's general purpose forces as being generally the right order of magnitude and composition.

This made it appear as though the Navy had gained its objectives without having undergone any trial by analysis. But appearances were deceptive. The major issue of policy was not so much the over-all size and composition of the Navy as it was the rate of its modernization. McNamara recognized the prob-lem.

I am well aware that the Navy faces a difficult problem of "block obsolescence" and that well over half of today's fleet was built during or just shortly after World War II. While it is true that these ships are now approaching the 20-year mark, the useful lives of many combatant types still can be extended by rehabilitation and modernization. Support and auxiliary types, in most cases, can be maintained in a serviceable condition much longer than 20 years.

In other words, even though he might not yet understand the basis for the Navy's requirements, McNamara refused to accept on faith the asserted dan-ger of "block obsolescence." On the contrary, he set out to analyze the validity of the concept itself.

Tentatively, one new attack carrier, conventionally powered, will be started every second year. The last carrier was included in the fiscal year 1963 shipbuilding pro-gram and, tentatively, the next carrier will be started in fiscal year 1965, and an-other in fiscal year 1967. If we were to carry through the Navy's long-standing pro-gram of one attack carrier every other year, the Midway-class carriers would be 30 to 32 years old by the time they were phased out of the force, clearly demonstrating that the 20-year rule-of-thumb is an artificial standard for measuring the useful life of naval vessels.

This kind of critical analysis no doubt was an inadequate substitute for a clear definition of functions and the establishment of a reasonably precise rela-tionship between the budgets, force levels requested, and the tasks that could be performed. But lacking such a device did not mean that McNamara would abandon his efforts to test, by all logical means, proposals coming up to him.

The area of research and development, with a budget for fiscal year 1964 of about $5.5 billion, called for still another style of analysis and decision-making. McNamara was not happy with the way the program had been going.

Of the 10 or 15 major systems I examined at one particular time, systems we have procured over the last three to five years, no one of them had an actual cost less than 300 percent of the original estimate, and several of them had final costs that were approximately 1000 percent of the original estimate. This represented a serious penalty to the Government, a penalty, I believe, that at least in part we can avoid.

That was not the only problem.

Research and development expenditures, whether measured in budget terms or in program terms, have been mounting steadily over the years, but too much of this effort is not producing useful results. What we want are weapons and equipment that the fighting man can use. We are not interested in supporting the intellectually challenging, but militarily useless, engineering "tour de force." If we are to make optimum use of our available scientific and engineering manpower resources, we must plan our program carefully and concentrate these resources where they will make the greatest contribution to our military posture.

As part of the effort to allocate resources more efficiently in the highly uncertain field of research and development, McNamara inaugurated what he called a "program definition phase."

This is the phase in which we, together with our contractors, do our thinking and planning—before we start "bending metal."

Very briefly, the program definition phase begins with the solicitation of proposals from industry and involves a number of early study contracts whose purpose is simply to define the program, prior to authorizing full-scale development. In the early stages of the program definition phase we do not attempt to establish rigorous specifications, preferring to encourage initiative and innovation on the part of our contractors or contractor teams. Indeed, where competing approaches present an unusually difficult choice, we may support more than one approach throughout the whole program definition period.

Working together, a contractor team can explore in depth the many unknowns which are present in any new effort. They can accomplish the overall system design, define the subsystems and major components and begin the early stages of laboratory experimentation and design. Most important, they can identify the critical problems and make good estimates of how long and how much money it will take to solve them.

With this information at hand, we are in a much better position to decide whether or not to proceed with full-scale development. And if we decide on full-scale development, the basic scientific and management team will have already been established, with a visible history of successful collaboration during the program definition phase. Finally, it will be possible to make the decision for full-scale effort with far greater assurance that the cost estimates are sound, that the performance of the system will meet the promise, and that the military requirement will be filled at the time needed.

Prior planning, and even feasibility testing of "pacing" components, are a lot cheaper than having to reorient, stretch out, or terminate expensive projects after they have been started. There are, of course, exceptions to this general rule. Where a development can add a new and unique dimension to our military capability like the A and H bombs and the ICBM, great costs and risks are justified. But such cases are rare. The typical development promises, if successful, to achieve a capability that can also be achieved in other ways or represents an improvement of but modest proportions in our total military capability. In these cases the urgency is not as great and the employment of a more measured and orderly approach to development and production is fully justified. In fact, I have observed that in most cases careful and comprehensive prior planning actually saves time as well as money and results in more effective and more dependable weapons.

McNamara gave the Congress two illustrations of weapon systems going through the program definition phase.

The mobile medium-range ballistic [missile] program . . . for which we are requesting large appropriations in fiscal 1964, has not yet progressed through the program definition phase. Until it does, we won't know for sure what we can accomplish with that weapon. After it passes through that phase, we may believe it is unwise to proceed further with it. Of course, next year we would come back and tell you that, why we arrived at that conclusion; and certain funds that might have been appropriated would remain unspent and, of course, you would wish to withdraw the appropriation.

Another project in the same status is Titan III. This is the large solid-propellant booster . . . which will have a capability of placing about 27,000 pounds in a low earth orbit. Its primary purpose is to give us a flexibility of solid propellants at a cost lower than the presently estimated costs for the liquid-fueled alternative, which is the Saturn booster.

. . . We have placed contracts with contractors to undertake the initial studies. . . . They run in the low millions. The total program is estimated to cost something on the order of $800 million. We are going to spend a few million dollars to find out what can be accomplished. As one of the committee members implied the other day, to complete it successfully will require technological developments which have not yet occurred.

McNamara summed up the role of different techniques of analysis and decision-making in his management of the Pentagon when he explained:

In adding to a defense budget as large as the one we now have, we begin to encounter the law of diminishing returns, where each additional increment of resources applied produces a smaller increment of overall defense capability. While the benefits to be gained from each additional increment cannot be measured with precision, careful cost/effectiveness analysis can greatly assist in eliminating those program proposals which clearly contribute little military worth in relation to the resource expenditures involved. We have applied this principle throughout our program and budget reviews.

McNamara derived several important benefits from the whole planning-programming-budgeting process with its emphasis on analysis done in terms of cost and effectiveness. Perhaps outstanding among them was that the system obliged both his military and civilian advisers to present and discuss major defense issues in terms that were readily comprehensible to him. It was now possible for the Secretary to discharge his legal responsibilities and choose knowledgeably among the many alternatives that confronted him. Moreover, the system—although by no means perfect in this respect—gave him a way of looking at functionally related aspects of the defense establishment, wherever these activities might be located organizationally. The ability to cut across organizational lines, and particularly to integrate both the complementary and competitive functions of the Services within the major program packages also permitted comparisons and a degree of efficiency which had been impossible with previous management techniques. This ability offered still another benefit; it reduced the need for the vast reorganizations that had shaken the Pentagon periodically since 1947. Responsibility for the management of the Department of Defense was clearly vested in the Secretary and he now had the

means, through the planning-programming-budgeting process, to exercise his authority in a systematic and orderly way. In effect, he had found a substitute for unification of the Services and establishment of a single Chief of Staff.
. . .

THE IMPACT OF ANALYSIS ON BARGAINING
IN GOVERNMENT *
William M. Capron

DOES the current addition to Washington's alphabetic vocabulary—PPBS —signify that a real and important change is occurring in the Federal government's decision-making process? Or do the techniques, devices, and ground rules summed up in the terms for which those initials stand—Planning-Programming-Budgeting System—merely represent a systematic eruption which will leave unaffected the real elements—and the actual results of—the "bargaining," or decision-making process, in government? . . .

Is Analysis "Anti-Political"? I would like to get one rather basic point out of the way at the outset: to my mind (and as far as I know, in the minds of others who helped to initiate PPB) there is no question that this system is very much a part of the political process. Indeed, if it is not—or at least does not become a political instrument—then it will be for naught. Professor Aaron Wildavsky, in a recent paper [1]. . . suggests that some of us at least do indeed view systems analysis as "superior" to the "ordinary" political process and antithetical to that process. I dissent from this view. Any suggestion that we are somehow degrading politics and political judgments, that we are substituting "rationality" for the "irrationality" of the political process lies only, as far as I can tell, in the minds of those who have made this charge. I will grant that I recognize that in the dialogue of the last 18 months and, indeed, going back over the last 10–15 years, there have been some advocates of a greater use of systematic analysis of one form or another who have perhaps given the impression that they were promoting an approach to public policy issues which was in some way antithetical to politics and to "political" decision-making. Perhaps some analysts have felt that this was what they were up to. But it seems to me a complete misunderstanding of the basic decision-making struc-

* From a paper delivered before The American Political Science Association in New York (September 1966), by William M. Capron of the Brookings Institution. Reprinted by permission of the author and the American Political Science Association. The views expressed herein are those of the author and do not necessarily represent the views of the Trustees, Officers, or other staff members of the Brookings Institution.

1. "The Political Economy of Efficiency: Cost-Benefit Analysis, Systems Analysis, and Program Budgeting," University of California, Berkeley: Institute of Urban and Regional Development, September 1966 (Preprint for limited circulation).

ture of our system of government and the role of the Executive, the Congress, interest groups, and the public at large to view the greater reliance on more formal analysis of policy issues and alternatives as in some sense basically (and necessarily?) changing the underlying process, relationships, and roles which are embedded in our system and have been throughout our history.

While accepting PPB as a part of the political process in this country, it seems to me perfectly consistent for me to go on to suggest that in my view, to the extent that this system is in fact accepted and becomes a fully working part of the budgetary and program decision-making process, it must certainly have a significant impact on that process. It may be perfectly true, as has been suggested, that a broad range of decisions will not be affected no matter how skillful and splendid the analysis provided by the Executive Branch: the pork barrel will still offer a rich and tempting diet of pork (though this "pork" is usually poured concrete) and we may still have Cross-Florida barge canals and Arkansas River projects—and even perhaps dams on the Colorado—even if we substantially improve the quality and sophistication of the "cost-benefit analysis" applied to evaluating such proposals.

Three Impacts of Analysis. Accepting this point, I would still assert three claims for the potential of the wider use of systematic analysis in government:

—the *dialogue* between the parties involved (the bureaus, the departments, the Executive Office of the President, the Congress, the private interest groups and "constituencies") will be conducted differently and will certainly be "impacted" by PPB

—*some* decisions will be different from what they otherwise would be without this approach

—and *some* of these decisions will be *better* than they would have been absent the use of more formalized analysis.

Of these three claims, the second is certainly more difficult to substantiate than the first, and the third incomparably more difficult to substantiate than the first or second. Indeed, until the art and science of political science and economics (and philosophy?) have advanced beyond their present stage of very rudimentary development, the last statement can only, in the final analysis, be defended as an individual value judgment and cannot in any meaningful sense be "substantiated."

I have used and will continue to use the term "budget process" and "budget decision" as a short-hand to encompass not only the dollars and cents decisions but also the *program* decisions and *policy* decisions which are affected by and reflected through the budgetary process. This is a usage which seems to me increasingly appropriate in Washington at least since 1961, since the Bureau of the Budget has become the focal point, as far as the Presidency is concerned, for the organization of the President's legislative program, a key part of which is the Budget itself. (As I recall my days (and nights) as Assistant Director of the Bureau of the budget, a very large fraction of my time was involved in dealing with policy and program issues which had only a peripheral connection and relation to expenditures in a quantitative sense.)

I am more than willing to adopt the basic framework and language to which Professor Lindblom first introduced me in order to consider the role of analysis and its impact in government decision-making. The Lindblom language is reflected, of course, in the title of this paper: "bargaining." And having for a while played a role in what can usefully be considered a bargaining process, I find this comfortable and relevant as a framework for considering the role of analysis. In this framework, I suppose the key question can be put as follows: is the bargaining *process* and/or the result of the "bargain" significantly affected if one or more of the "players" in the bargaining process employs systematic, explicit analyses of one variety or another? As I have already indicated, my tentative answer is "yes" to this question and, indeed, "yes" to both the *process* and *result* aspects of the question. Does this mean that judgment, intuition and "hunch" are downgraded or eliminated in the decision-making or bargaining process? To ask the question I think is to answer it, and this for two reasons. In the first place, I would be a poor advocate for the greater and greater use of analysis, and a poor supporter of efforts to expand the areas in which we develop a facility in using various analytic tools and an increase in the sophistication and breadth and reach of analysis, if I were to argue that analysis allows us to bring a kind of "neutral rationality" to government decisions so that we can turn to the computer to grind out the answers to policy issues untouched by human hands—or minds. I would be a poor advocate to try and argue this point because it is trivially easy to demonstrate it is a point with feet of clay—indeed, it is made of clay up to its armpits!

The Hierarchy of Decisions and of Analytic Forms: Cost-Effectiveness, Cost-Benefit, Systems Analysis. It is perhaps appropriate to say a word about terms like "systems analysis" and "cost-effectiveness" and "cost-benefit analysis." There is I think growing consensus on the use of these terms, though still a good deal of fuzziness in individual cases as to how a particular kind of analysis should be properly denominated. One convenient way of looking at the various art forms which go under the generic heading of "analysis" in this context is to recognize that we have a hierarchy of decisions which we can view either from the "top" or from the "bottom." Starting from the top, we have the very basic and broadest policy issues and policy choices. Should our marginal tax dollar be devoted to education or to transportation or to health or to an increase in the defense budget? Should a broad new Federal program be instituted not only to land a man on the moon but to attempt to start a whole civilization there—or perhaps on Mars? Questions at this pinnacle of the decision hierarchy may be (and, I would argue, should be) profoundly affected by the results of analyses at lower levels in this decision hierarchy but are not themselves the subject of useful formal and systematic analysis—at least at this stage. There are two reasons for this. First, the awesome complexity of comparing such alternatives, each with so many sweeping implications and ramifications for our society, is well beyond our capacity, given the status of the analytic art and the sciences this art employs, and I suspect this will be the case for a long, long time to come. Second, and more fundamental, these choices between basic and broad alternative public purposes and their rank order and weight depend so fundamentally on basic and illusive value judgments which (absent an explicit social welfare function) must be the personal judgment of each of us. As we move down the decision hierarchy, analysis becomes more manageable and also more directly influential and significant in the choices that are made. For example, once we accept, at least provisionally, the notion that the Federal government should give support to elementary and secondary education, the analyst can then—still at a rather high level of suboptimization—lay out alternatives for those who must make these decisions.[2] However, it is for this kind of choice that the impact of analysis on bargaining becomes rather easy to identify, namely, the way the alternatives are put and the explicit measures which are developed may be very much affected by the analysis—and the analyst (e.g., the choice between alternative techniques and levels of support to achieve "improvement in elementary and secondary education").

Analysis can only be said to "make decisions" at the very lowest level of suboptimization. Once an appropriation has been passed by the Congress and where a program's purposes are reasonably clear-cut and quantifiable, the choice of particular techniques to implement these programs may be made completely (or at least heavily controlled) by the results of one form of "analysis" or another. A clear-cut (though some may argue trivial) example is the job of air traffic control by the FAA. While human judgment still plays a significant role in the day-to-day, hour-to-hour, and minute-to-minute decisions of the air traffic controller, he relies more and more on automatic decision-making generated by various types of computerized and electronic gear and "analysis." And systems in the works may largely eliminate the human decision altogether. However, once one goes above this level—and in some programs one never gets down to this level—judgment plays a role and, as one moves up the hierarchy, judgment plays a more and more important role. At the middle and higher reaches, indeed, the judgment of the analyst is crucial, because at this level of "systems analysis" (or cost-benefit, or cost effectiveness), objectives are only given to the analyst in the vaguest form and, since typically more than one objective is involved, the analyst is required to make many judgments as to the way in which the multiple objectives— typically competing objectives (at least at the margin)—are to be melded and molded into the analysis. It has been suggested that some of the most significant efforts in systems analysis have actually been more important in the dis-

2. The phrase "those who make these decisions" and are potential customers of the analyst's output include, in the case of education (in ascending order), the Commissioner of Education, the Secretary of Health, Education, and Welfare, the President (rather, "the Presidency" which includes his key advisers, especially the Director of the Bureau of the Budget), and the relevant subcommittees and committees of the Congress, and finally the House and Senate. There are four relevant subcommittees and committees, the authorizing committees and the appropriating committees. To make the list complete, I should include a wide variety of interest groups such as the NEA, perhaps state school superintendents, major school superintendents, PTA groups, and so forth and so on at great length.

covery and specification of *objectives* than they have been in elucidating alternative *means* of reaching objectives.

Reasons for Introducing PPBS. In assessing the potential effect of government-wide use of systematic analysis, it is instructive to examine the motives of those who have played key roles in pushing the Establishment in this direction. I know from my own experience that one of the principal factors which motivated people in the Budget Bureau to insist on a greater use of analysis has been the fact that, typically, both program and budget recommendations coming to the President from the Departments and agencies have not contained any alternatives and have denied the President the option of making meaningful choices. The options have been screened out before the President has had an opportunity to choose among them. This great failure is frustrating to the Budget Bureau and to the President. Moreover, not only is the typical budget request as it comes forward to the Budget Bureau lacking in alternatives, but there is not even available to the Budget Director and the President he advises the kind of information which allows one to judge the effect on a given program of either a decrease or an increase in the funding level finally recommended to the Congress. The result of this is that the judgment of Budget Bureau staff is often superimposed on the judgment of those presumably much more knowledgable about the program. And the Budget Bureau inevitably acts, at least sometimes, in a very arbitrary fashion—arbitrary because those required, say, to cut X-hundred million dollars from a given program area have nothing before them to indicate the impact of that cut, or the impact of the manner in which they allocate that cut among various program elements. Equally significant to some of us has been the conviction that the application of systematic analysis to programs all across the board will not only encourage the examination of alternative ways of meeting program objectives, but will actually lead to the invention of new techniques for achieving public purposes. This, indeed, is the hallmark of a really good systems analysis, namely, that quite new ways of looking at problems have led in turn to the development of quite new *and better* ways of meeting problems)

Is PPB Revolutionary? Having mentioned some of the reasons lying behind the move to PPB, I would emphasize that I, at least, do not regard PPB and, more particularly, the emphasis on systematic analysis in the Federal establishment as really revolutionary. The whole system seems to me to be a quite natural *evolution* and the emphasis on analysis, while intense and ubiquitous, is, after all, neither wholly new nor revolutionary. Some sectors of Federal activity have for many, many years been subjected to systematic and regular procedures of analysis. In fact, one of the difficulties in getting enthusiastic support for this new emphasis on analysis is the deservedly bad repute in which some types of analysis have come to be held. The outstanding candidate for this role, in my view, is water resource cost-benefit analysis where, typically, the quality of analysis has been mediocre and the "guidance" to policy has been at best imperfect and irrelevant, at worst plain wrong. The fact that bad analysis can be done and the fact, moreover, that the water resource field is re-plete with examples of the manner in which the analyst can twist his assumptions to get the politically desired result is a powerful argument indeed for those skeptical of this whole effort. My response to this skepticism is the obvious one, namely, that because an approach and set of techniques have been abused in the past does not mean inevitably that they must be.

What can be done about "cheating" by the analysts who are directed to "make the case" for the projects and program the agency (and its constituency) have already decided they want? This will happen—witness the questionable assumptions (often hidden) in water-resource cost-benefit analysis. How can the abuse of analysis be handled? For one thing, elements in the organizational structure at echelons above the level at which the analysis is performed as well as "competing" agencies at the same echelon (especially, it is hoped, the Cabinet officer in whose department the program being analyzed is located) should insist that the analyst:

make *assumptions explicit*

carry out analysis with *alternative assumptions*

conduct *sensitivity analyses*

Occasionally, (perhaps on a sampling basis) the analyses will have to be redone independently to make sure the results are not biased by key hidden assumptions, quirks in the methodology, etc.

The Role of the Bureau of the Budget. The role of the Bureau of the Budget deserves a special word in this context. It is, of course, just another player in the bargaining process of Federal budget decision-making, but the Bureau, at least at its best, performs as the President's agent, which means that it takes a Presidential view of the decisions that come before it. Now, there is no question that the Presidential view is a very political view. But it is a political view which has by its nature a breadth which is lacking in almost any other player in the bargaining process: the bureau and department, the Congress (and particularly the Congressional Committee) and all the private interest groups. The very fact that the President must balance conflicting interests for his own political purposes in a sense places a requirement for a more systematic and analytic approach than is typical when one speaks as an advocate of a particular agency or interest group point of view. The fact that many values and the interests of many elements in the community must be taken into account in coming to final Presidential decisions lends added value to the use of an articulated systematic approach. As the President's major staff arm on program and budget matters, the Bureau sometimes likes to think of itself as, and to play the role of, "the taxpayers' counsel" at the government bargaining table. In particular, it is at the Budget Bureau level that the competition among major program areas comes to a head. At least one force for resisting the seemingly insatiable appetite for funds on the part of the advocates of many program areas is a simple fact which the Bureau and the President are required to recognize: if Program A gets more funds, other programs will get less. This is a fact of budgetary life, at least in the short run.

Does PPB Require Centralization? This leads me to comment briefly on the

organizational implications of PPB and to discuss more specifically the suggestion which has been strongly urged by Wildavsky (and less publicly by many
in Washington) that PPB requires a significant increase in the *centralization*
of the whole decision-making process. Briefly, this seems to me to be a complete misreading of PPB. Potentially, at least, PPB will permit, if properly implemented, a rationalization of the centralization-decentralization relationships
from the President to the Cabinet officer and major agency head to the bureau
and division level and down to the suborganization units which go to make
up the Federal hierarchy. As one moves up the hierarchy, if the inputs called
for in the PPB system are adequately developed, it would be possible for the
decision-maker at any level to make the choices among the elements for which
he has responsibility, but to a large extent to devolve on the decision-makers
below him responsible for each one of these elements the choices *within* each
of these elements. In the present system, unhappily, the cabinet officer is almost
compelled (if he wishes to really manage his department and to discharge the
responsibility which is nominally his) to "second guess" those way down the
line in his agency. Likewise, as I suggested above, the Bureau of the Budget,
because of the paucity of relevant information available to it under the pre-
PPB system for Presidential budget decision-making, is frequently compelled
to involve itself in detailed decisions which it is inherently less capable of
comprehending and properly deciding than those more directly involved in
the implementation and execution of the program. It seems to me, for
example, an excessive centralization when the Budget Director makes decisions with regard to the details of the staffing of regional offices of a given
Federal agency; and yet if he has no information before him which really indicates what that agency and what its individual offices are up to and yet is
constrained to keep some reign on expenditure levels, he is almost compelled
to make rather arbitrary (and, I am sure in some instances, capricious and
unfortunate) decisions. In short, the present system seems to me to lead to a
pernicious and promiscuous kind of centralization all the way up the line, and
it is this perverse centralization in the present system which hopefully at least
PPB will go some way to correcting. PPBS, when developed, can be a powerful force for a rationalization of the Federal decision structure and for *decentralization*.

PPB and Reorganization. Wildavsky and others who have commented in
the same vein are certainly right, it seems to me, in suggesting that the development of a sensible program structure does contain within it significant reorganization implications for the Federal establishment—even though not necessarily reorganization leading to greater centralization. Just to cite one example:
if there had not already been a strong move to establish a Department of
Transportation, I suspect that two or three years with PPBS would have provided the President and his chief advisors with a strong, if not compelling,
reason for moving to establish such a department. No matter what the program structure, however, there will continue to be, as there is in any budgeting system, the need for the central authority—the Presidency—to pay partic-

ular attention to what in today's jargon are identified as the significant "interfaces" among various major program categories. There is no question that the program budget, insofar as possible, should be structured so that the program categories, subcategories, and program elements make sense from a *program* standpoint. And for obvious reasons, a program budgeting system can operate much more effectively to the extent that the *organizational* structure corresponds more or less to the program structure. Since our present organizational structure reflects a whole series of "accidents of history," I agree with the suggestion that, over time at least, reorganizations will be, if not compelled, at least strongly encouraged by the development of a sensible program structure. But, I repeat, I see no reason to expect greater centralization to result.

Some of the inadequacies in the initial attempts to develop program budgets in the last several months have unquestionably resulted from the fact that present *organizational* structure in some areas has little relation to a sensible view of *program* structure. Since PPB must be viewed primarily as a tool and technique for improving Presidential budget decision-making and not primarily as a tool for guiding budget implementation (e.g., the actual expenditure of funds once appropriated by the Congress), it is very important, in my opinion, that the rationalization of the program budget be guided primarily by the development of sensible and viable program categories and components of those categories and that the demands of the organizational structure as it presently exists play a distinctly secondary role. I would add that in practice I recognize that compromises must be made to accommodate the existing organizational structure, at least until the necessary reorganizational moves have been made. One must recognize that even if we go to a structure which is more highly centralized than at present, there will always be difficult choices to be made as to where to place particular program subcategories and program elements since in at least some significant instances a case can be made that a given program belongs in two or more places in the overall structure. Finally, it would be foolish to ignore the fact that we are not starting from scratch, that important ties, loyalties and the strongly held views of groups represented at the bargaining table are going to leave us—no matter how hard we push in the direction that I'm suggesting—with some (to say the least) rather peculiar alignments of program and organization. This, though, is yet another instance which supports my basic thesis, namely, that the PPBS effort is bound to have an effect on the bargaining process and on its outcome, even though it will not in every instance control that outcome. Relationships which are now suppressed or ignored will be put on the bargaining table and may force people to recognize interrelationships (or, if you like, "interfaces") which up until now have conveniently been forgotten.

The Root vs. the Branch: Lindblom's View and Analysis. Another of Professor Lindblom's contributions to the discussion of government decision-making can be read to reject the notion that systems analysis can be of much use, except perhaps in very special cases. In "The Science of 'Muddling Through,'" he contrasts two approaches to public policy decision-making. One he identifies as the "rational-comprehensive" or root method; the other as the "successive limited comparisons" or branch approach. While recognizing and accepting many of the difficulties with the former (rational comprehensive) approach and further recognizing that more often than not the "successive limited comparisons" approach is what we observe in practice, it does not seem to me that an emphasis on articulate systematic analysis is inconsistent with Lindblom's preference for the successive limited comparisons approach, which he considers to be the more realistic and reasonable of the two methods. He points, for example, to the difficulty in starting out with a clearly articulated statement of the objectives before one begins empirical analysis. As I have indicated above, one of the hallmarks of good systems analysis as it has come to be practiced is that simultaneously with a definition and testing of alternative means is the refinement and specification of objectives. Furthermore, the *comprehensiveness* of any given systems analysis will depend on the ingenuity of the analyst, the kind of data available to him, and the amount of resources that are at his command in undertaking the analysis. I would urge even if Lindblom's preferred approach—successive limited comparison—is selected as appropriate to the case in hand, that it should be undertaken *systematically* with assumptions clearly specified. This is particularly necessary since in this approach, as he points out, many of the interrelationships with other parts of the system are ignored. It is important that those who will use the results of the "analysis" have called to their attention the limited nature of the analysis so that the limited, partial and incomplete nature of the argument will be understood. I am not so concerned with "comprehensiveness" or the lack thereof, but rather with the use of a very casual and inarticulate "analysis" in place of a specific, "spelled-out" analysis. The "consumer" of the results should be in a position to judge whether or not the particular analysis is in fact useful to him—whether he wants to be guided, in whole or in part, by the results of that "analysis."

Another idea associated with Lindblom's name and closely related to the above is his emphasis on "incrementalism" in public policy decision-making. Again, I would insist that this is *not* necessarily inconsistent with the philosophy underlying PPB. Most analyses will, indeed, be at the middle range of the decision hierarchy and will focus on relatively marginal changes in existing programs. However, there are occasions when it is appropriate to attempt a more ambitious analysis, an analysis which moves toward the end of the spectrum identified by Lindblom as the "rational-comprehensive" method. The use of a more sweeping, broader analysis (in the terms employed by some, "systems analysis" instead of "cost-benefit" or "cost-effectiveness" analysis) will be appropriate in at least two situations: first, where whole new program areas are being considered, that is, where the President, for example, is contemplating the initiation of Federal activity in an area in which the Federal government has not before performed. Very often in this situation there will be a number of options open to the President. It may very well be, and indeed in general I would urge that it is ordinarily the desirable strategy, that the first actual program moves be small and that experimentation characterize the initial efforts in a new area, since I fully share with Professor Lindblom and others skepticism at our ability through analysis to develop a very sure-footed understanding of the effect of government activity in an area where it has not been tried. This is so particularly because relationships are difficult to determine *a priori* in many instances and that in this situation we are largely working by analogy of one sort or another and have little or no directly applicable empirical evidence upon which to draw. However, it is in these instances of really new undertakings where a system-analytic approach, in the hands of a skilled analyst, often can lead us to be very inventive in developing new approaches and new techniques. The second area where a fairly broad sweep in a systems analysis is appropriate—where incrementalism won't do, at least as far as the analysis goes—arises where we have become seriously dissatisfied with the effectiveness of an existing program and where we wish to undertake major redirection and revision of a given Federal activity.

The Value of Obscurity on Objectives. I must refer to one other theme which is frequently emphasized by the skeptics,[3] namely, the value in many areas of government activity in *not* being explicit about objectives. Representatives of this view have pointed out that at least in some instances agreement on specific programs is possible, even though the interests of various affected groups in the program may be not only quite different but, in terms of their overall value schemes, antithetical. From this one *might* draw the inference that an attempt at articulating an analysis which identifies objectives will actually make agreement on programs and on budgets *more* difficult than reliance on implicit reasoning and bargaining to arrive at the program's contours and level. It is, moreover, pointed out that the implicit "analysis" in a bargaining system with various interests and values "taken care of" by the representation of these interests and values by one or more players at the bargaining table is a good and workable system. I would agree that, by and large, the system has been pretty good and pretty workable and I further agree that one can undoubtedly identify specific cases (especially where feelings run high) which might be put back rather than forward by an attempt to subject the program to an explicit analysis—or at least to make that analysis public. (But the Executive Branch can develop its position based on analysis without injecting analysis into public debate.) However, I am not persuaded by this view as a regular and basic guide. For one thing, the fact that there are different interests and different values concerned with particular programs does not mean that systematic analysis will necessarily make agreement on specific program decisions and specific budget decisions impossible. It is possible, for example, to reflect explicitly the degree and extent to which different objectives or values will be realized under different alternative approaches and different levels in a given program area. Thus, the interested parties will be able to identify the ex-

3. I had intended to identify this group as the "Yale School" but knowledgeable friends in political science warned me that this would be unfair to some at or from New Haven and also, perhaps, unclear.

tent to which *their* own particular interests—their own particular weighing of the outcomes—will be achieved. Furthermore, as I indicated at the outset, PPBS does *not* mean a basic nor drastic alteration in the bargaining system relationships. Nor does it signify the non-representation of all the present players in the game.

In brief, while I find much that is useful and insightful in the "skeptics" view of the governmental process, I think I can do so and still maintain a faith in the value and efficacy in an increased reliance on systematic analysis as an aid in making public policy choices.

PPB and Congress. Turning to another topic, it is frequently asked what will be the effect of PPBS on the relations between the Executive Branch and the Congress and on the authorizing and appropriating process within the Congress? I do not have the background or expertise to discuss this question with any kind of completeness—and I can certainly not speak from the Congressional point of view. However, there are several points that should be understood. In the first place, let me reiterate a point made above: PPBS was designed and is being pushed as a technique or set of techniques which will improve the *Presidential* budget decision process. The President, having made his decisions, can forward his recommendations to the Congress in a variety of forms. It is worth emphasizing that in any case the *implementation* of the President's budget once the Congress has authorized and appropriated funds requires expression of these budgetary decisions in the familiar "object class," input-oriented, and organizational-unit oriented terms of the traditional budget. There is no special difficulty or extra burden placed on the Executive Branch in translating the results of the program budget and the decisions reflected therein to the Congress in the familiar terms which they seem, at least up until now, to prefer. Thus, I see no particular technical difficulty in acceding to the apparent will of Congress that the familiar budget structure be maintained with regard to their deliberations.

There is, however, one central and sensitive point involved in the implications of PPB for Congressional-Executive relations: a key element in the new system is its emphasis on *multi-year* programming and budgeting. The standard pattern is that each program be developed in terms of a five-year program plan and that this be translated into a five-year financial plan. It has been suggested that this is in a sense impossible for a President to live with since he does not wish "to give up his options" (to use a phrase President Johnson has made familiar)—that he does not wish to tie his hands earlier than he must with regard to the future. The President need only make recommendations to the Congress with regard to the *next* year's appropriation levels, plus recommendations with regard to the new programs (or amendments to old programs) on which he is *now* (in the current session) requesting action by the Congress. Even though the President decides not to submit formally the five-year program and financial plans to the Congress, there is little question, given the facts of life in Washington, that the existence of these plans will not only be well known but that they will, one way or another—

above or below the table—come into the hands of the Congress. I recognize that there is a certain amount of risk for the President in this situation. Only by the repeated and steadfast reiteration of the fact that the plans for each program beyond the next budget year—the year for which he must make specific recommendations—are only tentative and do *not* represent any kind of Presidential determination or commitment, can he avoid creating the impression that he is committed for the future. And even if the President does this, he will occasionally and inevitably be embarrassed—but Presidents have been embarrassed by "commitments" for the future in the past, and have managed to survive this embarrassment. One way of minimizing the danger of an apparent premature commitment to funding levels and program development is to have program and financial plans (beyond the current and next budget year) presented in terms of two or more alternative funding and activity levels. It is worth noting that Secretary McNamara for the last several years has discussed the defense five-year program plan and force structure with the relevant committees of the Congress and has not been embarrassed especially that these plans have been revised from year to year. While the Secretary's relations with Senator McClellan, Congressman Rivers and other key figures on the Hill have not always been completely placid, it is not at all clear that his difficulties have been due to PPB!

My own forecast, for whatever it is worth, with regard to Congressional attitudes toward PPBS is that over the next several years in at least some areas, the Congressional committees (both substantive and appropriation) will come to discuss administration recommendations in terms of the dialogue of PPBS. In other words, I think that it will not only affect the bargaining *within* the Executive Branch (e.g., among the agencies and between the President and the agencies), but that it will also directly enter the bargaining dialogue between the Administration and the relevant focal points in the Congress— and the private constituencies. Indeed, already there are moves afoot on the Hill to develop staffing available to, and responsible to, the Congress to review systems analyses, program budgets and the like. Just as the Budget Bureau (at least on a sampling basis) must carefully review the various analyses performed within the agencies, so I think—even though it will make some of my former colleagues and associates very uncomfortable—it is desirable that on a sampling basis the Congress have available to it the necessary expertise to review in depth and very carefully the kinds of analyses being performed in the Executive Branch. Indeed, I see nothing inappropriate with the Congress itself initiating analyses of various programs, examining various alternative ways of accomplishing program purposes, and evaluating the effectiveness of existing undertakings.

Does PPB Matter: The McNamara Case Study. It would be too much to ask that I end this discussion without calling your attention to the best demonstration of many of the points that I have suggested above and, most importantly, the fact that an increasing reliance on systems analysis throughout the Federal establishment will indeed have a significant effect on the bargaining process and on the results of that process. This "evidence for the prosecution"—or rather, for the defense, since this is the American Political Science Association—is, of course, provided by the McNamara years in the Pentagon. While Wildavsky and others have questioned to what extent the use of a PPBS system has *really* had much effect and have pointed out that no one within the Establishment has yet laid out the case that this, in fact, has occurred, I find it hard to understand how even the most casual observer, dependent only on the *New York Times* as his information source, can question that at least the dialogue has been profoundly affected, if not the result. In the nature of the case, of course, it is impossible to establish in any irrefutable fashion that the results of the decision-making process have been affected by changes in that process since we are never able to develop an acceptable and rigorous test of the question—no specific decision is ever reached under the "pre" and "post" McNamara systems. The very fact that the Services have developed the capacity for performing very sophisticated systems analyses (perhaps in self-defense against the wiz-kid onslaught from on high) is certainly evidence of the impact which analysis has had on the bargaining process.

Has systems analysis within the defense decision area not only affected the dialogue in which the bargaining has been conducted between the Secretary and the Services) and particularly between the Secretary and the Joint Chiefs) but also affected the actual decisions which have been made? There is at least some evidence available to the outsider which strongly suggests that certain crucial decisions made in the last five years by Mr. McNamara and approved by the President have indeed been directly and even dominantly affected by the analysis. The most important of these analyses have been performed under the direction of Alan Entoven, now Assistant Secretary for Systems Analysis. It is my impression, for example, that the airlift-sealift decisions which have been made in the last year or two have been strongly influenced by systems analysis results. The decision to develop and acquire the C-5—a large logistics carrier—and the characteristics of that carrier were strongly influenced by analytic results produced in the last few years. The composition of the airlift-sealift forces—the "mix" of systems—has likewise been much influenced, if not dictated, by the analyses which have been performed both in the Office of the Secretary and by the Air Force and the Navy. And the still-disputed TFX decision was, from all indications, not unaffected by systems analysis.

Furthermore, I would offer in evidence the brief but incisive description of the development and implementation of PPB in the Defense Department in the period beginning in 1961 provided by Charles Hitch, until recently Comptroller of the Defense Department, in the Gaither Lectures, now available in book form under the title *Decision-Making for Defense*. It is clear that Mr. Hitch is anything but an unbiased witness. It is furthermore clear that this book does not pretend to be the kind of systematic "systems analysis" of the impact of systems analysis which apparently is called for by skeptics like Wildavsky. Yet, a reading of this work, making all the allowances for the undoubted prejudice with which Hitch understandably addresses this subject, offers a rather impressive dossier with regard to the radical changes in the dialogue, and perhaps in the quality and nature of the defense decisions taken in the period since 1961.

A final note on the McNamara revolution: While this phenomenon has been tied closely to the Secretary as an individual and has been in large measure a personal triumph, I am convinced that the McNamara-Hitch system will have a major impact on Defense decision-making for years to come. No successor could undo all McNamara has wrought—even if he wished to—and even if his successor is a person of the same rare quality.

Will It Work Across the Potomac? Will the same impact emerge—if we are willing to accept at least *some* impact from systems analysis on the defense scene in the last few years—over the coming five years on the domestic side as a result of President Johnson's dramatic memorandum of last August 25 announcing his determination to develop and apply PPB on a government-wide basis? It is too soon to tell and one would be foolish to make any kind of a flat forecast. We can perhaps, however, make some conjectural predictions. It is not too bold to suggest that we can be sure that the performance across programs will be very uneven. Indeed, within the defense decision-making arena itself, the impact of the systems analytic approach and the development of a program budget system has been uneven. Some problems and some program areas are more amenable to this approach, given the present state of our understanding and knowledge, than are others. And the same is obviously true on the domestic side of Federal activity. Furthermore, the aggressive and effective application of this new approach certainly depends on a number of factors. To cite just a few:

The viewpoint of the key players in the game. It is certainly clear, no matter how strong and insistent the exortation from the President and the Budget Director, that without the whole-hearted understanding and support of the Cabinet and independent agency heads the effect of PPB will be marginal. Certainly the major, or at least, a major reason for the effectiveness of PPB in the Defense context has been that the Secretary has grasped this (as Wildavsky himself has noted) as the major management tool by which he has "conquered" the Services and made himself the master of the Defense Department in a way far exceeding the degree to which any previous Secretary of Defense has ever exerted his authority and run his own show.

The effectiveness of the bureaucracy in alliance with its constituent groups and their representatives in Congress in resisting the effective implementation of PPB. There is little doubt on the part of those who have been in Washington in the last few months that there are certain loci of strong and effective resistance to changing the whole budgetary and program decision process. The success of this resistance will be very much dependent on the *de facto* control which the Presidency has over the activities in question and over the key personnel in the bureaucracy responsible for those activities. One can be sure that there will be certain program areas where resistance will continue to be more or less effective in blunting the attempt to make anything more than a pro-forma modification in the actual decision-making process and where only the most superficial and irrelevant attempts at analysis will be undertaken. I would suggest that this is not a peculiar characteristic of PPBS or systems analysis. Any attempt to modify significantly, the rules of the bargaining game will be strongly resisted by at least some elements of a bureaucracy as large and varied and, in some cases, as well entrenched as the Federal bureaucracy. As a first approximation, one can say that those who find the present arrangements comfortable and effective from their own self-interest and special interest view-point will resist changes of any kind, since change introduces uncertainty. The results of change for the individual bureaucrat, the individual agency, the individual Congressman and committee, and the individual special interest group may turn out to be good. They may also turn out to be bad. If things are reasonably satisfactory and comfortable now, the question facing these people and institutions is: "Why go along with attempts to rock the boat?" As an aside, I might add that one strong reason for supporting PPB lies precisely here: Quite apart from the intrinsic potential value of this new system should it be effectively implemented—or, put differently, even if it is not effectively implemented—there is real value in a periodic shake-up of the key centers in the Federal nervous system. And certainly if it has accomplished nothing else, PPB has already done this. It has forced people to rethink their own roles, the agency's roles; it is raising questions and providing a context in the bargaining framework in which questions can be raised which have largely been ignored in the past. All of this I submit is healthy and good as long, of course, as the boat-rocking is not to severe as to do more than ship a little water—we don't, after all, want to swamp the ship of State, just keep it responsive to changes in the currents, tides, and winds of government activity.

An assessment of the impact of analysis on bargaining in government must at this juncture be cautious and conjectural. I have tried to refrain from "overselling" or expressing wild optimism that the increased emphasis on analysis —and PPB *in toto*—will transform the quality of Federal decision and vastly improve public policy. On the other hand, I have indicated that I cannot share the view of those political scientists and old-hand Washington bureaucrats who think that PPBS is yet another passing fancy which will have no noticeable impact on anything—and will shortly fade away. Some representatives of this skeptical group seem to feel, in the absence of a violent revision in our basic governmental structure and process, that a modification as modest as PPB can have no impact. They appear to view the whole Federal decision process as involving "who is in what job and where is the real power" and "what will Mr. A do for Mr. B so that Mr. B will support A's pet project" and "what's in it for me, Jack?" This is not only a possible but sometimes useful way of looking at government. But viewed as the totality of the governmental process it is, I submit, badly misleading and incomplete. Even the most venal parochial party to governmental bargaining can be forced to take account of cogent systematic analysis—as long as some others at the bargaining table insist on making it part of the dialogue. My bet is that PPB (and its emphasis on analysis in particular) will have a far greater impact than the skeptics are ready to admit.

[*Editor's postscript:* A further note may be helpful on two important criticisms of PPBS that Capron glosses over. These are, first, that the system may lead (particularly in the hands of journeymen, rather than highly sophisticated, analysts) to the neglect of considerations which resist quantification; and second, that many programs have multiple and overlapping objectives which either cannot be weighted at all or cannot be weighted without incurring high political costs (in the form of offended constituents). Virginia Held, an enthusiastic observer of the PPBS "revolution," has recently described some of the efforts that are being made to overcome these problems.* Her report, in part, ran as follows:

In the Dorfman volume,† a paper by Ruth P. Mack and Sumner Myers . . . attempts to provide an analysis in cost-benefit terms that could be used to evaluate governmental expenditures on outdoor recreation. Benefits are calculated on the basis of what the authors call "merit-weighted user-days," which take into account various sorts of recreation for various sorts of people under varying conditions. The simple measure of "user-days"—a function of the numbers of people expected to use a park and of the lengths of time of their stays—is weighted to take account of evaluations that some user-days are better than others. The weighted figures include such judgments of social merit as that a day spent by a child in the wilderness has more lasting value than an adult's picnicking in a crowded, noisy park; that the marginal utility of additional recreation declines as larger amounts are made available; that equity requires government to provide relatively more recreational opportunities to those who most need them and can least afford private alternatives, plus many others. In ways too complex to examine here, alternative parks under consideration for a given expected number of users are then evaluated in terms of the "merit-weighted user-days" which they could be expected to provide. . . .

One of the most imaginative attempts to evaluate the effectiveness of programs with hard-to-assess objectives is a method devised by David Osborn, Deputy Assistant Secretary of State for Educational and Cultural Affairs. Built into this system, which is being programmed by the Franklin Institute Research Laboratory in Philadelphia, is the view that the agency's various activities have multiple and overlapping objectives, and that a conceptual structure delineating end programs aimed at through alternative means does not adequately reflect such overlapping. Osborn recommends a scheme of cross-multiplying the costs of the activities with a number representing the rank of its objectives on a scale. For instance, the exchange of Fulbright professors may contribute to "cultural prestige and mutual respect," "educational development," and gaining "entree," which might be given scale numbers

* "PPBS Comes to Washington," *The Public Interest*, Number 4 (Summer 1966), pp. 102–115. The quotations are from pp. 110, 112–113.

† Robert Dorfman, ed., *Measuring Benefits of Government Investments* (Washington, D.C.: The Brookings Institution, 1965).

such as 8, 6, and 5, respectively. These numbers are then multiplied with the cost of the program, and the resulting figure is in turn multiplied with an ingenious figure called a "country number." The latter is an attempt to get a rough measure of the importance to the U.S. of the countries with which we have cultural relations. It is arrived at by putting together in complicated ways certain key data, weighted to reflect cultural and educational matters, such as the country's population, Gross National Product, number of college students, rate of illiteracy, and so forth. The resulting numbers are then revised in the light of working experience, as when, because of its high per capita income, a certain tiny middle-eastern country turns out to be more important to the U.S. than a large eastern European one. At this point, country numbers are revised on the basis of judgment and experience, as are other numbers at other points. But those who make such revisions have a basic framework to start with, a set of numbers arranged on the basis of many factors, rather than single arbitrary guesses. As Osborn explains it: "We debate the numerical results we come up with but it becomes a revision process. The analysis gives us approximations to work with. If you break up your judgment into various parts you have something to talk about."

I leave you to assess the promise of these endeavors on your own.]

D.   Organization and Reorganization

THOSE characteristics of an administrative system that can be portrayed on an organization chart constitute only a small portion of its total character. Formal structure * is the easiest part of any organization to describe and control, however, and its relationship to the total organization does tend (except where the official leadership is exceptionally ineffective) to resemble that of bone structure to the total human body. For these reasons, writers about administration and chief executives of large organizations have always placed great stress on formal structure as an instrument of organizational control.

Through at least the 1930's, American students of public administration were almost totally preoccupied with formal structural arrangements. In addition, they were normatively oriented. They did little research, but on the basis of commonsense logic and reflection upon experience they elaborated "principles" to guide those responsible for shaping formal organizational patterns. On the whole, their prescriptions were mechanistic. They assumed that the human members of organizational systems would routinely interact as if they had all the properties, and only the properties, attributed to them by the organization chart. Most of those who wrote in this vein acknowledged that they were oversimplifying, but they believed that they had captured the essentials.

* Formal structure may be defined as those patterns of interaction and accountability within an organization that have been officially promulgated as decision rules to guide individual actors in the organizational system.

As noted elsewhere,† the "principles" of administrative management have been devastatingly attacked but not replaced in the last two decades. This is quite a serious matter, because practical men charged with organizing and reorganizing bureaucracies have to rely on *some* general ideas, even if the best available are recognized to be inadequate. Philip Selznick is one of the very few writers of the postwar period who has endeavored to go beyond the traditional "principles" on their own terms. That is, he has sought to develop a sociologically plausible general theory of how chief executives can shape their organizations into optimally serviceable instruments of their purposes. In the selection reprinted here, he emphasizes that the shaping of formal structure should be approached as an exercise in estimating the significance and "precariousness" of values, not as one of neatly grouping like activities with one another. In addition, he stresses that formal structure gains meaning only as it is supplemented by education, indoctrination, and practical experiences which give the subunit elites strong senses of collective identity and common purpose. Some of the questions you may wish to consider after reading this selection are the following: Would Herbert Simon consider Selznick's recommendations principles or proverbs? ‡ Is Selznick's theory, with its emphasis on elites, applicable to organizational systems in which democracy is a central value? Of what value is Selznick's analysis to students of the politics of administration?

Arthur Schlesinger, Jr. discusses the motives that appeared to lie behind Franklin Roosevelt's unorthodox administrative practices. He writes that Roosevelt favored the proliferation of new agencies, that he regularly gave his subordinates overlapping missions and jurisdictions, and that he had little use for the merit system during his first term. It is instructive to compare Roosevelt's practice with Selznick's theory. You may also wish to consider the difference between Schlesinger's celebration of pluralism and Lindblom's.

Ferrel Heady's article is a case study of the passage of the Reorganization Act of 1949. That act remains the basic statute governing federal reorganization procedures. Unlike Selznick and Schlesinger, who write from the chief executive's vantage point, Heady is primarily concerned with Congress' approach to the reorganization issue. His narrative makes clear that federal reorganization involves far more than shaping the bureaucratic instrument to serve the President's will.

INSTITUTIONAL INTEGRITY, PRECARIOUS VALUES, AND ELITE AUTONOMY *
Philip Selznick

ALTHOUGH every effective policy requires sustaining social conditions, the urgency of this need varies greatly. It is most important when aims are not

---

† Alan Altshuler, "The Study of American Public Administration," Section I-C.

‡ Simon's contention that the traditional "principles of administration" are mere proverbs has been outlined and reviewed on pp. 59–61.

*From Philip Selznick, *Leadership in Administration*, pp. 119–130. Copyright © 1957 by Harper & Row, Publishers, Inc. Reprinted by permission of the publishers.

well defined, when external direction is not easily imposed or easily maintained, when fluid situations require constant adaptation, and when goals or values are vulnerable to corruption. This open-endedness, we have argued earlier, generates the key problems of institutional leadership. Among these is the defense of institutional integrity—the persistence of an organization's distinctive values, competence, and role.

The integrity of an institution may be threatened, regardless of its own inner strength, if sufficiently great force is applied to it. But in diagnosis we are mainly concerned with points of special inner weakness. From that standpoint we may say that institutional integrity is characteristically vulnerable *when values are tenuous or insecure.* This variation in the strength of values has received little scientific attention. Yet it commands much energy and concern in practical experience. In the course of building an organization, and establishing its separate units, group responsibility is fixed. But these "custodians of policy" will not be equally capable of sustaining their distinctive aims and standards. We need to know something about the social conditions that affect this competence.

The ability to sustain integrity is dependent on a number of general conditions, including the adequacy with which goals have been defined. Here we shall consider a special problem, the relation between precarious values and professional or elite autonomy. Our primary aim is to illustrate the potential contribution of institutional analysis to administrative theory. Therefore it may be helpful if, before dealing with administration proper, we first consider some other applications of the general idea. To do this, let us examine three ideas and how they are related.

Elite. For present purposes, this term refers to any group that is responsible for the protection of a social value. Often this responsibility is accepted consciously, but that is not essential. There would be no great harm in substituting the term "profession" or "professional group" for "elite," so long as the definition is kept in mind. Both terms have been used to designate men who carry out this basic social function.

Social values are objects of desire that are capable of sustaining group identity. This includes any set of goals or standards that can form the basis of shared perspectives and group feeling.

Autonomy is a condition of independence sufficient to permit a group to work out and maintain a distinctive identity.

These definitions are hardly final or unambiguous, but they will permit us to make some progress. The basic relation to be considered may be formulated as follows: *The maintenance of social values depends on the autonomy of elites.* Let us turn to the bearing of this proposition on (1) the general problem of institutional integrity, as it is familiar to the historian of culture; (2) certain aspects of political organization, as revealed in the history of Communism; and (3) certain technical problems of administrative management.

1. *Elite autonomy and cultural viability.* . . . . It appears that what is critically necessary for the functioning of elites is enough autonomy to allow the

maturation and protection of values. The achievement of this autonomy is a central task of professional associations, "little magazines," specialized schools, and a host of other devices for self-insulation used by groups in society that wish to protect and promote a particular set of values. Private universities with large endowments are better insulated from day-to-day pressures than are many public institutions, sustaining the autonomy of their professors and scientists. Literary elites are hard-pressed from the standpoint of autonomy because of the high cost of publishing and the commitment of that industry to the mass market. Hence literary groups may seek the shelter offered by private colleges able to subsidize esoteric journals. In our culture, the legal and medical professions are well insulated, others much less so. Those who are concerned for the protection of political, educational, aesthetic, and religious values, must find ways of providing the conditions needed to sustain the autonomy of culture-bearing elites.

The point summarized here is quite familiar to the historian of culture. But the basic relation between value maintenance and elite autonomy may cast some light on rather different and more unfamiliar situations.

2. *Political isolation and the combat party.* In an earlier work referred to previously, the author attempted to analyze the organizational aspects of Communist strategy and to understand the inner dynamics of the "combat" party. Here is a characteristic elite phenomenon. The Bolsheviks attempt to build a leadership corps of "professional revolutionaries" that maintains a long-run dedication to the aims of Communism while engaged in the struggle for immediate power objectives. Any elite group, to maintain itself as such, must take special measures to protect its integrity. Among the most common of these measures are: (1) selective recruiting; (2) specialized training, as in the elite school; and (3) withdrawal from the everyday pursuits of mankind, especially from exposed competition in the marketplace. Each of these devices strengthens the isolation of the elite, its capacity to shape its own identity free of external pressures. All of these devices, among others, have played an important part in Bolshevik political and organizational experience. For the purpose of this discussion, a single illustration will suffice.

An important phase of Bolshevik political history took place during a period of "ultra-left isolation" from about 1924 to 1935. During these years the Communist parties throughout the world followed a policy of extreme (but mostly verbal) aggression against democratic and socialist forces. The latter were presented as "social fascists," against whom all means, including violence, were in order. This was a period of "dual" trade-unionism, in which the Communists disdained to work within the legitimate—"yellow"—labor movement but created their own "red" trade-unions. The latter usually included only Communist party members and their periphery, but they did lay the basis for later effective penetration of the mass unions.

The general effect of this ultra-left activity was organizational isolation. At first glance, this seems to have been self-defeating, and the later reversal might be understood as a corrective measure. The Communists did indeed isolate themselves from the main body of the workers, hence from any significant influence in society. Nevertheless, *this long period of isolation served to consolidate the power of the Russian party over the International, to test and train the party cadres, and to intensify reliance on conspiratorial methods.* Out of this period of ultra-left phrases, revolutionary adventures, splits, purges, and intensive indoctrination, there emerged a powerful political movement. This is not to say that the Communist leaders designed it so. But the modern Communist movement is a product of its history; it owes elements of strength, as well as of weakness, to the apparently irrational period of "social fascism" and "united front from below."

Specifically, this character-forming period readied the organization for a new period of propagandistic deception and organizational maneuver. After 1935, organizational isolation was definitively—and permanently—rejected. Open Communist propaganda was increasingly retired to the background, and the party turned to slogans of "unity," "peace," and similar generalities that might offer access to wider sections of the population. The "red" unions were abandoned and the party entered the legitimate trade-unions. The old aggression against "bourgeois" politicians was relaxed, and the party could support a Franklin Roosevelt when that was expedient. . . .

. . . In effect the conclusion was drawn that the day for worrying about the Communist integrity of the parties was past; the basic weapon had been forged; the time for wielding it effectively had arrived. Insistence on correct ideological formulae was to be exchanged for acceptance of more flexible slogans, and organizational practices were to be adapted to the conditions of the arena.

The period of ultra-left propaganda and organizational isolation was an *internally oriented* period, dedicated to preparing a weapon that would maintain its integrity when it was thrown into active political combat. It was this period of sharp break with the looser, more relaxed socialist traditions; of heavy emphasis on party discipline, on political orthodoxy, on conspiracy, and on intensive indoctrination that made possible the maintenance of the hard core of the party despite severe shifts in political line (as at the time of the Stalin-Hitler pact), and despite the heavy pressures on party members to become adapted to trade-unionist and reformist perspectives. Communist members could become *deployable agents* in other organizations—always serving the interests of the party—only as they accepted the authority of the party leadership. To create an organization able to exert such authority was a task that could not be accomplished without strenuous effort. Most of the early history of the Communist movement was devoted to that task of building "revolutionary cadres."

The Communist combat party, by assuming an ultra-left propaganda posture, preserved its autonomy as an elite, isolating itself from the pressures of the political arena *until it was ready to resist those pressures.* Put another way, the Bolsheviks wished to maintain an institution embodying a precarious value: a party competent to deploy members as disciplined agents. A period of organizational isolation, fostered by ultra-left propaganda, helped to contribute the sustaining social conditions. This only repeats, in a particular context, the generalization noted above, that the maintenance of values depends on the autonomy of elites. We have drawn here on a general institutional theory to help make sense of a particular historical development. The better developed such a general theory is, the more inferences can be drawn regarding the phenomena under analysis.

3. *Administrative autonomy and precarious values.* One of the perennial problems confronting the architect of organizations is administrative autonomy. When should an activity be thought of as distinctive enough to be allowed a relatively independent organizational existence? . . .

Applying the theory of professional or elite autonomy discussed above, we may recast the problem in the following way:

(1) When an organizational unit is set up, especially if it is large enough to have its own administrative staff, an elite is created in the sense that some men now become professionally responsible for the protection of a social value. Probably this elite function is the source of most organizational rivalry.

(2) It follows from our general theory that isolation is necessary during periods of incubation and maturation, but may be modified when this character-forming task has been accomplished. Moreover, the more readily subject to outside pressure a given value is, the more necessary is this isolation. (Roughly, this means that the more technical a function is, the more dispensable is organizational isolation. In highly technical fields, a large degree of *social* isolation is won simply by the use of esoteric techniques and language, and by the evident importance of professional criteria as to appropriate methods of work.)

(3) This provides us with a principle that can help in making decisions about administrative autonomy. We appraise the given value (be it intelligence, health, education, psychological warfare, or customer service) and consider (a) whether the elite function of value-protection is required, and (b) whether special safeguards against outside pressures are needed. This may lead to the conclusion, for example, that a new staff unit ought to be attached directly to a top-command echelon—not permanently, but during a period when its basic perspectives are being laid down, its distinctive mission being evolved. Or such a unit might be attached to one *quite different* in function (but institutionally strong) for the express purpose of offering a haven to an organization charged with defending and developing a precarious value. Strong groups with similar responsibilities, who might feel threatened by the new unit, would thus be restrained from attacking it too directly.

An approach to autonomy in these terms is a radical departure from the attempt to build organizations according to the logical association of functions. That principle—which will of course always be relevant—is often violated in practice, and for good reason. It must be violated whenever values are unequal in strength. Organization planning is unrealistic when it fails to take account of the differential capacity of subordinate units to defend the integrity of their functions. The theory of elite autonomy permits us to deal with this problem systematically and openly. This is important because many decisions that do in fact face up to this issue must now be justified obliquely, and be half-hidden, since there is no accepted administrative principle allowing organizations to be treated differently according to the strength of their respective values.

Let us apply this idea to the classic headquarters-field problem. Given a headquarters organization and a field organization, to whom shall subject-matter specialists (say in recreation, medicine, or personnel selection) be responsible? To the technical staff chief at headquarters or to the head of the local field organization? The dilemma is that the headquarters staff will be concerned over values (whether good accounting procedure or good medical practice), but the field executive will be under pressure to get an immediate job done while perhaps taking insufficient account of the long-run consequences of his decisions. One answer has been "dual supervision," in which certain officers are thought of as "administratively" responsible to one superior while "technically" responsible to another. This recognizes the special role of technical staff personnel in developing and defending values.

But "dual supervision" really presumes an optimum situation, in which a strong value-oriented elite (the technical staff) has had enough autonomy to lay down professional criteria that are accepted by the line officials. When, as in medicine and engineering, values have been effectively matured, dual supervision is relatively easy, for the boundaries within which the technical and administrative personnel may operate are reasonably clear-cut and are tacitly or even formally recognized as part of the code of proper behavior. Even in such fields, however, where the boundaries are unclear, as in the development of criteria for certifying military personnel fit for duty, it is to be expected that the professional group will be vulnerable to external pressure.

When we deal with *precarious* values—say an information and education program, or a political intelligence operation—special attention to the problem of elite autonomy is required. In such cases, we may accept a much closer relation between headquarters staff and field personnel than would otherwise be justified, because we recognize the need for intensive communication during character-forming periods. Such periods also require special measures to resist potentially corrupting external pressures, and this means a more intense professional self-consciousness. Suppose a government agency establishes a new labor relations policy, championed by the headquarters staff, but of necessity using line executives (say on construction jobs) who are not fully in sympathy with this policy. In the early days of the agency, we may expect a centralization of the labor relations program, perhaps manifested in a rule permitting workers to register complaints directly at headquarters and in the establishment of field labor relations specialists who conceive of themselves as self-conscious outposts of headquarters in an alien environment. This centralization permits the autonomous maturation of values; later, when the desired policies have been well established, a greater degree of decentralization will be in order. . . .

The theory of elite autonomy, thus applied, . . . leads us away from rigid rules of administrative organization, yet it helps to identify the key elements that need to be controlled and in terms of which guiding principles can be set forth.

ADMINISTRATIVE IMPROVISATION AND BUREAUCRATIC COMPETITION IN THE NEW DEAL *
Arthur M. Schlesinger, Jr.

TO guarantee the scope, Roosevelt had to revamp the structure of government. By orthodox administrative theory, the antidepression activities should have been brought in under the appropriate old-line departments—Agriculture, Commerce, Labor, the Treasury. But Roosevelt felt that the old departments, even with new chiefs, simply could not generate the energy and daring the crisis required. "We have new and complex problems. We don't really know what they are. Why not establish a new agency to take over the new duty rather than saddle it on an old institution?" Hence the resort from the start to the emergency agency, an essential instrument in the Rooseveltian technique of administrative improvisation. If the obvious channel of action was blocked and it was not worth the political trouble of dynamiting it open, then the emergency agency supplied the means of getting the job done nevertheless. And the new agencies simplified the problem of reversing direction and correcting error. "We have to be prepared to abandon bad practices that grow out of ignorance. It seems to me it is easier to use a new agency which is not a permanent part of the structure of government. If it is not permanent, we don't get bad precedents."

The New Dealers, particularly those of the Brandeis-Frankfurter school, talked a good deal about the importance of a first-class Civil Service on the British model. Roosevelt accepted this as an aspiration. "Public service," he said proudly in 1934, "offers better rewards in the opportunity for service than ever before in our history." But in practice the professional civil service often seemed an arsenal of obfuscation. It had become, said Tugwell, "a way of choosing and keeping 'the best of the worst,' of making certain that, barring revolution, war or economic disaster, the chosen dullards could have a long, uneventful, thoroughly secure working life." More than that, the Civil Service register for upper-grade positions reflected the generally Republican character of the professional and business classes. Mathematics thus indicated that

* From Arthur M. Schlesinger, Jr., *The Coming of the New Deal* (Boston: Houghton Mifflin, 1958), pp. 534–536. Reprinted by permission of the author.

staffing the New Deal through the Civil Service would fill key positions with anti-New Dealers. In consequence, the new agencies did their best to bypass the Civil Service. By 1936 the proportion of employees under the "merit system" had materially declined.

The new agencies were plainly indispensable. They tended to have an administrative dash and *élan* which the old departments, sunk in the lethargy of routine, could not match. Yet the theory could be pushed too far. At times Roosevelt acted as if a new agency were almost a new solution. His addiction to new organizations became a kind of nervous tic which disturbed even avid New Dealers. By 1936 we find Tugwell pleading with him not to set up new organizations. "My experience—and Harry's—is that it takes almost a year to perfect a country-wide administrative organization and that while it is being done there is political turmoil over the jobs, criticisms of procedure from the field, jealousy on the part of old organizations which fancy their prerogatives are threatened and other sources of irritation."

Each new agency had its own distinct mission. But in many cases jurisdictions overlapped each other and even spilled into cabinet departments. This was sloppy and caused much trouble. Yet this very looseness around the joints, this sense of give and possibility which Henry Stimson once called the "inherently disorderly nature" of Roosevelt's administration, made public service attractive to men of a certain boldness and imagination. It also spurred them on to better achievement. Roosevelt liked the competitive approach to administration, not just because it reserved the big decisions for the President, but perhaps even more because it enabled him to test and develop the abilities of his subordinates. How to tell which man, which approach was better? One answer was to let them fight it out. This solution might cause waste but would guarantee against stagnation. "There is something to be said," Roosevelt once observed, ". . . for having a little conflict between agencies. A little rivalry is stimulating, you know. It keeps everybody going to prove that he is a better fellow than the next man. It keeps them honest too. An awful lot of money is being handled. The fact that there is somebody else in the field who knows what you are doing is a strong incentive to strict honesty." One can see, for example, in the diaries of Harold Ickes how the overhanging presence of Hopkins and Morgenthau caused Ickes to spend hours and days in intrigue and invective. One can also see how the feuding stimulated him and them to more effective accomplishment and kept every part of the relief and public works effort forever on its toes.

Sometimes the competitive theory could meet political needs too. Roosevelt, as the leader of a coalition, had to keep a variety of interests satisfied, or at least hopeful. What better way than to give each representation where decisions were made? Some agencies seemed to be staffed on the ancient Persian theory of placing men who did not trust each other side by side, their swords on the table. Everywhere there was the need to balance the right and the left —let Cohen and Corcoran write the act establishing the Securities and Exchange Commission, but let Joe Kennedy administer it, but flank him with

Jim Landis and Ferdinand Pecora. Rather than sitting on creative vitality any-where, give each faction something of a head and try to cope with the results. "He had an instinct," wrote Frances Perkins with insight, "for loose, self-directed activity on the part of many groups."

Competition in government, inadequately controlled, would mean anarchy. Adequately controlled, it could mean exceptional creativity. One consequence under the New Deal was a darkling plain of administrative confusion, where bureaucrats clashed by night. Another was a constant infusion of vitality and ideas. In a quieter time, when problems were routine, there would have been every reason to demand tight and tidy administration. But a time of crisis placed a premium on initiative and innovation—and on an organization of government which gave these qualities leeway and reward.

THE REORGANIZATION ACT OF 1949 *
Ferrel Heady

IN belated response to urgent and repeated requests by the Commission on Organization of the Executive Branch and by President Truman beginning in January of this year, Congress in mid-June passed a new general reorganiza-tion act.[1] The immediate reason for this legislation was to make the time-tested presidential reorganization plan procedure available as a means for put-ting into effect many of the recommendations of the Hoover Commission. A longer range objective was to revive the reorganization plan technique as a continuing method of dealing with problems of federal executive reorga-nization in the future. Although patterned basically after the Reorganization Acts of 1939 and 1945, the Reorganization Act of 1949 differs from each of them in important respects. Designed originally to grant a much stronger re-organization authority to the President, the measure as ultimately enacted falls far short of the mark. The legislative history of the act reveals clearly that we have not yet established a recognized balance of responsibility between the President and the Congress for reorganization of the executive branch. The way leading toward executive reorganization is still more like an obstacle course than a well traveled road.

REQUESTS FOR A GENERAL REORGANIZATION ACT

The Hoover Commission, at the instigation of Commission members who had followed closely previous efforts at reorganization, agreed unanimously

* From the *Public Administration Review,* the journal of the American Society for Public Administration, Vol. 9 (1949), pp. 165–174. Reprinted by permission of the publisher.

1. Reorganization Act of 1949, Public Law 109, 81st Cong., 1st sess., approved June 20, 1949.

upon the necessity of asking Congress for a renewal of the grant of reorganization power to the President which had expired early in 1948. In its first communication to Congress, prior to submission of its reports containing reorganization proposals, the Commission requested a reenactment and broadening of the power previously granted to the President to initiate reorganization plans, in this way stressing the importance of this preliminary move to clear the way for action on its forthcoming recommendations. President Truman followed this up a few days later with his first special message to the Eighty-first Congress, in which he likewise urged the necessity of reviving the reorganization plan procedure and seconded the suggestions of the Commission for strengthening the basic legislation.

By the timing of its request, the Commission plainly indicated the desirability of early consideration, although it did not explicitly say so. The President particularly emphasized the urgency of prompt action, pointing out that reorganization plans would have to lie before the Congress for sixty calendar days of continuous session in order to become effective. "Unless the necessary legislation is adopted in the early weeks of the session," he stated, "it obviously will be impossible to make effective use of the reorganization procedure during the present session."

LEGISLATIVE ACTION

Identical bills were promptly introduced in the House and the Senate conforming in all essentials to the wishes of the Commission and the President. The House Committee on Expenditures in the Executive Departments conducted hearings beginning on January 24, and reported a substitute bill containing committee amendments early in February. This bill was debated and adopted by the House of Representatives with only one significant amendment on February 7 by a lopsided vote of 356 to 9.

In marked contrast, Senate consideration proceeded at a snail's pace. Hearings began on February 2 before the Senate Committee on Expenditures in the Executive Departments, headed by Senator McClellan of Arkansas, a member of the Hoover Commission. Although the hearings ended on February 15, the committee did not submit its report until April 7, and the bill as reported differed on major points from the version previously approved by the House. After another long delay without Senate consideration of the reported bill, President Truman dispatched a second special message on May 9, in which he reiterated the "compelling reasons" for enacting a general reorganization statute and again pointed out that the submission of reorganization plans during the current session depended upon early enactment because of the sixty-day waiting period. A week later, on May 16, by a unanimous voice vote after brief debate, the Senate accepted the committee revision of the House bill, with one minor amendment adopted during debate, and sent the measure to conference committee.

A deadlock among the conferees held up further action for exactly another month. During this time, the Hoover Commission released its *Concluding*

Report, in which it repeated its original recommendation for a reorganization bill, and the President issued a statement which called for redoubled efforts to carry out the Commission's proposed reforms and stated that he would submit a number of reorganization plans "if a workable reorganization act passes the present Congress in time."

When the conference committee did reach an agreement, involving a virtually complete acceptance of the Senate views, and submitted its report, both chambers on the same day accepted the bill as reported. The President signed the measure on June 20. In a special message the same day accompanying seven reorganization plans transmitted to Congress, he noted that the act did not conform entirely to his own recommendations and those of the Hoover Commission, but stated that he was "glad to proceed" under the measure although not completely satisfied with it.

Behind these legislative moves and countermoves leading eventually to the passage of a new reorganization act, there is an instructive story of honest disagreements over legislative policy regarding executive reorganization, combined with some artful camouflage of actual intent and what appears to have been deliberate procrastination to stave off the day of decision. Three main controversial issues emerged. Two of them sprang from joint recommendations of the Hoover Commission and President Truman which departed from the pattern of the 1939 and 1945 Reorganization Acts. These related to the permanency of the grant of reorganization power to the President and to the exemption of specified agencies from the scope of the reorganization plan procedure. The third issue, which did not become important until the bill reached the Senate, had to do with the method by which Congress would indicate its acceptance or rejection of reorganization plans submitted to it by the President.

TIME LIMIT

The first innovation jointly supported by the President and the Commission was that the power of the President to submit reorganization plans should not be limited as to time, as had been the case in the earlier acts, but that the grant should be made on a permanent basis. Pointing out that the reorganization plan procedure had proved itself in two limited trial periods within the last ten years, and that "the improvement of the organization of the Government is a continuing and never-ending process," the President in his message called for permanent reorganization legislation which would go beyond the immediate need for authorization to implement the recommendations of the Hoover Commission and facilitate needed future reorganizations as well. The Commission was less explicit, but did say that the power of the President to prepare and transmit reorganization plans "should not be restricted by limitations or exemptions," and Mr. Hoover testified in favor of permanent legislation before the House Committee.

Some doubt was raised at the House hearing as to the wisdom of this feature of the pending bill, and during the debate on the House floor later, Representative Hoffman offered an amendment which would have set January 20, 1953, as the termination date, thus limiting the grant to the current presidential term. This amendment was rejected without a record vote. Prior to the Senate hearings, Senator McClellan stated publicly that he favored a time limit, and that he would seek in committee to set April 20, 1953, as the terminal date. The Senate committee report did set an expiration date, but selected April 1, 1953. This feature of the Senate bill was retained by the conference committee, and appears in the Reorganization Act.

The primary justification given in the Senate for the insertion of this limitation was that it provided a guarantee that there would be a periodic reappraisal of the effectiveness of reorganizations undertaken. A much more important reason was mentioned in the House debate. Passage of a reorganization act without a termination date would have meant that the grant of reorganization power to the President could have been withdrawn only by the passage of new legislation. In the event of presidential opposition and veto of the repealer, a two-thirds vote in each house would have been required to override the veto and end the grant. A minor consideration mentioned in favor of a time limit was that it might spur the President to act promptly to submit plans well in advance of the expiration date set.

The limitation on the reorganization authority which actually was imposed should not be a serious handicap. The date selected provides President Truman with the grant throughout the remainder of his term, and extends into the term of his successor during the first session of Congress. Presumably if the grant is satisfactorily used, it could be periodically renewed thereafter at regular four-year intervals.

AGENCY EXEMPTIONS

A second issue of major importance was whether particular agencies should either be exempted altogether from the operation of the reorganization act, or at least be guaranteed preferential treatment. In both the 1939 and 1945 acts, a list of exempt agencies had been an integral part of the legislation. The earlier measure listed twenty-one such agencies. The 1945 law reduced the number of exempt agencies to seven, but provided special consideration to four more, and allowed no change in the status of any agency if Congress had established its status after January 1, 1945. Moreover, it contained a provision designed to protect the exercise of quasi-judicial or quasi-legislative functions by independent agencies.

The Hoover Commission came out flatly against any exemptions. "Once the limiting and exempting process is begun," the Commission declared, "it will end the possibility of achieving really substantial results." Within the Commission there had at first been some feeling that language should be retained to safeguard regulatory functions, but for reasons explained in the Commission's letter requesting new legislation, this idea was abandoned. Adequate protection against unwise reorganization plans, the Commission asserted, "lies both in a sound exercise of the President's discretion and in the reserved power in the Congress by concurrent resolution to disapprove any proposed plan." The message of President Truman was even more emphatic, insisting that the new reorganization act should be comprehensive in scope, and that "no agency or function of the executive branch should be exempted from its operation." The President pointed out that "such exemptions prevent the President and the Congress from deriving the full benefit of the reorganization-plan procedure, primarily by precluding action on major organizational problems. A seemingly limited exemption may in fact render an entire needed reorganization affecting numerous agencies wholly impractical." The President echoed the Hoover Commission in answering possible objections by stating that "the proper protection against the possibility of unwise reorganization lies, not in the statutory exemption from the reorganization-plan procedure, but in the authority of Congress to reject any such plan by a simple majority vote of both Houses."

This coordinated stand against exemptions was reflected in the original bills which contained no exemptions of executive agencies. Vigorous supporting statements on this point were made at the hearings by Mr. Hoover, Assistant Director Lawton of the Bureau of the Budget, and Comptroller General Lindsay Warren. Nevertheless, it soon became obvious that the most provocative issue was that of exemptions. Spearheaded by a procession of spokesmen for the Army Corps of Engineers, from both inside and outside of Congress, most of the time at the hearings in each House was taken up by a series of pleas that this and numerous other agencies should not be brought under the reorganization plan procedure.

That this movement for exemption would bear fruit for some agencies was indicated when, on January 25, top Democratic leaders in both Houses informed the President in a weekly legislative conference that at least four agencies would have to be excepted if the reorganization bill were to pass. A few days later, near the end of the House committee hearings, Chairman Vinson of the House Armed Services Committee offered a suggestion which was seized upon by the Committee on Expenditures as a convenient middle ground between outright agency exemptions and complete equality of treatment for all executive agencies. His request was that any reorganization plan involving any part of the National Military Establishment should be submitted to Congress in a "separate package." That is, any such plan would have to relate solely to the National Military Establishment, excluding any unrelated matters. Mr. Vinson made much of the point that he was refraining from making any request for exemption, and said that he was asking only for "a day in court" when Congress could exercise its judgment on national defense without the intrusion of extraneous considerations.

The committee adopted this means of protecting four agencies in the bill as reported out. These were the National Military Establishment, the Board of Governors of the Federal Reserve System, the Interstate Commerce Commission, and the Securities and Exchange Commission. In explanation, the committee stated: "Under this procedure the Congress may vote on the merits of the reorganizations affecting one of these agencies without being obliged to weigh the merits of such reorganizations as compared with the merits or demerits of reorganizations affecting other agencies."

This provision stilled somewhat the doubts of agency spokesmen, particularly those concerned about the civil functions of the Army Corps of Engineers, since Mr. Vinson had taken the position that the "separate package" treatment for the National Military Establishment adequately protected the Corps. Nevertheless, Representative Halleck, having previously failed in a bid to have agencies added to the list in committee, offered an amendment on the floor of the House to include nine more agencies. This amendment was rejected 86 to 151. Representative Bailey then offered another amendment, adding only the Railroad Retirement Board, National Mediation Board, and National Railroad Adjustment Board, which was adopted by a vote of 122 to 99. The bill passed the House in this form, with no completely exempted agencies but with seven agencies guaranteed "separate package" treatment.

In the Senate this provision for special treatment agencies was eliminated, and it was not revived by the conference committee, so that it does not appear in the act as approved. This was not because of any lack of attention in the Senate to agencies desiring to be shielded against reorganization. Indeed, the key figure in Senate consideration of the bill, Senator McClellan, was outspoken in his determination that the Corps of Engineers should either be exempted entirely or otherwise definitely made immune from transfer of its civil functions. The Senate hearings, under Senator McClellan's guiding hand, consisted primarily of statements on behalf of the Corps of Engineers, most of them maintaining that the "separate package" feature of the House bill did not give sufficient protection. Other witnesses appeared on behalf of the railroad agencies listed in the House bill, the Federal Deposit Insurance Corporation, the Comptroller of the Currency, and the Federal Security Agency, either asking that they be added to the list of "separate package" agencies, or maintaining that the "Vinson formula" was inadequate. In a key committee decision, a proposal by Senator McClellan for outright exemption of the Corps of Engineers was defeated by a close 5 to 4 vote. This precluded efforts to exempt other agencies. Moreover, the committee also abandoned the "separate package" plan of the House bill, and reported a "clean bill" without special consideration for any agencies. The only remnant of the "Vinson formula" was an amendment proposed by the Senate committee and accepted by the Senate declaring it to be the policy of Congress that each reorganization plan submitted by the President contain only related reorganizations. This amendment was eliminated in conference and does not appear in the act.

LEGISLATIVE VETO

The explanation for the abandonment of any attempt to protect designated agencies against reorganization lies in an agreement which was reached in the Senate committee to alter the procedure for legislative veto of reorganization plans. Both President Truman and the Hoover Commission had assumed that if new reorganization legislation were passed, it would follow the provisions of the 1939 and 1945 acts in this respect. These acts had provided that a reorganization plan submitted by the President could be prevented from becoming effective only by the passage by both houses of a concurrent resolution of disapproval within the sixty-day period following submission. This two-house veto requirement was written into the reorganization bills introduced in the 81st Congress.

Although this issue was raised during House consideration of the reorganization bill, it was only in the Senate that the matter assumed major proportions. Three lines of argument were used during the debates as justification for altering the previous arrangement. One was that the two-house veto procedure was unconstitutional or at least that its validity was under a cloud, despite the extensive use of it while the earlier acts were in effect. Another was that "sensitive" agencies should be safeguarded by requiring affirmative action by each house approving any reorganization plan affecting them. The third ground was that only by giving each house an opportunity to prevent any reorganization plan from becoming effective could a "clean bill" be enacted which would eliminate agency exemptions. This last consideration, accepted by the Senate and insisted upon by it in conference negotiations with the House, resulted in a tightening of the legislative veto procedure against the wishes of the Hoover Commission and of President Truman, and a consequent serious weakening of the new reorganization act.

The attack on the issue of constitutionality was pressed in the House by Representative Hoffman. Speaking on the floor of the House on the day committee hearings began on the reorganization bill, he charged that the bill "seeks to reverse the constitutional legislative process." He amplified this stand in a written statement submitted to the House Committee on Expenditures, of which he was ranking minority member. The committee report rejected these arguments, whereupon Mr. Hoffman transferred his efforts to the floor when the bill came up for consideration. An amendment offered by him to allow rejection of any reorganization plan by a majority vote of either house was rejected there after brief debate, by a vote of 95 in favor and 142 against.

Later, in the Senate debate, Senator McClellan also expressed some doubt as to the validity of the two-house veto, but this factor was not decisive in Senate abandonment of it. In view of the extensive use of this form of the legislative veto under two earlier acts, and the unchallenged grants of even broader reorganization powers to the President without any provision for legislative veto in 1933 and during both World War I and World War II, it is doubtful that serious credence can be given to the contention that the two-house veto involves an unconstitutional delegation of power.

Several suggestions were made that reorganization plans affecting "sensitive" agencies of special concern to the Congress should go into effect only if during the sixty-day period after submittal each house of Congress put itself affirmatively on record as favoring such a reorganization plan. This procedure of positive action by both houses is of course not substantially different from the ordinary process of legislation whereby the President can make suggestions for laws which may be enacted with the concurrence of the two houses. It is thus the equivalent of outright exemption from the reorganization plan procedure for the agencies designated. An amendment of this type, providing that no reorganization plan affecting the civil functions of the Corps of Engineers should take effect unless both houses passed a concurrent resolution in favor of the plan, was voted upon in the House of Representatives and rejected by a vote of 82 to 143.

The reason emphasized by the Senate committee for its rejection of the two-house veto which had been adopted by the House was that this offered the only feasible way of avoiding exemptions. The committee explained its action as follows:

> In order that the President might include essential Government reorganizations in conformity with the recommendations of the Commission on Organization of the Executive Branch, the committee was reluctant to include exemptions for specified agencies or to retain the House amendments placing certain of them in a restricted category, in the belief that such exemptions might interfere with realignments that would be desirable and in the public interest.
>
> It became increasingly apparent during the hearings on the pending legislation that, in view of the wide interest expressed in behalf of some of these proposed exemptions and restrictions, a number of them would be approved and included in the bill either in committee or on the floor of the Senate.
>
> It was determined that the most direct and effective way to eliminate the need for exemptions was to include an amendment providing that a simple resolution of disapproval by either the House or the Senate would be sufficient to reject and disapprove any reorganization plan submitted by the President.

Oral explanations supplementing this statement which were made on the floor of the Senate by Senators McClellan and Vandenberg apparently satisfied any skeptics regarding this change, for no opposition to it was expressed in the debate, even by Senator Lodge, sponsor of the act which created the Hoover Commission.[2] Consequently, the one-house veto was substituted for the two-house veto in the reorganization bill as passed by the Senate. This discrepancy between the House and Senate versions became the main issue to be threshed out in the conference committee.

Senator McClellan, who was to head the Senate conferees, pledged during debate on the bill that he would not yield to the House on the matter of the

2. Senator Vandenberg stated his attitude in these words: "I want to make it very plain that I think we are not free agents to write this reorganization formula without any limitations whatever. It is simply not in the cards to write that sort of a bill. We confront this choice of a bill which is a clean bill without agency exemptions, and a one-House veto, or a bill with a two-House veto and a list of exemptions as long as one's arm. Now, if the reorganization plans cannot justify themselves when submitted by the President in both Houses of Congress, then the presumption is, I should say, under the American legislative precedent and system, that the reorganization recommendations are not worthy of approval. That is the basis upon which we write laws. I have never heard of a system under which the House alone could enact a law. That is precisely what would be undertaken in reverse, except as the single-House veto as provided in the Senate recommendations were to be followed. . . . we have given the President carte blanche, without reservation or exemption, to make any recommendations he desires. We simply stand upon our ultimate legislative right to pass judgment in both Houses of Congress on the wisdom of what he proposes. That is the American system. That is the best way to get results from reorganization." 95 *Cong. Rec.* 6339 (May 16, 1949).

one-house veto, and in the ensuing month of negotiations, he was joined in this determination by his three Senate colleagues on the committee. The two Republican conferees from the House were more than willing to go along with them, but the three Democratic conferees on the part of the House held out for the House version which had been adopted by an overwhelming majority of that chamber. Various compromises were considered, including one proposal that rejection of a reorganization plan might be either by a two-thirds vote of one house, or by a majority vote of both houses. Eventually, as the price for getting any reorganization act on the statute books, the House conferees were forced to give way. The only significant concession won from the Senate was that the majority required in either house for a resolution of rejection would be a majority of the authorized membership of that chamber rather than a simple majority of those voting. Rejection would thus require a vote of either 218 members of the House or 49 members of the Senate.

CONCLUSION

In estimating the potentialities of the Reorganization Act of 1949 as a means of achieving needed reorganizations, the vital question is whether more was gained by the elimination of exempted agencies than was lost by the substitution of the one-house legislative veto for the two-house veto.

At first glance, the absence of exempted agencies looks like a substantial achievement. Equality of treatment for all executive agencies was one of the objectives sought by the President and the Hoover Commission. When linked with the one-house veto, however, this accomplishment may prove to be more apparent than real. Despite the laudatory sentiments expressed in the Senate concerning the virtues of a "clean bill," no one need be deceived that the favorite agencies of Congress have been thrown to the wolves by their congressional friends. For the half dozen or so agencies over which Congress has in the past been particularly unwilling to yield reorganization power to the President, the one-house veto will in practice be almost as effective a barrier to reorganization as outright exemption, and probably gives more protection than the "separate package" formula linked with the two-house veto would have provided. No exemptions in an act retaining the two-house veto would have been a pronounced improvement over previous acts. In an act permitting one-house veto, it is debatable whether there has been any gain worthy of mention. It is highly unlikely that a reorganization plan touching any agency to which Congress would have granted exemption will be acceptable to both houses.

The grave disadvantage inherent in the new procedure for legislative veto is that all reorganization plans must now face the additional hazard which was ostensibly introduced as a means of avoiding exemptions for a handful of agencies. It is of course impossible to predict what will be the ratio of acceptances and rejections under the new arrangement. That the chances of survival for any reorganization plan are drastically reduced may be inferred, however, from an examination of the record to see what effect the one-house veto has had, or would have had if applied, in past efforts at reorganization.

In our only previous experience with a similar provision for rejection of proposed reorganizations by action of one house, under the 1932 grant to President Hoover, the batting average for approvals was zero. Every one of the eleven proposals sponsored by President Hoover was rejected by the House of Representatives. Of the five reorganization plans which were submitted and went into effect under the 1939 act, one would definitely have been defeated had the one-house veto been operative. In three other instances, after the defeat in one house of resolutions of rejection, the success of the plans was assured whatever might have been the attitude of the second chamber, so we cannot be sure what outcome a one-house veto would have produced, although indications are that the other chamber was also in favor of each of these plans. The remaining plan definitely would have gone into effect even with a one-house veto, since neither house even considered a resolution of disapproval.

We do know definitely that of the seven reorganization plans submitted while the Reorganization Act of 1945 was in effect, only one would have been cleared if disapproval of one house had been sufficient to reject. As it was, three other plans did go into effect because one house accepted them although the other did not.

Perhaps the implications of these figures cannot be reliably applied to the present act. Presidents Hoover and Truman both had to contend with partially unfriendly Congresses. The requirement of a majority of the authorized membership to disapprove a reorganization plan in either house under the 1949 act will make rejection somewhat more difficult. Also, it may be expected that the impetus given currently to the movement for executive reorganization by the work of the Hoover Commission will put Congress in a favorable mood to accept reorganization plans designed to carry out the Commission's recommendations. Even with these factors taken into consideration, however, the prospects for clearance of the hurdle of congressional rejection are not encouraging. The Presidency and one or both houses of Congress may be controlled by different political parties again in the future. The "constitutional majority" requirement for disapproval will not be much more difficult to attain than a simple majority. Moreover, the attitude of cooperation is apt to fade when the more controversial recommendations of the Hoover Commission are sent to Capitol Hill, and the acid test will come when the current drive for reorganization is spent and future organizational problems have to be dealt with under this more hazardous procedure.

Sponsors of the one-house veto in the Senate gave as their reason for backing it that its adoption would make possible the elimination of agency exemptions. That this was not the sole consideration, even though it was the only one admitted openly, is indicated by the following exchange during the Senate debate:

MR. LUCAS. I am sure I understand the able Senator, but I desire to make the matter perfectly clear. In other words, if the House were to recede from the provisions that are now in the House bill with respect to the exemptions contained in it, and have no exemptions whatever in the bill, and if the House should agree to the provisions of the Senate bill, would the Senator from Arkansas under those conditions still insist on a separate veto by each House?

MR. MC CLELLAN. Yes. I would insist because I could not support the bill with exemptions out of it, if it required action on the part of both Houses to disapprove by concurrent resolutions.

This position reveals clearly that in the mind of Senator McClellan at least, and he probably was not alone, the real objective in inserting the one-house veto requirement was not just to get rid of exemptions, but to stiffen congressional powers of resistance to presidential reorganization plans. The success of this effort in the Senate to shift from the two-house veto to the one-house veto marks a definite withdrawal by Congress of effective reorganization powers which it had been willing to delegate in the 1939 and 1945 acts.

It is intriguing to speculate as to what might have been the outcome if the original reorganization bill based upon the recommendations of the President and the Hoover Commission had benefited from more vigorous and whole-hearted support from the Senate leadership. A primary reason for providing congressional representation on the Hoover Commission and for the appointment of the ranking majority and minority members of the Committees on Expenditures in the Executive Departments to the Commission was the expectation that members of the Commission would thus be in key positions to push Commission recommendations through Congress. Unfortunately, this did not happen in this instance. Senator Aiken, who had been chairman of the Senate Committee on Expenditures at the time the Commission was created, was not even a minority member of that committee in the Eighty-first Congress. Senator McClellan, who became the committee chairman in this Congress, used his strategic position not to support but to oppose the recommendations of the Commission concerning general reorganization legislation. Although he did not express disagreement with these recommendations when they were made to Congress by the Commission last January, he subsequently led the opposition to the joint stand taken by the Commission and President Truman on the three most important issues, and is more responsible than any other member of Congress for the form which the act finally took. He succeeded in inserting a time limit in the legislation. He frankly admitted that his primary concern was that the Army Corps of Engineers should be guaranteed against reorganization, despite the Commission's desire not to exempt agencies. He spearheaded the drive in the Senate for the one-house veto, and insisted in conference committee that it should remain in the bill. Moreover, the long delay in his committee before the reorganization bill was reported out largely accounts for its tardy enactment.

In view of the attitude of the House of Representatives, a reorganization bill substantially in accord with the views of President Truman and the Hoover Commission, with the possible deviation of providing "separate package" treatment for a few agencies, would in all probability have been enacted by Congress had a kinder fate provided a more friendly Senator as chairman of this vital Senate committee. In the Senate as in the House, the membership accepted the guidance of its Committee on Expenditures. The difference was that the House committee took a positive stand in favor of a strong reorganization bill, and the Senate committee did not.

[Editor's postscript: The 1949 act was, after its original expiration in 1953, extended for two-year periods in that year, 1955, and 1957. The 1957 extension, however, included an amendment of the Congressional veto provision. Whereas the statute had previously provided for veto by a majority of all members, the amended statute provided for veto by a simple majority of those voting. Subsequent extensions have retained this provision.

The act was allowed to lapse in 1959, but was reinstated for the new President in 1961. In 1962, President Kennedy aroused the wrath of many Congressmen when he submitted a reorganization plan—after a bill to achieve the same result had become bogged down in the House Rules Committee—to create a cabinet-level Department of Urban Affairs. Congress reacted by not only disapproving the plan, but also by refusing to extend the reorganization act in 1963.

After President Johnson's accession, Congress passed a one-year extension in 1964. It amended the law at this time, however, to bar the creation of new cabinet-level departments by reorganization plan. After his overwhelming landslide victory in the 1964 election, President Johnson proposed that the act as amended be made permanent. The House Government Operations Committee reported a bill embodying the President's request, but the Senate insisted on an expiration date of December 31, 1968. The House floor managers ultimately decided to obviate the need for a conference by pressing for House passage of the Senate bill. In this they succeeded. Needless to say, conditions were unlikely to be as favorable again to the passage of permanent legislation for many years.

E.   The New Federalism: Government by Contract and Grant-in-Aid

THROUGHOUT American history a high premium has been placed on avoiding unnecessary concentrations of power. Within the governmental system, the major expressions of this priority have been federalism, checks and balances, the Bill of Rights, and the lack of hierarchical discipline in both Congress and the national party organizations. In the social system as a whole, however, the most significant manifestation of this priority has been the national emphasis on minimizing the scope of governmental (and particularly federal) responsibility. During the nineteenth and early twentieth centuries, this objective was substantially achieved. The size of the public sector increased, but its rate of growth was scarcely more rapid than that of the total labor force and national income. More recently, the trend line has veered sharply upward. From 1927 through 1962, total public expenditures in the United States (federal, state, and local combined) rose from 11.6% of gross national product to 31.2%. Public employment levels rose a bit more slowly, from 6.7% of the labor force to 16.1%.*

The federal government has accounted for only about half this growth,† but it is the half that has involved armed force, esoteric technologies, extraordinary degrees of secrecy, and the capacity to make all society's other great institutions appear as pygmies beside it. Quite naturally, therefore, its half is the one that has preoccupied those concerned about the long-term threat of "big government" to American liberty and democracy. The primary way in which federal policy makers have sought to allay such fears has been to rely increasingly on state, local, corporate, academic, and other private nonprofit institutions to administer its programs.‡ In view of the wide distribution of political influence in the system, moreover, and the frequent mixing of the federal government's funds with those of its administrative "instruments," it has not always been clear just who was serving whom, and in what degrees. Some have argued that it could hardly matter less, so long as all parties find it beneficial to continue cooperating. In the free market, after all, one does not worry about whether buyer or seller is dominant so long as each is happy with their transactions.

To optimists about the future of American liberty and democracy, then, the picture has been one of the American genius for pragmatic improvisation in action. The cobwebs of dogma have been brushed away. New techniques of government have been devised to fit contemporary circumstances. The public and private sectors—and within the former, the federal, state, and local sectors—have been blending, but the distribution of power in the social system has remained more than adequately pluralistic to preserve liberty and democracy unimpaired. Some have argued, in fact, that as a result of increasing specialization, the very strong market position of highly trained men, and these new administrative devices, the trend is in the direction of more pluralism rather than less.

To pessimists, on the other hand, the picture has been one of the federal government extending its tentacles ever outward, subverting with a complex array of new financial lures the autonomy of the only institutions in the society that remained potential centers of resistance to its policies—and to its growth. The increases in public spending and employment, in this view, do not begin to measure the growth of federal power that has taken place over the past forty years. Power cannot be measured literally, but quite obviously the American system has been transformed. From one in which free enterprise, states rights, isolationism, antimilitarism, and legislative supremacy were the dominant themes, another has emerged in which the

---

* Frederick C. Mosher and Orville F. Poland, *The Costs of American Governments* (New York: Dodd, Mead & Company, Inc., 1964), pp. 141, 157. The latter comparison, it should be noted, is of 1929 with 1962.

† Federal spending rose from 3.5% of gross national product in 1927 to 20.4% in 1966. Federal employment, including the armed forces, rose from 1.6% of the labor force in 1929 to 7.3% in 1966.

‡ Allaying such fears is by no means the only advantage that an agency secures by contracting out. Several others of importance are the following: (1) contractors can frequently lobby with fewer inhibitions and greater effect on behalf of the agency's programs than mere divisions of the agency itself could; (2) private institutions, being able to offer higher salaries and better working conditions than the government, can employ many possessors of scarce skills who would otherwise be unavailable to the agency; and (3) contracting enhances the agency's flexibility, by permitting it to avoid long-term staff obligations and to choose among competitive bids whenever it has work that it wishes to assign.

economy is "managed," state and local tax revenues go largely to match federal grants, Presidentially defined national security requirements override all other political considerations, and Congress becomes perceptibly more passive with every passing decade.

Don K. Price, dean of the John F. Kennedy School of Government at Harvard, is probably America's foremost student of "science and public policy." As the following selection makes clear, he is one of the optimists. Price sees the new techniques of administration as very much within the American tradition, and he believes that they are highly appropriate responses to the problem of nationalizing support for programs without reducing pluralism. There is nothing in the nature of the new administrative system, he writes, to determine whether power will be increasingly concentrated at the center, or the center will increasingly fall under the multiple influences of its "instruments." In practice, he concludes, there is much less danger of central bureaucratic dictatorship in the United States than of excessive fragmentation, inattention to the broader issues of policy, and disregard of the public interest. You will do well to evaluate the case he makes for this proposition with the utmost critical care.

J. Stefan Dupré and W. Eric Gustafson analyze the Defense Department's relations with its contractors. Business is "by nature," they contend, oriented toward private interest rather than public responsibility; and the way to induce contractors to serve the public interest is to devise administrative controls which will simulate the constraints on sellers of free market competition. The burden of their analysis, however, is to emphasize the obstacles to, rather than the potential for, making progress in this direction. Since they wrote, Secretary of Defense McNamara has placed great emphasis on shifting from noncompetitive to competitive procurement. Even so, negotiated contracts, which accounted for 88% of all military procurement in fiscal 1961, still accounted for 82% in fiscal 1965. Several questions you may wish to consider after reading Dupré and Gustafson's article are the following: Is it clear that the aim of contract administration should be to approximate the market, as opposed to developing and utilizing a new ethos of business-government cooperation? What kinds of difficulties and risks might the latter objective involve? To the extent that the Defense Department avoids being influenced by its contractors and succeeds in controlling their administration of contracts effectively, is not the danger of excessive concentration of power vastly accentuated? If the dilemma thus posed is a real one, is there any way out of it?

The following selection is from a report by a Senate subcommittee on the attitudes of federal grant-in-aid officials toward the "new federalism" they administer. Although written rather colorlessly, it deals in concise and informative fashion with many of the most fundamental issues of contemporary intergovernmental relations, among them the following: Should the state and local recipients of grants-in-aid be left a wide area of discretion in determining how to spend them? To what extent, if any, should federal grant programs endeavor to offset disparities of wealth among the states? To what extent do federal aid officials and their local counterparts have divergent objectives and perspectives? To what extent are those administering the "new federalism" concerned with the impact of their endeavors on the overall intergovernmental relations system? In other words, is the objective articulated by Don K. Price—i.e., to nationalize the revenue base of our attacks on national problems without concentrating power at the national level—a living part of the intergovernmental relations system, or is it simply an academic rationale based on an idealized vision of reality? If you judge that the latter is true in significant degree, you might consider what would be involved in changing the system to more closely approximate Price's image of it.

THE DIFFUSION OF SOVEREIGNTY *
Don K. Price

"FACELESS technocrats in long, white coats are making decisions today which rightfully and by law should be made by the Congress," said Senator E. L. Bartlett of Alaska as he urged that Congress set up its own corps of scientific advisers. His complaint reflects a fear that is probably shared by many citizens. In view of the esoteric nature of the scientific processes that now seem to dominate our policies, can the elected representatives of the people maintain control over the major decisions of the government?

The typical liberal who supported the extension of governmental control over business in the early twentieth century was not very greatly worried about weakening the independent status of private property as a check on centralized power. To protect his freedom, he was inclined to trust the responsible processes of representative government. No matter how much power might be vested in the government, it would still be under popular control; the experts in the civil and military services would function only as the agents of policies that had been initiated by the processes of party leadership and legislative debate.

But now that great issues turn on new scientific discoveries far too complicated for politicians to comprehend, many people doubt that representative institutions can still do their job. The fear that the new powers created by science may be beyond the control of constitutional processes, and that scientists may become a new governing clique or cabal of secret advisers, has begun to seem plausible. The intellectual world in general, especially in Europe, is tempted to believe that modern man faces a political dilemma and is now obliged to choose between the two kinds of authoritarian governments that have taken over the control of many countries. One is the type that is guided by military or clerical leaders who affirm traditional values; the other is the type of dictatorship based on the materialist dialectic, professing science as its basic faith.

If American scientists, like American politicians, have generally not been persuaded that they had to choose either horn of this dilemma, it was probably because their actual experience was quite different from that of their counter-

* From Don K. Price, *The Scientific Estate* (Cambridge: Harvard University Press, 1965), pp. 57–81. Copyright, 1965, by the President and Fellows of Harvard College. Reprinted by permission. An earlier version of this chapter appeared in the *Proceedings* of The American Philosophical Society, Vol. 106, No. 3 (1962), pp. 235–245.

parts in many other countries. In most of Europe, the reactionaries and the radicals shared a basic assumption not only with each other, but also with the parliamentary liberals against whom they rebelled. That assumption was the idea of sovereignty, the notion that the government of a nation was in some sense an expression of a single authoritative national purpose, and the embodiment of a unified will. This sovereign will, or the parliament that expressed it, would define a set of policies, based on a coherent set of principles, to be administered by a coordinated and disciplined bureaucracy.

To any newspaper reader, it should be obvious how little this ideal of sovereignty corresponds to the actual nature of the American political system, although some scholars try to make the facts fit the ideal. Some of the most obvious differences appear in the different role of scientists, and in the organization of the new programs they have initiated. For American scientists have played a significant role in the development of a system of political responsibility that does not work on the principles of parliamentary government and does not work on the principles of the new dictatorships of either the right or the left that have been supplanting the parliamentary system in many countries. It is a system that—along with some considerable disadvantages—has one great advantage: it does not assume that within the government there must be a single sovereign will, and therefore additional functions can be given to government without adding to the concentration of power within society.

We need a theory of the relation of science to political authority that will more accurately reflect the American experience. Before we Americans try to outline such a theory—or at least an approach toward it—we need to take a careful look at the facts. We cannot understand science in relation to politics unless we understand the way scientists behave in relation to politicians, both individually and in the organizations to which they belong. We should therefore ask three elementary questions that seem relevant to any theory of political responsibility, and take special note of the role of scientists as we answer each of them: (1) What kind of men make a career of running the government? (2) Who initiates new policies? (3) Who controls the organization and procedures of the government departments?

SCIENTISTS AND PROFESSIONALS IN ADMINISTRATION

The classic parliamentary system is based on the collective responsibility of a cabinet to an elected assembly. Since that responsibility is collective—that is, all members of the cabinet are equally responsible for the policies of the government as a whole—it is necessary for the actual administration of the government to be under the coordinated control of a single disciplined administrative corps. It is hard to imagine such a corps composed of men whose education and early careers had been devoted to the intense specialization of the modern sciences. At any rate, none of the major nations whose governments are set up on the parliamentary model have ever tried to do without an elite corps of career administrators, and in such a corps scientists are rare indeed.

In the United States, on the other hand, men trained in the sciences, and in the professions based on the sciences, find it easy to move up into high administrative positions.

In Great Britain, which is the classic example of a parliamentary government, the Administrative Class, the top corps of the civil service, is still dominated by men trained in the humanistic and historical studies; not one man in twenty among these guardians of public policy has had a scientific or technical education. In spite of recurrent criticism of its role, the Administrative Class still maintains a professional monopoly (though in a studiously amateur and nonscientific way) over the organization of the government departments, and a major share of influence in the formation of national policy. It thus has no great interest in making it easy for scientists to move up into its membership, or the universities to work closely with it on its major policy problems.

Now that we are both constitutional democracies, it makes much less difference that Great Britain has a king and the United States a president, but a great deal of difference how we set up the professional group of men who actually run the government. Our Jacksonian revolution indeed destroyed the hopes of John Quincy Adams for a continuation of the Jeffersonian alliance between science and republicanism. At the same time, by wiping out the beginnings of a career system, it prevented the development of an elite administrative corps and thus cleared the channels of promotion for the scientists who, decades later, were to begin to move up in the civil service. The frontier radicalism of the day distrusted all forms of Establishment; this was the era in which state constitutions forbade clergymen to hold public office and prohibited educational qualifications for admission to the bar. But as the business of government got more complicated, the frontier had to admit that certain skills were necessary. Its essentially pragmatic temper insisted, as it became necessary to hire civil servants for merit rather than patronage, that the requirements be defined in terms of the needs of the specific jobs, rather than by general educational status. It was easiest to prove the need for special skills in technical fields, partly on account of the objective nature of the problem, partly because scientific societies were determined to raise and maintain their professional standards in the civil service as well as in private practice.

As a result, it was in the scientific and professional fields that the career civil service system was first pushed up to the higher ranks. As we developed our top civil service, we made it something quite different from a career Administrative Class; most of its members are not only nonpolitical, but nonadministrative as well, and they are not career officials in the same sense as a U.S. Navy officer or a British Civil Servant.

In recent years, scientists and engineers, though rare among those in high political office, have done reasonably well in the civil service. The program of Rockefeller Public Service Awards, recognizing distinguished achievement in the federal civil service between 1952 and 1960, gave two fifths of its awards to men engaged in scientific or technological programs, and having scientific or technical educations. Similarly, a recent study of 7,640 federal civil servants in the top ranks showed that as undergraduates a third of them had specialized in engineering, and nearly a quarter in the physical or biological sciences. By contrast, only 16 percent had specialized in applied studies like business, education, and administration, 16 percent in the behavioral sciences, and only 9 percent in the humanities. One tenth of them had doctors' degrees, and one quarter masters' degrees; among those who did graduate work, the proportion with training in the physical and biological sciences was even higher than at the undergraduate level. On their way up to administrative responsibilities, whether in government service or private life, many of these officials had served at length in the sciences and related professions; as late as fifteen years after starting their careers, 18 percent had been engineers, 8 percent scientists, and 2 percent medical doctors; only 3 percent had been lawyers.

The top positions within the career civil service, for administrative continuity and bureaucratic power, are those of the bureau chiefs. A study in 1958 of the 63 bureau chiefs showed that 9 of them had advanced degrees in the natural sciences, and 17 others had been trained in lesser ways as engineers or technicians. By comparison with these 26 from various branches of technology, there were 9 economists and only 8 lawyers, and 20 from miscellaneous administrative or business careers. Aside from the positions of bureau chief, the top career positions are the so-called "supergrade," which were added above the regular civil service grades to let the government compete for scarce talent. The favorite justification for creating these positions is the need to employ capable scientists and engineers, notably in the technical branches of the Defense Department and the National Aeronautics and Space Administration. Administrators have ridden along to higher salaries on the political coat tails of scientists.

Scientists who become bureau chiefs in the U.S. service are, of course, no longer practicing scientists; they are doing work that in the United Kingdom would be done by a member of the Administrative Class educated in history or the classics. Their training may not be ideally suited for their administrative duties, but neither was that of their English counterparts. Macaulay, after all, used to argue that he wanted to recruit university graduates in the classics not because they had been studying the classics but because the classics attracted the best minds which could adapt themselves to anything. And the scientific training of many American administrators puts them on a level with their English humanist counterparts in at least one respect: their lack of interest in management as a science, or sometimes at all.

THE INDUCTIVE INITIATION OF POLICY

Though the scientists in top civil service posts have not been deeply interested in administration, they have been interested in policy. And this is the second major way in which the scientific civil servant in the United States differs from his British or European counterpart: he takes a direct role in initiating policies and publicly advocating them.

In their influence on policy, as in their advancement in the hierarchy, the scientists in American government have had a special opportunity because they have not had to work under a tightly organized corps of administrators, or a tightly knit political leadership. After the Civil War, there was no strong conservative tradition based on a landed interest, and no national party with a coherent ideology to take control of the programs of government. As a result, policy tended to develop separately in every field. There was no one with sufficient authority to tell the scientific experts that they belonged in a subordinate role.

Indeed they were listened to all the more readily because they were usually not thought of as bureaucrats. There was no one from whom Congress wanted advice less than from the regular career service. But each group of scientists had one foot in government, so to speak, and one outside, and the policy views that the insiders developed would come back to the Congress from the National Academy or the scientific societies. In a government of limited constitutional powers, a research program could be justified in a given field when an action program could not. But the research ultimately seemed to lead to action, in spite of the lawyers' scruples and the party bosses' lack of interest in policy issues. Research was influential not merely because the politicians were persuaded by objective data; an even more important reason may have been that scientists (and in some fields, the economists) were the major organized communities of professional opinion with a continuous interest in specific public programs. This has been the pattern of the development of many new federal programs: you can trace it in agriculture, in natural resources, in the regulation of business, in labor and welfare, and we now see its beginnings in the support of education.

The most influential pattern was set in agriculture. Washington and Jefferson had been interested in fostering scientific improvements in agriculture, and in federal support of a national university. They were blocked by the lawyers' scruples about states' rights. But the agricultural scientists found a way to their goal by a different route—one that evaded constitutional barriers by merging federal and state interests through federal grants of either land or money to the states, and by building up a program on scientific and educational bases. The principal basis was, of course, the land-grant college; from it grew the experiment station, the extension program, and the whole interlocking system of institutions which has let the federal government play a more effective role in the agricultural economy than the government of any supposedly socialized state.

In all this development, the land-grant colleges and the associations of various kinds of agricultural scientists maintained an important influence on the Department of Agriculture, supplied most of its career personnel, and generally provided the intellectual leadership for national agricultural policy. Thus in effect they greatly weakened the old constitutional distinction between state and federal functions, but without subjecting the field of agriculture to the control of a centralized bureaucracy.

The pattern of grants-in-aid, with its new set of administrative relationships, met two cardinal needs: (1) to provide money, as well as national policy direction, from Washington, and (2) to enlarge the operating responsibilities of the states, while preserving a large measure of their autonomy. It accordingly became the basis on which new programs were developed—highways, public health, social security, welfare, housing, and others. This was what political scientists came to call the "New Federalism," which has given the scientists and specialists in each field of policy a chance to work out programs without too much constraint by any party doctrine.

The classic theory of parliamentary government calls for something like a deductive method in the formulation of policy. That is to say, it suggests that policy originates in the doctrines or platforms of the political parties, and that it is then expressed in the enactments of the legislature. The role of administrators and their scientific and technical subordinates is merely to carry out the predetermined policy, to deduce specific actions from the statutory general principles.

It was of course not the scientists, but the lawyers, who saved us from this dogmatic belief. Some people still think that the function of judges is simply to interpret and apply the laws that legislatures enact, and the function of administrators merely to administer such laws. This was the conception of the extreme doctrinaires of both the American and French revolutions; sovereignty was in the people, and could be expressed only through their elected representatives in deliberative assembly. So for a time in France, during the Revolution, judges were required to go back to the legislature and ask for guidance whenever they found a case not covered explicitly enough by statute. But the lawyers in the tradition of the common law never held with such nonsense. They knew that justice required a great deal of initiative and inventiveness from a profession with a corporate tradition. They knew that the political authority of a legislature would be destroyed, rather than enhanced, if the legal profession and the judiciary looked to it for all ideas and initiative, and failed to exercise their own.

In Great Britain the career administrators, for all their formal public deference to members of the cabinet, were soon accorded a powerful role in the initiation of policy, but the notion persisted rather strongly that the scientists were instruments for predetermined ends. In the United States, on the other hand, the politicians were rather more ready to accord to scientists than to general administrators the right to press their policy views.

The leaders of political parties or members of an elite administrative corps may like to look on scientists as properly subordinate, and science as a way of thinking that should deal with the means to support a policy, a tradition, or an ideology, rather than an end in itself. We can understand this relationship in other countries if we recall how, until recent years, our military services thought that civilian scientists in military laboratories should conduct their research only pursuant to "requirements" defined by military staff work. This notion was exploded as it became apparent that what scientists discovered by unrestricted research might be of greater military importance than the things the military officers thought they wanted—in short, that the means might determine the ends.

Weapons development provides the extreme (and almost the only conspicuous) example in American politics in which scientists have been faced with difficulties in getting a direct political hearing for their policy ideas. For members of Congress usually want their scientific advice on a specific problem undiluted by either party doctrine or the policy views of general administrators.

This attitude is something like an inductive approach to policy. It distrusts the deduction of specific decisions from general political principles, or from a party's ideology. It distrusts the presentation of facts by either bureaucrats or party managers who may distort them for their special purposes; it is afraid of the doctrine that the end determines the means, for it suspects that the politician does not really know in precise terms what is the chief end of man, and may be tempted to define it to suit purposes of his own. This approach may have been furthered, in American history, by the influence of scientific ideas along with rationalism during the Revolution. Later it may have been furthered by a dim realization that science, if not too much constrained by predetermined political ends (or, if you like, political teleology), could help develop a higher set of goals and purposes than had yet been dreamed of. But mainly, I suspect, it was given a chance because people were sick of the results of exaggerated party doctrine and of the Civil War to which it led.

So the President was not expected to run for office, or run his administration, according to a doctrinaire platform, or to coordinate his departments so closely as to suppress a certain amount of policy initiative from his technical subordinates. Similarly, the Congressional committees, which were fiercely partisan with respect to the spoils of office, became nearly nonpartisan, or at least weakly disciplined by their parties, in the consideration of new policies. And both the executive and the legislature developed the habit of turning for policy advice and assistance not only to the scientists in government, but to their colleagues in the universities and foundations. Both land-grant colleges and private universities were drawn into the processes of policy making, partly because they were, in the absence of a career bureaucracy, the main reservoir of expertise on which politicians could draw for advice, and partly in response to the influence of the philanthropic foundations.

By the 1920's, some of the major foundations had lost interest in the charitable alleviation of social problems, and had begun to hope that science might solve them. This idea led them to a strategy of supporting scientific research—and not only research but demonstration projects to test its application. After being tested, the research could be extended by the greater resources of government. The foundations' aid to scientific education and research is a familiar story in almost every branch of science. Equally important, they went on to help strengthen the professional organizations of scientists, to pay for the efforts of governmental agencies to reform their own systems of organization and administration, and to pay for research projects undertaken at the request of public officials who could not persuade legislatures to appropriate the necessary funds.

By the time of the Second World War, the leading scientists knew that a grant-making agency like a foundation could initiate nationwide programs by making grants to independent universities and governmental agencies. Hookworm control, the foundation of public libraries, and the reform of medical education had amply proved the point. And political leaders were inclined to turn to private funds to help them explore future policy opportunities, or experiment with them, as when President Hoover sought foundation financing for his Committee on Social Trends and for a National Science Fund. The Public Administration Clearing House provided the initial administrative costs for President Roosevelt's Science Advisory Board.

The process of responsible policy making is thus not something that begins with the definition of a political ideal according to some partisan doctrine, and concludes by using administrative and scientific means to attain that end. It is a process of interaction among the scientists, professional leaders, administrators, and politicians; ultimate authority is with the politicians but the initiative is quite likely to rest with others, including the scientists in or out of government.

POLITICAL DECENTRALIZATION OF THE EXECUTIVE

The presence of scientists and professionals in the civil service and their unusual degree of policy initiative are not the only differences that science has helped to bring about in the American constitutional system. The third difference is perhaps the most profound: the idea that the very organization of government itself is not something to be controlled by the insiders, but may be determined by the processes of open politics. Though the American scientific civil servant has policy initiative, and thus may seem to be tipping the balance of power against the politician, the politician more than makes up for it by assuming control over the internal structure of government organization and over its procedures.

The scientists were of course not the major influence in support of this tendency to open the inner workings of government to popular political control; that tendency came from many social and political sources. But it was encouraged by the early rationalism of the Jeffersonians, who believed that politics itself should be an experimental process. It was encouraged by the desire to give independent status within government to agencies with scientific functions, like the Smithsonian Institution, or agencies that were supposed to make their decisions more on technical than political grounds, like the regulatory commissions. And it was encouraged by the desire of scientific and professional services to have special status of their own apart from the general civil service, a desire which accounted for separate uniformed corps like those of the Coast and Geodetic Survey and the Public Health Service.

One of the classic principles of administration holds that with responsibility should go a corresponding degree of administrative authority. Within a limited managerial context, this is the proverbial wisdom, and sound enough. And at the political level, it is the key idea in the classic theory of parliamentary responsibility. The cabinet within the parliament, and the prime minister within the cabinet, were able to take control by saying, in effect, that they could not continue to carry the responsibilities of His Majesty's Government if not given full control over the means to their proposed ends. But in the United States the idea of authority commensurate with responsibility is contradicted by the history as well as the theory of our constitutional system.

For the Jacksonian revolution completed the efforts of the Jeffersonian rationalists to abolish all types of establishments. The Constitution had forbidden a national established church, and the Founding Fathers had moved rapidly to rely on the volunteer state militias rather than a national standing army. And the Jacksonians proceeded to root out the beginnings of a career administrative service, in order to prevent the democratic control of policy from being influenced by a vested interest within the government. In Great Britain, as A. V. Dicey was to point out, the civil servant (unlike his French counterpart) was kept subject to the same law and the same courts as the private citizen, in order to make sure that he did not exceed the authority granted him by law. The United States went one step further; the civil servant was kept, in effect, a part of the private labor market, rather than being made a part of a lifetime service with a corporate tradition. He worked for a bureau that was likely to be fairly independent of any general government policy, and rather more under the control of the particular Congressional committees to which it looked for legislative authority and for the appropriation of its funds. His Majesty's Civil Service was the embodiment of a national ideal; the U.S. Civil Service had only a nominal existence—it was only a set of rules and procedures that imposed negative restraints on a collection of nearly autonomous bureaus.

The President, in short, could not effectively demand control over the civil service or the form of organization of the executive departments, in order to control the means toward the ends legislated by Congress. For federal administration, like the process of policy making, was supposed to work on something like a parody of the inductive method. The existence of a general bureaucracy, committed to an integrated national purpose, was not to be taken for granted on general principles; each position in the civil service was supposed to be set up by law, or later by a formal proof of its necessity under a system of job classification, and the men recruited for their ability to fill these particular jobs were supposed somehow to constitute an organization capable of fulfilling a national purpose. The end did not determine the means; in Congressional procedure, the committee in charge of legislation defined the ends, and the appropriations subcommittee sometimes supplied the means.

This was the logical corollary of the peculiarly American assumption that it was just as appropriate for the voters and legislators to control the administrative organization and procedures of government as its policies, that is to say, to control the means as well as the ends. This was a radical departure from British or European assumptions. The parliamentary progression from conservatives to liberals to socialists never changed the fundamental European assumption that, although governments might be responsible to legislatures for the substance of their policies, it was better for politics and legislation not to meddle with internal administrative organization or the management of the bureaucracy. The socialist political leaders took the unity of the state and its bureaucracy for granted. If anything, they tended to make it all the more monolithic, and to push to its logical conclusion the tendency of Benthamite liberalism to abolish the privileges of guilds and public corporations.

But in the United States the current of radicalism ran in the opposite direction; after the age of Jackson, lobbyists and legislators were likely to concern themselves at least as much with the details of administrative organization as with major policies, generally with the purpose of creating centers of independence within government. Thus, in the nineteenth century, the states and cities adopted constitutions and charters that made them loose collections of independent agencies, with no responsible Executive.

This decentralizing tendency was pushed so far that it destroyed the unity of administration, and sometimes had disastrous effects on the competence and the political responsibility of government. But it also disproved the idea—often assumed both by those who admired and those who feared socialism—that an extension in the scope of governmental functions in the United States would automatically bring a corresponding centralization of power.

THE EXTENSION OF THE NEW FEDERALISM

Those three peculiarities of the American political system had made it possible, by the time of the New Deal, to bring the major programs of state and municipal government and the major programs affecting the agricultural economy within the scope of federal government policy, without destroying the operating autonomy of the states and cities or the land-grant colleges. The New Federalism, in short, had worked best in those aspects of public affairs in which the power of government and the power of the great industrial corporations were not in rivalry. Leaders of private universities and scientific institutions, partly with this example in mind and partly in view of their experience with the programs of private foundations, were beginning to wonder, a decade before the Second World War, whether they would have to accept some comparable relationship to the federal government.

The system of federal grants and contracts by which universities and industrial corporations now have been brought into a relation of dependence on federal policy and federal funds, but with a high degree of independence with respect to their internal affairs, was not the result of an immediate flash of wartime inspiration. Its essential idea can be traced back to the depths of the Great Depression. By that time the naive nineteenth-century faith in the contribution of science to democratic politics was less prevalent in the more important universities and the more advanced fields of science than in the agricultural colleges. Scientists in the major private universities were supported more by private corporations and foundations than by government, and leaders in the newer fields like nuclear physics and biochemistry had closer intellectual ties with their European counterparts than with the agronomists or engineers of the land-grant colleges. The scientists in institutions that derived their support from industrial wealth and were interested in problems of the industrial urban economy saw the constitutional model in a very different perspective. Among them, accordingly, were to be found both those conservative scientists who were most distrustful of government and those radicals who tended to take a Marxist view of the role of science in society.

It was from such institutions that the Science Advisory Board of 1934–35, set up by President Roosevelt to prepare a program to combat the depression, drew its rather conservative members. They came up with a report that shocked their colleagues, for they actually proposed government research grants to private institutions, citing as a precedent the previous programs of aid to the land-grant colleges. The federal government, however, or at any rate Public Works Administrator Harold L. Ickes, did not think it proper to give federal subsidies to private institutions, and rejected the proposal.

But the reluctance of private institutions to accept government support, and the reluctance of the government to grant funds outside the framework of complete political responsibility, broke down under the pressure of the Second World War.

The scientists who were then put in charge of the most advanced weapons programs (including some of the same leaders who had served on the earlier Science Advisory Board) were ready to work out a thoroughly pragmatic set of arrangements for the conduct of weapons research, based on the same procedures that had worked in the foundation programs with which they were familiar. The approach that they adopted in the two great scientific programs of the war—the Office of Scientific Research and Development (OSRD) and the Manhattan District of the Army Engineers—was simply to enlist institutions rather than individuals.

To those who expect wartime crises and military authority to produce a centralization of authority, this approach must have been as surprising as if the Army had used the war as an excuse to increase, rather than decrease, its reliance on the state militias. But in the hands of Vannevar Bush, James B. Conant, and Karl T. Compton, the government contract brought private corporations within the scope of a still newer and more flexible type of federalism, one that was founded on the government contract rather than the grant-in-aid. Under the OSRD, the Massachusetts Institute of Technology took on the responsibility for developing radar, and the California Institute of Technology rockets. Under the Manhattan District, the University of Chicago set up the first sustained nuclear reaction and the University of California fabricated the first atomic bomb, while Du Pont, General Electric, Union Carbide, and other industrial giants built the facilities to produce the fissionable materials.

The postwar extension of this system, already described, has brought private scientific institutions—universities as well as business corporations—into a connection with the federal government as intimate and active as that of any land-grant college. And in at least some parts of the industrial system it may now be bringing about a relation between government and business entirely different from the one that existed during the quarrels of the depression era, much as the grants-in-aid system transformed federal-state relations some decades after the Civil War. Indeed, it may now be breaking down the political opposition to federal programs even more effectively than did the system of grants to the states.

State and local governments and private corporations used to join in their jealousy of purely federal activities and to consider extension of them as socialistic. The federal grants to states in the field of agriculture, however, were no longer socialistic in the eyes of the governors and the farm bloc; they were a defense of the American way of life, even though they entailed government controls. And now that the atomic energy and space and military programs support such a large share of the nation's business, and so much of its enterprise and innovation spills over quite naturally and properly into related commercial fields, it is no wonder that private business corporations are less jealous of government. More accurately, their jealousy no longer takes the form of fighting socialism, but of haggling over the administrative provisions of contracts. A great deal of private enterprise is now secreted in the interstices of government contracts. In short, what the grants-in-aid programs did to the arguments for states' rights, the new contractual systems are doing to those for pure private enterprise.

The argument for a measure of independence from central authority still remains valid in either case, and so does the need to recognize that the fundamental responsibility of government cannot be delegated. Policy decisions remain the responsibility of government. But "policy" here means simply those aspects that government authorities believe ought to be controlled, either because they think them of major importance or because they realize that voters or Congressmen think so.

This means that they will consider as policy certain aspects of management (for example, fair employment practices or prevailing wage rates). But, so long as they retain ultimate control, they may act on the advice of contractors upon the most momentous new issues, or delegate major segments of the business whenever they can specify the purposes to be accomplished. The complex and costly nature of certain types of military studies, and the sophistication of the new techniques of operations research, make the possibility of such delegation very broad indeed. There is nothing in the nature of the contract itself (or the grant, which differs from it only symbolically and in technical detail) to determine whether a central bureaucracy will control every detail of the contractor's management or will leave him free to decide matters in secret that ought to be determined by the President and Congress.

But the general effect of this new system is clear: the fusion of economic and political power has been accompanied by a considerable *diffusion* of central authority. This has destroyed the notion that the future growth in the functions and expenditures of government, which seems to be made inevitable by the increase in the technological complexity of our civilization, would necessarily take the form of a vast bureaucracy, organized on Max Weber's hierarchical principles, and using the processes of science as Julian Huxley predicted to answer policy questions. Where scientists have shaped this development, its political and administrative patterns have reflected the way scientists actually behave rather than the way science fiction or Marxist theory would have them behave; they have introduced into stodgy and responsible channels of bureaucracy the amiable disorder of a university faculty meeting.

Take, for example, our oldest and least scientific federal agency having a large operational mission—the Post Office—and compare it with the Air Force or the Space Administration. The Post Office is a relatively self-contained hierarchy. The Air Force develops its policies and runs its programs with the advice and cooperation of several dozen of the most influential universities and industrial corporations of the country, whose executives and faculty members consequently have independent bases from which to criticize any policies, strategic plans, or administrative arrangements they dislike—and they can always find a Congressional committee to listen to them.

The role of science in this difference does not seem to be merely accidental. For one thing, the pursuit of science itself is a non-hierarchical affair; the best scientists either personally prefer, or are taught by their guilds that they should prefer, the university's combination of research, teaching, and undisciplined administration—and to get the best scientists the government took them on their own terms. But more important is the long-range and indirect connection; when the revolution of the Enlightenment proposed that the organization and procedures of government as well as its policies should be open to scientific inquiry and independent criticism, it started a process which has had deep effects on the constitutional system. These effects showed first in the relation of scientific administrators to their executive superiors and to Congressional committees, and later in the new structure of federalism, and in the new contractual relationships between the federal government and private institutions.

The involvement of scientists in these contractual relationships since 1945 has extended their earlier influence on our system of political responsibility.

In the first place, scientists have acquired an even higher degree of initiative and independence in policy. Scientists who advise government or carry on research for government, but are not primarily on the government payroll, have an even greater freedom of enterprise than scientists in the civil service. A government department that gets its research or its advice from scientists on the staffs of private institutions, and pays for it through a contract or grant, is not going to be able to train such men in the disciplined habits of anonymous discretion. On the contrary, these scientists have plenty of opportunity to take the initiative in policy matters and to further the contribution that research can make to the opening up of new political alternatives. The stories of the most awesome decisions of recent years—such as the decision to make the H-bomb, or to establish a Distant Early Warning system, or to try to work out an agreement with the Russians for ending nuclear tests—reveal a great deal of political enterprise on the part of scientists. Many of them were men whose primary formal status was with private corporations or universities.

In the second place, the developments since 1945 have given a new push to the decentralization of political responsibility. Already the American political concern with the means as well as the ends—the disposition to legislate (or even to establish by Constitutional provision) details of organization and procedure—had made it possible, within the framework of government, to decentralize administration even while centralizing our policies. What we did after the Second World War was to extend this process to a broader system that amalgamated public and private interests. For example, we have nationalized the support of research in the medical schools of the country through the grants of the National Institutes of Health. But administratively—which in this case means effectively—we have *denationalized* the process of controlling federal expenditures for this purpose. For Congress has by law provided that the principal control over medical research grants be exercised by a network of committees of scientists who are not primarily government officials.

If you think sovereignty is something real, this is not the way you will wish to run a government. You are more likely to deduce from the ideal of sovereignty the corollaries that the state is something like a person, and that its personality should be integrated and its ideas consistent with one another.

Since in the modern industrial world there is no way to keep government and business from being dependent on each other, this assumption of the reality of sovereignty, and the effort to find a system of legislative procedures and administrative institutions to translate its ideal purposes into actual practice, may lead to a continuous concentration of political and economic power. On what principles is that concentration to be controlled and held responsible?

Those who have abandoned the traditional value system of Western Europe, or who never held it, are likely to create a new ideology and a new elite to determine the ends of the state, and to control the entire society toward those ends. It may be argued (and this point will be considered later) that this is the way to let science control politics. But it is not a system of political responsibility, and need not be discussed now.

Those who hold to traditional values are likely to seek some new version of Plato's Guardians: the elite who are set apart from the rest of the citizens and trained and dedicated to the purposes of the state. The cruder way to do this, and the way that has been taken by a good many parliamentary democracies, is to rally round some military leader, or to give special responsibility to the career military corps. This is what has been done by those nations that lack the traditions and the skills of the nation that invented the parliamentary system. The United Kingdom can rely instead on its Administrative Class and its parliamentary leadership. The Administrative Class of its civil service is a corps that can continue to embody the purposes of the state as long as it is careful to avoid a role of authority or public responsibility. And the leadership of the House of Commons is a bipartisan group carefully self-schooled in the art of never letting the internal workings of Her Majesty's Government and Her Majesty's Services become objects of political or legislative determination. But under any type of Guardians—military, administrative, or parliamentary —the system of political responsibility is designed to test any new proposal in relation to the general purposes of the state, the ideal policies of the governing parties, or the effectiveness of the administrative establishment. It is not very much inclined to turn scientists loose to experiment with policy issues, or to license irresponsible private institutions to explore the inner workings of government, or to permit any of its parts to work at cross purposes with the rest.

In short, if you start by believing that sovereignty is something real, you are likely to design your constitutional system to focus political attention on the ends of the sovereign state, and to insist that the work of scientists supported by government be treated as a means toward the predetermined ends.

Politics in the United States has always seemed impossibly irresponsible to those who think from those premises. And this is perhaps because the United States started from a quite different premise. It not only abolished its allegiance to a particular sovereign, but abandoned the ideal of sovereignty, and treated it as only a word. Those who used the word most gave it the least reality. Those who talked most about the sovereignty of the several states were careful not to give the idea any administrative substance; if they had, they might have won the Civil War.

In the period of the American Revolution, its theorists appealed against the idea of sovereignty to both the past and the future. They appealed to the past when they asserted, with the lawyers, that the king was under the law, and that even the parliament itself did not have unlimited power to make law; indeed they were just as eager to set up Constitutional safeguards against unlimited legislative power as against executive authority. But the Revolution appealed also to the future, as men like Franklin and Jefferson sought to free both politics and science from the monarchical and ecclesiastical institutions that defined traditional values.

By consequence, democratic politics assumed the right to deal with the means of government as well as the ends, or even to put the means ahead of the ends. This meant that hardly anyone worried if neither the President nor the Congressional committees paid much attention to party doctrine in dealing with questions of policy, or to discipline and coordination in dealing with the administrative departments. This gave the scientists a chance to move back and forth between the government and private institutions, and from either base to take a lively initiative in matters of policy. And it made possible the development of more centers of dissent and criticism with respect to public policy even in those fields which government undertook to finance and direct.

This system makes it impossible to maintain an institutional distinction between ends and means, between policy decisions on the one hand and scientific research or administration on the other. Hence it makes party responsibility in the parliamentary sense impossible, and it greatly complicates the task of co-ordinating either policy or administration.

On the other hand, to blur the distinction between ends and means is a part of the scientific approach: no scientist likes to feel that his basic values and ob-jectives have been set by others so rigidly that he cannot follow where his re-search leads him. It may be even more necessary to blur the distinction be-tween ends and means, in an institutional sense, in the twentieth century, when it is the requirements of new ideology, rather than old orthodoxy, that threaten freedom. For science itself, by introducing so many complexities into public policy, destroyed the comfortable nineteenth-century notion that public issues could really be determined by the parliamentary competition of two op-posing doctrines. At the same time science, by developing new techniques of mass communication, made possible the means for producing disciplined sup-port of authoritarian government. If the structure of political institutions does not specifically encourage some social experimentation based on scientific ini-tiative, with some degree of deliberate freedom from the constraints of policy as determined by either partisan theorists or an administrative elite, it will nar-row the range of free scientific and political development. Perhaps our eighteenth-century Constitution, with its implied distrust of party discipline, will yet prove to be more adaptable to our scientific era than the classic nine-teenth-century parliamentary model of Walter Bagehot or Woodrow Wilson.

American scientists, who have tended to be a little disillusioned about their relationship with politicians ever since the Jacksonian period, are now entitled to look with a little more satisfaction on the system of political responsibility that they have helped to establish. For it is a system that is congenial to the pragmatic and inductive approach that appeals to most scientists, especially those who profess no interest in philosophy. It puts a premium on their quali-fications for promotion within the bureaucracy, and gives their policy views a respectful hearing. And it is based on principles quite different from either the classic parliamentary system or the single-party system that characterizes the new dictatorships.

But all this gives no grounds for self-satisfaction; it only helps us diagnose our troubles more accurately. It suggests that in the United States the main danger to political freedom and responsibility is not likely to come from the secrecy of scientific advice, or an excess of central executive authority, or a drift toward socialism. There is much less reason to worry that the great deci-sions of a scientific or technological nature will be secret than that they will be *popular;* the temptation of scientists to lobby for particular scientific programs, and to promise technological miracles in order to get funds for basic research may be a demoralizing one. There is much less reason to fear that the Execu-tive will dominate the Congress than that the Congress as a whole will sur-render its power to its own committees, and that they will be too obsessed with new technological toys to deal with broader issues of policy. And there is much less danger of a drift toward a socialist dictatorship than toward a sys-tem in which the government will pay all the costs of a series of expensive programs each of which will be contracted out to private corporations and managed in their private interests.

We do not need to believe in the traditional ideal of sovereignty to think that a modest measure of coherence in our national policies, and of discipline in our administrative system, may be desirable in the interest of political responsibility. Some argue that in order to attain those ends we need to strengthen the political influence of the traditional learning or religious values. Only by a return to traditional values, they argue, can party leaders be guided by moral and political theory, and career civil servants be trained in a philosophy of the public interest. Is this true? Or should we press ahead to a system in which science forms the basis for a new set of political dogmas, enforced by a new kind of establishment? Or do we have another and better choice?

The answers to these questions depend on the basic relation of the sciences to traditional values.

CONTRACTING FOR DEFENSE: PRIVATE FIRMS AND THE PUBLIC INTEREST *
J. Stefan Dupré and W. Eric Gustafson

ONE of the most challenging and costly imperatives of the Cold War is the need for constant innovation in weapons systems. Given the advanced state of defense technology, such innovation requires systematic research and development, which in turn call for sophisticated technical capacity, refined managerial skills, and flexible financial arrangements. Accordingly, the government has had to devise new standards in its contractual relationships with business firms. Essentially, the government now assumes the financial risk involved in innovation. Free competition no longer characterizes the process of bidding for government contracts. While private firms have thus been freed from the restraints of the open market, they have acquired new public responsibilities. They are no longer merely suppliers to the government, but participants in the administration of public functions. The capacity of private firms to promote the public interest in the absence of market forces poses serious conceptual and administrative problems.

GOVERNMENT AND THE CONTRACTOR: HISTORICAL

Contracting for goods and services in this country is of course as old as the United States itself. Close federal concern for the method of letting contracts goes back at least to 1809, when Congress directed that "all purchases and contracts for supplies and services . . . be made either by open purchase or by

* Reprinted with permission from the *Political Science Quarterly,* Vol. 77, No. 2, pp. 161–177.

previously advertising for proposals respecting the same." A later Attorney General's opinion limited open purchases to "situations of public exigency," and from 1829 the standard procedure for government contracting was one of open advertising for bids and its concomitant, a firm fixed price. This rule was more explicitly recognized in 1860, when Congressional legislation stipulated open advertising with but two exceptions: personal services and public exigencies necessitating immediate performance.

Peacetime defense procurement practices until after World War II were largely confined to competitive bidding.[1] During World War I there were substantial deviations, especially in the form of cost-plus-percentage of cost contracts, since declared illegal, in which efficiency was undermined by the fact that the contractor's profit was in direct proportion to the amount he managed to spend.

Deviation on a large scale from traditional contractual regulations came with World War II. The floodgates were opened by the first War Powers Act of 1941, which released agencies connected with the war effort from existing legal provisions regarding contracts. The widespread use of negotiated contracts with various forms of cost reimbursement dates from this time.

At the end of the Second World War, government contracting procedures needed overhauling. Wartime practices under negotiation had led to a number of abuses, many of which had been corrected by *ad hoc* legislation and special internal regulations. But it would have been difficult to return to the previously standard peacetime practice of advertising and fixed-price contracts. The rapid advance of military technology made it clear that there would have to be much contracting in the future for research and development, an area in which specification of the end product and advance estimation of costs are difficult. Yet open bidding on fixed-price contracts clearly requires both.

In the Armed Services Procurement Act of 1947, Congress attempted to frame a law to fit the new situation. It recognized the necessity for a large amount of negotiated (rather than advertised) contracts, but attempted to limit their use to seventeen more or less clearly defined situations which made advertised, competitive contracts cumbersome, expensive, or impossible. The Act thus gave the military departments fairly wide authority to contract without advertising—and the law contained little in the way of specifics to guard against abuses.[2] President Truman signed the Act in 1948 and at the same time wrote to the Secretary of Defense:

1. See John Perry Miller, *Pricing of Military Procurements* (New Haven, 1949), chap. III, for significant exceptions and for criticisms of the procedure. Dickson Reck, *Government Purchasing and Competition* (Berkeley, 1954), discusses parallel problems in purchasing civilian goods and services.

2. The Armed Services Procurement Act (10 USC 2301 *et seq.*) extends to the National Aeronautics and Space Administration as well as to the military departments. The Federal Property and Administrative Services Act (Title III, 41 USC 251 *et seq.*) permits the General Services Administration to delegate to nondefense agencies authority to negotiate which is almost as extensive as that open to the Armed Services. The military departments, however, remain by far the largest users of negotiated contracts. The Atomic Energy Act of 1954 also permits negotiated contracts.

This bill grants unprecedented freedom from specific procurement restrictions during peacetime. . . . To the degree that restrictions have been diminished, therefore, responsibility upon the Defense Establishment has been increased. There is danger that the natural desire for flexibility and speed in procurement will lead to excessive placement of contracts by negotiation and undue reliance on large concerns, and this must not occur.

The Armed Services Committee commented in a recent report that "The President's admonition . . . proved to be something of a prophecy."

In the past ten years, the need for flexibility and the pressures of uncertainty and complexity have further loosened contractual procedures. Private firms, unhampered by Civil Service regulations, can pay the going market rate for needed technical and managerial skills, charge them as a cost on contracts, and present the military departments with a technical and managerial package. The ultimate development has been for the military departments to let contracts for the design and production of entire weapons systems to prime contractors who are then responsible for the supervision, coordination and integration of the work of large numbers of firms on design and production of components for the system.

NEW CONTRACTING METHODS: GENERAL IMPLICATIONS

The position of the contractor under recently developed contractual methods can perhaps best be appreciated through a comparison of more traditional forms with the new. The advertised fixed-price contract lies at one extreme; the negotiated cost-plus-fixed-fee (CPFF) contract at the other.

The traditional firm fixed-price contract with open advertising is an attempt to bring full market forces into play. In order to use this system, the government must have a fairly exact idea of its requirements, and the items involved must be sufficiently standardized to enable a large number of firms to compete. In open advertising, the government lays down rigid specifications regarding the nature of the item it wishes to procure. With this information in hand, prospective suppliers submit bids which are publicly opened. The contract is automatically awarded to the qualified bidder who promises to meet the exact requirements for the lowest price.

Participating bidders are in open price competition. Their incentive is clear: to meet the government's requirements at the lowest possible cost. The lower their estimate of cost prior to bidding, the greater is the possibility of securing the contract. Once the contract has been awarded, the contractor's profit is greatest if he holds actual costs as far below his previous estimate as possible. The risk lies squarely on the contractor. He will reap its full rewards or (if his actual costs are higher than his estimates) suffer its full penalties.

By comparison with this classic concept of contracting, the newer forms are all deviations from the market mechanism. Contracts involving research, development and prototype production must by their very nature be handled differently from the procurement of routine items. It is impossible to secure firm bids in advance from which the winner could be chosen. The contractor is expected to find the solution to a problem and clearly the costs of doing so can only be roughly estimated in advance. The government thus agrees to re-imburse the contractor for the costs he incurs (subject to certain exclusions), and selects the contractor by negotiation on the basis of technical and mana-gerial facilities and know-how, rather than price. In addition, the government has had to provide a great part of the capital equipment involved in these efforts, since otherwise (so the argument runs) companies could not be in-duced to commit themselves to large-scale contracts with highly specialized equipment.[3]

As the pace of technological change has quickened in the military with the increasing dominance of advanced aircraft and missiles, a larger and larger share of procurement dollars has been spent on negotiated cost-reimbursement contracts. In fiscal 1952, 12.7 per cent of defense procurement dollars were tied up in cost-reimbursement contracts; by fiscal 1960, the proportion had risen to 42.6 per cent. In that year, the total value of military contracts was $22.9 bil-lion, over 86 per cent of which was negotiated. The disposition of a substantial fraction of our national income, therefore, is now the result of negotiation be-tween the military departments and the contractor.

WEAPONS-SYSTEM CONTRACTING

The mechanics of negotiated cost-reimbursement contracting will become somewhat clearer if we look at concrete examples. Negotiated cost-reimburse-ment contracting offers largely the same problems whatever the nature of the task or the amount of money involved. These problems appear in sharpest relief in weapons-system contracting in its single-manager form. Under this mode of organization, conceived by the Air Force, a single prime contractor is charged with the responsibility of developing and producing a complete weapons system including all components or subsystems, with the help of a widespread network of subcontractors.

A weapons system has its beginnings in the formulation of general oper-ating requirements by the Air Force, which then invites firms to submit de-signs and proposals. In the case of the B-70, currently in development, the Air Force invited six companies to submit designs in 1954. Late in 1957 North American Aviation won an intensive two-year competition after independent evaluations by the Air Research and Development Command, the Air Materiel Command, and the Strategic Air Command. As weapons-system prime con-tractor, North American was awarded a CPFF Phase I contract authorizing it to proceed with further design work and construction of mockups. Under

---

3. As an example, at the end of 1958 the Boeing Airplane Company had $239 million in plant and other facilities owned by the government; the company's own assets were $201 mil-lion. House Committee on Armed Services, Hearings on *Weapons System Management and Team System Concept in Government Contracting* (Washington, 1959), p. 195. For many other companies, the government-owned fraction of capital assets runs even higher. Cf. House Com-mittee on Armed Services, *Hearings Pursuant to Section 4, PL 86–89* (Washington, 1960), p. 604, for statistics on some Air Force contractors, a number with more then ninety per cent of their facilities government-owned.

normal circumstances this is followed by a Phase II contract (also usually CPFF) for completion of engineering and construction of prototypes and, finally, a Phase III contract for production.

What were the Air Force's principal considerations in awarding the prime contract to NAA? According to the company's President, James T. Atwood,

The primary factor in these determinations certainly is the design itself—the technical analysis, design and all the data that go toward the solution of the problem. . . . Other factors are considered, of course, general engineering capabilities and management capabilities are viewed, and production capabilities and certain program costs insofar as they can be determined in estimates, are considered.[4]

Complete estimates of costs are of course submitted. It is on these estimates that the fixed fee is based; in the case of the B-70, this was 6.5 per cent.

As prime contractor, North American received responsibility for the letting of subcontracts, subject to Air Force approval. For example, let us trace the negotiation of the subcontract for the B-70's auxiliary gyro platform subsystem. North American began by compiling a list of qualified bidders, using "recommendations from our own organization, listings in trade directories, suggestions from the various Air Force development laboratories, and direct requests from suppliers who wanted to be considered."[5] North American produced a list of thirteen qualified bidders which was approved by the Air Force.

North American sent invitations to bid to the listed firms and held a bidders' conference. Meanwhile, North American personnel toured the bidders' plants and made on-site evaluations. Subsequently, ten of the thirteen bidders submitted proposals, including a division of North American itself. North American, with Air Force approval, decided in favor of Sperry Gyroscope. An essentially similar process was used in the case of the other first-tier subcontractors. In addition, General Electric is developing the B-70 engine as an associate contractor. It holds a contract directly from the Air Force and reports to the government, except for certain aspects of technical coordination on which it has liaison with North American. All these contracts are on a CPFF basis.

North American maintains a resident representative in each of the subcontractor plants, charged with coordination and supervision. Subcontractors must furnish North American with regular reports comparing actual accomplishments with a predetermined timetable. They also submit monthly progress and cost reports which are checked against the technical and cost estimates laid out in the subcontract. As prime contractor, North American essentially takes the place that would otherwise be occupied by Air Force procurement personnel. Seventy per cent of the work on the B-70 is planned to be carried on by the subcontractors; thirty per cent will remain with North American

---

4. *Weapons System Management,* pp. 61–63. Those interested in examining weapons-system contracting in greater detail should consult M. J. Peck and F. M. Scherer, *The Weapons Acquisition Process: An Economic Analysis* (Boston, 1962), which became available after this paper was written.

5. *Ibid.,* p. 51.

itself, and even this is the result of competition with other possible subcontractors.

Each subcontractor enters into contracts with a second tier of subcontractors. These may be on a CPFF or a fixed-price basis, depending on the end item to be obtained. It is normally at this level that small businesses will begin to get some portion of the work. North American, with due regard to government regulations, takes steps to insure that small firms will be considered. First, all its subcontracts of $500,000 or more require the supplier to establish a small business subcontracting program as described in the Armed Services Procurement Regulations. Second, each subcontract of $100,000 or more requires that the subcontractor furnish North American with a quarterly report of all related small business contracting. Third, each subcontractor agrees to insert similar provisions in its own subcontracts of $100,000 or more. Fourth, all subcontracts exceeding $100,000 that appear to offer subcontracting opportunities are reported by North American to the appropriate regional office of the Small Business Administration and to the small business specialist of the appropriate military department.[6]

The entire subcontracting system, then, is based on continual administration and checking from top to bottom. Costs and economy are secondary considerations; technical efficiency and coordination hold prime importance. As each tier performs its managerial function, so do the fixed fees pyramid one on top of the other. Assuming a six per cent fixed fee to the prime contractor, and a similar fee to two levels of subcontractors, a second tier subcontract for $100,000 will involve payment of over $18,000 in fixed fees. The government thus procures management as well as hardware at all levels.

The single-manager concept of weapons-system contracting gives a particularly good example of multi-tiered contracting with major administrative responsibilities borne by private business. But there are many others as well. The associate weapons-system manager concept is an important modification. Here a number of prime contracts are let, with one of the primes as an integrator, the government retaining somewhat more managerial control. In the case of the Atlas missile, for instance, two Air Force units together with a hired consultant, Space Technology Laboratories, are system managers. North American Aviation, General Electric, Burroughs, American Bosch Arma Corporation and Convair are all prime contractors, with Convair holding responsibilities as integrator.[7] Somewhere between this system and the single-manager arrangement lies the Polaris Missile Program. Here the Special Projects Office of the Navy's Bureau of Naval Weapons is weapons-system manager. M.I.T. holds a prime contract for the development of the guidance system. The Lockheed Missiles and Space Division holds a prime contract as missile-system manager and has numerous subcontractors.[8]

These cases all illustrate government contracting in its various modern

6. *Ibid.*, pp. 98–99.
7. *Ibid.*, p. 306.
8. *Ibid.*, p. 129.

weapons-system forms, tying hundreds of firms together through various tiers to produce a single end item. The use of such complex contracting methods has created a set of problems of the utmost importance for public policy.

The new contracting methods create problems because they involve new concepts of the roles of government and business. Under our traditional contracting system, business firms are government suppliers whose responsibilities and performance are regulated by the competition and risk that characterize the market mechanism of the private economy. Government, for its part, plays a relatively passive role limited to assuring equitable competition for its business. Recently, however, there has emerged a mixture of the functions formerly considered "governmental" and "private" to the point where the old distinctions are inappropriate.

The result has been a number of problem areas in which old tools of control and old concepts prove ineffective in the modern context. Costs and performance are hard to regulate in the absence of the market discipline of competitive contracting; the requirements of the system have led to a concentration of business in a small number of hands, a situation which seems unavoidable under current practices; and the need for productive capacity has tied the hands of the Defense Department in terms of the sources of supply available to it and in terms of its ability to terminate its relationship with a contractor.

1. Costs. Negotiated CPFF contracts offer a marked contrast to the advertised fixed-price variety. First, while competition is not precluded, the number of competing firms is limited to those that receive government invitations to bid. Second, competition concentrates on proffered designs, technical and managerial competence, and the like, rather than estimated costs. Third, the assumption of the contract by the successful firm involves no element of risk; the government undertakes to reimburse costs. The contractor as a result is left with no market incentive to hold costs down; such incentives as there are to hold down the level of costs are purely administrative.

By contrast to the market-imposed controls of advertised fixed-price contracting, negotiated CPFF contracts are the result of a bargaining process in which government and business are at opposite ends. Here business firms have decided advantages. They will have an incentive to negotiate for high target costs and will be in a favorable position to do so; their personnel is more knowledgeable and better acquainted with cost determinants. The government's position is bound to be weaker in a situation where experience with thousands of components is needed. The advantages of the business firms in negotiation have been confirmed by numerous cases in which audits have revealed that negotiated fixed-price contracts have been overpriced. For instance, in a recent case before the Tax Court, it emerged that Boeing had initially submitted a bid on a contract of $540 million. After negotiation with the Air

Force, the price was reduced to $500 million. The FBI later turned up internal cost estimates made at the time by Boeing of only $460 million.

In an attempt to provide contractors with an inducement to hold costs down, the government has devised modified forms of contract. Cost-plus-incentive-fee and fixed-price incentive contracts permit the contractor to share in any cost reduction which takes place relative to negotiated target costs. (Contracts of this sort can normally be used only after research, development, and early prototype production.) In one frequent form, any savings on target costs go eighty per cent to the contracting military department and twenty per cent to the contractor. Incentive contracts, however, provide incentive for the contractor in two directions: to hold actual costs below target costs, but also to keep target costs as high as possible.

The effective operation of any of these contracting methods depends on the bargaining or "adversary" system which the contracting method assumes. The buyer must be an aloof and impartial decision-maker. Yet Defense contracting officials must now work hand-in-glove with their opposite numbers in the contractors' establishments. To a large extent, the standing of government personnel within their departments (and the standing of the military department itself, for that matter) depends on cooperation from the contractor. The result, as one might predict, is frequently a live-and-let-live situation when crucial decisions arise. This attitude can be especially damaging to cost control when emphasis is placed on time of delivery, while little attention is paid to cost. If the contractor is permitted to buy shorter delivery time with increased costs, and the reasonableness of these costs is not too closely scrutinized, the opportunities for inefficiency are multiplied.

2. *Concentration.* The number of firms which can participate as prime contractors has tended to be rather limited. Some of the reasons are obvious: few firms have the management, technical personnel, and industrial capacity to build complex and costly hardware and to manage sizeable contracts involving many subcontractors. Large firms have frequently done essential background research and development using their own funds or under other government contracts, and already hold government financed facilities. As the contract comes closer to the all-inclusive weapons-system concept, without provision for associate contractors, the number of firms which can possibly compete for the contract becomes smaller.

But also important is the fact that there are pressures in the contracting situation which tend to limit the number of firms which can participate in the process. As one small businessman phrased it:

All other things being equal, the average military procurement officer would rather give a contract to a big firm because he thinks it is safer and he takes less personal risk. If the contract doesn't work out, he always has the excuse that the big firm is well-known and well-established and should have performed better.

The result of these pressures has been to concentrate defense business in the hands of a relatively few large corporations. For example, in calendar year

1958, twenty-five corporations accounted for almost fifty-five per cent of DOD prime contract awards of more than $10,000. Furthermore, the concentration of contracts has tended to increase over time. During fiscal 1951, the 100 largest contractors received 61.2 per cent of DOD business. This percentage had increased to 73.8, by fiscal 1959.

From the point of view of certain segments of the business community, this problem of the concentration of contracts and the limitation on potential bidders for defense contracts is quite serious. The "play-it-safe" motivation in choosing contractors is not one about which much can be done; it is inherent in the situation (and indeed finds an exact counterpart in private business, according to many analysts of the corporation). But the weapons-system method of procurement ties up military spending in such large bundles that most otherwise suitable business firms are automatically disqualified as prime contractors because of their size. This is not only a problem for the potential contractor, of course, but one for the government as well, since limitation of competition is bound to lead to higher prices.[9]

3. Maintenance of Capacity. The limited number of large firms qualified to bid for prime contracts in the field of weapons systems has placed the government in a peculiar position. The market incentives for cost and good performance are of course weak, due to the necessity of using negotiated contracts. Nonetheless, there is another incentive which might normally operate. In the words of a Boeing Airplane Company representative, "a reputation for high costs is damaging to any contractor seeking to remain in the defense contracting industry."

Given the special nature of defense contracting, however, the threat of loss of business has considerably less meaning than it would in the context of the purchase of common use items from normal commercial suppliers and manufacturers. Many observers feel that defense officials are almost compelled to keep the large contractors in business in order to maintain the country's defense research and production capabilities and the defense establishment's investment in these facilities. Indeed, the Armed Services Procurement Act specifically provides that contracts may be negotiated without competitive bidding to maintain production facilities or "to maintain active engineering, research, and development." In recent fiscal years, this provision has been used as the explicit justification for more than one billion dollars' worth of negotiated contracts. Considerations of this sort undoubtedly play a role in many other contracts. As an illustration, the Robertson Committee found that "the need for maintaining the industrial base by spreading the work" was one reason why design competitions were used in only thirty per cent of the design

9. Some critics have suggested on both technological and economic grounds that lead-times would be shorter and costs lower if less contracting were done on a unified weapons-system basis, with more competition on components at the research and development level, the winner to be determined after prototypes have been produced by several different companies. The point is too complex for full exposition here, but see Burton H. Klein, "A Radical Proposal for R and D," *Fortune,* May, 1958, pp. 112–113, 218 ff., and Klein *et al., Military Research and Development Policies* (Santa Monica, 1958).

contractor selections by the Navy's Bureau of Aeronautics from 1947 to 1957.

The necessity of maintaining research and production facilities conflicts with an important underlying assumption of contracting. The assumption is that if a contractor does not perform to standard, his services need not be used in the future and the goods in question can be bought elsewhere from better qualified suppliers. Given the necessity for the facilities, however, and the fact that they have increasingly fewer alternative civilian uses, the freedom of the government to buy or not to buy from a given contractor is often fictitious. This inflexible situation is frequently compounded by political pressures from the geographical areas in which the large contractors are located.

4. *Private Benefit vs. the Public Interest.* The problems discussed so far are at their most severe in the areas where private benefit and public interest conflict. Such public goals as cost control, the insurance of competition, and protection for small business all come into conflict with the profit motive.

A good instance of the general problem caused by the quasi-governmental character of many of the defense contractors is the case of Space Technology Laboratories, a wholly-owned subsidiary of Thompson Ramo Wooldridge, which was technical director of the Air Force's ballistic missile program.

STL was barred from manufacturing activities related to its role as technical director, since these activities would have involved clear conflict of interest with its managerial responsibilities. Nevertheless, its status as a profit-making organization caused conflict between its public responsibility as technical director and its private interests, and because of conflict of interest with other firms involved, militated against its full effectiveness as coordinator of the missile program. The General Accounting Office in May, 1960, recommended that STL be absorbed within the Air Force on a number of grounds, most particularly the two we have pointed out. The GAO commented that, "As STL's know-how grows through continued systems engineering and technical direction, it would appear that the financial incentive to withdraw from the program would become increasingly dependent on the capability acquired by STL." The government could only hope that the possibilities for increased profit would not cause STL to leave the program. In addition, its effectiveness as coordinator was hamstrung by its profit-making nature, said the GAO. "The likelihood that the know-how being developed may be used by [STL] to compete for production in related fields and in future programs is a deterrent to full cooperation by the participating contractors." Manufacturers have "a natural reluctance" to make information that might lead to important patents [10] available to a potential competitor.

Many prime contractors for weapons systems seem to be in a position where similar problems would arise, and there is some evidence that they do. On the question of "make or buy"—to subcontract or not to subcontract—here seem to have been clear cases of conflict between the profit motive and "public re-

10. Comptroller General of the United States, *Initial Report on Review of the Ballistic Missile Program of the Department of the Air Force* (Washington, May 1960), pp. 27, 37, 39.

sponsibility" in instances where the guidelines were not at all clear.[11] The prime contractor's private interests (be they profit or merely the desire for a quiet life) may lead him to rely on a relatively small number of subcontractors, without encouraging the fullest possible competition. As Representative Curtis recently phrased it, "one of the things that the Small Business Committee is concerned about is this mother sow process where one big prime gets its favorite little piglets and that is a closed family party that keeps going on." In addition, small subcontractors have complained that the large primes are "proselyting the engineering and design know-how of the subcontractors, who after obtaining all the engineering and manufacturing know-how needed, proceed to build the products in their own shops."

To some, the solution for this conflict between private and public interest is quite clear: the management function should be returned to the Defense Department. In particular, the GAO made this recommendation with respect to Space Technology Laboratories.[12] Similar recommendations were made with respect to weapons systems from a small business point of view:

The only way . . . to genuinely increase small business participation in [weapons-system procurement] which is increasingly becoming the preponderant defense activity, is by eliminating the single-manager concept and giving the coordinating responsibility and contracting authority back to the Defense Department where it really belongs.[13]

The question of returning greater managerial responsibility to the military departments may be purely academic as long as the salary differential between public and private employment remains as large as it is. In the absence of marked salary differentials, there would still be problems: for many purposes, private organizations can act more flexibly than those bound by Civil Service procedures. But under present arrangements, government contributes to salary differentials through the funds it provides to contractors. Current proposals for making Civil Service salaries at executive levels competitive with those paid for comparable private jobs might enable the military departments to assume a greater portion of managerial functions. Nonetheless, such functions will continue to be shared by government and business to a certain extent because private firms enjoy a greater degree of flexibility than public agencies.

This brings us back to our thesis that public and private functions have be-

11. Senate Small Business Committee, Report on *Small Business Participation in Defense Subcontracting* (Washington, 1959), p. 12. This particular problem was avoided with STL because it was not allowed to manufacture.

12. The Air Force's solution to this problem has been to create a new nonprofit corporation, Aerospace Corporation, to take over STL's role as technical director of the missile program. The solution takes care of two difficulties: Aerospace's nonprofit status will minimize conflict of public objectives with private profit motivation, and its nongovernmental status will avoid Civil Service restrictions on personnel and their pay scales. The history of the controversy can be found in House Committee on Government Operations, Third Report, *Air Force Ballistic Missile Management: Formation of Aerospace Corporation* (Washington, 1961).

13. Sidney M. Kaplan, President of Systems, Inc., in Hearings on *Small Business Participation . . . *, p. 98.

come intertwined. Business is no longer merely a supplier but a participant in the management and administration of a public function. Negotiation and cost reimbursement have channeled public money into the private sector without the use of the market mechanism. Business, like government, must then become subject to noneconomic checks to avoid abuses. If they are to shoulder public responsibilities, private firms must ultimately become accustomed to close supervision with the resulting investigations, audits and other paraphernalia that accompany the spending of taxpayers' money. Finally, large firms administering subcontracts find themselves with administrative responsibilities toward their subcontractors similar to those the government holds toward them, and of allocating contractual funds with regard to such public policy goals as the sponsorship of small business, the relief of unemployment, "Buy-American," and nondiscrimination in hiring.

It is certainly tempting to read elements of federalism into this emerging system. This is particularly true if we think of the so-called "new federalism" of the last twenty-five years, under which federal grants have softened the traditionally emphasized legal distinctions of federalism in favor of federal-state cooperation in matters of broad public policy. Business retains its "autonomy" in the sphere of its purely commercial transactions, subject, of course, to existing regulations, just as the states have "autonomy" subject to the Constitution. But over-all business performance (investment patterns and so on) is affected by the availability of federal funds, just as state functions are affected by federal grants. In the contractual area itself, the business firm is subject to audits and administrative control but still retains a wide sphere of independence in the allocation of funds (for instance, salaries), again presenting a situation analogous to that of the states. Finally, efforts to allocate funds to small business and to labor surplus areas present a problem quite similar to the question of "fiscal need" (diversion of grant funds to resource-poor states) in federal finance.

To be sure, there is great danger in pushing the federal analogy too far. One could with greater safety speak in terms of a partnership, or of the industrial "public-mindedness" so cherished by the American business creed. Nevertheless, the term federalism brings at least one important item to mind—the fact that tax money is being spent on a decentralized basis and that the spenders, both "grantor" and "grantee," are subject to public accountability. But the involvement of private firms as opposed to institutions like state governments presents a distinct complication. Business is still not government; it is by nature oriented toward its private interests.

A major problem of our defense establishment, then, is to find effective contracting methods to enable private business to cooperate in public administration without conflict with its private interests. The tools and skills of administration must be further developed to ensure controls which will approximate the results of the market mechanism.

THE FEDERAL SYSTEM AS SEEN BY FEDERAL AID OFFICIALS *

INTRODUCTION

THE resolution creating this subcommittee charges it with the responsibility "to examine, investigate, and make a complete study of intergovernmental relationships between the United States and the States and municipalities. . . ."

At its first meeting, Senator Muskie discussed the subcommittee's objectives:

. . . What we hope to do in the work of this subcommittee is to give this . . . hidden dimension of government (intergovernmental relations) definition and identity—to understand what it is and what its potential is, and in what direction it is moving. . . .

It is clear that many Americans hold drastically conflicting views on the relative roles of the different levels of government, and it is our intention to give careful attention to every point of view to determine which pattern of interrelationships best serves the needs of the United States during this period of our history. . . .

More and more, the emphasis is on cooperation rather than competition among levels of government. We hear less talk about States' rights and more talk about States' responsibilities. . . .

There is no sense denying that the 20th century has seen the rise of revolutionary demands on the part of the people for the provision of services by the Government. What we are striving to achieve is a new balance of governmental activity which unshackles all levels of government to perform these tasks adequately. . . .

To this end the subcommittee has held hearings, considered legislation, issued reports and conducted research. The hearings have covered a wide range of topics exploring intergovernmental relationships in general, as well as specific problem areas. The subcommittee has also considered a number of bills to implement findings based on its hearings and on the reports of the Advisory Commission on Intergovernmental Relations and to carry out recommendations that emerged from subcommittee research studies.

One such research effort assayed the views of State and local officials on Federal-State-local relations. Through the distribution of a 97-item questionnaire a pattern of attitudes was identified, and valuable background information on various legislative proposals was amassed.

* From *The Federal System as Seen by Federal Aid Officials,* a study prepared by the U.S. Senate, Committee on Governmental Operations, Subcommittee on Intergovernmental Relations (committee print, December 15, 1965), pp. 1–2, 5–8, 21–22, 93–101.

The subcommittee now turns to Federal aid officials for their views on intergovernmental relations. These officials are responsible for the operation of some 125 programs of assistance to State and local governments, including grants-in-aid, shared revenues, technical assistance, and loans. Excluding loan payments and technical assistance, they disbursed close to $13 billion in fiscal 1964. Their views on the federal system clearly are of more than minor significance. . . .

FEDERAL AIDS

"The use of Federal grants-in-aid has been increasing both in variety and magnitude since the initiation of the device in 1862, and especially since the end of World War II." This was probably the least controversial statement in the 1961 report by the Advisory Commission on Intergovernmental Relations on grants-in-aid, and subsequent developments have only underlined the accuracy of their assessment. From the inauguration of President Kennedy to the close of the 88th Congress, 29 new grant programs were added to the ACIR's original list of 45. Federal expenditures for such assistance soared more than 41 percent during this same brief period. This remarkable increase provides additional evidence of the importance of grants-in-aid in the maintenance of our federal system during a period of significant domestic change. The use of grants strengthens federalism by promoting national goals within a cooperative framework. The grant device has, in effect, prevented the nationalization of functions by strengthening and preserving State and local government.

The grant-in-aid has been responsive to the changing needs of this country throughout its development. Land grants assisted the States and local governments as our Nation emerged. Money is now the measure of Federal support.

As grant programs and the administrative machinery have matured, the pattern has become more complex. The earlier subcommittee report, "The Federal System As Seen by State and Local Officials," stressed that this proliferation of grants and the continual amending of older grants have created confusion and a somewhat critical view of such Federal aids at the State and local levels.

In hearings held before this subcommittee, William G. Colman, Executive Director of the ACIR, cited one of the basic reasons for this attitude.

Grants-in-aid are increasing, in numbers and magnitude, at a rapid rate and we may come to a situation where grants-in-aid are an impenetrable jungle of legal, financial, and political and professional interlacings which will sorely try the minds of officials at all levels—Congressmen, Cabinet members, Governors, mayors, and county officials—in trying to maintain any kind of rational legislative and administrative direction of the areas of Government affairs in which grants play so large a part.[1]

1. U.S. Senate, Subcommittee on Intergovernmental Relations, Committee on Government Operations, *Problems of Federal-State-Local Relations*, 88th Cong., 2d sess. (U.S. Government Printing Office, September 18, 1962), p. 13.

This "impenetrable jungle" has been the subject of increasing examination since the first Hoover Commission dealt this topic a glancing blow in its 14-page report on Federal-State relations over 16 years ago. The Commission recommended that greater Federal attention be paid to the use of grants-in-aid and to revisions of the tax system.

Another early but more comprehensive report was prepared by the Council of State Governments for the Hoover Commission. This included a discussion of grants-in-aid. In addition to treating this topic generally the Council described the actual operation of 18 federally supported programs. Two sets of recommendations emerged from their analysis. Defects in the structure of State government formed the basis of the Council's suggestions for State consideration, while the use of grants-in-aid was the focal point of the recommendations for the Federal level. Several of the still unresolved questions raised in the Council's findings were covered in this survey of Federal executives.

The Council proposed that national grants be made for broad categories of public services. The subcommittee asked Federal administrators whether multipurpose grants, or permitting transfers of funds between grants, is desirable. The previous survey of State and local officials requested similar information. The Council also recommended that

Grant-in-aid programs should be based, in all cases, on close cooperation between the National and State Governments. In no event should the National Government attempt to deal directly in grant programs with the political subdivisions of the States or with individuals.[2]

This recommendation parallels questionnaire items 1 and 2 which deal with the channeling of aid requests and aid disbursements.

The Council urged the restriction of national supervision of the administration of grant programs to initial approval of overall plans, post-audit of expenditures, and technical assistance and guidance during operation. The implications of this broad statement apply to various questions asked in both subcommittee surveys, including a whole section of this study dealing exclusively with intergovernmental fiscal relations.

Finally, the Council recommended that "the present patchwork of grant-in-aid programs should be systematized, with provision for cooperative planning, appraisal, and administration on a continuing basis." This perennial problem received extensive coverage in both subcommittee questionnaires, including items 1, 2, and 5 in this survey.

These reports and recommendations lay dormant until the creation in 1953 of the Commission on Intergovernmental Relations, better known by the name of its second chairman, Meyer Kestnbaum. Unlike the Hoover Commission, this group confined its efforts specifically to intergovernmental relationships. The Kestnbaum Commission traced the use of grants-in-aid,

2. Council of State Governments, "Federal-State Relations," report of the Commission on Organization of the Executive Branch of the Government (Senate Doc. 81, 81st Cong., 1st Sess., Washington: Government Printing Office, March 25, 1949).

weighed their advantages and disadvantages, examined the operation of many particular grant programs, and measured the impact of this assistance on the functioning of State and local government.

This "blue ribbon" panel then discussed improvements in the operation of grant programs and the means of determining where such aid is needed. Three basic conclusions were reached:

(1) A grant should be made or continued only for a clearly indicated and presently important national objective. This calls for a searching and selecting test of the justification for national participation. The point has been made . . . that existence of a national interest in an activity is not in itself enough to warrant national participation. Related questions are the relative importance of the national interest and the extent to which it may be served by State and local action. Consequently, where the activity is one normally considered the primary responsibility of State and local governments, substantial evidence should be required that national participation is necessary in order to protect or to promote the national interest.

(2) Where national participation in an activity is determined to be desirable, the grant-in-aid should be employed only when it is found to be the most suitable form of national participation. It is important to compare the strong and weak points of the grant-in-aid device with those of other forms of national-State cooperation as well as with those of direct national action. It is likewise important to consider the types of objectives and situations for which the grant is best adapted. The probable effect on State or local governments is an important consideration.

(3) Once it is decided that a grant-in-aid should be made, the grant should be carefully designed to achieve its specified objective. This requires careful attention to the shaping of apportionment formulas and matching requirements, the prescription of standards and conditions, and the provision for administrative machinery and procedures. Objectives as varied as cancer control, old-age assistance, highway construction, and forest fire prevention call for imaginative use of varied types of standards, controls, and fiscal formulas. It is more important to shape these elements of the grant to a particular purpose to achieve complete uniformity among the programs. At the same time, in order to ease the impact of grants-in-aid on State and local government, as much uniformity should be striven for as is compatible with the achievement of specific objectives.[3]

Much of the present debate over grants-in-aid is still based on the work of this Commission. Consequently, many of the questions posed in the subcommittee's questionnaire find their roots in its final 1955 report to the President.

The Commission report had an impact on Washington. First, Meyer Kestnbaum was asked to stay on to work for the adoption of the proposals put forth by the first Hoover Commission and the Commission on Intergovernmental Relations. Later, President Eisenhower addressed the Governors' Conference on June 21, 1957. In this speech, he called for the creation of a task force to draw up an action program for congressional consideration. This Joint Federal-State Action Committee was assigned three tasks:

3. The Commission on Intergovernmental Relations, *A Report to the President for Transmittal to Congress,* House Doc. No. 198, 84th Cong., 1st Sess. (Washington: Government Printing Office, June 28, 1955), pp. 123–124.

(1) to designate functions that might be shifted from the Federal Government to the States;

(2) to recommend Federal revenue sources that might be turned over to the States to finance these functions; and

(3) to identify emerging problems that might require governmental action and recommend the appropriate division of Government responsibility for them.[4]

The recommendations adopted by this committee asked the States to assume responsibility for the vocational education program and construction of local waste treatment works. In return, the Federal Government was to give up a portion of the Federal telephone tax and to end its participation in the two aid programs.

The report was transmitted by the President to Congress, but the recommendations were not adopted. The two principal reasons for their rejection were highlighted during hearings held by the House Intergovernmental Relations Subcommittee. The subcommittee found that:

(1) Such an exchange would adversely affect the lower income States, which would lose far more in grants than they would gain in tax revenue. Many of the higher income States, on the other hand, would obtain substantially more revenue than needed to carry on the activities concerned.

(2) While grants purport to assist the States in supporting specific activities of national concern, it appears that many States would be unable or unwilling to carry on these functions alone. The result would likely be very uneven, with some States discontinuing or impairing programs because of their inability or unwillingness to impose the necessary taxes.[5]

This question of equalizing the differences between high and low income States is a perennial one. The return of taxes to the States in exchange for their assumption of a grant-aided program is also a longstanding issue. Question 3a of this study asks Federal administrators if their particular programs should reflect the variations in fiscal capacity among States and local governments. The earlier questionnaire also explored the desirability of recognizing disparities among the States in income or resources. State and local officials were asked if they favored the return of tax sources in exchange for the full responsibility of carrying out a program currently underwritten with grant funds.

Congressional interest in Federal-State-local relations (and the use of grants-in-aid in particular) increased when the House Intergovernmental Relations Subcommittee began its 3-year study of grants-in-aid in 1956. A comprehensive questionnaire to Federal agencies and State and local officials served as the basis for a series of public hearings. These proceedings were held both in Washington and in the field. The subcommittee wound up the investigation

---

4. Joint Federal-State Action Committee, Final Report to the President of the United States and to the Chairman of the Governors' Conference (Washington: Government Printing Office, February 1960), p. 2.

5. U.S. Congress, House of Representatives, Subcommittee on Intergovernmental Relations, Committee on Government Operations, 30th Report, *Federal-State-Local Relations, Federal Grants-in-Aid*, House Report No. 2533 (Washington: Government Printing Office, 1958), pp. 28–29.

with a consideration of the two recommendations of the Joint Federal-State Action Committee. Other broad findings and recommendations concerning Federal grants, as well as some valuable appendixes, are also included in this report by the House Committee on Government Operations. The subcommittee found general satisfaction with the use of grants-in-aid in its nation-wide survey and concluded that the grant-in-aid has been an important device in promoting cooperation among levels of government.

The creation of an advisory commission on intergovernmental relations was one of the major suggestions of this House report. Joint hearings were held on bills introduced by Senator Muskie and Representative Fountain to implement the proposal. On September 4, 1959, President Eisenhower signed an act creating a permanent, bipartisan Advisory Commission on Intergovernmental Relations.

The outstanding work of the Commission has brought the issue of Federal grants into sharper focus. The subcommittee has worked closely with it on this and other questions. The provisions of title III of S. 561, the proposed Intergovernmental Cooperation Act of 1965, for example, find their origin in the 1961 Commission report "Periodic Congressional Reassessment of Federal Grants-in-Aid to State and Local Governments." Specifically, this title requires that any new grant-aided program authorized for 3 or more years shall be reviewed with the following considerations in mind: (1) the extent to which the purposes for which the grants-in-aid are authorized have been met; (2) the extent to which such programs can be carried on without further financial assistance from the United States; and (3) whether or not there should be any changes in purpose, direction, or administration of the original program, or in the procedures and requirements.

The subcommittee has conducted its own probe of this subject. The first survey of State and local officials contained one section dealing specifically with grants-in-aid. The observations of these officials have assisted the subcommittee in its legislative efforts as well as in its research undertakings. In the present study Federal officials were asked for their opinion on the use of Federal aids. . . .

OVERALL QUESTIONNAIRE RESULTS

National domestic goals continue to be achieved through Federal programs of assistance to State and local governments and other public and private agencies, as well as through direct government activity. The expansion of the range and variety of these shared activities has reached the point now that it is difficult to find an area of public concern that does not involve government and, in turn, some form of Federal-State-local collaboration. The grant device, then, has become the foremost symbol of the partnership between and among the levels of government.

The historical pattern of this development has been irregular, however. From the beginning of the century to the great depression it was gradual and fairly uniform, with totals reaching approximately $200 million by 1932. By

1940 Federal grants reached more than $2.3 billion, but by 1946 they had slipped back to below $1 billion. From 1948 until the present, grant payments began to increase again at a fairly constant rate, as old programs were expanded and new ones were added. At the latest count, 10 executive departments of the National Government and 11 of its independent agencies are involved in administering some 143 general programs of Federal aid to State and local governments.

This development has produced a wealth of background material and a continuing debate on the role of grants-in-aid in our federal system. Yet it apparently has exerted little impact on many Federal program administrators. This section deals with four of the topics that have figured in this debate—channeling procedures, equalization provisions, suspension of payments, and the use of incentive grants. Several Federal officials provided hasty and superficial responses to these questions; some did not even bother to reply; and most of those who did respond seemed quite content with the present operation of their programs. Suggestions for change were few.

Whether the responding official administered a Federal-State, Federal-local, or Federal-State-local aid program, replies to the question on channeling and disbursement exuded satisfaction with present practices and provisions. These officials were equally sanguine when asked to comment on present equalization provisions (if any) found in their programs. Only 15 percent of the aid administrators and 21 percent of the grant officials who responded saw a need for greater recognition of differences in State and local fiscal capacity. Some of those answering "no change needed," of course, administer programs which permit the transfer of funds or sliding matching scales to reflect differences between wealthy and poorer States.

The question of incentive payments encountered general indifference from most of the survey's respondents. Sixty-three percent of those grant respondents answering saw little need for a provision of this type and only half of those conceding that it might be desirable felt that such a provision would improve the administration of their individual programs. In light of the personnel and planning problems cited by many in response to other questions, it is somewhat surprising that more of these officials did not see the use of incentive grants as a possible method of correcting some of these difficulties.

In general, only a few of the responding officials considered the four issues raised here in terms of the extraordinary growth in the number, cost, and significance of Federal grants-in-aid. Only a few considered the dynamic changes which State and local governments now are experiencing. Only a few analyzed the future of their individual programs in light of these developments. Most confined the scope of their answers to the administration of their own programs. Only a few, then, dealt with the questions posed in terms of a broader intergovernmental context. Indifference, standpattism, and a narrowly defined functionalism—these were the themes that dominated the majority of responses to these grant-in-aid questions.

This functional orientation has deep roots. The legislation establishing grants is usually initiated by a particular coalition of legislators, administrators, and special-interest groups who are deeply concerned with expanding existing programs or establishing new substantive ones. Concurrence of a substantial number of legislators is required in order to achieve congressional enactment. These factors insure that the program will be a matter of national concern.

But the approach followed throughout this legislative process is basically a functional one. It is geared to meeting specific, often urgent, problems. Relatively little consideration is given generally to the impact on other programs or on the State and local units which will administer it. Comparatively little thought is spent on such intergovernmental niceties as cooperative planning, appraisal, and administration. Program administrators, then, tend to have little awareness of questions of an intergovernmental nature because little in their mandate requires or promotes it.

Further, there is not much likelihood that interlevel problems will be explored at any length after a program's enactment. The aid administrator is called upon to carry out successfully the specific goals of his program. Many deviations from this course would place him in a precarious position. And the professional expertise that characterizes Federal administrators at this "upper-middle management level" also guarantees a preoccupation with the purposes of the program. The functional bias once again reveals itself as aid administrators and satellite interest groups fight to protect "the integrity of the program." They may view as intruders those legislative committees, top administrators, and commissions concerned with the broader problems of policy consistency, interlevel administrative procedures, interagency coordination, and structural reorganization.

Thus, program goals, professionalism, and clientele pressures, as well as the legislative process itself, combine to explain why Federal executives in general have neither the mandate nor the desire to assess their grant-in-aid programs in terms of their intergovernmental significance.

BUREAUCRACY AND FEDERALISM: SOME OBSERVATIONS AND PROPOSALS

This study began as a survey of the views of Federal aid administrators on some of the more troublesome issues confronting our federal system. As the study progressed, it also involved an analysis of some of the problems in contemporary public administration. As such, it became a study of middle management, since practically all of the survey's respondents are bureau chiefs or division heads.

The conventional wisdom of public administration holds that middle management is the principal home of the specialists—not the generalists—in the bureaucratic structure. This is not surprising, since the civil service classification system is still largely based on specialized principles and since appointment to this level usually comes to in-grade bureau personnel, not to outsiders. Further, the administrative unit which middle management executives head is the bureau or division. And this relatively homogeneous structure is built to perform one task or a series of closely related tasks. As such, it is a highly stable organizational unit that reorganization plans may shift around, but rarely abolish. Finally, most bureau chiefs and nearly all division heads have permanent tenure and thus are able to exert a continuing influence toward achieving unity and consistency in administering the programs falling under their jurisdiction. Stability based on tenure; professionalism based on technical training, experience, and program goals; and a narrow functionalism based on the relatively homogeneous program mandates of the bureau and division— these are the usual traits of middle management found in the lexicon of public administration experts.[6]

Four behavioral themes recur throughout the questionnaire responses of nearly all of the 109 administrators participating in this survey. These themes both correspond to and expand on the foregoing traits of middle management.

Functionalism, or the respondents' preoccupation with protecting and promoting the purposes of their individual programs, was the most important single conditioner of their comments regarding the items examined in all five parts of the questionnaire. This is in keeping with the normal role of an executive assigned to this administrative level and with the specific character of their program mandates. It is this norm that accounts for their intense desire to maintain clear channels of communication and to promote the closest possible relationship with their functional counterparts at the State and local levels. It is this norm that helps explain the aggressive defense of their programs' objectives. It is this norm that generates the special brand of politics—program politics—which successful middle management administrators so adroitly practice. And it is this norm that produces their general insensitivity to many of the diplomatic niceties required for more successful intergovernmental relations.

Professionalism, or the deep commitment to the merit system principle and to the technical and ethical standards of the specialized group to which they belong, dictated their answers to nearly all of the questions in the preceding chapters on State Organization and Intergovernmental Personnel. It is this norm that explains their keen interest in upgrading the expertise, tenure, and administrative capabilities of their counterparts at the State and local levels. It is this norm that explains their attempts to reduce to a minimum the meddling of "dilettante generalists" at any point in their administrative operations. It is this norm that explains their distrust of partisan intrusions into the administration of these programs. And it is this norm that explains their difficulty in arriving at a balanced definition of the public interest as it applies to the State or metropolitan level.

Standpattism, or the rigid defense of traditional practices, procedures, and principles, is a theme found in the great majority of their answers to the items

6. Leonard D. White, *Introduction to the Study of Public Administration,* Fourth Edition (New York, Macmillan Co.), pp. 88, 99; and Mary C. H. Niles, *Middle Management* (New York, Harper, 1949), *passim.*

covered in the chapters on Federal aids, financial administration, and metropolitan area problems. As the conservative defenders of administrative continuity and stability against innovating pressures from above, from below, and from outside, these middle management officials could hardly be expected to indicate that present channeling and disbursement practices, accounting and auditing procedures, and program activities in metropolitan areas are something less than sensible and sound. This norm, of course, is necessary to balance the impetus for change and to provide the proper administrative milieu for the implementation of any program. Yet, this norm and its adherents must also be recognized as the major obstacle to any reform in the problem areas reviewed in this survey.

The fourth behavioral norm—indifference, or the cavalier dismissal of serious questions and topics as being irrelevant or unimportant—was reflected in responses to every section of this questionnaire. Nearly every item produced a large percentage of "no opinion" replies, and several items produced "not relevant" comments from agency heads whose programs clearly were covered by the issue under examination. And even the clear-cut answers of many respondents indicated a complete indifference to the critical significance of the topic in question. This attitude, of course, is partly an extension of the three traits previously discussed. Middle management executives, with a strong functional, professional, and status-quo orientation, are not likely to approach broad questions of a multifunctional, interlevel, interagency, or coordinating nature with any great enthusiasm or concern. But this attitude also relates to other factors. It stems in part from the ignorance that only the narrow specialist can display toward broader questions of management, policy, and governmental operations. It stems in part from an acute awareness that their expertise is needed and that their administrative positions are fairly secure. It stems in part from their recognition that many of the larger intergovernmental questions can only be resolved by others more directly involved in the decisionmaking processes at the Federal, State, and local levels.

If the behavioral traits of this select middle management group conform fairly closely to the descriptions of authorities on public administration, their theory of federalism bears little resemblance to more familiar interpretations found in political addresses or in works dealing with intergovernmental relations.

The orthodox or conventional theory, now enunciated primarily by States righters, views the federal system as one in which competition is principally between or among the levels of government. The powers of the Federal Government and those of the State, so the interpretation runs, are and should be kept distinct from and independent of each other, and the activities at these levels should be confined to different spheres, with only incidental administrative collaboration. The ideal model, premised by this traditional theory, is one where "the functions of government are almost entirely assigned to a single one of the levels of government and the competitive friction is designed to preserve the insulation." In the familiar analogy from the pantry, the federal system ideally is like a layer cake, but the great contemporary problem is that the Federal layer now is not only on top, but is getting too thick. This clearly is not the view of the Federal aid officials.

The "marble cake" theory, developed by the late Morton Grodzins and further developed by Daniel J. Elazar and others, views the system as involving both competition and cooperation, but with an emphasis on the latter. The American federal system, then, is not and has never been a system of separated governmental activities. Whether cooperative federalism was intended by the Founding Fathers is difficult to prove, say these authorities. Events quickly demonstrated its necessity, however. "Governments operating in the same territory, serving the same people, generally sharing the same goals, and faced with the same demands, could not maintain a posture of 'dual federalism' (the separation of functions by levels of government)," Prof. Elazar contends.[7] By the 1960's, the principles and mechanisms of cooperative federalism have become an accepted part of the American governmental process and most of these came into being in the 19th century. The principles include "national supremacy, broad national legislative and appropriation powers, noncentralized government, and maximum local control." The mechanisms include "a nondisciplined, noncentralized party system; routinized legislative 'interference' in administration; regular intergovernmental consultation; and a system of grants-in-aid from higher to lower levels of government." This cooperative federal theory is not that of the survey's respondents, although it resembles their view more closely than the States righters' interpretation or the theory that follows.

A composite theory of federalism, which blends features of both the competitive and the cooperative concepts, emerged from the subcommittee's earlier survey of State and local officials. Four basic attitudinal positions were identified in this analysis: the Orthodox States Righters (ultraconservatives), who comprised 11 percent of the sample; the Neo-Traditionalists (moderate conservatives), who accounted for 43 percent; the Pragmatic Cooperative Federalists (realistic liberals), who represented 33 percent; and the New Nationalists (ultraliberals), who made up 13 percent of the total. The two middle groups differed in ideological emphasis, but shared a common viewpoint of many of the specific and practical problems confronting elected officials at the State and local levels. This fairly wide area of agreement permitted the piecing together of an operating or practicing theory of intergovernmental relations to which more than three-quarters of that survey's respondents adhered in the day-to-day carrying out of their official duties. The basic principles of that composite theory, which included both ideal and real features, were identified as follows:

1. As a practical matter, Federal, State, and local governments are viewed as loosely related parts of one overall system. Each level, however, vigorously

7. Daniel J. Elazar, "The Shaping of Intergovernmental Relations in the Twentieth Century," *The Annals,* Vol. 359, May 1965, p. 11.

maintains its separate institutional identity and freedom of action in policy-making.

2. The domestic functions of government are not neatly parceled out among the three levels; instead, several governmental activities are assumed jointly by each governmental level with significant and continuing responsibilities being assumed by all.

3. Decisionmaking in the intergovernmental process is shared fairly equally among various public bodies on the three planes, thus preserving a cardinal principle of traditional federalism.

4. The administration of programs of joint concern is a mutual under-taking. Such devices as joint boards, joint inspection, the sharing of specialized information, and use of another level's technical personnel reveal the benefits of this collaboration among equals; competition rather than collaboration, however, is produced when administrative regulations are unilaterally imposed without full consultation with another level's officials and without recognition of the merit of some administrative practices of other jurisdictions.

5. The Federal grant-in-aid is and will continue to be an inescapable and important feature of contemporary intergovernmental relations. It provides a necessary means whereby the three levels of government can collaborate to fulfill common purposes. If not encumbered with excessive administrative red-tape, it can also serve to strengthen State and local governments, since it utilizes the existing institutional framework for administering these activities of common concern.

6. Representative, responsive, and responsible State governments are vital for the proper operation of American federalism. They have a vital role in collecting a sizable proportion of total revenues, directly administering several important governmental services, providing vital assistance to their local units of government, and serving as political laboratories for testing new policies.

7. When properly empowered, financed, and aided, county and municipal governments singly and in voluntary association with one another can meet many of the challenges that ubiquitous urbanization has created.

8. Intergovernmental relations should be viewed primarily as a network of functional, financial, and administrative arrangements which seek to advance the commonweal. Parity with respect to the power positions of the various levels is an indispensable ingredient for successful collaboration in this area. Inequality, after all, undermines the voluntarism that is so essential for any full-fledged cooperative endeavor.

9. Every level has a fundamental duty to preserve the interlevel balance, but a primary responsibility for implementing this ideal rests with Congress. Its past enactments constitute the greatest single force shaping the federal system under which we live, and its future actions will exert no less an impact.

This composite, or hybrid, theory, which resembles a marble cake cut into layers, clearly is not that of the Federal aid administrators who participated in this questionnaire survey. But they would take fewer exceptions to this theory than to that of the States' righters.

What, then, *is* the theory of these Federal executives?

At no point did any of the respondents develop one. Nor was it expected, since middle management executives are supposed to be pragmatic administrators, not political theorists. Yet careful assessment of the answers to certain key questions indicates that the respondents do have a general idea of what intergovernmental relations are and how they should operate. In short, they have a theory of federalism, and more than three out of four adhere to the same interpretation of the system.

Few among the majority would recognize the elements of this theory as being the logical corollaries of their responses to one or more of the survey's questions. None probably would accept all of its provisions. Yet the following hypotheses are, in fact, the basic features of the theory of federalism which emerged from the majority's responses.[8]

(1) The Federal, State, and local governments are interrelated parts of a single governmental system; each level, however, must effectively discharge its mandated responsibilities if all of its rights as a member of this partnership are to be preserved.

(2) Most domestic functions of government are shared, but the Federal Government, as the senior, most progressive, and most affluent member of this partnership, has been forced to assume a disproportionate share of this responsibility.

(3) Policymaking in intergovernmental relations is a multilevel process, but obstruction—not collaboration—is as likely to be encountered from elected policymakers at the State and local levels.

(4) The administration of joint action programs is a mutual—and, ideally, a professional—undertaking. Their authorizing legislation establishes them on a functional basis, and the vertical lines of communication and collaboration between and among the functional specialists in Washington and their counterparts in the field must be kept clear and unbroken if the bases of genuine cooperation are to be maintained.

(5) The Federal grant and other aid devices are, and will continue to be, the most prominent and positive feature of contemporary federalism. They— not block grants, tax credits, or similar devices—provide the only time-tested techniques whereby the levels of government can collaborate effectively to fulfill common purposes and to meet certain national standards. Moreover, if not burdened with partisan or nonprofessional interference, they can also serve to strengthen the States and local units of government, since they rely primarily on these jurisdictions for administrative purposes and tend to upgrade the caliber of the civil servants employed by these levels. Efforts to achieve greater consistency and uniformity in the operation of aid programs ignore the basic fact that each program is designed to accomplish a specific public purpose; hence, administrative and financial practices and procedures must be geared to the needs of the individual program and not to any abstract standardized principles.

(6) Responsive and responsible State governments are vital for an effective

8. The minority differed primarily with the majority only with respect to the principles developed in items 6, 7, and 8.

federal system; yet most States do not possess these characteristics and are not likely to acquire them in the near future. Most States have failed to exert a maximum tax effort, to eliminate outdated limitations on the taxing authority of local units of government, to adopt statewide merit systems, to improve the salaries and professional opportunities of their civil employees, to establish greater order in their own metropolitan areas, and to revamp their political systems. In short, they have failed to achieve the minimum requirements of a democratic government in the mid-20th century. It is necessary, therefore, to continue those provisions in grant and other aid programs which minimize threats to effective collaboration among program administrators at the various levels.

(7) General units of local government, when properly empowered and financially aided by the States, can act as effective partners in Federal-State-local and Federal-local joint action programs. Special-purpose districts and authorities grow out of particular local and areawide needs and of the States' failure to strengthen the fiscal base of general units of local government; as such, they serve a useful purpose in helping to implement certain Federal aid programs.

(8) Rapid urbanization challenges traditional intergovernmental functional relationships; yet it is largely through strengthening these individual relationships, along with some increase in informal interagency contacts, that this challenge will be surmounted. Excessive preoccupation with regional or areawide principles and mechanisms can slow up the implementation of much-needed urban development and, in some cases, subject program administrators to additional political pressures.

(9) Intergovernmental relations are primarily a vertical and diagonal system of financial, functional, and administrative arrangements; the primary purpose of each and all of these relationships is to meet the demands of the American people for better or new public services. Intergovernmental relations, then, function as the essential means to this great end, not as an end in themselves.

(10) Successful intergovernmental relations are chiefly successful bureaucratic relations. Authorizing legislation, funds, and oversight come from legislative bodies. Policy directives, budgetary review and control, and administrative rules and regulations come from top management. And advice, assistance, and support, as well as complaints, criticism, and censure, come from officeholders at all levels, individual citizens, and interest groups. These basic forces of our pluralistic political system shape and sustain the broad, complex pattern of intergovernmental relations. The day-to-day conduct of these relations, however, falls to Federal middle management administrators, their field personnel, and their functional counterparts at the State and local levels. Well-intentioned but misguided reforms that ignore or undermine the team effort of these wheelhorses of federalism threaten the dynamism of the system itself.

These, in brief outline, are the features of the majority's rather unusual theory of American federalism. To revert to the kitchen, the ideal dessert of these respondents is not a layer or marble cake, and certainly not a marble cake cut into layers, but a large brick of harlequin ice cream containing 143 (depending on your aid count) flavors. And they want their end-of-the-dinner delight straight from the freezer with no melting at the bottom or top and no special syrup over it. With this theory of federalism, we leave the pantry and go to the refrigerator.

These contrasting analogies, of course, are based on contrasting emphases and principles. This theory's cooperative, functional, and anti-State-and-local-elected-official bias makes it completely unacceptable to the States' righters. Its nearly equal recognition of the role of competitive forces and its basic stress on the professional administrators as the real architects of cooperative federalism do not conform to the Grodzins-Elazar thesis. Its unsympathetic treatment of such topics as the power position of the States and general units of local government and their elected policymakers; more flexible regulations for aid programs; and Congress' role as strengthener of the federal system—to mention only three of the foremost differences—is in marked contrast to the positive positions taken on these issues by the majority participating in the previous survey. This, then, is an atypical interpretation of our federal system.

Like others, this "harlequin" theory both identifies points of tension within the system and creates tension points by the mere fact that its adherents occupy a critical position in contemporary intergovernmental relations. The basic problem areas highlighted in the theory are threefold.

First, there is tension horizontally between administrators at the various levels, created by the failure of the governments at the lesser levels to upgrade the professional capability of their civil employees.

Second, there is the tension vertically between the professional goals of administrators of intergovernmental programs and the political goals of the policymakers at the various levels of government.

Third, there is tension, both vertically and horizontally, between individual program administrators at every level and public administration authorities, some intergovernmental relations experts, and some sectors of top management. The latter, in their search for greater manageability, coordination, and simplicity and for less fragmentation, program insulation, and administrative pluralism, lose sight of the fact that these programs, and the larger system of which they are a part, are geared to serving the people's public needs, not the private or public needs of politicians, top administrators, or levels of government.

This theory of federalism also generates friction, since its proponents are major participants in the intergovernmental process and since its normative features—to a greater degree than its descriptive features—actually condition the official behavior of these respondents.

First, its unifunctional and professional bias, along with the normal motives for bureaucratic survival, tends to create tension among the Federal administrators of the various aid programs. This is especially true of the relations between the administrators of newer and those of older, more traditional programs.

Second, the theory's specialized program and bureau emphasis creates severe problems for departmental officials and various units in the Executive Office of the President. This occurs because top management and staff are charged with the duty of integrating the functions of individual bureaus and divisions with the national function of developing a coherent, timely presidential program based on scaled priorities; with the ultimate executive task of balancing the bias of particular administrative units with the general role of government as the "impartial instrument of a symmetrical national development," as Woodrow Wilson once phrased it.

Third, this theory's antipolitical and anti-innovation bias conflicts with, and even threatens, the efforts of policymakers and others at all levels who are seeking to bridge the communications and authority gaps at the Federal, State, and metropolitan levels, especially where the gaps impede the proper formulation and administration of urban development programs.

To sum up, the theory adhered to by three out of four of these Federal aid officials identifies three major sources of conflict in contemporary Federal-State-local relations:

(1) Professionalism at the higher level versus a lesser degree of professionalism at the other levels;

(2) Professional program administrators versus elected policymakers at all levels; and

(3) Administrators of individual aid programs versus intergovernmental reformers.

And because this "harlequin" theory of federalism is an operating precept as well as a descriptive interpretation, it produces its own areas of conflict:

(1) Professional administrators of one aid program versus the professional administrators of others;

(2) Specialized middle management versus generalized top management; and

(3) Conservative bureau heads versus innovators seeking to strengthen other components of the federal system—the States, our metropolitan communities, and the decisionmaking process at all levels.

III. PATTERNS OF CONFLICT AND ACCOMMODATION

THE focus of Part II was on mechanisms of asserting top leadership influence on the federal bureaucracy. That of Part III is on the strength and character of pluralism, and on mechanisms of lateral coordination, within the bureaucratic system.

Needless to say, the forces of separatism are unusually strong in the American system. The national society is large, new, and diverse. The citizenry is as free, and culturally prone, to organize as any in the world. The government is organized far more with a view toward checking than unifying power. In addition, most of the forces that make for separatism elsewhere are operative in high degree. Special interests press for insulation of their own programs from the general political process, so as better to ensure their control. Specialized skill groups maintain that they can do their jobs properly only if granted extraordinary degrees of autonomy. Officials develop perspectives based on their own program responsibilities, and tend to equate these with the overall public interest. As the scale of government grows, so do specialization and diversity within it. The need for coordination increases, but the knowledge required for *intelligent* coordination becomes ever more widely diffused. New methods of information handling can hold down the rate of increase in this disparity, but the need for lateral coordination—based on consensus and negotiation rather than authority—becomes inexorably greater.

Unfortunately, space permits only a mini-sampling of the literature on these themes below. Part III-A takes a look at one pole of the problem, reviewing the impact of special interests on the administration of some traditional domestic programs. Part III-B examines the other pole. It focuses on that branch of policy making in which the need for coordination is most widely recognized, and—not coincidentally—on the problem of reconciling diverse perspectives within the government rather than private interests.

A. Constituency Relations in the Domestic Arena

NO proposition is more generally accepted in the literature on American administrative politics than that every domestic agency bears primary responsibility for coming to terms with its own constituency of interested groups and congressional committees. (Most national security agencies are less "on their own," because Congress is far more persuaded of the need for central planning and unified direction in the security arena.) The accommodations that agencies reach in order to survive and prosper typically deflect them from their original conceptions of purpose, and render them less amenable to control from above. To those who value comprehensiveness, coordination, and consistency highly, these outcomes generally seem most unfortunate. Others consider them quite reasonable prices to pay for building responsiveness (to the demands of a wide range of interested publics) into the national administrative system, and for keeping it from confronting the rest of society as a monolith. The first three of the four selections which follow are case studies, chosen to illustrate the variety of ways in which these sets of values have confronted each other in concrete circumstances. The fourth is a highly provocative theoretical effort to specify the kinds of things that typically "go wrong" when American administrative agencies are charged with altering social and economic patterns.

Arthur Maass analyzes the modus operandi of the U.S. Army Corps of Engineers in its dominant peacetime role as a civil public works agency. The Corps is perhaps *the* classic example of an agency which has secured effective independence from its hierarchical superiors in the Executive Branch through its network of congenial relationships with the private groups and Congressional committees most interested in its work. The brazenness with which it has frequently exercised this independence is particularly striking when one considers that its leading officials are all members of a profession noted above all for its devotion to the ideal of hierarchical discipline. Maass concludes his article by calling for greater self-restraint on the part of Congress, and a greater orientation toward comprehensive water resources planning on the part of the Executive Branch. In the course of evaluating these suggestions, you may wish to consider such questions as the following: First, has Maass paid sufficient attention to the function of public works in the American legislative system as a policy arena in which side payments are made to facilitate accommodations on more important issues? Second, would comprehensive water resources planning really solve the problem of fragmentation? Water use, after all, is integrally related to land use; navigation improvements are only one kind of transportation investment; hydroelectric power accounts for only a portion of the nation's energy output, and so on. Third, what would the price of "comprehensiveness" be in terms of citizen participation and local flexibility in the policy planning process?

Grant McConnell recounts the embattled history of an agency which never succeeded in reaching a satisfactory accommodation with the interests most relevant to its fate. The Farm Security Administration's failure was not primarily one of incompetence. Probably no agency with its objectives could have long survived the New Deal period. One of the most remarkable features of the campaign to destroy FSA was its ostensible focus on issues of administrative form. This highlights the extent to which interest groups disable themselves politically when they concentrate on issues of "high policy" to the exclusion of administration. The leaders of such groups frequently have little choice, however. Many associations, particularly those which motivate their members by appeals to social conscience rather than to concrete self-interest, simply lack the capacity to shepherd favored programs through long years of struggle over apparently "technical" issues. Typical sources of such incapacity are limited staff resources, the multiplicity of issues competing for attention, and the value in organizational maintenance terms of focusing on easily dramatized controversies. After reading McConnell's case study, you may wish to consider whether American politics has altered significantly since the demise of the Farm Security Administration. The 1940's and 1950's were particularly unfavorable decades for welfare-oriented programs. While they lasted, it seemed to many observers of American politics that the confluence of circumstances that had permitted the Roosevelt Administration during its first half-dozen years to innovate in the welfare field had been unique in American history. McConnell wrote during this period of liberal discouragement. As this is written, early in 1967, the question of whether the American governmental system can sustain a meaningful "war on poverty" once again occupies the center stage of our domestic politics. In this context, the history of the Farm Security Administration is more than ever worth pondering, but there is also more room for disputing the validity (or precise nature) of its implications for the present.

The selection by J. Lieper Freeman is much more than a case study, but it is here classified as one for its focus on the Indian Bureau's history from 1933 to 1945. Freeman's study is one of the very few in the literature to focus upon an agency's effort to change its constituency base from one set of interests to another. He finds that the Indian Bureau was able to operate successfully as a protector of Indian interests so long as President Roosevelt had leisure to concentrate on domestic affairs and adequate political resources to dominate Congress. When these conditions ceased to be fulfilled, Roosevelt's appointee as chief of the Bureau became expendable, and the agency had little choice but to lapse into the pre-1933 pattern of permitting Congressmen from the affected areas (in which the great majority of voters were white, and frequently hostile to Indian interests) to set the limits of its commitment. This is not to say that in any period the Bureau's chief was totally without room for maneuver. It is rather to indicate how the scope of his discretion varied with changes in the general political situation. You are urged to consider the determinants of a bureau chief's range of discretion, together with the calculus of risks that may guide him within that range, more systematically, and for a wide variety of circumstances.

Louis Jaffe seeks to list and explain the most fundamental characteristics of economic regulation in the American system. His specific focus is on the independent regulatory commissions, but his theses are relevant to the whole subject of American governmental efforts to influence social and economic processes. Jaffe does not contend that the government's regulatory activities have been without effect. Rather, he endeavors to explain why the effects have frequently been different in character (for example, in their strong anticompetitive flavor) and have typically been less far-reaching than the original proponents of regulation would have forecast. In addition to his lucid analysis of the kinds of accommodations that regulators and regulated interests most often reach with each other, Jaffe provides an excellent critique of the case for detailed economic planning. Keep in mind as you read his article that it is a highly compressed piece of writing, and that its evidence bears mainly on regulatory outcomes rather than the mechanisms that produce them. If you find its argument persuasive, you will wish to think systematically about what these mechanisms are, and about the variables which influence their effectiveness in particular circumstances.

CONGRESS AND WATER RESOURCES *
Arthur Maass

SHOULD Twitch Cove, Maryland, be improved at Federal expense for the protection of the few crabbers who live near this Eastern Shore community? This past May, Congress decided yes; they confirmed a recommendation of the Chief of Engineers, U. S. Army. The United States Engineer Department, as the Corps of Engineers is called in the exercise of civil functions, recommended in favor of Twitch Cove after evaluating alternative plans of improvement and selecting that one which appeared to balance best the factors of "economic feasibility"—i.e., the ratio of benefits to costs, "engineering feasibility," and the "desires of local interests."

This last item is of interest for the moment. For any major improvement, even for Twitch Cove, there will be many groups of "local interests," and their "desires" will differ, may even conflict. Thus, the Engineers seek to adjust these interests and to come up with a recommendation that will maximize the total desires of the community.

Congress for a great number of years has followed a procedure of legislative self-restraint with respect to water resources developments. It will not authorize any improvement which has not received a favorable report from the Chief of Engineers. And since the Engineers attempt to maximize local desires, it may be said that Congress has transferred important responsibility for the adjustment of group interests from its own body to the U. S. Engineer Department, an executive agency.

The Engineers have recognized the nature of the responsibility which Con-

* From the *American Political Science Review*, Vol. 44 (September 1950), pp. 576–593. Reprinted by permission of the author and publisher.

gress has delegated to them. They have conducted their organization and operations in a manner designed to allow a rather full articulaion of local group interests. The project planning procedure, from the time Congress authorizes the Corps to undertake an examination of a given area, involves twenty distinct stages at which group interests are able to present their views to the Corps. At three of these twenty, public hearings are regularly provided for; at two additional stages, Engineer Department instructions require consultation with local interests; and at the remaining fifteen, the extent of consultation varies with particular circumstances, but the necessity of a constant awareness of the current attitudes of local interests is emphasized in all Engineer Department publications.

Recently, the Chief of Engineers said:

The authorization of a river and harbor or flood control project follows a definitely prescribed, democratic course of action. It is based upon the activation of the desires of local interests, who are most vitally interested. Local interests, as individuals or groups through the actions of their representatives in Congress, make request for an item to be included in a rivers and harbors or flood control bill (i.e., authorization to conduct an examination). . . . The District Engineer, mindful of the need for developing all public opinion, holds an open public hearing at which not only those interests that are active in obtaining the authorization of the proposed work but also all other views are obtained and encouraged. Having thus developed the desires of the local citizens, the District Engineer makes a study. . . .

I. PRESENT ARRANGEMENTS AND THE LEGISLATIVE PROCESS [1]

Several important consequences for the legislative process flow from this project planning procedure. These include the participation by members of Congress in the "executive" planning process; legislation by committee resolution; service by the Corps of Engineers as consultants to, and contractors for, the Congress, certain congressional committees, and individual members of Congress; by-passing of the President and friction among executive agencies; and the interlocking of pressure groups, the Corps, and members of Congress.

Though Congress as a group has largely disassociated itself from the process of project planning by transferring responsibility for adjustment of group interests to the Engineer Department, individual members of Congress have

1. Arrangements relating to Congress, the Corps of Engineers, and the President are discussed. No effort is made to deal in any detail with the relations of Congress and the Bureau of Reclamation because of space limitations and the fact that Corps arrangements constitute the more controlling factors in legislation for water resources. This has become more the case in the last few years. Where the Bureau and the Corps have been in competition since 1936, the Secretary of Interior has sought support of the President's office to offset support which the Corps has gotten from Congress. But even with the President's support, the Secretary has not had great success in getting his programs adopted. As a result, the Bureau of Reclamation and its supporters in Congress, the Western irrigation bloc, have begun to use the same legislative techniques which have meant such "success" for the Engineers. Adoption of these techniques has been limited, however, by the fact that support of the reclamation program of the Bureau is restricted in Congress to the Western bloc; whereas support of the navigation and flood control programs of the Corps is found in representatives from all areas.

not been so abstentious. Representatives and Senators, knowing they cannot obtain congressional authorization for the projects they are sponsoring without a favorable report from the Engineers, have attempted to pressure them into approving these projects by appealing to District Engineers and to the Board of Engineers for Rivers and Harbors in Washington in public hearings. . . .

If the Engineers submit an unfavorable or partially favorable report, the proponents of a project seek a reexamination, for the Congress will, as noted, not authorize an improvement without a favorable Corps recommendation. At the same time, the Corps by law may not initiate a survey unless Congress has specifically authorized it, usually in an omnibus rivers and harbors or flood control bill. However, to make it easier for members of Congress to require the Engineers to reexamine unfavorable reports in the hope that "changed conditions" may justify a favorable recommendation, the Congress has devised a truly unique procedure amounting to legislation by committee resolution.

After a report of the Chief of Engineers is one year old, any Representative or Senator may present a resolution to the appropriate congressional committee which, if adopted by the committee, requires the "Board of Engineers for rivers and harbors . . . to review the report with a view to determining whether any modification should be made at this time in the recommendation heretofore made." The committee resolution has the effect of law, and, it should be noted, is not subject to presidential veto.

Review resolutions have been quite common. As the Congressmen proposing the reviews enjoy no opposition to their requests in most cases, and as the Engineer Department has not been called upon often to report on the desirability of conducting reviews, the committees have been disposed to grant the requests, on occasion disregarding even the one-year waiting period. It is physically impossible for any one member of a committee to be informed on the history of all navigation and flood control projects. The Representative from Arkansas, for example, in all probability never heard of Mill Creek, Virginia, to say nothing of having any judgment as to whether or not the Engineers should be asked to review the report on this Creek; he will vote, Yes. Of 83 investigations completed by the Corps in fiscal year 1946, 20 were authorized by regular legislation and 63 were reexaminations submitted in response to committee resolutions.

The new House Committee on Public Works in 1947 resolved to cut down on this indiscriminate use of legislation by committee resolution. It adopted a rule extending the waiting period to three years and requiring the Chief of Engineers to report on the estimated costs of conducting the proposed reviews. The Senate Committee failed to follow suit.

It is difficult to evaluate the review resolution as a technique for pressuring the Corps to give its approval to the projects which the members of Congress desire. Available data, however, are rather impressive in showing the importance of the resolution in getting water projects approved, expanded in scope, or modified in terms of reducing the local contributions required.

The Congress, in its long history of legislating internal improvements, has developed close relations with the Corps. (The Corps was the engineering department of the Government which planned and executed the national internal improvement programs of the 1820's.) Congress considers the Corps to be *directly* responsible to it. By resolution Congress directs the Board of Engineers for Rivers and Harbors, an advisory board to the Chief of Engineers, to conduct reviews of surveys. It does not direct the chief executive officer, the President; nor does it even provide the President with an opportunity for veto.

The Corps concurs heartily in this relationship. The Engineers call themselves "the engineer consultants to, and contractors for, the Congress of the United States." The theoretical consequences of such a direct legislative-agency relationship are familiar to students of government and administration; they need not be repeated here.

As might be expected, Congress as a whole is not equipped to exercise direct responsibility over the conduct of Engineer Corps civil functions. It is rather certain congressional committees—those with competence over navigation and flood control matters—that attempt to hold the Corps accountable. It is to them that the Engineers are directly responsible. Witness the review resolution procedure in which Congress in effect allows a committee to legislate for it.

Traditionally members of Congress from the Mississippi delta area, where flood protection, drainage, and river navigation problems assume great importance, seek positions on the committees which handle Corps legislation. Through regular re-election they attain positions of seniority. Will M. Whittington of Mississippi, chairman of the House Committee on Public Works, was for years prior to the establishment of this committee chairman of the Committee on Flood Control. Judge Whittington, a hard hitting committee chairman, has always had Corps legislation closely under his control. More than anyone in the executive or legislative establishments, he is in close contact with, and almost in a position of supervision over, the Chief of Engineers and the USED. Until his recent death, John Overton of Louisiana was number one man in the Senate on navigation and flood control legislation.

Direct relations between these committees of Congress and the Corps have developed into a close identity of interests between the two. The Committees on Public Works feel a proprietary interest in the Corps of Engineers and in the direct relations which prevail. In terms of policies for the development of resources, the important consequences of this will be stated later.

In some respects the Engineer Department is more nearly responsible to individual members of Congress directly than to Congress as a whole or to certain congressional committees. It is the member of Congress who initiates the legislative proposal for survey; he is first contacted by the District Engineer to determine the scope of the desired improvement and interested parties; he is first to be informed of any change in the status of the investigation. The nature of the authorization process—the enactment of omnibus rivers and harbors and flood control bills—is such as further to encourage direct responsibility to individual Congressmen. When hearings are held by congressional committees on favorably reported projects to be included in omnibus bills, the testimony of the member of Congress from the district in which the project is located is usually corroborated and supplemented by the Army Engineer present at the hearing. All of these techniques have led to a sense of direct responsibility on the part of the Engineer Department to the individual member of Congress.

Direct relations between Congress and the Corps mean, of course, that the Engineers by-pass the President. This is obviously bad, for the only place where related executive functions can be coordinated effectively is in the President's office. Prior to the 1930's there was no major problem as most river improvements were for single purposes and did not impinge directly on the activities of other agencies. In the early '30's, however, the Corps began planning multiple purpose projects throughout the country involving flood control, power, irrigation, drainage, and other uses, and coordination in order to produce the best multiple purpose plan for the development of major drainage basins seemed essential. The history of resources legislation and of the development of planning procedures between 1934 and this date constitutes very largely the history of efforts by Presidents Roosevelt and Truman to break down direct agency responsibility to the Congress and to substitute for it a pattern of responsibility to the Chief Executive. Only in these terms can recent developments in the resources field be interpreted.

The agency with which the Corps has had greatest friction due to lack of coordination is the Bureau of Reclamation in the Department of the Interior. In this inter-agency feud, which has been really intense since 1939, the Corps, for reasons already indicated, has enjoyed the strong support of the Congress. The Secretary of the Interior and the Bureau of Reclamation, on the other hand, have received less consistent congressional support and have sought to balance the advantage of the Corps of Engineers in this respect by obtaining the support of the President and his Executive Office. The general pattern may be expressed as follows: Corps of Engineers+Congress v. Secretary of the Interior+Executive Office of the President.

The fact that Congress as a body has transferred to the Engineers responsibility for adjusting group interests in proposing water developments, but that individual members of Congress continue to take an active part in the planning and adjusting process is revealed in an interesting manner by the national water pressure groups—particularly the National Rivers and Harbors Congress. This comprehensive lobby counts in its membership the "local interests" (state and local officials, local industrial and trade organizations, contractors), the U. S. Congress (Representatives and Senators are honorary members), and the Corps of Engineers (officers of the Corps engaged in rivers and harbors work are all ex-officio members). The members of Congress, though they are in a real sense the lobbied, take a very active part in the Rivers Congress. Today, for example, the President is Senator John McClellan of Arkansas, a member of the Public Works Committee and of the subcommittee of the Committee on Appropriations which handles Engineer

Corps funds, and chairman of the Committee on Expenditures in the Executive Departments—to which the Hoover Commission recommendations proposing reorganization of the Corps of Engineers have been referred. McClellan, as a member of the Hoover Commission, dissented from those recommendations which would divest the Army of rivers and harbors functions. The national vice presidents of the pressure group are Senator Wherry of Nebraska, Republican floor leader and a member of the Appropriations subcommittee on Engineer Corps funds; Representative Whittington of Mississippi, identified earlier; and Representative Case of South Dakota, a member of the Committee on Appropriations and, at the time of his selection as vice president, of the subcommittee which considered appropriations for the Corps.

In the past the ex-officio members, officers of the Corps, also have taken part in the proceedings of the lobby, though today they are somewhat more circumspect. The Rivers Congress remains, however, the most active pressure group in support of the USED.

Perhaps the most interesting and important aspect of the Rivers and Harbors Congress is the work of the Projects Committee. When the National Congress was formed in 1901, its slogan was "a policy, not a project." The purpose was not to urge any specific waterway improvements but to interest the public and the Federal Congress in the development of waterways in general. In 1935, however, the Rivers and Harbors Congress reversed its policy, agreed to promote certain waterway improvements actively, and for that purpose organized a Projects Committee. The Committee meets once a year for several days preceding the annual convention to act upon all applications for endorsement. It holds hearings on each project, classifies it in one of several orders of priority, and presents its recommendations to the full Rivers and Harbors Congress for adoption.

Senators and Congressmen who are sponsoring waterway improvements in their districts appear before the Committee in order to obtain from that organization of which they are honorary members favorable recommendations for their projects. The following excerpts, in the April, 1940, issue of the *National Rivers and Harbors News,* are from a report of the annual meeting of the Projects Committee:

Congressmen Joe Hendricks of Florida presented testimony on the Cape Canaveral Harbor, which he stated will serve the $5,000,000 citrus fruit belt, which is now without proper harbor facilities.

Congressman John Jennings, Jr. of Tennessee, urged approval of the project for the construction of dams in the vicinity of Oakdale and Harriman, Tennessee.

Representative Edith Nourse Rogers, of Massachusetts, asked approval of the Merrimac River project. The project will help protect the city of Lowell, Massachusetts from disastrous floods, as well as the rest of that area, she said.

It is difficult to place a value on the general effectiveness of the Rivers and Harbors Congress because of the fact that it serves as a clearing house for uniting and coordinating the activities of local and sectional interests. The Congress itself puts forth bold claims as to its influence:

The influence of the National Rivers and Harbors Congress has been perhaps a more controlling force on legislation approved than that of any other organization. . . . Thus far there has been no adverse criticism of any of the recommendations made by the Congress in its resolutions and reports, and virtually every bill passed by the federal Congress for the improvement of harbors and waterways has been composed almost in toto of projects previously investigated and recommended by the National Rivers and Harbors Congress.

The [Rivers and Harbors] Congress is the country's oldest and largest water organization and occupies *semi-official status* by reason of its close liaison with the governmental agencies, legislative and executive, responsible for public works. . . .

Though the group may be correct in making these claims, we shall be content to accredit it with being certainly one of the most effective lobbies in Washington today.

II. THE NEGLECT OF WATER RESOURCE PLANNING

To this point we have considered consequences for the legislative process of the manner in which interests are adjusted in the planning of water projects. More fundamental, however, are the effects of these consequences in terms of best development of the nation's natural resources. The planning process has produced two important results: an absence of national plans and policies for water resources and an absence of executive branch arrangements that might develop such plans and policies.

Water planning to date has been characterized by continued emphasis on the localized aspects of individual water projects. This emphasis begins with the requirement that all surveys be authorized by Congress. The members of Congress who propose survey items for inclusion in omnibus navigation and flood control bills usually do so in response to requests of local interests in their districts. These interests often have not the ability to visualize the relationship of the improvements they desire to multiple purpose basin-wide development.

This local emphasis is accentuated by the Corps of Engineers. It seeks to limit the scope of investigations to what was intended by the Congressmen responsible for the particular authorizations. Further, the survey procedure of the Engineer Department is so oriented that each individual water development project is considered almost exclusively in the light of benefits to be derived by the area immediately adjacent to the improvement. This is most often what the local interests desire. Thus, for example, if the benefits from dredging a harbor channel to permit entrance of deeper draft vessels into an east coast Florida port are measured in terms of additional traffic and business for the localized port area, the project will be easier to justify economically than if the benefits were measured in terms of the general effects of the new project on all east coast ports in the vicinity; some of these ports might lose traffic to the newly developed one.

Finally, the procedure for authorizing improvements, the omnibus rivers and harbors and flood control bills, emphasizes individual projects—the pork barrel. Representatives and Senators appear before the appropriate congressional committees, seeking committee approval for projects in their districts which have received favorable Engineer Corps reports. At hearings on the omnibus rivers and harbor bill of 1949, 54 Representatives and Senators from 24 states testified or submitted statements to Representative Whittington's committee; on the flood control bill of the same year, 62 Congressmen from 25 states appeared.

It is not meant to say that there has been no basin-wide planning on the part of Congress and the Corps. In recent years there has been some improvement in this respect, especially for western river basins. But here the broader view on the part of the Corps is inspired primarily by competition with the Bureau of Reclamation, which has traditionally used the multiple purpose basin-wide approach. Concerning waterways legislation, President Truman said to Congress in May, 1950:

Finally, I urge the Congress to develop more satisfactory procedures for considering and authorizing basin-wide development programs. We are a long way still, both in the executive and legislative branches, from the kind of comprehensive planning and action that is required if we are to conserve, develop and use our natural resources so that they will be increasingly useful as the years go by. We need to make sure that each legislative authorization, and each administrative action, takes us toward—and not away from—this goal.

Today we have no rational national water policy, even apart from the unrelated consideration of individual projects. President Truman recognized this in January, 1950, when he set up a temporary Water Resources Policy Commission under Morris L. Cooke to develop one. Why is this true? Why are we spending hundreds of millions of dollars each year on water developments without a plan?

That ultimate responsibility rests with Congress, there can be no question. But Congress and congressional committees are not equipped to develop a national water plan out of whole cloth. They are admirably equipped to examine, approve, disapprove, and amend any intelligent programs presented to them which focus on the great issues. It is the Chief Executive who is best able to prepare such broad programs and assume responsibility for placing them before the elective body. For the greatest part of water development, however, the President has been short circuited. The Congress and the Engineers work together, but, as related, this combined labor has produced no plan.

The Corps of Engineers in reporting to Congress makes no special effort to point up the broad policy questions or to recommend or encourage the enactment of laws containing a careful definition of national policy in the water field. As the "Engineer consultants to and contractors for the Congress of the United States," they have, they say, no responsibility for initiating policies and broad programs; that is the function of Congress.

The following statement of Secretary of War Henry Stimson, in 1919, illustrates what we would put today into a broader framework:

When I was Secretary of War I found this situation, and I found that the reports of the Chief of Engineers which came to me were not "Is this an improvement which should be made in view of our particular funds this year—our particular budget this year—and in view of all the improvements in the United States taken at the same time?" but simply and solely "Is this an improvement of a waterway which should be made?" And the Chief of Engineers said he was directed by Congress to report in that way, and this was the way he was going to interpret that, not in comparison with other projects, but simply whether in the millennium it would be a good thing for the country to have that waterway improved. When I said "That does not suit me at all. You come in here with a lot of propositions which you have approved, and you want me to approve, to improve the navigation of such and such a river and such and such a creek and such and such a harbor. I want to know how does that compare with the situation of the whole?" He said, "I have nothing to do with that. I cannot have anything to do with it. Congress will not listen to me on that. They reserve the judgment to do that themselves."

President Roosevelt tried hard to fulfill what he considered his duty—to develop a national water policy and to submit this to Congress for action. He created and supported the National Resources Planning Board and its Water Resources Committee. But in this position the President enjoyed the intense opposition of the Congress and of the Corps of Engineers. The Corps failed to give full and genuine cooperation to the Water Resources Committee in its efforts to develop a policy. It dissented from most policy reports of the Committee, most notably from the important 1941 Report on National Water Policy. The Congress was always unsympathetic to the NRPB; refused, despite frequent personal appeals from the President, to give the Board permanent statutory status; and finally abolished it by denying appropriations in 1943. The single most important reason for congressional opposition to the Board was probably resentment on the part of the so-called rivers and harbors bloc in Congress to any effort by the President to interfere with the direct relations between Congress and the Corps. Furthermore, Congress failed to pay any heed to the policy recommendations of the Water Resources Committee which, though they contained dissents from the Corps, were supported by the President.

Herein lies a lesson for the new Water Resources Policy Commission. The acceptance of its recommendations may turn on the support they can get from the Corps and the congressional Committees on Public Works. The members of the Commission seem well aware of this.

III. CONGRESS AND EXECUTIVE BRANCH ORGANIZATION

The fact that organization for water resources development is so inadequate today is in large part a result of the congressional attitudes we have outlined.

Theodore Roosevelt, Herbert Hoover, Franklin Roosevelt—all have tried to bring rationale into administration of water functions. And all have failed,

failed because Congress will brook no interference whatsoever in its direct relations with the Corps. As one writer has said, "The civil functions of the
Army Corps of Engineers constitute a veritable Rock of Gibraltar against all
executive attempts to introduce any organizational integration of flood control
and river development with the land use, irrigation, and electric-power activities of other federal agencies."

In recent years the Bureau of the Budget, as a coordinating agency for the
President, has tried to break into the direct channel between the Corps and
Congress. It has required that survey reports (in the same manner as proposed legislation) be submitted to the Executive Office of the President,
prior to submission to Congress, so that the Corps can be informed of the relationship of the reports to the program of the President. But when the Executive Office informs the Corps that a project does not conform with the President's program, the Engineers pay no heed. They recommend to Congress,
nonetheless, that the project be adopted.

The Budget Bureau is the source of statistics to back up this conclusion. Between January, 1941, and September, 1948, the Corps of Engineers submitted
to the Budget Bureau 436 reports favorable to construction of federal improvements. Three hundred and sixty were cleared with no objections to the authorization of the projects, and 76 were (a) held by the Bureau to be wholly
or partially not in accord with the President's program (44 reports) or (b)
were the subject of specific reservations stated in special comments by the Bureau (32 reports).

With regard to the 44 reports held not in accord with the President's program, the Corps of Engineers transmitted reports on all of these projects to
Congress with favorable recommendations. Congress authorized 38. Of the
total of 76 projects on which the Bureau made some reservations and comments, Congress authorized 62; seven were either abandoned, or considered by
Congress and rejected, while seven projects had not yet been formally considered by Congress. The projects authorized by Congress upon which the Bureau had expressed reservations or full opposition had a total estimated cost in
1947 of $2 billion; those not authorized by Congress, a cost of about $500 million.

Senator Douglas' recent publicized effort to reduce by $840 million the au-
thorizations contained in the 1950 rivers and harbors and flood control bill
provides another illustration. Most all of the projects which Douglas attacked
had been given low priority or held not in accord by the Bureau of the
Budget. Yet the Senate, like the Senate and House Committees on Public
Works and the House of Representatives before it, adopted the recommendations of the Chief of Engineers and disregarded those of the President.

Under the present planning pattern, the water experts of all agencies of the
Federal government do not cooperate to prepare reports on the best uses of
water in any drainage basin. Rather the Corps of Engineers (or the Bureau of
Reclamation, as the case may be) undertakes a survey for which it assumes
sole responsibility. It may or may not call in experts of other agencies during

the conduct of the survey. When the report has been completed and tentative recommendations announced to the local interests, then the report is referred to other agencies for comment; but experience has proved that clearance occurs too late in the planning process for effective coordination.

This pattern of uncoordinated planning was set by Congress in enacting the first two national flood control bills in 1936 and 1938. Although it was known, certainly by 1938, that the President, the National Resources Planning Board, the Budget Bureau, and the Agriculture and Interior Departments all preferred provisions for genuinely cooperative planning, Congress preferred to assign the planning responsibility directly to the Corps, not to the executive branch as a whole through the person of the President.

The NRPB recommended that the President veto each of these bills for this failure, among other reasons. The President approved them, but in each instance stated his opposition to the uncoordinated planning provided and his determination to alter this within the executive branch. He said in 1938:

I have approved this bill with some reluctance. . . .

It is not a step in the right direction in the setup provided for general government planning.

I am in doubt as to the value of some of the projects provided for and it is unwise to place recommendations to the Congress solely in the hands of the Engineer Corps of the Army in some cases and of the Department of Agriculture in other cases.

Coordination of all such public works involves a wider survey and the examination of more national problems than any one bureau or department is qualified for.

In these respects future legislation will be vitally important, in order to give to the Congress and to the country a complete picture which takes all factors into consideration.

For the coming year, however, I shall try to obtain this coordination by asking for complete consultation between all groups and government agencies affected. In this way the whole of the problem can be made more clear. I have, however, approved the bill because it accomplishes a number of good things, with, however, the reservation that its deficiencies should be corrected as early as possible.

The President was unsuccessful in this resolve, due largely to those congressional-Corps relations we have been discussing. The same obstacle prevents the President from consolidating important resources functions. Theodore Roosevelt recommended to Congress in 1908 that responsibility for water development be centralized. Congress, expressing full confidence in the Corps of Engineers, failed to implement his recommendation. Herbert Hoover proposed to Congress in 1932 that the civil functions of the Corps of Engineers be transferred to the Department of the Interior. His reorganization plan, submitted under the Economy Act of 1932, was roundly defeated in the House. The members of the House Committees on Flood Control and on Rivers and Harbors, Democrats and Republicans alike, opposed the reorganization. Franklin Roosevelt in 1937 proposed that Congress enact legislation permitting him to effect reorganizations within the executive branch. No agencies of Government were to be excluded. When in 1939 Congress finally passed the Reorganization Bill authorizing the President to submit plans to Congress which would become law unless vetoed by both Houses of Congress within 60 days, the Corps of Engineers was one of a very few purely executive agencies placed beyond application of the legislation. Harry Truman in 1945 asked that Congress reenact reorganization legislation (it had lapsed some years previously) and that no agencies be exempted from its provisions. Congress did exempt some eight agencies, seven of them independent commissions or boards, and the eighth, the Corps of Engineers.

The Hoover Commission in 1949 proposed that the water resources functions of the Corps of Engineers and the Bureau of Reclamation be consolidated in a Water Development and Use Service and that this Service be organized within the Department of the Interior or, as three commissioners urged, within a new Department of Natural Resources. In proposing this consolidation, the Commission's task force on Natural Resources said:

> Perhaps the most imposing argument against transferring the civil functions of the Corps of Engineers to another agency is found in the intense opposition with which any such proposal is likely to be met. There is no need to emphasize the powerful local and congressional support of the Corps. . . . The history of past reorganization efforts reveals the difficulties encountered when measures have been proposed involving any change whatsoever in the civil functions of the Army Engineers.

To implement this proposal and many others, President Harry Truman and former President Herbert Hoover urged Congress in 1949 to enact a general reorganization bill. The legislation was to be similar to earlier reorganization bills in that plans submitted by the President would become law unless vetoed by both Houses of Congress within 60 days. It was to differ from earlier legislation in that both Truman and Hoover insisted on a "clean bill," one containing no exemptions, and on a permanent bill, not one that expired within a few years.

The supporters of the Corps of Engineers, both in and out of Congress, objected strenuously to the proposed legislation. Herbert Hoover lashed out at these supporters and their demand for exemption for the Corps. Despite considerable opposition, the House passed the bill with no outright exemptions. The Senate, too, passed a "clean bill," no exemptions. But the Senate bill has a joker, one to which the House had to agree to get any bill at all. This joker provides that any reorganization plan submitted by the President shall become law unless vetoed by a constitutional majority of *one* House. This constitutes a major reverse for administrative reorganization; the bills of 1939 and 1945 had required veto by both Houses.

Why did the Senate insist on this change? Because the congressional supporters of the Corps of Engineers announced that they would forego outright exemption for the Corps *only if* Congress would agree to a one-House veto. They were sure that any proposed transfer of the Corps could not get through Congress under these conditions. And to make sure that future changes in the complexion of Congress might not alter this situation, they provided that the bill expire at the end of Truman's present term of office. The ease with which Congress, under this scheme, can defeat reorganization plans of the President has been demonstrated recently with grim reality.

Continued congressional opposition to Valley Authorities has been in part a consequence of the traditional legislative handling of water business. Congressional supporters of the Army Engineers, particularly members of the congressional committees to which the Engineers report, have been among the most violent opponents of Valley Authority legislation. They argue that the Engineers are doing a fine job and should not be diplaced by independent corporate organizations.

It will be remembered that in 1937 President Roosevelt sent to Congress his famous message on regional authorities—the "8 little TVA's," as it came to be known. This much misunderstood proposal called for dividing the nation into eight regional areas for the purpose of developing integrated plans for resources development and management. At least in the early years, regional authorities with responsibilities broader than just planning would be set up or continued in only three areas. These were the TVA, the Columbia Valley Authority, and the Mississippi River Commission.

A careful reading of the hearings on this legislation before House and Senate committees reveals that almost all opponents of the bill, no matter whether their hostility to the legislation was inspired principally by opposition to hydroelectric power, by fear that the favored position of navigation interests in river development might be adversely affected, or by other causes, expressed complete confidence in the Engineer Department and an unwillingness to see any tampering with its duties in regard to rivers and harbors and flood control.

Significantly, the only Valley Authority legislation which has passed the Congress, that creating the TVA, was not handled by the committees which write navigation and flood control legislation, but rather in the Senate, by the Committee on Agriculture and Forestry, and in the House, by the Military Affairs Committee. These committees, particularly the Senate Committee on Agriculture, have been infinitely more sympathetic to Valley Authorities than the committees with which the Engineer Department has cooperated. Thus the fate of Valley Authority legislation, at least in so far as getting a sympathetic committee hearing is concerned, has depended in large part on the committee of reference.

The classic example is the legislation proposed by the President, and introduced by Senator Murray, to create a Missouri Valley Authority (S. 555, 79th Cong., 1st Sess. [1945]). Senator Murray wished this bill referred to the Committee on Agriculture which had handled TVA legislation. The opponents of an MVA wished it referred to the Committee on Commerce, which then handled navigation and flood control. The Committee on Irrigation and Reclamation was also interested. Senator Murray lost, and this meant sudden death for the MVA. In an almost unprecedented action, the Senate adopted a resolution (Sen. Res. 97, 79th Cong. 1st Sess. [1945]) referring the bill to all three committees—*first,* for a period of 60 days to the Committee on Commerce with respect to navigation and flood control; *second,* for an equal period, to the Committee on Irrigation and Reclamation with respect to their competence; *last,* to the Committee on Agriculture. Within 60 days the Commerce Committee had reported back unfavorably; some five months later the Committee on Irrigation reported unfavorably. There was no necessity for the Agriculture Committee either to hold hearings or to make a report—the bill was dead.

Responsibility for TVA legislation was apparently shifted to the Committees on Public Works in the Congressional Reorganization of 1946. Thus, when President Truman's Columbia Valley Administration proposals were introduced, they were referred to these committees, the very ones which work most closely with the Corps. CVA legislation has received a most unsympathetic hearing on both sides of the Capitol. Indeed, with the exception of Senator Sparkman, an Alabama supporter of TVA, it is hard to find conscientious CVA proponents on either committee.

IV. THE PROPER ROLE OF CONGRESS

What function *should* Congress perform in water resources development and how *should* this function be organized? . . .

. . . Keeping in mind both the functions for which the legislature is best equipped and the acknowledged necessity for holding the bureaucracy in close check, an ideal solution for authorization would appear to be this. Congress should pass a basic law setting out in some detail the standards to be met by any proposed water project desirable of development. The executive water development agency should then be authorized to undertake any investigation, not having to rely on Congress to authorize each survey, and to approve for construction any project that meets the standards of the basic law. For any project not falling clearly within the standards, but highly desirable in the eyes of the executive agency, a recommendation for special authorization should be submitted to the Congress. Congress would always have the authority to disapprove by legislation any project approved by the agency under this general authorization.

The basic law should further set forth criteria for establishing priorities among approved projects. The manner in which the agency applies its appropriations against project priorities, established in accordance with standards of the basic law, would, of course, be reviewed yearly by the Appropriations Committees. Finally, Congress should insist that the basic law be reconsidered periodically, and that the executive agency adopt a continuing program for reexamining, on the basis of experience, the operation of the law and recommending to Congress revisions of standards.

. . . Adjustment of group interests occurs throughout the administrative and legislative processes. In this instance, the integration and coordination of group interest which is required in setting the basic statute will be a responsibility of the Congress; that required for developing individual projects, a responsibility of the executive agency.

This proposal for very broad delegation of responsibility for interest group adjustment should not aggravate the already bad consequences we have noted from a more limited delegation. On the contrary, it should bring improvements in the existing situation. The very fact that, within the limits of standards set in the basic act, full, rather than incomplete, responsibility would be transferred should remove much of the pressure on Congress. Thus, for example, the technique of the review resolution would not be available. The executive agency would no longer look to Congress for the authorization of specific investigations. There would be no hearings on omnibus authorization bills at which interested members of Congress and the representative of the Chief of Engineers form a team in support of projects.

To be sure, individual members still would seek approval for investigations and projects in their districts. But they would be more on their own; they would not be supported in the same way by congressional committees. And the members of the committees themselves would not continue to occupy the same highly preferred positions they have now with respect to the conduct of the water agency. . . .

A number of other revisions in legislative organization and procedure might, of course, be mentioned. But space permits the mention of only one relating to committees. Jurisdiction over major water resources programs is split in both Houses of Congress between two committees—those having supervision over the Corps of Engineers and other public works and those concerned with the Bureau of Reclamation and other programs of the Department of the Interior. This is a major source of difficulty and unless remedied may well preclude any significant improvement in the conduct by Congress of its water business.

Finally, a great many of the difficulties in water legislation today are a consequence of, or in an important way related to, the division of water development responsibilities in the executive branch between the Corps of Engineers, the Department of Interior, and other agencies. From the point of view of Congress, therefore, significant improvements in the legislative handling of water resources may well be impossible without executive reorganization.

THE FARM SECURITY ADMINISTRATION *
Grant McConnell

I

. . . "Agricultural policy" over the years preceding the depression had come to mean an area of controversy in which prices were the central issue. As the

* From Grant McConnell, *The Decline of Agrarian Democracy* (Berkeley: University of California Press, 1953), pp. 84–89, 93–111. Reprinted by permission of the author and publisher.

economic crisis deepened, agricultural credit came to share somewhat in the concerns of farm leaders, educators, and administrators. Yet it is remarkable how rarely the agricultural spokesmen exhibited any awareness of problems outside these two orbits. . . . The main orientation of public policy lay in the discovery of methods of efficient production and their diffusion. True, various regulatory and other auxiliary activities combined to swell the tasks of the government with regard to agriculture. Here and there, discussions were held on tenancy, corporation farming, and soil conservation, but the attention attracted to them was hardly such as to suggest that these were proper concerns of agricultural policy. The most significant fact, however, was that the important agricultural organizations did not seem greatly concerned with any problem other than that of prices.

When the new administration took office in 1933, one of the most pressing problems was sheer relief. Both the energy with which the problem was attacked and the confusion in methods form chapters in a familiar story. Poverty and acute distress were to be found everywhere, both in cities and on farms. The administrative structure, swiftly thrown together, was one of multiple agencies, overlapping jurisdictions, and chaotic action.

Strangely enough, the vast (for the time) establishment of the Department of Agriculture and its auxiliaries had little part in this strenuous activity. It was tacitly admitted that the department's custodianship of the country's agrarian foundations did not extend to the direct relief of poverty upon the land. . . .

The great task of providing care for the distressed fell to emergency agencies. Of these the one which carried the most importance for subsequent developments in rural life was the Federal Emergency Relief Administration. The changes which swept through this agency were many and kaleidoscopic and cannot be recounted here.[1] One change, however, was of great importance. This was the early shift of emphasis from immediate relief to long-term rehabilitation. In itself, the change was a recognition that the problems with which the emergency agency was dealing were more than transitory. In 1934 a program of loans to distressed farmers was added to the system of outright doles. It did not supplant direct relief, but rather supplemented it, and was combined with grants when these were required for individual recovery. This was the origin of "rural rehabilitation," which eventually found its way, willynilly, into the Department of Agriculture.

A second device that appeared in the early New Deal derived from sources that could more properly be described as agricultural. This was the idea of subsistence homesteads. It originated in part, no doubt, from the somewhat spontaneous back-to-the-farm movement.[2] This movement was deplored by

1. For a lively account see Robert E. Sherwood, *Roosevelt and Hopkins* (New York, Bantam ed., 1950), vol. 1, pp. 46–94.

2. Among the sponsors of the movement was Henry Ford. In the main, however, it was unorganized. Even in the depression, 1932 was the only year in recent times which saw a net migration from cities, towns, and villages to farms. Cf. Report on H.R. 369, Interstate Migration,

farm leaders. More important was the urging of M. L. Wilson, a reflective "farm leader" who had played an early part in the development of the Extension system and who had great influence on Roosevelt and his farm advisers. The idea had apparently been suggested to Wilson by the success of some private projects in Utah, and at the meeting with the president-elect in which the plan for the A.A.A. was discussed, he brought forth the homestead scheme; it met with Roosevelt's approval.

The new administration, then, adopted the subsistence homesteads idea and made it a matter of public policy. Unlike other parts of the new rural program, authority for which was often vague, the subsistence homesteads scheme was given a definite legislative base. It is characteristic of the origins of the New Deal program on rural poverty that this authority was placed not in the new agricultural legislation but in the National Industrial Recovery Act. In part, this was a reflection of the belief that homesteads would help relieve urban poverty. In all likelihood, however, the absence of enthusiasm in the Department of Agriculture or among the external farm groups was equally important. This inference is supported by the fact that administration of the homesteads was placed in a special division of the Department of the Interior. Thus, the seeds of New Deal policy on rural poverty—rural rehabilitation and subsistence homesteads—were both germinated outside the Department of Agriculture.

Administration of these two projects was transplanted on April 30, 1935, to a new agency, again one that was independent of the Department of Agriculture. This was the Resettlement Administration, headed by Rexford Tugwell, who was concurrently Under Secretary of Agriculture. Tugwell thus served as a link between the established agricultural hierarchy and the new rural programs. However, the choice of Tugwell emphasized the divergence of the new agency's programs from the rest of agricultural policy; while within the house of agriculture, he was definitely not of it.

The life of the Resettlement Administration was short and spectacular. The problems which confronted the agency were many and difficult to integrate in a coherent administrative scheme. Just to list them will indicate their lack of unity: resettlement, rural rehabilitation, settlement from urban areas, soil erosion, stream pollution, seacoast erosion, forestation and reforestation, flood control, loans to purchase land and equipment by farmers, tenants, croppers, and farm laborers, and migratory labor camps (the first federal public housing).

The administrative materials for the new agency came from three sources: rural rehabilitation from the Federal Emergency Relief Administration, subsistence homesteads from the Department of the Interior, and land policy from the Department of Agriculture. These divisions had become going concerns and had developed their own points of view. As the new agency grew

House Select Committee to Investigate the Interstate Migration of Destitute Citizens (Tolan Committee), 77th Cong., 1st sess., 1941, table, p. 287.

on top of these three units—which it did in dramatic fashion—the possibilities for confusion became nearly unlimited.[3] Almost continual reorganization characterized its internal life.

Nevertheless, the Resettlement Administration represented the development of a fairly coherent point of view on the problem of rural poverty. As its name suggested, the agency concentrated on the detrimental effects of cultivating submarginal land. To take farmers off land that should be used for pasturage of forests and to reëstablish them upon good land that would support a decent standard of living—this was the ideal solution of the agency. The limitations of the approach are now obvious: they were the limitations upon the availability of good land itself. However, it is probably unfair to condemn the agency on this score, since its life was short and it did contain tendencies which led in other directions as well. The emphasis was important in one regard, however. This was its evocation of an old tenet of the American creed, the belief that the small independent landholder is the backbone of the nation. So far as this aspect of the Resettlement Administration's program was emphasized, the agency was standing firmly upon an old tradition.

This concern for the small landholder was reflected during this period by a drive to secure federal legislation to reduce farm tenancy. In 1935 Senator John H. Bankhead sponsored a bill for this purpose which passed the Senate but failed in the House. Various outside groups devoted their energies to dramatizing the problem and making it known. Their success was sufficient to persuade both political parties to include statements on tenancy in their platforms. Soon after the election, the President appointed a special committee to study the problem.

The Resettlement Administration had come under sharp political attack, partly because of the personality of Tugwell. In order to save the program, Tugwell resigned, and the agency was transferred bodily into the Department of Agriculture. This shift, which preceded the report of the President's Committee on Farm Tenancy by six weeks, was but the preliminary to a general reorganization which came with passage of the Bankhead-Jones Farm Tenancy Act of 1937. This act, which was designed, at least in the eyes of some, to place a legislative foundation under the entire program dealing with rural poverty, emerged from Congress primarily as an act to assist farm tenants to become landowners. It authorized short-term loans for rehabilitation and a program for retirement of submarginal land. It carried no appropriation for the rehabilitation program, and the appropriations for the other two functions were small. As the foundation for a long-term program dealing with the problem of rural poverty, the act was disappointing. Soon after the passage of the act, the Secretary of Agriculture abolished the Resettlement Administration and created the Farm Security Administration (F.S.A.) to take its place.

This complicated history of bureaucratic organization and reorganiztion

3. Before it was superseded, the Resettlement Administration assembled a staff of approximately 18,000, more than 13,000 of whom came from the old state rural rehabilitation corporations. The term "Unsettlement Administration" came to be a byword in bureaucratic circles.

has a meaning that goes beyond the search for sheerly efficient media of administration. A big issue was at stake: the establishment of a federal program directed to the problem of rural poverty as part of the nation's public policy. It is fairly clear that there was little hope for the development of such a program within what might have appeared the logical part of the federal establishment, the Department of Agriculture. Initiative for such a program came from neither the department nor the external organization to which the department looked for its own support before Congress.[4] The program had to be nurtured outside the department, and then, when the political climate appeared threatening to the life of the program, it was brought into the department in which superficially it appeared to belong. This was, in general, the logic of the often bewildering series of changes in the administrative structure of the program. The appointment of the President's Committee on Farm Tenancy, the resignation of Tugwell, the movement of the Resettlement Administration into the Department of Agriculture, the Bankhead-Jones Act, and the creation of the F.S.A. were all parts of a coherent plan to establish the program on rural poverty.

This administrative history has a number of interesting features. First, the program did not originate with the usual farm sources. Second, it grew large very quickly. Third, the success of a relatively few liberal New Deal leaders in starting the program is remarkable. Their achievement was made almost wholly without organized support outside the administration. Because of the lack of powerful external organization, much in the program had to be carried on without specific congressional sanction. Fourth, the decision to place the program in the Department of Agriculture was something of a Hobson's choice; the program might not have survived as long as it did without this compromise. . . .

In general, the F.S.A. was the residual legatee of nearly every human problem of rural life that was not solved by increasing the prices of a few "basic" commodities. To no other place in the federal establishment, least of all to other agencies in the Department of Agriculture, could such problems be assigned. The F.S.A. welcomed the responsibility. One of the remarkable—and unfortunate—features of the organization was that its programs were carried out under vague and scattered fragments of legislative authority. This permitted flexibility of operation, but it made the whole agency an administrative adventure. It may be said that this was an example of a familiar pattern of bureaucratic aggrandizement. Such a statement would be inaccurate; other agencies which might have assumed the responsibility in fact did not. Moreover, assumption of these particular responsibilities carried its dangers. The fate of the F.S.A. is sufficient evidence of this.

The sheer fact that the agency held the torch of rural welfare was its major significance—not that this method or that was employed. The chief critic of the family-size farm idea has suggested that the F.S.A. embodied in the New Deal revival of "the Jeffersonian ideal" (i.e., the family-size farm). This is

[4. The "external organization" referred to was the American Farm Bureau Federation. Ed.]

thoroughly to misunderstand the significance of the F.S.A. program. Whether or not the family-size farm is the sole means of curing the ills of rural poverty, support of it was an expediency forced upon the agency by the political circumstances in which it developed. Purchase of family farms for tenants was a possible method of assisting some of the rural poor, and it was employed.

The problems of rural poverty in which the F.S.A. became involved were themselves exceedingly varied. They varied, first, by regions. It might almost have been possible to organize the work of the agency by regions and thereby to have achieved much the same approach to its problems. The most distressed area of the nation was, of course, the South. In the words of President Roosevelt, the South presented "the Nation's number one economic problem—the Nation's problem, not merely the South's." As a result, the F.S.A. was heavily oriented toward the South. Many on the agency's staff were Southerners. This focusing of energies was also reflected in the distribution of rehabilitation funds: 38 per cent of all borrowers were located in twelve Southern states.

In the South, economic distress was particularly severe among the Negroes. In the bleak picture of discrimination against Negroes in the South, as Gunnar Myrdal saw it, one of the few bright spots was the fact that Negroes shared in the F.S.A. program to a degree almost corresponding to their proportion in the population.[5] Success in achieving this degree of fairness in administration required no little political courage.

The problems of the South were not limited to those arising from the racial issue. Low standards of health, of education, of housing, of farming practice were to a peculiar degree Southern problems. The F.S.A. made some kind of attack on most of them. The point of importance here is not so much that the F.S.A. was energetic and alert in attacking these problems but that, in so doing, it directly antagonized powerful organized interests. This may be illustrated by the crusade of F.S.A. workers to cure one of the worst characteristics of cotton farming, the practice of planting the crop right up to the doorstep. In teaching its "clients" to plant gardens and to shift to dairying as a means of livelihood, the agency was earning the displeasure not only of landlords who favored exploitative methods of farming but also of the commercial dairy interests of the North.

A second regional concentration of F.S.A. efforts was in the Great Plains area, where drought and dust storms during the 'thirties had caused acute suffering, on the scale of a national disaster. Payment of emergency rehabilitation grants under the F.S.A. centered almost wholly in the Great Plains area. Loans were made also to coöperatives in order that they might buy grain elevators whose operators had failed. Again the agency incurred the hostility of important interests—the large private grain dealers of Minneapolis.

The most serious effects of migrancy were felt in areas having heavy seasonal

5. Gunnar Myrdal, *An American Dilemma* (New York, Harper and Bros., 1944), pp. 274–275. Myrdal expressed surprise that this should be so, for, at the time his study was made, F.S.A. loans were subject to approval by local committees consisting of "big" farmers. Myrdal rightly assessed the general significance of the committee system, but seems to have been unaware that the committees only recently had acquired power to pass on eligibility for loans.

demands for field labor. In California, where the problem has always been at its worst, there was a long-standing tradition of exploiting farm workers. By seeking to alleviate the degraded conditions in which these workers moved, the F.S.A. appeared to be impairing the system by which the shifting army of farm labor was kept docile and cheap.

This catalogue of political liabilities of the F.S.A. was serious. However, it was almost insignificant compared to the scale of the problem of rural poverty. Out of the activities of the F.S.A. and the many special studies of rural life in the 'thirties, a few great facts emerged: first, the depth and extent of rural poverty; second, the low level of productivity of the poorer farms. It was apparent that rural poverty was not only grave but that it was a long-term problem and not merely a product of the business cycle. The farmers who were most afflicted, moreover, were generally excluded from the benefits provided in the principal schemes of agricultural policy. And, from the standpoint of economic efficiency, too many people were trying to live on the land.

The policy of the F.S.A. was open to serious doubts arising from these implications. So far as it sought settlement on the land, the policy had limited application. So far as this succeeded, there were questions whether it was not restricting farm income and adding to rural unemployment. These questions grow pale, however, before the fact that the F.S.A. had as its potential burden the welfare of a part of the farm population which at times approached one-half. Measured on this scale, the effort was pitifully inadequate. In the absence of other efforts, though, the F.S.A. (together with its predecessors) represented the greatest innovation in agricultural policy since the passage of the Homestead Act. . . .

II

In mid-1941 the Farm Security Administration came under an attack that has seldom been equaled for bitterness. By mid-1943 the F.S.A. was dying; by the end of 1946 it was dead.

The story of this attack is one of the bleakest in the history of agricultural politics. In itself, it constitutes one of the most important pages of that history. The struggle seems in retrospect to have been conducted behind a veil of obscurity woven out of superficial complexities and war distractions. The battle was fought over seemingly trivial matters of administrative organization. However, that alone cannot explain the virulence of the assault; its meaning was much deeper. And yet the paradox remains that administrative organization was the crux of the entire battle. This was frankly, even bluntly, stated, and the attack was subtle only in the sense that the import of administrative form was grasped by few outside the circles of the antagonists themselves.

The American Farm Bureau Federation was the agency which destroyed the F.S.A., and bureau leadership directed the attack. Auxiliaries were marshaled into the battle, but it nonetheless remains true that this was a Farm Bureau campaign. Accordingly, it is important to trace the attitude of the Farm Bureau in the period preceding the outbreak of hostilities.

In its official publications the federation has occasionally taken credit for the F.S.A., although it has avoided the claim of outright sponsorship. When Farm Bureau responsibility for the death of the F.S.A. is mentioned, the response is that F.S.A. was simply "a good idea that went wrong"; the bureau had no fault to find with the intentions of the agency or even with the people who supported it or benefited by it. The F.S.A. had become a wastefully administered bureaucracy which was imposing upon the people in need of its help; the Farm Bureau intervened only when the situation became serious. As a matter of fact, however, the bureau did not actually begin its campaign from outside the federal bureaucracy until 1941. The F.S.A., before this, had been under constant pressure to conform to the peculiar outlook of the Department of Agriculture, and to a degree it had conformed. What happened in 1941 was not that the F.S.A. had become hostile to the ways of the department or the farm leaders, but that the Farm Bureau found this moment opportune for attack. The F.S.A. by this time had traveled a long way in its own "agriculturalization." The family-size farm was becoming increasingly its central tenet.

Actually, the Farm Bureau had never been a supporter of the F.S.A. in any sense. Before the creation of the F.S.A., the Farm Bureau had not played any significant part in calling attention to the prevalence of rural poverty except as it was useful to do so in securing government support of prices. The struggle which culminated in the "purge" of 1935 and the entrance of the Resettlement Administration into the Department of Agriculture involved little effort by the Farm Bureau as an organization. Not all the moves made in this period are visible now, but it is likely that events were influenced by pressures which were partly generated from sources close to the Farm Bureau and that the change in the status of the Resettlement Administration was made in anticipation of more drastic action. For a time, the concession of placing the problems of rural poverty in the care of the Department of Agriculture was adequate.

O'Neal was one of the members of the President's Committee on Farm Tenancy. His inclusion in this group, which he can hardly have found congenial, was perhaps made in the hope that he might be persuaded to lead the American Farm Bureau Federation toward a socially enlightened policy for agriculture; if so, the hope was doomed. O'Neal refused to approve the report of the committee without qualification. His statement was restrained and contained no general condemnation of the findings or the plan. However, in view of later developments, his statement is significant. He made six points; the first three require quotation in full:

1. The law should be administered by the Secretary of Agriculture through the directors of extension in the various States, who will carry out the provisions of the act under rules and regulations prescribed by the Secretary.

2. Administration in county or region should be by an appointee of the Secretary, selected from a list supplied by the director of extension in the State. All appointees should meet qualifications set up for county agents in the State.

3. To pass on the eligibility of applicants for aid under the proposed law in each

county or region, a nonsalaried committee of three members should be appointed by the Secretary from a list supplied by the extension director. In case the Secretary is unable to select a full committee from the first list submitted, he should be empowered to ask for additional names. All committee members must be men whose chief interest and experience have been in agriculture. This committee should be permanent and should act in an advisory capacity to the local administrator and the director of extension.

The remaining three points were that assistance should be confined to worthy young farmers who were unable to get credit from other agencies, that tenants purchasing farms under the plan should get title at an early stage, and that loans from the Secretary should be permissible only in the period before transfer of title. In his letter, O'Neal added, "I have grave doubts that credit can carry the burden of such a program."

When the Bankhead-Jones farm tenancy bill came up in Congress, the Farm Bureau parade of witnesses usual in hearings on agricultural legislation was absent. The Farm Bureau was represented only by a letter from O'Neal. It took but a single page in the record. O'Neal urged such a law despite his belief that "a fair price system" would do more than anything else to prevent loss of farm homes through foreclosure. He then repeated verbatim the points made in his statement to the President's committee. Thus the Farm Bureau would not support the bill; neither would it openly oppose the bill.

This position, taken on what proved to be the blueprint for the F.S.A., was consistently maintained by the Farm Bureau during the next few years. The F.S.A. did not have the approval of the Farm Bureau; when the showdown came, the first three points stated by O'Neal in 1937 were the ones which the Farm Bureau sought to establish. At the same time, the statement contains no hint of the strong hostility that was to appear in 1942 and 1943, after the F.S.A. had been in existence for a number of years. Articles on the F.S.A. appeared occasionally in the Farm Bureau's chief publication, and these were quite objective. As late as July, 1940, the organization included in the agricultural platform which it offered to both political parties a recommendation that rehabilitation of farm families and help for tenants and migrants should be continued by the F.S.A. This was perhaps the high-water mark in Farm Bureau tolerance of the F.S.A.

Any responsible person who took this statement as being meaningful, however, was disappointed. The Farm Bureau was willing that the recommendation should go into political platforms, but it was not willing to give the political support which this seemed to imply. When Farm Bureau delegations appeared before congressional appropriation committees they gave no support to F.S.A. appropriation requests. This was true in both 1939 and 1940. On the whole, the Farm Bureau was merely indifferent to the F.S.A. during this period.

In 1940, however, Farm Bureau leadership was increasingly uncertain of its relationship with Secretary Wallace and, indeed, with much of the Department of Agriculture. The F.S.A. continued as a large unit of the department;

it was clearly outside the Farm Bureau sphere of influence. The department was making strenuous efforts to instill vitality and independence into the county committees charged with production control and planning. Wallace and "liberal" elements in the administration succeeded in getting a reorganization of the independent agencies dealing with farm credit which brought these into the department in a more centralized administration. The previous decentralization had been amenable to control by elements friendly to the Farm Bureau. This last was probably the precipitating issue that decided the Farm Bureau leadership to wage a campaign to remake the Department of Agriculture.

When the annual convention of the Farm Bureau met in December, 1940, the usual list of resolutions was revised and the first two places were given to national reorganization and state administration. The former was a plan that would deal with most of the so-called "action" programs. The latter was a commendation of the Extension services of the land grant colleges as administrative agencies. One of many points under this heading was the recommendation that the Extension Service should be responsible for the home and farm management phases of the F.S.A. programs. Another heading covered farm credit. Independence in administration was the objective sought here. The last specific recommendation under this head was, "We favor placing the loaning activities of the Farm Security Administration as a separate Department under this Board." This was the declaration of war.

The attack was opened in 1941 with a full-scale offensive on the Department of Agriculture at the crucial appropriation hearings. The Farm Bureau leadership was well aware that its influence was stronger in the House than in the Senate; so the opening battle was fought solely before the former. The most favorable ground for Farm Bureau purposes would have been the House Committee on Agriculture, but this could not be chosen because the wartime situation forbade consideration of any new farm legislation. The Senate committees, whether on Agriculture or Appropriations, were less favorable to the Farm Bureau than either House committee. The House Committee on Appropriations was accordingly the best possibility at hand, and the Farm Bureau concentrated upon it.

The campaign of 1941 was the most ambitious of the entire period. O'Neal brought in a total of fourteen state Farm Bureau heads, each with a set speech and a point to make. Among them, they presented a coherent statement of the Farm Bureau plan for reorganizing the Department of Agriculture. Since the Farm Bureau was striking for complete victory at one blow, the full story of the year's campaign properly belongs in another chapter. What is relevant here is that the plan for breaking the F.S.A. in two was forcefully stated: the farm and home management services should be given to the Extension Service and the loaning functions should be given to the Farm Credit Administration.

In this the Farm Bureau overreached itself. The House subcommittee refused to be made the vehicle for such a sweeping change. In terms of narrow objectives, however, the Farm Bureau scored a success—the achievement of getting a rider to the appropriation bill effectively keeping F.S.A. personnel out of Civil Service. This was an important step, for the federal government was then undergoing a rapid reorganization in preparation for war. Experienced government workers were in great demand in the new agencies, and many incentives were offered people in the older agencies to take new jobs. Moreover, the Ramspeck bill, which authorized presidential "blanketing-in" of workers outside the Civil Service, was under consideration. It was expected to result in Civil Service status for almost all government personnel still unprotected; those in the F.S.A. shared this hope. When the rider forbade such action, agency morale plummeted and many resignations followed. This is precisely the sort of tactic by which an alert pressure group can accomplish far-reaching results in an inconspicuous manner. Here the effect was seriously to cripple the F.S.A.

The Farm Bureau also engaged in widespread efforts to generate support for its plan. O'Neal mentioned "a great many discussions in groups and regions; South, Midwest and East and all around." Wherever possible, other organizations were brought into the campaign. The Washington office of the Farm Bureau requested the state organizations to seek out evidence to be used against the F.S.A. This was apparently the result of a decision made after the large-scale attempt had failed, to strike for a narrower objective. The material gained in this manner was inadequate and seems to have consisted mainly of vague complaints that nevertheless yielded a few tactical hints.

Although the decision had been made to concentrate on the F.S.A., the Farm Bureau leadership was unprepared when its opportunity came in December. The Byrd Committee, a joint committee on reduction of nonessential governmental expenditures, began its hearings at this time. The F.S.A. was one of the first agencies summoned to justify itself before the committee. The initial hearing went off quietly and without any display of congressional skepticism. The watchful legislative department of the Farm Bureau, however, quickly improvised a course of action. The very purpose of the Byrd Committee gave an excellent clue to the most promising line of attack. But the Farm Bureau lacked ammunition for the purpose.

The national convention of the Farm Bureau met just before Christmas. The resolutions passed were somewhat different in form from those of previous years in that they had to deal with wartime conditions. However, they placed curtailment of nondefense spending in a conspicuous place. The administrative program was unchanged, although it was stated less concretely. There was no mention of the F.S.A.

In January, 1942, the inner circle of the national board of the Farm Bureau met and directed O'Neal to seek out the material needed for a hearing before the Byrd Committee. He, in turn, ordered the legal staff of the national organization to investigate F.S.A. operations. The general counsel, Kirkpatrick, sent six investigators into eight different states, with instructions to get what they could quickly. O'Neal specified the types of information to which they should pay special attention:

1. Check organization and policies of F.S.A. coöperatives.
2. Large socialized farming projects.
3. Solicitation of clients for rural rehabilitation loans and farm tenant plans.
4. Grants of money to improve status of delinquent borrowers.
5. Cases of excessive costs saddled on borrowers—unnecessary equipment, etc.
6. Cases of farm management programs in conflict with AAA or extension programs.
7. Excessive overhead expense in administration.
8. Duplication and unnecessary expense in Soil Conservation Service. Examples of high costs and results attained by Extension Service.

Because of limited time, only the first five points received attention. Beyond this, the investigators were given to understand rather clearly that the objective was to find material on which criticisms of the F.S.A. could be based.[6]

The bureau's "investigation" of the F.S.A. took place between January 7, the date of the decision to make the search, and February 6, when the findings were presented to the congressional committee. The analysts sent to the Northern states had little success and O'Neal was not able to use their reports except to mention that the inquiry had touched the states mentioned. But the investigator sent into the Southern states, William G. Carr, a Chicago attorney, struck an area in which F.S.A. operations were more extensive. His report was made to carry the burden of the Farm Bureau charges. This was the substance behind O'Neal's confident assurance to the committee that "Our counsel, Mr. Kirkpatrick, has made a very complete study of this whole agricultural program."

The Farm Bureau performance before the committee was opened with a flourish that indicated a flair for the dramatic. O'Neal, in his long career as impresario at congressional hearings, had acquired a good sense of the gestures likely to arrest attention. Accordingly, he introduced first a Southern judge who had discovered that F.S.A. supervisors regarded the poll tax as a legitimate item on the allowable list of expenditures in the farm and home plans on which loans were based. The point was made that the F.S.A. was paying poll taxes. Thereafter, O'Neal had his audience well in hand.

After a tribute to the purposes of the committee, O'Neal began: "While we thoroughly agreed that the activities under the farm-tenant purchase program and the Farm Security program should be drastically and severely curtailed, we believe that at least part of the work of these agencies [sic] should not forthwith be abolished." However, most of the work of the F.S.A., he continued, was now unnecessary, and the remainder of its activities should be parceled out among other agencies. He then outlined the Farm Bureau case against the F.S.A. The charges must be summarized if the sweeping nature of the condemnation is to be appreciated. These were:

6. This was brought out inadvertently and Senator La Follette secured its inclusion in the record. One of the investigators wrote to his chief as follows: "Enclosed you will find detailed report of observations in Shelby County and evidence secured for some criticism made. Also what we were able to locate and find out in Clark County. If this is in line with what you had hoped to receive, or if there are other suggestions you might have after looking over these notes, I hope you will do so and notify me."

1. F.S.A. assignment of quotas of clients in order to spend funds appropriated by Congress "and to maintain personnel employed by the agency."

2. Solicitation of clients to meet quotas.

3. Burdening of clients with excessive loans.

4. Establishment of impractical collective farming projects.

5. Giving grants to enable repayment of loans "rather than using such funds to relieve destitution."

6. Use of renewal notes and variable payment plans to disguise low payment on loans.

7. "Flagrant attempts to build pressure groups to maintain congressional appropriations."

8. Instances of refusal to accept payment of indebtedness in full.

9. Rigid control of business and farming plans of clients.

The evidence supporting these charges came mainly from the Carr report to O'Neal and Kirkpatrick. For the most part it consisted of a series of indefinite citations of individual cases supplemented by Carr's own summaries of public opinion in the states he visited. Thus, he found that the general public of Arkansas was against the F.S.A. This discovery was made on the basis of a few days' visit. Most of the material presented in the Carr report was hearsay, and even the number of examples cited was not impressive. Despite the evident unreliability of the material, a fact which much of the committee seems to have appreciated, the Carr "documentary material," as O'Neal called it, was inserted in the record.

The remainder of the Farm Bureau evidence was in the form of articles and statements by F.S.A. employees. One news story quoted a statement by an assistant administrator to the effect that fee-simple ownership accounted for many of the ills of the American land. Although much the same statement could have been found in the Report of the President's Committee on Farm Tenancy, the idea proved shocking to Congress in 1942 and 1943. Even the ghost of the old antagonism to Tugwell was invoked against the F.S.A.

It is unlikely that the Farm Bureau case—a tissue of scattered instances reported in colored language and of large generalizations—would have been granted a hearing had it not been for the determination of groups in Congress such as the Byrd Committee, which were using the war situation to dismantle as much of the New Deal as possible, and the peculiar structure of the congressional committee system which permitted the rehearing of discredited charges before different bodies.

The Farm Bureau repeated the nine charges and the Carr material so extensively and so often that these came to acquire an aura of truth. After the Byrd Committee had seen and heard them, they were presented to the Senate Committee on Appropriations and the House Committee on Appropriations. These committees, which had to examine the requests of governmental agencies each year, were thus treated to reviews of the Farm Bureau material in both 1942 and 1943. The Senate committee had been fortunate that it had not been selected to serve as a sounding board in 1941. The Farm Bureau added little new material in support of its charges through these hearings.

Slowly, however, an organization was improvised to defend the work of the F.S.A. The list of groups was impressive, but frequently their spokesmen failed in the acid congressional test: they could rarely show that they were real dirt farmers. They ranged all the way from labor unions to the Y.W.C.A. Only one of these assorted groups can be said to have been truly effective—the Catholic Rural Life Conference, represented by a remarkable priest, Monsignor John O'Grady. Monsignor O'Grady made by far the most forceful and persuasive appeal in the entire round of hearings, asking not only the continuation but also the extension of the F.S.A. His efforts were nevertheless insufficient to still the charge that the F.S.A. was communistic.

The campaign against the F.S.A seemed to follow some developmental law of its own nature. Each time the attack was renewed before a different committee, the charges and the material with which they were supported were much the same. Yet the shortcomings (from the Farm Bureau point of view) of previous hearings seemed to dictate that the charges should be made more shrilly and that the recriminations should become more bitter. It was inevitable that personal hostilities should grow, but it was scarcely necessary that the Farm Bureau's dislike of the F.S.A. should extend to the latter's clients. This occurred.

As O'Neal and his assistants sought charges that would goad Congress to action, the emphasis insensibly was shifted. At first the Farm Bureau had taken the ground that F.S.A. clients were not receiving enough help, but by 1943 O'Neal was insisting that the latter should be cut off from any help. His argument was that the "2,000,000 smallest farms consumed on the average about one-half of the production of these farms and sent only $100 worth of products to market. This group produced only about 3 per cent of the marketed crops. They do not have the land, facilities, or labor to produce large quantities of food." The statement was interesting not only for its dubious inference—this was contested by such authorities as John D. Black and Howard Tolley—but for the double indication of Farm Bureau awareness of the existence of rural poverty and Farm Bureau unwillingness that anything be done to relieve it.

By 1943 the Farm Bureau had found allies who brought an important new set of reasons for the elimination of the F.S.A. The president of the Irrigated Cotton Growers charged that the F.S.A., in administering the program by which Mexican labor was brought into the United States under terms of a formal agreement signed by the two governments, had insisted that a minimum wage of thirty cents an hour be paid for cotton picking.

The reverberations from the F.S.A. policy extended to the Old South. Oscar Johnson, president of the National Cotton Council of America, came before the same committee and testified that the F.S.A. was "impeding" the cost of production, lowering worker morale, threatening disruption of economic and social conditions and relationships, and promoting class distinctions, hatred, prejudice, and distrust. He presented a copy of a letter from Philip Murray to various unions urging support of the F.S.A. as evidence of "a direct tie-up between the C.I.O. and the F.S.A." If there was any doubt in regard to Mr. Johnson's meaning, this was removed by a resolution passed by the Cotton Council which he read:

We contend that Farm Security Administration, as it now operates, with few exceptions is in direct violation of our position as stated above and that it threatens the foundations of American agriculture and, through their contention for a minimum wage per hour for cotton picking, threatens to disrupt a fair and satisfactory system that has successfully operated in the Cotton Belt for over 100 years.

The outcome of the struggle was decided in the summer of 1943. The Farm Bureau's campaign before the existing committees of Congress resulted in the setting up of still another committee, a subcommittee, commonly known as the Cooley Committee, of the House Committee on Agriculture to investigate the activities of the F.S.A. The committee was in existence for more than a year and provided an open forum for all who cared to bring charges against the F.S.A. The committee itself was amenable to Farm Bureau suggestions in its probing, and either was unaware of the objectives of the F.S.A. or was hostile to them. The investigation made by the committee was not characterized by any sense of proportion or, indeed, by any sense of the realities of rural poverty.

One of the inevitable results of this prolonged series of investigations was to build up a case for the prosecution, not merely because the prosecutors had been active but because grievances tended to pyramid. In this hearing, the voice of the National Grange was added to that of the Farm Bureau and its close allies. Curiously enough, the motivation of the Grange came as much from its hostility to the Farm Bureau as from any concern about the F.S.A. itself. The Grange had always resented the close relationship between the Extension Service and the Farm Bureau. In the Farmers' Union defense of the F.S.A., the Grange saw a comparable relationship developing between the F.S.A. and the Farmers' Union. There was some truth in this view. The Farmers' Union had had representatives on hand at each one of the hearings to support the F.S.A. Ever since the accession of James Patton as president of the Farmers' Union, the affinity between the F.S.A. and his organization had been growing. F.S.A. officials conferred frequently with Patton but never with O'Neal. Baldwin, in fact, mentioned that O'Neal avoided the F.S.A. office. Patton did not.

A real question exists whether the F.S.A. personnel deliberately attempted to "build up" the Farmers' Union. James Maddox, who was in a position to know what was going on, says that some help was given to Farmers' Union organize.. in certain areas and that such assistance was discussed in one or two other regions. However, his judgment is that the F.S.A. hardly got beyond toying with the idea. At any rate, it seems doubtful whether the friendliness of the Farmer's Union was an asset to the F.S.A. during its trial.

Whatever the truth of the matter, Albert Goss, Master of the Grange, believed that his organization suffered from the affinity existing between other farm organizations and segments of the Department of Agriculture. Accordingly, when he appeared before the Cooley Committee, he lashed out in both directions. He necessarily dealt most with the Farm Bureau-Extension relationship, but the net effect was to add the weight of the Grange to the Farm Bureau's campaign against the F.S.A.

The purposes of the Farm Bureau were served in another manner by the succession of hearings. Each of those preceding the Cooley hearing were, so to speak, rehearsals for this, the showdown battle. There had been abundant opportunity to observe the relative effectiveness of the various charges. The accusations were substantially the same as hitherto, but the emphases were noticeably different. In the Farm Bureau presentation, first place was now given to the resettlement projects. The costliness of the projects, their numerous weaknesses of operation, and the analogy that could be drawn with the collective farms of Soviet Russia were stressed. Grouped with the projects were the more recent efforts of the F.S.A. to help many farm families which had been rendered homeless by military acquisitions of land. The F.S.A. had bought tracts of land to deal with this problem, and these purchases were presented as evidence of deliberate intention to evade the will of Congress that the resettlement project idea should not be extended.

While the Cooley Committee covered virtually all the familiar ground as well as some that was new, the issue of the total objective of the F.S.A. was lost in that of the resettlement projects. Without question, the agency had been weakest in this part of the program. For one thing, Congress was antagonistic to anything that smacked of coöperative farming. Then, too, the F.S.A. for a number of years had lost faith and interest in some of its own projects. This was the clearest indication of the agency's "agriculturalization." The problem presented by military relocation had brought the entire issue of F.S.A.'s basic approach to the surface again, but the policy actually remained the traditional family-size farm. Moreover, few of the F.S.A. projects seemed to be operating successfully, although here the evidence is probably inadequate as a basis for judgment. The agency had unwisely arranged for ninety-nine-year leases of certain tracts. This was seized upon as the best possible evidence of F.S.A.'s contempt for the concept of fee-simple ownership of land. Accordingly, much of the committee's time and energy was directed to this phase of the F.S.A. program.

The hearing went beyond its predecessors in the degree to which scurrility was tolerated. The Carr "documents," which had been rejected by some of the previous committees, were brought forth again and O'Neal was asked leading questions which permitted further rehearsing of the old charges. Perhaps the low point came when the committee appeared in Phoenix and gave hearing to the suggestion that the F.S.A. regional director, who had helped negotiate the labor agreement with Mexico and who was married to "a lady of Mexican extraction," by some curious theory of international relations thereby betrayed "communistic" leanings.

The fate of the F.S.A. had been determined long before the committee made its report, but there is nonetheless some significance in the language with which the findings were clothed.

The committee has sought to determine whether or not those charged with the responsibility of administering the affairs of the Farm Security administration have violated the true intent and meaning of the several acts of Congress by virtue of which the agency has been permitted to function, and further to determine to what extent, if any, in the management of the affairs of the agency, there has been a departure from traditional American policies and well-established laws and customs. . . . [the F.S.A. was] financing communistic resettlement projects, where the families could never own homes, or be paid for all that they made or for all the time they worked, and was supervising its borrowers to the extent of telling the borrower how to raise his children, how to plan his home life and, it is strongly suspected in some cases, how to vote.

The committee found the F.S.A. guilty on two major counts throughout: the F.S.A. was treating its clients badly; the F.S.A. was doing too much for its clients. Although most of the discussion covered the resettlement projects and the labor program, the recommendation was for liquidation of both the projects and the rural rehabilitation program (the labor program had already been taken from the F.S.A.).

A number of features in this long series of congressional inquiries are worthy of comment. First is their progressively degraded character. Second is the absence of any searching investigation into the total operations of the F.S.A. or the guiding concepts of its administration. The latter certainly was needed. The F.S.A. had never faced the basic dilemma of its policy. Binding people to the land in a time of rapid technological change, whether by rehabilitation, tenant purchase, or resettlement projects, could not insure a standard of living commensurate with that in other segments of the population for the large mass with which the F.S.A. had to deal. Some F.S.A. operations had a definite odor of paternalism about them. This the various committees caught, but they discussed it in such terms that the merits of the matter could never be learned. Third is the readiness with which the committees—and Congress as a whole—allowed themselves to be manipulated by the lobbyists of the Farm Bureau.

The F.S.A. disintegrated before the Cooley Committee was through. The defense housing activities of the agency were transferred to the National Housing Administration in December, 1941. This was a reasonable change, but it did remove a highly specialized corps of builders. A year later the F.S.A. was placed in the War Food Administration headed by Chester Davis, a friend of the Farm Bureau. The labor program was removed, and a new law prohibited a minimum wage and housing or security of working conditions for government-transported American workers; funds were denied for additional farm labor camps, and immigration restrictions were waived.

The 1944 appropriation for the F.S.A. was withheld in 1943 and in the fall of that year Baldwin resigned as administrator. Most of the policy-making staff followed. Frank Hancock, a former North Carolina congressman, was appointed to Baldwin's position and did his best to meet the requirements of the Cooley Committee and the Farm Bureau. One of the measures of his success is the swiftness with which he dispersed the agency's personnel. When Hancock was through, little was left of what Secretary Wickard had once called the "specialized zeal" of th F.S.A.[7]

The F.S.A. was formally ended late in 1946. Under the terms of an act passed in that year, the agency was liquidated and the Farmers' Home Administration was set up to carry on the "good" parts of its work. The successor had three functions: to continue the farm ownership program started under the 1937 Bankhead-Jones Act, to manage the water facilities program, and to make production loans. The first two had been parts of the F.S.A. program; the third was a former program of the Farm Credit Administration. The act specified that preference must be given to veterans. In practice, this has meant that the Farmer's Home Administration is primarily a veterans' agency.[8] The agency has given sufficient evidence of its reliability for Congress to entrust a new program to its care; it may now make loans to "bona fide fur farmers." Such is the resolution of the problem of rural poverty.

THE POLITICAL ECOLOGY OF A BUREAU *
J. Lieper Freeman

. . . IN order to understand how issues are resolved and national policies are made, one must view the system as something other than a well-geared monolith. . . . Historically, although the federal government has accumulated great power and reached huge proportions in the course of the nation's development, it has done so relatively slowly and usually against considerable resistance from various special interests. Many groups directly or indirectly urge specific expansions of power favorable to themselves but oppose either general expansions or increases of authority specifically favoring other groups. Furthermore, increases in federal power have usually been realized only after limitations imposed by the federal sysem, by the separation of powers, and by checks and balances have been reasonably satisfied. Perhaps the most significant point, in the last analysis, is that the growth of the federal government has most frequently occurred when new activities have been urged on Con-

* Condensed from J. Lieper Freeman, *The Political Process: Executive Bureau-Legislative Committee Relations* (New York: Random House, Revised Edition, 1965), pp. 4–7, 70–76, 80–94. © Copyright, 1955, 1965, by Random House, Inc. Reprinted by permission of the publisher.

7. F.S.A. personnel by years: 1942, 19,045; 1943, 14,862; 1944, 11,176. Hancock gave his objective for 1945 as 9,514. He more than achieved this.

8. In the first year of operation of the Farmers' Home Administration, three-fifths of the loans for purchase of farms went to veterans. In 1950, 93 percent of these loans went to veterans.

gress and the Administration by special segments of the population. If there is any creeping socialism in American government, it has come and is coming largely as an accompaniment of what might be called "creeping pluralism," that is, the gradual growth of political groups especially concerned with the protection and promotion of particular interests. The kind of government which has evolved is far from being a tightly knit leviathan.

THE AIMS AND UTILITY OF THIS STUDY

The present study endeavors to focus attention upon and to state some propositions about the interactions of certain key participants in this pluralistic leviathan. The actors are members of political subsystems centering upon executive bureaus and legislative committees. The chief value to be derived from the study should be a greater understanding of the patterns of policy-making *within* these subsystems. The major focus, beyond an examination of the relations between the general political setting and the participants in the subsystem, is upon relations among subsystem actors from the bureaucracy, from congressional committees, and from interested segments of the public. The value of studying the patterns of influence within executive-legislative subsystems has been well-stated by Professor Ernest S. Griffith, who called them "whirlpools." Griffith said, in part:

. . . It is my opinion that ordinarily the relationship among these men—legislators, administrators, lobbyists, scholars—who are interested in a common problem is a much more real relationship than the relationship between congressmen generally or between administrators generally. In other words, he who would understand the prevailing pattern of our present governmental behavior, instead of studying the formal institutions or even generalizations in the relationships between these institutions or organs, important though all these are, may possibly obtain a better picture of the way things really happen if he would study these "whirlpools" of special social interest and problems.

In a recent most valuable book, Douglass Cater has similarly analyzed power in Washington in terms of "sub-governments" which are essentially the same as the whirlpools depicted by Griffith. These phenomena are neither new, surprising, nor devious. Rather they are so numerous and increasingly specialized that the mass of the citizenry has difficulty in following them. And as Cater points out, no part of the national political framework can effectively control all of them.

Similarly, a closely related additional value of the study may be a better understanding of the plural patterns of power and decision-making within the national government as they mirror the functional specialization and diversity of American society. This diversity of interests—of groups concerned with special values—has a host of sources deeply rooted in the nation's experience. Geographic dispersion, cultural heritage, religious belief, economic status, technological specialization, and traditions of individual and group self-seeking are but an important few of these sources. The groups arising from them have demanded the attention of special units of Congress and of the Administration and have thereby contributed to the diversity and complexity of the federal government while simultaneously attaining protection from it and niches for themselves within it. At the same time, Congress and the Administration, organized under legal norms which encourage permissiveness and particularism through their many sub-units, have tended to accommodate these interests. Furthermore, they have tended to encourage, aid, and abet their political activity and their very survival. The leaders from the official sub-units have become involved in relationships with leaders of the interest groups and have tended to take over major decision-making functions officially allotted to the government as a whole. By observing how and under what conditions specialists in certain areas of public policy are important determinants of that policy for the overall political system, one may sharpen his understanding of the importance of bureau-committee subsystems in the larger legislative-executive political setting. . . .

Using Top-Level Support. The proposals of bureau leaders . . . can be either endorsed or mediated by the higher echelons of the Administration of which the bureau is a part, especially in major issues of policy where the points under consideration are crucial to the Administration. In such an instance, the head of the department and other top leaders are likely to become involved. . . . Of course, the rule of limited intervention in lower echelon affairs usually applies to the Secretary and other top leaders of a department, as well as to the President, although in lesser degree. The Secretary does not intervene in every skirmish between one of his bureaus and a congressional committee any more than the President intervenes in every battle between a department and congressional leaders. Leaders of the Administration can be "supporting artillery" for a bureau chief, and the more crucial the target, the larger the "gun" that is brought to bear upon it.

The effect of the use of this strategy by a bureau leader was generally illustrated in the legislative relations of the Bureau of Indian Affairs during the New Deal, when high-level support from the Administration seemed to enhance the ability of the Bureau's leaders to gain acceptance of their recommendations and to defend themselves against attacks from committees and interest groups. During the earlier years of the New Deal, Commissioner Collier of the Bureau was successful on numerous occasions in getting Secretary of the Interior Ickes to communicate with or to testify before committees of Congress in support of the Bureau's viewpoint. In these instances the Secretary made the Commissioner's battles his own, with the characteristic Ickes vigor, and he usually helped to subdue critical committee members.

As has already been indicated, this state of mutual reinforcement does not appear uniformly in the relations of bureaus with the Administration. Yet every bureau chief to some degree has a choice as to the extent to which his efforts will be identified with the goals of the Administration and a choice as to how much he will exploit the power symbolized by the Secretary of his department or by the President. The case of Collier, Ickes, and Roosevelt was extreme, perhaps, in two ways: first, in the long span of their simultaneous incumbencies in office and second, in the degree of their interest and ideological proximity. All three men saw the New Deal through from its inception. All three were committed to the "progressive" point of view, sometimes looking with disdain upon the conventional political parties, but always strong for the "New Deal party." Ickes was put forward at first for the office of Commissioner of Indian Affairs under the New Deal, at which time he was supported by Collier and others. Roosevelt instead selected Ickes—almost sight unseen—to be Secretary of the Interior. Forthwith, Ickes, the party maverick in the Cabinet, gained the President's support and confidence, something he succeeded generally in holding for the next twelve years. The Secretary in turn got Roosevelt to appoint Collier as Commissioner, beginning a similar pattern of relations between the Bureau chief and the Department head. This was reinforced by the interest in Indians held by Anna Wilmarth Ickes, the Secretary's first wife, and by her assistance to Collier.

The Commissioner followed the strategy of using the backing of these leaders of the Administration to a maximum degree, and in turn utilized his own talents for promoting the New Deal in areas not particularly germane to his own Bureau. In securing the passage of the comprehensive Indian Reorganization Act of 1934, the Commissioner obtained the close support of the Secretary plus two endorsements from the President. He also used the prestige of the President in explaining the purposes of the bill to Indians in Oklahoma, telling them:

> You know that at the present time President Roosevelt controls both Houses of Congress. When the President wants a piece of legislation, he gets it from Congress. The bill we are going to discuss today is an Administration measure. It is a President Roosevelt measure. The majority of the members of Congress do not pretend to understand the Indian question in detail at all. The majority of the members of Congress have nothing to gain or lose by any Indian legislation. In other words, if the Administration had wanted to put this bill through quietly and quickly, understand they had the power, and they have the power to do it. The Administration, as I stated before, has adopted a new policy, which is the policy of bringing all the Indians into consultation on the bill, even though it entails, or may entail delay.

Needless to say, many committee members do not appreciate bureaucratic attempts to exploit the halo which sometimes attends presidential leadership, especially when the bureau spokesman infers that Congress can be pushed around by a strong President. Senator Elmer Thomas berated Collier for making the above statement. He said:

> You told *my* Indians down at *my* home that it made no difference what Congress thought about it, that you would pass the bill if you wanted to, and would do it quickly.

Also at issue here was another legislative norm: the sanctity of the local state or district against "outside" interference, especially "meddling" by the executive branch without consulting the lawmaker from that constituency. In using presidential support in this way the Commissioner evidently chose to bet that, given the popularity of the President, the exploitation of his support would in the long run more than offset the hostility aroused in the Senate Committee by violating some of the norms of its members. In this case the bill was passed, although Senator Thomas succeeded in delaying its application to his Indians in Oklahoma until he personally could investigate the need for it.

In the years between the advent of the New Deal and the advent of World War II the Commissioner secured the support of the Secretary in many other situations despite Ickes's preoccupation with Public Works and with the rarefied intrigues around the President. For example, Collier got the Secretary to issue a memorandum to Bureau employees telling them, in effect, either to quit criticizing the new policies in Indian affairs or to resign, and that if they persisted in their criticism without resigning, they would be dismissed. The Commissioner also cited the Secretary in standing up against congressional criticism of Indian Bureau publicity tactics and of the use of an official Indian Service periodical to organize support for the new policies. Collier told members of the House Committee on Indian Affairs:

. . . We are promoting many things which, for their success, depend upon a friendly and informed opinion. We should properly cultivate public opinion, and we will continue to do that.

I need only to add that I think this committee ought to know by this time that neither Secretary Ickes nor I hesitate to speak. We can always put out a release and we do so.

The two officials also joined in fighting certain groups which brought charges against them before the Dies Committee on Un-American Activities and before the Senate Committee on Indian Affairs. They also joined in warding off constant attempts to repeal the Indan Reorganization Act or to undermine it by cutting its appropriations. The Commissioner in turn extended his activities to take part not only in the propaganda battle in behalf of the President's Supreme Court plan, but also in the early attempts to counter the growth of the America First movement, two courses of action which reinforced strong interests of the Secretary's as well as of the President's.

In thus identifying with and using the endorsements of the Administration "above and beyond the call of duty," the Commissioner was often able to maximize his influence in the subsystem of Indian affairs by associating his recommendations with the prestige of higher officials. At the same time, however, he enlarged the range of controversy in the subsystem, and both he and his Bureau were recipients of retaliations that otherwise might not have come their way.

The other side of the coin of a bureau leader's attachment to higher symbols in the Administration and his exploitation of their prestige was demonstrated later when the support of Roosevelt and Ickes for Collier's Bureau was not so easily obtained and when it was not so effective, even though obtained. The Bureau headquarters were moved to Chicago during World War II to make room in Washington for wartime activities. Close communications with the

Department of Interior and the White House were severely curtailed. The attention of the Administration was turned almost entirely from domestic policy to the war. In fact, it was doubtful if the New Deal was at that time the basis of the Administration's support so much as was the unifying objective of defense and victory.

During this period the Bureau chief became increasingly unable to stave off attacks from congressional committees. He was able to help the Bureau survive, but little else. Part of his difficulty in keeping committee members interested in Indian welfare and rehabilitation arose from the temporary mitigation of his Bureau's problems by the increase in Indian income due to wartime employment and by the relief furnished by the money sent home by many Indian servicemen. Part of the Commissioner's difficulty with some committees came from long-standing personal differences. Yet a crucial factor was his record of consistent fighting for the views of the New Deal and the use of the Administration's power to protect the policies installed in Indian affairs early in the New Deal. Lacking the continued strong reciprocal support of the Administration during the war period, the Commissioner was no longer able to maintain a favorable equilibrium. . . .

Choosing Alternative Committees. Among the strategies of influence which a bureau leader can use is that of playing one committee against another. Every bureau deals with at least four committees of Congress, and frequently with more than four, giving the bureau leader a range of alternatives along this line. We have already observed the tendencies of the Senate Appropriations Committee to counterbalance the House Appropriations Committee. In addition, appropriations committees can and do alter policies enacted by substantive committees, both in setting the amount of money available for authorized programs and in altering the conditions under which money can be spent by the administrative unit. It is also possible that one investigating committee may counteract another in inquiries covering much of the same ground. All of these situations furnish possibilities in strategy for bureau leaders.

The last of these possibilities was used with some success by Commissioner Collier in the early 1940's. At that time the Investigating Subcommittee of the Senate Committee on Indian Affairs, which had been operating since 1928, brought out one of its most damaging indictments of the Bureau's policies and personnel. Shortly thereafter the Commissioner arranged with the leaders of the House Committee on Indian Affairs for a subcommittee of that unit also to investigate the Bureau, limiting its probe to specific, mutually acceptable points of inquiry to be covered in a stated length of time. Largely under the direction of Congressman Karl Mundt this was done, and a report was published which was considerably at variance with the Senate Subcommittee's report. Temporarily, the Bureau received some respite from the hostility emanating from the Senate Committee on Indian Affairs.

Exploiting Committee Hearings. Despite recognizable limitations, committee hearings furnish important channels of influence for participants in a subsystem, especially for bureau leaders. . . . Most hearings, especially those which are not televised and which are not given extensive press coverage, provide opportunities for some relatively unguarded communication among the policy-makers of the subsystem, as well as the opportunity to extend and exploit the proceedings for propaganda purposes.

Bureau leaders can frequently build up an impressive case for their side in the record. This furnishes documentation for those committee members who would be inclined to argue for the bureau's viewpoint, either in executive session where committee votes are taken, before the whole legislative body, or in public speeches. On occasion, a strong presentation in a hearing by bureau leaders may influence neutral or less-involved committee members. Yet often the most vital factors in communications in committee hearings, as in other small-group assemblages, are the methods and the disposition of the communicator plus his listeners' attitudes toward him and what he symbolizes, rather than the alleged facts presented and the logic used. Thus, among busy committee members who do not like to be snowed under by official or technical talk, bureau spokesmen can, by the strategies they employ, create or reinforce in the hearings sentiments about themselves and their organizations which have a lasting and controlling effect on the decisions of committees. It may be most important to the legislator whether he feels that the bureaucrat: (1) "knows what he's talking about" (e.g., speaks with confidence, answers questions simply and often categorically); (2) "plays it straight" (e.g., does not appear to evade, admits to imperfection, keeps the committee informed); and (3) "cooperates" (e.g., seems amenable to suggestions from committee members, shows them proper deference, does not try to put them on the spot with the press or with their constituents, and does not play his initiative too heavy-handedly). . . .

The Use of Publicity. In addition to the opportunities for making news in committee hearings, there are other important facets of publicity (or propaganda) activities of bureau leaders which are critical. In general, these practices are natural outgrowths of needs for certain types of communications in our political system and overall legal attempts to limit them have been impracticable. Consequently there are usually abundant opportunities for bureau leaders to exploit the media of mass communication. A bureau's information office regularly gives out press releases (usually under departmental auspices) which, while dealing mainly with the facts of the bureau's business, nevertheless furnish a means of keeping the organization and its officials constantly on the news wires. If the bureau chief has an exceptional item to give out, he can usually get a reporter's ear without difficulty. From time to time radio and television opportunities come his way, as well as requests to write articles. Also, there is usually a network of friendly media only too willing to help carry the propaganda battle for the bureau leaders, to serve as vehicles of semi-official tests of public sentiment, and to be favored in turn with inside stories. Finally, there is the array of official publications and reports, many of which can serve not only as information devices but as media supporting the bureau's policies and goals. . . .

The bureau leader may not have to propagandize a tremendous number of people in order to have an effect. First, the general public is not usually consistently interested in a subsystem. Second, the leading participants—committee members, clientele leaders, group leaders, and bureau employees—are the ones who are most sensitized to the propaganda of the subsystem. This means first that general-circulation media can usually be effectively used only to condition in a general, nontechnical way the sentiments of the public at large and their leaders toward the affairs of the subsystem, and second that "trade" or special-audience media will usually be more effective in mobilizing and sustaining the sentiments of the "insiders" or the informed and interested publics of the subsystem and their leaders.

In the publicity battle of Indian affairs, Commissioner Collier had either access to or considerable support from the following: *Indians at Work,* an official periodical of the Bureau in which he frequently editorialized about current issues of policy; the publications of the American Indian Defense Association, of which Collier had formerly been executive director, and the publications of its successor, the Association on American Indian Affairs; and *The Nation* and *New Republic,* two liberal periodicals which frequently devoted space to articles by friends of the New Deal Indian program. Also, *Collier's* magazine occasionally presented articles by feature writers who tended to convey the Bureau's viewpoint in popularized form, and *The New York Times* and *The Washington Post,* in giving comprehensive coverage to national events, would devote space occasionally to Commissioner Collier's program. Moreover, releases from the Commissioner's office were sometimes printed in those local Western newspapers whose readers were likely to be involved. The above types of publicity were supplemented from time to time with various articles and addresses by the Commissioner. The Bureau and its chief were unusually well-fortified for the propaganda battle both among the general public and within the limited public of the subsystem.

There were counterparts of the Bureau's channels of publicity and propaganda in which the opposition could have its say—with the notable exception of official Bureau publications. Naturally enough, it was over the use of official publications that Collier had some of his greatest difficulty with committee members and with hostile group leaders. Frequently, they took statements from the Bureau's periodicals and introduced them as examples of unfair or unwarranted use of public facilities and of official status. Committee members warned Collier against such tactics, and subsequently on several occasions members took the matter of the Commissioner's publicity activities to the floor of the House or the Senate. Collier declined to alter his publicity activities, stating that he would never "hesitate to speak out." As a result, his capacity for exploiting the means of publicity seemed to reinforce his immediate influence in the subsystem; however, it also fed a smouldering resentment among those committee members who perceived him as "a good propagandist but a poor Commissioner," and it probably contributed to their increased opposition to Collier in the long run.

INTERACTIONS BETWEEN BUREAU LEADERS AND GROUPS

Bureau leaders so often take the initiative in drafting and proposing policy changes that they must come to the committees of Congress buttressed by the favorable sentiments of significant groups represented in the subsystem, or at least of the spokesmen for these groups. The groups usually most intimately concerned with the affairs of a subsystem by virtue of their internal relationship with the bureau are its employees and its so-called clientele. Though the two are distinguishable, they often have much in common. In the first place, both depend upon the bureau: the employee for his livelihood and for other job-related satisfactions and the client for services, goods, or direction. Both in some measure are concerned about the organization's rules, goals, and resources. They are further likely to share certain loyalties, to have established certain particular mutual friendships, and perhaps to have identified with common symbols peculiar to that area of policy. Both groups will "know the lingo" of the organization, just as veterans come to know about the certificates of eligibility handled by Veterans Administration employees, or as both farm leaders and Agriculture Department personnel are conversant about parity and price supports. Finally, it is often the case that many employees of a bureau were, or are, clients as well.

Of course, neither the interests of clientele nor those of employees are uniform, and most bureau leaders are content to get major segments of each group, or perhaps only the most vocal ones to concur. This amount of employee and clientele support is well-nigh the crucial minimum for a bureau chief's success in dealing with committees. If he seems to lead and to represent these two groups, his case is likely to carry considerable weight with committee members, other things being equal, because the legislators often view the employees and the clients as considerable molders of what may be called the grass-roots sentiment in their constituencies as well as people who "know what it's all about." The employees are regarded as molders of sentiment partially because they represent the official side of the subsystem in the field. Often they can deliberately help (or fail to help) friends of committee members in the course of the performance of their duties for the bureau. Similarly, clientele leaders will be regarded as opinion molders insofar as they can voice satisfaction or dissatisfaction for the "folks back home" to hear.

Bureau attempts to mobilize employee support do not meet with uniform success, however. Committee members are likely to be highly suspicious of testimony or opinions conveyed to them under what appears to be some organized campaign from bureau headquarters. Furthermore, groups of employees themselves are likely to resist official attempts to coerce them. The case of the previously mentioned order handed down by Secretary Ickes at Commissioner Collier's request, directing employees of the Indian Bureau to refrain from criticizing new policies, was subsequently aired before a committee by certain unhappy employees, and it was used to cast the shadow of bureaucratic coercion over expressions of opinion by Bureau personnel. The cry of "gag rule" leveled at leaders of the bureaucracy has seldom helped their standing with legislators, and in this instance Ickes and Collier appeared to lose status.

Similarly, bureau leaders usually have to be circumspect about organizing the clientele. Congressmen resent this kind of "public relations," especially in their own territories, and more especially if they are not parties to it. Usually the clientele groups are sufficiently diverse so that some of the clientele who are opposed to the bureau will see to it that committee members are kept well-informed of their views as well as of the opinion-forming operations of the bureaucrats. . . .

Relations Between Bureau Leaders and Non-Internal Groups. All groups participating in a subsystem are not necessarily so "internal" to the bureau as are the employees and the clientele. There are likely to be those who are simply in sympathy with the interests of the clientele and the services performed by the bureau. Others are likely to be in competition with or hostile to the clientele. In Indian affairs, a variety of non-Indian groups took interest in the policies of the Bureau apparently because they were primarily concerned about the welfare and the future of Indians as underprivileged people. Of course, other motives may have stirred their members, such as a desire to be socially active, to do good, to be identified with charitable enterprise, and so forth. Nevertheless, these groups were noted for their concern with the problem generally stated as "Indian welfare" or "Indian rights" or "Indian rehabilitation." Yet, despite this general bond of interest these groups often disagreed. For example, church and missionary groups felt that some Indian welfare organizations took too secular an attitude toward the definition of Indian advancement. However, all groups of the welfare type tended to oppose those groups which competed with Indian economic interests or which were actively engaged in trying to pry Indians loose from some of their property or privileges.

To a considerable extent, those non-clientele groups which were sympathetic toward the Bureau's clientele as a class were possessed of what may be called a cosmopolitan outlook. They drew their values from rather universal systems of ethics which were not generated primarily by particular relationships within the subsystem. They had memberships composed of people from diverse geographic and occupational categories. Some of their strongest bonds seemed to be ideological. On the other hand, the groups competing with the Indians or hostile toward the Bureau's protection of its clientele frequently seemed to be what may be characterized as more local or grass-roots in nature. Their systems of values arose from particular situations in "Indian Country." Their objectives were largely economic advantage for themselves and their kind, and their bonds were often geographic or occupational.

In gaining support for his policy views—especially to get backing before the congressional committees—the Commissioner of Indian Affairs found the cosmopolitan groups more amenable to his ideological approach. Insofar as his philosophy appealed to them, these groups were likely to support his concrete plans. The catch was, of course, that cosmopolitan groups lacked to some extent the ingredients for affecting non-Indian sentiment at the grass-roots where committee members might most likely be touched via the ballot box. Of course, cosmopolitan groups did have considerable field contact with Indians, with whom they could often make their views felt, but Indian opinion was often not the controlling one in a Western constituency, and most Committee of Indian Affairs members were from the West. Cosmopolitan groups were usually more skilled and effective in the battle of the mass media, the hearing room, and the colloquium than in the battle for local votes.

On the other hand, the local, anti-protection groups were usually less amenable to the Commissioner's views and were more likely to oppose him before the legislative committees as long as his major efforts were to guard energetically the economic interests of his clientele and to promote extensively their security through government aid. Frequently it was possible for leaders of these groups to convince committee members that they carried great weight in Western constituencies, since their memberships included more non-Indians of the West. Moreover, it was often characteristic of some grass-roots organizations that they would adopt ideological positions which would question basically the integrity of Bureau leaders and the philosophy behind their programs. Characteristic of the ideological warfare waged by these more extreme local interests was a weaving of examples of the Bureau's red tape and statements and actions of officials taken largely out of context into a pattern of interpretive innuendo. The result of this attack against the Bureau, somewhat irrespective of its intent or content, was basically to reduce congressional and public confidence in the Bureau's policies and personnel. To some extent this made it easier to assert local non-Indian interests over against those of Indians as seen by the Bureau, as well as to add strength to the anti-Administration forces in general. In fact, the more extreme members of certain of these local groups built up a considerable record of association with the more rabid, "super-patriotic," isolationist groups which fought the emerging internationalism of the New Deal from 1937 to 1941. . . .

THE EFFECTIVE LIMITS OF THE
ADMINISTRATIVE PROCESS *
Louis L. Jaffe

MANY of the still current attitudes about the administrative process, and certain of the doctrines of administrative law, at least in their form and intensity,

* From the *Harvard Law Review*, Vol. 67, No. 7 (May 1954), pp. 1105–1123, 1127–1135. Copyright, 1954, by the Harvard Law Review Association. Reprinted by permission of the author and publisher.

have been powerfully influenced by the immediate historic role of the administrative process. That history began, let us say, with the adoption of the Interstate Commerce Act of 1887. It reached its culmination in the New Deal with the creation of the Labor Board and the Securities and Exchange Commission. The administrative process was thought to have an inherent political or social orientation. There was more or less agreement as to its significance between those who hailed it and those who hated it. It was seen with hope by the one and fear by the other as capable of working continually progressive modification of the economy and the society. Supplanting private industry, it would take over the role of leadership in the "public interest." This was not, as we can see now, a just historical estimate if we were to push history far enough back. But it is both the strength and the weakness of the American that he is not history-minded. Very few great societies have had less history to contend with and have been so emboldened to bank upon an unmortgaged future. Our faith in a vigorous application of the administrative process has borne fruit. If we use the hopes of their proponents as the measure (not to try at this time to make absolute evaluations), the National Labor Relations Board and the Securities and Exchange Commission, to name but two, have been successful. They have, in their fields, made remarkable contributions to the reorientation of American society. They are only two evidences of a legislative and administrative movement which has profoundly changed our society, a change which can be set down beside the English Reform Movement of the nineteenth century as one of the great historical jobs of law-making. In taking stock of the administrative process today, it would compound the shortsightedness of the thirties if we forgot these achievements. But to accomplish this miracle with an unfettered, unquestioning spirit it may have been necessary to misunderstand the basic nature of our economy and to overlook the fact that history does not grant to any institution a fee in perpetuity. A long look at the administrative process might show some inherent potentialities, certain persistent functions, at least certain patterned recurrences and reincarnations, but it would also show that it can serve "reaction" as well as "progress," stability as well as change. Indeed those of us who took hope from the SEC were even at the time appalled by the Immigration Service, but this was not permitted to infect our general outlook. And now there are signs that we are readying ourselves for a Great Disillusion. There may be cause for disillusion, but I am afraid that we are in danger of drawing the wrong conclusions.

Let us begin by recalling how in 1938 a representative scholar was coming to envisage the role of the administrative process. I take an example from Dean Landis' eloquent series of lectures, *The Administrative Process*. Landis, speaking of the SEC, draws an analogy between its development and the ICC's: "As in the case of the Interstate Commerce Commission, it was not long before it became evident that the mere proscription of abuses was insufficient to effect the realization of the broad objectives that lay behind the movement for securities legislation. The primary emphasis of administrative activity had to center upon the guidance and supervision of the industry as a whole."

"[R]esort to the administrative process," he continues, "is not . . . simply an extension of executive power. . . . In the grant to it of that full ambit of authority necessary for it in order to plan, to promote, and to police, it presents an assemblage of rights normally exercisable by government as a whole." It thinks, he says, "in terms of the economic well-being of an industry." "If the railroads are 'sick' we listen eagerly to what Commissioner Eastman may have to say upon the subject. . . . [T]he ills of the industry have become . . . [the ICC's] bailiwick. The policies they must formulate must now be directed toward broad and imaginative ends, conceived in terms of management rather than of police." Thus the administrative process is seen evolving through two stages, one merging imperceptibly into the other: first the identification of the administrative process with the protection of the economically weak and unorganized against the oppression of the economically powerful; and then, because private industry has appeared to fail in its organizing function, the assertion of government responsibility to plan for the well-being of industry. This was the ultimate view that enthralled the New Dealer. This was the horrid specter that terrified the world of private industry.

We have come to see that both the thrill and the chill failed to take into account basic factors limiting the managing and "planning" potentialities of the administrative process. These factors are inherent in our industrial organization, in our conceptions of regulation, and in our political machinery. The planning thesis took almost no account of the character and the psychology of our administrators, a psychology which is a complicated product of these social factors, of the pattern of human nature in America, and of the special attitudes developed in the regulator by the fact of regulation itself. Let us turn then to a consideration of these factors.

I

The regulated and client groups exert an effective pressure on the administrative agency in proportion to the importance of their economic function and to their organizational cohesion.

I confess at the outset that this thesis is not demonstrable. An administrative action which "favors" an industry or some defined portion of it can usually be adequately explained as expressing a "correct" application of the statute or a theory of regulation which is administratively rather than industry determined. The thesis is rather a way of pointing to a significant current phenomenon, explain it as you may. This phenomenon is present where the administrative action reflects predominantly the solution desired by the industrial group. There is widespread recognition of the so-called "industry-oriented" agency. But the criticism implied in this recognition is in my opinion inadequate and misleading. There are those who say that the ICC is "railroad-minded," as if actions of the ICC favorable to the railroads were a deviation from the expectable and relevant norm. The criticisms of the ICC are tendentiously documented and ultimately evasive.[1] There can surely be no question

1. The most elaborately documented thesis to this effect is Huntington, *The Marasmus of the ICC: The Commission, the Railroads, and the Public Interest*, 61 YALE L.J. 467 (1952).

that it was an essential element of the philosophy of the Motor Carrier Act to protect (as the drafters saw the problem) the *regulated* railroad from the *unregulated* motor carrier by subjecting both types of carrier to the same regime of regulation. In the words of a Senate Committee at a somewhat later date (1939), this was not a "railroad philosophy" but a "transportation philosophy." Obviously the implementation of this philosophy as against the previously unregulated motor carrier would favor the railroads. It may be that the ICC is more "railroad-minded" than "motor carrier-minded," but recent criticism has failed to distinguish to what extent it goes beyond the likely consequences of the kind of regulation which presently obtains in this field. The criticism pinning the blame on the ICC, and proposing perhaps this or that reshuffling of administrative power, refuses to face the problems created by regulation as such.

There is also the fact that the ICC is an old agency, that it has rigidified. This I call the arteriosclerosis theory. It is a very valuable and important theory.[2] When the evil which gives rise to a reform has been somewhat alleviated, the initial dynamism is dispersed. There is a newly evolved status quo. It requires an exceptional effort of concern and attention to maintain human energies at high pitch, to keep courage screwed to the sticking point. Only a

There is a reply to this in Morgan, *A Critique of "The Marasmus of the ICC: The Commission, the Railroads, and the Public Interest,"* 62 YALE L.J. 171 (1953). The ostensible thesis of the Huntington article is that the ICC has lost its "viability," its political support, that it is withering away ("marasmus" means a gradual withering away) because it has become identified with the railroad interest and *for that reason,* that is, its loss of viability, "it should be abolished as an independent agency," and the motor carrier, water carrier, and railroad regulatory functions divided among three agencies. Morgan, chief carrier analyst of the ICC, replies in an article that is at many points naive but throws grave doubts on the disinterestedness of Huntington's scholarship. For one thing, at many crucial points Huntington's documentation stops at 1942; nearly all of it is inadequately analyzed from the point of view of its faithfulness to the statutory standard. Huntington disingenuously replies that he is not concerned with "the economic or social wisdom . . . of these actions" or whether they are "wrong," "erroneous," or "nefarious," that Morgan mistook a "descriptive proposition . . . for a normative proposition concerned with the desirability of that policy." *The ICC Reexamined: A Colloquy,* 63 YALE L.J. 44, 48 (1953). But this simply will not wash. It is not only that the whole tone of the article implies an almost violent disapproval of the ICC and a breach of duty by it, but the very last paragraph of the article explicitly charges the ICC with a "prolonged failure to adhere" to the norms of public policy as laid down by the Supreme Court. The ICC must be abolished and be replaced "by other instrumentalities better able to act in the public interest." 61 YALE L.J. at 509.

2. It was very astutely foreseen as long ago as 1892 by Richard Olney, the Attorney General under Cleveland. In reply to his friend Charles E. Perkins, President of the Chicago, Burlington and Quincy Railroad, who had recommended that Olney press for the abolition of the Interstate Commerce Commission, Olney wrote as follows: "My impression would be that looking at the matter from a railroad point of view exclusively it would not be a wise thing to undertake . . . . The attempt would not be likely to succeed; if it did not succeed, and were made on the ground of the inefficiency and uselessness of the Commission, the result would very probably be giving it the power it now lacks. The Commission, as its functions have now been limited by the courts, is, or can be made, of great use to the railroads. It satisfies the popular clamor for a government supervision of railroads, at the same time that the supervision is almost entirely nominal. Further, the older such a commission gets to be, the more inclined it will be found to take the business and railroad view of things. It thus becomes a sort of barrier between the railroad corporations and the people and a sort of protection against hasty and crude legislation hostile to railroad interests . . . . The part of wisdom is not to destroy the Commission, but to utilize it."

limited number of urgent problems can enlist this effort at any one time; the remaining problems must be handled on a routine, stand-by basis until the status quo once more becomes intolerable.

Under normal conditions, as I shall try to show, private management is inevitably the dominant *organizing* force. When the industry, after a period of reform, has been stabilized at a new level, management direction becomes the primary influence. Paradoxically, this phenomenon may be reinforced by a vague, broad delegation of administrative power! Such a delegation is a source of administrative strength in the initial reform period. The implied objectives, the climate of opinion give directing significance to the generalities of the statute. But when these objectives are realized, the statutory vagueness may no longer yield a sense of mandate. External forces rush in to fill the vacuum. The arteriosclerosis theory, however, does not explain why the CAB, only 16 years of age, is fully as "industry-minded" as the ICC—in the opinion of some, more so. Perhaps, as with the ICC in recent years, the answer lies in the genesis and concept of the regulation. The "evil" to which the legislation was directed was the "instability" of the airline business. Congress wished to promote the development of the industry. The legislation was passed to attract capital and enterprise into the industry. The aim has been brilliantly achieved though sometimes despite rather than because of the regulation.

A few examples will illustrate the general thesis of effective pressure. The Civil Aeronautics Act was passed in 1938. It was an administration bill designed to develop the airline industry by a generous policy of deficit guarantee in the form of air mail pay. It was, of course, ardently supported by the airlines. There were at that time twenty airlines operating 32,335 miles of routes. The twenty were shortly reduced by failure and merger to sixteen and are now only thirteen. The CAB, though it has enormously expanded the domestic route miles to 130,000, has never certified a new domestic trunk line carrier. From 1946 to 1948 the airlines somewhat mysteriously lost $20,000,000, but since then their earnings have been dazzling: $19,000,000 in 1949 (5.9% on book assets); $41,000,000 in 1950 (12.4%); $52,000,000 in 1951 (14.9%); $59,365,000 in 1952 (14.3%). The average for 1939–1952 is 8.3%.[3]

The certificated airlines as a unit have until recently set their face against reduction of fares to attract a substantial volume of new business; air travel in their view was a luxury, a "first-class" commodity. In this they were seconded by the CAB, which, from time to time, put obstacles in the way of the introduction of coach fare. The situation has been radically changed by one of the most bizarre and illuminating chapters in the history of regulation.[4] A class of air carriers sometimes known as "irregulars," sometimes as "nonscheduled" ("non-skeds") were exempted by the CAB from the certification requirements. Immediately after the war there was a great supply of discharged military aviators and obsolescent equipment. The CAB concluded that the two

3. General Passenger Fare Investigation, Order Ser. No. E-7376, at 205 (CAB 1953).

4. The story is told from a point of view somewhat hostile to the CAB in two reports of the Senate Small Business Committee. Sen. Rep. No. 540, 82d Cong., 1st Sess. (1951); Sen. Rep. No. 822, 83d Cong., 1st Sess. (1953).

might be put to work doing the odd jobs of air carriage ("contract" flights of one sort or another). But the planes were too large to be thus profitably employed. The non-skeds more and more scheduled semiregular flights over the more profitable long-distance routes (New York-Miami, New York-Los Angeles). They cut rates drastically and took the velvet off the first-class service, establishing a so-called "coach service." There was no question that their conduct violated the terms of their authorization. But it has taken years to put them out of business. Many of them had numerous "letters." [5] When one was cancelled, another "was taken out from under the desk" and the operation continued. Furthermore, the Small Business Committee has championed the non-skeds and occasionally abated or postponed the CAB doom. The certificated carriers have finally capitulated and now about 30% of their traffic is coach at coach fare. The few remaining "non-skeds" are seeking certification over the principal long-distance routes on a non-subsidy basis, but all signs point to a rejection of their applications. The CAB is completely committed to the existing certificated carriers; the non-skeds have done the job of putting air service on a greatly expanded lower price basis. Like the highest flying drone, having fertilized the queen bee, they must now die.

Last year the certificated carriers requested permission to surcharge each passenger $1.00 per flight in order to even out the overhead costs of the short flight. The CAB gave temporary permission but instituted a general passenger fare investigation. When the certificated carriers moved to dismiss, the CAB split 2–2. The Board waited for a new appointment. The new member, reputedly after some vacillation, voted to dismiss; but the $1.00 surcharge survived. The dissenters pointed to the present high level of profits and to the fact that the CAB has never completed a single investigation of the general rate level and has never announced a rate principle. The majority believed that the high profit might be a temporary consequence of the traffic generated by the Korean War and that any tampering with the general rate level might discourage experimentation with low coach rates.

The reader is not here intended to judge the soundness of these actions; excellent arguments can be offered to support them. The matters are intricate and the material for decision cannot now be canvassed. One clue to what may seem to some a rather baffling story is the traumatic experience of 1946–48. The CAB was then told by a chorus of scolds that this slump was a consequence of its excessive certification of new routes. It was embarrassed by the heavy subsidies required to bail out the airlines. It will now do nothing at all likely to produce a recurrence. At this point, however, our only purpose is to point out that policy tends to flow along the channels congenial to the dominant certificated carriers. We shall discuss below in a related connection other examples from the ICC experience.

This phenomenon is most prominent in the completely regulated industries such as transportation. But it is not unknown in others. It has been an oft ob-

5. The nonscheduled airlines need not have certificates of public convenience and necessity, but they must obtain "letters of registration." 14 CODE FED. REGS. § § 291.2–.21 (Supp. 1952).

served characteristic of agricultural price and production control through the so-called marketing agreements that the farmers, more exactly the cooperatives and the distributors, have largely determined the character of those agreements. The consumer was no doubt recognized as setting a price limit somewhere, primarily on the theory of what the market could bear. The NLRB was "captured" by the CIO from 1935–1940. I suspect that the FTC's enforcement of the Robinson-Patman Act reflects the fact that the FTC's chief political, specifically Congressional support is from the small business interest represented by Midwestern, Southern, and Western congressmen. These last two instances are obviously marginal to the argument. The balance of forces, the alliances involved are not stable, not so fixed a segment of the general social and economic structure. The type of regulation is narrow in its impact, and spasmodically applied. It does not, therefore, give rise to such relationships as exist under the Aeronautics and Transportation Acts.

It is the "planning," the industry-regulating, all-purpose administrations which are most typical of our thesis. In these situations the phenomenon loosely and invidiously described as "industry orientation" is much less a disease of certain administrations than a condition endemic in any agency or set of agencies which seek to perform such a task. It is a product of our political philosophy with its insistence on representation and the procedure through which representation functions, of our legislatures which are organized to register all functionally and socially significant groups, of our statutes which grant powers so wide that solutions will be much more the consequence of group interaction than of legislative formulation, of our theory of regulation which divorces legal command from managerial responsibility, of our dynamic industrial and economic economy which outruns prophecy and prescription, and of our administrators whose character and psychology is perforce the type of the good American.

II

The administrator develops a presumption in favor of regulation.

The charge against the ICC and the CAB is that they are "industry-minded." I would say that they are "regulation-minded" and that industry-mindedness is as much an effect as a cause. It was, for example, very clear in 1935 to Joseph Eastman, whose office, significantly enough, was Federal Coordinator of Transportation, that motor truck competition with the railroads and within the trucking industry itself must be dealt with by extending the existing system of railroad regulation. The initial impetus in the 19th century for railroad regulation came from consumer interests which demanded a curb on the monopoly power of the railroads. But there was little or no consumer demand for truck regulation. The nub of the problem was not monopoly but a too vigorous competition. The railroads, joined by rail labor, quite understandably if regulation of railroad competitive power was to continue, demanded a limit on truck competition. And in time the large trucking corporations made common cause with the railroads. In this controversy it was clear to the ICC led by Eastman (and also, it has been said, to the state commissions) that the answer was more rather than less regulation. Commissioner Eastman had recommended that air transportation be regulated: "It is believed that regulation of the kind indicated would accomplish much toward straightening out and stabilizing the industry, making it thereby a more efficient and responsible public servant. Against these advantages are to be set a possible dampening of the initiative and a partial loss of flexibility in the conduct of the industry. Much depends, of course, on how and by whom the regulation is administered." And he proposed that the ICC administer it as well as the regulation of water and motor transportation. It made for a "logical rounding out."

He made similar proposals for regulation of motor carriers: "There are some who think that the thing to do is to let down the bars and allow the competitors to fight it out to the finish. . . . The eventual result might be a kind of coordinated system of transportation, achieved through survival of the fittest, but the greater competitive strength of the railroads would be likely to distort the results. The fact is that this plan of free-for-all competition has never worked successfully, either here or elsewhere. It has been tried and found wanting." "While some shippers gain temporary advantage from unstable and unpublished rates, the greater present good and the long-run good of all require that the transportation factor in the cost of doing business be known and predictable." "Constructive coordination" is to be preferred to "destructive competition." "Stated more concretely, the question is whether it is sound public policy to encourage duplication of facilities and warfare all along the line, or to find the work which each form of transportation can do best and endeavor accordingly to build up a national transportation system in which the various agencies will function with more regard to correlation and less to competition and with a minimum of waste."

In this thinking competition becomes the equivalent of "chaos," of "waste," and of "destruction"; regulation will assure neat, explicable, rationalized ordering of transportation resources, each with its duly appointed role. Note the static implication in the proposal to "find" what each form of transportation "can do best." Should we not anticipate this reaction? We cannot say, of course, that Eastman was wrong. Granting, however, that the question was at least arguable, the whole experience of the ICC has predisposed it to see solutions in terms of its methods. One by one it had been given powers first to fix maximum rates to protect the shipper from the railroad, then to fix minimums to protect the railroads from each other, then to decide concerning any proposed rate whether it would make the traffic "move" (that is, whether it would be good business), and then to control entry and exit, financing, and safety. The Commission itself had developed many of the governing concepts. Could we expect men so conditioned to face a drastic reorientation without emotion? [6] If the railroads are suffering from too much truck and water com-

6. When in 1940 the railroads proposed to restrict ICC power over rates, particularly the power to make a judgment as to whether a new rate was wise from the business view (would make traffic "move"), the ICC replied with a suggestion of resentment that this would make it "mere computers, a conclusion which we repudiated in Reduced Rates, 1922, 68 I.C.C. 676." Of this Dearing and Owen say: "This statement seems only to obscure the central issue. The

petition, the answer is more regulation. Eastman did not, for example, pin-point the evils and propose limited powers to deal with them. The proposals were for the nearly full panoply of powers, the new layer of regulation to be superimposed upon the old. There were exemptions for contract carriers and most significantly for "agricultural commodities." This last illogical exemption (illogical, that is, in terms of the thesis underlying the legislation) was the political price to be paid to the most powerful shipping interest, and it might be inquired whether the exception did not disprove the rule. In short, this whole scheme, I think, is as much regulation-minded as railroad-minded. In-deed, were railroad regulation to be abandoned or recast in much more lim-ited form, there would have been little call for truck regulation.

Immediately upon the passage of the Motor Carrier Act, the ICC encour-aged, indeed in some measure insisted upon, the conference agreement method of rate-making. In its 1936 report the Commission said: "We believe that the motor carriers of property should be encouraged in their efforts to bring a greater degree of order and stability into the rate structure through confer-ences. . . ." And the first director of the Bureau of Motor Carriers is reported to have said in a speech: "The Commission wants to work with the industry . . . but we can't work with the industry if there are 57 varieties of rates in the industry. The result of that is going to be that if you folks don't get together yourselves in the interest of uniformity of rates, you may get by with it ini-tially but a little later the Commission is going to have to prescribe them for you." And in *New England Motor Carrier Rates* the Commission said: "It is clear that the motor common carriers in New England have labored val-iantly . . . to bring about some stability of rates, through a process of organi-zation and joint effort intelligently conceived. . . . Much of value has been accomplished, but the desired stability is still elusive, principally because the degree of cooperation . . . has not been sufficiently complete. Disaster threat-ens, and the only remaining recourse is to the power of the Government."

The Commission then proceeded, as the private rate bureaus finished their work, to put into effect a series of minimum rate orders throughout the coun-try. It is said that individual dissenters who proposed particular lower rates found it very difficult either to get by the private rate bureaus or to convince the Commission. The story in railroad rate-making is similar. The Supreme Court in *Georgia v. Pennsylvania R.R.* came close to holding that joint rate-making (conferences or bureau methods) violated the antitrust laws. The railroads, with the active cooperation of the Commission, secured statutory approval of rate conferences and bureaus.

What we see here is as much Commission as industry leadership. A mo-

fact that the ICC in 1922 repudiated the role of rate computer is irrelevant to a solution of the issues posed by the carriers in 1939. The Commission has repeatedly acknowledged that the near-monopoly once held by the railroads has been replaced by intensive and almost uni-versal competition. Even at current high levels of traffic, interagency competition is so effective that the railroads hesitate even to *propose* general rate increases that would provide adequate revenue." NATIONAL TRANSPORTATION POLICY 298 (1949).

ment's thought makes it evident that unless the industry organize a cooperative mechanism for rate-making, the administrative agency would sink into
the Slough of Despond under the sheer mass of activity required to evolve and
test a rate system. It is the theory of regulation which dictates the result. "A
rate structure," the Commission has said, "is not simply a loose aggregation of
separately established rates, but is a single entity composed of interrelated
rates." "There is no alternative to procedures calling for such initial joint consideration of proposed rate changes that would not involve, on the one hand,
cutthroat competition . . . or, on the other hand, placing a work load on us
which could not be carried to the satisfaction of carriers or shippers." If "constructive coordination" is to be "stability" it becomes administratively necessary
to use a cooperative industry mechanism.

There are latter day manifestations of ICC regulation mania which under
the circumstances seem rather pathetic. In 1951 the Commission "let its hair
down" and wept bitterly. And it is indeed a curious story which it had to tell.
In 1940 its total appropriations were $7,867,000. In 1952 its appropriations for
"general expenses" were $8,784,935. This and other more subtle influences
brought about a shrinkage of personnel from 2,439 to 1,682. It experienced
great recruitment difficulty even in jobs for which it had the funds. In the
meantime the amount of trucking had increased enormously. ICC jurisdiction
had been extended to inland water carriers and freight forwarders, though certain aspects of its more traditional business had perhaps diminished. The
Commision explained that its enforcement activity, its preparation of cases, its
research must all suffer from this reduction of personnel. The Commission
would have to rely on private party presentation. Its critical and initiatory role
of expert would be severely handicapped. This, incidentally, though the Commission did not make the point, would increase agency dependency on "industry."

"Although," says the Commission, "the Congress has since 1940 repeatedly
expanded the Commission's regulatory functions, deregulation is increasing
through the gradual but steady reduction of the appropriations for the Commission each year. The resulting slow but steady attrition of the staff, aggre-
gating in too many instances actual decimation, which more recently has increased with alarming speed, is reflected in deterioration of morale and increasing difficulty of recruitment. The net result to date is an impairment of
efficient administration, a growing inability to perform the functions and duties required by the statute, and a weakening of the Commission's regulatory
authority which has already assumed serious proportions. All this leaves the
general public more and more helpless and defenseless." Yet these pages are
preceded and followed by proposals for legislation giving the ICC additional
supervisory powers to plug up minor leaks in the regulatory dike, to control
practices which it would appear amount to no more than covert competitive
chiseling.

III

The planning thesis gave too little weight to the dynamism of the industrial system.

Much of the thinking of the thirties was based on the notion that the industrial system was "mature" or even senescent. "If the railroads are 'sick' we listen eagerly to what Commissioner Eastman may have to say upon the subject." Administration was a branch of geriatrics. This thinking was a not unnatural reaction to the terror of the depression. In 1933 we could see that our resources and our already developed plant were immensely productive, capable of providing an unprecedented standard of living. On every hand it was said that our problem was one not of production but distribution. It is not easy at any one time to direct intellectual and moral energies to more than one major term of a problem. To deal with the distribution problem we assumed a given level of output and a given organization of resources for producing it. This, at least, was the implicit psychology of the planning thesis. To a shattered nation the gospel of salvation by competition was a devilish irony.

The Eastman thesis saw price competition primarily as a destructive tactic of business-getting under relatively static engineering and organizational conditions. The Commission was to "find" the best use of each transportation agency. This thesis took too little account of the basic character of scientific research and its progressively drastic innovatory character. It failed to realize that a managerial price decision even though meant as a mere market tactic may be an intuitive response to profound changes in the employment of resources. Norbert Wiener in a fascinating paper tells us that an invention is popularly conceived of as a mere substitute for a particular operation in a given total process. Electricity at first substituted for water in driving an elaborate system of shafts. But the significance of electricity was that it could be directly delivered to individual machines in any desired amount. The overhead shafts and belts have disappeared. The entire factory layout has been reorganized. Cotton displaced flax because it was more easily worked by machine. New machines may bring flax back. Wiener foresees that with the increasing rationalization and institutionalizing of research, the logic of invention will be more and more zealously pursued. This may accelerate the rate of change to a point where it is a profound threat to personal and social stability.

Changes in commodity transportation may not be so dramatic as in other fields, but they are sufficiently large to have created tremendous problems for any regulation directed to stability. The rail made over-the-road carriage and canals relatively obsolete. The motor truck has become a major threat to the rails but only, it has been said, for short hauls. Recently, however, longer and longer hauls appear to be economically feasible. But now comes the "piggyback." Trailers are brought by the trucker to railway flat cars and picked up again by trucks at the other end of the line. Neither the railway nor trucking industry has any idea where this will lead. Highway congestion too may set another limit to over-the-road transport. Not only the airplane's speed but radio, radar, and improved airfields with their increases in safety may make obsolete long-distance railroad carriage of passengers. I do not suggest that economic performance here and now is the only determinant of public policy. It may be necessary to maintain marginal economic forms of transportation for war and emergency. We shall wish to preserve the efficiency and attractiveness of our highways. It may be advisable to stabilize the rate of change in order to protect human personality from the disintegrating effects of excessive instability. Commissioner Eastman perhaps saw this as the prime function of regulation. The tendency "to a radical change in the rate structure," he said, "might be tempered and controlled under public regulation to an extent impossible under free competition. However, the private truck sets definite limits to any policy of modification. . . . The prospects are that there will be disruption of the rate structure in any event, but there is more chance of keeping this tendency within reasonable limits with comprehensive regulation than without."

The air carrier story detailed above offers much that is instructive for our thesis and also certain qualifications of it. It must first be recognized that Congress did (in some measure) understand the dynamic character of this industry. Stability and safety of investment was here to be provided in order to encourage development. This was most significantly manifested by the choice of a separate agency rather than the ICC. The CAB in determining the need for new air routes gives little weight to the existence of good surface transportation. Indeed the presence of exceedingly good train service between two points is sometimes used to explain the need for better air transportation than presently exists. One can imagine that the ICC with its thesis of "constructive coordination" would handle these cases somewhat differently. Dean Landis has stated well the point involved: "The creation of a new Commission also permitted freedom in shaping its internal organization. Overhanging habits and traditions of operation that had developed as a result of association with a different problem did not mold the new growth. Furthermore, it was not essential to approach the new problems in a way that required their synthesis with preexisting policies, as would have been the case had such new regulating duties been intrusted to an established body." But almost from the start restrictive impulses tended to assert themselves. It has already been noted that to this day no new trunk carrier has been certified. In the beginning the Board was indisposed to certify a competitor over an already certified route where the existing carrier was adequate. But it very soon reconsidered its position and as a consequence introduced and increased competition on all the main trunk routes. It enormously expanded the certified air routes (32,000 to 130,000 miles). Then after the war came the Great Slump with its $20,000,000 deficit. No one quite knows what hit the industry. But travel did fall off; the grounding of the DC-6's after a number of catastrophes shook public confidence and piled up losses. But companies and critics were most inclined to blame the CAB because it had overcertified. The point of criticism was that this together with the greatly increased capacity of the new DC-6's created excessive competition. The route pattern and the system of carriers were, it was said, "unbalanced"—a few powerful companies with rich long-distance routes and then in descending order carriers with overcompetitive or scrawny undernourished routes. The Board took this to heart, and all of its actions since have been governed by the fear of another depression. This fear is reinforced by the obligation of the Board to subsidize carrier losses. It is particularly in the last two years that this policy has been more strikingly exemplified. The most important new route proposal has been turned down in a decision which places a heavy burden of proof upon any application proposing new competition and which discounts heavily any prognosis of additional business adequate to support the application. These actions came when the Great Slump of 1946–48 had been turned into the Golden Harvest of 1951–52. Finally the CAB has expended enormous energies fighting the most important development in the industry—the cheap coach fare service.

Does this seem fantastically perverse? Not at all. It is quite understandable. It exemplifies more pointedly perhaps than is customary the pitfalls and traps of regulation. . . .

It is difficult to avoid preoccupation with the mistakes of the past. It takes time for emergent problems to be observed, to be diagnosed. When a regulatory concept is finally evolved to deal with a problem, a new unforeseen problem may render the current concept obsolete. This is the peculiar hazard of regulation as compared with competition, which in its ruthless, unwitting, unrationalizing fashion is constantly creating fresh solutions—solutions which may, of course, be thoroughly unacceptable to the social conscience. The Board's reaction to the coach fare is particularly interesting as an example of official regulatory thinking. The orthodox creed was that air travel was a luxury, and it was nowhere more strongly entrenched than in the CAB, where it served as part of the regulatory structure. It cannot be said that the non-skeds in the beginning consciously held to a different view. They did not, like Henry Ford, have a vision of the revolutionary possibilities of cheap mass production and high wages. Their price cutting was a tactic of desperation. But that is the peculiar virtue of competition. It does not require high motives in its practitioners to bring about extraordinarily useful economic consequences. . . .

IV

The dynamism of American industry presents peculiar problems for a regulatory scheme under which government makes decisions in the area of management but does not accept managerial responsibility.

When an industry is static, when invention and innovation dry up, when empiricism decays, when business restricts production and maintains high prices, then the managerial function shrinks to caretaking along customary lines. Where these conditions are reversed, management, if the enterprise is to survive and prosper, must be imaginative and bold. In this process capital outlay and price decisions, both in quantity and in time, may be crucial, though it is no doubt possible to exaggerate the significance of speedy readjustment over the long pull. Our railroad and trucking regulation has, of course, more and more impinged on the area of responsibility for capital outlay and price deci-

sions. Landis went so far as to say: "[A]s responsibility for the efficient functioning of the railroads is assumed in greater degree by the nation, the Commission possesses less the appearance of a tribunal and more that of a committee charged with the task of achieving the best possible operation of the
railroads." During the twenties and thirties the Commission in passing on rate
increases took into account, over management protest, the probable revenue
consequences of increases; and in 1933 Congress specifically authorized the
Commission to consider the effect of rates on the movement of traffic. Professor Locklin admits that the carriers should be in a better position than the
Commission to make this judgment, yet, quoting Professor Sharfman, he crit-
icizes the carriers for their failure to present the Commission with well-consid-
ered "good faith" proposals. He indicates that this may make it doubtful
whether the carriers would exercise their freedom properly. But this criticism
takes no account of the well-known phenomenon of "bargaining." The administrative process being itself prone to operate by compromise, an applicant asks
for more in order to get what he needs. "Good faith" is a shadowy idea where
the operator does not make his own decision. And where the entrepreneur has
the power to decide, "good faith" is meaningless. Responsibility gives him the
opportunity to respond intelligently or incur the consequences of failure. The
railroads, of course, still hold important monopolistic positions in certain
commodities—coal is one—and some control of maximum rates is necessary. It
must be confessed that this poses a dilemma. The solution may be a much
more selective method of control. In any case, because the Commission does
not guarantee the effect of its veto it is right that it should accord great deference to proposed management decisions, particularly insofar as the management factor is involved. This is one more aspect of what will be invidiously
identified as 'industry-mindedness," but it is the necessary attitude with our
version of regulation. A similar and of course more acute problem is involved
in the crucial area of regulating minimum competitive rates. Here is the true
growing place of innovation and of managerial responsibility, but it is also
the place where the Commission's—and the statute's—theory of "constructive
coordination" is most seriously and constantly challenged. Commissioner Eastman's concept of "tempering" the rate of change would seem preferable to any
systematic—and doomed—attempt to "rationalize" the industry. The veto should
be invoked only against obvious raiding tactics which do not promise the
establishment of new economic levels.

The Government through the air mail subsidy *does* accept some responsibility
for managerial decisions in airline carriage. Curiously, however, the CAB had
been somewhat less intrusive than the ICC, at least in the last few years. We
have told the story of the *General Passenger Fare Investigation*. We see here perhaps a case where the CAB, having managerial responsibility and having created
many of the current situations, has identified itself rather completely with its
managers. It may be haunted not only by the specter of 1946–48 but by the
plight of the railroads. It does not want to "upset the apple cart." Again, under
a somewhat different guise, we observe the psychological hazards of regulation. . . .

V

The adequate staffing of the regulatory agencies, particularly the federal, presents certain peculiar problems.

The plight of the ICC has already been mentioned. In 1943 its appropriation for general expenses was $8,169,900. In 1953, with money buying only about three-fifths as much, its appropriation was $9,600,000. There has been a shrinkage of personnel of about 1000. This is not an isolated instance. In 1943 the appropriations of the FCC were $7,884,914, in 1953 $7,400,000. It is always possible to argue that in any particular case the earlier appropriations were excessive, but with the increase in both the price level and other sections of the budget the evidence would seem to support the proposition that the regulatory budgets after reaching a certain point have become stabilized at levels which discourage vigorous and adventuresome administration. One can do little more than guess at reasons. In a large sense they are just those reasons which we have already explored. Given the performance of their economic system, the American people have no enthusiasm for regulation. In the presence of general breakdown or glaring evils they will respond with regulation, but their concern will not survive the resolution of the crisis. The reader may insist that no more explanation is needed than the pressure of defense on the civil budget. This is important and, unfortunately, it is probably a long-term factor. The amounts, however, involved in the regulatory budgets are relatively so small that their vulnerability to this pressure is another expression of the agencies' political weakness. When, for example, Congress chose to expand the NLRB jurisdiction to outlaw labor as well as employer practices, there was no difficulty in securing substantial budgetary increases.

Our federalism sets limits to the size and effectiveness of a federal agency. These arise in part from the going conception of an agency as a group of men, few enough at the top level to function as a vigorous unified command. . . . This situation may be reinforced by an ill-defined states' rights sentiment which resists a completely rationalized application of federal power.

But the personnel problem has aspects much more deep-seated and ineradicable than that of size. Because the dynamo of our system is still predominantly private, private management is more attractive to the majority of able men, at least at the higher levels, than public service. For this there is a variety of reasons. Remuneration is still greater despite income tax restrictions. There is in private business a broader area of individual initiative. Public life, with its complex and contradictory demands on his loyalties, is morally confusing to the ordinary man. Finally, continuation in high public office depends on political favor. In sum, many commissioners look upon their term of office as a novitiate for a business career or an interim between jobs in industry. The Government is not wholly the loser. On these terms it is able to secure the services of able men. Furthermore, for the most part these men have sufficient stature and pride to envisage and act upon a conception of independent public service; nor does such a man spoil his chances in industry by zeal for the public service. As long as he is not motivated by hatred of those whom he regulates he may be more sought after by business than the complaisant administrator. Nevertheless, where the regulator expects ultimately to spend his days representing the other side, his philosophy is apt to reflect this fact. The great turnover of top men, particularly in certain agencies, is much deplored, but it is questionable whether long tenures are preferable. Can it be said with any assurance that the members of the FTC and the ICC have been better than those of the FCC or the SEC, that they have displayed more courage, more ingenuity, more flexibiliy? If the life tenure man is more expert he may at the same time be more tradition-bound, less energetic. His very tenacity may indicate that he is less able to command his pick of jobs and that he stands somewhat in awe of the business tycoons. If he is greatly concerned with reappointment he is careful not to offend political figures. Finally, the *homo Americanus* likes to be liked by everyone from the President down to his own office boy. Hostility arouses his anxiety; he wants to give everyone as much as possible. If being a "good fellow" is an avocation with the ordinary man, it is almost the business of the administrator. . . .

CONCLUSION

It is not then my purpose here, nor am I prepared, to draw out the conclusions from what has gone before. Professor Schwartz in a recent article has noted some of the same phenomena. He points particularly to the fact that the agencies appear to adopt official industry attitudes of a monopolistic character. This, he argues, is contrary to our official philosophy. He suggests that the courts adopt a general rule of law that an agency can approve the lessening of competition only where the objectives of its statute cannot be otherwise achieved. This rule would be enforced by judicial review of the agency's action. This seems to me questionable. If what I have said so far is sound, much of what the agencies do is the expectable consequence of their broad and ill-defined regulatory power. The fault, if fault there be, is at least as much in the statutory scheme as in the administration. Has Congress proclaimed its commitment to competition in airlines, motor carriers, railroads, ships, agriculture, labor? Once given the power to regulate all rates, minimums and maximums, all entries and exits, does the system lend itself to analysis in terms of the competition-monopoly dichotomy? I do not mean to imply that competition cannot and should not operate within this system. I, too, would appreciate an administration that resolved debatable issues in favor of competition. But it is much less clear that each of the various statutes embodies a mandate for competition which is judicially discoverable and enforceable. Let us not forget that the Motor Carriers Act was born under the constellation of "constructive co-ordination" and that an agency may quite legitimately conclude that its stars require a trajectory of agency-industry harmony. Can we who for so many years belabored the courts for usurping the realm of discretion, in good conscience place upon them now the responsibility for enforcing a rule of competition which is without statutory warrant?

What then? Should we not reexamine at the statutory level the concept of "constructive coordination"? We have, perhaps, succumbed too easily to the siren song of regulation, or rather, let us say, of comprehensive regulation.[7] We may have been too easily moved by notions of rationalized completeness. If some regulation was good, more was even better. It is the way of the regulator to be mightily irritated by the peripheral which lies just beyond his grasp because what goes on there appears to him to be precisely the cause of trouble in his own bailiwick. And, of course, it may be. But it does not follow that the trouble is great enough to be worth the cost of trying to suppress it. We should, in short, look for the *strategic control,* for that control which is the least we can get along with and the most effective for our urgent need. . . .

B.   Civil-Military Relations

NEARLY all American political thought has been liberal, and one of the central themes of liberal thought has always been antimilitarism. Liberal hostility to the military has been based on a sense that military institutions are inherently undemocratic and antilibertarian; that professional soldiers are unsympathetic to the values of civilian life; and that they are highly prone to overvalue force as the way to deal with both international and civil conflict. Conceivably these fears have been misplaced,* but it is undeniable that they have had a great impact on the history of American military institutions. Among the specific elements of that history to which they have made powerful contributions are the following: the citizen army ideal (expressed, *inter alia,* in terms of a predominant role for the state militias and resistance to professionalization of the officer class in the nineteenth century, in terms of support for the National Guard and a high-turnover army of draftees in the twentieth); the nation's refusal to support more than skeletal peacetime armed forces until after the Korean War; and the fragmented organizational structure of the defense establishment. Let us focus on the last of these.

Defenders of American military pluralism have generally emphasized its contribution to civilian control. This is far from saying, however, that American intramilitary rivalries have been devised or structured in accord with some coherent civilian strategy of dividing the military to rule it. The original separation of the army and navy, to cite just one example, simply followed conventional eighteenth century practice. It was sustained by a century and more of insulation from the affairs of

---

* For a brilliant argument that they have been, see Samuel P. Huntington, *The Soldier and the State* (Cambridge: Harvard University Press, 1957), especially Chs. 3, 4, 17.

7. It is extremely interesting that the British in once more opening up trucking to private industry are going to rely on unregulated rate competition between trucks and the government-owned railroads. Only in situations in which the shipper has no choice as to means of transport can railroad rates be attacked by shippers as too high or discriminatory. Transport Act, 1953, 1 & 2 ELIZ. 2, c. 13, § 22.

Europe, during which time the army's primary mission was to fight Indians in the continental heartland, while the navy concentrated on protecting trade and providing a shield against potential (though highly improbable) invaders. Over time, of course, vested interests and elaborate theories grew up to reinforce the separation, but their part in shaping it had been quite minor.

Similarly, it is worth keeping in mind that military pluralism has not always produced direct confrontations of views. As Huntington emphasizes below, the army and navy typically ignored each other in periods of "peace" until the onset of the Cold War. Interservice rivalries are not traditional; they are rather a product of recent efforts to coordinate service plans and operations. Throughout most of American history, therefore, it has simply not been the case that the army-navy separation has highlighted options for top level civilian controllers. These latter, in any event, were themselves organized solely along service lines until the position and office of the Secretary of Defense were created after World War II.

Most twentieth century controversies over military organization have focused on whether "more" or "less" integration was desirable, taking the existing pattern of subunit roles and jurisdictions for granted. Only in the past few years has a concerted effort been made to pattern the work processes of the Defense Department, and subunit roles within it, so as deliberately to infuse the whole with an optimal combination of intelligence, innovative energy, esprit de corps, flexibility—and civilian control. Increased attention has also been paid in recent years to patterning military careers so that professional officers who achieve the highest ranks will have transcended narrow loyalties and perspectives. It is with such trends as these, along with the new dilemmas they pose, that this section is concerned.

Samuel Huntington confronts the popular view that interservice conflicts produce waste, impede "objective" assessments of national military requirements, and (by spurring the services to pursue political support ever more aggressively) threaten effective civilian control. Even more usefully for a sophisticated audience, however, he reviews the changing nature of intramilitary rivalries from the end of World War II to 1960. He finds that each service increasingly sought to diversify its capacities, so that it would not lose too severely when policy-makers shifted emphasis from one kind of warfare (or strategic conception) to another. The result has been that intraservice rivalries, and rivalries in which the lines of conflict and alliance cross service lines, have become increasingly common. The consequences of these trends, Huntington concludes, have been to increase the number of options available to civilian leaders, to enhance the adaptability of the armed forces to changing conditions, and to keep the military highly attuned to civilian values. He also judges that unification of the military establishment in the most meaningful sense is more likely to come from the further proliferation of intramilitary conflict than from its elimination.

As you evaluate these provocative theses, you may wish to consider a problem that is closely related to them. To what extent is it reasonable to assume, as most writers on military organization implicitly do, that whatever enhances civilian control also serves the broader values of liberal democracy? Recent developments highlight the relevance of this question. During the tenure of Secretary McNamara, pluralism within the military establishment has increasingly been structured, and the resultant controversies have been channeled into collective evaluation processes, with the aim of multiplying the options available to the Defense Department's civilian leadership. In this sense, the cause of civilian control has been served. On the other hand, the subunits have been restrained with increasing effectiveness from taking their cases to Congress and the press. How might one go about evaluating this sort of "mixed" result?

Gene Lyons maintains that the concept of civilian control has little relevance in the contemporary Pentagon. Although it is highly centralized and civilian dominated, the most striking recent trends within it have been the "civilianization" of its military leadership and the "professionalization" of its civilian leadership. It is on these developments that analysis ought to focus. Today's high civilian officials in the Defense Department have typically devoted many years to administration or scholarship in the national security arena. Moreover, they are numerous enough to have a major impact on defense planning, and they can call on a growing body of civilian specialists in military affairs employed outside the government (by universities, "think" organizations such as RAND, etc.) for special studies and advice. On the other side of the ledger, today's highest military officers are likely to have had a wide variety of experiences in such "civilian" activities (within the Defense Department) as financial management, research administration, diplomacy, congressional liaison, long-range planning, and public relations. Consequently, Lyons writes, the perspectives of the Defense Department's top military and civilian leaders, viewing each group collectively, have all but merged. He concedes implicitly that this merging of perspectives has not solved the problem of attuning military programs to the broad requirements of foreign policy. His stress on the "professionalization" of the Pentagon's civilian leaders, moreover, suggests the possibility that they may be a very special breed of civilians, who have been socialized into thinking on many subjects like military professionals. Whether this is a real problem, and if so, whether it is susceptible of alleviation without impairing the nation's security, are questions left to you.

The final two items in this section illustrate the directions in which civilian leaders of the military establishment have recently sought to move the professional officer class. Edward Katzenbach argues—before an audience of West Point cadets —that today's first-rate officer possesses a broad fund of knowledge, a highly analytical turn of mind, and a capacity to absorb education throughout his career. Secretary of the Navy Nitze states as official policy that naval officers selected for promotion to flag rank should be men who have shone in a wide variety of roles, not simply one—even if that one has been operational command.

INTERSERVICE COMPETITION AND THE POLITICAL ROLES OF THE ARMED SERVICES *
Samuel P. Huntington

"CONVENTIONAL wisdom" (to purloin a phrase from Galbraith) holds that interservice competition necessarily undermines economy, efficiency, and

* From the *American Political Science Review*, Vol. 55 (March 1961), pp. 40–52. Reprinted by permission of the author and publisher.

effective central control in the military establishment. The remedy is further unification, possibly even the merger of the services into a single uniform. The conventional wisdom also holds that political action by military groups necessarily threatens civilian control. The remedy is to "keep the military out of politics." The pattern of American military politics and interservice rivalry since World War II, however, suggests that the conventional wisdom may err in its analysis of their results and falter in its prescription of remedies.

I. THE ROOTS OF INTERSERVICE RIVALRY

Service political controversy between the world wars had two distinguishing characteristics. First, on most issues, a military service, supported, perhaps, by a few satellite groups, struggled against civilian isolationists, pacificsts, and economizers. The Navy and the shipbuilding industry fought a lonely battle with the dominant forces in both political parties over naval disarmament. The Army lost its fight for universal service after World War I, and throughout the Twenties clashed with educational, labor, and religious groups over ROTC and with other groups over industrial mobilization preparation. In the annual budget encounters the issue usually was clearly drawn between service supporters who stressed preparedness and their opponents who decried the necessity and the legitimacy of substantial military expenditures. To the extent that the services were in politics, they were involved in conflicts with civilian groups. Behind each specific opponent of the moment was that broad and deeply ingrained anti-military sentiment which had characterized American society since the eighteenth century. By the end of the Coolidge administration this sentiment was so far in the ascendancy that the appropriations for the Army and the Navy together had been whittled to about $750 million in a total annual budget of just under $4 billion.

Second, each service waged its own political battles independently of the other. Throughout the 1920s and 1930s, the services cooperated in strategic planning through the Joint Board and in a few other enterprises. Strategic planning, however, involved no immediate claims upon scarce resources. It produced some disagreement but no real political conflict. The most significant intramilitary controversies involved the efforts of the two semi-services, the Air Corps and, to a lesser extent, the Marine Corps, to achieve greater autonomy and *de jure* recognition as services. The two major services, however, seldom fought each other politically and virtually never helped each other. They were distinct departments. Separate legislation, handled by separate Military and Naval Affairs Committees in both houses, established and organized them, authorized their strengths and prescribed their systems of promotion and recruitment. Separate appropriations subcommittees provided their funds in separate supply bills. The political successes and failures of one service had little implication for the other: the National Defense Act of 1920 boded neither good nor ill for the Navy; the Vinson Acts of the 1930s neither assumed nor precluded an increase in the Army. Each service struggled along in its own world with its peculiarities and preoccupations, its own friends and enemies. . . .

. . . World War II destroyed the separate political universes of the services. The development of new weapons and the emergence of a new role for the United States in world affairs meant a change in their old functions and activities. Service futures were now interdependent. The concerns which each service felt for the future tended to focus into a concern over the effect of the other services on that future. A unified defense organization meant competition over organizational position and strategic doctrine. A unified appropriations process meant competition for funds. The interservice battle over unification between 1944 and 1947 was not only a model of battles to come, but it also shaped the nature of those battles. Interservice rivalry was the child of unification. Both reflected the unity and complexity of modern war, and without the one, the other would never have come into existence. . . .

The rise of interservice rivalry had a direct impact on civil-military relations. Potential conflict between civil and military institutions was sublimated and deflected into conflict among the services. Interservice controversy substituted for civil-military controversy. Two crucial foci of civil-military relations in modern states have been between the foreign office and the military, on the one hand, and between the military and the budgetary agencies, on the other. American civil-military relations in the postwar decade, however, were characterized by the relative lack of sharp conflict between a united military establishment and either the State Department or Budget Bureau. Service rivalry permitted the civilian agencies to pick and choose. When the State Department wanted to reinforce Europe in 1950, elements in the Air Force took a skeptical attitude, but the Army moved in to help develop and merchandise the policy. Conversely, when the Secretary of State later spoke of massive retaliation, the Army dissented, but the now-favored Air Force congratulated the diplomats on their military common sense. When the budget was reduced in Fiscal 1954, Vandenberg made his futile protests while the Army and Navy sat on the sidelines. When it was reduced in Fiscal 1955, the Air Force was pleased with the new emphasis, and the Army fought alone against the cuts. Civil-military relations before and after the Korean War would have been far different if the frustrations generated by the Johnson and Wilson budgets had not in part been dissipated in decrying other services and other strategic doctrines. Indeed, at no point after World War II were the President and his Budget Bureau confronted with a truly joint, integrated military program, publicly announced and supported by all military men as the indispensable minimum for national security. The *imprimatur* which the Joint Chiefs bestowed upon force-level recommendations was seldom more than *pro forma*. The "minimum" programs were service minimum programs for 70, 143, or 137 wings; for one *United States,* ten *Forrestals,* or a series of nuclear carriers; for twelve, twenty-four, or twenty-seven divisions. Each service chief tended to attack not the overall ceiling on the military budget but rather the allocation of the budget among the services. The oft-commented-upon failure of the

American military to have a distinctive "military viewpoint" on national policy after World War II was not unrelated to the presence of distinctive service viewpoints.

In almost every modern state, the division of the military forces into two or more separate groups has been used to bolster civilian control. Totalitarian states create SS or MVD troops to check their regular forces. The Founding Fathers provided for both a militia and a regular army. After World War II, interservice rivalry played a similar role. "I want competition," Representative Vinson is quoted as declaring. Interservice rivalry not only strengthened civilian agencies but also furnished them with a whipping boy upon whom to blame deficiencies in the military establishment for which just possibly they could be held responsible.

Interservice controversy rendered unlikely any military rejection of the civilian world and its values, such as occurred in the late nineteenth century and between the two world wars. Civilian agencies were now more frequently arbiters than opponents, and each service was impelled to adjust its values and interests to those of influential civilians or to risk falling behind its rivals. Interservice conflict stimulated a politicization of the military which meant both a less military attitude in dealing with civilians and more sophisticated political techniques in dealing with other military groups. Implicitly, service activity directed at other services was more acceptable than service activity directed at civilians. The services themselves found it easier and more virtuous to tangle with each other than to challenge civilian groups and arouse the hallowed shibboleths of civilian control.

Despite these functions which it apparently served, interservice rivalry nevertheless was often denounced by civilians as the source of many evils in the Department of Defense. Interservice harmony, the elimination of duplication (rational organization), reduced costs, and greater unification were often seen as directly related; and the achievement of interservice harmony, it was argued, was a step toward the achievement of the others. If this were the case, however, it is indeed strange that political and military leaders so persistently refused to realize these values. Why wallow along with interservice bickering, duplication, needless expenditure, and administrative disunity, if they could all be eliminated or reduced together by taking a few simple steps? The relations among these goals were considerably more complex than they superficially appeared to be.

Interservice competition was not so much a cause of decentralization, duplication, and increased expenditures as it was the result of the desire to eliminate these supposed evils. More harmony among the services could be bought at the price of disunity, duplication, higher costs. It is generally conceded, for instance, that the less money there was in the military budget, the more intense and bitter was the competition of the services for it. Similarly, interservice competition in the postwar decade originated in unification, and efforts to increase unification usually tended to produce greater interservice competition. . . . In comparable fashion, duplicating ambitions were a cause of interservice rivalry; duplicating programs and functions a means of reducing that rivalry. Both the Army and the Air Force wanted to develop, produce, and operate intermediate range ballistic missiles. This conflict of ambitions was, in part, mediated by allowing both services to produce their respective missiles. In one sense, duplication was a result of interservice rivalry, but it was a result which tended to reduce its cause, and efforts to decrease duplication tended to increase interservice tensions.

Interservice harmony could thus be achieved at the sacrifice of reduced expenditures, rationalized organization, and greater unification. In addition, interservice peace would probably have certain costs in decreased civil-military harmony. Conversely, the achievement of these other values was only possible by accepting a considerable degree of interservice competition. One suspects that the real cause of the sustained deprecation of interservice competition was not its direct association with other evils in Defense Department management, but rather because it was a discomfort which had to be endured if these other evils were to be reduced. What people identified as the consequences of interservice competition were in reality the alternatives to it. Interservice competition became an ubiquitous, inherent, and permanent feature of the defense establishment because it would simply cost too much to eliminate it.

For the services, interservice competition was a justification for, as well as a cause of, service political activities. Traditionally, and again immediately after World War II, service appeals to their officers to be public relations-conscious stressed the close interrelation of political and military affairs and the general responsibility of military officers to enlighten the public on the needs of national security. Increasingly, however, the stress on the public relations responsibility of the officer assumed a service-oriented approach. Exhortations to political action were couched in terms of putting the service view across— informing the public of the indispensability of sea, air, or land power to national security. Competitive emulation thus provided the impetus for the multiplication of service political activities. "The Jupiter," as Wernher von Braun explained, "involves several hundred million dollars of the taxpayers' money. One hundred percent security would mean no information for the public, no money for the Army, no Jupiter. . . . The Army has got to play the same game as the Air Force and the Navy."

Each service, with the notable exception of the Marine Corps, developed an image of itself as the "silent service," politically underprivileged, misunderstood by the public, incapable of competing equally in the public arena with its more articulate and dramatic rivals. Each service's feeling of inadequacy was undoubtedly real, and the ritualistic deploring of its inferiority furnished a perfect rationale for, and incentive to, political action. Contrary to what one might expect, however, the stronger a service was, the more it tended to deplore its inferiority. Perhaps the greater its power and the more extensive its activities, the more the service felt the need to justify them by stressing how weak it was. Conceivably, too, feelings of inadequacy derive more from the gap between a service's power and its aspirations than from its power relative to its rivals. Or, it may be that bemoaning the state of one's public relations is itself an inherent part of public relations activity and increases as the latter increases. In any event, by almost any standard, the Air Force was the strongest service politically during the postwar decade. It consistently outscored its rivals, for instance, in public opinion polls, and after 1951 it regularly received the lion's share of the Defense Department budget. Yet the Air Force undoubtedly complained the most about its political weakness. The Air Force, one of its generals declared, had "a special problem in public relations" because most Americans did not understand the basic concepts of strategic air power and believed air power to be too expensive. "The Vice Chief of Staff," an Air Force journal reported in 1954, "is convinced that the Air Force had failed to keep the public properly informed." A distinguished lawyer and brigadier general in the Air Force Reserve compiled an imposing list of obstacles to the development of American air power:

Air power is the victim of cultural lag. . . . The military commentators were brought up in the older services. . . . The Air Force lacks representation in the Office of the Secretary of Defense. . . . The Congressional relations of the Air Force are inferior to those of the other services. . . . The Air Force is really the silent service. Its senior commanders do not write books and articles. . . . Those responsible for the development of national air power have not made use of the basic instrumentalities of information and enlightenment to get the public behind them.

The *Air University Quarterly Review* endorsed these conclusions and pointed out other deficiencies. Both the Army and the Navy had regular TV programs; the Air Force had none. Fewer movies were made about the Air Force than about the other services. The *Review* found just one area of Air Force superiority. "Only in the mass medium of the comics does the Air Force come out ahead, with 'Steve Canyon' and 'Terry and the Pirates' far outstripping any competition in that field of communication and public relations." The complaints of the other services differed only in quantity, not in quality, from those of the Air Force.

II. THE POLITICAL CASTELLATION OF THE SERVICES

Interservice competition tended to weaken the military as a whole but to strengthen the military services. Challenging the services, the rivalry also toughened them and forced them to develop the mechanisms and support necessary for survival in the pluralistic world of American politics. The expansion of their political activities tended to resemble a process of castellation. Building out from its inner keep, each service slowly constructed political, institutional, and legal defenses, after the fashion of an elaborate medieval castle with inner and outer walls, ramparts and barbicans, watchtowers and moats. The services, in short, entrenched themselves on the American political scene, as countless other interest groups, private and public, had done before them.

Expansion of Public and Congressional Relations. Service emphasis upon reaching the public and Congress was concretely reflected in the elevation of these activities in the formal administrative hierarchy. During the 1920s and the 1930s, the Army and Navy public information sections occupied subordinate positions in the Intelligence branches of the services. Inevitably the outlook and values associated with the collection and interpretation of intelligence were not those which encouraged the collection and dissemination of news to mass media of communication. Congressional liaison responsibilities were dispersed among a number of bureaus in the Navy and assigned to the information offices in the Army and Air Force. By 1956, however, all three major services had similar organizational arrangements for public information and legislative liaison: two distinct offices at the highest level directly responsible to the service secretary.

The elevation of these offices was accompanied by an expansion and diversification of their activities. The Army Chief of Information, for instance, opened a branch office in Los Angeles in 1952 to improve relations between the Army and the movie industry, and another in 1956 in New York, designed, in the words of the Chief of Staff, to "assist in getting its story across to the public" through all the available news media. At the same time, the Chief of Staff pointed with pride to the award by the American Public Relations Association of three citations to Army organizations for outstanding public relations. Public relations was included in the Army Program System. Public information objectives were established quarterly, covering "those critical areas for which the Department of the Army particularly desires emphasis during the period." The parallel between the military services and the large industrial corporations was pointed out, and the military were urged to adopt the public relations philosophy of industry. General Ridgway's call in 1954 for the "creation of a public relations-conscious Army" had its counterparts in similar exhortations by the other services. Increased activities meant increased funds, and, reportedly, total military expenditures for legislative liaison doubled between 1953 and 1958.

"Backstop" Associations and the Articulation of Service Interests. A second aspect of the growth of service political activities in the postwar decade was the increased number, membership, and activities of service "backstop" organizations, private associations concerned with the support of the services and the articulation of their programs. The Navy League, oldest of the major associations, was formed by a group of civilians in 1902 to counter-balance the reaction against the Navy in the years after the Spanish-American War. Prior to World War II, the League was an active and devoted advocate of the Navy, but never a very large, affluent, or influential one. The unification controversy of 1945-1947, however, gave the League a new role to play, not in fighting anti-Navy midwesterners, but in fighting anti-Navy soldiers and airmen. The Air Force Association was organized in 1946 and the following year it took over the publication of the monthly *Air Force* magazine, previously published by the Army Air Force. In 1959, it had 55,000 members. The Association of the U.S. Army was formed in 1950 by the merger of the Infantry and Field Artillery Associations. In 1955 it assimilated the Antiaircraft Association, and by 1958 it had a membership of 50,000 and almost a hundred chapters.

The development and vitality of the "backstop" associations was particularly relevant to one major problem of service behavior in the postwar period: the definition and articulation of service interests. Normally the leaders of a group are its natural advocates and defenders. With the services, however, this is not necessarily true. To be sure, the role of the service secretary differs little from that of the secretary in a civilian department. In most civilian agencies, however, the definition, articulation, and promotion of the agency's interests are also a function of the top career leaders of the agency, those whose work-lives are continuously identified with it. The freedom of the military leaders to perform this function, however, is restricted by their presumably instrumental character. The Department of Agriculture, for example, has a responsibility for and to the farmers of the country as well as a responsibility to the President and Congress. The military, on the other hand, are responsible only to the higher political authorities of government: their representative role is minimal; this is the essence of "civilian control." Thus, the top military leaders of a service—those who might be presumed to be most active and influential in the defense of its interests—are normally among those who must act with the greatest circumspection in this area. The "backstop" association, however, is uniquely able to perform this function. As a private group, it can openly criticise the Administration while service leaders limit themselves to oblique suggestions under the prodding of sympathetic congressmen. The Chief of Staff speaks for his service but also for the Administration and the Department of Defense. The service association speaks only for the service.

In addition, the association can engage in political tactics and methods which are denied to the service. The Regular Army, for example, in its struggles with the National Guard Association and the Reserve Officers Association, is, as one scholar has pointed out, handicapped "by its inability to throw charges—either reckless or responsible charges—into the headlines as its opponents frequently do." Service associations are under no such restraints, and the less directly they are associated with the service, the greater their freedom. On the other hand, they cannot become completely detached; if they are too distant from the service, they decrease their authority and responsibility and may misjudge the service's interests.

Preserving the balance poses problems with respect to membership. From the start the Navy League protected its freedom of action by barring from membership military men on active duty. The Air Force Association permitted active personnel to be members only in a non-voting, non-office-holding capacity. In contrast, the Army Association was originally composed largely of active officers. In 1956, however, it was reorganized, and the leadership was transferred to individuals not on active duty "so that the Association may exercise its right to express its own independent opinions." While they may in consequence have the freedom to do so, the service associations rarely, if ever, take stands opposed by the leaders of their service. The resolutions and programs adopted by the service associations at their annual conventions represent approximately what the leaders of the services would ask for if they were freed from Administration restraints. In 1959, for instance, the Administration advocated an Army of 870,000 men, the Chief of Staff one of 925,000 men, and the Army Association one of a million men.

Usually the service recognizes the unique position of the service association and the special relations which exist between them. At the same time, it also stresses the independence of the association. The Navy League, the Secretary of the Navy declared in 1958, is "the civilian arm of the service." Two months later, however, Admiral Burke told a Navy League audience that the Navy "has absolutely no control over your fine organization." Air Force sources have informally referred to the AFA as "our lobby," and in 1949, General H. H. Arnold even described the Association as "Air Force-controlled." Yet its private character is also emphasized. The Secretary of the Army has declared that the relationship between the Department and the Association "although unofficial, must be close and cooperative." The "success of the Association," he said, "is a matter of vital interest to the Department of the Army."

Cultivation of the "Grass Roots." The postwar period was also marked by increased service activities designed specifically to reach public opinion at the "grass roots." Service installations and activities, of course, were spread across the face of the land. A clear distinction existed, however, between the interest of a community in a particular installation and its interest in the service as a whole. The congressman from Charleston is an ardent supporter of the Navy —until the Navy proposes to cut its operations at the Charleston Navy Yard. Unlike many private associations and a fair number of governmental agencies, the services could not easily mobilize sentiment across the country in support of a national program. The problem which they faced was not dissimilar from that confronted by the large industrial corporations. Both the corporation and the service are national and highly centralized institutions. Political power in America, however, is to a large extent channeled through local organs. Individual political influence depends upon prolonged local residence and participation: the employees of the corporation and the service are continually on the move. On the one hand, the economic health of the local community may depend upon decisions by a General Staff in Washington or a board of directors in New York. On the other hand, the small community normally possesses direct access to state and local governing bodies, and frequently to Congress, in a way which is denied to the national organization.

Corporations have attempted to adjust to the decentralization of political power by supplementing their general public relations activities with other efforts specifically designed to reach local publics. The armed services have done likewise. Among them, the Army has been most active; more than the other services, it is apt to be concerned with issues where grass roots support is important. Shortly after World War II, for instance, when confronted with the need to stimulate recruiting and to arouse support for UMT, the Army sponsored the creation of Army Advisory Committees in numerous communities, each committee made up of leading local figures in business, religion, education, the press and radio, and civic organizations. "[I]nformation on our actual policies and actual plans," the Army's Chief of Information declared in 1947, "can be disseminated down through these advisory committees to all the various agencies that affect public opinion right out in the 'grass roots.' That is very important." Antedating the Committees, but subsequently closely associated with them, were the civilian aides to the Secretary of the Army. Their duties included advising the Secretary on matters relating to the public standing of the Army, investigating specific problems at his request, and cooperating with the local Army commanders in furthering their programs. The Navy's counterpart to the Army Advisory Committees was the Advisory Council on Naval Affairs, sponsored by the Navy League. The members of the Advisory Council were appointed by the commandants of the various naval districts and furnished the Navy with a means of reaching local opinion groups. In addition to these broadly purposed programs, all the services emphasized the importance of "community relations" to the commanders of their posts and installations and urged them to carry on an active program of visits, support of local charities and projects, and sympathetic consideration of local interests.

The reserve structure was another means of reaching local public opinion. The reserve organization, and, to an even greater extent, the National Guard were influential with Congress simply because they were organized locally. As more than one congressman has noted, in contrast to the service "backstop" associations, the reserve organizations "have the votes." "Because the National Guard Association represents the fifty-one states and territories," as one National Guard leader put it, "and is able through its membership to bring considerable pressure to bear on Congress, it has consistently enjoyed a high respect from Congress." The strength of the Guard, he continued, lies both "in the state representation" and in "the potential vote represented by the 500,000 and their families." Army spokesmen and supporters frequently urged that efforts be made to utilize the reserves to put across the Army viewpoint. The very power of the reserve organizations, however, made them less susceptible to use by the service leadership and more likely to have interests different from those of the service. The Guard, for instance, was politically stronger than the Army reserve, but also more independent of the Regular Army.

Industrial Bulwarks. The high level of military spending required by the Cold War and the heavy concentration of that spending on complex weapons brought into existence a significant peacetime munitions industry for the first time in American history. In their search for support in civil society the services could hardly overlook their contractors. In mobilizing industry the Navy and the Air Force started with two advantages over the Army. Both the Navy and the Air Force furnished a substantial portion of the total demand for the products of two distinct industries. The shipbuilding industry would always encourage a larger Navy, and the aircraft industry a substantial Air Force. The Army, in contrast, had no such concentrated source of industrial support. Secondly, the research, development, and, in some cases, the production of Army weapons was traditionally handled in government arsenals. The Navy made greater use of private industry, and the Air Force came into existence with little organized experience in research and development and hence depended very heavily upon the private aircraft companies. Army arsenals could generate support from the congressmen of their districts, but the aircraft companies could do this and also engage in all the public relations and propagandizing activities which their private status and funds permitted. "The aircraft industry," Senator Goldwater observed, "has probably done more to promote the Air Force than the Air Force has done itself."

Interservice rivalry stimulated industrial competition, and industrial competition, in turn, fanned the flames of interservice rivalry. In 1959, as the conflict between the Army Nike and the Air Force Bomarc came to a head, Boeing took newspaper and magazine ads to counter the "misinformation" spread about Bomarc, and Army officials urged Western Electric to increase its advertising on behalf of Nike. On the other hand, as General Gavin said, "what appears to be intense interservice rivalry . . . in most cases . . . is fundamentally industrial rivalry." Trade journals, Wernher von Braun declared, engage in "active instigation of interservice rivalry." They "often seem to feel that they owe it to their advertisers to go to bat for them" and to "publish quite frequently some rather vitriolic articles, taking a very one-sided stand in favor of one of the services." In nationwide advertisements, Chrysler proudly heralded the Army's successful Jupiter C space shot. Two weeks later Douglas retaliated with ads declaring that the Air Force Thor was "already in mass production." The Army Director of Special Weapons replied by referring caustically to a missile with "an apogee of four feet." The Air Force struck back by leaking information concerning its new solid-fuel Minute Man missile and at the same time deprecating the expense of the Navy's solid-fuel Polaris missile. The Navy replied that Polaris was less vulnerable and much closer to operation than Minute Man. "Thus a publicity contest between two corporations," as William S. Fairfield observed, ". . . now involved the uniformed personnel of all three services."

The Thor-Jupiter controversy was perhaps a classic example of how interservice rivalry initially can open a choice to the top civilian leaders of the defense establishment and then, in effect, shut off that choice through the competitive castellation of services. Thor and Jupiter were, as one general said, "about as alike as the Ford and the Chevrolet." The Secretary of Defense repeatedly asserted that only one or the other would be put into production. He delayed his decision, however, and in the end choice was impossible. "If the Defense Department suggested canceling the Air Force's Thor program," a former Pentagon official declared, "a Congressional delegation from California would be down our necks. And elimination of the Army Jupiter program would have half the Alabama delegation plus a couple of representatives from the Detroit area fighting us."

The shift from aircraft to missiles tended to broaden the ties of the aircraft industry with the services. The Navy, of course, had always been a significant purchaser of aircraft, and increasingly in the 1950s the Army also turned to the aircraft companies for its missiles. "The aircraft industry," one Air Force legislative liaison officer is quoted as saying in 1958, "just isn't likely to be as good a source for lobbying as it was two years ago." In the conflict between Jupiter (Chrysler) and Thor (Douglas), Douglas Aircraft was on the side of the Air Force. In the conflict between the Air Force Bomarc (Boeing) and the Army Nike (Douglas), however, Douglas was presumably on the side of the Army. As the major defense contractors in missiles and electronics increasingly held contracts with two or more services, the lines of industrial competition did not always coincide with and sometimes perhaps blurred those of interservice competition.

The Proliferation of Doctrine. After World War II, interservice competition contributed to increased service concern with, and output of, doctrine. Every bureaucratic agency, military and civilian, tends to develop a "bureau philosophy" or "ideology." The armed services differ from most civilian groups, however, in the extent to which the bureau philosophy becomes formal, self-conscious, and explicit. The philosophies of civilian agencies may be just as real as those of the military, but they are seldom codified into written statements of "doctrine." The importance of doctrine stems from the extent to which the military groups are perceived to be and perceive themselves to be simply the instruments of a higher national policy. The armed services explicitly rationalize their existence in terms of a higher national end, and each activity and unit is justified only by its contribution to the realization of the prescribed hierarchy of values and purposes. This instrumentalism is reflected in the emphasis, peculiar to the military, on the concept of "mission," and it manifests itself most concretely in the elaboration of doctrine.

Prior to the 1930s, doctrine was reasonably well developed in the Navy, somewhat less so in the Army. The rise of airpower, however, was a powerful stimulant to the military quest for ideology. Lacking secure organizational existence or general acceptance during the 1920s and 1930s, the supporters of airpower, like any new, crusading group, were tremendously concerned with the development of an intellectual rationale. The existence of the surface forces might be taken for granted; the need for an air force had to be demonstrated. Moreover, no longer was it possible for a service to elaborate a doctrine defining its importance to the nation and its relation to national policy without explicitly—and not just inferentially—defining the position of the other services also. Mahan had constructed a doctrine of seapower without specifically denigrating landpower. For the supporters of airpower, however, the attack on the surface forces was unavoidable. Once the Air Force was established, the intensity of its doctrinal concern perhaps moderated somewhat, but by this time the other services had felt compelled to reply in kind. Just as unification led to interservice political conflict, so it also stimulated interservice doctrinal conflict, and with the same power goals in view: jurisdiction, appropriations and influence.

The historical output of political theory, it has been suggested, correlates rather well with the presence of political crisis, turmoil, and conflict. So also,

when vital controversies arise, military doctrine flourishes. After 1945, it pro-
liferated in a variety of forms in manuals, speeches, journals, regulations, War
College theses, and staff studies. The competitive spur to its formulation was
concretely reflected in the creation of special staff units specifically designed to
develop doctrine and arguments for use in the interservice debates, such as the
Navy's "Op-23," headed by Captain Arleigh Burke during the B-36 hearings,
and the Army's Policy Coordinating Group, the head of which retired shortly
after the interservice blow-up in the spring of 1956. Each service also attempted to formulate concise statements of doctrinal guidance for its members
and persuasion for its potential supporters.

III. THE CHANGING CONTEXT OF INTERSERVICE COMPETITION

Interservice competition and the castellation of the services continued
throughout the fifteen years after World War II. The content and the significance of the competition, however, changed markedly. In the immediate postwar period fundamental issues of service existence and strategy were at stake.
After a major war, military policy is in a state of flux. The cake of custom,
bureaucratic routine, and sustained habits of behavior—executive, congressional, and popular—are broken. Change is not only possible, but expected. In
such periods, existing organizational units have the most to fear from major
threats to their existence, and new organizational units have the best prospects
for an easy birth or growth.

After World War II, each service and hoped-for service was anxious to
carve out a role for itself suitable to its ambitions and self-conceptions before a
postwar equilibrium was established and the patterns of organization and behavior jelled into enduring form. The unification battle involved the general
pattern of postwar organizational relationships for all the services and, specifically, the formal recognition of the separate existence of the Air Force.
Closely linked with this were the legitimate fears of the Navy and Marine
Corps for their future being. "Why should we have a Navy at all?" asked the
commanding general of the Army Air Forces, and answered himself by declaring that "There are no enemies for it to fight except apparently the Army
Air Force." Similarly, the then Chief of Staff of the Army, Dwight D. Eisenhower, made it quite clear that the Marines ought to be maintained as only a
minor landing force. The uneasiness these views inspired in the sea-going services was not allayed until their functions were carefully defined in the National Security Act and the Key West roles-and-missions paper, the Forrestals
floated forth on the flood of Korean War appropriations, and the Marine position was sanctified in the Marine Corps Act of 1952. By 1952 the United States
had four recognized services instead of the two it had had in 1940. After 1952,
whatever the vicissitudes of budgets and strategy, the existence of no service
was in serious danger from another. An equilibrium had been reached.

The strategic debates of the late 1940s seemed equally momentous for the
services. All agreed that the next war would be a total war. They did not
agree how that war should be fought. In the Air Force image, the war con-

sisted of an initially decisive—or airpower—stage in which victory would be irretrievably won or lost, and then a second mopping-up stage in which the other services might be of some use. The Army view (and essentially the Navy view, too) was that the initial air exchange would be indecisive until the surface forces had been built up to the point where they could move forward to seize bases and territories close to the enemy. After they had done their work, the air attack might play a somewhat more important role. But the final *coup de grace* would still be administered by ground forces moving in, defeating the enemy's land armies, and occupying enemy territory. Between these two concepts of a future war and the way in which it should be fought, no compromise seemed possible.

The debate, however, soon became obsolete. The war whose strategy the services were debating never occurred. Instead, the Korean War and the development of thermonuclear weapons changed the framework of strategic thought. It became less and less likely that another war would be World War II plus nuclear weapons. The Air Force no longer stressed the decisive aspect of airpower, but rather its deterrent quality. The experience of the other services in Korea was codified into a doctrine of limited war. Previously, the Air Force concept and the surface forces' concept of how to fight a general war had been completely incompatible. Deterrence and limited war, on the other hand, were complementary and competitive but not incompatible. Previously, any increase in the effectiveness of strategic airpower meant a decrease in the probable roles of the other services. Now, the more effective the massive deterrent became, the greater the probability of the smaller-scale disturbances with which the other services were primarily concerned. To be sure, the debates still continued over how much of the effort should be devoted to one purpose and how much to the other. All the services, however, accepted the necessity of devoting some resources to each. What had been conflicting images of a single-contingency future were replaced by general agreement on a multiple-contingency future, although the priorities and probabilities of the various contingencies remained in dispute.

In the middle 1950s, interservice debate was just as prevalent and intense as it had been previously. Strategic questions, however, had become less important and proprietary issues more important. The question was less what should be done than how it should be done and who should do it. Neither the fundamental existence of the services nor fundamental alternatives of national strategy were main issues, but rather marginal gains and losses of weapons and functions. Major strategic issues were still debated, but the debate was not so strictly along service lines. In 1949, the Navy attacked the entire theory and practice of strategic air warfare: ". . . the threat of instant retaliation," Admiral Radford had declared, "will not prevent it [war] and may even invite it." In 1956, the Army and the Air Force tangled neither over the doctrine of retaliation nor the need to develop strategic missiles to implement that doctrine, but rather over who would build the missiles, who would operate them, and how much would be spent on one missile against another. Service enthusiasts might be as passionate as ever, but their disputes involved proprietorship, not principle. . . .

The lines of strategic cleavage thus diverged from the lines of interservice competition. The strategic functions of the Cold War—massive deterrence, defense of Western Europe, continental defense, preparation for limited wars, construction of a general war mobilization base—fell within the domain of no single service. One service might be more interested in one strategic mission than another, but the differences were differences in degree rather than kind. The Army played a major role in the defense of Western Europe and in the maintenance of a general war mobilization base. It also, however, had the three-division Strategic Army Corps for limited war, and devoted perhaps fifteen percent of its budget to continental defense. During the mid-1950s, also, the Army developed Redstone and Jupiter missiles for strategic deterrence and the exploration of space. Similarly, the Navy contributed to a variety of missions: naval forces in the Atlantic and Mediterranean to the defense of Europe; naval aviation and Polaris submarines to strategic deterrence; warning aircraft, radar ships, and increasingly, antisubmarine warfare to continental defense; carrier task forces and the Marine Corps to limited war needs. The major combat commands of the Air Force, in turn, were concerned with strategic deterrence, continental defense, and the tactical support of limited war forces.

The diversification of service functions had several important consequences. First, it tended to foster intraservice conflict. In the late 1950s a continuing debate went on within the Army over the extent to which it should aspire to a role in strategic deterrence. "For $5 billion worth of troop equipment," one division commander remarked in 1959, "I'd trade Huntsville away in a minute." Similarly, the Army commitment to the defense of Europe necessarily limited its effort to develop the Strategic Army Corps. Within the Air Force, officers of the Strategic Air Command openly attacked the recommendations of the Air Force-sponsored Project Vista on tactical nuclear weapons and of Project Lincoln on continental defense. In 1949 Air Force fighter pilots reportedly stimulated press leaks unfavorable to the B-36, and junior officers of the Air Defense and Tactical Air Commands later repeatedly warned of the dangers of giving overriding priority to strategic retaliation. On retiring in 1959, General Weyland, commander of the Tactical Air Command, "warned that the Pentagon's preoccupation with strategic bombing and long-range missiles may soon leave us unprepared to fight a limited war." Within the Navy intraservice struggle was muted because of the variety of functions to which individual naval weapons might contribute. Nonetheless, like the Army in the mid-1950s, the Navy in the early 1960s was tending to divide between those who favored increased emphasis upon strategic deterrence and those favoring greater attention to the naval weapons and forces useful in limited and conventional warfare.

Intraservice rivalry, however, never rivaled interservice rivalry. The services were like nation-states: loyalties to them tended to override sectional or class affiliations and also to be stronger than transnational loyalties. Normally it is easier to change sectional or class affiliations within a nation-state than to change citizenship from one state to another. Changes in the former, moreover, can be partial and gradual, while changes in the latter are usually abrupt and clearcut. Similarly, within the military, the lines between functional groupings within a service were seldom as clearcut as the lines between services. If the Navy withered away, naval officers could not easily become citizens of the Air Force. On the other hand, if one naval function declined, no insuperable barriers prevented the transfer of officers associated with that function to other functions. The officers of a service were united in a common hierarchy, advancement through a common promotion list, identification with common symbols, allegiance to a common high command, and, to an increasing extent, attendance at a common undergraduate academy. The institutional ties probably precluded intraservice controversy from becoming as intense as interservice controversy.

The relation of the services to fundamental issues of strategy in a sense tended to resemble the relation of the political parties to fundamental issues of national policy. The two parties have different centers of gravity with respect to policy, and yet each includes groups representing almost all viewpoints on the political spectrum. Similarly, while the outlook and doctrine of each service differs somewhat from that of the others, each service also has interests all across the strategic spectrum. . . . The argument that the United States is well off to have non-ideological parties and that it would be unfortunate if the division between left and right coincided exactly with the division between Democrat and Republican may also hold true with respect to the services and strategy. . . .

The Cold War thus replaced the simple pattern of service-*vs.*-service rivalry by a complex matrix of rivalry between service and service, service and function, function and function. The multiplication of the lines of conflict also tended to minimize its intensity. In this, the evolution of military politics followed a classic American path. Overlapping memberships in interest groups moderate group conflicts. The conflict of interest groups within and across party lines moderates the party struggle. Party conflict across institutional boundaries moderates executive-legislative conflict. Similarly, in the military area, just as interservice rivalry moderated the potential conflict between military services and civilian agencies, the emergence of conflicting functional programs tends to moderate interservice rivalry. A society, as E. A. Ross said, "which is riven by a dozen oppositions along lines running in every direction, may actually be in less danger of . . . falling to pieces than one split along just one line. For each new cleavage contributes to narrow the cross clefts, so that one might say that society *is sewn together* by its inner conflicts." Experts in military organization often argue that "unification" requires either the merger of the four services into a single uniform or the abolition of the services and organization of the Pentagon purely on a functional basis. The former proposal, however, is blindly utopian in rejecting the inevitability of pluralism, and the latter could intensify conflict to the point where it would be unbearable. "Unification" is more likely to come not from the reduction or elimination of intramilitary controversy but from its multiplication.

Diversification of function also gave the services organizational flexibility and balance by freeing them from identification with and dependence upon any single strategic concept or functional mission. "The Army," its Secretary declared in 1957, "cannot—and indeed assiduously seeks not to—commit itself to any particular doctrine, strategy, or tactic." Noncommitment was the means of self-preservation. Shifts in emphasis in national policy from massive retaliation to limited war to continental defense would affect the relative standing of the services, but it was unlikely that they could threaten the existence of any service. The new role of the services was formally recognized in the Reorganization Act of 1958: the interservice and functional commands became clearly responsible for combat, the services for personnel, training, and logistics. By reducing the combat functions of the services, the act insured their continued existence.

If this tendency continued, eventually the services would end up as English regiments on a grand scale—administrative organizations rather than fighting organizations. Thus, at the very time when interservice competition was forcing the services to develop doctrinal justifications, the evolution of strategy was depriving them of their traditional source of doctrine. As a result, the doctrinal issues debated among the services often seemed to have but minor relevance outside the locus of interservice competition. Not infrequently they assumed a certain metaphysical quality, in arguments over whether landpower or airpower was the dominant force in modern war and whether guided missiles were aviation or artillery. Such issues had little practical consequence for policy, except—and it is a vital exception—so far as the future of the service was concerned.

The value of the services thus stemmed precisely from their incomplete commitment to any single doctrine. An organization such as SAC or the Continental Defense Command, which exists for only one strategic purpose, cannot be receptive to changes in its purpose or to the creation of new organizations embodying competing purposes. The functional commands of today are the vested interests of tomorrow. So long as the existence of no service, however, depends upon any single strategic purpose, no service has reason to oppose intransigently changes in strategic purposes. Organizational permanence is the partner of strategic flexibility. Thus the unified and specified commands may become the instruments of strategy, and yet the political castles of the services may also continue to stand, with their storied keeps of service loyalty and tradition, their inner and outer walls in the executive and Congress, their towers and barbicans in industry, their moats flowing with the currents of public opinion. Perhaps, at some point, a major political or military innovation may, like gunpowder, bring these political structures down in a heap of broken masonry. The experience of other established organizations in American politics, however, suggests a different fate: that the castles of the services, like many of their medieval counterparts, will remain in existence, battered but untaken, long after the decisive battles—both political and military—have shifted to other fields.

THE NEW CIVIL-MILITARY RELATIONS *
Gene M. Lyons

HISTORICALLY the character of civil-military relations in the United States has been dominated by the concept of civilian control of the military. This has largely been a response to the fear of praetorianism. As recently as 1949, for example, the first Hoover Commission asserted that one of the major reasons for strengthening the "means of exercising civilian control" over the defense establishment was to "safeguard our democratic traditions against militarism." This same warning was raised in the report of the Rockefeller Committee on defense organization in 1953. While the overriding purpose of the committee's recommendations was to provide "the Nation with maximum security at minimum cost," the report made it clear that this had to be achieved "without danger to our free institutions, based on the fundamental principle of civilian control of the Military Establishment." Finally, during the debate on the reorganization proposals of 1958, senators and congressmen used the theme of a "Prussianized" military staff to attempt to slow down the trend towards centralization in the military establishment.

Despite this imposing support, the concept of civilian control of the military has little significance for contemporary problems of national security in the United States. In the first place, military leaders are divided among themselves, although their differences cannot be reduced to a crass contrast between dichomatic doctrines. Air Force leaders who are gravely concerned over the need to maintain a decisive nuclear retaliatory force are by now acknowledging the need to develop a limited war capability. At the same time, Army leaders are quite frank to admit that "flexible response" requires both strategic and tactical power of sizable strength, although they are particularly committed to developing a large tactical force. If these differences appear to be only differences in emphasis, they are nonetheless crucial in a political process within which priorities must be established and choices must be made. Without firm agreement on priorities, there is little reason to expect that the military can control government policy even if civilian authorities abdicate responsibility for basic decisions. The most that can result is a compromise between different military positions. Commonly, military disagreement, if exposed, is an invitation for civilian intervention.

* From the *American Political Science Review*, Vol. 55 (March 1961), pp. 53–63. Reprinted by permission of the author and publisher.

Secondly, the concept of civilian control of the military ignores two other factors that complicate civil-military relations. On the one hand, the military themselves accept the principle of civilian supremacy; on the other, they have been thrown into a political role in the formation of policy. The resignation of General Gavin over the budgetary restrictions of the "New Look" strategy is a case in point. The General disagreed with the judgment of his civilian superiors but, like General Ridgway before him and General Taylor after him, held his most violent fire until he was out of uniform and freed from the limits of professional restrictions.[1] His case dramatically illustrates the dilemma of the military as they move into the center of defense policy-making. Here they have to struggle between the non-partisan tenets of their creed and the requirements of effective participation in the political process. Their advice as experts is not only used by the Executive to bolster its case, but is eagerly courted by Congress and the public as a basis for testing the caliber of executive action. In one respect the political role of the military tends to dilute their own professionalism. But in another, it affords them more than one opportunity to maintain a balance between their professional code and the individual conscience. The nature of the American political system thus provides an outlet for frustration which, in other settings, has been the catalyst to set off an outburst of militarism.

In its broadest sense, the concept of civilian control of the military means military responsiveness to the policies of politically responsible government. But this too needs to be reinterpreted in the light of revolutionary changes that have greatly complicated the formation of defense policy. Preparedness is as much the product of civilian expertise in science and engineering and of civilian decisions on the allocation of national resources as it is of military planning. At the same time, it is very often the military who put defense policy to the test of political accountability by exposing the bases for decisions to congressional and public inquiry. As a result, there is a constant reversal of traditional roles, a situation that has brought civilians and military into a new set of relationships. These relationships have been reflected only in a limited way in recent organizational changes that have strengthened the central agencies of the defense establishment. To appreciate their full significance, it is also necessary to understand changes in the character of both civilian and military leadership in defense affairs. Civilians are becoming "militarized" and the military "civilianized" and it is these changes that reflect more clearly than organization alone, a fundamental break with tradition in the evolution of civil-military relations.[2]

1. The views of all three Generals have been documented in books they published shortly after they retired: James M. Gavin, *War in Peace in the Space Age* (New York, 1958), Matthew Ridgway, *Soldier* (New York, 1956); and Maxwell D. Taylor, *The Uncertain Trumpet* (New York, 1959).

2. For a theoretical statement of the concept of civilian control of the military, together with references to other major analyses of the subject, see Samuel P. Huntington, "Civilian Control of the Military: a Theoretical Statement," in Eulau, Eldersveld and Janowitz (ed.), *Political Behavior* (Glencoe, Ill. 1956), pp. 380 ff.

I. THE EVOLUTION OF DEFENSE ORGANIZATION

Like many institutions in American political life, a highly centralized, civilian-dominated Pentagon has developed in response to changing forces and conditions. Had the Joint Chiefs of Staff been able to function as a collegial unit rather than as a divided group of service representatives, it is possible that reorganization trends might have taken different directions. Centralization, however, was probably inevitable in one form or another. Increasing defense costs made centralized budgeting and programming a necessity. The bite of military expenditures in the total federal budget makes it impossible to ignore the impact of defense on the national economy, the government's tax program and the whole range of complex problems of resources allocation. The impact of technology has also been a centralizing factor. Indeed, work on the military applications of atomic energy had already been centralized in the Atomic Energy Commission. But work on missiles had been left in the separate services and the duplication of effort in three competitive programs brought on demands for greater coordination in propulsion programs in the late 1950's. Finally, both these areas of financial management and of research and development require skills that are "civilian," in essence, and are not yet possessed by many high ranking military officers. Thus it might be argued that "civilianization," as well as centralization, was inevitable given the nature of the problems that needed to be solved.

The growth of central civilian authority has nevertheless come in stages. The first Secretary of Defense, James Forrestal, had been opposed to the development of a large central staff even after he had come around to accept the concept of an overall defense chief. As a former Navy Secretary he was committed to the retention of strong civilian leadersihip in the individual services, first, to avoid a situation that might lead to the domination of a single strategic doctrine and, second, to keep civilian authority lodged at the operating levels of the military departments. He insisted that the Secretary "must be free to concentrate his efforts on the establishment of broad policy" and in so doing "must look to the secretaries of the military departments for the information and data upon which his policy is to be based and then look again to them for the execution of these policies." Within these guidelines, he was reported to want only "a very small executive force for the single Secretary to consist of [a total of] 15 to 25 '$10,000-a-year men' and officers."

The National Security Act of 1947, highly influenced by Forrestal's views, thus created a federation of military departments with little authority in the office of the Secretary of National Defense. In little more than a year, however, Forrestal himself recommended a number of statutory changes that mark the second step in the strengthening of centralized civilian authority. The critical problem he had faced was the absence of any military consensus upon which to develop strategic programs. He therefore sought to develop independent staff at the Defense Department level, including an Undersecretary of Defense, a Chairman for the Joint Chiefs of Staff and a larger Joint Staff. He also called for greatly clarified responsibility over the military departments to enable the Secretary to settle controversies over the roles and missions of the separate services and the allocation of budgetary resources.

Forrestal's recommendations, largely reinforced by the report of the first Hoover Commission a year later, were the basis for the National Security Act Amendments of 1949 which created a Department of Defense where only a coordinating mechanism had hitherto existed. The Secretary, however strengthened his position became, was nonetheless still forbidden, by law, to encroach upon the "combatant functions assigned to the military services." Congress deliberately used this basic prohibition to maintain the essential identity of the individual services, a tactic that has been retained in subsequent major reorganizations in 1953 and 1958. Nevertheless, this restriction has become less limiting on the authority of the Secretary of Defense as major strategic decisions have turned on problems of weapons development and financial management rather than directly on the controversy over roles and missions.

The reorganization plan of 1953 went another step in centralizing authority in the civilian leadership by creating assistant secretaries of defense with responsibilities in functional areas, such as supply and logistics, and manpower and personnel. These posts were established with the understanding that "they should not be in the direct line of administrative authority between [the Secretary] and the three military departments, but instead should assist in developing policies, prescribing standards, and bringing to the Secretary of Defense information on which he may base his decisions." Under these terms, the authority of the assistant secretaries was ambiguous. Administration witnesses were always cautious to assure congressional committees that the assistant secretaries of defense had no operating authority and were exclusively advisory to the Secretary. While this was theoretically so, actual practice was often to the contrary since they were frequently in a strong position to recommend that service positions be over-ruled. And the authority of the Secretary of Defense to delegate powers to his assistant secretaries was confirmed under the 1958 Act, apparently clearing away the ambiguity.

The growth of centralized civilian authority has thus been related to the decline in the authority of the service secretaries. Forrestal himself had found at an early stage that the service secretaries could not administer the individual departments and still act as his deputies in the formation and execution of overall policy. As service heads they were obliged to support major positions developed by their military chiefs or risk losing the main leverage they had to be effective in their jobs. The policy process is largely a process of bargaining and persuasion. Without the confidence of the military leaders, a civilian secretary cannot hope to persuade them to alter their views. At the same time, he has little chance to gain their confidence unless he largely supports the positions they have developed. He thus plays a dual rule, representing the Defense Department at the Service level and the military department at the Defense level. Under the pressures of inter-service competition for limited resources and the development of a large secretariat in the Department of Defense, the service secretary has become more and more a spokesman for his service's position and less and less a positive instrument in the formation of policy by the Secretary of Defense.

But by far the greatest part of the increase of authority gained by the civilian leadership in the Defense Department has accrued because of the inability of the Joint Chiefs of Staff to come to agreed positions on the military requirements of national security. The far-reaching provisions of the 1958 Act were largely in direct response to the wide range of problems raised by service disagreement. Under the Act, the Secretary of Defense can exercise direct authority over unified commands, transfer weapons systems from one service to another and maintain centralized direction of all military research and development through the Director of Research and Engineering. The practical impact of these powers is to give the Secretary considerable influence over the roles and missions of the services which are still prescribed by law within the broad and flexible categories of land, air, and sea forces. The concept of unified commands and the sweeping authority over weapons development now enable the Secretary to bring about *de facto* unification of the armed services even within the framework of a three-departmental system.[3] But to accomplish this, he has a total civilian staff of almost 2,000—a far cry from the "15 to 25 '$10,000-a-year men' and officers" that Forrestal had wanted less than 15 years ago.

II. THE "DEPOLITICALIZATION" OF THE DEFENSE DEPARTMENT

The increasing authority of civilian leadership has not been granted without misgivings. Several aspects of this trend have been viewed with concern: the turnover of civilians in the Pentagon;[4] the inability of civilians to come to grips with problems which have no exact parallel outside the military establishment; the tendency for the Defense Department to evolve into a fourth operating agency of the military establishment; the pre-occupation of Defense officials with budgetary matters; and delays in military programs as result of the need to obtain clearances from a thickening layer of "functional" chiefs. Indeed, Senator Henry Jackson has commented that ". . . at one time we worried about a German General Staff setup in the Pentagon. I think we are at the point of a civilian general staff. . . ." Senator Jackson was not, however,

---

3. Almost two years after the passage of the Reorganization Act of 1958, the *Army, Navy, Air Force Journal* (May 28, 1960) summed up some of the ways Secretary of Defense Gates "is using the full powers of his office . . . to achieve increased unification within the terms of existing legislation." These included centralization of missile test ranges, centralization of toxicological research, and establishment of an All-Service Defense Communications Agency. In addition, early in 1960, Secretary Gates sent a memorandum to the Chairman of the JCS, stating: "It is requested that I be promptly informed regarding any issue on which a difference of opinion is developing within the Joint Chiefs of Staff. I intend that either the Secretary of Defense and/or the Deputy Secretary of Defense will promptly meet with the Joint Chiefs at such times as they consider the issue in qeustion . . ." (reprinted in *Army, Navy, Air Force Journal*, January 16, 1960).

4. The problem of turnover has been the subject of a proposed Senate resolution "that it is the sense of the Senate that nominees appearing before its committee shall indicate their willingness to serve so long as the President desires" (S. Res. 338), 86th Cong., 2d sess. . . .

critical of the establishment of new duties in the Office of the Secretary, but rather of "a failure to exercise these functions properly."

The problem of "proper" performance in top defense positions is necessarily complex. Many administrators have held top positions over long periods— longer indeed than many military officers who are subject to rotation in assignment at frequent intervals. Others have had equally long tenure although they have hedge-hopped from position to position. It has, however, been difficult to attract first-rate people into high defense posts. Charles Wilson, for example, reported that, just before he took over the post of Secretary of Defense in 1953, out-going Secretary Lovett said to him: "Charlie, do not be too critical of some of these men that are here to help you do this job, because in some cases they are the thirty-third men I propositioned to come before I could get anyone." In the final analysis, the caliber of leadership in high positions will depend on the President and the kind of men he wants as advisers and his willingness to use his persuasive powers to bring them into government. It will also depend, though to a lesser degree, on the pressures the Senate puts on the Executive.

When the Eisenhower Administration took office in 1953, there was an almost complete turnover in civilian leadership (and, indeed, in military leadership as well). With the exception of the Defense Comptroller, Wilfred McNeil, all of the top Pentagon posts changed hands. This changeover was perhaps more disrupting than usual since it marked the advent of the first Republican president in twenty years. But the turnover was also very deliberate for the new Administration had almost completely divorced itself from the foreign and military policies of the Truman Administration during the presidential campaign. The new President and his chief advisers looked for a loyalty to their leadership and policies that they felt few Truman aides could muster. It is nevertheless instructive to note that by the end of the second Eisenhower Administration most civilian leaders in the Pentagon had spent periods of 4 to 8 years in defense work, if not in the same post.[5] At the same time Thomas Gates, the last Secretary of Defense under Eisenhower, and Robert Lovett, the last Secretary under Truman, were both urging that high defense posts be protected from partisan politics and that both parties agree to maintain effective continuity in the civilian leadership of national security programs.

5. For example: Thomas Gates, the Secretary of Defense, had served (with one short break) since October 7, 1953, as Undersecretary and Secretary of the Navy, as well as Deputy Secretary and Secretary of Defense; James Douglas, Deputy Secretary of Defense, had served continuously since March 3, 1953, as Undersecretary and Secretary of the Air Force, as well as Deputy Secretary; Herbert York, Director of Defense Research and Engineering, came to this post (and was the first incumbent in 1958) after long experience in defense work with the Advanced Research Projects Agency, various scientific advisory committees, and non-profit institutions engaged in defense activities; Charles Finucane, the Assistant Secretary of Defense for manpower affairs, had served as Assistant Secretary and Undersecretary of the Army for almost four years when (after a short break in service) he was brought back to the post at the Defense level in 1958; similarly, the three service secretaries, Brucker in the Army, Franke in the Navy, and Sharp in the Air Force had all had almost continuous Pentagon service for at least five years.

The recommendations of Secretaries Gates and Lovett are symptomatic of the change that has slowly been developing in the character of civilian leadership in the Pentagon in spite of the sharp setback in 1953. It is marked by what might be called a "depoliticalization" of the Defense Department, that is, an emphasis on standards of competence and experience in making appointments. Appointive posts in all federal departments are, of course, subject to both political and non-political considerations. Indeed, in the areas of foreign and military policy, the motivation of national interest operates to counteract the political forces of geographic distribution, party balance and pressure groups that dominate top appointments in other departments. Non-political considerations regarding background and ability thus largely govern the selection process.

Most appointive posts in the Pentagon break down into three general groups. There is, first of all, the Secretary of Defense and his immediate staff. Here the needs and thus the will of the President himself will certainly dominate, for the prime importance of the Secretary is as a top presidential adviser. His constant occupation is to serve as a deputy to the President in the performance of his constitutional duties as commander-in-chief of the armed forces. Indeed, as the problems of national security have come to absorb so much of the President's time and energy, the Secretary of Defense has come to be one of the most prominent members of both the President's cabinet and his inner circle.

But below the Secretary and his personal staff are a group of appointive posts at the Defense and military department levels, in which functional or "program" rather than constitutional or presidential, responsibility is emphasized. These include posts in the fields of financial management, manpower, and procurement and logistics. What is often as necessary as practical experience in the subject field itself, is an ability to manage complex enterprises and a deep understanding of the political and governmental processes. Thus, experience in public service is of prime importance. Men chosen for these posts might come from several sources. They might be men who possess these qualities and are also important figures in the President's party; their appointment can thus perform two functions at once—bring a professional hand to high office and meet the party's requirement for patronage. They might also be men whose identity with one of the major political parties has been incidental but whose experience with problems of public policy has made them wise selections for office regardless of party. Finally, they might be high-ranking civil servants whose records are outstanding and who are willing to give up the security of tenure for the political risks of appointive positions. Where a choice is possible, the determining factor will be the importance with which the President and his principal advisers view the balance of interests that are involved.

Finally, there are appointive posts that require a high level of specialized expertise but cannot be included within civil service categories. This is especially true in the field of research and engineering. The incumbents will often act as policy advisers and, even within the bounds of their own professional integrity, must be in basic agreement with the political dimensions of the President's defense program. At the same time, the civil service cannot provide the high degree of expertise that is required for top direction. The background and experience which the evaluation of complex weapons systems requires can rarely be gained by working in government agencies. It is more usually found in men whose prior experience has been developed in university and industrial laboratories.

Several factors can thus be identified as vital qualifications for high Pentagon posts below the Secretary of Defense himself: the benefit of government experience; the need for expertise; and the desirability of continuity. These traits have been increasingly recognized and their recognition is operating to develop a "depoliticalization" of these posts. "Depoliticalization," nevertheless, has limits. National security issues cannot (and indeed should not) be entirely taken out of politics. Top presidential advisers must be prepared to defend the choices they make before congressional and public criticism. At the same time the President needs to have the alternative of changing his close advisers if the sense of purpose and the support that he feels is necessary to his program are missing. Capable men available for such posts, no matter how broad the recruitment sources are becoming, will, moreover, continue to be few; and many of those who agree to accept political responsibilities will be under pressure to return to private life. For that matter, some turnover in the top echelons is desirable to bring a continual freshness and critical direction to government administration. Thus, no matter how far "depoliticalization" goes, political appointees will not always be able to provide the continuity and stability in government that are the principal contributions of career professionals.

"Depoliticalization" is, however, only one of the characteristics of the larger trend towards a professionalization of civilian leadership in defense affairs. Professionalization is taking other forms as well—the influence of career executives in the development of major policy decisions, innovations in administration which have brought outside experts into government through a variety of institutional devices, and a growing interest in military affairs among civilians outside government. All of these, taken together, contribute to the changing character of civilian leadership that is, in turn, influencing the character of civil-military relations.

III. THE PROFESSIONALIZATION OF CIVILIAN LEADERSHIP

The importance of continuity and stability in government is emphasized when the nature of the policy process is clearly understood; it is likelier to be appreciated more toward the end than at the beginning of any particular Administration. Policies are usually developed with a long history of conjecture, false starts and negotiation. Very often they take shape from a series of operational responses or the byplay of a number of viewpoints rather than from a single breakthrough of brilliant analysis. Within such situations, the influence of careerists, military and civilian, is enormous. It is equally impressive in moments of crisis when only professionals have the background and experience to respond quickly. The military professionals wield their greatest influence within the military departments; a large and burgeoning staff of civilian careerists exert similar powers in the Department of Defense. They perform staff work in connection with establishing budgetary and manpower priorities, supply the background material for new programs and have usually developed a network of informal contacts that make them invaluable in inter-departmental negotiations. Indeed, General Gavin recalled (perhaps with some bitterness) that ". . . the Civil Service employees . . . in the Department of Defense . . . probably have more impact on decision-making . . . than any other individual or group of individuals, military or civilian."

The hazy line that divides policy from administration and the influence of career professionals on decision-making are familiar themes in the literature of public administration. In the Defense Department, professional influence has been increased by the tendency to seek solutions to problems at a technical level in order to minimize differences over vital matters of policy. In such cases, the guides for policy become efficiency and empirical verification rather than intuition and inspiration; and in any such atmosphere technicians and arbitrators play a critical role. Such tactics often reduce policy to a compromise between opposing positions, a practice that is often stultifying. In many cases it is nevertheless an inevitable consequence of policy-making within the democratic process, particularly in the field of national security. For within the goldfish bowl of American politics, there is a limit to the risks a political leader is willing to take in approving defense programs that can be argued in terms of national survival and for which there is no indisputable solution.

But like the "depoliticalization" of appointive posts, there are limits to the contribution that increased civil service influence can make to the professionalization of civilian leadership in the Pentagon. Some of these limits have already been suggested. For one thing, few civil servants possess the degree of specialized expertise that is required for technical staff work in fields such as research and engineering. Nor, for that matter, does the bureaucracy offer the environment in which careful study and reflection on basic problems, such as strategic doctrine, is encouraged and indeed rewarded. At the same time, there is little chance that the top layer of the American civil service can be transformed into an administrative class like that in Great Britain; neither the social structure nor the political system to support such a class is present.

Within the special context of American governmental institutions, a series of innovating techniques have therefore been developed to bring professional competence to bear on matters of public policy where neither political nor career executives can fully meet the demands. They include *ad hoc* and standing advisory committees, contractual arrangements for consultative services, the assignment of broad investigations or actual operations to outside institutions, and government-financed independent agencies set up outside the formality of the bureaucracy.[6] These administrative techniques perform a number of functions. They bring creativity to the public service in areas where it is often discouraged by the routinization of bureaucratic procedures or the dangers of interservice and political disagreement. They offer political executives (and congressional leaders) alternative sources of expert advice to the career services, civilian and military. They permit the kind of experimentation, reflection, flexibility, and deep probing that the complex problems of national security require but that the regular federal service cannot completely accommodate because of its size, its need for standardization, and its emphasis on current operations.

The strides taken in recent years to develop new modes of government administration have largely been forced by the demands of technology. The scientific programs during the second world war and the industry-based programs of the Air Force in the postwar years established precedents for government contracting in areas that now extend beyond technological projects to projects in the social and behavioral sciences. Each of the services has created a "think" organization to which it can farm out problems—the RAND Corporation of the Air Force, the Operations Research Office of the Army and the Operations Evaluation Group of the Navy. Within the Department of Defense a variety of advisory panels are available to the Secretary and his assistants—on research and development, on psychology and the social sciences and on education and manpower. In addition, the Institute of Defense Analyses has been established "to create machinery for putting a segment of the nation's intellectual resources more effectively at the disposal of the national security effort." Originally established in connection with the evaluation of competing weapons systems, the scope of the Institute now encompasses broad areas of military strategy where the support for judgments on weapons evaluation is very often to be found. Indeed the close connection with strategic issues has been the link that has extended research on military operations into the far reaches of national policy.

These innovations in administration project the professionalization of civilian leadership in defense far beyond the confines of government itself. That they extend as widely as they do is, in many ways, an indication of the response of industry, science and private scholarship to the problems of national security. Like government-sponsored research, research in industry has begun to go beyond technical subjects. General Electric, for example, publishes a *Defense Quarterly* that is devoted to the broad issues of technology and foreign and military policy. It has also established a "think" group of its own, as have other corporations such as General Dynamics, IBM and many of the large aircraft companies. While most of these "in house" divisions are set up for scientific research and development, many of them dig into military and social

6. For a general discussion of the development of such innovations in government administration, see Don K. Price, "Creativity in the Public Service," *Public Policy*, Vol. IX (1959, Cambridge, Harvard University Press), pp. 3 ff. . . .

problems affected by technological advances. At the same time, many industrial companies contract out their research activities with institutions such as the Stanford Research Institute, a non-profit corporation which has moved into the fields of military and foreign policy in the wake of its primary interest in the frontiers of technological change.

In addition, since 1950 there has been an outpour of books and articles on national security from scholarly sources. Some have actually been made possible through association with Defense Department projects or under contract with congressional groups investigating various aspects of the defense program. But a very high number of these efforts have been undertaken on private initiative, with or without foundation or university support. The subjects of these studies have ranged from the broadest issues of military strategy to more specialized problems of military organization and education. They include Kissinger's *Nuclear Weapons and Foreign Policy,* Osgood's *Limited War,* Huntington's *The Soldier and the State,* Brodie's *Strategy in the Missile Age,* the books by Walter Millis, the monographs of the Princeton Center of International Studies, the studies of the Rockefeller Brothers Fund and the volumes that have come out of the research projects conducted at the Center for International Studies at the Massachusetts Institute of Technology. In all cases, these works have plunged deep into military problems. Indeed there are indications that some military leaders are concerned that "there has been too little solid contribution from military pens to national security policy thinking for this new age . . ."

The practical consequence of all of these activities is that professional advice, studies and investigations on complex military issues are being made available to responsible officials from sources other than the military themselves. Civilian leaders need no longer rely entirely on the military services for the bases for policy decisions. Their own experience in service, the solid contribution of career professionals and the wide new sources of research and reflection, together with the multi-dimensional nature of defense problems, permit them to be more critical, more questioning and more constructive in their own right. Needless to say, all that has been discussed are tendencies, trends that can be perceived as we analyze the course of civil-military relations during the last ten years. Nevertheless, it seems safe to predict that these trends will continue to gain momentum—the "depoliticalization" of appointive posts, the influence of career executives, innovations in government administration and an interest in military affairs among writers, scientists and scholars. They are also bound to contribute to a growing professionalization of civilian leadership in military affairs and, in turn, this professionalization will have important repercussions on the nature of civil-military relations.

IV. THE CHANGING CHARACTER OF MILITARY LEADERSHIP

The significance of the professionalization of civilian leadership cannot be judged without some consideration of the changing character of military leadership. When General Maxwell Taylor retired in mid-1959, a veteran Washington reporter commented that this marked "the point at which the Old Army is drawing to the end of its mission—and even of its relevance." He called Taylor "the last great captain of the old hunters . . ." and his successor, General Lyman Lemnitzer, "an intellectual, a staff officer of vast experience, a kind of professor of the new kind of war." The contrast is perhaps overdrawn, for it is difficult to think of the military—without its "heroic leaders," left to the impersonal calculations of the "military managers." It nevertheless catches the essence of a fundamental change in the character of military leadership.

Military leadership is changing under the impact of two forces: the revolutionary developments in weapons technology; and the close relationship between military programs and foreign and economic policies. The management of a missile program or a test range, the constabulary duties of an overseas assignment, the pseudo-diplomatic function of a military assistance advisory group, the planning involved in a Pentagon or a NATO slot—these are the tasks for which the military must prepare the officers of the future. At the same time, the threat of war, total, nuclear, limited or conventional, and the demands that open hostilities make on military leadership, are ever present. Thus the old attributes of "heroic leaders," the qualities of discipline, courage and command ability, cannot be forgotten. In this respect, the new responsibilities of military leaders have not so much altered their fundamental make-up as they have added new dimensions to their character and made them more complex human beings. This new complexity is being reflected in a number of changes in the military profession. Three of these are particularly important: the broadening base for officer recruitment; the development of higher military education; and new policies for selection and promotion to higher rank.

To a large extent, the broadening base for officer recruitment is a matter of arithmetic. In recent years the services have had to draw in more than 40,000 new officers every year, with a good percentage of these needed on a career basis. At the same time, the service academies graduate only about 1,500 new lieutenants and ensigns. As a result, the services have had to look to other sources for career officers, particularly civilian colleges and universities. This development has more than quantitative significance, however. It is also qualitative. The broadening recruitment base for young officers is bringing into the services men with new outlooks and new areas of technical competence that serve to meet the widening range of military responsibilities.

The elaborate structure of higher military education is also responding to the broadening character of military responsibility. Curriculum changes in undergraduate programs at the service academies and in military programs in civilian colleges and universities are moving in two directions: first, they are incorporating new material to expose the students to the expanding technology that is making such an impact on military life; and, second, undergraduate courses are becoming less vocationalized and are taking the form of preprofessional education to lay a solid intellectual base for future career development. At the post-commissioning schools—from the command and staff colleges through the service war colleges to the Industrial College of the Armed Forces and the National War College—there is an increased emphasis on the problems of international politics, the dilemmas of war and peace brought on by nuclear weapons, the impact of defense on the national economy and the complexities of life in a world of allies, international organizations and uncommitted nations. There are still weaknesses in military education: there is a tendency to be highly technical and vocational, even in dealing with social science material; service-organized programs also tend to be parochial, emphasizing the narrow views of the service itself; and the image of the world scene that is projected in military teaching is static and over-simplified. The advancements in the last fifteen years have nevertheless been striking and have taken military education far beyond the traditional emphasis on "loyalty, precedent, specific technical skill, and a gentlemanly code of conduct." [7]

Traditions, however, die hard. In the transition from one generation of military leaders to another, the qualities of the "heroic leader" continue to have primary importance and significance for those older officers who grew up in the "old Army," in the "black-shoe Navy" or even in the "propeller-driven Air Force." These are the officers, moreover, who control the machinery for selection and promotion. Here the struggle between the old and the new takes place. While assignments to the war colleges and long tours of duty in technical posts seem to be good preparation for the new roles military men are undertaking, they are not always the best routes to higher rank. Loyalty, length of service and the number of tours on sea and command duty are very often the qualifications that members of a military selection board look for. A few years ago, the Secretary of the Navy, in an attempt to break down these traditional barriers to advancement, instructed the selection board to accelerate the promotions of officers who were "head and shoulders" above their colleagues. The reverberations of these orders are still shaking the Navy's high command. Accelerating promotion means advancing officers in grade because of "potential" rather than actual performance. It thus involves an exercise of judgment about human behavior, as well as future military requirements, that is, at best, difficult to make. It is more difficult during a transition period when the old consensus on military qualities is breaking down and a new concept of military leadership is evolving.

More recently, the Secretary of Defense, in December 1959, issued a directive that "all officers . . . will serve a normal tour of duty with a Joint, Combined, Allied or OSD [Office of Secretary of Defense] Staff before being considered qualified for promotion to general or flag officer rank." Significantly, the directive makes an exception of Army and Air Force officers "whose proposed advancement and qualifications for promotion are based primarily upon their scientific and technical achievement and proposed utilization in that specialty." This emphasis on planning and technical experience and the deemphasis on

7. John W. Masland and Laurence I. Radway, *Soldiers and Scholars* (Princeton, 1957), p. 5. This work is a study of the response of military education to the widening policy role of military leadership.

parochial views were also underscored in the instructions of the Secretary of the Navy to the Flag Selection Board in 1960. Acknowledging the traditional concern for "a thorough seagoing background in the Line of the Navy," the Secretary brought the Board's attention to the need for "high performance on the planning level and a keen discernment of future operational requirements." He then went on, at some length, to explain that "the explosive technology of our modern weapons systems requires a high degree of concentration and knowledge in particular areas and precludes, to a great degree, the rapid rotation from job to job of many of our most outstanding officers for the purpose of qualifying them in all phases of naval warfare in the pattern of the past."

Both these actions reflect the concern of civilian leaders with the new dimensions of military leadership. Nevertheless, however "civilianized" military officers may become, the profession itself will continue to be anchored in the distinct nature of its trade, the process that has so succinctly and meaningfully been called the "management of violence" by Harold Lasswell. And, in the fulfillment of their mission, the military will continue to be highly influenced by the particular tools of their craft. Indeed, without this distinction what is the meaning of the military profession as a separate group in society? And what do military leaders have to offer that physicists, engineers, diplomats and economists cannot do to meet the requirements of national security? The answer, obviously, is nothing. At the same time, within the framework of its primary and unique contribution, the military profession is dramatically changing. At the moment, it is in a state of transition from the old to the new with the dimensions of the new still unformed, still taking shape, still resembling the contours of an earlier day.

V. TOWARD A NEW CONCEPT OF CIVIL-MILITARY RELATIONS

The nature of civil-military relations is thus being changed through the strengthening of central organization in the Department of Defense, through the professionalization of civilian leadership and through the broadening character of the military profession. These trends might also be expressed as the "militarization" of civilians and the "civilianization" of the military. When extended to their logical conclusion, they suggest new relationships between civilians and military based on a more complex division of labor than has heretofore existed. These relationships, however, are responsive to the new shape of national security in which military affairs are no longer a monopoly of the military and a clean-cut division between matters of war and peace, between foreign and military policies, is a false and misleading notion.

It is nevertheless as essential as ever that defense planning be attuned to the broader perspectives of national policy. This is a problem which can no longer be met through civilian control of the military, however. We need to be concerned with the whole complex of professional direction in defense planning and the dilemma of relating the problems of security to the goals and values of national policy. In this task there are limits to what organizational techniques can accomplish. The spectrum is too broad. There is also the danger of accepting institutional devices as a solution without pressing forward along other lines as well. These include arousing enthusiasm for public service in the leading professions in our society, developing a sense of the stakes involved in national security among the general public, encouraging the study of foreign and military policy in educational programs, strengthening the civil service, urging new recruitment and educational standards for military careers and continuing innovation in government administration. In this context the purpose of organization is not so much to control as it is to create the machinery through which to bring the full force of our intellectual resources to bear on the complex issues we have to meet.

THE MILITARY MIND *
Edward L. Katzenbach, Jr.

A FAVORITE subject of mine is the military mind. One of the reasons this is so is because there is so much mileage in it these days, what between "Fail Safe," "Dr. Strangelove," and "Seven Days in May."

Other less facetious reasons for my interest in the military mind are its importance to the nation and the cost of its preparation and education. . . . We have in school at any one time up to 300,000 or between ten and fifteen percent of the total military population of the United States. All of these people aren't learning to take apart machineguns and nuclear missiles and radar sets or one thing and another. Many are studying at universities. One Service, for example, has graduate students at 88 different universities in this country and abroad. Consequently, I would imagine that today the Armed Forces are as well an educated profession in terms of the number of years they spend in school as any other. This fact is impressed upon me every morning when I come in and see the Air Force Colonel who is my Director of Education Programs because he has not only a Bachelor of Science Degree from West Point, but also a Master of Public Administration from Harvard, a Master of Business Administration from George Washington, and a Doctor of Education from the University of Denver.

But what does this erudite military mind really think about? Few people, I suppose, know or even profess to know. The military mind, of course, really isn't unlike other professional minds. It deals with intellectual problems in basically the same way that an academic mind or a medical mind or an engineering mind or a legal mind attack their respective problems. It deals with very real, intellectual problems concerning the profession of arms. Ones which

* From a speech delivered at West Point (April 24, 1964). Reprinted by permission of the author.

I imagine most of you haven't thought about before. I'd like to illustrate one in the very simplest possible terms, the machine gun, a weapon which is in some degree familiar to all of us.

Consider for a moment the problem of being confronted for the very first time with a weapon that can shoot at so many rounds per minute, that can traverse and go up and down and shoot overhead, that takes a large amount of ammunition, that heats after a certain period of time and then freezes with heat. How would this thing be used? Do you use it on attack? Do you use it on defense? Do you mount it on something? Do you use it on the flanks? How do you supply it with ammunition? Does its firepower allow for a reduction in conventionally armed troops? It took as bright a group of intellectuals as the world has really known eight years to figure out these programs in terms so that they're willing to buy machine guns. That was the German General Staff at the turn of the century. But now, of course, military people's problems have increased a good deal more than that in intellectual terms. Have you ever thought about the history of, say, the thousand years between 847 and 1847 and then 1847–1947? That thousand to a hundred year span and then that in terms of the ten years just between 1947 and 1957. Between 847 and 1847 was the period of castles and crossbows and longbows and big Swiss pikes and gunpowder and cannons and the new engineering. Compare that to the period from 1847 to 1947 in terms of battleships, oil, gasoline, repeating weapons, tanks, planes, and the atomic bomb, and then think of it in terms of the ten years after that—automation, miniaturization, hydrogen bomb, missiles, space. You have about a thousand to a hundred to ten ratio of technological compression.

Now, what's the military problem? The military problem is to think in terms of the usage in terms of power of a technology which is changing in these kinds of terms. In other words, the military today has the problem of turning into social terms the fastest-changing technology that the world has ever seen. This is what the military mind is occupied with. It is occupied, in other words, with a world in which over a twenty-year span there has been the most enormous paradox that there ever has been in history. They are dealing with a world which technology has shrunk until it is so small that we can go around it in hours and communicate with one another through outer space. Yet, at the same time, the world over that period of time has been growing as fast as it has been shrinking in social terms. It has been getting larger in terms of numbers of countries. It has been getting larger in terms of numbers of people, and it has been getting larger in terms of the numbers of people that we care about.

So what does the military mind think about? The military mind thinks about the relationship between this technology, as I suggest, and its impact socially and psychologically and economically and politically on the world in which they live. But they have to take a step beyond this. The military today also has to be able to think in terms of training missions the world over, a more complicated problem than is faced in any other profession because he may be training at one time in South America, at another time in the Far East, and at still another in Africa or in Europe. He has got to know more than most economists know in terms of international economics—he must know village economics, and he must know how people eat, and he must know village sociology, and he must know village politics, and he must know the history of regions, and he must know the prejudices of regions, the theology of peoples, what motivates them, what they think about; he must know what they want to be so that he can help them to be the kind of people they really want to be.

This, then, is the world of the military. There is no profession which is more intellectual than this one, and that is why I suggest that the military mind really doesn't have very much time on its brain cells so to speak, to be worrying about taking over the government or starting world wars. It is really much more concerned with meeting the ever-increasing demands and responsibilities thrust upon this nation.

THE SELECTION OF NAVAL OFFICERS
FOR FLAG RANK *
Paul H. Nitze

REAR ADMIRAL GRIFFIN: In giving consideration to the responsibility I have for participating in the process of selection of officers for flag rank, I have come to the following views.

1. Far more important than anything I may write or say upon this subject is the designation of a selection board, consisting of members in which I have the utmost confidence that they will be wisely responsive to the requirements of the naval service. For this reason, I gave personal attention to this aspect of the selection process. It is my conviction that in this year's board we have members who are attuned to the changing nature of the requirements for flag officers, who will be able to determine from the performance of officers within the duty patterns of their past years, those who are best fitted to provide leadership in an appreciably different future.

2. Having said that, I should nevertheless like to record my view of how the requirements of the past may have differed from the requirements of the future and the effect this should have on your approach to the selection process.

3. I believe that it continues to be most important for the Navy to select officers of flag rank who will be superb leaders in sea-going commands. This does

* From a letter to Admiral Charles D. Griffin, President of the FY 1965 Navy Flag Selection Board (May 18, 1964).

not mean, however, that we need to place so much emphasis upon competence in sea-going billets that we fail to give substantial emphasis to competence to provide leadership in critical positions involving technical and management responsibilities. I believe that it should be possible to identify those officers whose performance at sea has given evidence that they will be brilliant leaders of task forces and fleets, but who have demonstrated those additional characteristics of leadership that qualify them for positions of greatest responsibility ashore.

4. I shall not presume to try to describe for you, who are far more experienced in Naval operations than I, the characteristics that mark a man as a potentially great operational commander. I do believe that I have had the professional experience to provide guidance and insights in regard to those additional qualities which would be most likely to provide great benefit to the Navy in assignments other than at sea.

5. You will have been briefed by the Chief of Naval Personnel on those billets which can best be filled by officers of various sub-specializations. I have the view that these sub-specializations are most important and that this fact should be recognized by each selection board and given serious, but not overriding weight. By that I seek to emphasize that I do not consider it mandatory that any given board endeavor to provide selections from all specializations which require flag officers, but, rather, that we should expect that over a period of several years the law of averages will permit us to fill required specializations while giving major emphasis to the selection of more broadly qualified leadership.

6. After giving careful consideration to qualification for sea command and required specializations, I believe the selection board should place great stress on seeking evidence, in the past performance of prospective flag officers, of the qualities of flexibility of mind, analytical thought processes, creativity and imagination which will best qualify them to compete with the increasingly professional and intellectual civilian leadership within an increasingly integrated Defense Department. I think that the evidence of such qualifications can be found in many categories of billets. However, I can think of none where the naval officer is put to a greater test of ability to rise above his background and possible prejudices than by demonstrated outstanding performance in Joint and International Staffs and Agencies. It is here that the common dogma of any one service must give way to the give and take of analysis from differing perspectives. It is here that he must rely less on the lessons of past experience and more on his basic qualities of intellect and thoughtfulness.

7. It seems to me that still another method of getting at the qualities mentioned in paragraph 6 above is through scrutiny of the manner in which the prospective flag officer has adapted himself to changes in professional billets involving distinctly different skills. That is, an officer who has performed brilliantly in a series of positions of related skills may not be as broadly capable of the kind of performance we need in the Navy of the future as one who has demonstrated similar performance in a series of different skills.

8. As a separate matter, if the Navy is to make its proper contribution to those councils where more than one military service is represented, it is important for the program of early selection of the past several years to continue in conformity with the general guidance provided by the Chief of Naval Personnel and approved by me. At the same time, in order that motivation to continue sustained performance in the more senior years may be provided, I consider it important that there be conformity also to the general guidance for numbers to be selected in the more senior categories.

9. I hope that the results of this board will provide a balance through a range in seniority, a range in specializations, and most importantly, a strong leavening of line officers broadly qualified to provide not only brilliant operational command but also unique intellectual leadership in any new and different positions—Navy, Joint, or International—into which they may be ordered.

Sincerely,

PAUL H. NITZE,
Secretary of the Navy

Adm. CHARLES D. GRIFFIN,
Commander in Chief,
U.S. Naval Forces, Europe,
Fleet Post Office, New York, N.Y.

IV. CAN THE PUBLIC CONTROL THE BUREAUCRATIZED STATE?

IS democratic control of the federal government in jeopardy? One's answer will depend largely upon the trends he emphasizes. Quite clearly, numerous strands of recent American history lend themselves to the view that democracy is ascendant. Malapportionment, suffrage restrictions, and election frauds have all been attacked with a high degree of success; free speech guarantees have progressively been extended; cultural barriers between regions, ethnic groups, and classes have been declining; and the educational level of the electorate has been rising.

On the other hand, those who actually govern the nation are probably less constrained by public opinion with every passing decade. The diversity and complexity of modern governmental activities overwhelm the electorate's capacity to develop strong opinions. To a lesser, but profound and increasing, degree, Congressmen are similarly disarmed. The pace or change is such that even specialists who spend their lives working in a single policy area frequently lose their capacity to "keep up" well before retirement age. The possessors of valued skills typically organize themselves into professions, and then bend their efforts to securing insulation from public scrutiny and control. Public agencies are increasingly bold in their endeavors to build favorable public images by controlling the flow of information about their activities. The litany might be extended, and the individual propositions refined, almost indefinitely.

This section is concerned with trends of the latter type: those which contribute to the apparently widening gulf between the public's independent opinions and the political system's policy outputs.* Its purpose is to stimulate your thought, first,

* For simplicity's sake, the term "independent" is here employed to include all opinions but those which policy-makers can treat as manipulable over the short run.

about how fundamentally these trends are altering the political system, and second, about how the system is compensating for them. Among the more optimistic lines of interpretation that you may wish to explore—selected on the premise that pessimistic examples will readily occur to you—are the following: (1) Perhaps the chain of command from the public to its governors has become longer, more indirect, and more difficult to trace precisely, without becoming substantially less effective. (2) Perhaps what should be emphasized is that even as the democratic influence has been declining within the government, the government has been increasing its influence on the rest of society. The net result may well be a gain in terms of democracy's impact on the social system as a whole. (3) Perhaps theory should focus on the ever-increasing significance of professionalism as a supplement to democracy in the checking of bureaucratic arbitrariness. (4) In the same vein, perhaps the taking-off point for analysis should be that Americans have never considered responsiveness to be the sole criterion of a good governmental system. On the contrary, their most characteristic position has been that in excess democracy leads to mischievous results, and that it is best conceived as a process for imposing broad constraints upon government—not for controlling its activities in detail. (This approach should lead to a consideration of the precise kinds of constraints that the electorate *can* now impose upon the government, and whether their effectiveness is dangerously on the wane.)

Section IV-A, which immediately follows, is essentially a case study. Secrecy and news management are but examples, though among the most important ones, of the factors that many believe are progressively chipping away at the electorate's capacity to constrain the federal bureaucracy. Section IV-B, by contrast, has an extremely broad focus and a normative orientation. Its subject is general approaches to domesticating the modern national bureaucracy's power potential.

A.   Secrecy and News Management

DEMOCRATIC forms unaccompanied by free political inquiry and discussion are hollow shells. This view has traditionally pervaded both the theory and practice of American government. Program for program (a qualification which involves, *inter alia,* taking account of this country's unusual security responsibilities), the American political system is one of the world's most open. The American press is remarkably vigorous in its pursuit of "inside" stories. And the American people are perhaps the freest in the world to criticize their incumbent governors of any moment.

Still, there are grounds for disquiet about the future of political criticism in American democracy. Knowledge is power; and the disparity between the bureaucracy's knowledge and that of its potential critics (not excluding Congressmen) is constantly growing. In part, this trend is simply a product of the knowledge explosion and the fantastic proliferation of government programs. Increasingly, however, it is also a product of policy. The justifications for keeping some information about public activities out of the public domain are persuasive: national security, the need to protect confidential sources, individual rights of privacy, etc. The likelihood that the bureaucracy will become obsessed with the need for secrecy, however, is great; and the implications for democratic control if it does are ominous. The prospect is not totally far-fetched of discussion being left *free,* while gradually being rendered *ineffectual as a mechanism of democratic control* by the government's systematic distortion of its information base.

Full-scale "news management" entails much more, of course, than simply leaving a void where there might be news. It also involves filling that void, by releasing information selectively, and by employing a whole panoply of public relations techniques to ensure that it is both sympathetically interpreted and widely disseminated. High level officials typically maintain (1) that they do not try to manage the news, (2) that they could not even if they would, and (3) that the proof of the pudding is the extent to which their policies are criticized. Perhaps the selections which follow will help you to assess these arguments when you run across them in future.

Harry Howe Ransom judges that the central problems posed by secrecy are two: how to balance the people's need to know with the dangers of disclosure, and how to keep those charged with deciding what information should be released from employing their authority as a political weapon. He concludes that the forces of secrecy are overwhelming those of openness, not as a result of cool appraisals of national needs but rather in consequence of biases in the decision structure. If you find his case persuasive, you will wish to consider whether (and, if so, how) these biases might be remedied, and whether outsiders generally have any means of distinguishing between legitimate and politically inspired uses of secrecy.

By contrast with Ransom, Douglass Cater maintains that few secrets of political relevance are successfully kept in the American system. He attributes this "failure" to the lack of centralization in American government, coupled with the importance of publicity as a weapon in interagency power struggles. Other writers on this theme have hypothesized two additional causes: first, that great numbers of high level administrators have spent most of their working lives in the private sector, with the result that their internalization of public service professional norms is weak; and second, that the liberal ideal of disclosure has always been unusually strong in the American tradition. By way of illustrating the latter point, it is significant that the reporter who publishes a secret document commits no crime in the United States. The public official who "leaked" it is culpable, but conclusive evidence as to his identity is generally impossible to secure.

Although unworried about the public's capacity to obtain all the raw data that it needs, Cater believes that the methods by which much information is released pose serious threats to the public's capacity to *evaluate* the news. After reading his brief for this definition of the news management "problem," you may wish to consider such questions as the following: Are you persuaded that secrecy *per se* is a false issue? How might the news media help the public to evaluate unattributed news? How should the law deal with officials who "leak" and news media which disseminate classified information? What do you think of the proposal (reviewed by Cater) to have an independent judicialized agency monitor excesses of secrecy and news management? If you reject this proposal, have you any alternative ideas on how the balance between openness and other national values should be drawn?

From May 1962 through March 1964, John Mecklin helped "manage" the news from Saigon. In the end, he lost faith in his role, resigned, and wrote a book describing his experiences. The selection reproduced here constitutes both the core of his story and a case study of one of the bitterest disputes between officialdom and the press in American history. Reviewing the outcome of this battle, Mecklin concludes that the government side suffered a rout. Although few officials had serious compunctions about misleading them, the best reporters on the spot managed to piece together a fairly accurate picture of events. If anything, Mecklin believes, their stories were biased in the direction of *excessive* skepticism toward official pronouncements. Moreover, they treated the Administration's lack of candor as itself a major story, with the result that public confidence in the Administration's veracity declined.

The capstone of this debacle was that—by subconsciously "willing" greater consistency between its knowledge, its policies, and what it wished the press to believe —the U.S. Mission in Saigon came to believe its own misrepresentations. It reported them faithfully to Washington, which was also taken in—though, to repeat, the best reporters covering the war were not. The remarkable thing about Mecklin's account is that it makes this syndrome comprehensible. This is not to say that effective news management is always, or even usually, impossible. The single situation Mecklin observed was full of peculiarities, including the radical nature of the disparity between official optimism and the observably deteriorating war situation. Even in this situation, moreover, the Administration succeeded in taming most of the press most of the time. The vast majority of journalists in Vietnam reported the U.S. Mission's handouts uncritically, and some of the others (including at least two who resigned from *Time* magazine in protest) regularly had their dispatches rewritten by editors back home who were determined to print only facts and interpretations compatible with the official line. Thus, it is well to keep in mind that the effectiveness of news management is a matter of degree. Mecklin considers the effort he describes to have been a failure, but this judgment conveys more information about the high standard of success that had come to be taken for granted than about what actually happened. Taking off from Mecklin's analysis, however, you may wish to reflect more generally than he does on the circumstances in which news management is likely to be most effective, and on those in which it is most likely to be frustrated.

SECRECY, DEFENSE, AND DEMOCRACY *
Harry H. Ransom

I

A PRINCIPAL distinction between a free and a totalitarian society is that in the latter the government controls the formal media of communication. But even in a free society government-imposed secrecy for intelligence operations and reports is regarded as acceptable practice and traditional necessity. There have always been legitimate military and state secrets in a democracy, not only in wartime but in the conduct of peacetime defense and diplomacy. The number of state secrets tends to vary in proportion to the government's concern about threats to the common defense.

Since World War II government secrecy has been extended far beyond the traditional peacetime boundaries. Democratic man's "right to know" about what his government is doing is now challenged by a new concept of "need to know" and by the government's increasing ability, in the name of national security, to manipulate the news as an instrument of policy. The burden of proof has shifted from government, once required to defend its secrecy, to Congress, the press, or the individual citizen in or out of government, who now must prove a "need to know" certain categories of information.

An ever-expanding secrecy, or its corollary—state management of the flow of critical information—is not the result of the Cold War alone. Certainly the Communists' Iron Curtain around strategic information has provoked the American government, whatever the party in power, to retaliate with greater domestic secrecy than ever before. But beyond this, the growing role of government in American life and the increasing complexity in the forms and functions of the great Federal bureaucracy impose their own secrecy requirements—not always, it must be said, to the detriment of individual freedom.

* From Harry H. Ransom, *Can American Democracy Survive Cold War?* (New York: Doubleday, 1963), Anchor paperback edition, pp. 196–199, 208–219, 224–227. Copyright, 1963, by Harry H. Ransom. Reprinted by permission of Doubleday & Company, Inc.

The national security label has become a convenient one to apply to almost any category of information the Administration in power wants to protect from disclosure, even though at times the only "security" sought may be the security of the party in power.

Because information about defense plans, policies, programs and weapons systems, if prematurely disclosed, can be of great strategic value to a potential enemy (including domestic "enemies" of policies in the planning stage), the government has created an elaborate security system for classifying documents according to degrees of secrecy required. Such a system is not without its costs. It can actually endanger security by hampering scientific progress, alienating allies, and making difficult the existence of a well-informed electorate, or, at the very least, a knowledgeable, attentive public.

The problem was once concisely summed up by Dr. Vannevar Bush as that of "distinguishing between information which rightly and properly belongs to every man and information which for the safety and security of every man must be protected." It is far easier to state the problem than to solve it.

In the contemporary atmosphere the pressures for secrecy are overpowering the pressures for disclosure. The size and scope of national security programs extend the arguments for secrecy beyond those that normally attend the growth of a giant bureaucracy, and unbalance the Executive-Legislative relationship. The expanding role of government in the economic life of the nation, bringing into government files a massive amount of confidential data on corporations, institutions, and individuals, has inevitably increased the amount of bureaucratic secrecy. The expansion of the civil service, especially in an era that has been characterized by widespread "loyalty" investigations, has produced highly personal information on the lives of millions of Americans. The increasing number of bureaucratic organizations has multiplied the amount of intragovernmental flow of confidential, privileged communications. The enormity of the task of interdepartmental coordination of defense plans and policies greatly augments the number of documents stamped "Secret."

Another factor nurturing secrecy is the fact that government agencies have become "public relations" conscious. This has led to a centralization of the public-information function in the various departments and agencies, in the hope of manipulating the departmental image in the public mind. Joseph and Stewart Alsop have termed this a "progressive *embourgeoisement*" of government departments, stemming from their desire to put up a good front and to expand their size and service. Behind the penchant for secrecy and good public relations lies the belief of most bureaucrats—this term is used here in its objective sense—that Congress and the public cannot comprehend crucial issues of public policy and should not be informed until decisions have been made. These bureaucrats also recognize that information is one of the most powerful of weapons in the interdepartmental competition over the allocation of national resources. Both the FBI and the Navy, to take random examples, would like the public to believe that their services represent the nation's "first line of defense."

Centralizing public information tends to establish an agency "party line," restricting the flow of objective information. Information is selectively released by press agents. Congressman John Moss, Democrat, California, has described one particular tactic: "Not only has the Pentagon invented dozens of ways of keeping information secret, but it has full time platoons of press agents managing news and attempting to dull reporters' senses through floods of hand-outs." [1]

Attempts to strike a balance between public disclosure and secrecy have taken the form of an elaborate system of classifying privileged information into three major categories, TOP SECRET, SECRET, and CONFIDENTIAL. There are also higher categories whose classifying labels are themselves secret. One wag has suggested that the highest security classification is: "Burn Before Reading." And there is a complex informal system for maintaining the secrecy of internal administrative information, not necessarily sensitive in the military security sense, but thought to be *privileged* in the administrative sense. By means of Executive Orders, directives, and regulations, elaborate systems now exist for prior review and censorship or clearance of information emanating from the Department of Defense, the military services, and associated national security agencies. . . .

III

The Cold War has coincided with the new cult of government public relations and with dramatic developments in communications technology. At the same time, the bipolarization of world power, an accelerating technology, the commitment to the concept of collective allied security, and the massive machinery for national defense have resulted in the most restrictive government information policies in peacetime history.

While government control of information during "hot" wars met with the general cooperation of the mass-communications media, such a high degree of press self-restraint cannot be expected in periods of ill-defined "Cold" War. Since World War II editors and reporters have complained loudly and often that the sources of independent information within the government are drying up, and that the government has been flooding the press and the public with "managed" information.

James Reston has referred to government officials' "growing tendency to manage the news," [2] and Marquis W. Childs commented in 1954:

Among working reporters in Washington there is a growing concern over what appears to be a concerted effort to suppress legitimate news—and with a system of rewards and punishments to see to it that only news which is favorable, or is reported

1. Address, October 8, 1960, at Reno, Nevada. Many of these points are cogently discussed in Francis Rourke, "Secrecy in American Bureaucracy," *Political Science Quarterly,* December 1957, pp. 544–48.
2. Testimony in *Hearings,* Subcommittee on Government Information, House Committee on Government Operations, November 7, 1955, Part I, p. 25. For a more recent description of conditions, see Clark R. Mollenhoff, *Washington Cover-Up,* Garden City, New York, Doubleday, 1962.

in a favorable light is given to the public. Partly this is a carry-over from the big and little wars of the past fifteen years, when propaganda was an instrument of warfare. Partly it reflects the tensions of the cold war and the continuing struggle against Communist imperialism.[3]

It was, however, from a different angle that President Kennedy viewed the problem after the CIA-sponsored attempt to invade Cuba in April 1961 had failed. Speaking to the American Newspaper Publishers Association he said that this time of "peace and peril" creates a threat to national security never exceeded even at the height of any of our past wars. He observed that America's foes have "boasted openly of acquiring through our newspapers information they otherwise would hire agents to acquire through theft, bribery or espionage." Such information—on our covert intelligence preparations, on the strength, location, and nature of our forces and weapons, and details on secret missile tracking mechanisms—would never have been revealed by the press under the conditions of a declared emergency or war. But the President at this time declared no such emergency. Rather he pleaded with the mass communications media to exercise discrimination between the "facts the public deserves to know" and the news it doesn't, and to exercise voluntary self-restraint. Short of declared war, can such a formula be expected? The President's response is revealing: "Perhaps there is no answer to the dilemma faced by a free and open society in a cold and secret war."

Official policies have attempted to resolve the dilemma, but the balance has been increasingly weighted on secrecy's side. Following "unification" of the armed forces in 1947, the first Secretary of Defense, James Forrestal, issued a memorandum on October 10, 1947, which dealt with public relations. In addition to restricting security information, Mr. Forrestal directed that only data "not inimical to the national security shall be released." He added that the Unification Act of 1947 established a unity principle and "the conduct of public relations is to conform to the spirit of the law." It is surprising now to read his further decree that public disclosures of "interservice controversies are to be avoided."

To this end he required *prior approval* by his office of announcements on subjects (principally general policies, budget making, and interservice disputes) that were his responsibility as Secretary of Defense. Included under this directive was any news release affecting more than one department unless the release had the agreement of all departments concerned.

Forrestal's "unity" directive was supplemented on February 4, 1948, by another memorandum to the Secretaries of the three services and the Joint Chiefs of Staff, stipulating that no speech, press release, or article touching upon a controversial subject could be released either by them or by the Under Secretaries, Assistant Secretaries, Deputy Chiefs of Staff or the Vice Chief of Naval Operations without prior clearance from the Defense Secretary's office. This directive, he said, was "intended to promote a closer and more harmonious integration of the armed forces by preventing the inevitable differences of opin-

3. United Features syndicated column, December 3, 1954.

ion about policy matters from becoming topics of public debate and controversy." Anyone who has followed military affairs between 1948–62 knows that the directive has been something less than effective.

To administer control of such information Secretary Forrestal established, on July 19, 1948, an Office of Public Information within the National Military Establishment. A director was made specifically responsible for "developing and coordinating over-all public information matters." On March 17, 1949, Secretary Forrestal further centralized all public information activities of the military establishment within the Office of the Secretary of Defense. At the same time, he assembled various media representatives to discuss the problem of departmental "leaks" and the more prompt release of non-security technical information. He urged upon representatives of the press "an assumption . . . of their responsibility in voluntarily refraining from publishing information detrimental to our national security." He advocated a "security advisory council" of six media representatives to advise the Secretary and guide the press, but when he was unable to persuade the press of the necessity and feasibility of this proposal, he abandoned the idea and designated the Office of Public Information as "the sole agency for the National Military Establishment as the seat of government for dissemination of information to media of public information." Secretary Forrestal retired from office soon after this and his successor, Mr. Louis Johnson, on April 14, 1949, announced an even more restrictive policy termed by the press a "gag rule." This was subsequently rescinded on June 4, 1949.

By June 1950, the United States was at war in Korea, and some of the atmosphere that had prevailed during World War II returned. Voluntary censorship was attempted in Korea but soon gave way to field press censorship following unfriendly press relations between General Douglas MacArthur and some of the war correspondents. In December 1950, President Truman directed prior White House clearance of policy statements by high military officials. It was this requirement that Mr. Truman accused General MacArthur of disobeying when he relieved him of his command the following April.

Since 1950 the concept of security has expanded far beyond the military establishment. The Truman Executive Order No. 10-290 of September 24, 1951, spelled out censorship regulations based largely upon State Department and military censorship codes for all Federal Departments, and empowered heads of Federal agencies to designate persons within their organizations authorized to classify information.

This order drew sweeping condemnation from such organizations as the American Society of Newspaper Editors, the Sigma Delta Chi journalistic fraternity, and the managing editors of the Associated Press, on the grounds that: it extended to non-military agencies what was essentially a military classification scheme; it failed to define the precise criteria for the various categories of classification; it invested agency heads with power to delegate classifying responsibilities; it provided no system for reviewing the decisions of classifying officers; and it established no appeal system from such decisions.

President Truman, in promulgating Executive Order 10-290, admonished government officials not to abuse their new authority or use it to cover up maladministration or dishonesty. He promised that his own White House press office would handle any complaints of overclassification or other abuses. The press did not rest easily with these assurances and criticism continued.

The Truman order also incurred the ire of the President's political opponents in the Senate. On October 2, 1951, Senator Styles Bridges of New Hampshire and twenty-four other Republican Senators issued a statement, in part, as follows:

We . . . pledge to the American people that we shall fight to guarantee that in the difficult days ahead, no man's voice shall be silenced. We shall vigorously resist any attempt to conceal the facts from the American people. We shall defend to the utmost the fundamental right of free, unlimited discussion of controversial questions in government. We shall rally to the defense of any person against whom reprisals are directed as a result of his constitutional right of freedom of speech.

Later, on September 18, 1952, the staff of the Republican Policy Committee of the United States Senate issued a long report, "The Growth of Federal Censorship under 20 Years of Democratic Administration." And the 1952 Republican Party platform contained the pledge: ". . . not to infringe by censorship or gag order the right of a free people to know what their government is doing."

Despite this pledge most segments of the press seem to agree that during the period 1953–60, secrecy in the Executive branch became more pervasive than ever. Revelations of continued progress in Soviet science and technology and of Soviet espionage activities convinced many persons that American information security was not tight enough. Many assumed, incorrectly, that the chief basis for Soviet technological achievement was information carelessly revealed by, or stolen from, the United States.

President Eisenhower attempted to correct the worst abuses of Truman's Executive Order 10-290 by substituting another Executive Order, Number 10-501, on November 6, 1953. This deprived twenty-eight Federal agencies of power to classify information on security grounds, restricting classification powers to seventeen agencies; limited the authority of agency heads to delegate this responsibility; attempted to define the various security classifications more clearly; and made provisions for appeal and review, allowing the press, for example, to appeal to higher authority an official's decision to deny access to specific information.

Although most critics believed that the new order was an improvement over prior regulations, a number felt that it was no more than "window dressing." Allen Raymond, spokesman for the press, put it this way: "Actually all this new Eisenhower order did was to placate some of the editors, temporarily, and eliminate a few of the more glaring absurdities in President Truman's directive." [4]

4. Allen Raymond, Report to the American Civil Liberties Union, October 24, 1955, p. 39. This report is an excellent review of the secrecy issue during this period.

The fires of controversy were to burn still brighter in the two years that followed. Fuel was added by two actions of the Executive branch, one in 1954, the other in the year following.

The 1954 action came on November 5, when Secretary of Commerce Sinclair Weeks announced that at Presidential direction, as recommended by the National Security Council, the Office of Strategic Information was to be established within the Department of Commerce to work with the business community in "voluntary efforts to prevent unclassified data from being made available to those foreign nations which might use data in a manner harmful to the United States." In the interest of national security, restrictions were placed upon the release to news media of certain kinds of industrial information. This provoked immediate protests from the press, from the technical and trade publications chiefly affected, and from journalism societies.

A public relations specialist, R. Karl Honaman from Bell Laboratories, was named Director of the Office of Strategic Information. Mr. Honaman had to try to balance two conflicting requirements: the need for interindustry communication—so important to technological progress—and the presumed need to protect information of strategic importance. This move by the government to institute, in effect, a fourth classification—*Strategic Information*—was criticized, particularly from within the journalistic fraternity, on a number of specific counts: a new classification had been added by an Administration pledged to freer flow of information from the Executive branch; no clear-cut definition of "strategic information" was made; danger existed that the system could be used to discriminate against some companies while showing partiality to others by giving out information on a "need to know" basis; a new kind of censorship, albeit voluntary, was to be instituted on non-military information; and such a system would inhibit and stifle technological progress.

Commenting on the NSC-Presidential directive creating the Office of Strategic Information, Walter J. Murphy, editorial director of the Applied Journals of the American Chemical Society, told Congress:

There seems to be a childlike belief on the part of a great many people in this country—people who should know better—that (1) we have all, or practically all, of the scientific and technical brainpower of the world residing in this country. (2) If each night we lock up our store of scientific and technical reports, we will thereby curtail the scientific and technological advances of other countries.
. . . If we padlock our scientific and technical knowledge, we will be withholding it from our own scientists and technologists just as much as from a potential enemy. Anyone who has had the slightest contact with science knows it is an elementary fact that a report of one piece of progress catalyzes further advances.
. . .[5]

Under a barrage of similar criticism, the Office of Strategic Information went out of existence on June 30, 1957, perhaps because it represented a misguided effort with the unintentional consequence of effecting a closed society.

5. From *Hearings* of April 27, 1956, in *25th Intermediate Report*, House Committee on Government Operations, *Report* No. 2947, 1956, p. 23.

The immediate cause of its demise was the failure of the Administration to obtain appropriations for its continuance in the face of strong Congressional opposition, organized and led by Democratic Congressman John E. Moss of California and his House Subcommittee on Government Information of the Government Operations Committee.

The new public relations spirit appeared to be predominating when, on March 29, 1955, Secretary of Defense Wilson issued a directive requiring officials of his department to adhere to new regulations for prior review and clearance of material to be published. The directive stated in part:

Such review and clearance shall be related not only to a determination of whether release of the material would involve any technical or substantive violation of security but also to a determination of whether release or publication of the material would constitute a constructive contribution to the primary mission of the Department of Defense.

This "positive thinking" directive specifically required that manuscripts, speeches, and news items to be released to the public through news media by military or civilian personnel of the Department of Defense be submitted for review and clearance not less than three days in advance of public release, and required all Defense Department personnel to assume responsibility for their speeches, articles, and information releases being "consistent with the national security and the policies and objectives of the Department of Defense."

The Defense Secretary simultaneously issued a memorandum directing each service secretary to supplant military officers with civilians as public information chiefs, and to reduce sharply service public-information personnel. These new regulations were believed to be the result of the Secretary's growing impatience with publicity about interservice rivalries. They were also apparently the result of White House pressure. President Eisenhower had become incensed on a number of occasions about the amount of unauthorized information on new weapons and defense planning appearing in the press.

The orders produced more loud protests from the press. Hanson W. Baldwin wrote in *The New York Times* that "A new kind of iron curtain, Pentagon model, is being tried out in Washington this week." American journalistic societies, particularly the Freedom of Information Committee of the American Society of Newspaper Editors, made formal protests to the Pentagon, demanding a clear definition of what would constitute a "constructive contribution." The main point of the criticism was that it is the press and the public, after all, who decide what is, in fact, "constructive." Many press representatives protested vigorously at a designation of a "gray area" in security information, implying the existence of information that is not legitimately a military secret but might prove helpful to a potential enemy, particularly when collated with additional facts.

The nub of the matter was that secrecy had been extended beyond any legitimate or necessary boundary. A striking example of the unnecessary secrecy that was being practiced is the fact that for some years the velocity at which an intercontinental ballistic missile could travel was considered secret information. Yet the word "ballistic" and the freely announced missile's range of, say, 6000 miles almost automatically spells out this velocity to anyone with the knowledge of how to calculate it.

The Harvard Library case is another example. During World War II, Harvard scientists undertook secret research for the armed services. More than a decade later the Harvard Library found itself burdened with a mass of material still labeled secret. Not only was this unavailable to Harvard scientists, there was no one on hand with "clearance" to examine the material which continued, year after year, to occupy badly needed space. Storage cost ran to $1200 per year. Congressman John E. Moss, attempting to remove the albatross, appealed to the Secretary of Defense:

Harvard . . . is burdened with the cost of storing and protecting secret material which no one at Harvard can look at and which Harvard can't get declassified, can't return to the Government, can't give away, and can't burn. At the same time, material which would be of value to scientists and scholars is padlocked beyond their reach.[6]

A sensible classification system would be one in which such data was automatically declassified by a certain date, unless a deliberate decision were made to keep it secret. Risks would be involved in such a policy, no doubt, but gains would very likely outweigh loss.

A more difficult problem is the bureaucrat's tendency to overclassify in the initial step. Without a basic change in attitude it will be unrealistic to expect an individual officer to resist this temptation. No one is punished for overclassification, but there are reprimands for underclassification. The only incentives for releasing information are the protests of scientists, newsmen, or Congressmen. Until this is changed and fewer persons (over a million in 1960) have the authority to classify, the mountainous mass of documents, some perhaps permanently secret, will grow.

Many of these problems were emphasized in the Democratic Party's successful drive to capture the White House in the 1960 election. Once in office and having felt the sharpness of the dilemma's horns, the President called attention, after the Cuban fiasco of April 1961, to a "challenge of our times" which imposes "two requirements that may seem almost contradictory in tone, but which must be reconciled and fulfilled. . . . the need for greater public information and . . . the need for greater official secrecy."

In a directive on May 31, 1961, Secretary of Defense McNamara promulgated four "principles" of public information policy: (1) In a democratic society the public must be kept informed of major issues, including the arguments on both sides of any major controversy. The public also is entitled to know about mistakes and ineffective administration and operations. "The public has at least as much right to bad news as to good news." (2) However, information that can materially assist the enemy must not be disclosed. And toward this end "it is equally as important to avoid overclassification—when in

6. Letter of May 24, 1957, quoted in House Committee on Government Operations, 27th Annual Report, House *Report* No. 1884, June 16, 1958, p. 118.

doubt underclassify. In no event should overclassification be used to avoid public discussion of controversial issues." (3) Public statements by Pentagon officials, civilian and military, which appear to reflect Department of Defense policy must reflect that policy in fact. (4) In their public statements, all Defense officials should confine themselves to defense matters. Specifically they must avoid foreign policy matters, a field reserved to the President and the Secretary of State. Otherwise there is danger that when military officers state their opinions on foreign policy matters, their words may be taken as the policy of the government. . . .

IV

. . . In 1822, James Madison wrote:

. . . a people who mean to be their own governors must arm themselves with the power knowledge gives. A popular government without popular information or the means of acquiring it is but a prologue to a farce or a tragedy or perhaps both.[7]

In 1956 Walter Millis, commenting on the Eisenhower years, observed: "We have cloaked the operations of the Executive Branch of Government in veils of secrecy unknown to any previous epoch of our history." [8]

The sharp contrast between the comments of Madison and Millis raises at least two fundamental questions: whether all the principles of the Founding Fathers meet the requirements of national security in the nuclear-missile age; and whether recent government leaders, in their preoccupation with security, have forgotten the importance of a free flow of information in a democratic system.

A major bulwark of liberty is a citizenry sufficiently informed about the major issues of public policy to participate in a meaningful way in self-government; and a prime requisite for progress is a high degree of freedom of information in science and its application. Democracy and progress can both be debilitated if leaders unnecessarily enshroud government operations with a curtain of secrecy. Expert witnesses before the House Special Subcommittee on Government Information testified in 1956 that there would have been no development of nuclear power if the security regulations of 1956 had been in force in 1939.

But the democratic way of life may be destroyed in another way—by disclosing to a potential enemy, openly or inadvertently, special categories of information that will enable him to surpass, surprise, or deter us with modern instruments of force. And enlightened innovations in public policy can, in the discussion or planning stage, perish in the harsh glare of premature publicity. In the consensus-building process of American policy making, there are always those opponents to change of any kind who can use bits of distorted information as a weapon to maintain the *status quo*.

A central problem for democratic government, then, is to discover precisely

7. Letter to W. T. Barry, August 4, 1822, *The Complete Madison*, ed., Saul K. Padover, New York, Harper, 1953, p. 337.
8. *Arms and Men: A Study in American Military History*, New York, Putnam, 1956, p. 360.

what types of information truly deserve secrecy, and when. A high price must be paid for secrecy, perhaps an incalculable amount—in civil liberties, speed and diffusion of scientific development, and knowledge and public understanding of the realities of world politics. There is also a calculable direct dollar cost: hundreds of millions of dollars annually for guards, security measures, personnel investigations, codes, and other special procedures. These expenditures must be balanced against the potential costs of disclosure of secret data that might dry up sources of information about potential enemies, increase the efficiency of enemy weapons and countermeasures, and in general solve many of the potential enemy's strategic problems.

Aside from national security considerations, an obsession with secrecy seems to be a natural stage all bureaucracies eventually reach if they are permitted to follow their inherent tendency without adequate counterpressures. Bureaucracies err on the side of secrecy. Democratic leadership must strive to thwart this tendency.

In America's past wars, the censorship and secrecy required have been effected through the cooperation of most elements in our society. Each war, nevertheless, has left its large residue of secrecy. In the Cold War, national consensus on policy and strategy are often absent. Both the nature of the threat and the best means of meeting it are highly debatable. National purpose and objectives are variously defined by different groups, this condition being, in fact, a prime characteristic of the democratic idea.

In the Cold War most of the pressures and many of the strongest arguments have been for greater government secrecy. But as these pressures have increased, they have fortunately had to contend with ever-present counterpressures . . .

SECRETS, SCOOPS, AND LEAKS *
Douglass Cater

. . . FOR the Washington reporter there is a note of unreality about much of the outcry over security and secrecy. He feels that it fails to get at the heart of the matter—the method and the motivation for the leakage of secret information to the press. Comparatively little of the traffic is in classified documents. The stuff of the news is not composed of such documentation. The Alsop brothers, who have disclosed more than their share of secrets over the years, claim that neither one has read a classified document since 1947. "Furthermore, if anyone now made us a present of a classified document,"

* From Douglass Cater, *The Fourth Branch of Government* (Boston: Houghton Mifflin, 1959), Vintage paperback edition, pp. 121–130, 138–141. Reprinted by permission of the author and publisher.

they have testified, "we should reject it as firmly as we should reject a pot of poison."[1]

How does the press acquire its secrets? The techniques of the "scoop" in this field are varied. First of all, the astute reporter learns a good deal by intu-ition. He reflects quietly on the processes that must be going on within the government in response to a given situation. Senator Paul Douglas once likened this cerebration to the explanation by the idiot boy of how he found the stray blind horse. "I shut my eyes and asked myself where I'd go if I were a blind horse; I went, and the horse was there."

The reporter follows his hunches, picks up a piece of the story here, another piece there. He plays one source off against another. Soon the pattern of a story—not necessarily the complete story—begins to emerge. In this field of projective analysis, James Reston has few peers. The details of the way he broke the news of the thirty-day Korean Armistice Plan in 1951 illustrates his technique:

Last fall [Reston] began to feel disturbed about some background aspects of our negotiations. First there was the endless bickering over Kaesong, which seemed to him a trivial point. Then there were some leaks at the Pentagon about the stra-tegic disadvantages involved in signing a truce, emphasizing, for example, the fact that Chinese armies would be released for operations in Southeast Asia. Next came Colonel Hanley's statement about the massacres of American prisoners. And finally, Acheson, who was in Paris, made what seemed to Reston a maladroit talk calling the Chinese "sub-barbarians." With this circumstantial evidence at hand, Reston began calling on the embassies of some of the UN countries with troops in Korea, expecting to find them skeptical of U. S. sincerity in the truce negotiations. "I turned out to be wrong," he recalled later. "When I took my suspicions to the em-bassies, I found out that some kind of plan was in the works. Then I was able to get a confirmation at the Department—so I got a one day beat."[2]

Part of the technique comes from a reporter's sense of timing—the calcula-tion of the exact moment when pressure applied at a precise point in the gov-ernment will yield results. The late Anthony Leviero, of the *New York Times,* revealed extraordinary talents in this. His exclusive story giving details of the Truman-MacArthur conference on Wake Island in 1951 was a case in point. Leviero has left a first-person description of how he got this story:

It is not possible to tell all details of how the Wake Island story was obtained. It has to be done with some gobbledegook as to sources. On a rented television set on April 19, we watched and listened in the bureau office as MacArthur spoke before Congress. It soon became obvious that the speech would have a terrific impact and when it was over I said to Luther Huston that the country seemed to have for-gotten that Truman and MacArthur had met at Wake and were supposed to have agreed on almost everything.

I said I thought I ought to go after the Wake Island conference report. Huston told me to go ahead. (This disposes of the stories about a "plant," although I or

1. Joseph and Stewart Alsop, *The Reporter's Trade* (New York, 1958).
2. From "The Troubled Press," in *Fortune,* February 1952.

any other Washington correspondent would gladly accept a planted authentic document.)

I put in a call to source No. 1; he was out. Source No. 2 was in a conference, and that was also the story on source No. 3. I left a message in each instance and then it was a matter of waiting. The numbers have no significance as to the importance of the sources; they merely indicate the order in which they were called . . .

All afternoon I monitored my telephone and if I went to the men's room I told the switchboard girl that if anybody called to keep him on the wire until I returned. No. 3 called back first, after 7 P.M. I put the proposition to him that perhaps now was the time to tell the story of the Wake conference. I said I would have to see the whole story and promised to use discretion in covering up my method of obtaining it.

No. 3 promised to see what he could do, as he had to go to higher authority. About an hour later No. 1 called. I told him the proposition I had made to No. 3 and asked his support if he saw fit. At 11 P.M., while still in the office doing a Sunday story, No. 3 called and I told him what I had told No. 1.

When I arrived at the office at 11 A.M. next morning I found an urgent message to call home. Having just moved into a house, I could only think that the boiler had exploded, or the roof caved in. But Mrs. Leviero said that No. 3 had called to say that I should call No. 2.

No. 2 told me to come to such-and-such place at noon. I filled two fountain pens and went. He put the source material before me in its original authenticated form. I horrified him by asking if I could use a typewriter. So I used the pens, using up one and part of the other in two hours of feverish scribbling. I had lunch and returned to the office, my arm still numb with writer's cramp.

A final word on the claims of discomfited rivals that this was an Administration "plant." Without conceding the story came from the White House, I can say that never in more than three years of covering the place did a member of the President's staff offer me a story. But I often scored by asking at the right time. I believe that at least a dozen reporters for rival newspapers, if they had figured out the prevailing mood of Administration sources that day and made the right approach, could have had the story.[3]

But the reporter's intuition and sense of timing are only one side of the business of transmitting the secrets of government. Leviero would never have got his story if a government official had not decided to provide him the information. What causes the leak? One veteran reporter has written, "The leak or exclusive story is rarely an example of a reporter's persistence and skill. More often it is simply an evidence of the harassed necessity of some official to put a situation before the public with a spurious sense of drama in order to gain attention for it."[4] On occasion, of course, human frailties—vanity, desire for vengeance or recognition—have led an official to disclose secrets that he ought not to have. But the primary cause for the almost constant revelation of behind-the-scenes episodes of government is the power struggle that goes on within the government itself or among the governments doing business in Washington.

3. Anthony Leviero, "Wide Awake on Wake." in *Times Talk*, May 1951.
4. William S. White, "Trying to Find the Shape—If Any—of the News in Washington," in *Harper's Magazine*, August 1958.

On matters of foreign policy, the correspondent finds the foreign embassy in Washington is often a good peephole on what is happening behind the closed doors of the State Department. The embassy is not bound by purely American classifications about what is secret and what is not. But leakage does not end with the embassies. On national security matters, secrecy is repeatedly violated in the conflict among the great rival subgovernments in Washington—Air Force vs. Army vs. Navy; State vs. Treasury vs. Defense vs. the numberless special agencies and special assistants dealing in security matters. And, of course, there is the constant conflict between the Executive and Congress. These are not petty disputes. They represent the clash of major issues and ideas concerning the fate of the nation. Measured against the penalties incurred by a violation of secrecy, the benefits to be gained from publicity are at times irresistible to the partisans. . . .

This is the way our government works and will likely continue to work even in a time of national peril. The misguided official who attempts to clamp an iron-handed control on the flow of information is doomed to frustration. Congress, far from tightening the laws on secrecy, has been more disposed to investigate and expose excessive security imposed by the Executive departments. A more fruitful course for government would be to consider how the flow of information may be better timed and coordinated so that the public receives a balanced story. Too often the real damage caused by public disclosures comes from the fact that the information is partial and biased.

On the other hand, the serious observer on the Washington scene must agree that certain secrets should be kept secret for at least a calculated interval of time. It is possible by premature publicity to disrupt the whole process of policy formulation. Particularly during the preliminaries to diplomatic negotiation, it can be harmful to the country's interest for other governments to be tipped off in advance about our government's bargaining position. Sometimes even the method in which a story is broken can be disastrous. The United Press's sensational disclosure of "Fail Safe," the story of our Strategic Air Command's operations in the Arctic, was a case in point. It should have been possible to describe our military precautions without resorting to the phony dramatics about bombers headed toward Moscow which alarmed our allies and provided propaganda material for the Soviets.

From time to time members of the press and government alike have come up with proposals for boards of impartial umpires to pass judgment on the more serious clashes over secrecy. Its powers could be limited. Indeed, the punishment of public censure ought to be adequate enforcement authority for a board sufficiently prestigious and unprejudiced. It would go a long way toward curtailing the excesses of secrecy in the government and sensationalism in the press.

Despite the various proposals for a public monitor in this field nothing has ever come of it. James V. Forrestal, the first Secretary of Defense, gave long and serious consideration to the problem. He felt that a system could be made to work if a government advisory committee could be established that the press and public would accept as "above self-serving." But, according to a newspaperman who knew him well, "Forrestal never could envisage a committee with that acceptance in peacetime."[5] It is a sad and sobering thought that Forrestal may well have been right.

. . . For the average citizen, who can be expected to bring only so much sophistication to the business of reading his newspaper, . . . unattributed news can be a highly confusing matter. Take, for example, one of the most notable instances of this practice. It happened during the spring of 1955 when there was one of the recurrent crises with the Chinese Reds over the islands in the Formosa Strait. On Saturday, March 26, the reader found a three-column thirty-six-point headline in the upper right-hand corner of page one in the *New York Times:* U.S. EXPECTS CHINESE REDS TO ATTACK ISLES IN APRIL; WEIGHS ALL OUT DEFENSE. Three days later, the reader found another headline in the same position, same type: EISENHOWER SEES NO WAR NOW OVER CHINESE ISLES.

If he studied the accompanying stories closely, he noted one similarity amid the contradictions. Neither had a single word to indicate who had presumed to speak in the first instance for the United States or in the second for President Eisenhower. The reader was obliged to take the word of the reporters, in these two instances highly reliable men, that their awesome stories were based on fact.

In point of fact, the source of the first story was Chief of Naval Operations Robert B. Carney, speaking to a select group of reporters at a background dinner. The second was none other than the White House press secretary, James Hagerty, who attended a hastily called second background conference in order to repudiate the stories arising out of the first.

During that particularly troublesome winter and spring, the citizen was obliged to accept a sizable quantity of news in this fashion. He was told that the evacuation of the Tachen Islands was a retrenchment designed to prevent a situation in which the Chinese Nationalists might involve us in fighting for some comparatively worthless real estate. Later he learned, via the headlines, that a "China Stalemate Foreseen by US in Formosa Policy" with a continuing situation of neither war nor peace. He was subsequently given lengthy and varying descriptions of the timing, the extent, and the conditions of potential war in the Far East, but always without being told who was making these life and death judgments. One newspaperman catalogued five basic contradictions in the stories emerging during a few days of late March 1955. It was truly a period of the background story gone wild.

But it was by no means a unique period. Cloaked news has become an institutional practice in the conduct of modern government in Washington, part of the regular intercourse between government and the press. During periods of high tension when formal channels of communication such as the President's and the Secretary of State's press conferences are cut off, it often becomes the major means by which important news is transmitted. In the words of one newspaperman describing the time of the Middle East crisis in 1956, "During the most critical period in recent months, at a time when any word out of

5. Arthur Krock, in the *New York Times,* July 2, 1957.

Washington was considered of international significance, what had developed, it appeared, was government by leak." . . .

Inevitably, the case against cloaked news gets down to the fundamental concepts of reporting. What is the reporter's responsibility? Is he an intelligence agent for his paper and via it the American public? Or is he to be made a tool of the government's counterintelligence operations? Arthur M. Schlesinger, Jr., has posed the alternatives in fairly stark terms: "Washington newspapermen today hardly know whether to believe the Secretary of State, because they do not know if he is speaking to them as reporters or seeking to use them as instruments of psychological warfare. . . . What is the responsibility of a newspaperman when he discovers that some rumored development of policy is really only a psychological warfare trick? Should he print the truth at the risk of wrecking the plans of the Secretary of State? Or should he suppress the truth, betray himself, and deceive the American people?" [6]

In this, as in much that concerns reporting in Washington, the absolutist position has little relevancy to the reporter's workaday world. He cannot narrowly demarcate his sphere of operations. He is caught and intimately involved in the ceaseless battle of intelligence versus counterintelligence. He can remove himself from the battlefield only at the risk of negating his role as a reporter.

A more fruitful inquiry may be directed into the conditions that should be imposed on cloaked news as a technique of communication. On the government's part, there needs to be a clearer recognition of the limits to which this practice can go. No matter how compelling the exigencies, the press in a free society should not be turned into the government's propaganda instrument. A fine line has to be drawn between the diplomatic and the deceitful. The government went over that line when, during the Quemoy-Matsu crisis of August 1958, Secretary Dulles issued a public statement of official policy, then immediately afterward proceeded to make more sweeping pronouncements to reporters on a not-for-attribution basis. He was transferring an unfair burden to the reporter.

The main responsibility in guarding against the misuse of counterintelligence, however, lies not with government but with the press. Just as government must take the initiative in safeguarding its essential secrets, so the reporter must in the first instance decide what is proper and what is improper practice in the handling of the leak.

There are good grounds for thoughtful review in this field. In his eagerness to get at the inside news, even the good reporter frequently loses the keen discrimination he shows in his more open reporting. As William S. White has written, "Often reporters handle a leaked story with a solemn uncriticalness. The documents, or whatever, are ceremoniously produced for the public—which at times must scratch its head in perplexity as to what the devil they are

6. Arthur M. Schlesinger, Jr., "Psychological Warfare: Can It Sell Freedom?" in *The Reporter,* March 31, 1953.

all about. The motivation for the leak usually is not mentioned, although that may be the most significant part of the story." [7]

One example of this: the reader needed to know in order to understand the Admiral Carney story that this attitude toward an inevitable war in Asia was nothing new on Carney's part. Indeed, after the fall of Dienbienphu ten months earlier, Carney had made a similar exhortation in a public speech, comparing the situation to that of Munich. No news story could have been complete without mentioning this long standing attitude of the man or the fact that others, even among the Joint Chiefs, disagreed with him. Instead, the sudden publication of the unattributed stories in many of the major newspapers made it look as if all official Washington had arrived simultaneously at the prediction of war.

The reporter is guilty of deceits in the business of cloaking the news. He refers vaguely to "informed circles" implying a plurality of opinion when in fact he may be quoting the views of one person. He plays leaks with an importance they would not deserve if their sources were made known.

There is no reason why the rules for cloaked news cannot be made to fit the needs of honest reporting. For example, when anything of a highly controversial nature comes forth at a background session, the moratorium should be extended long enough to enable the reporter to check other sources. Few instances occur when anonymity need be carried to the point that the reporter must deliberately confuse his reader about what is being related. The reporter's first obligation is to present a clear and balanced story.

This war of intelligence *versus* counterintelligence is likely to remain one of the perplexing phenomena of the Washington scene. Though limits may be imposed on its excesses, there is no possibility of ever declaring a permanent truce. The conditions that give rise to it are basic to the American system of government and the free condition of American society. For the reporter, few hard and fast rules can be laid down to serve him as a permanent code of conduct. Instead he must be governed in his daily work by sound and subtle judgments. It is one more measure of the creative role he has to play in the political life of Washington.

MANAGING THE NEWS IN VIETNAM *
John Mecklin

I

AS public affairs officer of the U.S. Mission, I was the Ambassador's chief advisor on relations with the newsmen in Vietnam. I was also assigned to ad-

* From John Mecklin, *Mission in Torment* (Garden City: Doubleday, 1965), pp. 99–119. Copyright © 1965 by John Mecklin. Reprinted by permission of Doubleday & Company, Inc.
7. In "News in Washington," *Harper's Magazine*, August 1958.

vise the Vietnamese Government on press relations. I can hardly claim success. Ambassador Nolting went home under a barage of press attacks such as few if any American diplomatists had experienced. The Diem regime collapsed cursing the American press with its dying words.

The so-called "press problem" in Vietnam was overshadowed by the "news-management" furor resulting from the Kennedy Administration's treatment of the Cuba crisis, but in many ways our problem was more significant. It contributed to a breakdown of dialogue between the U.S. Government and the American people on our policy and operations in a critical area at an exceptionally critical time. It was partly responsible for the public confusion, and suspicions, about Vietnam which became an issue in the 1964 presidential campaign.

The newsmen who worked in Vietnam in 1962–63 charged that the U.S. Mission deliberately lied to them about the war and the Diem regime.

Charles Mohr of *Time* (who later resigned to join the *New York Times*) complained that the Mission attempted to portray defeats as victories and otherwise was "deliberately misleading." Stanley Karnow of the *Saturday Evening Post:* "It became part of American policy to camouflage the shortcomings of the Diem oligarchy." David Halberstam of the *New York Times:* "The U.S. Embassy turned into an adjunct of dictatorship. In trying to protect Diem from criticism, the ambassador became Diem's agent." Neil Sheehan of *United Press International:* "A tremendous amount of misinformation (was) put out."

"The harsh facts of the war in South Vietnam," said a *New York Times* editorial on May 21, 1964, "were only brought to public notice through the enterprise of American newspapermen on the spot." Despite its look-ma-no-hands tone, this was true, but the case against us was more complex than the sin of falsehood.

The root of the problem was the fact that much of what the newsmen took to be lies was exactly what the Mission genuinely believed, and was reporting to Washington. Events were to prove that the Mission itself was unaware of how badly the war was going, operating in a world of illusion. Our feud with the newsmen was an angry symptom of bureaucratic sickness.

Part of the explanation was simple bumbling, and inexperience with this kind of war among some of our top people. We made the error of basing critical judgments of both the political and military situations on information provided mainly by the Vietnamese Government. This was sometimes prettied up to keep the Americans happy. Mostly it was just plain wrong. Indeed one of the main reasons the Diem regime was losing the war was the fact that it never understood what was happening in the countryside.

The U.S. Mission made little effort to distinguish between information provided by Vietnamese sources and the reports of American advisors in the field. If the V.C. attacked a hamlet, for example, information on what happened would be reported initially by the hamlet chief, who quite possibly heard about it from an illiterate, teen-age peasant militiaman, who was as terrified of the hamlet chief as he was of the Viet Cong. From the hamlet chief it would pass through a succession of military commanders who were often political appointees, who owed their jobs to the continued pleasure of the palace, and who knew that Diem frequently fired commanders who reported unpleasant news, or took too many casualties. The U. S. Mission often accepted this kind of information as fact. Much of it was material that even an unscrupulous gossip columnist would regard as doubtful.

The government figures on Viet Cong casualties—which the Mission accepted—became a joke around Saigon. It was a V.C. practice—like other high-caliber fighting men, such as the U. S. Marines—to try to carry away not only their wounded but also their dead, even at great hazard, during a battle. This made it easy for government forces to claim victories when they had only three or four V.C. bodies to show, on the grounds that dozens more were "carried away." Similarly the fact that V.C. guerrillas often masqueraded as simple peasants made it easy to claim as "V.C." the innocent civilians killed by the government forces through indiscriminate bombardments of hamlets.

The Mission was equally sanguine about the casualty claims of Vietnamese and American pilots who attacked supposed V.C. concentrations. These were usually labeled PI-REPS (pilot reports) but nevertheless accepted as reasonably accurate. Many a "victory" thus was based on the claim of a pilot flying at 150 or 200 mph over a battlefield, often under fire from the ground, that he had counted 50 or 100 "V.C." bodies.

In the field of political information the Mission's shortcomings were more consequential, and revealing of a basic error in our approach to the problem of Vietnam. This was our inclination to treat the problem like any other war. There was a commendable effort to keep track of political developments on the enemy side, e.g. such questions as the effect of the Sino-Soviet split on the Vietminh leaders in Hanoi. But our knowledge of what was going on inside the Vietnamese Government, and among its officials in the provinces, was casual and incomplete. In effect we treated the Diem regime like any other ally —for example, the British in World War II—whose effectiveness and determination were beyond doubt, and who therefore should not be spied upon. A heart-warming glimpse of American good faith perhaps, but unrealistic in the circumstances.

Similarly there was little effective effort to keep tabs on the political attitudes of the Vietnamese people, despite the known fact that our adversary gave first priority to this. The Mission paid lip service to the fact that the objective in this kind of war was the support and control of the people, instead of the control of territory which determines the outcome of classic warfare, but failed to mount a reliable watch on popular opinion. This was no less inexcusable than neglecting to find out where the enemy forces are located geographically in conventional combat, or a political party neglecting to find out what the voters think.

Instead we made a heroic effort to fit the problem into the standard military mold, expending countless man-hours and reams of paper to reduce the question of who controls what to charts and graphs. One result was a "measles" map of South Vietnam purporting to show this by different colorings. Another exercise was a line graph to show the progress of the strategic hamlet program in terms of numbers of hamlets under the regime's control. Both efforts turned out to be meaningless because of the basic fallacy in assuming that the war could be profiled in geographical terms.

General Harkins was not unaware of the problem. One of his favorite acts with visitors was to tap his head with a finger and say "the real strategic hamlet program is up here," meaning that what counted was what the people thought about it, which was certainly the fact. Yet American advisors in the field operated under standing orders not to raise political questions with the villagers or even with their Vietnamese counterparts—for fear of annoying the Diem regime. Instead the U. S. Mission accepted the judgment on such things of a government that had so desperately lost contact with its own people that its very survival now depended on U. S. aid.

Inexperience with this kind of war and poor intelligence were, however, only part of the explanation of the illusions inside the U. S. Mission. There was another and perhaps more significant factor—our own psychological blinders.

There was truth in the remark of one senior official, long after he had left Saigon, that "we were too involved subjectively." This was often blamed on Ambassador Nolting and General Harkins as the dominating personalities of the Mission. They were indeed "subjective," but so were most of the top people in Washington, including the men who gave orders to Nolting and Harkins—McNamara, Taylor and Rusk, for example. It was a euphoria that went far deeper than individual officials.

The root of the ailment was the fact that the U. S. had bet all its chips on Diem. There was no alternate, fall-back policy if Diem failed us.

This was not as inexcusable as similar one-crop policies that the U. S. had attempted elsewhere. It could not be compared, for example, with our stubborn, unimaginative and needless support for Premier Adnan Menderes of Turkey in 1958–59 when he was unmistakably running his country into the ground. In Turkey there was an immediate, responsible, anti-Communist alternative in Ismet Inonu and his Republican Party, who eventually did come to power to the distinct betterment of U. S. interests. In Vietnam there was no visible Inonu.

On the contrary, even the severest critics of Diem conceded merit in the argument that "dumping" him would not necessarily produce a successor regime that would be an improvement. The Communists had long since drained off many of the ablest Vietnamese leaders. The French and/or Diem had suppressed many of the remainder, or driven them into exile. The senior officers in the armed forces—the only people who could overthrow Diem, as they eventually did—were mostly political appointees of uncertain character and intelligence, in many cases unthinkable as candidates for national leadership.

There was very real danger that collapse of the Diem regime could lead to a power vacuum and an immediate threat of a Communist victory. This, in turn, would confront the U.S. with two equally unpalatable choices: (1) to seek a "neutral" solution on the pattern of Laos, which probably would only delay a Communist takeover and thus would amount to a step toward surrender, or (2) to bring in American combat forces to continue the fight, which would be unpopular with the American public—and might not work anyway. This was almost exactly how things developed after Diem was ousted in the coup d'état of November 1, 1963.

U.S. support for Diem thus was not a whim, nor based in ignorance. It could be argued that the Mission persisted too long in this support, in the face of mounting evidence that Diem was a failure. But our critics were equally at fault in concluding that Diem had to be unseated long before there was adequate evidence that this critical gamble was justified. Whether he should have been unseated at all, in fact, was still a political issue more than a year after Diem was gone.

The psychology behind U.S. policy was compounded by special emotional considerations that were unique to Vietnam. As mentioned earlier, a large portion of the American community in Vietnam privately disliked and distrusted the Diem regime, and doubted that it could prevail. Among those of us who felt that we nevertheless should keep trying, in the absence of an acceptable alternative, this tended to create a complex of defensiveness. I hope it is not presumptuous to suggest that this in turn created an underlying feeling, perhaps subconsciously, of guilt vis-à-vis the American people because we were politically bankrupt, failing to serve their interest well in a critical situation. This, in any case, was the way I felt. Failure became unthinkable.

At the Washington end, all this was further convoluted by the recent spectacular failure at the Bay of Pigs, and President Kennedy's resulting sensitivity to any suggestion of a similar outcome in Vietnam. Washington was also acutely aware that it had seriously damaged the security of South Vietnam by accepting the "neutralization" of Laos at Geneva in mid-1962, more or less removing all hope of effective action against Viet Cong infiltration through Laos. The possibility of still another retreat in Vietnam thus was political dynamite.

We were stuck hopelessly with what amounted to an all-or-nothing policy, which might not work. Yet it *had* to work, like a Catholic marriage or a parachute. The state of mind in both Washington and Saigon tended to close out reason. The policy of support for Diem became an article of faith, and dissent became reprehensible.

In its dealings with newsmen, the U.S. Mission thus was often wrong about the facts, in a situation of utmost importance to the U.S. national interest, in support of a controversial policy that was costing the lives of American servicemen. Even if conditions had otherwise been normal, this was incompatible with the inquisitive, skeptical nature of American journalism, and trouble would have been inevitable. Unhappily conditions were not otherwise normal.

II

The breakdown of communication between the U. S. Mission and American newsmen, and thus the American public, was further exacerbated by the special political considerations that enveloped our operations in Vietnam like a terminal-care oxygen tent.

For one thing the U. S. decision in 1961 to intervene massively in Vietnam amounted to outright abrogation of the Geneva Agreement of 1954. (The U. S. was not a signatory but it pledged itself unilaterally to honor the agreement.) The agreement provided that there be no increase in foreign forces in Vietnam above the level at that time. In the case of the U. S., this was some 685 men. There was also a provision limiting introduction of armaments which was similarly dumped in the trash can of history.

It was characteristic of the schoolbook morality that so often inhibits U. S. foreign policy that the Kennedy Administration was extremely uneasy about this, despite the fact that the Communists flagrantly violated the agreement years before we did.

Secondly Washington was worried about the propaganda and diplomatic ammunition that U. S. intervention in Vietnam would provide the Communists, not only in Southeast Asia but globally. This no doubt resulted in part from the fact we had been so badly burned so recently in the Bay of Pigs, but it was an unrealistic concern. Any increased American effort in Vietnam was certain to stir a storm of Communist talk about American "imperialism," and so on, and there was nothing we could hope to do about it—except to make it work, which would more than cancel out the damage of any amount of Communist propaganda.

Thirdly the Kennedy Administration knew that U. S. support for Vietnam had never been popular among American voters, and it feared that increased "involvement" might lead to damaging domestic political repercussions. President Kennedy was one of the most politically sensitive men who ever occupied the White House, making this consideration particularly important.

The problem was further compouunded by the attitude of the Vietnamese Government toward the press. Columnist Joseph Alsop described it as "idiotic." The Diem regime reacted to newsmen as though they were a foreign substance in the bloodstream, in uncontrollable convulsions.

Ambassador Nolting called the problem a "clash of cultures," as indeed it was. It was also a clash of centuries: the twentieth versus, let's say, the sixteenth. To the Ngo Dinh family with its Mandarin background, and its feudalistic form of government, the average freewheeling American newsman seemed both incomprehensible and dangerous. The family could not understand why the American press would publish anything that was derogatory to an ally locked in battle against an enemy who was also an American enemy. It demanded the same blank-check support from the press that it was receiving from the U. S. Government.

After a good many years of trying, the Americans persuaded Diem early in

1961 to hire a professional public relations consultant. The contract went to a New York agency, at a reported fee of $100,000. An American expert turned up in Saigon, but the experiment fizzled. One reason was a morass of financial complications. Another was the suspicion among some newsmen in Saigon that one of the expert's functions was to keep track of their activities for the palace.

This was all before my time, but I suspect the expert also failed because the palace regarded him as a form of technical assistant, expected to make the newsmen be good, just as an insecticide specialist would wipe out malaria. The root of the trouble was beyond the reach of specialists. This was the Ngo Dinh family's unshakable belief in its own infallibility. It regarded public relations as the mere process of communicating the word. Newsmen were expected to listen and be swayed, like the audience of the Saigon radio, which turned out to be equally unswayed. Diem and the Nhus sincerely believed that it was not only insulting for newsmen to seek information from sources other than the palace, but that such information could not possibly be accurate in any case.

The regime was not malicious, nor particularly self-seeking about this. The palace seldom lied intentionally to the press. It often tried to persuade reporters to accept absurdities, but it usually believed them itself—and regularly tried to sell the same absurdities to the U.S. Mission, often, unhappily, with greater success.

Almost nothing was done to provide essential working facilities for newsmen. Vietnam was a nation at war, yet the only official spokesman for the Vietnamese armed forces was an obscure Lieutenant Bang, who could seldom be found. Military developments were reported in a daily communique, but it was regularly three or four days behind the news, and always played down setbacks. It was largely ignored. There were three or four relatively competent civilian information officers, but they too were difficult to find, especially when the news was bad.

The newsmen, of course, found other sources for the news, and increasingly treated the regime's communiques with the contempt they invited. This, in turn, outraged Diem and the Nhus, who tended to blame the U.S. Mission. Like politicians all over the underdeveloped world, they believed that the U.S. Government controlled the American press, just as they controlled the Vietnamese press. No amount of patient explanation could persuade them of the reality that the American newsmen not only were wholly independent of government control but in fact regularly transmitting dispatches that the U.S. Mission considered to be damaging to the U.S. interests.

This created a dangerous vicious circle. The Diem regime, recognizing that it could not persuade the newsmen, sought to control them. It tried to limit their movements around the country, to block their sources, and to keep them under surveillance. It lifted their dispatches out of the cable office—in violation of international communications codes—and had them translated for private circulation inside the government. And it protested vigorously to the U.S.

Mission about everything it disliked in the newsmen's reports, sometimes calling us on the carpet for dispatches that had not yet been published in the newspapers to which they were addressed. The protests would often interfere with negotiations between the Mission and the regime on more important issues.

This still further poisoned the Mission's attitude toward the newsmen. We rationalized our attitude like this:

1. Success of the struggle against the Viet Cong depended importantly on persuading the Diem regime to heed U.S. advice.

2. The regime believed, however wrongly, that the U.S. press reflected the views of the U.S. Government and therefore blamed the U.S. Government for press reports that it disliked.

3. Such reports angered the regime and made it reluctant to accept American advice on matters of importance to the war effort.

4. Newsmen who wrote such dispatches were therefore damaging the U.S. national interest. To put it another way, it became unpatriotic for a newsman to use an adjective that displeased Mme. Nhu.

Completing the vicious circle, this kind of thinking led the Mission to react with sympathy to the regime's complaints, in the understandable human hope that by doing so we could get on with other business. Occasionally it worked that way. More often our sympathy simply tended to encourage the regime to more complaints. This also tended to identify the Mission with the regime's hysterical attitude toward the press, including eventually even its physical reprisals against newsmen.

Together all these special considerations led to an official U.S. policy on press relations that attempted on one hand to discourage publicity of any sort about our operations in Vietnam, and on the other to pamper the Diem regime.

At the outset, in 1961 and early 1962, the American buildup was treated like a clandestine operation, producing some memorable absurdities. When the aircraft carrier *Core* tied up at a dock in the Saigon River, for example, newsmen at the rooftop bar of the Majestic Hotel across the street could almost flick a cigarette down among the helicopters cluttering her flight deck. Yet if one of them asked if that was an aircraft carrier across the street, the official reply was supposed to be "no comment." The Mission was forbidden to discuss arrivals of military personnel or materiel of any sort.

This kind of foolishness quickly stirred the wrath of newsmen working in Vietnam, especially when the Viet Cong began killing Americans who were clearly engaged in combat missions. Excessive American secrecy became a news story in itself and was widely reported, with the implication that the U.S. Government was cheating on its own people, trying to fuzz up a policy that was costing the lives of American servicemen. The main result of the secrecy was considerably more publicity than the U.S. buildup would otherwise have generated. It also provoked indignant editorials and, more importantly, queries from congressmen.

By early 1962 difficulties with the press had reached a point where Washington ordered a reexamination of information policy. The result was a new directive, State Department cable No. 1006 of February 21, 1962—two months before my arrival—which was supposed to "liberalize" the policy. It was "liberal" in the sense that it recognized the right of American newsmen to cover the war in Vietnam, but it was otherwise little more than codification of the errors the Mission was already committing.

The text of the cable, which was classified, was not released, but it was shown to members of the House Subcommittee on Foreign Operations and Government Information headed by Rep. John E. Moss, Democrat, of California. The Subcommittee's report on October 1, 1963, paraphrased the cable as saying:

News stories criticizing the Diem government "increase the difficulties of the U.S. job."
Newsmen "should be advised that trifling or thoughtless criticism of the Diem government would make it difficult to maintain cooperation" with Diem.
Newsmen "should not be transported on military activities of the type that are likely to result in undesirable stories."

The Subcommittee's report commented: "The restrictive U. S. press policy in Vietnam . . . unquestionably contributed to the lack of information about conditions in Vietnam which created an international crisis. Instead of hiding the facts from the American public, the State Department should have done everything possible to expose the true situation to full view."

Cable No. 1006 was the policy I was expected to carry out as public affairs officer.

III

Feuds between newsmen and government officials had long been commonplace. During a World War II press conference, for example, President Roosevelt contemptuously presented a Nazi Iron Cross to an unfriendly reporter, implying that his reporting had been helpful to Hitler. Conflict was built in under the American system of checks and balances—the clash of the people's fundamental right to know versus the government's duty to guard secrets that would help the nation's enemies.

In Vietnam the feud reached a degree of bitterness such as I had never before encountered in some twenty years of foreign duty.

I was treated to a disconcerting glimpse of the official attitude toward newsmen on my first morning in Saigon. My advice was invited on a press conference to be given later that day by two American sergeants who had just been released after several weeks in the jungle as prisoners of the Viet Cong. The Communists had given them a fistful of propaganda leaflets to distribute among their comrades—the standard claptrap appealing to peace-loving Americans to cease participating in this dirty imperialist war against the peace-loving Vietnamese people and go home.

To my surprise an American military officer suggested that the sergeants be ordered not to tell the press about the leaflets. "Why should we help the V.C. circulate their propaganda?" he asked. He seemed to be saying that he thought American newspaper readers might be swayed by it. I objected and argued that, as a matter of principle, the sergeants should be instructed to withhold only sensitive military information of possible help to the V.C. In any case, I said, Americans don't take that kind of propaganda seriously, just as we all had laughed at Tokyo Rose and Axis Sally during World War II.

Came the press conference. After the sergeants had recounted their adventures, Peter Kalischer of the Columbia Broadcasting System asked: "Did the V.C. give you anything to bring out?" One of the sergeants looked Kalischer in the eye and replied: "No, sir."

It was an evident falsehood, obviously on orders, in equally obvious disregard of my recommendation. As is usually the case, the lie didn't work. Kalischer had visited the spot where the sergeants had come out of the jungle, talked to the American authorities there and heard about the leaflets. He even had a copy of one of them in his pocket when he asked the question. The lie was duly reported by newspapers, TV and radio all over the United States the next morning.

For some officials of the U.S. Mission, misleading a newsman was almost instinctive, if only as a way to get rid of him. It was a curious phenomenon, not necessarily malicious. These officials were men of high personal integrity, who would never dream of deceiving their wives or a colleague, or a friend. They seemed to regard a journalist as a natural adversary who was deliberately trying to sabotage the national interest, or as a child who would not understand and should not be asking about grown-up affairs in any case. Once in a press statement, for example, a senior American officer—I think inadvertently—used a figure on Viet Cong casualties that was absurdly inflated. I asked one of his aides to consider issuing a correction. "That would only draw attention to it," he replied, closing the matter.

To the best of my knowledge, no responsible U.S. official in Saigon ever told a newsman a really big falsehood. Instead there were endless little ones. They were morally marginal and thus difficult to dispute.

One day in 1962 a delegation of angry newsmen came to see me to complain that the U.S. Mission had been lying to them. I asked for examples. They could think of only two. One was our report that an American soldier was drowned when he fell from a boat on an "outing," when in fact the boat had been fired on by Viet Cong. The second was an official announcement that Vietnamese forces had rescued the American crew of a downed aircraft, when in fact they had been rescued by an American search party. I explained that in both cases our initial reports had been based on erroneous information from our own people, and I said I thought these were poor examples to support an accusation of lying.

What I did not say, could not say in my position, was that I understood their point exactly, that there had been so many little deceptions that they no longer believed anything we said on any subject.

A man from Mars admitted to official inner circles in both Vietnam and Washington could have been excused if he got the impression that the newsmen, as well as the Viet Cong, were the enemy.

At a meeting in Saigon one day it was reported that a V.C. bullet had missed the foot of a reporter riding in a helicopter by only an inch or two. A senior officer snapped his fingers in disappointment, like a man who had missed a putt on the golf course. Everyone laughed. At a meeting in Washington, a "negative" story by Homer Bigart in the *New York Times* was under discussion. A senior official cracked that "Mr. Bigart spells his name wrong," meaning that it should be "bigot." Everyone laughed. Among newspapermen, Bigart was one of the most respected men in the trade.

There was a patronizing, holier-than-thou tone in the official attitude toward the press. We repeatedly received cables from Washington using expressions like "tell the correspondents" to do so and so, or "explain how they were wrong" to write such and such. This was like trying to tell a New York taxi driver how to shift gears. Newsmen the world over are extraordinarily jealous of their prerogatives, often suffer from an inferiority complex, and react violently to any kind of pressure on their reporting.

Still worse was the frequent official suggestion that a "negative" reporter was somehow un-American. Visiting Saigon on one occasion, Admiral Felt was asked a difficult question at a press conference. "Why don't you get on the team?" he snapped at the offending reporter. The local press corps was outraged. Similarly Ambassador Nolting once asked a newsman to "give President Diem the benefit of the doubt," implying that the press had been slanting its dispatches against Diem. The point was not entirely unjustified, but Nolting was never forgiven the remark.

This was characteristic of the whole sorry mess. Neither Felt nor Nolting was deliberately trying to needle the newsmen, nor even aware that what he said would be so strongly resented. With one or two exceptions the same insensitivity was true of the other senior officers in Saigon. There was a self-righteous witlessness about the official attitude toward newsmen that was hard to explain in men of such long and varied careers in the public service.

The Mission persisted in the practice of excessive classification, under the secret fraternity doctrine of State Department Cable No. 1006, to a degree that denied newsmen access to whole segments of U.S. operations in Vietnam. During the time I was there, whether or not napalm (jellied gasoline) was being used against the Viet Cong was technically classified, despite the fact that *Life* Magazine in early 1962 published a cover photograph in color of a napalm attack in Vietnam. The classification presumably was removed after Secretary McNamara, in a press conference on April 24, 1964, admitted that napalm was being used, though he insisted this was only "very rarely."

Newsmen were forbidden (until mid-1964) even to visit the airfield at Bien Hoa, outside Saigon, where an important part of the U.S. Air Force effort in Vietnam was based. (This was the same base so disastrously hit by Viet Cong mortars in November 1964.) This was part of a near total ban on publicity about the Air Force. Inevitably it backfired.

Much of what the Air Force was doing was "blown" by Captain Edwin Gerald ("Jerry") Shank, a T-28 fighter-bomber pilot who was killed in Vietnam, in letters to his wife that were widely published in the spring of 1964.

There was eloquent comment on the U. S. Mission's policy toward the press, and how it affected many of the Americans out there, in this passage (*U. S. News & World Report,* May 4, 1964) of a letter dated January 20, 1964:

"What gets me most is that they won't tell you people what we do over here. I'll bet you that anyone you talk to does not know that American pilots fight this war. We—me and my buddies—do everything. The Vietnamese 'students' we have on board are airmen basics (raw recruits). The only reason they are on board is in case we crash there is one American 'advisor' and one Vietnamese 'student.' They're stupid, ignorant sacrificial lambs, and I have no use for them. In fact, I have been tempted to whip them within an inch of their life a few times. They're a menace to have on board. . . ."

Surely it would have made more sense to invite the press to report the life and activities of Captain Shank and the other American fliers in Vietnam, and thus to give them some of the credit they so richly earned, than to have the story appear in this bitter, sensationalized form, coupled with an accusation from a dead hero that the U. S. Government had misled the American public about his work. Shank's letters were dramatic proof of a basic reality, that secrets don't keep in a situation as confused and controversial as Vietnam.

Excessive classification infected newsmen with distrust of everything we did and said on the understandable assumption that we probably were not telling the whole truth.

One of the spectaculars of the American performance in Vietnam was the compulsive official optimism about the state of the war. This was partly explained by the common ailment of "career involvement," a man's natural inclination to make his work look good. It was partly caused by the fact that Diem liked to be praised, and was inclined to regard as an enemy anyone who failed to praise him. Praise became part of the "advisory" technique. Mainly, however, the unrealistic optimism about Vietnam in both Washington and Saigon was defensive, a silly effort to counter hostile press reporting—in some ways like the losing candidate on election night who keeps pleading for everyone to wait for the upstate returns.

There were some memorable extravagances. Lyndon Johnson, who visited Vietnam in 1961 as Vice-President, compared Diem publicly with Winston Churchill. Secretary McNamara called him "one of the great leaders of our time." After a visit in 1962 General Taylor claimed to have found "a great national movement" that was crushing the Viet Cong. Ruefully I must confess helping to draft a speech by Ambassador Nolting in 1962 forecasting that "the Republic of Vietnam will take its place in history as the country where the tide of Asian Communism was reversed and the myth of Communist invincibility forever shattered." McNamara, Felt and Harkins repeatedly predicted publicly that the war would be in hand by 1964 or 1965, often coupling their remarks with disdainful references to "slanted" or "irresponsible" press reporting from Saigon.[1]

1. A ditty, sung to the tune of "Twinkle, Twinkle, Little Star," circulated through American

In early 1963 Senator Mike Mansfield visited Saigon and departed *without* commenting on the war at all. Things had reached such comic opera proportions that the newsmen regarded this as news and reported it widely.

Way-out official optimism and public abuse of the press often led the newsmen to look for more bad news to justify their previous reporting, further outraging the VIP optimists. Official restrictions on fresh, unedited news, under Cable No. 1006, similarly led the newsmen to look for private sources of their own. They were plentiful, and many of them were malcontents: resentful aircraft crews who were taking most of the American casualties, incompetent officials seeking recognition that had been denied in the public service, neurotics whose vanity was massaged by the attention of reporters from big-time organizations, or sincerely indignant officers who believed the Kennedy Administration was leading the U. S. to disaster in Vietnam and were willing to risk a jail term (by compromising secrets) to appeal their case to the U.S. public.

To protect such sources as these the newsmen used terms like "informed Americans" or "American observers" or "knowledgeable American sources" in their dispatches. Just as regularly each such story would provoke a protest from the Vietnamese Government, or Washington, or both, and the Mission would receive instructions to prevent any further stories attributed to "American sources." This was roughly like trying to prevent a reporter visiting a city of twenty thousand population from talking to anyone, yet some very important people in Washington apparently believed it could be done. The usual result was, first, a massive security investigation which always failed to uncover the source of the story; second, a directive reiterating previous instructions on how to talk to newsmen without saying anything; and third, a rash of indignant stories accusing the Mission of trying to "intimidate" news sources.

There was a particularly spectacular leak in late February 1963. It concerned a change in the rules of engagement for helicopter gunners. The principle was that they could open fire only in self-defense. Previously this had been interpreted to mean they could only fire when fired upon from the ground. The new order said that gunners now could fire if they observed the V.C. preparing to shoot, i.e. the Americans could shoot first in self-defense. It was a sensible but also sensitive order, first because the change would be of great interest to the V.C. and, second, because it suggested further U. S. "involvement" and thus invited political repercussions.

It leaked so rapidly that stories appeared in the press before the new rules had even taken effect. This was hardly surprising. The order had to be circulated among something like a thousand persons, most of them young, embittered helicopter crewmen who had lost buddies to V.C. fire, and many of

---

field messes in Vietnam. I can recall only the first two verses:

We are winning;	If you doubt me,
This I know.	Who are you?
General Harkins told me so.	McNamara says so too.

whom were close personal friends of newsmen. It should have been obvious from the outset that it could not be suppressed and that the only hope for avoiding page-one headlines was to call in the newsmen, tell them about it and appeal for it to be played down. Most of them would have cooperated. Instead the attempt to keep it from them led to sensationalized publicity all over the world.

Altogether the Mission's press policy tended to encourage soreheads while it outraged the newsmen. Its gumshoe investigations of leaks poisoned the American community with doubt and suspicion of colleagues, further depressing morale in an extraordinarily difficult situation. And it was unworkable anyway.

B.   The "Responsible" Exercise of Discretion

THE politics-administration dichotomy, by suggesting that goals and means were clearly divisible, discouraged serious thought about the political significance of bureaucratic discretion. In a well-ordered governmental system, students of administration assumed, bureaucratic discretion would involve little more than experimentation with techniques of cost reduction. As the politics-administration dichotomy came under scholarly fire in the thirties and forties, however, attention suddenly focused on the vast degree of bureaucratic freedom that the effective conduct of public business required, and on the enormous value implications of the decisions that many administrators made.

As the profession took a careful look, it became apparent (1) that all realistic goal choices were based heavily on assumptions about their feasibility, and about the acceptability of the means that their implementation would require; (2) that means invariably affected many values other than those they were designed to serve, with the result that few but the lowest level means choices were purely technical; and (3) that consequently the distinction between means and ends normally dissolved the more closely one examined specific choice situations. Among the practical effects of these abstract propositions, it developed, were the following: (1) that a high proportion of all statutes originated in the bureaucracy; (2) that politicians charged with evaluating legislative proposals typically relied heavily on bureaucratic advice; (3) that bureaucrats were exremely active "sellers" of ideas to both elective policy-makers and the general public; (4) that most laws left room for a wide range of interpretations (frequently not less than the Constitution's "due process" clauses), and that the courts typically treated administrative interpretations that were remotely plausible as authoritative; and (5) that the vast multitude of statutes left many public agencies substantial discretion about which to emphasize and which to treat as dead letters.

How were these findings to be reconciled with the ideal of democratic control?

Some of the most interesting normative writings ever produced by the American political science profession have been addressed to this problem over the past thirty-odd years. A few of the more provocative lines of attack that have been suggested are highlighted in the selections which follow.

Carl Friedrich proposed, in several essays published between 1935 and 1940, that the path to control of the bureaucracy in those realms where full answerability to political superiors was unfeasible lay in the development of professionalism. Professions, he maintained, might encourage the progress of knowledge, develop criteria for judging the work of individual practitioners, and cultivate the consciences of their members. To the extent that they performed these functions well, the threat of arbitrary government would be erased. The public will, normally vague and highly general in content, would be elaborated faithfully and implemented effectively. Government would be "responsible" in the fullest possible sense. Herman Finer, then teaching at the University of London,* vehemently criticized nearly every aspect of Friedrich's argument in two articles which appeared respectively in 1936 and 1941. Their debate is probably the most famous single episode in the whole history of the "administrative responsibility" controversy. The selections reprinted here are from the final summations of each.

Norton Long's concern is the power potential conferred on the bureaucracy by its knowledge. Among the questions with which he grapples are the following: How can the bureaucracy's capacity to shape public, and even congressional, opinion through its command and interpretation of the "facts" be disciplined? Can its expertise be employed in salutary fashion to constrain the demagogic instincts of politicians? During the gestation period of policy proposals originated by the bureaucracy—at which stage most are eliminated, and the rest are decisively shaped—how can consideration of the widest possible range of values most effectively be encouraged? Long's recommended answers are highly controversial, but they are worthy of the most serious consideration.

A number of books and articles published over the past decade have attempted to outline nearly all the important positions that have emerged in the administrative responsibility controversy, and to point out the major weaknesses of each. My policy in selecting for this volume has been to eschew such articles, on the ground that they encourage pseudosophistication, an unwarranted sense of superiority to those who have dirtied their hands in the fray. For much of its length, Glendon Schubert's article is clearly in the surveying-debunking tradition. Schubert does have a viewpoint, however, and it is an intriguing one. He believes that the public interest can and should be defined in such a way as to satisfy the following criteria: (1) be "democratic" but otherwise value-free, (2) be sufficiently precise to permit empirical measurement of the extent to which it has been served in particular cases, yet (3) be sufficiently general to guide the exercise of most discretion. Nor does Schubert confine himself to listing criteria; he also outlines a specific conception of the public interest on which he believes the developmental effort should focus. I have deleted the portions of Schubert's essay in which he merely reviews viewpoints to reject them. What remain are the passages in which he develops his own position. You may judge for yourself whether his proposed criteria are adequate for a definition of the public interest, and whether the specific definition he recommends is susceptible of development to a point where it can fully satisfy them.

* He subsequently moved to the University of Chicago. Friedrich was, and is, a professor at Harvard.

Perhaps the most striking thing about Schubert's definition is that it is procedural. Most other writers on the public interest have aspired to define it in terms of
substantive value content, so that it might guide shapers as well as servants of the
public will. Controversy has focused on whether the public interest is susceptible of
such a definition, and if not, whether it is a meaningful concept at all. Schubert
clearly answers the former question in the negative. Roland Pennock, by contrast,
maintains that the public interest does have widely understood substantive meaning,
though he admits the impossibility of pinning this meaning down verbally. You
may be tempted to dismiss Pennock's argument as mystical, but he contends that
the theory of knowledge on which it rests is at least as reasonable as any other. His
article should challenge you to consider not only whether it is useful to conceive the
public interest as something distinct from the democratic will, but more generally
how precise a term has to be in order to be meaningful. If you find yourself drawn
to Pennock's approach, you will also wish to consider the obstacles to employing it
objectively in the evaluation of concrete administrative acts.

PUBLIC POLICY AND THE NATURE OF ADMINISTRATIVE RESPONSIBILITY *
Carl J. Friedrich

RESPONSIBILITY AND POLICY FORMATION

THE starting point of any study of responsibility must be that even under the
best arrangements a considerable margin of irresponsible conduct of administrative activities is inevitable. For if a responsible person is one who is answerable for his acts to some other person or body, who has to give an account
of his doings (Oxford English Dictionary), it should be clear without further argument that there must be some agreement between such a responsible
agent and his principal concerning the action in hand or at least the end to be
achieved. When one considers the complexity of modern governmental activities, it is at once evident that such agreement can only be partial and incomplete, no matter who is involved. Once the electorate and legislative assemblies
are seen, not through the smoke screen of traditional prejudice, but as they are,
it is evident that such principals cannot effectively bring about the responsible
conduct of public affairs, unless elaborate techniques make explicit what purposes and activities are involved in all the many different phases of public policy. It is at this point that the decisive importance of policy determination becomes apparent. Too often it is taken for granted that as long as we can keep

* From Carl J. Friedrich and Edward S. Mason, eds., *Public Policy: 1940* (Cambridge: Harvard University Press, 1940), pp. 3–14, 19–24. Copyright 1940, by the President and Fellows
of Harvard College. Reprinted by permission.

the government from doing wrong we have made it responsible. What is more important is to insure effective action of any sort. To stimulate initiative, even at the risk of mistakes, must nowadays never be lost sight of as a task in making the government's services responsible. An official should be as responsible for inaction as for wrong action; certainly the average voter will criticize the government as severely for one as for the other.

Without a well-defined and well-worked-out policy, responsibility becomes very difficult to bring about. Yet such policies are the exception rather than the rule. Many of the most severe breakdowns in contemporary administration, accompanied by violent public reactions against irresponsible bureaucracy, will be found to trace back to contradictory and ill-defined policy, as embodied in faulty legislation. There are numerous familiar illustrations. . . .

. . . In the light of the large amount of legislative work performed by administrative agencies, the task of clear and consistent policy formation has passed . . . into the hands of administrators, and is bound to continue to do so. Hence, administrative responsibility can no longer be looked upon as merely a responsibility for executing policies already formulated. We have to face the fact that this responsibility is much more comprehensive in scope.

POLICY-MAKING AND POLICY EXECUTION

It has long been customary to distinguish between policy-making and policy execution. Frank J. Goodnow, in his well-known work, *Politics and Administration,* undertook to build an almost absolute distinction upon this functional difference.

There are, then, in all governmental systems two primary or ultimate functions of government, viz. the expression of the will of the state and the execution of that will. There are also in all states separate organs, each of which is mainly busied with the discharge of one of these functions. These functions are, respectively, Politics and Administration.[1]

But while the distinction has a great deal of value as a relative matter of emphasis, it cannot any longer be accepted in this absolute form. Admittedly, this misleading distinction has become a fetish, a stereotype in the minds of theorists and practitioners alike. The result has been a great deal of confusion and argument. The reason for making this distinction an absolute antithesis is probably to be found in building it upon the metaphysical, if not abstruse, idea of a will of the state. This neo-Hegelian (and Fascist) notion is purely speculative. Even if the concept "state" is retained—and I personally see no good ground for it—the idea that this state has a will immediately entangles one in all the difficulties of assuming a group personality or something akin to it.[2] In other words, a problem which is already complicated enough by itself —that is, how a public policy is adopted and carried out—is bogged down by a vast ideological superstructure which contributes little or nothing to its solu-

1. Frank J. Goodnow, *Politics and Administration* (New York: Macmillan, 1900), p. 22.
2. See Carl J. Friedrich, *Constitutional Government and Politics* (New York: Harpers, 1936), pp. 29ff. and elsewhere.

tion. Take a case like the AAA. In simple terms, AAA was a policy adopted with a view to helping the farmer to weather the storm of the depression. This admittedly was AAA's broad purpose. To accomplish this purpose, crop reduction, price-fixing, and a number of lesser devices were adopted. Crop reduction in turn led to processing taxes. Processing taxes required reports by the processors, inspection of their plants. Crop reduction itself necessitated reports by the farmers, so-called work sheets, and agreements between them and the government as to what was to be done, and so forth and so on. What here is politics, and what administration? Will anyone understand better the complex processes involved in the articulation of this important public policy if we talk about the expression and the execution of the state will? The concrete patterns of public policy formation and execution reveal that politics and administration are not two mutually exclusive boxes, or absolute distinctions, but that they are two closely linked aspects of the same process. Public policy, to put it flatly, is a continuous process, the formation of which is inseparable from its execution. Public policy is being formed as it is being executed, and it is likewise being executed as it is being formed. Politics and administration play a continuous role in both formation and execution, though there is probably more politics in the formation of policy, more administration in the execution of it. In so far as particular individuals or groups are gaining or losing power or control in a given area, there is politics; in so far as officials act or propose action in the name of public interest, there is administration.

The same problem may be considered from another angle. Policies in the common meaning of the term are decisions about what to do or not to do in given situations. It is characteristic of our age that most legislation is looked upon as policy-deciding. Hence policy-making in the broad sense is not supposed to be part of administration. While these propositions are true in a general way, they tend to obscure two important facts, namely, (1) that many policies are not ordained with a stroke of the legislative or dictatorial pen but evolve slowly over long periods of time, and (2) that administrative officials participate continuously and significantly in this process of evolving policy. To commence with the latter fact, it is evident that in the process of doing something the administrator may discover another and better way of accomplishing the same result, or he discovers that the thing cannot be done at all, or that something else has to be done first, before the desired step can be taken. In our recent agricultural policy, examples of all these "administrative" policy determinations can be cited, as likewise in our social security policy. The discussions now taking place in both fields amply illustrate these points. What is more, such administrative participation alone renders policy-making a continuous process, so much in a state of flux that it is difficult, if not impossible, to state with precision what the policy in any given field is at any particular time. But, if this is true, it follows as a corollary that public policy will often be contradictory and conflicting in its effects upon society. Our myth-makers, of course, remain adamant in proclaiming that this should not be so, and let it go at that. It is hard to disagree with them, but we still have to face the question of responsibility, seeing that policies are in fact contradictory and conflicting. Who is responsible for what, and to whom? To what extent does such responsibility affect the actual conduct of affairs? A complex pattern appears when we attempt to answer such questions.

Some time ago I pointed out that administrative responsibility had not kept pace with our administrative tasks. In relying upon the political responsibility of policy-making persons and bodies, we had lost sight of the deeper issues involved. At that time I wrote:

. . . autocratic and arbitrary abuse of power has characterized the officialdom of a government service bound only by the dictates of conscience. Nor has the political responsibility based upon the election of legislatures and chief executives succeeded in permeating a highly technical, differentiated government service any more than the religious responsibility of well-intentioned kings. Even a good and pious king would be discredited by arbitrary "bureaucrats"; even a high-minded legislature or an aspiring chief executive pursuing the public interest would be thwarted by a restive officialdom.

An offended commentator from the British Isles exclaimed loudly that if I imagined that to be true of England I was "simply wrong." But I think it would be easy to show that the officials of a seventeenth-century prince were more responsible, i.e., answerable, to him, their sovereign, than the officials of any modern democracy are as yet to the people, their supposed sovereign. In the comparison there was no judgment as to the positive amount of responsibility found in either. Admittedly, many commentators have dwelt at length upon the frequently irresponsible conduct of public affairs in Great Britian and elsewhere.

THE NEW IMPERATIVE: FUNCTIONAL RESPONSIBILITY

It is interesting that the administrators themselves attach so little weight to the influence of parliamentary or legislative bodies. Leading Swiss officials—and Switzerland has as responsible a government service as any country in the world—told the author that "responsibility of the public service in Switzerland results from a sense of duty, a desire to be approved by his fellow officials, and a tendency to subordinate one's own judgment as a matter of course. Still, in a case like the arrival of Social Democrats into the Federal Council, it might happen that official conduct would be slow to respond to the new situation." They also felt that officials are not unwilling to allow a measure to lapse, although actually provided for in legislation, if considerable opposition is felt which the public might be expected to share. Thus a wine tax was quietly allowed to drop out of sight, just as the potato control act remained a dead letter in the United States.[3] There are, of course, ways by which the legislature secures a measure of control that enables it to enforce responsibility, usually of the negative kind which prevents abuses. Legislative committees act as watchdogs over all expenditure.[4]

3. See Schuyler C. Wallace, "Nullification: A Process of Government," *Political Science Quarterly*, vol. XLV, no. 3 (September 1930), p. 347.

4. See George C. S. Benson, *Financial Control and Integration* (New York: Harpers, 1934).

What is true of Switzerland and the United States without "parliamentary responsibility" seems to be equally true of England and France. In both countries complaints against the increasing independence of officials are constantly being voiced. In a very important discourse, Sir Josiah Stamp called attention to the creative role the civil servant is called upon to play in Great Britain. "I am quite clear that the official must be the mainspring of the new society, suggesting, promoting, advising at every stage." Sir Josiah insisted that this trend was inevitable, irresistible, and therefore called for a new type of administrator. An editorial writer of *The Times,* though critical of this development, agreed "that the practice, as opposed to the theory, of administration has long been moving in this direction." He added, "In practice, they (the officials) possess that influence which cannot be denied to exhaustive knowledge; and this influence, owing to the congestion of parliamentary business and other causes, manifests itself more and more effectively as an initiative in public affairs." Testimony of this sort could be indefinitely multiplied; and as we are interested in practice, not in ideology, we must consider the question of responsibility in terms of the actualities. Such cases throw a disquieting light upon the idea that the mere dependence of a cabinet upon the "confidence" of an elected assembly insures responsible conduct on the part of the officials in charge of the initiation and execution of public policy, when those officials hold permanent positions. It is no accident that the Goodnow school should fully share such illusions. After pointing out that the British Cabinet unites in its hands power of legislation and administration, and thus both formulates and executes policies, Goodnow remarks:

> So long as their action meets with the approval of Parliament . . . there is none to gainsay them. If, however, they fail to gain such approval . . . they must resign their powers to others whose policy is approved by Parliament. . . . In this way the entire English government is made responsible to Parliament, which in turn is responsible to the people.[5]

This is no longer very true. It is objectionable to consider administrative responsibility secure by this simple device, not merely because of interstitial violations but because there is a fundamental flaw in the view of politics and policy here assumed. The range of public policy is nowadays so far-flung that the largely inoperative "right" of the parliamentary majority to oust a Cabinet from power belongs in that rather numerous group of rights for which there is no remedy. The majority supporting the Cabinet may violently disagree with this, that, and the other policy advocated and adopted by the Cabinet, but considerations of party politics, in the broadest sense, will throttle their objections because the particular issue is "not worth a general election" and the chance of the M.P.'s losing his seat.[6] As contrasted with the detailed and continuous criticism and control of administrative activity afforded by Congressional committees, this parliamentary responsibility is largely inoperative and

5. Goodnow, *op. cit.,* p. 154.
6. See Ramsay Muir, *How Britain is Governed* (New York: Richard R. Smith, Inc., 1930), pp. 81–91, 120–132.

certainly ineffectual. When one considers the extent of public disapproval directed against Franklin D. Roosevelt's Congressional supporters who were commonly dubbed "rubber stamps," it is astonishing that anyone extolling the virtues of British parliamentarism should get a hearing at all. For what has the parliamentary majority in Britain been in the last few years but a rubber stamp of an automatic docility undreamt of in the United States?

THE MODERN PHASE: ADMINISTRATIVE DISCRETION

British observers are not unaware of this development. Indeed, the Committee on Ministers' Powers, whose able report has already been cited, was created in response to widespread criticism of the irresponsible bureaucracy which was supposed to be developing. While Lord Hewart's *The New Despotism* undoubtedly exaggerated, his critical attack upon the growth of discretion allowed administrative agencies corresponded to a widespread sentiment. Unfortunately, his views were expressive of an unrealistic nostalgia for legal traditions which the forward march of social development has irrevocably assigned to limbo. Like Beck's *Our Wonderland of Bureaucracy,* Lord Hewart's denunciation of policy-determining officials failed to take into account that this "bureaucracy" had arisen in response to undeniable needs, and that therefore the real problem is how to render these functionaries responsible, not how to take all power away from them. The Committee on Ministers' Powers addressed itself to the real task. They set out to reduce the extent of the rule-making power of administrative agencies and to subject the making of such rules and regulations to a measure of parliamentary control. A standing committee of each house was to scrutinize bills with a view to whether they contained any such delegated legislative power, and, if so, to report upon the provisions in the light of given standards. Without going into the details of these recommendations—for they have not been put into effect—it must be said that they fail to cope with the decisive issue, the responsibility of officials for the policy adopted. No doubt technical improvements would result here and there, errors would be corrected, and mistakes avoided. But wherever the acquisition of discretionary rule-making power would be considered desirable by the government in power, of its exercise in a particular instance justifiable in terms of its policies, it is scarcely probable that under the British parliamentary system a committee composed of a majority of the government's party would cause any real difficulties. Either in getting such discretionary power on the statute books, or in exercising it as the permanent officials see fit, the government's view is more than likely to prevail.

The Report itself is illuminating on this score, though it soft-pedals the real trouble. The Report states that tactical considerations of party politics will play a role, and that, as realists, the committee members recognize it. An interesting illustration is afforded by their discussion of the so-called "Henry VIII Clause." This clause bears its nickname reminiscent of Tudor absolutism because it empowers the appropriate minister to modify the provisions of an act he is called upon to administer so far as may appear to him necessary for the purpose of bringing the act into operation. A number of important statutes in the last few decades contain such a clause. By way of illustrating the inevitability of such a clause, the Report remarks that the Committee had been assured that the National Insurance Act, 1911, could never have been brought into operation without the powers conferred by the Henry VIII Clause. Furthermore, it says:

We have been told, rightly or wrongly, that if that Bill had not passed into law in 1911, the chance of it passing the Parliamentary ordeal with success in 1912 or 1913 would have been small; with the result that a social measure . . . of far-reaching importance would never have passed at all. In other words, the practical politician has to seize the tide when it serves or may lose his venture. We admit this truth: and because we admit it, we consider that the Henry VIII clause is a political instrument which must (*sic*) occasionally be used.[7]

The Committee recommended, of course, its sparing use and all that, but the only sanction they could think of was a parliamentary standing committee dominated by the government's majority. Evidently, a monarch could count on his officials' acting more nearly responsibly and in accordance with his will than the people can under such arrangements.

A DUAL STANDARD OF ADMINISTRATIVE RESPONSIBILITY

But are there any possible arrangements under which the exercise of such discretionary power can be made more responsible? The difficulties are evidently very great. Before we go any further in suggesting institutional safeguards, it becomes necessary to elucidate a bit more the actual psychic conditions which might predispose any agent toward responsible conduct. Palpably, a modern administrator is in many cases dealing with problems so novel and complex that they call for the highest creative ability. This need for creative solutions effectively focuses attention upon the need for action. The pious formulas about the will of the people are all very well, but when it comes to these issues of social maladjustment the popular will has little content, except the desire to see such maladjustments removed. A solution which fails in this regard, or which causes new and perhaps greater maladjustments, is bad; we have a right to call such a policy irresponsible if it can be shown that it was adopted without proper regard to the existing sum of human knowledge concerning the technical issues involved; we also have a right to call it irresponsible if it can be shown that it was adopted without proper regard for existing preferences in the community, and more particularly its prevailing majority. Consequently, the responsible administrator is one who is responsive to these two dominant factors: technical knowledge and popular sentiment. Any policy which violates either standard, or which fails to crystallize in spite of their urgent imperatives, renders the official responsible for it liable to the charge of irresponsible conduct.

In writing of the first of these factors, technical knowledge, I said some years ago:

7. Committee on Ministers' Powers, *Report* (London, 1936; Cmd. 4060), p. 61.

Administrative officials seeking to apply scientific "standards" have to account for their action in terms of a somewhat rationalized and previously established set of hypotheses. Any deviation from these hypotheses will be subjected to thorough scrutiny by their colleagues in what is known as the "fellowship of science." . . . If a specific designation were desirable, it might be well to call this type of responsibility "functional" and "objective," as contrasted with the general and "subjective" types, such as religious, moral and political responsibility. For in the former case, action is tested in terms of relatively objective problems which, if their presence is not evident, can be demonstrated to exist, since they refer to specific functions. Subjective elements appear wherever the possibility of relatively voluntary choice enters in, and here political responsibility is the only method which will insure action in accordance with popular preference.[8]

Similarly, John M. Gaus writes:

The responsibility of the civil servant to the standards of his profession, in so far as those standards make for the public interest, may be given official recognition. . . . Certainly, in the system of government which is now emerging, one important kind of responsibility will be that which the individual civil servant recognizes as due to the standards and ideals of his profession. This is "his inner check." [9]

Yet this view has been objected to as inconceivable by one who claimed that he could not see how the term "responsibility" could be applied except where the governed have the power to dismiss or at least seriously damage the office-holder.[10] Thus, with one stroke of the pen, all the permanent officials of the British government, as well as our own and other supposedly popular governments, are once and for all rendered irresponsible. According to this commentator, political responsibility alone is "objective," because it involves a control by a body external to the one who is responsible. He also claims that its standards may be stated with finality and exactitude and its rewards and punishments made peremptory. For all of which British foreign policy leading up to Munich no doubt provides a particularly illuminating illustration.

It seems like an argument over words. The words, as a matter of fact, do not matter particularly. If you happen to feel that the word "objective" spells praise, and the word "subjective" blame, it may be better to speak of "technical" as contrasted with "political" responsibility, or perhaps "functional" and "political" will appeal. Whether we call it "objective" or "functional" or "technical," the fact remains that throughout the length and breadth of our technical civilization there is arising a type of responsibility on the part of the permanent administrator, the man who is called upon to seek and find the creative solutions for our crying technical needs, which cannot be effectively enforced except by fellow-technicians who are capable of judging his policy in terms of the scientific knowledge bearing upon it. "Nature's laws are always

8. Carl J. Friedrich, "Responsible Government Service under the American Constitution," *Problems of the American Public Service* (New York: McGraw-Hill, 1935), p. 38.

9. John M. Gaus, "The Responsibility of Public Administration," *The Frontiers of Public Administration* (University of Chicago Press, 1936), pp. 39–40.

10. Herman Finer, "Better Government Personnel," *Political Science Quarterly*, vol. LI, no. 4 (December 1936), pp. 569ff. esp. pp. 580ff.

enforced," and a public policy which neglects them is bound to come to grief, no matter how eloquently it may be advocated by popular orators, eager partisans, or smart careerists.

POLITICAL RESPONSIBILITY

The foregoing reflections must not deceive us, however, into believing that a public policy may be pursued just because the technicians are agreed on its desirability. Responsible public policy has to follow a double standard, as we stated before. We are entirely agreed that technical responsibility is not sufficient to keep a civil service wholesome and zealous, and that political responsibility is needed to produce truly responsible policy in a popular government. Discarding the wishful thinking of those who would tell us that Great Britain has solved this difficult problem, it is first necessary to repeat that such truly responsible policy is a noble goal rather than an actual achievement at the present time, and may forever remain so. All institutional safeguards designed to make public policy thus truly responsible represent approximations, and not very near approximations at that. One reason is the intrusion of party politics, already discussed; another is the tremendous difficulty which the public encounters in trying to grasp the broader implications of policy issues, such as foreign affairs, agriculture, and labor today. Concerning unemployment, all the general public really is sure about is that it should disappear. . . .

SHALL WE ENFORCE OR ELICIT RESPONSIBLE CONDUCT?

. . . Responsible conduct of administrative functions is not so much enforced as it is elicited. But it has been the contention all along that responsible conduct is never strictly enforceable, that even under the most tyrannical despot administrative officials will escape effective control—in short, that the problem of how to bring about responsible conduct of the administrative staff of a large organization is, particularly in a democratic society, very largely a question of sound work rules and effective morale. As an able student of great practical experience has put it:

This matter of administrative power commensurate with administrative responsibility, or the administrator's freedom from control, is not, under our system of government, anything absolute or complete: it is a question of degree. . . . Nothing which has been said should be construed to mean that preservation of administrative freedom, initiative and resourcefulness is not an important factor to be considered in organization: quite the contrary, it is one of the major factors.[11]

The whole range of activities involving constant direct contact of the administrator with the public and its problems shows that our conception of administrative responsibility is undergoing profound change. The emphasis is shifting; instead of subserviency to arbitrary will we require responsiveness to commonly felt needs and wants. The trend of the creative evolution of American democracy from a negative conception to a positive ideal of social service posits such a transformation. As the range of government services expands, we

11. Lewis Meriam, *Public Personnel Problems* (Washington: Brookings Institution, 1938), p. 340.

are all becoming each other's servants in the common endeavor of operating our complex industrial society.

It seems desirable to consider one further problem of especial significance in this area, and that is the role and the importance of satisfactory relations of the government to its employees of all ranks and classes. Private employers are becoming increasingly aware of the decisive role which all their employees must play in the public relations of business concerns. Competition through service is becoming an ever more important factor, and the contact of the general public with particular businesses is through their employees. It is evident that the government through its expanding services is placed in a similar position. The Postal Service has long recognized this and has evolved careful regulations concerning the dealings of its employees with the public. As a result, the letter carrier has become a symbol of cheerful service. By contrast, the arbitrary official of authoritarian regimes abroad has always been acknowledged as the antithesis of democracy. Although such conduct was often condoned as part of administrative efficiency, we know today that this view is mistaken. Just as morale within the service is of decisive importance in bringing about responsible administration, so likewise morale should extend beyond the confines of the service itself.

The most serious issue revolves around the problem of the employees' right to organize, to bargain collectively, and to strike if their demands are rejected. . . . It is obvious that in lieu of the possibility of bringing their complaints and grievances forcibly to the attention of their employer, the government, government employees must be provided with exceptionally well-ordered institutional safeguards for mediation and arbitration. Such mechanisms have a fairly long tradition in some countries; they are rapidly developing in this country. . . . [Democracy] cannot possibly hope to develop and maintain responsible conduct unless it accords its employees a status at least equal in dignity and self-respect to the status its labor laws impose upon and demand from private employers. In short, even though the government did not feel justified in conceding the right to strike, it should not discriminate against employees who join an organization which advances this claim. For merely to demand this right is not a crime, since reasonable men may differ as to the right answer. Employees who are denied the rights of ordinary citizens cannot possibly be expected to remain loyal and responsible public servants.

The right policy is to be sure that all necessary disciplinary rules are loyally accepted by the entire staff, irrespective of what organization they belong to. This formula works well as long as those responsible for the rules respect the rights of the persons working under them. It must be kept in mind, however, that there are quite a few difficult border-line cases, where the infraction of a given rule has been due to faulty behavior or hostile attitudes on the part of the higher-ups. . . . The possible frictions of this type are endless; it is evident that adequate representative organization of the employees is the only possible way of coping with the situations as they arise.

Another important problem which is closely related to the foregoing, and equally controversial, is the right of officials to talk and write about issues of general public policy, more particularly those on which they themselves possess exceptional information and understanding because of their official position. There was a time when officials were supposed never to speak their mind in public. But the American and other democratic governments have gradually relaxed these restrictions. It must seriously be doubted whether technical responsibility, which, as we have shown, is coming to play an ever more important role in our time, can be effectively secured without granting responsible officials considerable leeway and making it possible for them to submit their views to outside criticism. The issue is a very complex one. Opinions vary widely. People try to escape facing these difficulties by drawing facile distinctions, such as that officials might discuss facts but not policy. It might cogently be objected that facts and policies cannot be separated. Any presentation of facts requires a selection, and this selection is affected by views, opinions, and hence bears upon policy. What is worse, in many of the most important matters intelligent and well-informed students disagree frequently on what are the facts.

The simplest solution, and one to which the authority-loving politician has recourse without much hesitancy, is to forbid such public utterances altogether. It is undeniable that great inconveniences might and often do result from technical authorities' bringing out "facts" which make the official policy appear in a questionable light. Hence instances of "gag rules" are quite frequent. At one time a federal department head ruled that no official in his organization was to give any more interviews, because one of them had annoyed him. Thereupon six reporters proceeded to that department and got six different stories, all of which were printed and sent to the administrative head to show him that his rule had been foolish and could not really be enforced. In this case the power of the press forced the abandonment of an unsound policy which would seriously interfere with making the administration responsible in the formulation and execution of policy. While many cautious administrators will aver that an official should not discuss policy, it seems wiser, in a democracy, to avoid such a gag rule. Many officials will hesitate to express themselves, anyway, for obvious reasons. A great deal depends upon the nature of the case. In matters of vital importance the general public is entitled to the views of its permanent servants. Such views may often provide a salutary check on partisan extravagances. Such views should be available not only to the executive but to the legislature and the public as well. Gag rules seek to insulate the specialist so that he is no longer heard. A large benefit is thus lost. Irrespective of what one thinks of the particular policies involved, a presidential order not to talk against administration bills to Congress is particularly doubtful, for Congress certainly is entitled to the advice and expert opinion of permanent officials of the government, who may be presumed to have a less partisan viewpoint on particular policy proposals. In fact, the rule can easily be circumvented by an official determined to make his views known: he can prime Congressional questioners to ask the right questions, and, as the officials must answer, their views become available to whole committees. This is true, but while it is alleged that no president would dare punish a man for what he says in answer to a Congressional query, it may often seem to the official undesirable to incur the presidential wrath. Hence no such rule should be allowed at all.

What applies to enlightening Congress really applies likewise to a wider field. It seems inexcusable that highly trained professional economists, for example, should be handicapped in addressing themselves to their colleagues in a frank and scientifically candid manner. Even when they are permitted to do so, they will be only too prone to be overcautious. The only sound standard in a vast and technically complex government such as ours is to insist that the public statements of officials be in keeping with the highest requirements of scientific work. If a man's superiors disagree with him, let them mount the same rostrum and prove that he is wrong; before the goddess of science all men are equal.

CONCLUSION

The ways, then, by which a measure of genuine responsibility can be secured under modern conditions appear to be manifold, and they must all be utilized for achieving the best effect. No mere reliance upon some one traditional device, like the dependence of the Cabinet upon majority support in Parliament, or popular election of the chief executive (neither of which exists in Switzerland), can be accepted as satisfactory evidence. At best, responsibility in a democracy will remain fragmentary because of the indistinct voice of the principal whose agents the officials are supposed to be—the vast heterogeneous masses composing the people. Even the greatest faith in the common man (and I am prepared to carry this very far) cannot any longer justify a simple acceptance of the mythology of "the will of the people." Still, if all the different devices are kept operative and new ones developed as opportunity offers, democratic government by pooling many different interests and points of view continues to provide the nearest approximation to a policy-making process which will give the "right" results. Right policies are policies which seem right to the community at large and at the same time do not violate "objective" scientific standards. Only thus can public policy contribute to what the people consider their happiness.

ADMINISTRATIVE RESPONSIBILITY IN
DEMOCRATIC GOVERNMENT *
Herman Finer

. . . My chief difference with Professor Friedrich . . . is my insistence upon distinguishing responsibility as an arrangement of correction and punishment

* From the *Public Administration Review*, the journal of the American Society for Public Administration, Vol. 1 (1941), pp. 335, 344–350. Reprinted by permission of the publisher.

even up to dismissal both of politicians and officials, while he . . . believes in reliance upon responsibility as a sense of responsibility, largely unsanctioned, except by deference or loyalty to professional standards. . . .

I

. . . Professor Friedrich begins his article in *Public Policy* with some remarks on the Munich Pact, with the intention presumably of showing that administrative responsibility to Parliament is ineffective. He offers it as evidence that "pious myth-makers" have no right to accept the claim that the formal dependence of the Cabinet upon the confidence of the House of Commons effectively insures responsible conduct of public affairs by officials, high and low. (He reverts to this example later also.) As a matter of fact, this example proves the exact converse of Professor Friedrich's intention. The Munich Pact only too well carried out the will of Parliament. Mr. Harold Nicolson, M.P., now Under Secretary to the Ministry of Information, even jeopardized his career by denouncing the hysteria with which the invitation to Munich and peace was received by Parliament. It is true that thereafter, as the consequences came to light, Parliament and people felt that the Government had been wrong—but they too were completely implicated. The revulsion of feeling caused the Government, under parliamentary pressure, to give up its appeasement policy and push on with civil defense preparations and rearmament. . . .

Professor Friedrich has somehow come to believe that "parliamentary responsibility is largely inoperative and certainly ineffectual." Is he referring to the policy-making powers of administrators, or the acts of the Cabinet? His criticism seems to apply to the Cabinet, and not to the subject of his essay, viz., the responsibility of *officials,* for, citing the case of Munich and "the last few years," he seems to be concerned mainly with a foreign policy of which he did not approve but of which a large majority of his "ineffectual" Parliament emphatically did. And then he claims the benefit of this demonstration, I suppose, for the thesis that in England the civil service is out of hand?

On this point there are two records which might be summed up as follows. On questions of foreign policy, the Government, misguided as it may have been (in my view as well as Professor Friedrich's), was steadily supported by a large majority in Parliament, and I should guess a large one in the country. As for control over the administration, has Professor Friedrich heard of Parliament's actions on the Unemployment Regulations of 1934, the reform of the Post Office, the reform of the constitution of the B.B.C., the special areas, the preparation of the scheme of civil defense, the partial success in getting a Minister for the Coordination of Defense, the overthrow of Sir Samuel Hoare, the speeding up of arms production? And, during the war, the successful pressure of Parliament for the removal of certain ministers, e.g., from the Ministry of Information, for more reasonable use of the powers of interning refugees, its control over government contract methods, over appointments in the civil service, over the Defence Regulations proposed by the Home Secretary, over economic and fiscal policies and administration, and, finally, over the very existence of the Chamberlain Government itself? I have listed only a few of the outstanding successes of Parliament in controlling (a) the government in general, and (b) the proposals of administrators and their parliamentary chiefs before they were "made" into policy by Parliament.

The conclusion of this section of the essay reads: "Admittedly, many commentators have dwelt at length upon the frequently irresponsible conduct of public affairs in Great Britain and elsewhere." This is of course true; they have; and they have been right. But that does not mean that the examples are many, important, or long continuing. Nor would any person claim perfection for any system. You do not prove the value of your enthusiasm by showing that there are some flaws in existing political arrangements. Rather is political science a comparative weighing of the imperfections of alternative consequences. Even so, this should hardly lead the author to the conclusion that runs like a scarlet thread throughout the entire treatment, that if political responsibility is imperfect it is to be cast out in favor of a sense of responsibility in the bosom of the official: "a sense of duty, a desire to be approved by his fellow officials, and a tendency to subordinate one's own judgment as a matter of course," a point that Friedrich cites with evident approval from shaky evidence given to him orally by a Swiss official. Without the existence of the Federal Assembly, for how long does Professor Friedrich think the Swiss civil service would remain in tune with the humor of the people and responsive to its wants?

Professor Friedrich then turns to that agitation against the civil service which was summed up in Lord Hewart's book, *The New Despotism.* Alas, for the thesis of the author! *The Report of the Committee on Ministers' Powers,* while showing that, certainly, our civil service was very useful, showed that only in a few respects, and those not very important or deep-seated, were its members escaping control. He seems to harbor an objection to the power which the parliamentary majority would have over the rule-making authority of the administrator though submitted to a committee of the House for sanction. What is wrong with this? Even if a special scrutinizing committee is organized, why should not the majority views of the whole House prevail? What is wrong with the majority? . . .

In the effort not to let reconsideration correct his first misconception of "responsibility," Professor Friedrich finds himself compelled to adopt quite an undemocratic view of government, and to throw scorn upon the popular will. I do not think for a moment that he really is antidemocratic, but his line of argument presses him to enunciate views which might lead to this suspicion. The error in his conception leads to an error in the consequence; and the error in the consequence is precisely what officials (not constrained by principle and institutions to the dictates of political responsibility) would begin to use as an argument to justify their irresponsibility: conceit of themselves and scorn of the popular will. Thus

The pious formulas about the will of the people are all very well, but when it comes to these issues of social maladjustment the popular will has little context, except the desire to see such maladjustments removed. A solution which fails in this regard, or which causes new and perhaps great maladjustments, is bad; we have a right to call such a policy irresponsible if it can be shown that it was adopted without proper regard to the existing sum of human knowledge concerning the technical issues involved; we also have a right to call it irresponsible if it can be shown that it was adopted without proper regard for existing preferences in the community, and more particularly its prevailing majority.

The answer to this argument is this. It is demonstrable that the will of the people *has* content, not only about what it desires, but how maladjustments can be remedied, and some of its ideas are quite wise. The popular will may not be learned, but nevertheless the public's own experience teaches it something, the press of all kinds teaches it more, and political parties and the more instructed members of the community play quite a part. "The people" consists of many kinds of minds and degrees of talent, not of undifferentiated ignorance and empty-mindedness. Legislative assemblies created by election, in which political parties play a vital part, also exist; and they are not so dumb. Their sagacity is not to be ignored or derided. Second, a policy which is based upon an incomplete or faulty grasp of technical knowledge is *not* an irresponsible policy, for to use the word "irresponsible" here is to pervert it by substituting it for the words "incomplete" or "faulty" or "unwise." It is surely wisest to say that the full grasp of knowledge is to be used by the official within the terms of the obligation and policy established for him by the legislature or his departmental superior; otherwise it looks as though an independent position were being claimed for the official. Nor is it wise to make responsibility to "the community" an addendum to a "proper regard to the existing sum of human knowledge, etc., etc." And, by the way, the state seems to have cropped up again in the word community!

"Consequently," continues Professor Friedrich, "the responsible administrator is one who is responsible to these two dominant factors: technical knowledge and popular sentiment. Any policy which violates either standard, or which fails to crystallize in spite of their urgent imperatives, renders the official responsible for it liable to the charge of irresponsible conduct." But just as surely there is no responsibility unless there is an obligation to someone else; no one is interested in a question of responsibility as a relationship between a man and a science, but as it involves a problem of duty—and the problem of duty is an interpersonal, not a personal, matter. Responsibility in the sense of an interpersonal, externally sanctioned duty is, then, the dominant consideration for public administration; and it includes and does not merely stand by the side of responsibility to the standards of one's craft in the dubious position of a Cinderella. If the community does not command, there is no call for the technical knowledge whatever; and, however magnificent the grasp of technical knowledge and the desire to use it, it must be declared irresponsible whenever it becomes operative except under a direct or implied obligation. Many a burglar has been positively hated for his technical skill.

There is another consequence of his thesis which Professor Friedrich would not like, I feel certain, if he had developed its implications. He declares: "Administrative officials seeking to apply scientific 'standards' have to account for their action in terms of a somewhat rationalized and previously established set of hypotheses. Any deviation from these hypotheses will be subjected to thorough scrutiny by their colleagues in what is known as the 'fellowship of science.'" What is the force of the phrase "have to account for their action?" Exactly to whom? By what compulsion? Does this phrase mean only that there is left to the official the vague, tenuous reaching out of his qualms in view of the known or possible public opinions of the men with whom he studied or those who are the present leaders of the profession? Suppose he despises their grasp of knowledge and scorns their judgment—is he therefore irresponsible? Suppose that they are conservative, while he is one of a minority of progressive practitioners? When is he responsible and when irresponsible? When he follows the ancients or marches with, perhaps even leads, the pioneers?

This question takes us directly into the history of these professional organizations of colleagues, "the fellowship of science," the associations, the guilds, of medical men, engineers, accountants, lawyers, and others. Even if such fellowship were fully organized to implement Professor Friedrich's wish, whom could the ordinary man trust for a better deal, the great osteopath, Mr. (later Sir as a mark of popular gratitude) Herbert Barker, or the elders of the British Medical Association, the organization which banned him; Whistler, Charles Ricketts, or the Royal Academy; an Epstein or the stone chippers favored by the Society of Sculptors? I do not err, I believe, in thinking that there are analogous instances in American experience, which Professor Friedrich could supply better than I can. But there is before us the judgment of the District Court of the District of Columbia regarding the American Medical Association's action against medical practitioners—their expulsion because they participated in a group medicine clinic. Which criterion: groupist or antigroupist?

I do not deny all value to such guild organization; I affirm and applaud some of these organizations. Yet, appraised from the very angle of the theory which I am here opposing, they must be seen as broken reeds in a long-run view of governmental devices to keep men in the van of social progress, technically defined, and still less to satisfy progress as the populace, the consumer, asks for it. Professor J. M. Gaus, who is quoted in support of the claim that responsibility is professional, is by no means so zealous in the service of the notion as Professor Friedrich who quotes him, for he says: "The responsibility of the civil servant to the standards of his profession, *in so far as those standards make for the public interest,* may be given official recognition." I have italicized the proviso, and it is essential, I am sure, to Professor Gaus's view.

Who would define the public interest—who could define it? Only the public, I believe, or its deputies.

Professor Friedrich seems to be so obsessed by modern technology, and the important part which the knowledge of it must play in the establishment of policy, that he seems to forget how old this problem is, and what the answer of the ages has been to the very problem he poses. Does he think there was no question of "technical needs" three hundred years or three thousand years ago, or of the relationship of those who provided the knowledge and service to those members of the public who were its consumers? Governments owned warships, weapons, sewers, baths, roads, and irrigation works, and even had mines and forests to administer, and domestic and foreign trade to regulate. The relationship of the public to the mysteries of religion and ecclesiastical procedures—a very important technique in the context of good living—was for centuries one of the most critical problems in the history of political responsibility. "The creative solutions for our crying technical needs," as Professor Friedrich calls them, have for centuries been offered by the experts of various kinds, and the verdict of mankind has been that they need the expert on tap and not on top. All important questions are begged by throwing in the word "creative." It is no news to tell us, as we are told here, that nature will have her revenge if her laws are not understood and followed in any particular piece of administration. Of course that is so. But there is a wider concept of nature than that which relates to interest in the "technical"; there is also the nature of man as a political animal. We are entitled to believe, from the reading of his millennial administrative history, that *his* nature, as well as physical nature, is thwarted where the primacy of public responsibility is challenged by blurred interpretations, theoretical and practical, of the term responsibility.

Nor is there any novelty in the fact that political responsibility (the importance of which Professor Friedrich admits in a scanty oasis of one paragraph in twenty-four pages) acts by its power on the official mind in anticipation of action by the sanctioning organs of popular control. In pursuance of his denigration of the British system of political responsibility he rather misinterprets the function of questions in the House of Commons. Their principal function is not to inform ministers of public reaction to policy, but to discipline administration. Ministers know already through other procedures. Questions are a *force*. Only ask the officials who prepare the information for the ministers whether they are not in an anxious sweat until the House is appeased!

Why, this is almost the ideal instrument for exercising that power of anticipation over the officials' mind, and therefore upon his sense of obligation to the community, which indirectly implies an obligation to the expertness he commands. I say this with diffidence, since the article seems a little severe on British experience. Nor am I an idolator of every item of parliamentary technique as it now operates. It should certainly be improved; but it ought not to be scouted.

There are occasions when Professor Friedrich seems to admit the fundamentality of political responsibility, but the relapse certainly and fatally follows. Thus he says: "The whole range of activities involving constant direct contact of the administrator with the public and its problems shows that our conception of administrative responsibility is undergoing profound change. The emphasis is shifting; instead of subserviency to arbitrary will we require responsiveness to commonly felt needs and wants." Whose is the arbitrary will? The parliamentary assembly's emanating from popular election? . . .

I come now to the last matter in which I care to take issue with Professor Friedrich, the relationship between administrative responsibility and the doctrine of official anonymity.

Professor Friedrich believes:

It must seriously be doubted whether technical responsibility, which, as we have shown, is coming to play an ever more important role in our time, can be effectively secured without granting responsible officials considerable leeway and making it possible for them to submit their views to outside criticism. The issue is a very complex one. Opinions vary widely. People try to escape facing these difficulties by drawing facile distinctions, such as that officials might discuss facts but not policy. It might cogently be objected that facts and policies cannot be separated.

The rejoinder to this statement in the first place is that it is possible in some cases at any rate to distinguish facts and policy quite clearly. For example, the government or the representative assembly in seeking a policy to deal with rural water supplies might properly expect to receive from an official a description of the existing situation, in terms of the total water resources of the country, the supplies and the sources of supply in various rural vicinities, what those supplies cost per thousand gallons, whether the nearest supplies beyond the jurisdiction of each unit need pumping stations or whether the water will come down by being piped, what are the costs of pumping and distribution in various other areas, and so on. What the assembly shall do about it, once these facts are before it, is a matter of policy. A wise civil servant, careful to preserve his own usefulness and that of his colleagues, and not reckless in the face of the always imminent cry of bureaucracy and despotism, would not urge a policy upon it. Still less would he use public advocacy to spur on his political chief or connive with reformist groups having a purposeful policy. He would rather confine himself to frank private demonstration of the alternatives and their advantages and disadvantages, to his political chief, or where the political system requires, to the committee of the assembly at their request.

That, however, is not all. If Professor Friedrich really believes that the severance of fact and policy is impossible, then a fortiori the civil servant should preserve his anonymity, on pain of bringing himself and his colleagues into partisan contempt. And Professor Friedrich does really seem to contemplate a war of all against all. He seems to approve of the fact that six reporters proceeded to a federal department whose head had ruled that his subordinates were not to give interviews and violated the chief's rule by getting six different stories. Is this the way to promote official responsibility to the chief? To the technical standards? To the "fellowship of science"? Does Professor Friedrich approve of this piece of press impudence? Has he ever investigated what such impudence cost the T.V.A. in prestige, morale, and administrative efficiency in the old days? Nor can I view with equanimity the grave consequences of such proposals as this: "In matters of vital importance the general public is entitled to the views of its permanent servants. Such views may often provide a salutary check on partisan extravagances. Such views should be available not only to the executive but to the legislature and the public as well."

This doctrine surely is to set up the official against the political parties, to make the official the instrument of conflict between the "general public" (which I thought had already been thrown out of court earlier in Friedrich's article) and the legislature. He would set the official, I suppose, against the chief executive also, for he has been elected by the general public, and may utter as many "partisan extravagances" as he pleases in the course of a four-year term. It is not clear whether Professor Friedrich thinks that the civil servant shall pursue moral responsibility as far as a crown of thorns, whether once he has embroiled parties and public and legislature he must resign. As matters are, he would certainly be kicked out by the legislature or chief executive, and it would serve him right. For democracy is ill served by and justifiably abhors those who, appointed to be its servants, assume the status and demeanor of masters.

II

. . . Never was the political responsibility of officials so momentous a necessity as in our own era. Moral responsibility is likely to operate in direct proportion to the strictness and efficiency of political responsibility, and to fall away into all sorts of perversions when the latter is weakly enforced. While professional standards, duty to the public, and pursuit of technological efficiency are factors in sound administrative operation, they are but ingredients, and not continuously motivating factors, of sound policy, and they require public and political control and direction.

The public and the political assemblies are adequately sagacious to direct policy—they know not only where the shoe pinches, but have a shrewd idea as to the last and leather of their footwear: and where they lack technical knowledge their officials are appointed to offer it to them for their guidance, and not to secure official domination; and within these limits the practice of giving administrative latitude to officials is sound.

Contemporary devices to secure closer cooperation of officials with public and legislatures are properly auxiliaries to and not substitutes for political control of public officials through exertion of the sovereign authority of the public. Thus, political responsibility is the major concern of those who work for healthy relationships between the officials and the public, and moral responsibility, although a valuable conception and institutional form, is minor and subsidiary.

PUBLIC POLICY AND ADMINISTRATION: THE GOALS OF RATIONALITY AND RESPONSIBILITY *
Norton E. Long

I

No problem is more momentous for the modern democratic state than its capacity to develop rational, responsible, goal-oriented policy. In many fields, including the most crucial ones, foreign policy and defense, the staff work on which well conceived public policy must depend can scarcely be supplied elsewhere than in the great government departments. To only a somewhat lesser degree this is true of agriculture, finance, commerce, and labor. Accordingly, a major task of administration is the formulation of policy proposals for consideration by the political executive and the legislature. The capacity of our administrative organizations to perform rationally and responsibly the task of formulating the policy alternatives for politically responsible superiors is the major criterion of organization efficiency. The beginning of wisdom in administrative analysis consists in a realistic assessment of the capacity of the organization to think.

The conception, now formally abjured, of the separation of policy and administration has obscured the vital "thinking" role of organized bureaucracy in government. The doctrine of the political supremacy of the elected over the nonelected branch of the government has inspired the delusion that to be politically supreme the legislature must not only make final decisions on policy but must also have primacy in the whole process of policy formulation—that the bureaucracy should be an instrument rather than a brain. The necessities of the case have forced the abandonment of this view save as folklore and political metaphysics. In practice it must be recognized that the bureaucracy is a part, and a highly important part, of the collective brain that somehow thinks or emotes a government policy.

The attempt of some writers, influenced by logical positivism, to construct a value-free science of administration may well have the unintended and logically unwarranted result of reviving the policy-administration dichotomy in new verbiage. Policy would become a matter of determining values, a legislative-political matter; administration would consist in the application of the values set by the political branch to sets of facts ascertained by the administra-

* From the *Public Administration Review*, the journal of the American Society for Public Administration, Vol. 14 (1954), pp. 22–24, 27–31. Reprinted by permission of the publisher.

tive. In this reasoning, administration could arrive at determinate answers without being sicklied o'er by the pale cast of policy thought. . . .

But, alas, we know this institutional divorce, however requisite for a value-free science of administration, does not exist. And, with deference, it seems rather doubtful that much would be gained by altering the facts to fit the theory—if, indeed, there were any remote chance that the public and publicly responsible officialdom would consider it. Instead, we may be wiser to seek so to structure our administrative operations as to reflect the values and the facts that, given the nature of our society and its problems, should enter into the formulation of the policy alternatives to be considered and adopted by the legislature and the political executive.

If one of the most important tasks of administration is conceived to be the formulation of policy proposals to solve problems, interesting consequences for organization follow. In this view, the rational organization of government would reflect the major problem areas whose boundaries have evolved from and been defined by socially felt needs and the state of relevant technology for meeting them. Organization would be structured to ask the questions and provide the facts necessary for solutions. Thus, analysis of the administrative adequacy of State Department organization would concern itself in part with the capacity of that organization to develop and test the theories implicit in its foreign policy proposals and to extract meaning from the experience with those proposals when they were put into practice. Adequate organization would require that every major question have an institutional protagonist, the securing of every important piece of factual information be an assigned responsibility, and every important point of view have a spokesman built into the proposal-formulating process.

The nature of the policy to be formulated implies the theoretical, factual, and value premises necessary for its rational and responsible development. The institutional structure can then be considered in terms of personnel possessed of values, drives, and skills so structured as organizationally to simulate a reasoned inquiry. The test of organizational rationality is the capacity of the organization to make explicit and controlling the theory on which its actions depend, to spell out and test the crucial hypotheses involved in the theory, and to amass and focus the facts needed to test the hypotheses. Such an organization can have experience that approximates the self-correcting discipline of a science. From the point of view of goal-oriented behavior and problem-solving capacity, it is an ideal.

In the political context, and because it is politics we are dealing with, the model of scientific procedure—the formulation and testing of hypotheses—is only partially relevant. Politics is not a science, but to be consequent it must employ science and logic in the pursuit of its purposes. The structuring of organization must be concerned with the reflection of values and their implementation. Much of the implementation and a great deal of the critical work in the shaping and reshaping of values will depend on scientific determination of relevant factual propositions. But values cannot be verified as can propositions of fact, and therefore an enterprise so importantly concerned with the process of valuation as is administration requires an organization differently structured from the sciences and yet disciplined to the utilization of their results. . . .

III

Once the fact is faced that the bureaucracy is not, and cannot be, a neutral instrument solely devoted to the unmotivated presentation of facts to, and the docile execution of orders from, political superiors, a more realistic picture of its problems and potential can be had. Constitutionalism itself demands that the political will be limited by procedure. An important addition to the constitutional arsenal lies in the potentialities of administration. The concept usually applied to political superiors vis-à-vis administration has something in it of the metaphysics of free will: only unchecked supremacy is compatible with sound doctrine. Power must be commensurate with responsibility. Simon has assailed this concept, but it persists. Actually, unfettered freedom is incompatible with the growth of technology. Knowledge expands power, but in doing so, imposes limitations. In one sense, a well-conceived personnel policy is a limitation on managerial freedom, but its adoption removes other limitations and so enhances freedom of action in desired directions.

For good or ill, we know the fund of knowledge in the bureaucracy will be a source of power. Damning or denying this power accomplishes little toward the major task of increasing the probability that public policy will be informed and responsible. The whole purpose of the Weather Bureau would be subverted if superiors dreamed they could give any orders they pleased. The Bureau of Labor Statistics was badly mauled because of suspicion of the integrity of its cost of living index. The Council of Economic Advisers became so openly an instrument of presidential propaganda as to minimize its value as a means of securing consensus on basic economic data and the approximate dimensions of our economic problems. The recent assault on the Bureau of Standards in the name of the policy supremacy of the Secretary of Commerce has critically impaired the agency's capacity to present a common ground of scientific fact within the government and for the broad public. Ability to stipulate with confidence the kind of basic facts these agencies were intended to provide is essential to even the beginning of rational policy discussion. As Walter Lippmann has wisely said:

. . . when full allowance has been made for deliberate fraud, political science has still to account for such facts as two nations attacking one another, each convinced that it is acting in self-defense, or two classes at war each certain that it speaks for the common interest. They live, we are likely to say, in different worlds. More accurately, they live in the same world, but they think and feel in different ones.

A common and rationally warranted conception of the world—the relevant facts—is basic to communication and rational discussion in government as elsewhere. Without some accepted means of stabilizing the conception of the environment with which policy is intended to deal, we are lost in the world without coordinates of Orwell's *Nineteen Eighty-four.* To be sure, this is a free-wheeling world of rhetoric and emotion that many find congenial and that most politicians are adept at exploiting—a world in which solid facts evaporate and special devils and angels exercise occult or heavenly powers. The elimination of this world of the comic books, with its moralistic technology of "the good guys and the bad guys," from its predominant role in the rhetoric of public policy formation is a major requisite for the rational and responsible development of policy.

Administration has a great contribution to make in providing an alternative view of reality to the tempting, popular, and presently politically rewarding comic-book interpretation of history. The gradual restriction of mythical thinking in the field of politics seems no more insuperable a problem in principle than that which has been met with considerable if imperfect success in medicine. It is possible to build administrative structures whose accounts of the facts will provide a salutary limitation to the range of policy proposals that politicians will find it politic to espouse. To the extent that the procedures used in developing the facts attain public acceptance, as may for instance the statistical work of the Bureau of Labor Statistics, public support of these procedures and the accounts they provide will in turn compel debate on agreed facts and so limit alternatives by some meaningful test of feasibility.

The enormous power that substantial control of the accepted version of the facts gives to any group must be faced. Even with the best intentions, facts are rarely presented in a fashion that is neutral to all the parties at interest. Indeed, if they are to do any useful office in clarifying the real alternatives of public policy, they must foreclose some alternatives, and in doing so give umbrage to their proponents. The danger that the fact-gathering process will be corrupted is always present. Such remedy as we have is a consensus that there is integrity in procedures and that these procedures exert a control over the practices and values of personnel engaged in the enterprise. That such consensus is possible, to a degree at any rate, is exemplified by the bar and the bench. Reliance on hierarchical control by interested political superiors, except within house-keeping limits and in case of provable breach of professional behavior, would taint with misplaced partisanship a function whose success depends on a general consensus of lack of such bias.

Fact-finding agencies may be established that can achieve some broad acceptance and confidence. The process is slow. But at least in principle we may recognize the necessity of structuring into administration the means to provide a neutral summary of the facts that can serve as the common ground for rational discussion. While this is of exceeding importance for collaboration between the executive and the Congress and for the general realism of public debate, it is also of great concern for coordination of activity within the executive itself. Each agency is prone to develop its own research and intelligence section, not merely to be informed, but even more, to avoid being controlled by a source of facts that is suspect and to provide a rationalization for its own policy preferences. A great forward step in coordination would result from the development within the executive of institutions capable of providing a minimum factual consensus in terms of which policy differences would have to be argued.

One leader, one President, is no substitute for one view of the world with which administration must deal. Structuring a hierarchy is no substitute for structuring a reasoned consensus in the facts. While it is an understandable feature of interagency rivalry that each agency should fabricate its own figures and at times throw dust in the air, it would seem, though difficult, the part of wisdom to reduce these competing versions of reality to as near a consensus or a clear statement of differences as accepted technology will permit. It is doubtful that this can or should be accomplished by hierarchical command alone, but there are fruitful possibilities that what cannot be accomplished by fiat may be accomplished by a professional consensus that will permeate all the agencies and in time extend to press and public.

It may be accepted that the integrity of the expert's role as the source of fact should be protected, though how and to what extent remains a problem. But when the reality is faced that the facts produced may not be politically neutral, and that in consequence political superiors may well wish to control their production, a grave problem is presented: in what degree should political superiors be compelled by custom and/or institution to run the gauntlet of facts produced by personnel who are professionally and procedurally, but not politically, responsible? The question is twofold. First, should they be compelled? And second, if they should be, how is it politically feasible to do so? There seem strong reasons for believing that, if properly structured, an enforced confrontation of policy proposals with a professional estimate of relevant reality would be salutary. If public acceptance developed it would be feasible. It is already practiced in varying degrees in particular areas of government operation. Taking a point from administrative law, though one in which there has been more form than substance, one might strive for acceptance of the view that policy should be grounded on substantial evidence and that evidence should be the product of professional procedures.

While any rigid dichotomy between fact production and policy proposal is bound to prove tenuous, there is a reasonably clear distinction between such agencies as the Weather Bureau, the Bureau of Labor Statistics, and the Bureau of Standards, on the one hand, and the State Department, the Department of Defense, and the Department of Agriculture, on the other. The former labor under very little pressure to produce major policy proposals; the latter are expected to produce answers to the most significant problems of our times. Interpretation of a most significant sort is required of the second group, as well as production of crucial facts.

The policy proposals which the departments present to the President and the Congress are, except for end runs, initially policy proposals made within the departments to political superiors. The structuring of this process to insure, to the extent feasible, conscious and reasoned choice among carefully worked out alternatives should be a major objective of administrative technology. Today, the dominance of political superiors and a tight chain of command are the normal emphases of political theory. If, however, political superiors and their subordinates can be looked upon as a problem-solving team engaged in working out the terms of a continuing adjustment of group values to a dynamic environment, a new view of the most helpful role of subordinates may be achieved. The roles of subordinates in the policy-formulating process are determined by the ability of our technologies to grasp the environment and the nature of the problems that determine the tasks of the administrative organization. The technologies and the objective problems provide, within limits, some element of determinativeness to what kind of organization would be most likely to cope effectively with a given set of objectives.

IV

The progress of administration as an applied science depends on its capacity to influence the climate of relevant opinion in the direction of political superiors disciplining themselves to restraints on their area of choice. In recent years the fear has been expressed that the men of the Kremlin would be deceived into dangerous adventures by agents falsely reporting to them what the agents believed agreeable to their masters' views. The disciplining of the desires and inclinations of the superiors to the unpleasant realities is a job for administrative structure, staffing, and procedure. It requires the building into the organization of a system of values and procedures that will enforce the presentation at the highest level of all the relevant facts—and their most significant possible interpretations.

Actually, an organization capable of presenting to political superiors an objectively controlled picture of the facts and a fair range of possible problem solutions, whose feasibility had been tested so far as practicable, would greatly increase the superiors' real range of choice—although it should be noted that psychologically the awareness of alternatives exercises constraint as well. This constraint in our value system, however, should be salutary. The slow but hopefully constant pressure of Project Lincoln, the Marvin Kelly Report, and Project East River indicates both the possibilities and the limitations of the presentation of unpleasant realities to political superiors. The organizing, strengthening, and regularizing of this process is a major task that consists in large part of creation of public expectation and elite public pressure.

If the problems and the existing state of technologies are important determinants of the desirable structure of organization, the values of the community that enter into public opinion are equally significant facts to be considered. Indeed, to get a fair representation of the alternatives an *advocatus diaboli,* and one acting more than pro forma, will be necessary for a reasoned decision among all the alternatives. Even the most convinced anticommunist Secretary of State might wish sources of information on China beyond those provided by the orthodox supporters of Chiang Kai-shek. While final decisions must and should rest with political superiors, by custom and practice they should come only after the painful and salutary routine of examining alternatives and objections. To get these, organization must be structured for variety of points of view so that significant values in the community are necessarily considered in the formulation of policy proposals.

In his richly perceptive article on "Legislative-Executive Relationships in Budgeting as Viewed by the Executive," in the Summer, 1953, issue of this *Review,* Frederick J. Lawton describes interest and value representation in the budgetary process. As described, this process is a good example of at least an embryonic structuring of organization rationality. Hierarchy is accorded a major function of introducing perspectives and priorities appropriate to the various levels of administration into the budgetary process. The process is described in terms of a dynamic interaction between levels, organizations, programs, and interests. Ideally the resulting work program and allocation of the nation's resources would represent proposals that have been arrived at after a full hearing of competing claims, views, and the relevant facts. Few, however, who have struggled with the process of budget formulation in Washington would believe that there exists a well-structured, self-conscious, going concern for the clear formulation, on the one hand, of the "program of the President" and, on the other, for the formulation and testing of estimates from below in terms of diversified community needs, political demands, and objective facts.

. . . What are the consequences of this constitutionalizing of hierarchy? What implications does it have for the theory . . . that a new administration should have administrative power commensurate with its programmatic responsibility?

The answers to such questions may be highly conservative, smacking of Burke, the Federalists, and John Stuart Mill. The phrases that leap to mind are "a permanent settled will over a transient inclination," "constitutional settlement," "due process," "balance of interests." These constitutional arrangements we think of as ordinarily being embodied in the separation of powers, judicial review, and federalism. However, if we recognize the bureaucracy as becoming increasingly the policy-maturing, policy-proposing branch, both in the initiation of legislation and budget estimates and in the discretionary administration of legislation, the advisability of building constitutionalizing elements into the bureaucracy will seem of prime importance. The deficiencies of the legislature as both a thought and a will organization in Graham Wallas' sense lead to the growing power of the executive. The inevitability of this development leads straight to the consideration of the adequacy of the executive branch for performing the political, policy function of proposing an agenda to Congress.

We would all recognize the deficiency of a one-party legislature, yet many of us would applaud, and are applauding, a one-party top-level bureaucracy. It may seem a forcing of the analogy to suggest that a loyal opposition in the upper levels of the bureaucracy could serve a function well nigh as socially useful as that performed by the loyal opposition in Parliament. We have only begun to think of how best to staff and organize administration if a major part of its job is to propose policy alternatives—alternatives that have run the gauntlet of facts, analysis, and competing social values built into the administrative process.

If it is sound to present political superiors in the departments with alternative problem solutions and to structure organization so to do, it might be well to consider the implications of this arrangement for executive-legislative relations. Much congressional frustration seems due to the lack of ability to make a choice in deciding programs. Congress can wreck a program, it can whittle one down, but it cannot have a well-worked-out program unless it accepts the one program presented to it by the executive. The same reasons that dictate that political superiors in the departments should be compelled to make a choice between reasoned alternatives may well apply to departmental presentations to Congress. If Congress is to make reasoned choices it would seem that it should have before it the reasoned alternatives. However, political necessities may preclude the executive from presenting anything but one program to the Congress. If this is the case, and it well may be, a vital part of rational decision and community representation must be structured into administration if they are to occur at all.

"THE PUBLIC INTEREST" IN ADMINISTRATIVE DECISION-MAKING: THEOREM, THEOSOPHY, OR THEORY? *

Glendon A. Schubert, Jr.

... A THEORY of "the public interest" in administrative decision-making ought, one supposes, to describe a relationship between a concept of the public interest and official behavior in such terms that it might be possible to collect data for the purpose of attempting to validate hypotheses concerning the relationship. If extant theory does not lend itself to such uses, it is difficult to comprehend the justification for teaching students of public administration that subservience to the public interest is a relevant norm of administrative responsibility.

ADMINISTRATIVE REALISM

For Arthur Fisher Bentley, the public interest and the general welfare were "mind-stuff," appropriately discussed by writers of fiction who spun phantasies, but with no place in the reality which it was the business of the social scientist to explore. As Richard W. Taylor puts it, "The ghosts of 'national in-

* From the *American Political Science Review*, Vol. 51 (June 1957), pp. 346, 357–358, 360–362, 367–368. Reprinted by permission of the author and publisher.

terest' and 'general welfare' are unfrocked; these phrases come to have no more authority over inquiry than a divested priest has over the faithful."[1] The essence of Bentley's theory is distilled, in his own words, in the statement that:

As for political questions under any society in which we are called upon to study them, we shall never find a group interest of the society as a whole. We shall always find that the political interests and activities of any given group—and there are no political phenomena except group phenomena—are directed against other activities of men, who appear in other groups, political or other. The phenomena of political life which we study will always divide the society in which they occur, along lines that are very real, though of varying degrees of definiteness. The society itself is nothing other than the complex of the groups that compose it.[2]

As applied to administrative decision-making, this meant for Bentley that discretion (in the subjective sense of an attribute of the administrator) was an illusion. What was *really* happening was that the field within which the interest groups concerned might maneuver in their attempts to maximize their influence over the administrator was contracted or expanded. The administrator's decision, in actuality, was an expression of the action necessary to bring about a new equilibrium among the groups whose interests were in conflict:

It is so with every public official in every function. Perhaps he has little discretion and we can easily watch the pressures operating through him. Perhaps he has great discretion, and we have difficulty to keep ourselves from being led astray by his prominence as a technical process. But in either case we must push the analysis down to the groups represented and in either case we shall on the test find that our fullest and richest statement of the law is in terms of the group activity tending to spread itself, with allowance for the differences of technique in the governing organ through which it functions.[3]

The implications of Bentley's views on the public interest were spelled out, much more clearly than Bentley himself had done, by his disciple, David B. Truman. Truman describes the administrator's mediatory role in precise accord with Dean Leys' third category of "discretion as ambiguity":

The administrator's position in controlling the access of competing interest groups is made the more difficult if the terms of his mandate from the legislature are highly ambiguous. . . . Where compromise in the legislative stage is the alternative to temporary failure and where the imperative to compromise is accepted by some participants as a means of avoiding the open frustration of expectations widely held in the community, the terms of legislative settlement are almost bound to be ambiguous. Such compromises are in the nature of postponement. The administrator is called upon to resolve the difficulties that were too thorny for the legislature to solve, and he must do so in the face of the very forces that were acting in the legislature, though their relative strength may have changed. Note that it is not the

1. Richard W. Taylor, "Arthur F. Bentley's Political Science," *Western Political Quarterly*, Vol. 5, p. 215 (1952).
2. Arthur F. Bentley, *The Process of Government* (Bloomington, Ind., 1949), p. 222. [This book was originally published in 1908.]
3. *Ibid.*, p. 292.

ambiguities in the law that make difficult the question of what groups shall have privileged access to an administrator. Almost all legislative declarations are ambiguous in part. It is rather the causes of the ambiguity that make the difference. If the administrator holds out for an interpretation of these controverted ambiguous provisions that is not in itself a compromise, he invites the affected groups either to denounce his 'dictatorial' methods and his 'unscrupulous assumption of powers not granted to him' or to expose his 'sell-out' of the 'public interest.'[4]

Truman's restatement of the Bentlian view of the public interest is that:

Many . . . assume explicitly or implicitly that there is an interest of the nation as a whole, universally and invariably held and standing apart from and superior to those of the various groups included within it . . . such an assertion flies in the face of all that we know of the behavior of men in a complex society. Were it in fact true, not only the interest group but even the political party should properly be viewed as an abnormality. . . . Assertion of an inclusive 'national' or 'public' interest is an effective device in many . . . situations. . . . In themselves, these claims are part of the data of politics. However, they do not describe any actual or possible political situation within a complex modern nation. In developing a group interpretation of politics, therefore, we do not need to account for a totally inclusive interest, because one does not exist.[5]

. . . Probably the best known study of the relationship between pressure groups and administrative decision-making is that of Pendleton Herring. Herring seems to have developed his hypotheses and frame of reference for this study in ignorance, or at least in independence, of Bentley's work, since he neither cites nor otherwise acknowledges Bentley. Herring's book is based upon a series of case studies of so-called regulatory agencies. His work has the virtue, for present purposes, of evincing intellectual concern with the problem of the administrator confronted with a maelstrom of group pressures and feeling both a legal and an ethical obligation to reconcile them in accordance with the public interest. This is in fairly sharp contradistinction from the bland optimism with which Bentley and Truman contemplate the impact of the group struggle upon public policy. Although he arrives at similar conclusions, Herring at least worries a bit in the process:

Under democracy the public interest is based not upon the welfare of one class but upon a compounding of many group interests. We assume the possibility of achieving a balance of forces, social and economic. . . .

This increase in administrative discretion, while making possible the more understanding application of rules to concrete situations, nevertheless places a heavy duty on the administrator. The words of the statute delimit his scope, but within the margin of his discretion he must write his interpretation of state purpose. . . . What criteria are to guide him? The *public interest* is the standard that guides the administrator in executing the law. This is the verbal symbol designed to introduce unity, order, and objectivity into administration.

This concept is to the bureaucracy what the 'due process' clause is to the judiciary. Its abstract meaning is vague but its application has far-reaching effects. The

4. David B. Truman, *The Governmental Process* (N.Y., 1951), p. 443.
5. *Ibid.*, pp. 50–51.

radio commissioners were to execute the law in the 'public interest, convenience or necessity.' The trade commissioners are to apply the law when they deem such action 'to the interest of the public.' Congress has frequently authorized boards and quasi-judicial commissions to determine the public interest.

Although it is clear that the official must balance the interests of the conflicting groups before him, by what standards is he to weigh their demands? To hold out the *public interest* as a criterion is to offer an imponderable. Its value is psychological and does not extend beyond the significance that each responsible civil servant must find in the phrase for himself. Acting in accordance with this subjective conception and bounded by his statutory competence, the bureaucrat selects from the special interests before him a combination to which he gives official sanction. Thus inescapably in practice the concept of public interest is given substance by its identification with the interests of certain groups. . . . [T]he public interest can be realized only through promoting certain special interests. . . .

The task of government in a democracy, we assume, is the adjustment of warring economic and social forces. The public interest is the standard that supposedly determines the degree to which the government lends its forces to one side or the other. Without this standard for judgment between contenders, the scales would simply be weighted in favor of victory for the strongest.[6]

What "standard of judgment"? By his own repeated testimony, Herring has assumed the role of an oath-helper for Thrasymachus. Waldo is of the same view, noting that Herring's

evidence strongly supports the 'resultant-of-forces' hypothesis. In practice the 'public interest' is given meaning only by the pulling and hauling of private interests— mitigated occasionally by the personal views of the Good Society held by some regulatory commissioners. Admirable as these analyses are, Herring advances us little in the search for a substantive content for the 'public interest.' [7]

Although several of the pressure groups theorists so far considered have spoken of "balance" and "equilibrium," the first to attempt a concise statement of an equilibrium theory was Avery Leiserson. And implicit in Leiserson's theory is an operational definition of the public interest: an administrator best serves the public interest when his action creates or restores all equilibrium among all of the affected group interests, or if this is not possible, when the disequilibrium following his act is minimized. Quite to the contrary of the "countervailing force" role postulated for bureaucracy by the advocates of administrative engineering, equilibrium theory posits an essentially negative, conservative task:

Is there any objective test of such a capacity [the facility for judgment in which the administrative expert's policies and decisions are guided by the test of optimum satisfaction on the part of the groups affected by his administrative acts]? Hypothetically, we shall formulate this test as the acceptance of administrative decisions and policies by the group interests affected or concerned by them. . . . In other words, the political formula or agreement, expressed in legislative enactment, is a suspen-

6. E. Pendleton Herring, *Public Administration and the Public Interest* (N.Y., 1936), pp. vii, 8, 23–24, 259, 377.
7. Dwight Waldo, *The Administrative State* (N.Y., 1948), p. 13, and also p. 93.

sion of overt political conflict between group interests—a period in which admin-istrators are given the opportunity to devise policies, under and within the law, which influential parties to the political conflict for the most part accept as a work-ing *modus operandi*. These policies are exposed to public (multigroup) scrutiny and may be said to have become accepted if the affected groups no longer agitate before the legislature to obtain amendments or repeal of the law.[8]

Dean Leys seems to express the same idea when he says that "The problem is to relate an immediate and pressing interest to a mass of other interests in such a way that the immediate interest somehow 'fits into the picture.'"[9] For the administrator who functions as a charismatic leader of the unorganized public, group equilibrium theory would substitute the democratic adminis-trative politician. The latter image seems to be the one which is in closer ac-cord with common experience.

While equilibrium theorists focus upon the dynamic environment con-fronting the administrator, psychological realism focuses upon the administra-tor himself, as a discrete human being rather than as a statistical mean. This suggests, as an initial insight, that "legitimacy," from the point of view of the individual, is a subjective rather than an objective phenomenon:

To the extent that democracy means to an administrator the formal processes of courts, legislatures, and hierarchy, his democratic beliefs make him responsive to these processes *even beyond* their power to hold him formally accountable. To the extent that the administrator has some conception of a popular will, a general inter-est, or natural rights that goes beyond the formal political processes, his democratic beliefs may actually make him less responsive and more resistive to judicial, legis-lative, and hierarchical accountability. Each policy that is imposed on the adminis-trator will be interpreted and executed by him in terms of *his* conceptions of legit-imacy.[10]

CONCLUSION

. . . The Administrative Realists have defined the problem of the adminis-trator in terms of the political process rather than in terms of administrative efficiency or natural law. The principal difficulty of their theory lies in its gen-erality, for they describe wondrous engines (including the human mind) into which are poured all sorts of miscellaneous ingredients which, after a decent period of agitation, are spewed forth from time to time, each bearing a union label which reads: "Made in the Public Interest in the U.S.A." But their hero is neither the Charlie Chaplin of *Modern Times* nor Prometheus unbound; he is the administrative counterpart of the politician described by Herring in *The Politics of Democracy*. The statements of the administrative due process theor-ists do suggest the possibility of the construction of more detailed models of the structure of specific decisional processes in particular agencies with identi-fiable functions to perform. Such models (whether as descriptions of existing

8. Avery Leiserson, *Administrative Regulation* (Chicago, 1942), p. 14.

9. Wayne A. R. Leys, *Ethics for Policy Decisions* (N.Y., 1952), p. 68.

10. Simon, Smithburg, and Thompson, *Public Administration* (N.Y.: Knopf, 1950), pp. 551–552. Italics supplied.

agencies, or as blueprints for reorganized or new agencies) would lend themselves, at least in principle, to empirical verification. Moreover, Leiserson has suggested a pragmatic test of the extent to which a specific decision, or set of decisions, have been "Made in the Public Interest."

If we assume that the peaceful adjustment of conflicting interests is not only the consummate art of the politician, but that it is also the fundamental task of all policy processes in a democratic polity, then a model of administrative due process would be empirically verified if, in practice, the decisions actually made resulted in the maximal accommodation of the affected interests, in comparison with the relative capacities of alternative structures for making the same decisions, and measured by a reciprocally minimal recourse to other centers for public policy change (i.e., the legislature, the chief executive, courts, etc.) I would not wish to underrate the great difficulties to be overcome in doing what I have suggested. There would be technical problems in the construction of realistic models, and there would be practical problems in inducing political support for the translation into actuality of any models that went beyond the description of existing agencies and processes. Indeed, as research on the Inter-University Case Program public administration cases has demonstrated, there are difficult problems in inducing sufficient political support to make possible the realistic description of existing or historical processes. But I submit that this is a step forward along the long road that needs to be travelled if we ever are to have a political *science,* and if theory in political science is to have a significant impact upon practice and rise above the level of dilettanteism.

THE ONE AND THE MANY: A NOTE ON THE CONCEPT OF THE PUBLIC INTEREST *
J. Roland Pennock

. . . I WISH to deal briefly with two of the many issues clustering around the concept of "the public interest": (1) is it a valid concept? and if it is (2) is the public interest different from the sum of private interests? Many students have been led to question the usefulness and even, in some sense, the validity of the term because of its vagueness. Others seem to feel that it must have a single, precise meaning waiting to be found out and that if only we could discover it administrators, legislators, and others who are called on to act in the public interest would be aided in the performance of their duties. It appears to me that both are mistaken.

* From Carl J. Friedrich, ed., *Nomos V: The Public Interest* (New York: Atherton Press, 1962), pp. 177–182. Copyright 1962, Atherton Press. Reprinted by permission.

That the term is vague cannot be denied. For certain purposes this indeterminacy may deprive it of usefulness. But this is by no means to say that it is not a valid concept in the sense of one that conveys meaning. Our language and ability to communicate would be impoverished indeed if we were to outlaw all words and phrases that are inherently vague. Take the word "beauty." The dictionary definition confirms our intuitive recognition of its vagueness: "the quality attributed to whatever pleases or satisfies in certain ways, as by line, color, form, texture, proportion, rhythmic motion, tone, etc." Students of esthetics are in notorious disagreement as to what constitutes beauty. Yet when it is a matter of applying the concept to a particular kind of thing, or in a particular context, there is frequently wide agreement as to the appropriate standards. To take an example about which every man is his own expert, and yet on which there is a considerable measure of agreement at least within a given culture, consider the term "a beautiful woman." We may agree or disagree with the verdict of the judges of a beauty contest, but no one would dream of *defining* "a beautiful woman" procedurally (or "operationally"), that is, as "one who wins a beauty contest"! Nor would one deny that there is such a thing as a beautiful woman. As a matter of fact, while even acknowledged experts may disagree as to which one of a bevy of beauties should be judged "Miss America" the measure of agreement far exceeds the range of conceivable dispute. We can be sure that the winner will not be one whose curves have turned to bulges, that her teeth will be regular and gleaming, her complexion clear, her nose straight, and so on and so forth. . . .

Sometimes we contrast the public interest with private rights. It is then the residuum after private rights are exhausted that part of the general welfare is not included in acknowledged private claims. What is it that is thus contrasted with the private? Something different? or only private interests that have not crystallized as "rights" or that might otherwise be overlooked? In other words, is the public interest more than the sum of private interests? About this question there seems to be much misunderstanding. I should like to hazard four propositions with which, on reflection, I believe there will be general agreement; and to suggest that they largely, if not wholly, eliminate the problem. First, the public interest is not confined to interests that are recognized by those whose interests they are. We frequently recognize that a person has interests (often calling them "real" interests) of which he is not aware or which he even denies. Even speed laws are partly in the interest of the very people whose activities they curb. Second, the public interest includes the interests of persons who are not yet born. How far the present generation should save for the benefit of its successors is always a difficult question. But nearly all parents have, and feel, an interest in providing for the future of their own children (living or prospective) at some expense to themselves. When society makes this choice, the problem is not essentially different. Both public interest and private interest, in other words, include future interests.

The last point suggests that private interests may be conceived narrowly or broadly and that when the public interest is said to include more than the sum of private interests it may be at least partly because private interests are at that moment being conceived rather narrowly. My third proposition grows out of this same fact. It is that private interests must be conceived as including the individual enjoyments, satisfactions, fulfillments, and so on that come only in and through society. When one thinks what a life of solitude would be like it is apparent that most of our interests are dependent upon society. And if we think of the pleasures of each other's company and of conjoint activity we see that many of our interests are directly social. Society, and its supporting structure, government, become the sources of satisfaction of so many of our interests that we even come to value them, as we say, for their own sakes. That is to say, we acquire an interest in the preservation and further development of society and government as essential means to the satisfaction of many different and more specific interests. As is frequently the case with such generic means to valued ends, we come to think of society and even of the state as valuable in themselves. Anything that injures the society or the state injures us. Yet of course the society, and specifically its government, may injure our personal interest in a way that makes us contrast the two.

Finally, however, I would say that anything that is part of the public interest must be capable of recognition by individuals as an interest that they share in the sense that they wish to see it furthered or think it ought to be furthered. Nor do I believe that this limitation rules out anything that those who protest against identifying the public interest with the sum of individual interests would think ought to be included.[1]

In summary, when anyone, whether judge, administrator, legislator, or private citizen, seeks to make a decision in accordance with the public interest, he must weigh a number of factors. He must consider the claims of private rights. These claims may appear as limitations upon the public interest, as when one tries to balance national security needs against the right of the individual to be able to cross-examine opposing witnesses; or they may appear as part of the public interest, as when the individual in the case just cited contends that it is in the public interest that the right to privacy or the right to fair trial be protected. When it is a matter of interpreting the law, he must consider the apparent purpose of the law and the lawmakers, the interests which the legislation appears to have been designed to protect or advance, the current notions of the "public interest" as applied to the matter at hand, and also his own ideas of the real interest of the public. Judges and others will differ as to the relative weights that ought to attach to these sometimes conflicting claims. Frankfurter will stress the conscience of the community and Hand the conscience of the judge, while others will feel bound by the inten-

---

1. Cf., for instance, Gerhard Colm, "In Defense of the Public Interest," *Social Research*, 27 (1960), 295–307. Actually, as appears at various points in his argument, what Colm is concerned about is the identification of "public interest" with the sum of individual "self-interests." But there is no reason for identifying "interest," with "self-interest." For an excellent discussion of this subject, emphasizing the inevitably normative quality of the term "interest," see S. I. Benn, "Interests in Politics," *Proceedings of the Aristotelian Society*, 60 N.S. (1959–1960), 123–140.

tion of the lawmakers, at least where that can be determined with any assurance. But few will deny all relevance to any one of these elements. Fewer still will claim that the weighing process is necessarily completely arbitrary, although the verdict may always be surrounded by a penumbra of doubt.

What then is the "public interest"? In general, it is a spur to conscience and to deliberation. It is a reminder that private rights are not exhaustive of the public interest and that private interests include much more than self-interests. A term that plays this role, even though it lacks precision, is as valuable as it is inescapable. Moreover, in many particular applications, the context of the situation gives the phrase greater definition. For such uses it has the special virtue that it serves as a receptacle for accumulating standards. A legislature that delegates to an administrative agency the power to regulate in accordance with the public interest is not merely "passing the buck"; it is providing the means for applying a dynamic and increasingly precise policy based on experience, continuing contact with special interests, and freedom to pursue the general welfare as they come to see it.

BIOGRAPHICAL DATA ON CONTRIBUTORS

ALAN A. ALTSHULER is Associate Professor of Political Science at the Massachusetts Institute of Technology. He previously taught at Cornell University (1962–1966). He is the author of *The City Planning Process: A Political Analysis* (1965).

WILLIAM M. CAPRON is a member of the Senior Staff of the Brookings Institution. From 1962 to 1964 he served on the staff of the Council of Economic Advisers, and from 1964 to 1965 as Assistant Director of the Bureau of the Budget.

DOUGLASS CATER has been a Special Assistant to the President of the United States since 1964. Prior to this, he was for many years chief Washington correspondent and an editor of *The Reporter*. His most recent books are *The Fourth Branch of Government* (1959) and *Power in Washington* (1964).

HARLAN CLEVELAND has been United States Ambassador to the North Atlantic Treaty Organization since 1965. From 1953 to 1956 he was successively executive editor and publisher of *The Reporter*. From 1956 to 1961 he served as Dean of the Maxwell School of Citizenship and Public Affairs at Syracuse University, and from 1961 to 1965 he was Assistant Secretary of State for International Organization Affairs. Among his publications are *The Obligations of Power: American Diplomacy in the Search for Peace* (1966) and (co-author) *The Overseas Americans* (1960).

J. STEFAN DUPRÉ is Professor of Political Economy and Director of the Centre for Urban and Community Studies at the University of Toronto. He taught previously at Harvard University. He is co-author of *Science and the Nation: Policy and Politics* (1962).

RICHARD F. FENNO, JR. is Professor of Political Science at the University of Rochester. He is the author of *The President's Cabinet* (1959) and *The Power of the Purse* (1966). In addition, he co-authored *National Politics and Federal Aid to Education* (1962).

HERMAN FINER is Professor Emeritus of Political Science at the University of Chicago. Among his many books are *The Presidency: Crisis and Regeneration* (1960), *Dulles Over Suez* (1964), and *Major Governments of Modern Europe* (Second Edition, 1961).

J. LIEPER FREEMAN is Professor of Political Science at Vanderbilt University. He is the author of *The Political Process: Executive Bureau-Legislative Committee Relations* (Second Edition, 1965).

CARL J. FRIEDRICH is Eaton Professor of the Science of Government at Harvard University. His most recent books are *Man and His Government* (1963), *Transcendant Justice* (1964), and *An Introduction to Political Theory* (1966).

ALVIN W. GOULDNER is Max Weber Research Professor of Social Theory at Washington University. His publications include *Patterns of Industrial Bureaucracy* (1954) and *Enter Plato* (1965). He is the co-author of *Modern Sociology* (1963) and *Notes on Technology and the Moral Order* (1962).

W. ERIC GUSTAFSON is Assistant Professor of Economics at the University of California at Davis. He has previously taught at Harvard and served two years (1963–1965) as Research Advisor at the Pakistan Institute of Development Economics in Karachi. He is co-author of *Made in New York: Case Studies in Metropolitan Manufacturing* (1959).

PAUL Y. HAMMOND is a member of the Social Science Department of the Rand Corporation. He has previously taught at Harvard, Columbia, Yale, and Johns Hopkins universities. He is the author of *Organizing for Defense* (1961) and the co-author of several works including *The United States in a Disarmed World* (1966).

FERREL HEADY is Academic Vice President at the University of New Mexico. He was formerly Director of the Institute of Public Administration and Professor of Political Science at the University of Michigan. His publications include *Public Administration: A Comparative Perspective* (1966) and *State Constitutions: The Structure of Administration* (1961).

SAMUEL P. HUNTINGTON is Frank G. Thomson Professor of Government at Harvard University. From 1959 to 1962 he was Associate Director of the Institute of War and Peace Studies at Columbia University. His publications include *The Soldier and the State* (1957), *The Common Defense* (1961) and (co-author) *Political Power: USA/USSR* (1964).

LOUIS L. JAFFE is Byrne Professor of Administrative Law at Harvard University. Among his publications are *Cases and Materials on Administrative Law* (Second Edition, 1961) and *Judicial Control of Administrative Action* (1965).

EDWARD L. KATZENBACH, JR. is Director of the Commission on Administrative Affairs of the American Council on Education. He has previously been Director of the Harvard University Defense Studies Program (1955–1959) and Deputy Assistant Secretary of Defense for Education and Manpower Resources (1961–1964).

HERBERT KAUFMAN is Professor of Political Science at Yale University. Among his publications are *The Forest Ranger: A Study in Administrative Behavior* (1960), *Politics and Policies in State and Local Government* (1963) and (co-author) *Governing New York City* (1960).

WILLIAM W. KAUFMANN is Professor of Political Science at the Massachusetts Institute of Technology. He has previously taught at Princeton and Yale, and been Head of the Social Science Department of the Rand Corporation. His publications include *British Policy and the Independence of Latin America* (1951) and *The McNamara Strategy* (1964).

CHARLES E. LINDBLOM is Professor of Economics and Political Science at Yale University. He is the author of *The Intelligence of Democracy* (1965) and co-author of *Politics, Economics, and Welfare* (1953) and *A Strategy of Decision* (1963).

NORTON E. LONG is James Gordon Professor of American Community Government at Brandeis University. He has served as Assistant to the Administrator of the Office of Price Administration (1942–1946), Assistant Administrator of the National Housing Administration (1946–1948), and staff consultant to the Governor of Illinois (1961–1963). He is the author of *The Polity* (1961).

GENE M. LYONS is Orvil E. Dryfoos Professor of Public Affairs at Dartmouth College. He is the author of *Military Policy and Economic Aid: The Korean*

Case 1950–53 (1961) and co-author of *Education and Military Leadership* (1959) and *Schools for Strategy* (1965).

GRANT McCONNELL is Professor of Political Science at the University of Chicago. Among his publications are *The Decline of Agrarian Democracy* (1953), *Steel and the Presidency—1962* (1963), and *Private Power and American Democracy* (1965).

ARTHUR MAASS is Frank G. Thomson Professor of Government at Harvard University. His publications include *Muddy Waters: The Army Engineers and the Nation's Rivers* (1951) and (co-author) *Design of Water-Resource Systems* (1962).

DEAN E. MANN is Associate Professor of Political Science at the University of California at Santa Barbara. He is the author of *The Politics of Water in Arizona* (1963) and co-author of *American Democracy in World Perspective* (1967) and *Men Who Govern* (1967).

JOHN MECKLIN was a *Time* foreign correspondent from 1948 to 1961, and is now a *Time* bureau chief. Between 1961 and 1964 he served successively as Public Affairs Advisor of the United States Mission to the Organization for Economic Cooperation and Development (OECD) and Public Affairs Officer of the United States Embassy in Saigon. He is the author of *Mission in Torment* (1965).

RICHARD E. NEUSTADT is Associate Dean of the John F. Kennedy School of Government, Director of the Institute of Politics, and Professor of Government at Harvard University. He was an Assistant to the President of the United States from 1950 to 1953, and has been a consultant to Presidents Kennedy and Johnson since 1961. He is the author of *Presidential Power* (1960).

PAUL H. NITZE is Deputy Secretary of Defense. He has previously been Director of the State Department's Policy Planning Staff (1950–1953), President of the Foreign Service Educational Foundation (1953–1961), Assistant Secretary of Defense for International Security Affairs (1961–1963) and Secretary of the Navy (1963–1967).

J. ROLAND PENNOCK is Professor of Political Science at Swarthmore College. Among his publications are *Liberal Democracy: Its Merits and Prospects* (1950) and (co-author) *Political Science: An Introduction* (1964).

DON K. PRICE is Dean of the John F. Kennedy School of Government and Professor of Government at Harvard University. His publications include *Government and Science* (1954), *The Political Economy of American Foreign Policy* (1955) and *The Scientific Estate* (1965).

HARRY H. RANSOM is Professor of Political Science at Vanderbilt University. His publications include *Central Intelligence and National Security* (1958) and *Can American Democracy Survive Cold War?* (1963).

ARTHUR M. SCHLESINGER, JR. is Albert Schweitzer Professor of Humanities at the City University of New York. From 1946 to 1961 he was a member of the History Department at Harvard University. From 1961 to 1964 he served as Special Assistant to the President of the United States. Among his numerous books are *A Thousand Days: John F. Kennedy in the White House* (1965) and *Bitter Heritage: Vietnam and American Democracy 1941–1966* (1966).

GLENDON A. SCHUBERT, JR. is Professor of Political Science at the University of North Carolina. From 1952 to 1967 he was a member of the Political Science Department at Michigan State University. His publications include *The Public Interest* (1960), *Constitutional Politics* (1960), *Judicial Policy Making* (1965), and *The Judicial Mind* (1965).

Philip Selznick is Professor of Sociology at the University of California at Berkeley. His publications include *TVA and the Grass Roots* (1949), *The Organizational Weapon* (1952), *Leadership in Administration* (1958), and (co-author) *Sociology* (Third Edition, 1963).

Theodore C. Sorenson is a member of the New York law firm of Paul, Weiss, Rifkind, Wharton and Garrison. He was a legislative assistant to Senator John F. Kennedy from 1953 to 1961, and Special Counsel to the President of the United States from 1961 to 1964. He is the author of *Decision Making in the White House* (1963) and *Kennedy* (1965).